DRUG AND SUBSTANCE ABUSE AMONG OLDER ADULTS

Drug and Substance Abuse Among Older Adults provides a timely, comprehensive overview and analysis of the silent epidemic of drug and substance abuse involving elderly Americans. Combining the authors' individual 50-plus years of formal academic and clinical experience, the book presents a critical reflective analysis and synthesis of the published research associated with older adult psychotropic drug use and abuse in the United States. Chapters delineate related causes and consequences and provide the reader with guidance on how to minimize and effectively deal with this significant and growing problem. Related professional reminders throughout each chapter emphasize and remind readers of important basic content and principles, while common misbeliefs regarding specific abusable psychotropics and their use by older adults are debunked and corrected. Also included are carefully developed figures and tables to supplement chapter content along with explicit guides and tools to facilitate the assessment and diagnosis of abusable psychotropic dependence or use disorder.

Health and social care professionals in the U.S. will learn to assess and diagnose abusable psychotropic dependence or use disorders among older adults and to provide clients quickly and accurately with appropriate, efficacious, and empirically validated treatment.

Louis A. Pagliaro is currently a Professor Emeritus, University of Alberta, and Co-Director of the Substance Abusology and Clinical Pharmacology Research Group. He was formerly a tenured, full professor in the Department of Educational Psychology, as well as in the faculty of Pharmacy and Pharmaceutical Sciences, at the University of Alberta where he taught for over 30 years.

Ann Marie Pagliaro is currently a Professor Emeritus, University of Alberta, and Co-Director of the Substance Abusology and Clinical Pharmacology Research Group. She was formerly a tenured, full professor in the Faculty of Nursing at the University of Alberta where she taught and supervised undergraduate and graduate students for over 30 years.

DRUG AND SUBSTANCE ABUSE AMONG OLDER ADULTS

Identification, Analysis, and Synthesis

Louis A. Pagliaro and Ann Marie Pagliaro

Routledge
Taylor & Francis Group
NEW YORK AND LONDON

Cover image: © Getty Images

First published 2022
by Routledge
605 Third Avenue, New York, NY 10158

and by Routledge
2 Park Square, Milton Park, Abingdon, Oxon, OX14 4RN

Routledge is an imprint of the Taylor & Francis Group, an informa business

Library of Congress Cataloging-in-Publication Data
Names: Pagliaro, Louis A., author. | Pagliaro, Ann Marie, author.
Title: Drug and substance abuse among older adults : identification, analysis, and synthesis / Louis A. Pagliaro and Ann Marie Pagliaro.
Description: New York, NY : Routledge, 2022. | Includes bibliographical references and index. | Identifiers: LCCN 2021041442 (print) | LCCN 2021041443 (ebook) | ISBN 9780367445515 (hardback) | ISBN 9780367445508 (paperback) | ISBN 9781003010333 (ebook)
Subjects: LCSH: Older people—Drug use—United States. | Psychotropic drugs—United States. | Drug abuse—Treatment—United States.
Classification: LCC HV5824.A33 P34 2022 (print) | LCC HV5824.A33 (ebook) | DDC 362.29084/60973—dc23
LC record available at https://lccn.loc.gov/2021041442
LC ebook record available at https://lccn.loc.gov/2021041443

ISBN: 978-0-367-44551-5 (hbk)
ISBN: 978-0-367-44550-8 (pbk)
ISBN: 978-1-003-01033-3 (ebk)

DOI: 10.4324/9781003010333

Typeset in Times New Roman
by Apex CoVantage, LLC

DRUG AND SUBSTANCE ABUSE AMONG OLDER ADULTS

Identification, Analysis, and Synthesis

Louis A. Pagliaro and Ann Marie Pagliaro

Routledge
Taylor & Francis Group
NEW YORK AND LONDON

Cover image: © Getty Images

First published 2022
by Routledge
605 Third Avenue, New York, NY 10158

and by Routledge
2 Park Square, Milton Park, Abingdon, Oxon, OX14 4RN

Routledge is an imprint of the Taylor & Francis Group, an informa business

Library of Congress Cataloging-in-Publication Data
Names: Pagliaro, Louis A., author. | Pagliaro, Ann Marie, author.
Title: Drug and substance abuse among older adults : identification, analysis, and synthesis / Louis A. Pagliaro and Ann Marie Pagliaro.
Description: New York, NY : Routledge, 2022. | Includes bibliographical references and index. | Identifiers: LCCN 2021041442 (print) | LCCN 2021041443 (ebook) | ISBN 9780367445515 (hardback) | ISBN 9780367445508 (paperback) | ISBN 9781003010333 (ebook)
Subjects: LCSH: Older people—Drug use—United States. | Psychotropic drugs—United States. | Drug abuse—Treatment—United States.
Classification: LCC HV5824.A33 P34 2022 (print) | LCC HV5824.A33 (ebook) | DDC 362.29084/60973—dc23
LC record available at https://lccn.loc.gov/2021041442
LC ebook record available at https://lccn.loc.gov/2021041443

ISBN: 978-0-367-44551-5 (hbk)
ISBN: 978-0-367-44550-8 (pbk)
ISBN: 978-1-003-01033-3 (ebk)

DOI: 10.4324/9781003010333

Typeset in Times New Roman
by Apex CoVantage, LLC

To all older adults in the U.S. who have been harmed by their abusable psychotropic use—before and during—the new millennium. It is our hope that the information presented and discussed in this reference text will:

1. Help to generate a greater awareness and deeper understanding of the nature and extent of abusable psychotropic use among older adults during the third decade of the new millennium;
2. Significantly assist health and social care professionals—as they tirelessly strive to stem the ever-growing tide of abusable psychotropic dependence and use disorders among older adults across the U.S.—lessen the associated pain and suffering experienced by these older adults and their families and communities.

LAP/AMP

CONTENTS

GOAL, OBJECTIVES, MAJOR FEATURES AND BENEFITS, AND UNIQUE CONTRIBUTIONS OF THIS REFERENCE TEXT

GOAL

To present a coalescence of our findings from a formal, comprehensive, systematic review and critical reflective analysis and synthesis of the published research associated with older adult abusable psychotropic use in the U.S. during the first two decades of the new millennium.

OBJECTIVES

To assist health and social care professionals in the U.S. to:

1. Understand the pharmacology, psychology, and sociology of abusable psychotropic use by older adults—particularly, that involving alcohol, amphetamines, caffeine, cannabis, cocaine, nicotine, prescription opiate analgesics, and prescription sedative-hypnotics;[1]
2. Be aware of new millennial trends, both current and forecast, in abusable psychotropic use among older adults (i.e., baby boomers) in the U.S.;
3. Quickly and accurately assess and diagnose abusable psychotropic dependence or use disorders among older adults;
4. Provide older adults with appropriate, efficacious, and empirically validated treatment for abusable psychotropic dependence or use disorders.

MAJOR FEATURES, BENEFITS, AND UNIQUE CONTRIBUTIONS OF THIS TEXT

1. Written explicitly and specifically for health and social care professionals at a post-graduate level;
2. Content is current, thoroughly researched, and documented by reference citations;
3. Focuses specifically on older adults in the U.S. with abusable psychotropic dependence or use disorders, including those with one or more related (i.e., contemporaneous, concurrent, comorbid) diagnoses;

---

1. Thus, this reference text is not significantly concerned with and, consequently, does not comprehensively address legal/forensic issues related to abusable psychotropic use. Thus, while some related data are presented (e.g., drug dealing and trafficking by older adults in the U.S.), we have not addressed, for example, the incidence or rates of arrest or incarceration for older adults in general or for specific subgroups of older adults in the context of drug-related crimes.

   In this regard, it is extremely important to recognize that, even if all of the abusable psychotropics, which are discussed in this text, were made entirely legal for recreational use across the entire U.S., it would not significantly affect the data presented in this text. That is to say that while the reported incidence of use and the frequency of undesired, or harmful, effects and toxicities would undoubtedly change, the core data (i.e., pharmacology; pharmacokinetics; toxicology; and assessment, diagnosis, and treatment of related dependence or use disorders) would not change.

4. Provides and utilizes carefully developed illustrations—both figures and tables—throughout each chapter to: (1) compliment the prose; and (2) facilitate better understanding of the chapter content;
5. Includes generic names, brand/trade names, street names, and common related street argot for all abusable psychotropics used by older adults;
6. Provides "Related Professional Reminders" throughout each chapter to emphasize and remind readers of important basic content and principles that: (1) are often missed or forgotten; and (2) require particular emphasis;
7. Identifies specific varied cultural, genetic, racial, and socioeconomic factors that can protect against, or mitigate, abusable psychotropic dependence or use disorders—and/or response to treatment;
8. Draws attention to—and corrects—common "Old Misbeliefs" regarding specific abusable psychotropics and their use by older adults;
9. Addresses major iatrogenic causes of abusable psychotropic dependence or use disorders with attention to practices/strategies that can be used to minimize this significant problem for older adults;
10. Provides explicit guides and tools (e.g., psychometric tests) to facilitate the assessment and diagnosis of abusable psychotropic dependence or use disorder among older adults, as well as presentation of and discussion related to DSM-5 criteria;
11. Clearly identifies, presents, and discusses pharmacotherapeutic and psychotherapeutic/counseling treatment approaches, which have been empirically validated among older adults;
12. Extensively uses cross-referencing throughout the text to: (1) integrate data and analysis; and (2) facilitate coverage and discussion of issues;
13. Utilizes a writing style that commonly cites direct quotes referenced from authors in order to provide readers with both a "flavor" of the research and examples of direct representation—without bias or interpretation;
14. Integrates the unique combined knowledge of the authors regarding abusable psychotropic use among older adults, which is based on over 50 years of academic and clinical experience for each author;[2]
15. Includes an extensive, cross-referenced index to facilitate data retrieval for readers.

---

2. The authors identified over 40 years ago that the formal study of drug and substance abuse required its own faculty as a separate and unique transdisciplinary university level of the various sciences, and, subsequently, established the first Substance Abusology Research Unit (SARU) in North America at the University of Alberta—with attention to the education of a diversity of transdisciplinary undergraduates, master's, doctoral, and post-doctoral students from education, medicine, nursing, psychology, and other faculties.

ABOUT THE AUTHORS

Louis A. Pagliaro is currently a Professor Emeritus, University of Alberta, and Co-Director of the Substance Abusology and Clinical Pharmacology Research Group. He was formerly a tenured, full professor in the Department of Educational Psychology, as well as in the faculty of Pharmacy and Pharmaceutical Sciences, at the University of Alberta where he taught and supervised undergraduate and graduate students in the areas of abusable psychotropic use and the biological basis of both clinical pharmacology and clinical psychology for over 30 years. As a registered psychologist, he served a three-year elected term as President of the College of Alberta Psychologists. His area of specialty clinical psychology practice is the treatment of adults who have refractory alcohol or other dependence or use disorder(s).

Ann Marie Pagliaro is currently a Professor Emeritus, University of Alberta, and Co-Director of the Substance Abusology and Clinical Pharmacology Research Group. She was formerly a tenured, full professor in the faculty of Nursing at the University of Alberta where she taught and supervised undergraduate and graduate students, for over 30 years, in the areas of theory development and clinical practice with a primary focus on the prevention and treatment of abusable psychotropic dependence or use disorders across the lifespan—with particular attention, in this reference text, to older adults of varied ethnic, genetic, racial, and socioeconomic backgrounds. Her specialty area of research continues to be the epistemological study of human abusable psychotropic use.

The Pagliaros—full-time members of the academic staff at the University of Alberta from 1977 to 2008—taught thousands of students, published over 300 professional scientific articles, and extensively consulted for numerous governmental and professional organizations, locally and nationally—including the White House Office of Drug Abuse—and internationally. Seven of their previous clinical pharmacology and therapeutics textbooks have focused explicitly on drug and substance abuse, including: *Pagliaros' Comprehensive Guide to Drugs and Substances of Abuse* (1st and 2nd editions), which were published by the American Pharmacists Association in 2004 and 2009, respectively, and *Women's Drug and Substance Abuse* (1st and 2nd editions), which were published by Brunner/Mazel and Routledge (Taylor & Francis) in 2000 and 2018 respectively. *Child and Adolescent Drug and Substance Abuse: A Comprehensive Reference* (2020), was the 19th—and most recent—textbook that the Pagliaros have co-edited or co-authored since 1979. Almost 40 years ago, in 1983, they developed and co-edited *Pharmacologic Aspects of Aging*, which was published by C. V. Mosby, and was one of the first clinical pharmacology and therapeutics texts in North America to focus exclusively on older adults. Several of their texts have received prestigious publishing awards—including, in 2013, the "Choices Award" as an outstanding academic title from the Association of College and Research Libraries. *Drug and Substance Abuse Among Older Adults: Identification, Analysis, and Synthesis* is their 20th textbook. The Pagliaros have been married for 50 years.

4. Provides and utilizes carefully developed illustrations—both figures and tables—throughout each chapter to: (1) compliment the prose; and (2) facilitate better understanding of the chapter content;
5. Includes generic names, brand/trade names, street names, and common related street argot for all abusable psychotropics used by older adults;
6. Provides "Related Professional Reminders" throughout each chapter to emphasize and remind readers of important basic content and principles that: (1) are often missed or forgotten; and (2) require particular emphasis;
7. Identifies specific varied cultural, genetic, racial, and socioeconomic factors that can protect against, or mitigate, abusable psychotropic dependence or use disorders—and/or response to treatment;
8. Draws attention to—and corrects—common "Old Misbeliefs" regarding specific abusable psychotropics and their use by older adults;
9. Addresses major iatrogenic causes of abusable psychotropic dependence or use disorders with attention to practices/strategies that can be used to minimize this significant problem for older adults;
10. Provides explicit guides and tools (e.g., psychometric tests) to facilitate the assessment and diagnosis of abusable psychotropic dependence or use disorder among older adults, as well as presentation of and discussion related to DSM-5 criteria;
11. Clearly identifies, presents, and discusses pharmacotherapeutic and psychotherapeutic/counseling treatment approaches, which have been empirically validated among older adults;
12. Extensively uses cross-referencing throughout the text to: (1) integrate data and analysis; and (2) facilitate coverage and discussion of issues;
13. Utilizes a writing style that commonly cites direct quotes referenced from authors in order to provide readers with both a "flavor" of the research and examples of direct representation—without bias or interpretation;
14. Integrates the unique combined knowledge of the authors regarding abusable psychotropic use among older adults, which is based on over 50 years of academic and clinical experience for each author;[2]
15. Includes an extensive, cross-referenced index to facilitate data retrieval for readers.

2. The authors identified over 40 years ago that the formal study of drug and substance abuse required its own faculty as a separate and unique transdisciplinary university level of the various sciences, and, subsequently, established the first Substance Abusology Research Unit (SARU) in North America at the University of Alberta—with attention to the education of a diversity of transdisciplinary undergraduates, master's, doctoral, and post-doctoral students from education, medicine, nursing, psychology, and other faculties.

ABOUT THE AUTHORS

Louis A. Pagliaro is currently a Professor Emeritus, University of Alberta, and Co-Director of the Substance Abusology and Clinical Pharmacology Research Group. He was formerly a tenured, full professor in the Department of Educational Psychology, as well as in the faculty of Pharmacy and Pharmaceutical Sciences, at the University of Alberta where he taught and supervised undergraduate and graduate students in the areas of abusable psychotropic use and the biological basis of both clinical pharmacology and clinical psychology for over 30 years. As a registered psychologist, he served a three-year elected term as President of the College of Alberta Psychologists. His area of specialty clinical psychology practice is the treatment of adults who have refractory alcohol or other dependence or use disorder(s).

Ann Marie Pagliaro is currently a Professor Emeritus, University of Alberta, and Co-Director of the Substance Abusology and Clinical Pharmacology Research Group. She was formerly a tenured, full professor in the faculty of Nursing at the University of Alberta where she taught and supervised undergraduate and graduate students, for over 30 years, in the areas of theory development and clinical practice with a primary focus on the prevention and treatment of abusable psychotropic dependence or use disorders across the lifespan—with particular attention, in this reference text, to older adults of varied ethnic, genetic, racial, and socioeconomic backgrounds. Her specialty area of research continues to be the epistemological study of human abusable psychotropic use.

The Pagliaros—full-time members of the academic staff at the University of Alberta from 1977 to 2008—taught thousands of students, published over 300 professional scientific articles, and extensively consulted for numerous governmental and professional organizations, locally and nationally—including the White House Office of Drug Abuse—and internationally. Seven of their previous clinical pharmacology and therapeutics textbooks have focused explicitly on drug and substance abuse, including: *Pagliaros' Comprehensive Guide to Drugs and Substances of Abuse* (1st and 2nd editions), which were published by the American Pharmacists Association in 2004 and 2009, respectively, and *Women's Drug and Substance Abuse* (1st and 2nd editions), which were published by Brunner/Mazel and Routledge (Taylor & Francis) in 2000 and 2018 respectively. *Child and Adolescent Drug and Substance Abuse: A Comprehensive Reference* (2020), was the 19th—and most recent—textbook that the Pagliaros have co-edited or co-authored since 1979. Almost 40 years ago, in 1983, they developed and co-edited *Pharmacologic Aspects of Aging*, which was published by C. V. Mosby, and was one of the first clinical pharmacology and therapeutics texts in North America to focus exclusively on older adults. Several of their texts have received prestigious publishing awards—including, in 2013, the "Choices Award" as an outstanding academic title from the Association of College and Research Libraries. *Drug and Substance Abuse Among Older Adults: Identification, Analysis, and Synthesis* is their 20th textbook. The Pagliaros have been married for 50 years.

ACKNOWLEDGMENTS

First, we would like to share our appreciation and thank our many colleagues, students, and older patients (including, in numerous cases, their adult children), who helped us to achieve a better understanding of the real-life experiences and the ramifications of the exposure to, or use of, abusable psychotropics among older adults. We have attempted to share this understanding with the readers of this text. In this regard, we have been guided by the mottos of the two universities that have played a significant role in our academic lives: (1) the University of California (Berkeley and San Francisco Medical Center campuses—Schools of Medicine, Nursing, and Pharmacy), "FIAT LUX" (*Let There Be Light*); and (2) the University of Alberta (Faculty of Education, Department of Educational Psychology), "QUAECUMQUE VERA" (*Whatsoever Things Are True*).

The published clinical and other research cited in this reference text, and the lived experiences shared with us by older adults over the past 40 years, have provided us with an appreciation of the truly devastating nature and extent of abusable psychotropic use among older adults in the U.S. during the new millennium. We are both inspired and motivated by the significant therapeutic outcomes that can be achieved by older adults and their families and communities with the attention of appropriate prevention and treatment strategies by a variety of caring and competent health and social care professionals.

Second, we would like to share our appreciation to the dedicated staff at Routledge (Taylor & Francis), who directly contributed to the development and production of this reference text, particularly Amanda Devine, Grace McDonnell, Marie Louise Roberts, and Chris Mathews.

EPIGRAPH[1]

Do not regret growing old. It is a privilege denied to many.

(Anonymous)

REFERENCE

Pagliaro, L. A., & Pagliaro, A. M. (1983). *Pharmacologic aspects of aging*. St. Louis, MO: CV Mosby.

1. We used this anonymous quote in our first text that dealt exclusively with older adults (i.e., Pagliaro & Pagliaro, 1983) and, now almost 40 years later, we chose to use it again. However, additionally, in the context of the subject matter of this text, we would add that if we, as health and social care providers, allow our elderly patients to be propelled into what Dylan Thomas referred to as "that good night" broken, scarred, and defeated by drug and substance abuse, then we—in reference to the work by Ernest Hemingway—"need not know for whom the bell tolls"—it tolls for us.

CHAPTER 1

ALCOHOL

Whether obtained from a loving son as a special gift for his father's birthday in a nursing home, enjoyed at a granddaughter's wedding, or used to celebrate a holiday with family and friends, alcohol is used by many older adults to, for example:

1. Achieve a desired dose-dependent disinhibition euphoria (i.e., for "pleasure");
2. Attain a sense of well-being;
3. Be like "everyone else," who needs "a drink or two;"
4. Cope with "life's pains, disappointments, and impossible tasks;"[1]
5. Decrease social and sexual inhibitions;
6. Fit in with other members of their social groups (e.g., bowling team, golf foursome);
7. "Have fun;"
8. Relieve anxiety, tension, or stress.

Unfortunately, when compared to all of the other drugs and substances of abuse used by older adults, alcohol is the most commonly used and, for this age group, it is associated with more harm than all of the other drugs and substances of abuse combined (Barry & Blow, 2016; Kuerbis, Sacco, & Blazer, 2014; Pagliaro & Pagliaro, 1992b, 2018; Ross, 2005). As noted by the CDC (2020a, p. 1):

> Excessive alcohol use is responsible for more than 95,000 deaths in the United States each year, or 261 deaths per day. These deaths shorten the lives of those who die by an average of almost 29 years, for a total of 2.8 million years of potential life lost.

In this chapter, we present and discuss alcohol use among older adults with attention to its chemistry, pharmacology, and patterns of use in the U.S. during the new millennium. The chapter concludes with a thorough discussion of the assessment, diagnosis, and treatment of alcohol dependence or use disorder (AUD) among older adults.[2]

Pharmacologically, alcohol is classified as a psychodepressant that belongs to the "sedative-hypnotic" subclass, which also includes prescription sedative-hypnotics

---

1. The related full quote from Sigmund Freud (2005, p. 20) is:

   > Life as we find it, is too hard for us; it brings too many pains, disappointments, and impossible tasks. In order to bear it we cannot dispense with palliative measures. . . . There are perhaps three such measures: powerful deflections, which cause us to make light of our misery; substitutive satisfactions, which diminish it; and intoxicating substances [e.g., alcohol], which make us insensible to it.

   For older adults, these "pains," "disappointments," and "impossible tasks" vary widely and may include, for example: cancer diagnosis, death of a loved one, severe arthritis pain, and retirement and its associated: (1) loss of prestige; (2) reduced monthly income; and (3) social isolation—or just being "old" and never being "young" again.
2. The terms, "alcohol dependence" and "alcohol use disorder" (i.e., AUD), subsume and replace all of the older established related terms, including "alcohol abuse" and "alcoholism."

DOI: 10.4324/9781003010333-1

(e.g., benzodiazepines; z-drugs).[3] However, we decided, for several reasons, to separate alcohol from the prescription sedative-hypnotics and discuss it in its own chapter. The reasons for this decision include the:

- Long history of medical and nonmedical/recreational use of alcohol in the U.S.;
- Identification of alcohol as a human neurotoxin;
- Cultural inculcation of the use of alcohol into celebrations, parties, and social gatherings in the U.S.;
- Potential for significant alcohol-related physical, mental, and social harm;
- Current use of alcohol by more than 70% of older adults in the U.S.;
- Abuse of alcohol by more than 15% of older adults in the U.S.

We begin with a brief review of the basic chemistry and pharmacology of alcohol.

CHEMISTRY

In this section we present and discuss the basic chemistry of alcohol, which, in the science of chemistry, is defined as any organic compound that has a hydroxyl (-OH) functional group bound to a carbon atom, including beverage alcohol—ethyl alcohol or ethanol (C_2H_5OH) (Figure 1.1).[4] Throughout this reference text, we use the word, "alcohol," to refer exclusively to beverage alcohol.

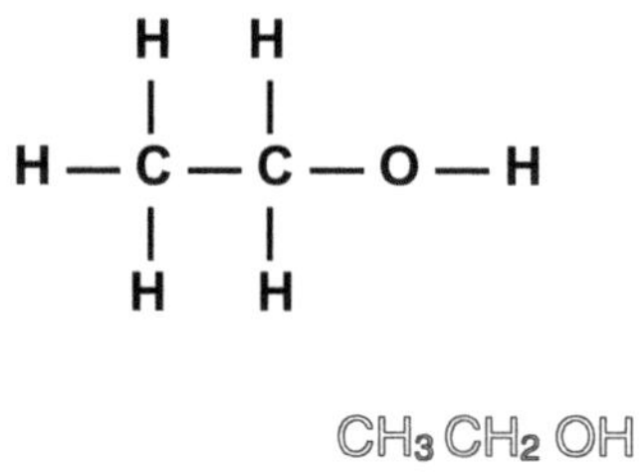

Figure 1.1 Chemical Structure of Alcohol

Beverage alcohol[5] is a colorless, flammable, and volatile liquid that is produced by fermenting various carbohydrate foodstuffs, including fruits, grains, and vegetables with the use of yeasts.[6,7]

3. See the related discussion in Chapter 6, *Prescription Sedative-Hypnotics*.
4. Methanol, methyl alcohol or wood alcohol, which is used industrially as an antifreeze, fuel, or organic solvent, contains a methyl group linked with a hydroxyl group (i.e., CH_3OH). It is extremely toxic causing, for example, metabolic acidosis and ophthalmic toxicity ranging from blurred vision to blindness. Additionally, methanol is commonly added (generally in 5% to 10% concentration) to ethanol to denature the ethanol (i.e., make it unfit for human consumption) and, thereby, make the resultant product ineligible for alcohol-related governmental control and taxation (for example, to produce some hand sanitizer in response to the COVID-19 pandemic).
5. This form of alcohol is also used as: (1) a fuel; (2) an industrial solvent; and (3) a vehicle for various prescription and non-prescription drugs. These uses of alcohol are not further discussed in this chapter.
6. Yeasts are single cell fungi (genus, *Saccharomyces*) that are capable of fermenting (i.e., digesting or decomposing) carbohydrates (e.g., cellulose, starches, sugars) to ultimately produce alcohol, carbon dioxide, and water.
7. The concentration of the alcohol that is produced by fermentation is limited to approximately 16% because higher concentrations kill the yeast and, consequently, halt the fermentation process. To increase

PHARMACOLOGY

In this section, we highlight the basic pharmacology of alcohol with attention to its:

1. Pharmacodynamics—mechanism of action and blood alcohol concentrations;
2. Pharmacokinetics—absorption, distribution, metabolism, and excretion;
3. Potentially significant drug-drug interactions;
4. Undesired, or harmful, effects and toxicities;
5. Physical and psychological dependence;
6. Overdosage/unintentional poisoning.

Pharmacodynamics: Mechanism of Action and Blood Alcohol Concentrations

Old Misbelief: Alcohol is used and abused for its psychostimulant actions.

False. In fact, although "paradoxical excitation" may accompany alcohol use, alcohol is classified as a sedative-hypnotic as supported in the following subsections—"Mechanism of Action" and "Blood Alcohol Concentrations." Like other sedative-hypnotics, alcohol produces a progressive dose-related depression of the central nervous system (CNS) that ranges from mild sedation to deep sleep. Coma may rarely occur and can be fatal. These psychodepressant effects are generally predictable and depend on three major factors:

1. Type of the alcoholic beverage ingested (e.g., beer versus whiskey);
2. "Proof" (i.e., the equivalent to double the percentage concentration of the alcoholic beverage—for example, 40 proof indicates 20% alcoholic concentration);
3. "Amount" of the alcoholic beverage ingested (e.g., one can of beer or a six-pack of beer) per unit of time (e.g., hour, day, or week).

Mechanism of Action

As recently as the last century, alcohol was erroneously identified as a "psychostimulant" that was commonly used by older adults for such desired effects as to "warm-up after coming in from the cold." It also was medically used for a variety of indications, from reviving someone who had fainted to treating the fatigue and weakness associated with cachexia. Although this belief was supported by lay and medical observations that drinking too much often resulted in apparent "psychostimulant-mediated" behaviors—such as throwing one's clothes on the floor and dancing naked on a table in a bar or getting into a violent fight at a party—alcohol possesses no psychostimulant actions (see the following subsection, "Related Blood Alcohol Concentrations"). Empirical findings in support of the psychodepressant actions of alcohol include the general observation that, as more alcohol is ingested

---

the alcohol concentration, for example, to 18%, as is done to produce sherry and other fortified wines, more alcohol is simply added to the already fermented product. Even higher concentrations of alcohol (e.g., concentrations of 30%, or higher) can be obtained by distilling the fermented product to obtain such distilled spirits as brandy and whiskey.

during a drinking episode, drinkers do not become more awake, they become drowsier and, inevitably, uniformly fall asleep.

> Mrs. D. said her father, an 82-year-old former maintenance worker, meets [daily] with his friends for cocktails at about 3 or 4 [in the afternoon] and then passes out, which he calls a nap.
> (Ellin, 2014, p. 2)

The exact mechanism of action by which alcohol depresses the entire CNS remains a mystery. However, research over the last several decades has resulted in two major plausible theories:

1. Alcohol readily crosses the blood-brain barrier (BBB), disrupting the function of brain membrane lipids and glucose metabolism;
2. Alcohol primarily acts at two specific receptor sites in the brain: (1) gamma aminobutyric acid ($GABA_A$) receptor sites; and (2) N-methyl-D-aspartate (NMDA) receptor sites (Brower, 2001; Deitrich, Dunwiddie, & Harris, 1989; Gonzales & Jaworski, 1997; Pagliaro & Pagliaro, 2009; Peoples, Li, & Weight, 1996; Valenzuela, 1997).

While either theory may contribute to the actual mechanism of the action of alcohol, research in glucose metabolism supports the first theory, which also explains the effects of alcohol on learning and memory. Research in support of the second theory suggests that alcohol acts to enhance GABAergic inhibition primarily by modifying the membrane environment of the $GABA_A$ receptor complex. This action significantly increases the affinity of the $GABA_A$ receptor complex for both endogenous sedative-hypnotics (e.g., GABA) and exogenous sedative-hypnotics (e.g., benzodiazepines; z-drugs), thus, enhancing GABAergic inhibition.[8] (For additional related discussion regarding the GABA receptor, see Chapter 6, *Prescription Sedative-Hypnotics*, and the benzodiazepines pharmacology subsection—"Pharmacodynamics: Mechanism of Action.")

In addition, alcohol appears to inhibit the activity of glutamate, which is a naturally occurring excitatory neurotransmitter that functions largely at the NMDA receptors, as well as alpha-amino-3-hydroxy-5-methyl-isoxazoleproprionic acid (AMPA) and metabotropic glutamate receptors (mGluRs) (Gonzales & Jaworski, 1997). The regular, long-term use of alcohol by older adults results in "up-regulation" of the NMDA receptors. These receptors, based on data obtained from laboratory animal studies, are posited to play a significant role in both:

1. Alcohol-induced neurotoxicity;
2. The alcohol withdrawal syndrome, particularly the occurrence of withdrawal-related seizures (Chang-Mu, Jen-Kun, & Shing-Hwa, 2010; Charlton, Sweetnan, & Fitzgerald, 2002; Hoffman, 1995; Hoffman & Tabakoff, 1994; NIAAA, 2005).

Related Professional Reminder**: *Alcohol induces sedative-hypnotic effects largely by reducing excitatory neurotransmission—specifically, that involving the excitatory amino acids aspartate and glutamate.***

8. These posited actions of alcohol involving the $GABA_A$ receptor complex may also help to explain the: (1) development of tolerance to alcohol; and (2) cross-tolerance that is noted between alcohol and other sedative-hypnotics, specifically benzodiazepines, as well as the efficacy of these drugs in preventing/treating alcohol withdrawal (see the related discussion in the later pharmacotherapy subsection, Physical and Psychological Dependence—"Alcohol Tolerance" and "Alcohol Withdrawal Syndrome").

Other factors also have been identified as contributing to both the pharmacological and toxicological effects related to alcohol use and withdrawal (Vezali Costardi, Teruaki Nampo, & Lourenco Silva, 2015). For example, serotonin (5-HT) has been frequently related to the positive pleasure and rewarding effects associated with alcohol use and, consequently, the preference for alcohol, regulation of alcohol intake, and development of alcohol dependence (Muller & Homberg, 2015; Sari, Johnson, & Weedman, 2011; Schweighofer, Bertin, & Shishida, 2008).

Specifically, regarding the serotonergic system:

1. Serotonin release and transmission are increased in the CNS by the acute phase of alcohol use, while chronic alcohol use causes an overall decrease in serotonin neurotransmission;
2. Regular long-term, or chronic, use of alcohol leads to: (1) adaptive changes to the serotonin 5-HT_2 receptors (i.e., "up-regulation"); or (2) an increase in the number of 5-HT_2 receptors;
3. Direct activation of the 5-HT_3 receptors, which are localized in cortical and subcortical regions of the brain, appear to contribute to acute alcohol intoxication;
4. Alcohol withdrawal is associated with a reduction of serotonin levels (see the related discussion in the later subsection, Undesired, or Harmful, Effects and Toxicities, Physical and Psychological Dependence—"Alcohol Withdrawal Syndrome").

(Lovinger, 1997; Sari et al., 2011; Marcinkiewcz, 2015; Tollefson, 1989)

Blood Alcohol Concentrations (BACs)

Regardless of the actual mechanism of action, BACs associated with the amount of alcohol ingested during a drinking episode highly correlate with the direct and progressive depression of the CNS (Pagliaro & Pagliaro, 2009) (see Table 1.1).[9]

Lower BACs associated with the initiation of a drinking episode are often accompanied by excitement, happiness, and increased mental and physical activity. In fact, historically, these observed behaviors led researchers to commonly misclassify alcohol as a "psychostimulant" (see the earlier related discussion). However, the stimulant-like behaviors were later found to be due to alcohol's general depression of the CNS—resulting in "disinhibition euphoria."

The relatively low BACs, which are, for example, achieved at the beginning of a drinking episode, diminish the control of the medulla oblongata over the higher cortical (i.e., executive functioning) centers of the brain and, consequently, impair thinking and psychomotor performance. Social norms and related inhibitions, such as being polite or wearing clothes in public, also are impaired. There also is an incremental loss in concentration, conscious

9. The ingestion of a typical serving of alcohol (i.e., 12 fluid ounces of beer; 5 fluid ounces of wine; 1.5 fluid ounces of 80-proof distilled spirits) increases the BAC by approximately 0.02 gram % (i.e., 20 mg/100 ml of blood) in the average older adult—it should be noted that this approximation was traditionally calculated based on a 21-year-old male of European continental descent weighing 70 kg. Consequently, variation in BAC is to be expected among older adults, particularly older women and all obese older adults (see the related discussion in the following section, "Pharmacokinetics").

Table 1.1 Blood Alcohol Concentration (BAC) and Associated Physical and Mental Effects Among Older Adults[10]

BAC (gram % or grams per 100 ml)	PHYSICAL EFFECTS	MENTAL EFFECTS
0.01 to 0.03	Generally, normal/usual appearance	Generally, normal/usual behavior
0.03 to 0.06	Feel warm and relaxed with mild impairment of coordination and diminished ability to perform fine motor tasks	Mild euphoria (e.g., feelings of intense excitement and happiness) with decreased inhibitions and increased sociability and talkativeness Mild decreases in alertness and concentration
0.06 to 0.08	Increasing loss of coordination with a slight loss of both balance and speaking ability	Mild impairment of reasoning and memory with intensification of emotions Increased disinhibition euphoria with apparent "stimulant effect" on behavior and extroversion Lowered interest in sex
0.08 to 0.10	Mild impairment of hearing, speech, and vision	Mild impairment of both judgment and self-control with increased risk for and incidence of accidents
0.10 to 0.15	Continued loss of coordination with marked impairment of balance, slowed reaction time, and slightly slurred speech	Increased emotional instability with euphoria being increasingly replaced with the opposite feeling of dysphoria Significant impairment in judgment and ability to make good decisions with up to ten-fold increase in the probability or incidence of accidents
0.15 to 0.20	Significant drowsiness, slurred speech, and prolonged reaction times Significant visual impairment with blurred vision, reduced glare recovery, and decreased peripheral vision	Significant impairment of perception Gross intoxication with further deterioration of judgment and up to a 30-fold increase in the probability or incidence of accidents
0.20 to 0.30	Severe motor and speech impairment with an appearance of a "sloppy drunk"—appears "smashed" May require assistance to stand upright or to walk	Significant mental confusion—may be dazed or disoriented Loss of normal understanding Significant pain tolerance ("feeling no pain")

10. The BACs listed and their associated effects are meant to provide a general guideline. Variability from one older adult to another does occur and can be significant, particularly in relation to the varied contexts of age, gender, genetics, health status, and acquired tolerance. Consequently, older adults can be generally expected to experience the noted physical and mental effects at the lower end of the BAC range (Pagliaro & Pagliaro, *Clinical Patient Data Files*).

BAC (gram % or grams per 100 ml)	PHYSICAL EFFECTS	MENTAL EFFECTS
	Impaired gag reflex with risk of choking on food or own vomitus Risk of serious injury related to falls, walking into traffic, being attacked, robbed (i.e., being "rolled"), or raped	Memory loss and alcoholic blackouts May become stuporous, or achieve a state of near unconsciousness ("a drunken stupor")
0.30 to 0.35	Total loss of motor control Significantly depressed or absent reflexes Incontinence, or loss of voluntary bladder control, "totally pissed" Significantly slowed heart and respiratory rates	Level of consciousness diminishes to a state of stupor, a complete lack of mental alertness or a condition of significantly impaired ability to respond to external environmental stimuli Level of consciousness diminishes to coma, or an extremely deep stupor—a condition in which the person cannot be aroused by external environmental stimuli (e.g., talking to the person, calling the person by name, or gently shaking the person to arouse him or her) Total lack of response to painful stimuli, such as pinching the skin or pricking the skin with a pin or needle (i.e., level of surgical anesthesia)
0.35 to 0.40+	Impaired circulation of the blood throughout the body Death, usually due to respiratory arrest LD_{50} = 0.4 grams %	Severe CNS depression and unconsciousness

Modified from: Pagliaro & Pagliaro, 2020.

control over behavior,[11] discrimination, fine motor movement, and memory performance. Wide fluctuations in mood, with frequent emotional outbursts, also may occur.

As the BAC increases, the state of disinhibition euphoria is progressively impaired as the actions/control of the cerebral cortex are increasingly diminished.[12] As a consequence, "bar fights" and other aggressive behavior may occur. In this regard, older women, when

11. The behavioral reaction to disinhibition, occurring at lower doses, is unpredictable and is determined by individual factors, including an older adult's mental set and the setting in which the drinking occurs. Mental set and environmental setting become less important when increasing amounts of alcohol are ingested because sedation dominates and behavioral activity decreases. As alcohol ingestion increases, all drinkers experience progressive psychomotor incapacitation. Thus, for example, at low alcohol dosages/BACs, some drinkers may appear as "happy drunks," get on a table in a bar, take off their clothes, and dance or sing naked without a care in the world. However, as alcohol BACs increase, all drinkers become "sleepy drunks" and soon fall asleep, or "pass-out."
12. The nature and extent of these psychodepressant actions depend upon factors such as gender, genetics, hepatic function, lean body weight, and tolerance to alcohol.

compared to older men, are equally at risk for physically assaulting someone when they are drinking (Timko, Moos, & Moos, 2009).

Instances of domestic violence or intimate partner violence (IPV) often involve alcohol use—both acute intoxication and chronic drunkenness associated with regular, long-term use (Pagliaro & Pagliaro, *Clinical Patient Data Files*; Pagliaro & Pagliaro, 2018; Stuart, Meehan, & Moore, 2006; Stuart, Moore, & Ramsey, 2004; Stuart, Temple, & Follansbee, 2008). These incidents of violence, are significantly influenced by:

1. Pharmacological actions of alcohol;
2. Perpetrator's innate personality or predisposition to engage in violent behavior;
3. Environmental circumstances.

Alcohol use—at any level—generally does not increase, or improve, cognitive or psychomotor performance.[13] With moderate to heavy alcohol ingestion: (1) visuospatial performance bias, which generally favors older men, disappears; while (2) episodic memory performance bias, which generally favors older women, is maintained. These observed actions may be mediated by the effects of alcohol on sex hormones (e.g., the facilitation of the conversion of testosterone to estrogen) (e.g., Yonker, Nilsson, & Herlitz, 2005).

When the BAC exceeds 0.1 gram %—usually within the first one to two hours after initiating a drinking episode (or approximately four drinks for older women and five drinks for older men)[14]—further psychodepression occurs, resulting in impaired judgment, decreased coordination, slowed reaction time, and blurred vision. For this reason, the legal limit of intoxication in the U.S. is a BAC of 0.08 gram % (i.e., 0.08 grams of alcohol per 100 ml of blood) (for further related discussion, see the later subsection, "Drinking and Driving").

It is interesting to note that the psychodepressant actions associated with the ingestion of alcohol appear to be more marked when the BAC is increasing rather than when it is decreasing.[15] As the ingestion of alcohol increases, the function of the CNS becomes progressively impaired as a general anesthesia ultimately prevails.

Acute alcohol ingestion also can affect other body systems resulting in changes in respiratory function, temperature regulation, sexual performance, and urinary output. See the later pharmacology subsection, "Undesired, or Harmful, Effects and Toxicities."

---

13. A noted exception is the case of an older adult who is experiencing the alcohol withdrawal syndrome. In this case, "a bit of the hair of the dog that bit her" (i.e., an alcoholic drink) would increase BACs, relieve the signs and symptoms of the alcohol withdrawal syndrome, and, consequently, improve performance—at least temporarily. Thus, an experienced surgeon or pianist might perform better in this context "with a drink" rather than "without a drink," but not better than if sober—and free of withdrawal symptoms (Pagliaro & Pagliaro, *Clinical Patient Data Files*).
14. In the U.S., a standard drink is typically considered to be 0.5 ounces, or 15 grams, of absolute (i.e., 95% to 100%) alcohol. In relation to commonly consumed alcoholic beverages, this amount of alcohol is roughly equivalent to 12 ounces (360 ml) of beer, 5 ounces (150 ml) of wine, or 1.5 ounces (45 ml) of 80-proof distilled spirits. Given these equivalencies, it is easy to see the truth in the adage, "a drink is a drink is a drink" (i.e., ultimately, the type of alcoholic beverage older adults drink matters less than the number of standard drinks consumed during a drinking episode).
15. This is probably due to the body's attempts to preserve homeostasis, or equilibrium, within the body (i.e., a state of dynamic equilibrium in response to both internal and external environmental changes). As such, it is more difficult to accommodate, or adapt to, new changes (e.g., increasing BAC in the body) rather than to those which occur after the body has adapted—already made necessary changes (e.g., when BAC is decreasing).

Pharmacokinetics: Absorption, Distribution, Metabolism, and Excretion

Alcohol displays interesting and unique pharmacokinetics—from absorption to excretion. These processes are discussed in the following subsections.

Absorption

About 90% to 100% of alcohol is absorbed from the gastrointestinal (GI) tract with small amounts of alcohol (i.e., 10% to 20%) being directly absorbed from the stomach. Absorption from the small intestine is rapid and virtually complete with any remaining amounts of ingested alcohol being absorbed in the colon (i.e., 80% to 90%). The time from the last drink of alcohol to the maximal BAC usually ranges from 30 to 90 minutes—depending on gastric emptying time.

Gastric emptying time can be prolonged by the type and amount of food present in the stomach and, thus, can slow both the rate by which alcohol is released into the small intestine and, in turn, the rate by which the BAC increases. The presence of food in the stomach also can slow the absorption of alcohol by diluting the alcohol and blocking absorption by covering some of the gastric mucosa through which alcohol is normally absorbed. In contrast, gastric emptying time can be shortened by ingesting an alcoholic beverage with a carbonated beverage (e.g., a "shot of whiskey" followed by a "beer chaser," "gin and tonic," or "rum and coke"). This conscious approach to drinking allows drinkers to achieve higher BACs and associated desired effects more rapidly by:

1. Distending the stomach;
2. Relaxing the pyloric sphincter between the distal end of the stomach and the small intestine;
3. Promoting the rapid release of stomach contents into the small intestines—where alcohol is primarily absorbed.

However, regardless of the rate of absorption, any amount of alcohol that is ingested, under normal conditions, is virtually completely absorbed. This rule may be a deadly one regarding older adults who participate in "drinking games" with their friends or grandchildren, or try extremely risky methods of alcohol ingestion, such as "funneling" (i.e., pouring large amounts of alcohol through a funnel attached to a tube held in the mouth).[16]

16. "Funneling" large amounts of alcohol, rarely, may also be accomplished by gay men who insert the funnel rectally (Pagliaro & Pagliaro, *Clinical Patient Data Files*). A somewhat related method of alcohol use came to our attention around 3 am on a Saturday morning when an older man was admitted to the emergency department (ED) with the broken off top of a long-neck beer bottle stuck in his anus. As he explained, he was playing a drinking game with some younger male friends to get each other drunk by inserting the uncapped bottles of beer into one-another's anus as they helped each other to stand on their head. Because of the jagged nature of the broken beer bottle, its proximity to the rectal vein, and lack of expert surgical services at the country hospital at that time in the early morning—the man was made comfortable, sedated, and, as soon as it was possible, transported by ambulance with an ED nurse to the nearest medical center hospital, 50 miles away, for treatment. Visiting the ED a week later, he said he was a bit embarrassed, but "they did a good job getting the neck of the bottle out."

Distribution

Alcohol is a small molecule (see Figure 1.1) that is hydrophilic and is not protein-bound.[17] Thus, it easily crosses biological membranes. For example, alcohol crosses from the GI tract into the bloodstream and from the bloodstream across the BBB into the CNS (see Figure 1.2).

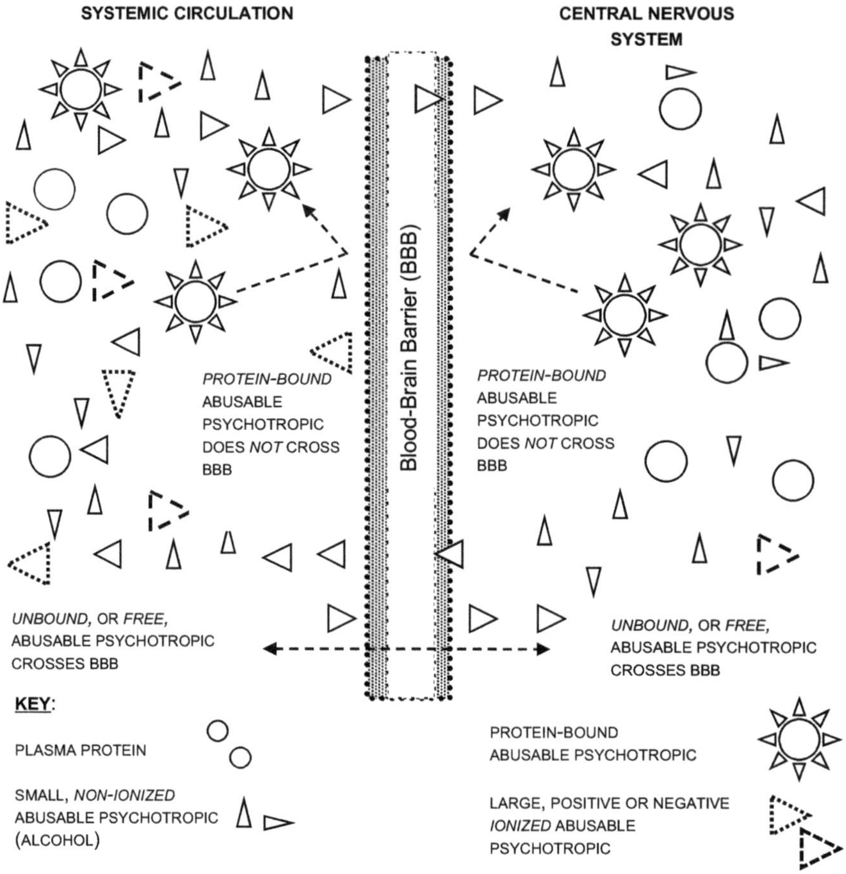

Figure 1.2 Abusable Psychotropic Transfer Across the Blood-Brain Barrier

Although highly soluble in water, alcohol is not well-distributed into fatty (i.e., adipose) tissues. Thus, the distribution of alcohol is generally different for older women when compared to older men.[18] As emphasized by Cederbaum (2012, p. 667), generally, for all body

17. Consequently, the decreased serum albumin concentrations for older adults do not affect the volume of distribution of alcohol (Gomi, Fukushima, & Shiraki, 2007; Pagliaro & Pagliaro, 1983; Weaving, Batstone, & Jones, 2016).
18. Because of sex hormone-related differences, women, on average, have higher levels of body fat than do men—even when factors, such as age, height, weight, and physical condition are controlled for.

tissues the equilibrium of alcohol within a tissue depends on the water content, rate of blood flow, and tissue mass.

Metabolism and Excretion

A relatively small amount of alcohol is metabolized in the stomach by alcohol dehydrogenase (ADH),[19] thus preventing or reducing its systemic absorption. The nature and extent of this effect is related to several factors, including the:

1. Length of time that the alcohol remains in the stomach, which itself depends on several factors including the presence of food (see the previous subsection, "Absorption");
2. Activity of ADH, which is influenced by age and genetics.[20,21] (Cederbaum, 2012)

Approximately 90% to 95% of ingested alcohol undergoes hepatic metabolism at a constant rate (Pagliaro & Benet, 1975) (see Figure 1.3), which is mediated by ADH[22] and cytochrome P450 CYP2E1 (Chan & Anderson, 2014; Lieber, 1999).[23,24] The remaining 5% to 10% of ingested alcohol, which is not metabolized in the liver, is excreted in unchanged

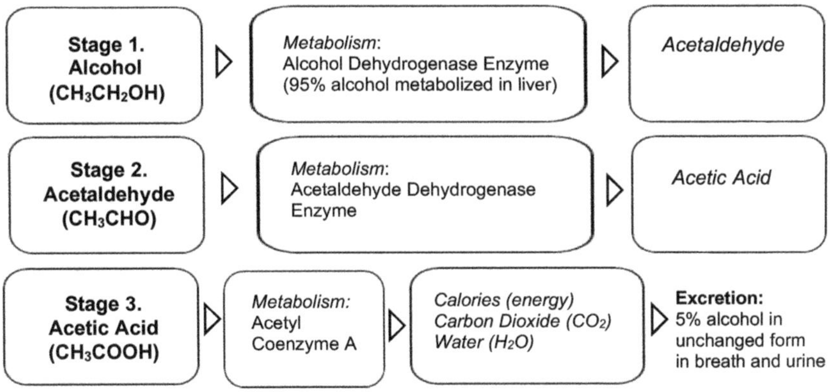

Figure 1.3 Alcohol Metabolism

19. Of the ten different variants (i.e., isoenzymes) of ADH, four (i.e., ADH3*1, ADH5, ADH6, and ADH7) are present and particularly active in the stomach (Zakhari, 2006).
20. N.B. ADH activity is lower among adults with alcohol dependence or use disorder, particularly older adults.
21. For example, Bosron and Li (1986) originally identified that the genetic polymorphism of the human alcohol dehydrogenase enzyme may contribute to an up to three-fold variation in alcohol elimination rates.
22. Six of the isoenzymes of ADH (i.e., ADH1, ADH2*1, ADH3*1, ADH4, ADH5, and ADH6) are present and particularly active in the liver (Zakhari, 2006).
23. CYP2E1 is also primarily responsible for the hepatic metabolism of fatty acids and xenobiotics (Chan & Anderson, 2014).
24. The activity of the enzymes responsible for alcohol metabolism (i.e., alcohol dehydrogenase, acetaldehyde dehydrogenase, and cytochrome P450 CYP2E1) decreases among older adults, particularly those of advanced age, and, consequently, may significantly reduce their capacity to metabolize alcohol, resulting in apparently more severe intoxication among these individuals with the ingestion of lower amounts of alcohol (Meier & Seitz, 2008).

form in the breath,[25] sweat, and urine. The energy released per gram of alcohol is approximately 7 kilocalories (kcal). However, because alcohol has no nutritional value (e.g., vitamins and minerals) and is not "stored" in the body for later needed energy, it is considered to only provide "empty" calories when metabolized.

The rate of alcohol metabolism is linear with time and is minimally affected by variations in blood concentration.[26] For the average 21-year-old, 70 kg male of European continental descent (i.e., the subjects of the initial studies of alcohol metabolism), the rate of metabolism is approximately 10 to 20 ml of 100% alcohol per hour. Thus, it takes approximately one hour to metabolize a "typical drink" (i.e., approximately 30 ml of whiskey or another distilled spirit; 150 ml of wine; or 360 ml of beer).[27] If a larger amount of alcohol is ingested per hour than is capable of being metabolized, the BAC increases along with its corresponding psychodepressant actions, including desired and undesired, or harmful, effects and toxicities (see Table 1.2).

> Old Misbelief: An older adult, who is drunk, can quickly "sober up" by drinking several cups of strong coffee.

False. In fact, the process of "sobering up" is directly related to the half-life of elimination of alcohol (i.e., the equivalent number of drinks that is eliminated per hour). There are several factors (e.g., ingestion of fructose, or fruit sugar, and some vitamins) that may, theoretically, alter the rate of alcohol metabolism and, thus, increase its rate of elimination. However, none of these factors has demonstrated clinical significance when used in this context and, consequently, none have received United States Food and Drug Administration (FDA) approval.[28] Thus, even though it is commonly thought that drinking "strong" coffee, taking a cold shower, or walking around can increase the elimination of alcohol and, thus, "speed-up" the process of "sobering-up" after a heavy drinking episode—they do not.

It also is commonly thought that caffeine in coffee (or energy drinks) can counteract drunkenness or prolong the desired effects of alcohol. The only thing that these actions consistently accomplish is to change a drowsy drunk into a wide-awake drunk. Of course, the more time that is devoted to these activities, the more time passes in which alcohol can be slowly, but steadily, eliminated and, thus, make these ineffective activities sometimes appear to be effective.

Presently, in the U.S., there is no practical way to increase the rate of alcohol metabolism. Once alcohol is ingested, absorbed, and distributed throughout the body, its ultimate elimination from the body primarily depends on its slow and steady rate of metabolism by the liver. This process may be impaired among adolescents who have liver disease (e.g., cirrhosis of the liver) or genetic polymorphism of both alcohol dehydrogenase and

---

25. Thus, the physiological basis for the validity of the "alcohol breathalyzer test."
26. This form of metabolism is often referred to as "capacity limited," "dose-dependent," "zero order," or "Michaelis-Menten" kinetics (Holtzman, 1983; Pagliaro & Benet, 1975; Winek & Murphy, 1984).
27. N.B. See the caveat regarding the diminished alcohol metabolism in older adults (i.e., earlier footnote [# 23]).
28. Metadoxine (Metadoxil®), pyridoxine-pyrrolidone carboxylate, is an ion pair of pyridoxines (i.e., vitamin B_6 and pyrrolidone-2-carboxylate). It is used either orally or intravenously for cases of both acute and chronic alcohol intoxication in Europe. Metadoxine appears to work by several mechanisms of action, including increasing the enzymatic activity of acetaldehyde dehydrogenase. Consequently, the metabolism of alcohol and acetaldehyde are increased and the half-life of elimination of alcohol is decreased (Addolorato, Ancona, & Capristo, 2003; Diaz Martinez, Diaz Martinez, & Villamil Salcedo, 2002; Shpilenya, Muzychenko, & Gasbarrini, 2002; Vonghia, Leggio, & Ferrulli, 2008). Metadoxine has not received FDA approval.

Table 1.2 Acute, Chronic, and Acute/Chronic Toxicities Associated with Alcohol Use Among Older Adults

ACUTE TOXICITIES	CHRONIC TOXICITIES	ACUTE/CHRONIC TOXICITIES
Decreased social inhibitions	Alcohol dependence or use disorder	Absenteeism from work—sick days increase
Diminished eye movements	Alcohol withdrawal syndrome	Accidents (e.g., drownings; falls; MVCs)
Hallucinations	Anemia	Abusive and aggressive behavior—physical and psychological
Hangover	Cardiac dysrhythmias	Alcoholic "blackouts"
Homicide—perpetrator or victim	Cardiovascular disease	Alcoholic ketoacidosis
Hypokalemia	Contemporaneous diagnosis	Amnesia
Hypothermia	Decreased immune response	Cognitive dysfunction/impairment
Peripheral vasodilation, or "flush"	Diabetes mellitus	Coma
Psychomotor impairment	Hypertension	Criminal behavior
Psychosis	Hypertriglyceridemia	Gastritis
Respiratory depression	Malnutrition (e.g., thiamine deficiency)	Guilt—increased
Risk-taking behavior—increased	Neuropathy	Hypoglycemia
Sexual activity—increased	Peripheral neuropathy	Impaired relationships with adult children and other family members, co-workers, employers, or friends
Sexual dysfunction (men)	Physical dependence	Memory dysfunction—short- and long-term memories
Sexual inhibitions—decreased	Psychological dependence	Mental depression
Sexually transmitted diseases—increased		Neurotoxicity
Short-term memory impairment		Partner/spousal abuse—physical and psychological
Slurred speech		Self-neglect—increased
Vomiting		Social problems (e.g., absence from work or arguments with family members)—increased
		Suicide, attempted or completed—increased
		Victimization (e.g., physical assault or sexual assault)—increased
		Violent behavior (e.g., homicide, physical assault, and rape)—increased
		Work productivity—decreased

aldehyde dehydrogenase (i.e., enzymes involved in the hepatic metabolism of alcohol and in the occurrence of the "Asian Flush") (see Figure 1.3.). Genetic polymorphism also may account, in part, for the variations in alcohol metabolism and elimination rates observed among older adults of certain continental and other descents (e.g., Jewish versus American Indian or Alaska Native) (Pagliaro & Pagliaro, 1992a) (see also the earlier related discussion in this subsection).

Drug-Drug Interactions

When compared to any other age group, drug-drug interactions involving alcohol are most likely to occur among older adults. There are several reasons for this observation including:

1. 70% of older adults drink alcohol;
2. More than 90% of older adults use one or more medications, both prescription and non-prescription, on a regular basis.

As noted by Zanjani, Allen, and Schoenberg (2018, p. 261), "Almost 90% of adults aged 60 and over take at least one medication, and over 75% take two or more." Additionally, these interactions are more likely to result in adverse consequences (e.g., therapeutic failure; toxicity) because of the following conditions associated with aging, including age-related:

- Diminished reserve capacity;
- Decreased renal and hepatic functions;
- The increased incidence of serious chronic medical conditions (e.g., cardiac dysrhythmias, chronic kidney disease, congestive heart failure, chronic obstructive pulmonary disease [COPD], diabetes, and hypertension). (Pagliaro & Pagliaro, 1983; Pagliaro & Pagliaro, *Clinical Patient Data Files*)

In their review of the published literature regarding the potential risks for alcohol drug-drug interactions among older adults, Moore, Whiteman, and Ward (2007) found that, on average, approximately 25% of older adults are at risk for a significant alcohol-related drug interaction. Further, in this context, Qato, Manzoor, and Lee (2015, p. 2324), in their nationally-representative population-based study of 3,000 older adults, found that older adult men with multiple chronic conditions had the highest prevalence of potential drug-alcohol interactions.

Several clinically significant drug-drug interactions have been associated with the concurrent use of alcohol, involving, for example:

- Other psychodepressants (e.g., opiate analgesics, prescription sedative-hypnotics);
- Other drugs that may be associated with depression (e.g., opiate analgesics, prescription sedative-hypnotics);
- Psychostimulants (e.g., caffeine, nicotine);
- Alcohol abstinence maintenance drugs (e.g., disulfiram, Antabuse®; fomepizole, Antizol®).

These alcohol drug-drug interactions are presented and briefly discussed, in alphabetical order, in the following subsections.

Alcohol and Antihypertensives

The orthostatic hypotension associated with the use of antihypertensives (e.g., clonidine, furosemide, methyldopa) in older adults can be exacerbated by alcohol consumption. Consequently, the risk for falls and associated harm (e.g., fractured hip) increases.

Alcohol and Caffeine

See the later drug-drug interactions subsection—"Alcohol and Psychostimulants."

Alcohol and Disulfiram

Disulfiram (Antabuse®) is an inhibitor of aldehyde dehydrogenase. Consequently, when used concurrently with alcohol, the metabolism of alcohol is blocked at the stage of acetaldehyde production (see earlier pharmacology subsection, pharmacokinetics—"Metabolism and Excretion"). The resultant accumulation of acetaldehyde causes the unpleasant signs and symptoms—including facial flushing, hypotension, nausea, tachycardia, and vomiting—collectively referred to as the "acetaldehyde syndrome" or "Antabuse® syndrome." The occurrence of this alcohol drug-drug interaction is therapeutically used for the management of alcohol abstinence maintenance (see the related discussion in the later subsection, Alcohol Abstinence Maintenance—"Disulfiram [Antabuse®] Pharmacotherapy").

Alcohol and Fomepizole

Fomepizole (Antizol®) is a potent inhibitor of the enzyme alcohol dehydrogenase. It is therapeutically used for the treatment of ethylene glycol and methanol poisonings (see the related discussion in the later subsection, "Alcohol Overdosage/Unintentional Poisoning"). Fomepizole, because of its mechanism of action, can significantly increase the half-life of elimination of alcohol (Kraut & Mullins, 2018). (See also the related discussion in the earlier pharmacology subsection, Pharmacokinetics—"Metabolism.")

Alcohol and Metformin

Heavy alcohol consumption may increase the risk of metformin (Glucophage®)-induced lactic acidosis, particularly among older adults with chronic kidney disease. It may also increase the incidence and severity of metformin-related GI distress (e.g., diarrhea, dyspepsia). Additionally, the ingestion of alcohol can cause hypoglycemia, particularly when in a fasting state that is exacerbated by metformin.

Alcohol and Metronidazole

The concurrent use of alcohol and metronidazole (Flagyl®) may result in a disulfiram-like reaction. See also the earlier alcohol drug-drug interaction subsection—"Alcohol and Disulfiram."

Alcohol and Nicotine

Alcohol and nicotine are often used together, and each can influence the use of the other. Contemporaneous diagnoses of an AUD and nicotine use disorder (NUD) reinforces the operant, or cue mediated, use of both alcohol and nicotine. Although, not completely understood, the mechanism of these interactions appears to involve both "the stress hormone systems" and "adaptations" within the mesolimbic dopamine system (Little, Barron, & Prendergast, 2007; Ostroumov, Thomas, & Dani, 2015; Verplaetse & McKee, 2017). In summary:

- Concurrent alcohol and nicotine use (i.e., e-cigarette vaping; tobacco smoking, or other nicotine use—chewing nicotine gum or using other nicotine replacement products):
    - Increases nicotine craving between nicotine use sessions;
    - Decreases the time between nicotine use sessions;
    - Increases the amount of nicotine vaped, tobacco smoked, or otherwise used per use session.
- Concurrent nicotine and alcohol use (i.e., drinking beers, liqueurs, whiskey, wines, and other alcoholic beverages):
    - Increases craving for alcohol;
    - Decreases the subjective effects associated with alcohol use;
    - Increases the overall amount of alcohol ingested per drinking session.

(See also the later drug-drug interactions subsection—"Alcohol and Psychostimulants.")

Alcohol and Other Psychodepressants

The concurrent use of alcohol and other psychodepressants (e.g., opiate analgesics, prescription sedative-hypnotics, and volatile solvents and inhalants) results in additive effects. These additive effects can significantly increase both the incidence and severity of the undesired, or harmful, effects and toxicities associated with alcohol use, including risk for falls, respiratory depression, and death. (See the related discussion in Chapter 5, *Prescription Opiate Analgesics and Heroin*, and Chapter 6, *Prescription Sedative-Hypnotics*.)

Alcohol and Psychostimulants

The concurrent use of alcohol and psychostimulants (e.g., amphetamines, caffeine, and cocaine) may reduce or ameliorate, respectively, the contributory psychodepressant and psychostimulant actions of both alcohol and the psychostimulant. However, in most of these cases, researchers have found only negligible results, while others have found mixed results. For example, Barkla, McArdle, and Newbury-Birch (2015) found—regarding the use of psychostimulant drugs used for the management of attention deficit hyperactivity disorder (ADHD) (e.g., methylphenidate [Ritalin®]) and alcohol—"only a minimal increase in side-effects when ADHD medication (therapeutic doses) was taken with alcohol" (p. 270). Similarly, regarding psychostimulants and alcohol, McKetin, Coen, and Kaye (2015) found, "insufficient evidence" to conclude that mixing caffeinated energy drinks with alcohol, "led to increased alcohol consumption or altered the nature of alcohol-related harm." (See also the earlier drug-drug interactions subsection—"Alcohol and Nicotine.")

Alcohol and Warfarin

Warfarin (Coumadin®) metabolism is impeded by heavy, episodic alcohol consumption. Consequently, the risk of major bleeds/hemorrhage increases, particularly in association with injuries commonly sustained by older adults, including falls. (See, for example, the earlier drug-drug interactions subsection—"Alcohol and Antihypertensives.")

> ***Related Professional Reminder:*** ***The clinical significance of drug-drug interactions involving the abusable psychotropics depends on several factors including the:***
>
> 1. ***"Drug"—the drug or substance of abuse that is used, including dosage/ amount and method of use;***
> 2. ***"Set"—personality characteristics and general mental and physical health of the user;***
> 3. ***"Setting"—the context of use.***[29]

Undesired, or Harmful, Effects and Toxicities

> A medical colleague referred a 67-year-old woman to me with mild depression, weakness, and complaints of short-term memory loss. Her physician told her there was no clear medical explanation for her symptoms, given that her physical exam, exhaustive lab tests and brain M.R.I. were all normal. . . . The problem, I soon discovered, was that her alcohol consumption had tripled since the death of her husband a year earlier. She did disclose to her internist that she drank but minimized the amount. She turned to alcohol, self-medicating her grief, but it only worsened her mood and impaired her memory, typical of alcohol's effects on the brain.
>
> (Friedman, 2013, p. 1)

Toward the end of the second decade of the new millennium, Delker, Brown, and Hasin—based on their epidemiologic overview of alcohol consumption in the U.S.—concluded that:

> In the United States, AUD accounts for a high and potentially preventable proportion of overall disability and mortality.
>
> (2016, p. 13)

Additionally, as reported in the Global Burden of Disease (GBD) study:

> Alcohol use is a leading risk factor for death and disability . . . [and concluded] our results show that the safest level of drinking is none.
>
> (GBD, 2018, pp. 1, 12)

> People aged 45–74 had the highest rates of death [in the U.S.] related to alcohol.
>
> (NIAAA, 2020a, p. 1)

29. See Zinberg (1986) for the original related discussion of "drug," "set," and "setting."

Effects of Alcohol on Body Systems

With its desired psychotropic actions (e.g., disinhibition euphoria), and certain other positive qualities (e.g., legal availability; pleasant color, taste, and bouquet; satisfying thirst), it is surprising to some—and often overlooked by many others—that alcohol use is associated with more harm than all of the other drugs or substances of abuse combined (Pagliaro & Pagliaro, 2009). Consequently, alcohol consumption has been consistently cited as the third leading cause of death in the U.S. (CDC, 2004, 2012a; NIAAA, 2020b). In addition to direct physical effects, these deaths are mediated by alcohol-related accidents (e.g., motor vehicle crashes [MVCs]), HIV infection, and suicides. See also the related discussion in the later pharmacology subsection, Undesired, or Harmful, Effects and Toxicities, subsections—"Mental Depression and Suicide," "Risky Drinking and Driving," and "Sexual Assault."

The general effects of alcohol on many body functions often are not recognized, including its effects on body temperature, executive processes, respiratory function, sexual behavior, sleep, and urination—all of which are directly affected by BAC (see also the earlier related discussion in the pharmacology subsection, Mechanism of Action and Blood Alcohol Concentrations—"Blood Alcohol Concentrations").

Regarding "body temperature," alcohol ingestion generally causes peripheral vasodilation—along with a characteristic warm "flush"—and a decrease in body temperature.

> Old Misbelief: When older adults come inside from the winter cold, a "little sip" of brandy or whiskey can warm them up right away!

False. In fact, unfortunately, they will only get a warm feeling in their stomachs. The vasodilation associated with alcohol ingestion, particularly that of blood vessels located near the skin surface, cools the body down in a manner similar to the automotive radiator cooling coils that cool an engine down. Thus, coming in from the cold and taking a drink of alcohol to "warm up" is a fallacy.

Regarding "executive processes," Bickel, Moody, and Mueller (2013, p. 1) noted "significant executive dysfunction" among alcohol-dependent subjects. The decrease in executive functioning contributes to many adverse consequences, including domestic violence (Kaysen, Dillworth, & Simpson, 2007; Pagliaro & Pagliaro, 2018; Stuart et al., 2004; WHO, 2006).[30]

Regarding "respiratory function," moderate amounts of alcohol may stimulate or depress respiratory function.[31] In addition, the ingestion of large amounts of alcohol (e.g., BAC = 0.4 gram %, or higher), can be fatal due to associated severe respiratory depression and negative cardiac effects.

---

30. N.B. However, it should be noted, and we would like to emphasize—based on our clinical experience—that alcohol use alone (i.e., in the absence of contributing personality and situational factors) does not appear to significantly increase domestic violence.
31. However, health and social care professionals should be cognizant of the fact that both the: (1) "protective" effect of carbon dioxide on breathing—the increase in ventilation induced by the decreased availability of oxygen supply to the body tissues (i.e., hypoxic ventilatory response/drive); and (2) increase in ventilation induced by the increased levels of carbon dioxide in the blood (i.e., hypercapnic ventilator response/drive), are always depressed by alcohol intoxication (Roeggla, Roeggla, & Roeggla, 1995; Sahn, Lakshminarayan, & Pierson, 1975; White, Lindsey, & Vincente, 1981).

Regarding "sleep," the ingestion of alcohol slows the electroencephalogram (EEG) activity toward slow-wave sleep, depresses rapid eye movement (REM) sleep, and inhibits dreaming. The sleep induced by drinking alcohol is not always restful and peaceful—one reason, among others, why alcohol is not medically recommended as a sedative-hypnotic, even though it reduces sleep onset latency. In fact, large amounts of alcohol ingested at bed-time, as well as patterns of regular, long-term alcohol use that continue throughout the day, and that are characterized by finally "falling down drunk," have been associated with several sleep-related problems including:

- Lower slow-wave sleep;
- Poor quality of sleep, particularly later in the night;
- Reduced REM sleep, particularly later in the first part of sleep;
- Sleep apnea;
- Urinary incontinence.

In addition, alcohol withdrawal is associated with: (1) decreased total sleep time; (2) problems falling asleep; and (3) REM rebound (Brower, 2001; Coltrain, Nicholas, & Baker, 2014; Ebrahim, Shapiro, & Williams, 2013).

Finally, regarding "urination," the use of alcohol exerts a diuretic effect by two principal mechanisms:

1. "Directly" by its suppressant action on the production and secretion of the antidiuretic hormone by the hypothalamus and pituitary gland, respectively, which increases the reabsorption of water in the distal convoluted tubules of the kidneys;
2. "Indirectly" by the large quantity of liquid ordinarily ingested as alcoholic beverages, particularly beer.

Although, these actions and effects may result in urinary incontinence, alcohol does not appear to directly cause permanent harm to the physical structure or physiological function of the kidneys.[32]

---

32. The urinary incontinence that is often associated with heavy drinking episodes occurs primarily as a direct result of the psychodepressant actions of alcohol (i.e., drinkers fall into a deep sleep, or "pass out," and losing urinary bladder control, experience urinary incontinence—hence, the basis for the derivation of the associated drinking phrase, "getting pissed") (Pagliaro & Pagliaro, *Clinical Patient Data Files*). These alcohol-related effects are most often noted among older drinkers who are living "on the street" (i.e., homeless) (Pagliaro & Pagliaro, *Clinical Patient Data Files*).

A related vignette, which we observed in our clinical practice when visiting a rural treatment facility, involved an older man with alcoholism, who was homeless and staying at a group facility for recovering alcoholic men. The previous evening, he "slipped out" to visit a local bar in the small town located near the facility. Returning in the early morning hours, he was found near the administration building by one of the attendants, face down and frozen to the walkway, where he had apparently passed out and subsequently urinated himself as he slept. Fortunately, after he was freed from his overalls, which were frozen to the walkway and had to be cut off, he was reoriented to where he was and "warmed up"—without any severe related sequelae.

Additionally, as shared by one of our patients, an older man who, for over 10 years, lived "as a drunk" on "skid row" in the downtown area of a major city:

> When I went on a bender—usually on a cash payday for casual labor—I would sleep in the bathtub of the motel room until I pissed myself and woke-up. Even in inner city hotels for transients they kick you out for peeing the mattress!
>
> (Pagliaro & Pagliaro, *Clinical Patient Data Files*)

As identified in Table 1.2, there are many undesired, or harmful, effects and toxicities—both acute and chronic—that are "directly" and "indirectly" associated with alcohol use by older adults. According to the National Institutes of Health (NIH):

> 28% of adults, aged 18 and older consume alcohol at levels that put them at risk for developing alcoholism, liver disease, and other medical and psychosocial problems.
>
> (Costin & Miles, 2014, p. 157)[33]

Numerous non-exclusive molecular mechanisms have been suggested by various researchers (e.g., Bao & Shi, 2010; Cederbaum, 2012; Most, Ferguson, & Harris, 2014; Rusyn & Bataller, 2013; Seitz & Stickel, 2007; Zakhari, 2006) as possible explanations for these alcohol-related undesired, or harmful, effects and toxicities that occur—during both intoxication and withdrawal. These mechanisms include:

- Acetaldehyde formation;
- Adduct formation (both stable and unstable);
- Alcohol-responsive transcription factor activation (e.g., the transcription factor cyclic AMP response element-binding protein [CREB]);
- AMPA/kainate receptor inhibition;
- Apoptosis (induced cell death);
- Brain-derived neurotrophic factor (Bdnf) mRNA levels increased;
- Cytokine formation;
- DNA damage (e.g., alteration of methylation and impairment of DNA repair);
- Dopamine reward pathways activation with acute alcohol use;
- Epigenetic alterations;
- Equilibrative nucleoside transporter 1 (ENT1) inhibition;
- Fatty acid ethyl esters (FAEEs) formation;
- $GABA_B$ receptor splicing effects;
- Glutamate receptor upregulation;
- Glutathione (GSH) depletion;
- G protein-coupled receptor interaction;
- Hypodopaminergic state with chronic alcohol use;
- Hypoxia (i.e., oxygen deficits in the liver);
- Immune actions;
- Inhibitory $GABA_A$ signaling activation;
- Kupffer cell activation;
- Ligand-gated chloride ion channel interaction;
- Membrane disruption;
- MicroRNA expression changes;

33. N.B. In a large study involving almost 600,000 adult current drinkers (without previous cardiovascular disease) from 19 high-income countries, Wood, Kaptoge, and Butterworth (2018) found that minimum all-cause mortality risk was associated with the consumption of 100 grams, or less, of alcohol (i.e., approximately seven standard drinks) per week.

- Mitochondrial damage;
- Molecular neuroadaptations;
- NAD/NADH ratio redox state changes;
- Neuroimmune system activation;
- NMDA receptor function inhibition;
- Oxidative stress;
- Phosphodiesterase (PDE) inhibition;
- Phospholipid phosphatidyl ethanol formation;
- Protein kinase A (PKA) activation;
- Reactive molecule (e.g., acetaldehyde) production;
- Reactive oxygen species (ROS) (e.g., acetaldehyde) formation;
- Synaptic neuroadaptation (e.g., decreased dopamine concentrations, reduced number of D_2 receptors, reduced GABA activity, and reduced serotonergic activity).

In the following subsections, nine particularly serious harmful effects and toxicities, which are commonly associated with alcohol use by older adults, are presented and discussed in alphabetical order:

1. Alcohol-Related Cancers;
2. Alcohol-Related Cardiovascular Disease;
3. Alcohol-Related Dementia;
4. Alcohol-Related Liver Disease (i.e., cirrhosis of the liver);
5. Alcohol-Related Mental Depression and Suicide;
6. Alcohol-Related Osteoporosis;
7. Alcohol-Related Physical and Psychological Dependence;[34]
8. Alcohol-Related Risky Drinking and Driving;
9. Alcohol-Related Sexual Assault, Acquaintance/Date-Rape, and Intimate Partner Violence.

Alcohol-Related Cancers

Alcohol use is directly associated with increased risk for several types of cancers, particularly:

- Breast cancer (in women);
- Colorectal cancer;
- Esophageal cancer;
- Gastric cancer;
- Laryngeal cancer;
- Liver cancer;
- Oral cavity cancer;

34. This topic is discussed in the later section—"Physical and Psychological Dependence."

- Pancreatic cancer;
- Pharyngeal cancer.

(Jiao, Silverman, & Schairer, 2009; LoConte, Brewster, & Kaur, 2018; Ma, Baloch, & He, 2017; Matejcic, Gunter, & Ferrari, 2017; NCI, 2018; Seitz & Stickel, 2007; Tanaka, Yamamoto, & Suzuki, 2010; Zhang & Zhong, 2015)

Of concern and relevance, approximately 70% of all new cases of cancer in the U.S. are diagnosed among older adults, 60 years of age or older (White, Holman, & Goodman, 2019). Additionally, it has been noted that tobacco smoking, which is commonly associated with alcohol use (see Chapter 3, *Caffeine and Nicotine*), significantly increases the risk for developing cancer, particularly cancers of the esophagus, larynx, lung, oral cavity, pancreas, and pharynx (e.g., NCI, 2018).

Breast Cancer The mechanisms involved in the development of cancer may differ from one form of cancer to another. Among women, for example, the ingestion of two or three alcoholic drinks daily increases their estrogen blood concentration, and consequently, also increases their risk for breast cancer by 20% (Hamajima, Hirose, & Tajima, 2002). Other researchers (e.g., Allen, Beral, & Casabonne, 2009) found that for every alcoholic drink consumed per day by women in developed countries, the incidence of breast cancer (for women up to 75 years of age) increased by approximately 11 per 1,000, or 1%. More recently, from a comprehensive review of the effects of alcohol ingestion on the development and incidence of breast cancer among women, Freudenheim (2020, p. 9) concluded that:

> Given the strength of the evidence linking alcohol to breast cancer, increasing awareness of risk is critical. It is time for a clear public health message identifying the role of alcohol in breast carcinogenesis and indicating that there is no apparent lower threshold of effect. Consumption levels of less than one drink per day are associated with increased risk. Further, drinking alcohol affects risk at all phases of life, including early and late life. The science is consistent and clear, but awareness is low. It is time for a focus on developing public understanding of alcohol, which is a very common exposure, and its connection with increased risk of breast cancer.

Colorectal Cancer For colorectal cancer (CRC), the underlying mechanisms and contributions associated with alcohol consumption are much more varied and complex. As identified by Rossi, Anwar, and Usman (2018, p. 44):

> Alcohol's consumption and metabolism can have multiple molecular consequences that can instigate colon carcinogenesis. Its oxidative and non-oxidative metabolism, and formation of byproducts, such as ROS [reactive oxygen species] and metabolites, can lead to a constellation of genetic, epigenetic, cell signaling, and immune processes. Interaction of these various mechanisms can affect cancer characteristics like proliferation, angiogenesis, stemness, EMT [epithelial to mesenchymal transition] oncogenic expression, and altered immunity.

Ovarian Cancer Kunzmann, Coleman, and Huang (2018), in their analysis of data from the *Ovarian (PCLO) Cancer Screening Trial*, which involved 99,654 participants, 55 to 74 years of age, found that "positive linear associations were observed between lifetime alcohol consumption and cancer-related mortality and total cancer incidence" (p. e1002585). However, overall, the results of various studies and literature reviews (e.g., Chang, Canchola, &

Lee, 2007; Yan-Hong, Jing, & Hong, 2015; Zhu, Jiang, & Niu, 2020), which have evaluated the relationship between alcohol consumption and ovarian cancer, have, to date, yielded negative or inconsistent mixed results.

Alcohol-Related Cardiovascular Disease

Available published data regarding the effects of alcohol on cardiovascular health are conflicting and inconsistent. Age (e.g., 50 years of age versus 65 years of age or older), amount ingested, gender, genetics, length and pattern of use, race, and type of alcoholic beverage consumed (e.g., beer versus red wine)—as well as the potential cofactors of obesity and tobacco smoking—have produced significantly different results in a myriad of studies. However, overall, it appears that heavy drinking or abusive or compulsive alcohol use is significantly associated with:

- Atrial fibrillation;[35]
- Nonischemic dilated cardiomyopathy;
- Reversible hypertension, particularly among older adults;
- Stroke, both hemorrhagic and ischemic.

(O'Keefe, Bhatti, & Bajwa, 2014; Rehm & Roerecke, 2017; Roerecke & Rehm, 2014; Wakabayahi & Araki, 2010)

The long and often reported potential benefits of low to moderate alcohol use on cardiovascular function are based on the varying results of several epidemiological studies. Consequently, as quantified by Piano (2017, p. e-16):

> Because there are no randomized controlled trials [associated with the beneficial effects of alcohol consumption in humans], health care professionals should not recommend alcohol consumption as a primary or secondary lifestyle intervention.

We strongly and unreservedly agree with this observation and recommendation.

Alcohol-Related Dementia

Alcohol-related dementia (ARD) is generally believed to be a direct consequence of the neurotoxicity that is clearly associated with alcohol use (e.g., Costin & Miles, 2014; Gupta & Warner, 2008; Newman, 2018). As such, ARD is clinically distinct from other dementias, diseases, or syndromes, including: (1) Alzheimer's Disease; (2) vascular dementia; and (3) Wernicke-Korsakoff's Syndrome, which is caused by a deficiency of vitamin B1

---

35. Regarding the relationship between alcohol use and atrial fibrillation, several interesting research findings have been reported over the past decade:

    1. Alcohol abstinence is beneficial for preventing the recurrence of atrial fibrillation;
    2. Moderate, weekly alcohol use (e.g., one or two drinks daily for five or more days per week) is a significant risk factor for new-onset atrial fibrillation;
    3. Excessive alcohol use (e.g., binge drinking) is a significant risk factor for atrial fibrillation.

    (Kim, Han, & Choi, 2019; Larsson, Drca, & Wolk, 2014; Paddock, 2019) (i.e., thiamine) associated with decreased intestinal absorption and reduced consumption that is prevalent among long-term "alcoholics," particularly those who are homeless and living on the streets. This thiamine deficiency is caused by both decreased intestinal absorption and reduced consumption that is prevalent among long-term "alcoholics," particularly those who are living on the streets.[36]

ARD has been widely associated with the loss of brain tissue, which is observed among older adults who are chronic alcoholics, particularly in relation to a reduction in white matter in the frontal cortex (e.g., Zahr & Pfefferbaum, 2017). As noted by Yarnell, Li, and MacGrory (2020, p. 226):

> At the time of autopsy, 78% of individuals diagnosed with alcoholism have evidence of brain pathology.

Mechanistically, on a molecular level, it has been suggested that:

> Chronic alcoholism inhibits N-methyl-D-aspartate (NMDA) causing upregulation of the NMDA subtype of glutamate receptors in the frontal cortex, probably reflecting alcohol-induced chronic neurotoxicity with increased intracellular calcium (mediating oxidative stress) along with loss of cholinergic muscarinic receptors. This may be related to the clinical symptoms of alcohol withdrawal and altered seizure activity in the brain.
>
> (Gupta & Warner, 2008, p. 351)

However, some researchers (e.g., Moriyama, Mimura, & Kato, 2006; Ridley, Draper, & Withall, 2013) question the identification of ARD as a distinct condition arguing that the: (1) lack of definitive diagnostic criteria; and (2) possibility of repeated subclinical episodes of the Wernicke-Korsakoff Syndrome, may actually account for ARD. We tend to concur. That is to say that, although ARD appears to occur among older adults who are alcoholics, alcohol use is better characterized as a contributory factor (i.e., it may exacerbate Alzheimer's Disease and other dementias—making related signs and symptoms more readily identifiable and problematic), but it is not a sole, direct cause of what is commonly called "ARD" (Pagliaro & Pagliaro, 1983; Pagliaro & Pagliaro, *Clinical Patient Data Files*). For example, Kivimaki, Singh-Manous, and Batty (2020, p. e2016084), in a multi-country cohort study designed to determine the relationship between alcohol consumption and risk of future dementia among adults, concluded that:

> The findings of this study suggest that alcohol-induced loss of consciousness, irrespective of overall alcohol consumption, is associated with a subsequent increase in the risk of [all

---

36. In a related context, over 30 years ago we were invited to address, "Drug Therapy in the Elderly: Interaction of Diet and Nutrition," at a holistic gerontology conference held at a large psychiatric hospital (Pagliaro & Pagliaro, *Clinical Patient Data Files*). Over our luncheon break, we were presented with a case involving one of their recently admitted patients. This older man was described as a loving grandfather who had lived with his daughter's family including her husband and two young daughters. He had lived with them for five years since the death of his wife. Quite suddenly, over a short period of time, he started to make inappropriate sexual remarks about his young granddaughters. Appropriately concerned, the parents requested an evaluation of his mental status.

    In summary, he was diagnosed with dementia and admitted to the psychiatric hospital for custodial care and treatment. We were also informed that his history was fairly unremarkable but did include congestive heart failure, diabetes, and a long history of alcohol abuse. In response, we suggested that a thiamine (vitamin B_1) deficiency test be performed. The results indicated extremely low B_1 levels. We were later informed that, after two weeks of twice daily 100 mg thiamine injections (as per our recommendation), both his B_1 levels and mental status had returned to normal. He was subsequently continued on daily oral thiamine, discharged after a few weeks, and returned to live with his family.

> forms of] dementia [i.e., Alzheimer's disease; atherosclerotic-related dementia; early-onset dementia; late-onset dementia].

Alcohol-Related Liver Disease

Alcohol consumption is one of the leading causes of chronic liver disease in the U.S. (Anantharaju & Van Thiel, 2004). Alcoholic liver disease (ALD) occurs in three, often overlapping stages:

1. Fatty liver disease (i.e., steatosis);
2. Alcoholic hepatitis;
3. Fibrosis/cirrhosis.

(Allampati & Mullen, 2016; Gutierrez Garcia, Blasco-Algora, & Fernandez-Rodriguez, 2015; Mann, Smart, & Govoni, 2003; Osna, Donohue, & Kharbanda, 2017)

Effective intervention for advanced alcohol-induced liver disease is limited. Abstinence remains the most important therapeutic intervention. Hospitalizations for ALD in the U.S. occur significantly more often for men than for women (Shirazi, Singal, & Wong, 2021). Liver transplantation is considered in severe cases.

Among older adults who have developed ALD, a linear correlation generally exists between the amount and duration of alcohol use and the development and extent of the disease. Additionally, both genetics and the environment play major roles in the development of ALD, but the exact nature of these roles has not yet been clearly established (Anstee, Daly, & Day, 2015). However, as identified by Maddur and Shah (2020, p. 1):

> Certain populations, including those with genetic predispositions (e.g., presence of the *PNPLA3* genotype), are more susceptible to end-stage effects of alcohol-related liver injury.

Additionally, their review of alcohol-related liver disease concluded that:

> It is quite evident from currently available literature that women, compared to men, have an increased risk of end-stage liver disease from alcohol use.
>
> (p. 6)

In their comprehensive review and analysis of U.S. mortality data from the National Center for Health Statistics over the first two decades of the new millennium, White, Castle, and Hingson (2020) found that 30% of alcohol-related deaths were from liver disease.

Alcohol-Related Mental Depression and Suicide[37]

Alcohol use, both acute and chronic, can cause, or exacerbate, mental depression (Pagliaro & Pagliaro, 1999, 2009).[38] It has been commonly noted that DSM-5 diagnoses of AUD and

37. See also the related discussion in the later subsection—"Alcohol Overdosage/Unintentional Poisoning."
38. N.B. Genetics appears to play a major mediating role in this relationship—which, can be cyclical in nature—with depression leading to alcohol dependence and alcohol dependence leading to depression (Pagliaro & Pagliaro, *Clinical Patient Data Files*).

major depressive disorder (MDD) frequently occur contemporaneously among regular, long-term drinkers (e.g., Pagliaro & Pagliaro, 2018; Sher, Stanley, & Harkavy-Friedman, 2008). This combination of disorders has long been highly correlated with the risk for suicide attempts and completions (Pagliaro & Pagliaro, 1990). As noted by Bailey, Patel, and Avenido (2011, p. 614), "Individuals with severe clinical depression and alcohol use disorder are at high risk [for suicide] if untreated."

For example, Agrawal, Tillman, and Grucza (2017), in their analysis of data from the prospective cohort study, the *Collaborative Study of the Genetics of Alcoholism*, found that "suicide attempts are associated with increased likelihood of substance [alcohol] dependence" (p. 96). As we have observed in our own clinical practice, the relationship between alcohol dependence and mental depression appears to equally occur, on an individual basis, as either a precedent or consequence of alcohol use (Pagliaro & Pagliaro, *Clinical Patient Data Files*). In either case, abstaining from alcohol use is a precedent for further therapeutic interventions. Generally, a single day, to a couple of weeks, of abstinence from alcohol use can result in a significant improvement in alcohol-related depressive signs and symptoms. As explained by Conner and Bagge (2019), the suicidal behavior related to acute alcohol use is associated with dose-dependent lowering of inhibitions and promoting suicidal thought. Thus, even a brief period of abstinence may significantly reduce the risk of suicide.

In summary, as suggested by McHugh and Weiss (2019), the high rate of the co-occurrence of AUD and MDD presents in three, non-exclusive pathways:

1. AUD increases the risk for MDD;
2. MDD increases the risk for AUD;
3. Both AUD and MDD share pathophysiology or have common risk factors.

***Related Professional Reminder*: The co-occurrence of AUD and MDD is consistently associated with greater severity and poorer prognosis for both mental disorders.**

> There is sufficient evidence that AUD significantly increases the risk of suicidal ideation, suicide attempt, and completed suicide.
>
> (Darvishi, Farhadi, & Haghtalab, 2015, p. e0126870)

> AUD is the second most common identified mental disorder among suicide decedents worldwide (the most common is mood disorder).
>
> (Conner & Bagge, 2019, p. 1)

Suicide attempts[39] are typically five to ten times higher in association with acute alcohol dependence. In addition, as noted by several researchers (e.g., Pagliaro & Pagliaro, 1990; Pagliaro & Pagliaro, *Clinical Patient Data Files*), suicide associated with alcohol use is significantly affected by other variables, in addition to mental depression—particularly,

39. Suicide is generally thought of as involving an "acute" event (e.g., drug overdosage, gunshot wound, hanging, or poisoning). However, we have also conceptualized a "chronic" aspect of suicide that includes chronic, problematic abusable psychotropic use, particularly in the context of alcohol or opiate analgesic abusive or compulsive use (Pagliaro & Pagliaro, *Clinical Patient Data Files*). For example:

> [An] elderly family member who fell on difficult times. He'd lost his spouse, and soon after, had to put his dog down as well. . . . At age 82, he just decided to drink himself to death.
>
> (McGuinness, 2019, p. 1)

gender and racial/ethnic affiliation. For example, as identified by Chartier, Vaeth, and Caetano (2013, p. 231):

> Recent alcohol use was reported among suicides in 46 percent of Native Americans, 30 percent of Hispanics, 26 percent of Whites, 16 percent of Blacks, and 15 percent of Asians.

***Related Professional Reminder:* Suicide is the result of a complex interaction of biological, environmental, psychological, sociological, and spiritual factors. In fact:**

- ***Suicide is largely a uniquely individual behavior (i.e., the contributing factors associated with suicide, as well as their significance, may differ from one older adult to another);***
- ***Retrospective analysis allows the determination of significant correlations between suicide and several possible major contributing factors (e.g., pattern of alcohol use or length of mental depression);***
- ***Suicide cannot be predicted a priori with any significant degree of certainty (i.e., validity and reliability).***

Alcohol-Related Osteoporosis

A number of factors, in addition to excessive alcohol use or heavy drinking, contribute to the risk for developing osteoporosis, including: lack of physical activity, low calcium intake, postmenopausal status for women, small body/bone frame, and tobacco smoking. Alcohol use, itself, can contribute to osteoporosis by:

- Decreasing estrogen levels in older women;
- Decreasing testosterone levels in older men;
- Disrupting calcium balance;
- Increasing cortisol levels;
- Interfering with vitamin D production. (Kogawa & Wada, 2005; Luo, Liu, & Liu, 2017; Maurel, Boisseau & Benhamou, 2012; Pagliaro & Pagliaro, 2018; Sampson, 2002)

Additionally, the cognitive and psychomotor impairment associated with alcohol use, particularly among older adults who have osteoporosis, can contribute to falls resulting in hip and vertebral fractures (Kaukonen, Nurmi-Luthje, & Luthje, 2006). As emphasized by Yuan, Dawson, and Cooper (2001, p. 1089):

> Alcohol-related disease increases the risk of hip fractures significantly and reduces long-term survival.

Alcohol-Related Risky Drinking and Driving

> In 2016, there were almost 42 million licensed drivers ages 65 and older in the United States. Driving helps older adults stay mobile and independent. But the risk of being injured or killed in a motor vehicle crash [MVC] increases as people age.
>
> (CDC, 2017, p. 1)

Major factors that increase the risk of being injured or killed in MVCs, for older adults include:

- Cognitive impairment;
- Decreased vision;
- Diminished hearing;
- Psychomotor impairment;
- Slower reactions times.

Generally, these factors are the consequences of concurrent: (1) normal aging processes; (2) medical conditions; and (3) medical and/or nonmedical/recreational abusable psychotropic (e.g., alcohol) use.

Adult drivers in all 50 states are currently prohibited from operating a motor vehicle if their BAC is equal or greater than 0.08%. Several countries, including Austria, Denmark, and Japan, have lowered the BAC associated with impaired driving to 0.05% (e.g., Teutsch, Baldwin. & Degutis, 2018). The U.S. National Highway Traffic Safety Administration sponsored a study entitled, *Getting to Zero Alcohol-Impaired Driving Fatalities*, which was conducted by The National Academies of Sciences, Engineering, and Medicine. In January 2018, the committee released its formal report that included a recommendation to modify the BAC associated with impaired driving in all 50 states from 0.08% to 0.05% (AP, 2018; Teutsch et al., 2018).

One of the most significant examples of alcohol-related "preventable disability and mortality" among older adults involves drinking and operating, or being a passenger in, a motor vehicle—including all-terrain vehicles (ATVs), boats, cars, snow mobiles, and trucks (e.g., Li, Brady, & Chen, 2013; Pagliaro & Pagliaro, 2003, 2018).[40] As identified by Brady and Guohua (2013, p. 104)[41] in their review of data from the *Fatality Analysis Reporting System* for 2005–2009:

> Alcohol was the most commonly detected substance present in 40.2% of the fatally injured drivers [in the U.S.], followed by cannabinols (10.5%).

In this context, it should be noted that an even greater number, who do not die, are seriously injured (e.g., experience/suffer from brain damage, loss of a limb, or quadriplegia) in alcohol-related motor vehicle accidents each year in the U.S. Unfortunately, this number is increasing and is largely due to "distracted driving" (e.g., "texting" while driving). As noted by Wilson, Stimpson, and Tibbits (2013), "Alcohol use is quickly increasing as an important factor behind distracted driving fatality." Additionally, a strong association has been noted between binge drinking and alcohol-impaired driving (e.g., Flowers, Naimi, &

40. In addition, a significant number of injuries and death incurred by bicycle riders and pedestrians are associated with alcohol impairment (Harada, Gangi, & Ko, 2015).
41. Reportedly, the percentage of fatally injured drunk drivers in the U.S. decreases with increasing age. For example, the IIHS (2018), based on an analysis of data from the U.S. Department of Transportation, found that among drivers (with BACs greater than or equal to 0.08%), who were killed in a MVC: (1) 35% were 16 to 59 years of age; (2) 18% were 60 to 69 years of age; and (3) 8% were 70 years of age or older. In a similar analysis of fatal crashes involving drivers with a BAC greater than or equal to 0.08 g/dl, the NHTSA (2018) found that, for older adults: 15% were 55 to 64 years of age; 9% were 65 to 74 years of age; and 6% were 75 years of age or older.

Brewer, 2008; Naimi, Nelson & Brewer, 2009). (See the related discussion in the later subsection, "Binge Drinking.")

> ***Related Professional Reminder:** **All health and social care professionals should keep in mind that older adults, in general, are more susceptible to the CNS sedation and psychomotor impairment associated with the pharmacological actions of alcohol. Consequently, even at relatively low levels of alcohol consumption (i.e., one to two drinks), the risk for accidents, including falls and MVCs, significantly increases—particularly for older adults.***

Alcohol-Related Sexual Assault, Acquaintance/Date-Rape, and Intimate Partner Violence

Sexual performance generally decreases as a direct response to increases in alcohol ingestion.[42] However, of all the commonly used drugs and substances of abuse, alcohol is by far the one that is most often used for the perpetration of sexual assault, including acquaintance/ date rape (A/DR) and IPV (e.g., Anderson, Flynn, & Pilgrim, 2017; Madea & Musshoff, 2009; Slaughter, 2000).

> Conservative estimates of sexual assault prevalence suggests that 25 percent of American women have experienced sexual assault including rape. Approximately one-half of those cases involve alcohol consumption by the perpetrator, victim, or both.
>
> (Abbey, Zawacki, & Buck, 2001, p. 43)[43]

Acquaintance/Date Rape Acquaintance rape is the perpetration of rape by a person who is known to the victim (e.g., care giver, co-worker, employer, family member, friend, or neighbor). Although briefly discussed in the preceding subsection, date rape, as a form of acquaintance rape, generally involves some aspect of "romance."[44] Both are frequently alcohol-related

---

42. As noted by Shakespeare in his play, *Macbeth*:

    It ["much drink"] provokes the desire, but it takes away the performance.

    (Act 2, Scene 3, 1606)

43. Although published related data concerning older adults are extremely limited (e.g., Bows & Westmarland, 2017; Cook, Dinnen, & O'Donnell, 2011), our clinical experience would indicate that the statistics concerning older adults (overwhelmingly, women, but also including men) are very close to those reported for younger women in the U.S. However, in comparison, we have noted three differences between older adults and younger women:

    1. Suspicion, and related inquiry by health and social care workers regarding the rape of older adults, is much lower than that for younger adults and, consequently, it is often infrequently and inadequately formally addressed;
    2. Perpetrators are usually younger than their victims;
    3. Assaults usually occur within the victim's residence (e.g., own home, hospital setting, or nursing extended-care facility). (Pagliaro & Pagliaro, *Clinical Patient Data Files*)

44. Over the last decade, we have identified a significant increase in reported cases of sexual assault of older women in the context of an increasing use of dating/romance websites. These websites (e.g., "JDate," "Silver Singles, and "Senior Friend Finder") have specifically been designed for and directed (e.g., marketed in both Internet and television advertisements) toward "older adults." In the overwhelming number of cases that have been reported to us, women are the primary victims (Pagliaro &Pagliaro, *Clinical Patient Data Files*).

crimes that deserve additional specific attention by health and social care professionals. Alcohol, the original acquaintance/date rape drug, continues to be the most widely used drug for acquaintance/date rapes (see Chapter 6, *Prescription Sedative-Hypnotics*, for discussion of other drugs that are commonly used to facilitate acquaintance/date rape).

Alcohol use by either, or both, perpetrators and victims, plays a significant role in facilitating this criminal behavior. A serious concern of researchers over the last four decades (e.g., Pagliaro & Pagliaro, 2004, 2018), this abhorrent violence is neither rare nor restricted by population group, although statistics vary.

Alcohol use facilitates acquaintance/date rape through many of its direct psychodepressant actions, including:

- Decreasing social inhibitions;
- Impairing cognitive functioning, including judgment and risk assessment;
- Encouraging misinterpretation of friendly cues, both verbal and nonverbal, with "sexual invitations;"
- Reducing the ability to avoid, or ward-off, a potential or actual attack.

(Pagliaro & Pagliaro, 2004, 2018; Pagliaro & Pagliaro, *Clinical Patient Data Files*)

One of the many interesting forensic cases that we have consulted on, and which involves all of these factors, was that of an older Native American Indian woman, who was an alcoholic. She was picked-up by a truck driver while hitchhiking at night on a highway near her reservation. The pair shared some drinks from an open whiskey bottle inside the cab of the truck. Subsequently, the woman became alarmed that the truck driver was getting her drunk so that he could rape her and, even more concerning to her, that he might be the man who had raped and murdered several native women in that same general geographical location over the past year. After consuming all of the alcohol, the two began to fight. When the truck slowed down, she jumped out to "save her life." The truck driver stopped his vehicle completely, jumped out, and ran after her.[45] Subsequently, during our clinical interview, she shared with us:

> I thought I was dead. I thought I'm gonna be the next Indian woman killed by this maniac. Then, as I lay on the ground and looked up at the dark night sky, I knew I would be okay. I saw a bright light and giant bottle of Jack Daniel's[46] coming down from the sky in the bright light toward me and I knew I would be saved.
>
> (Pagliaro & Pagliaro, *Clinical Patient Data Files*)

While some older women are willing to report their related experiences, it should be noted that many—very likely most—of these victims choose not to report the incident of acquaintance/date rape for several reasons, including:

- Being embarrassed or ashamed over the incident;
- Being labeled as an acquaintance/date rape victim or other undesired label (i.e., fear of being stigmatized);

45. The previous data were included as part of the official police report.
46. During the clinical interview, "Jack Daniel's" was revealed to be her favorite alcoholic beverage.

- Concern that they will be unable to prove that the sexual act was nonconsensual;
- The incident did not match their "beliefs" regarding sexual assault (e.g., the perpetrator did not fit their stereotype of a rapist/sexual predator; physical violence, or threats, did not occur);
- Fear of job loss or the jeopardization of job promotion (e.g., if the perpetrator was their boss, co-worker, or superior at work);
- Fear of retaliation by the perpetrator;
- Fear of social isolation, or ostracism, from family and/or friends;
- Not wanting the perpetrator to be severely punished;
- Repression of the event (i.e., denial that it ever occurred);
- Self-blame for drinking and/or placing themselves in a risky situation;
- Suffering from associated post-traumatic stress disorder (PTSD);
- Unfamiliarity with details of the state laws concerning rape.

(Pagliaro & Pagliaro, *Clinical Patient Data Files*)

In these situations, older adult victims often resort to rationalization to deal with the sexual assault by labeling it as "bad sex," "miscommunication," or "a learning experience" (particularly, if they are just returning to "dating" after many years).

Intimate Partner Violence Intimate partner violence (IPV)—economic, emotional, physical, sexual, and/or verbal abuse—usually occurs in the home. IPV is most often perpetrated by a current or former spouse or partner, who is in an intimate relationship with the victim and has been highly correlated with alcohol and/or other abusable psychotropic use among older women—and their intimate partners (Afifi, Henriksen, & Asmundson, 2012; Pagliaro & Pagliaro, 2018) (also see related discussion in Chapter 2, *Amphetamines and Cocaine*). Acute alcohol intoxication, or a history of AUD and/or substance use disorders (SUDs), are strongly associated with IPV (Smith, Homish, & Leonard, 2012). As suggested in several studies (e.g., Devries, Child, & Bacchus, 2014), there is a distinct possibility of a bi-directional relationship involving these factors. For example, in some cases, older adults, who experience IPV, may use—in turn—alcohol to "self-medicate" (i.e., cope, or deal with) a traumatic experience associated with IPV.

PHYSICAL AND PSYCHOLOGICAL DEPENDENCE

Alcohol has a high abuse potential and is associated with the development of both physical and psychological dependence. Physical dependence is characterized by: (1) the development of tolerance; (2) the occurrence of an alcohol withdrawal syndrome when regular, long-term use of increasing amounts of alcohol is abruptly discontinued; and (3) immediate withdrawal relief with resumed alcohol use. Physical dependence, previously identified as the medical disease, "alcoholism," has been more recently identified in the DSM-5, by the American Psychiatric Association (APA, 2013), as the "alcohol use disorder" (i.e., AUD). Psychological dependence accompanies physical dependence and is associated with intense "craving"—longing, hunger, or thirst—for alcohol that contributes to the "loss of control" over its use.

Old Misbelief: The ability of older adults to "hold their liquor" indicates a developed "immunity," or resistance, to alcoholism, AUD, or physical and psychological dependence on alcohol.

False. In fact, the ability to "hold one's liquor," is an indication of acquired tolerance—a characteristic sign of physical dependence (i.e., AUD or "alcoholism").

The extent to which physical and psychological dependence develop—as well as associated physical, psychological, and social consequences—is directly related to the specific pattern and context of alcohol use. Infrequent use, or low to moderate "social use" of alcohol in small amounts—one or two drinks on holidays and special occasions, or less than 5 drinks a week for older adults is generally associated with few or no harmful effects.[47] However, for abusive and, ultimately, compulsive use, associated harmful effects and toxicities become increasingly more apparent and significantly more troublesome.[48]

Alcohol dependence or use disorder is inherently complex in nature. It typically occurs insidiously with the regular, long-term moderate to heavy drinking of alcohol over months to years and is characterized by the development of tolerance to alcohol (i.e., older adults find themselves drinking more frequently, and in larger amounts, in an attempt to achieve the desired effects that they initially achieved with infrequent, low to moderate drinking). Severe alcohol dependence, or use disorder, is also characterized by the need to drink alcohol throughout the day to prevent, or ward off, the signs and symptoms associated with decreasing BAC, and the resultant alcohol withdrawal syndrome.

Consequently, we have, for several decades, considered alcohol dependence or use disorder to be more accurately considered as a syndrome characterized by many specific related signs and symptoms, as well as varying levels of harm and/or associated risk. Most of these signs and symptoms are reflected in both the DSM-5 criteria for AUD and associated items/questions that have been constructed to detect older adult alcohol dependence (see also the related discussion in the later subsection, "Quick-Screen Psychometric Tests"). Typically, common signs and symptoms include:

- Alcoholic "blackouts"—being unable to account for specific periods of time when drinking;
- Concealing alcohol in a Thermos® or water bottle in order to drink at work or during a local BINGO game with friends;
- Displaying negative affect or personality changes;
- Drinking alone;
- Drinking in the morning or "starting the day" with a drink;[49]

47. Exceptions include, for example, older adults who are: (1) alcohol dependent, but who are now abstinent (i.e., have achieved a pattern of resumed nonuse); and (2) receiving disulfiram (Antabuse®) pharmacotherapy for alcohol abstinence maintenance (see the discussion in the later treatment subsection—"Pharmacotherapy"). Additionally, ingesting all five drinks, respectively, during the same drinking episode would be harmful "binge drinking" (see the related discussion in the later subsection—"Drinking Estimates and Trends in Binge Drinking").

48. Genetics has been estimated to contribute to approximately 50% of the risk for developing alcohol dependence or use disorder (AUD). Polymorphisms in isoforms of alcohol dehydrogenase and acetaldehyde dehydrogenase (see related discussion in the earlier pharmacology subsection, "Pharmacokinetics—Metabolism") have been implicated in this risk, but specific loci of responsible genes have not yet been identified (e.g., Costin & Miles, 2014).

49. This behavior is usually engaged in to deal with a hangover as a result of heavy drinking the preceding evening (see related discussion in the following subsection, "Alcohol Withdrawal Syndrome—Hangovers").

- Experiencing signs and symptoms of withdrawal due to decreasing BAC when alcohol use is "cut-down" or suddenly discontinued;[50]
- Feeling increasingly "guilty" about drinking behavior and/or associated effects;
- Gulping down drinks to rapidly increase BAC;
- Sneaking drinks;
- "Stashing" alcohol under a workbench in the garage, in a golf or knitting bag, or in another hiding place;
- Tolerance to alcohol—and, consequently, increasingly, drinking more alcohol, more frequently, to achieve initial desired effects.

> "When you try to hide your drinking from your grandchildren, you do whatever you can," said Ms. Dobrow, 81, a mother, grandmother and great-grandmother living in Stockton, Calif.
>
> (Ellin, 2014, p. 1)

Alcohol Tolerance

As previously noted, tolerance (i.e., acquired tolerance) is an essential component of the development of physical dependence. It is simply defined as a "diminished response to the actions of a drug"—particularly, alcohol or other drug or substance of abuse. Tolerance develops with the repeated, prolonged exposure to increasingly higher drug doses that are needed in an effort to achieve the initial intensity of the desired effects that were reached with lower doses. From both an evolutionary and physiological perspective, the development of tolerance can simply be interpreted as the body's response, or attempt, to maintain homeostasis in reaction to the effects of administered drugs.[51]

Several types of tolerance have been identified, including the following seven types: "acute tolerance," "behaviorally-augmented tolerance," "environment-dependent tolerance," "extrinsic tolerance," "functional tolerance," "intrinsic tolerance," and "metabolic tolerance."

1. ***Acute tolerance***. Acute tolerance refers to the observation that alcohol-induced impairment is greater when measured soon after beginning alcohol consumption in comparison to that measured later—at the same BAC. For example, when the BAC is rising in comparison to when it is declining;
2. ***Behaviorally-augmented tolerance***. Behaviorally-augmented (learned) tolerance refers to tolerance associated with performing a task (e.g., performing at a music concert or performing surgery while "under the influence" of alcohol);
3. ***Environment-dependent tolerance***. Environment-dependent tolerance refers to the accelerated tolerance (i.e., a form of Pavlovian conditioning) that occurs when alcohol is routinely ingested (in some cases, always) in the same environment that produces the same repeated cues that reinforce/support alcohol consumption—while watching

---

50. N.B. Consequently, health and social care professionals are cautioned to carefully monitor all older adults for signs and symptoms of alcohol withdrawal whenever they are admitted for any indication to a hospital or a long-term care facility (see the following subsection—"Alcohol Withdrawal Syndrome").
51. Over the new millennium, several researchers have utilized the term "allostasis" in lieu of the term "homeostasis." We consider the change to largely be a "distinction without a difference." Consequently, we continue to routinely use the original term, "homeostasis."

sports on TV from their living room at home while sitting in their favorite chair; at the local neighborhood pub with the same group of friends every Friday evening;

4. ***Extrinsic tolerance.*** Extrinsic tolerance refers to tolerance that results from alterations in compensatory neural circuits;
5. ***Functional tolerance.*** Functional tolerance refers to the ability to perform a psychomotor behavior (e.g., driving a car, playing a piano, or riding a bicycle) while at a specific BAC;
6. ***Intrinsic tolerance.*** Intrinsic tolerance refers to tolerance that results from changes within the neurons controlling a specific behavior/effect (i.e., molecular tolerance that occurs within the primary neural circuit);
7. ***Metabolic tolerance.*** Metabolic tolerance refers to the tolerance that is associated with an increased rate of alcohol metabolism/elimination (see the earlier related discussion in the pharmacology subsection, Pharmacokinetics—"Metabolism").

(NIAAA, 1995a; Pagliaro & Pagliaro, 1998, 2004; Pagliaro & Pagliaro, *Clinical Patient Data Files*; Pietrzykowski & Treistman, 2008)

Five non-exclusive molecular mechanisms of tolerance were identified by Pietrzykowski and Treistman (2008):

1. Epigenetic cytoplasmic mechanisms (e.g., microRNA regulation) of channel message stability;
2. Genetic factors;
3. Interactions with auxiliary proteins (e.g., regulatory subunits of channels);
4. Interactions with the lipid microenvironment;
5. Post-translational modifications of existing phosphorylated channels.

Alcohol Withdrawal Syndrome

> Depending on the amount of alcohol consumed and the duration of an individual's drinking habit, alcohol withdrawal syndrome can range from *minor* symptoms such as irritability, agitation, anxiety, headache, anorexia, diaphoresis, palpitations, insomnia, nausea and vomiting, and tremors; to *moderate* symptoms, including confusion and autonomic hyperactivity; to more *severe* symptoms, including muscle rigidity, seizures, and delirium tremens.
>
> (Costin & Miles, 2014, p. 8)

> Approximately 50% of patients with alcohol dependence experience alcohol withdrawal.[52]
>
> (Schmidt, Doshi, & Holzhausen, 2016, p. 389)

> The alcohol withdrawal syndrome is characterized by a period of "rebound hyperexcitability," which may be quite severe and, consequently, may be fatal—particularly, for regular, long-term heavy drinkers, who abruptly discontinue alcohol use.
>
> (Hoffman & Tabakoff, 1994)

52. Interestingly, Dixit, Endicott, and Burry (2016, p. 797) further noted that:

> Approximately 16–31% of patients in the intensive care unit (ICU) have an alcohol use disorder and are at risk for developing alcohol withdrawal syndrome.

As noted in the earlier pharmacology subsection, "Mechanism of Action," the regular, long-term use of alcohol is associated with up-regulation of the NMDA glutamate receptors. Hence, during alcohol withdrawal, excess excitatory glutaminergic function significantly contributes to the signs and symptoms associated with the alcohol withdrawal syndrome (Gonzales & Jaworski, 1997; Hoffman, 1995)—including, related seizure activity.

The use of alcohol, like many other sedative-hypnotics, can suppress epileptic seizures. However, when regular, long-term alcohol use is abruptly discontinued, this anticonvulsant action may be followed by seizure-related hyperexcitability that lasts for several days. Older adults who have alcohol dependence or use disorder and abruptly discontinue their regular, long-term, moderate to high use of alcohol, commonly experience seizures during withdrawal—usually tonic-clonic, or grand mal, seizures.[53] During alcohol withdrawal, the associated seizures typically peak approximately eight to 12 hours after their last drink.

The seizures associated with alcohol withdrawal are generally resistant to standard anticonvulsant pharmacotherapy (e.g., carbamazepine [Tegretol®] or phenytoin [Dilantin®]). However, associated seizure risk and actual seizures respond well to benzodiazepine pharmacotherapy (e.g., diazepam [Valium®]), both in terms of prophylaxis and active treatment, respectively. (See also the later discussion in the "Treating Older Adult Alcohol Dependence or Use Disorder," pharmacotherapy subsection—"Alcohol Withdrawal Syndrome.")

Hangovers

Fortunately, for most older adults who drink alcohol, a milder form of the alcohol withdrawal syndrome—commonly, known as a "hangover"—occurs. Hangovers are typically identified by the following characteristic signs and symptoms that generally follow heavy drinking episodes:

- Anxiety;
- Cognitive deficits (particularly deficits in attention and memory);
- Depressed mood;
- Dry mouth;
- Fatigue;
- General malaise;
- Headache (often severe);
- Hypersensitivity to light and sound;
- Nausea;
- Thirst;
- Vomiting.

As identified by several researchers (e.g., Ling, Stephens, & Heffernan, 2010; McKinney, 2010; Prat, Adan, & Perez-Pamies, 2008), hangovers also are commonly associated with:

- Impaired job performance;
- Potentially dangerous situations involving daily activities (e.g., driving a car or operating heavy machinery);

53. In some cases, partial seizures may also occur.

- Reduced productivity;
- Workplace absenteeism.

Many of the signs and symptoms of a hangover are often self-managed by drinkers. For example, a commonly used remedy is to take "a little hair from the dog that bit me."[54] Others may have a "Bloody Mary" cocktail (tomato juice and vodka) for breakfast or a "Screwdriver" cocktail (orange juice and vodka)—to which vitamins, protein powder, and a raw egg may be added (Pagliaro & Pagliaro, *Clinical Patient Data Files*). These and other approaches that are used to self-manage hangovers are *not* recommended because they tend to promote, or reinforce, harmful drinking patterns that are likely to result in, or sustain, alcohol dependence or use disorder (Piasecki, Robertson, & Epler, 2010).

Alcohol Overdosage/Unintentional Poisoning[55]

Alcohol overdosage is generally self-limiting for older adults who are regular, long-term heavy drinkers because they usually end their heavy drinking episodes by simply falling asleep (for related discussion, see also the earlier pharmacology subsection, Pharmacokinetics—"Absorption").[56]

A troubling trend, over the last two decades, is the increasing number of fatalities associated with the concurrent use of alcohol and other psychodepressants. As reported by Jones, Paulozzi, and Mack (2014), working on behalf of the FDA and The Centers for Disease Control and Prevention (CDC), "alcohol was involved in 22.1% of opiate pain reliever and 21.4% of benzodiazepine drug-related deaths" (p. 881). The synergistic psychodepressant actions of alcohol—particularly respiratory depression—exacerbated by the concurrent use of other psychodepressants, such as opiate analgesics (e.g., oxycodone) and prescription sedative-hypnotics (e.g., benzodiazepines), account for these increased mortality rates. (See also the related discussion in the earlier pharmacology subsection—"Alcohol Drug-Drug Interactions.")

Signs and symptoms of "alcohol poisoning" (i.e., severe alcohol overdosage), in addition to those associated with alcohol intoxication (see Table 1.2, "Blood Alcohol Concentration [BAC]" and Associated Physical and Mental Effects Among Older Adults) include:

- Apnea;
- Bradycardia;
- Confusion;
- Cyanosis;
- Delirium;
- Hypothermia;

---

54. This common expression for treating a hangover originated from the related folklore and practice of treating a rabid, or other, dog bite by placing into the wound, "some hair from the dog that bit you."
55. See also the related discussion in the earlier Undesired, or Harmful, Effects and Toxicities subsection, "Alcohol-Related Mental Depression and Suicide."
56. Also, commonly associated with acute, non-fatal overdosages of alcohol are hangovers that occur during the post-drinking recovery phase. (See additional related discussion in the previous alcohol pharmacology subsection, Undesired, or Harmful, Effects and Toxicities—"Hangovers.")

- Seizures;
- Stupor;
- Unconsciousness;
- Vomiting.

***Related Professional Reminder*: Upon presentation to the ED—after the provision of urgent care, including respiratory support—it is highly recommended that the following laboratory analyses be obtained: (1) BAC, in order to document the extent of the alcohol overdosage; and (2) a full toxicology screen in order to determine, or rule out, the use of other drugs and substances of abuse and/or the presence of other co-intoxicants.**

Although the incidence of mortality associated with alcohol overdosage/unintentional poisoning is relatively low in comparison to that associated with the toxic alcohols, deaths associated with overdosage/unintentional poisonings do occur in the U.S.[57] As identified by the CDC (2015, p. 1):

> An average of 6 people die of alcohol poisoning each day in the U.S.

No specific antidote is available to treat alcohol poisoning. Treatment consists of symptomatic, supportive care. For example, in addition to maintaining respiratory function, older adults with alcoholic ketoacidosis require IV infusion of dextrose 5% in water (e.g., D_5W) and normal saline (NS) in order to restore volume deficits and prevent hypoglycemia. Other common measures include: (1) thiamine that may be required for the correction of vitamin B_1 deficiency; and (2) a urinary catheter to manage incontinence and monitor urinary function. Hemodialysis effectively removes alcohol from the blood and should be considered, particular in severe cases with BAC exceeding 400 mg/dl (see the related discussion in the earlier pharmacology subsection, Pharmacodynamics, Mechanism of Action and Blood Alcohol Concentrations—"Blood Alcohol Concentrations") (Atassi, Noghnogh, & Hariman, 1999; Newman, 2017; Quispe Gonzales, Gomez Giralda, & Ruiz-Zorrilla Lopez, 2011).[58]

NEW MILLENNIAL TRENDS IN OLDER ADULT ALCOHOL USE

For most older adults, their alcohol use began before the beginning of the new millennium during which selected patterns of alcohol use were developed—patterns that may or may not be influenced by new trends in alcohol use during the new millennium. Thus, we begin this section with an overview of nine patterns of older adult alcohol use. This section is followed by specific, new millennial trends in alcohol use, including the medical, nonmedical, and personal, or "recreational," use of alcohol.

57. The lethal dose of alcohol for adults is, approximately, 3–5 gm/kg (Hovda & Jacobsen, 2016).
58. Although not FDA approved, see also the discussion of metadoxine in the earlier pharmacology subsection, Pharmacokinetics—"Metabolism and Excretion."

Nine Patterns of Older Adult Alcohol Use

This section presents and discusses nine patterns of older adult alcohol use. It is followed by an overview of the trends identified in older adult alcohol use during the new millennium. The use of alcohol (and other abusable psychotropics) can be characterized by nine patterns of use from "nonuse" to "resumed nonuse" (see Figure 1.4).

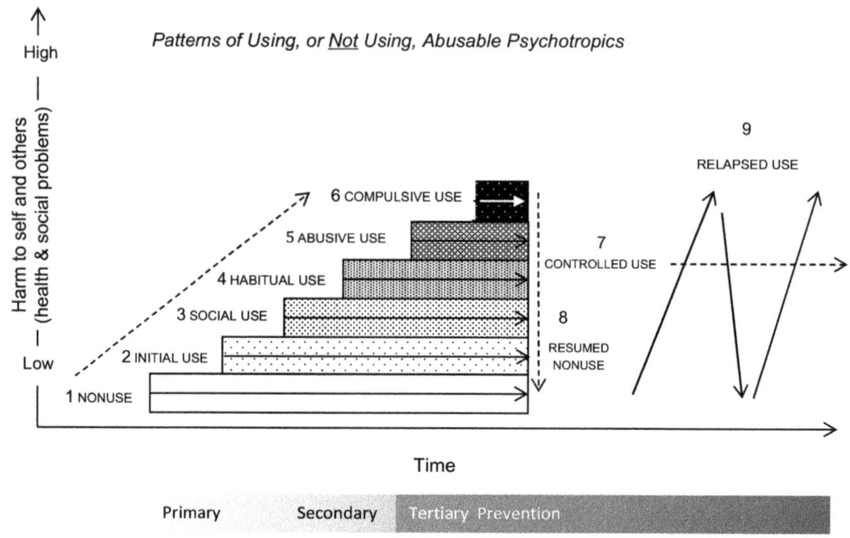

Figure 1.4 Nine Patterns of Abusable Psychotropic Use

Each of these patterns of use, which we identified and developed over the last 30 years, generally relate to the use of all abusable psychotropics (Pagliaro & Pagliaro, 1992b). They are presented and discussed in the following subsections, using alcohol as the example. It should be noted that a number of individual factors, as well as interacting factors, have been postulated as contributing to the various patterns of use, including nonuse. For example:

> Protective effects of high neighborhood co-ethnic density on HED [heavy episode drinking] are stronger for US-born than for foreign-born Latinos and Asians in California.
>
> (Tam, Lui, & Karriker-Jaffe, 2021, p. 74)

> The probability of older persons reporting increased drinking was much greater among those with poor mental health.
>
> (Capasso, Jones, & Ali, 2021, p. 1)

> Women with psychological distress were over 4 times more likely to have an AUD.
>
> (Verplaetse, Peltier & Roberts, 2021, p. 1)

> Higher racial-ethnic identity buffers the effects of discrimination on illicit drug [and alcohol] use for Latinx, but not for Black respondents.
>
> (Reyes, Treitier, & Peterson, 2021, p. 1)

Major factors, which are related as both causes and consequences of alcohol use among older adults, are presented in Figure 1.5.

Figure 1.5 Various Factors Identified as Causes or Consequences of Habitual, Abusive, or Compulsive Alcohol Use Among Older Adults

We begin with "nonuse."

Nonuse

Nonuse, the first pattern of use, characterizes older adults who have never consumed an alcoholic beverage—or who are currently abstinent following earlier periods of use (i.e., "Resumed Nonuse").[59]

Initial Use

Initial use of alcohol among older adults may have occurred during childhood in association with religious ceremonies (i.e., Holy Communion) or because of curiosity (e.g., when a child takes a sip of beer—often provided by a parent—to "see what it tastes like"). For example, Jackson, Barnett, and Colby (2015), in their related study of initial alcohol use, found that: (1) approximately 30% of surveyed students "sipped" alcohol by the sixth grade; (2) in most cases the "sip" of alcohol occurred in their own homes; and (3) the primary

59. Of the 20% of people in the U.S. who currently do not drink alcohol (i.e., those who are "nonusers" and/or "resumed nonusers"), approximately one-half abstain for religious reasons (e.g., Church of Jesus Christ of Latter-Day Saints [Mormons]; Fundamentalist Moslems [Religion of Islam]; and Seventh-day Adventists) and the remaining one-half abstain for medical reasons. Included in the latter group are those who are recovering from alcoholism and who subscribe to the principles of Alcoholics Anonymous (AA) or other similar 12-step programs. See the related discussion in the later diagnosis and treatment subsection, Psychotherapeutic/Counseling Approaches—"Alcoholics Anonymous."

However, except for the factors of gender, genetics, and frequency/quantity of use, most of the proposed relationships have either been insignificant and/or unreproduced. Specific exceptions have been noted throughout the chapter.

supplier/source of the alcohol was a parent. Others experienced their first use of alcohol later during adolescence.[60] The remaining older adults who consume alcohol had their first drink in adulthood—including older adulthood.

Social Use

The most common form of alcohol use among older adults is "social use," which involves the ingestion of alcohol, in the form of beer, wine, and distilled spirits (i.e., liqueurs, vodka, and whiskey) at celebratory and other social situations with others (e.g., back yard barbeques, birthdays, divorces, holidays, job promotions, retirements, sport team victories, and weddings). The social customs of various cultural/ethnic groups in the U.S. significantly affect older adult drinking at this level. Other factors include:

- Alcohol availability;
- Continental descent, including genetic predisposition to tolerate the use of alcohol (e.g., older adults who are Jewish), or lack thereof (e.g., sensitivity of Asian older adults to alcohol as characterized by the common "Asian Flush");[61]
- Family history of alcohol or other dependence or use disorder(s);
- Gender;[62]
- Legal or religious restrictions;
- Personal preferences;
- Sexual orientation.[63]

Habitual, Abusive, and Compulsive Use[64]

Once the use of alcohol begins, it generally continues throughout life and is characterized by habitual use (e.g., regularly having a glass of wine with dinner, drinking a couple cans of beer while watching a televised sporting event, or having a "nightcap" before going to bed) and is generally not associated with serious problems. However, many older adults, whose alcohol use is associated with characteristic patterns of abusive use (e.g., intermittent heavy drinking), increasingly suffer undesired, or harmful, effects and toxicities that, for some, may be fatal. Interestingly, approximately one-third of older adults, who develop harmful patterns

---

60. 90% of Americans who consume alcoholic beverages begin use by 21 years of age.
61. The "Asian Flush" is also known as the "Asian Flush Syndrome" or the "Oriental Flushing Syndrome." The characteristic "flushing," or "blushing," of the skin associated with drinking alcohol usually involves the face, neck, and shoulders. This reaction is caused by the accumulation of acetaldehyde in the circulatory system associated with a deficiency of acetaldehyde dehydrogenase—the enzyme primarily responsible for the metabolism of acetaldehyde in the body. This genetically controlled, or inherited, deficiency is particularly common among older adults of Asian continental descent—thus the name, "Asian Flush."
62. N.B. Previously, men significantly outnumbered women in virtually every alcohol use category. However, gender differences, in the incidence of alcohol use in the U.S., has virtually been eliminated during the new millennium (Pagliaro & Pagliaro, 2018).
63. Among all age groups in the U.S.—including older adults—bisexuals, gays, lesbians, and transsexuals have significantly higher rates of alcohol use in comparison to their heterosexual, age-matched cohorts.
64. See also the related discussion in the later subsection, "Recreational Use by Older Adults—Drinking Estimates and Trends in Binge Drinking."

of alcohol use, do so after 50 years of age. This pattern of alcohol use is commonly referred to as "late-onset AUD" (Emiliussen, Sogaard Nielsen, & Andersen, 2017; Rigler, 2000).

> [Sixty-nine-year-old] Rep. Ann Kirkpatrick, an Arizona Democrat, announced on Wednesday that she will seek treatment for "alcohol dependence" after suffering a serious fall. . . . "I do, however, have another challenge I must face, which was the underlying cause of my fall. Beginning next week, I will receive treatment that I have struggled to ask for, to treat my alcohol dependence," she said.
>
> (Foran, 2020, p. 1)

It has long been recognized that harmful patterns of habitual, abusive, or compulsive use are more frequently encountered (i.e., up to 25%) among the lesbian, gay, bisexual, transgender, and queer/questioning (LGBTQ) community (Pagliaro & Pagliaro, 2018, 2020). Generally, among older adults, in the U.S.—of all sexual orientations—the incidence is approximately 10%. However, among those with a LGBTQ orientation, this incidence may be doubled. For example, as found by Bryan, Kim, and Fedriksen-Goldsen (2017, p. 595), utilizing data from the *2014 Aging with Pride: National Health, Aging, and Sexuality/ Gender Study (NHAS)*:

> Approximately one-fifth (20.6%) of LGB older adults [e.g., 50 to 98 years-of-age] reported high-risk drinking, with no significant differences in rates between men (22.4%) and women (18.4%).

We now turn to new millennial medical and nonmedical/recreational alcohol use among older adults.

Medical Use by Older Adults

Since its introduction to North America by European explorers and traders, alcohol was used to treat such varied conditions as the common cold and "rheumatism." Until approximately 80 years ago, alcohol was medically classified as a "psychostimulant" and was administered by nurses by the "syringeful" to their patients when "rapid stimulation" was required (Pagliaro, 1986, p. 10). It also was thought to possess nutritive and other benefits.

For the last 50-plus years, the only medical use for alcohol, other than its use as a topical antiseptic at injection sites,[65] has been its use as a vehicle for the preparation of various pharmaceutical formulations (i.e., alcohol-containing solutions and elixirs). In response to both public and health care provider demands for alcohol-free liquid pharmaceutical products, particularly those formulated for children and older adults, the use of alcohol for the preparation of various pharmaceutical products has decreased significantly during the new millennium.[66]

65. Typically, isopropyl alcohol (i.e., C_3H_8O) is used in this context, primarily because of price—including the absence of a "liquor tax." However, with the COVID-19 pandemic, this changed rapidly and significantly to allow ethanol (i.e., "drinking alcohol") to be used as the principal active ingredient in hand sanitizers usually without the addition of any denaturing agent and generally in concentrations between 60% and 95% (i.e., 120 and 190 proof) (CDC, 2020b).
66. A corresponding reduction in the alcohol content of personal care products (e.g., aftershave and mouth wash) also occurred during the new millennium. This reduction was aimed at deterring the use of these products by older adults and other regular, long-term users of alcohol, who were generally homeless, "living on the street," and who primarily used these alcohol products when they were unable to obtain their usual wine, whiskey, or other alcoholic beverages, to prevent, or self-manage, the alcohol withdrawal syndrome (i.e., to avoid "getting sick") (Pagliaro & Pagliaro, *Clinical Patient Data Files*).

However, several pharmaceutical formulations—for prescription and non-prescription (i.e., over-the-counter) use—currently contain alcohol (5% to 15%), including several:

- Liquid cough and cold formulations, such as Ambenyl®, Benylin®, Dilaudid, Cough Syrup®, Novahistine®, Robitussin®, and Vicks®;
- Liquid vitamin drops, such as Ce-Vi-Sol®, Geritol®, and Nu-Iron®;
- Mouth washes, such as Cēpacol® and Listerine®.

Health and social care professionals require an awareness of the alcohol content of these and other pharmaceutical drug products, particularly when working in settings[67] where regular, long-term users of alcohol may substitute these products when beverage alcohol is unavailable to them (e.g., when they are unable to purchase alcohol or obtain some from a friend, or are restricted from using it when jailed or enrolled in drug treatment programs). In addition, it is particularly important for health and social care professionals to be aware of these alcohol-containing products if older adults, who have been diagnosed with alcohol dependence or use disorder, are initiating or being treated with disulfiram (Antabuse®) pharmacotherapy, which requires a total restriction of the use of alcohol because of the associated possibility of triggering an alcohol-induced "disulfiram reaction." (See also the related discussion of disulfiram [Antabuse®] in the earlier pharmacology subsection—"Alcohol Drug-Drug Interactions," and the later treatment section, Pharmacotherapy and Psychotherapy/Counseling—"Pharmacotherapy.")

Recreational Use by Older Adults

The nonmedical/recreational use of alcohol among older adults during the first two decades of the new millennium are discussed in the following subsections with attention to drinking estimates and trends in binge drinking.

Drinking Estimates and Trends in Binge Drinking

Most studies indicate that approximately 65% of older adults in the U.S. regularly ingest alcoholic beverages. Since the beginning of the new millennium, the habitual/abusive pattern of "binge drinking"—traditionally defined as the ingestion of five or more alcoholic drinks per drinking episode (generally within a two-hour time frame) for older men, and four or more alcoholic drinks per drinking episode for older women (Pagliaro & Pagliaro, 2018)—has significantly contributed to mortality in the U.S.:

Unfortunately, the limited availability of personal care products that contain alcohol, led to another related concern—drinking, for the same reasons, household cleaners and food products that contain alcohol. These products, and their various methods of use, include: "decanting" pressurized cans of Lysol® Disinfectant Spray (80% alcohol) and drinking the liquid solution, and drinking Chinese cooking wine (18% to 25%) or pure vanilla extract—which contains 35% alcohol (Pagliaro & Pagliaro, *Clinical Patient Data Files*). (See also the related discussion in the previous footnote.)

67. These settings include, for example: convenience stores, grocery stores, and pharmacies—particularly those located in, or near, alcohol-free Indian reservations and inner-city neighborhoods with significant homeless populations (Pagliaro & Pagliaro, *Clinical Patient Data Files*).

> Binge drinking was responsible for more than half of the estimated 79,000 deaths and two thirds of the estimated 2.3 million years of potential life lost as a result of excessive drinking each year in the United States during 2001–2005.
>
> (CDC, 2010, p. 1274)

As identified by the U.S. Surgeon General:

> In 2015. . . over 66 million people in the U.S. reported binge drinking in the past month.
>
> (USDHHS, 2016, p. ES-1)

Finally, as noted by the NIAAA (2021, p. 2):

> Binge drinking is on the rise among older adults—more than 10 percent of adults ages 65 and older reported binge drinking in the past month and the prevalence is increasing.

However, it is important to note that binge drinking estimates in the U.S. display significant variability for several reasons as discussed later in this chapter. For example, as found by Solomon, Laditka, and Forthofer (2021, p. 100):

> Hispanic and African American women were more likely to engage in binge consumption than whites.

Regardless of this variance, the incidence of the occurrence of binge drinking episodes has increased significantly over the past two decades and appears to be continuing to increase across the U.S. (Pagliaro & Pagliaro, 2009, 2018). Specifically, regarding older adults in the U.S., alcohol abuse, including binge drinking, significantly increased during the second decade of the new millennium (Han, Moore, & Sherman, 2017; NIDA, 2020; Reinberg, 2019; Span, 2017) and baby boomers drove this increase (Achenbach, 2018; Cho, Bhimani, & Milapkumar, 2018; Kuerbis et al., 2014; Mattson, Lipari, & Hays, 2017).[68] The related morbidity and mortality (e.g., cognitive impairment, MVCs, or violent behavior) also contribute to many significant related harmful effects for the families, friends, co-workers, and communities of older adult binge drinkers—and monetary costs, which are frequently overlooked, including those related to decreased workplace productivity, criminal justice costs, and health care costs.

Related Professional Reminder: ***The adverse health consequences associated with binge drinking can be significantly increased by comorbidities; environmental pollution; genetics, including being a woman; and polypharmacy. These contributory factors are exacerbated among older adults, placing them at particular risk for the occurrence of adverse health consequences associated with binge drinking.***

The highest rates of binge drinking in the U.S. are reported for the Northern states along the Canadian border—excluding Washington state—and the states of Alaska and Hawaii (Sacks, Gonzales, & Bouchery, 2015). Approximately 80% of these binge drinkers are males (Han, Moore, & Ferris, 2019; Kanny, Naimi, & Liu, 2018). Additionally, over 10% of adults in the U.S. who are older than 65 years of age engage in binge drinking (Han et al., 2019;

68. Additionally, as identified by White et al. (2020), alcohol consumption has increased at a significantly higher rate in the U.S. among older adults (i.e., 50 years of age and older) in comparison to younger age groups.

National Institute on Drug Abuse (NIDA), 2020; Reinberg, 2019).[69] These percentages are consistent with those reported a decade earlier by Blazer and Wu (2009), who, in their analysis involving over 4,000 U.S. respondents 65 years of age and older, found that "more than 14% of men and 3% of women reported binge drinking" (p. 1162). Similarly, Han, Moore, and Sherman (2018), based on an analysis of data from the *National Survey on Drug Use and Health* for 2005 to 2014, found that 14.4% of older adults, 50 years of age and older, "reported past-month binge drinking" (p. 48).

Regarding the number of binge drinks consumed per year in the U.S., Kanny, Naimi, and Liu (2020, p. 30) found, in their analysis of data from the *Behavioral Risk Factor Surveillance System* (BRFSS) on behalf of the CDC, that:

> The age-adjusted total annual number of binge drinks per adult who reported binge drinking increased significantly from 472 in 2011 to 529 in 2017. Total annual binge drinks per adult who reported binge drinking also increased significantly from 2011 to 2017 among those aged 45–64 years (23.1% from 428 to 527).

However, overall, several researchers (e.g., Lee & Sher, 2018; Moss, Schutte, & Brennan, 2010; Pagliaro & Pagliaro, *Clinical Patient Data Files*) have identified a significant, virtually linear decline in harmful drinking behavior—including binge drinking—over the adult lifespan (i.e., from a higher level for those in their early 20s to a lower level for those 65 years of age and older). This "desistance" has been recognized by Lee and Sher (2018) as being explained primarily by two theoretical processes, "maturing out" and "natural recovery."[70]

The data supporting the former theory (i.e., "maturing out") appears to be: (1) particularly related to developmental role changes (e.g., full-time employment, living on one's own, and marriage); and (2) particularly relevant for those at the early end of the adult age continuum. The latter theory (i.e., "natural recovery") is primarily viewed as the result of experience derived from the personal consequences of problem binge drinking (e.g., arrest for drunk driving, divorce, job loss, or physical illness). This experience, and its associated "learning"—in turn—can result in:

- Personal reappraisal of drinking behavior;
- Self-identification of the problem (i.e., as occurs in the context of AA, "My name is [person's first name] and I'm an alcoholic");
- Willingness and specific efforts by the drinker to modify aversive drinking habits/behaviors.

Natural recovery appears to be particularly relevant for those in "middle" adulthood.

The patterns of binge drinking by older adults may be influenced, to some extent, by aspects of both "maturing out" and "natural recovery." In comparison to younger adults, aversive health consequences (see earlier related discussion) appear to be the predominant

69. This represented an increase from 7%, which was reported in 2006, and is consistent with the overall increasing abusable psychotropic use noted among older adults from the "baby boomer" generation (Ducharme, 2019; Pagliaro & Pagliaro, *Clinical Patient Data Files*; Reinberg, 2019; Yarnell et al., 2020).
70. Other researchers have used other theories to explain this phenomenon. For example, Moss et al. (2010) cite: (1) social learning theory; (2) stress and coping theory; and (3) social control theory. The various theories posited to explain this phenomenon generally reflect the "theoretical orientation" of the researcher and frequently contain elements of significant overlap with other related theories.

factor associated with the decrease in binge drinking among older adults (e.g., Pagliaro & Pagliaro, *Clinical Patient Data Files*; Rigler, 2000; Schutte, Moos, & Brennan, 2006). However, additional factors must also be taken into account.

For example, Villalonga-Olives, Almansa, and Shaya (2020, p. 108099), in their longitudinal analysis of the relationship between social capital and binge drinking among older adults in the U.S., found that "negative social support [i.e., lack of positive social interactions/relationships] favored binge drinking." Race and sexual orientation are additional factors that also can play a significant role in both the incidence of and continuation of binge drinking—as reported by Greene, Jackson, and Dean (2020, p. 462): "Black and Hispanic sexual minority women reported the highest prevalence of binge drinking (45.4% and 43.4%, respectively), followed by White sexual minority women (35.7%) and White heterosexual women (23%)."

DIAGNOSIS AND TREATMENT OF ALCOHOL DEPENDENCE OR USE DISORDER AMONG OLDER ADULTS

> Pamela Noffze was 58 when she arrived at Hazelden's center in Naples [Florida] for treatment. At her worst, she was drinking a case of light beer a day, but she didn't think she had an issue until her daughter threatened to ban her from seeing her grandsons again unless she sought help. "That's when I knew I had to do something," said Ms. Noffze.
>
> (Ellin, 2014, p. 2)

This section focuses on assessment and diagnosis of alcohol dependence or use disorder among older adults and age-related treatment approaches. We begin with assessment and diagnosis.

Assessment and Diagnosis of Alcohol Dependence or Use Disorder

Related Professional Reminder: ***The assessment of alcohol dependence or use disorder includes a thorough history—both past and present—for the use of alcohol and its patterns of use, including concurrent use with other abusable psychotropics. If alcohol use is reported, then specific questions should be asked for alcohol, as well as for each of the other abusable psychotropics used, including:***

- ***Age of initial use;***[71]
- ***Context(s) of use (i.e., "set/setting");***
- ***Desire to address current alcohol or other dependence or use disorder(s) (i.e., "readiness to change");***

71. These data are of relevance—even when dealing exclusively with older adults—because it has generally been identified that older adults, who have alcohol dependence or use disorder, differ according to "age-of-onset" with approximately 66% beginning harmful alcohol use often much earlier in life (i.e., "early-onset alcoholism") while approximately 30% begin their harmful alcohol use later in life (i.e., "late-onset alcoholism").

- ***Duration of use;***
- ***Experience of adverse consequences associated with alcohol use including signs and symptoms of withdrawal;***
- ***Family history of alcohol dependence or use disorder;***
- ***Frequency of use;***
- ***Method(s) of use;***
- ***Positive experiences/benefits reportedly (believed to be) associated with alcohol use;***
- ***Previous intervention, or treatment, for alcohol dependence or use disorder and outcomes;***
- ***Quantity of use;***
- ***Severity of alcohol and other dependence or use disorder(s);***
- ***Usual circumstances of use.***

The use of alcohol, as well as other abusable psychotropics, by older adults in the U.S., reached significant and alarming proportions during the new millennium. However, only a small proportion of family physicians include an adequate assessment of alcohol dependence or use disorder during routine annual physical examinations or other office visits (Aspy, Mold, & Thompson, 2008). As claimed by Ross (2005, p. 32):

> Since the vast majority of older adults have regular contact with physicians, there are ample opportunities to screen for AUDs. However, many patients are not adequately screened due either to lack of training on the part of physicians or bias that such disorders are not worth treating in this population.

Yarnell et al. (2020, p. 226), in a related systematic review, noted the following "main finding of this study:"

> With the Baby Boomer generation aging into the geriatric cohort, they bring with them a lifetime of experiences and habits, including substance use disorder. Despite this, substance use disorders in the elderly remain underestimated, under identified, underdiagnosed, and undertreated.

Unfortunately, this lack of attention to screening for alcohol or other dependence or use disorders occurs among the vast majority of all health and social care professionals (e.g., nurse practitioners, physicians, psychologists, and social workers) who are involved in promoting the health and well-being of older adults. Consequently, during the first two decades of the new millennium, alcohol dependence or use disorder was often "overlooked" among older adults both by family members and health care professionals (NIA, 2017; Pagliaro & Pagliaro, *Clinical Patient Data Files*; Yarnell et al., 2020). Thus, for many older adults, alcohol and other dependence or use disorder(s), are left unidentified and remain untreated until associated personal and social problems escalate (see Table 1.3). For example, as described by the National Institute on Aging:

> Uncle George always liked his liquor, so his family may not see that his drinking is getting worse as he gets older. Grandma Betty was a teetotaler all her life until she started having a drink each night to help her get to sleep after her husband died. Now, no one realizes that she needs a couple of drinks to get through each day.
>
> (NIA, 2017, p. 1)

Table 1.3 Alcohol or Other Dependence or Use Disorders: Missed Physician Diagnoses and Patient Responses

PERCENTAGE AND TYPE OF PHYSICIAN RESPONDENTS	PHYSICIAN DIAGNOSTIC BEHAVIOR
94% **Primary Care Physicians**	**Fail** to diagnose alcohol abuse when presented with early signs and symptoms in older adult patients
58% **Physicians**	**Fail** to discuss the use of drugs and substances of abuse with older adults because they believe that they lie about it[72]
41% **Pediatricians**	**Fail** to diagnose illicit use of the drugs and substances of abuse when presented with a classic description of a "drug-abusing" older adult
35% **Physicians**	**Fail** to treat a patient who abuses the drugs and substances of abuse because of time constraints
30% **Physicians**	Identify that they are prepared to diagnose drug abuse
20% **Physicians**	Identify that they are prepared to diagnose alcoholism
17% **Physicians**	Identify that they are prepared to diagnose illicit drug and substance abuse
11% **Physicians**	**Fail** to treat a patient who abuses drugs and substances of abuse because they are concerned that they won't be reimbursed for the time necessary to screen and treat the patient
PERCENTAGE OF PATIENT RESPONDENTS	**PATIENT REPORTS OF PHYSICIAN BEHAVIORS**[73]
75%	Say their primary care physician was *not* involved in their decision to seek treatment for an alcohol or other dependence or use disorder
54%	Say their primary care physician did *nothing* about their addiction

Sources: Center on Addiction, 2000; Wood, Samet, & Volkow, 2013.

Assessment and diagnosis of alcohol dependence or use disorder among older adults can be facilitated by the use of:

1. The Screening, Brief Intervention, and Referral to Treatment (SBIRT) model;
2. The Diagnostic and Statistical Manual of Mental Disorders (DSM-5) Criteria;
3. Specific quick-screen psychometric tests.[74]

72. Approximately 58% of patients agree that they lie (i.e., minimize, or are not entirely truthful) about their illicit/nonmedical drug and substance use/abuse.
73. The typical patient respondent had a drug or substance use problem for 10 years before receiving treatment.
74. Specific screening tests for detecting other abusable psychotropics (i.e., amphetamines, caffeine, cannabis, cocaine, nicotine, opiate analgesics, and sedative-hypnotics) are presented, respectively, in each of the following chapters.

Each of these screening approaches are discussed in the following subsections. However, we first consider the importance of screening.

Importance of Screening

It has long been recognized that delayed intervention or treatment can result in increasingly harmful consequences that are largely preventable. Selected screening offers health and social care professionals an accurate, economic, and efficient means for identifying older adults who are in need of immediate intervention for alcohol or other dependence or use disorders (Eberhard, Nordstrom, & Hoglund, 2009), including, as needed, referral to other appropriate health and social care providers (Searight, 2009) (see Figure 1.6). Additionally, we and others (e.g., Crome, Bloor, & Thom, 2006) have long recognized that alcohol or other dependence or use disorders—particularly when left unidentified or undiagnosed—can exacerbate, predispose, mask, or otherwise interfere with the diagnosis and management of other mental and physical disorders (see also the later section in this chapter, "Contemporaneous Diagnoses").

By the end of the first decade of the new millennium, the U.S. Preventive Services Task Force (USPSTF) recommended "screening for unhealthy alcohol use in primary care

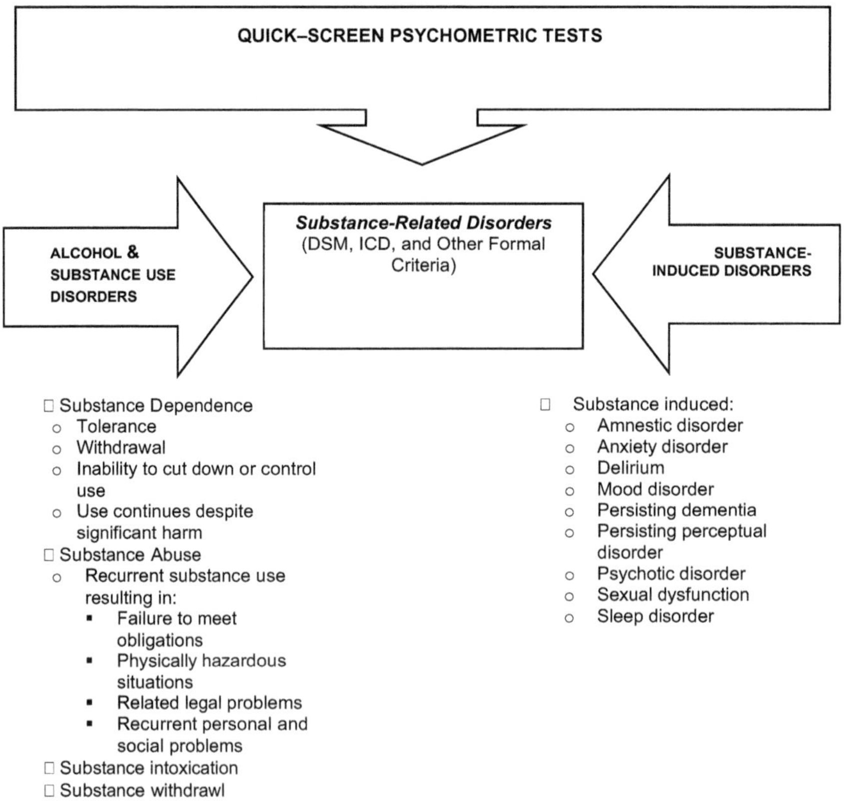

Figure 1.6 Diagnosing Alcohol or Other Dependence or Use Disorders

settings for adults" (USPSTF, 2019, p. 770a). Later, Jones et al. (2014)—in the context of the millennial opiate analgesic epidemic in the U.S.—identified that alcohol was involved in 22% of deaths and 18% of ED visits associated with opiate analgesic use in 2010. As a result of these findings, the CDC (2018) recommended the use of alcohol screening and brief intervention (ASBI) for all patients who consume alcohol and use opiate analgesics (i.e., a focused special application of the widely known, "Screening, Brief Intervention, and Referral to Treatment" [SBIRT] model—see the following subsection).

In June 2020, the USPSTF updated its earlier recommendation:

> The USPSTF recommends screening by asking questions about unhealthy drug use in adults 18 years or older. Screening should be implemented when services for accurate diagnosis, effective treatment, and appropriate care can be offered or referred.
>
> (USPSTF, 2020, p. 2301)

However, as noted by Orciari Herman (2020, p. 1) in a *Physician's First Watch* report on the USPSTF recommendation:

> In an accompanying editorial, Dr. Richard Saitz—an addiction medicine specialist and associate editor with *Physicians First Watch*—advises several cautions for clinicians who implement screening. Among them: "Given that any evidence for efficacy is limited to individuals seeking treatment, screening becomes less relevant, and clinicians should focus on treatments for those seeking help."

To us, this extremely cavalier and dismissive attitude toward those with abusable psychotropic-related problems is both appalling and woefully uninformed. Even if, for the sake of argument, one were to concede that "evidence for efficacy" was limited to "those seeking help," this would not invalidate the fact that significant clinical benefits for patients can still accrue from systematic screening. For example, early detection of hazardous problematic patterns of the use of abusable psychotropics may preclude the development of full-blown alcohol dependence or use disorder as well as related sequelae. Additionally, "screening adults for unhealthy drug use" can often help detect a related contemporaneous diagnosis. Finally, recognizing the significant incidence of alcohol dependence or use disorder among older adults and inconsistent and inadequate use of related screening, the CDC—most recently in 2021—urged all healthcare providers to "screen all adult patients for excessive drinking" (CDC, 2021, p. 2).

The Screening, Brief Intervention,[75] *and Referral to Treatment (SBIRT) Model*

In an effort to assist health and social care professionals, including physicians, psychiatrists, psychologists, and other health and social care providers, to assure the accurate and timely diagnosis and management of alcohol or other dependence or use disorder(s), several approaches for SBIRT have been developed and implemented (e.g., Babor, McRee, & Kassebaum, 2007; Madras, Compton, & Avula, 2009; SAMHSA, 2011; Searight, 2009).

75. For additional details regarding brief intervention, see the later subsection, "Psychotherapeutic/Counseling Approaches: Brief Intervention (BI)."

Although data are limited, several studies (e.g., Schonfeld, Hazlett, & Hedgecock, 2015) have demonstrated the efficacy of SBIRT among older adults.

The Substance Abuse and Mental Health Services Administration (SAMHSA) has defined SBIRT as:

> A comprehensive, integrated, public health approach to the delivery of early intervention for individuals with risky alcohol and drug use, and the timely referral to more intensive substance abuse treatment for those who have substance abuse disorders.

"Screening, brief intervention, and referral to treatment" is a treatment model that was developed early in the new millennium. It represents a major shift in the focus of the assessment and treatment of alcohol or other dependence or use disorder, from a focus on patients experiencing patterns of "abuse" or "compulsive use," to include a focus on "initial," "social," and "habitual use" of alcohol and other drugs and substances of abuse (i.e., it targets those who have not yet developed significant related problems). As explained by SAMHSA (2013, p. 1):

> One of the strengths of the SAMHSA SBIRT model is that it screens all patients regardless of an identified disorder, allowing healthcare professionals in a variety of settings to address the spectrum of such behavioral health problems even when the patient is not actively seeking an intervention or treatment for his or her problems.

Generally, the SBIRT model functions at the intersection between "prevention" and "treatment" (see Figures 1.7, The SBIRT Model, and 1.8, The SBIRT Flowchart).

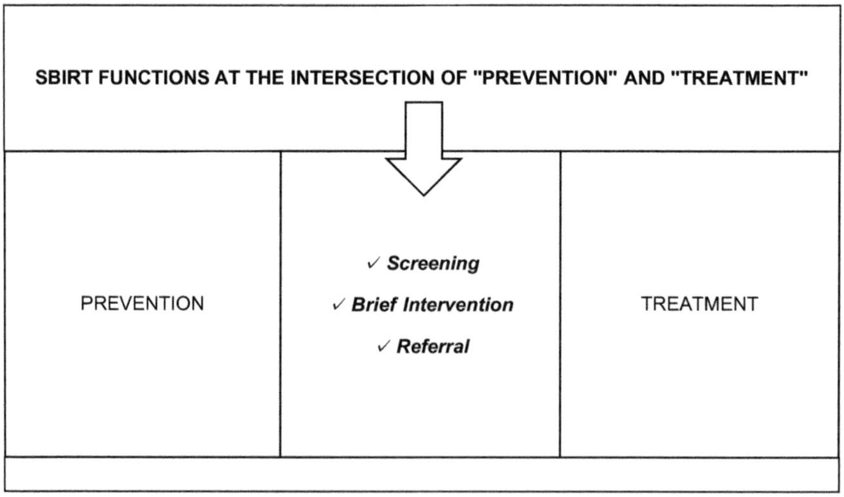

Figure 1.7 The Screening, Brief Intervention, and Referral to Treatment (SBIRT) Model

As noted by SAMHSA (2011, p. 7):

> There is substantial evidence from review studies and meta-analyses of randomized clinical trials that show the effectiveness of SBIRT in reducing hazardous drinking in patients presenting in primary care and other health care settings.

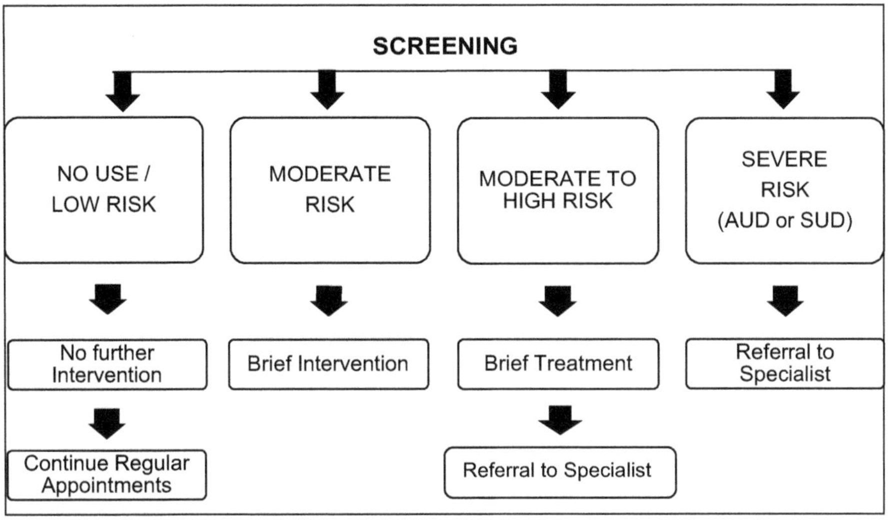

Figure 1.8 The Screening, Brief Intervention, and Referral to Treatment (SBIRT) Flowchart

The SBIRT model has also been found to be effective in ceasing or decreasing tobacco use (SAMHSA, 2011). However, for other abusable psychotropic dependence or use disorders, results have been mixed. SAMHSA (2011) has identified the following three factors that appear to be the major contributors to the observed variability in results:

1. Characteristics of the provider;
2. Specific environmental setting;
3. Patient population.

The SAMHSA SBIRT model is characterized by six major elements (SAMHSA, 2013):

1. ***Brevity.*** The initial screening is accomplished quickly (modal time is about five to ten minutes),[76] and the intervention and treatment components, indicated by the screening results, are completed in significantly less time (i.e., usually one to five sessions) than traditional specialty alcohol or other dependence or use disorder(s) care;
2. ***Universality.*** All patients, clients, retirees, or other target populations are screened as part of other standard intake processes;
3. ***Focus.*** One or more specific behaviors are targeted. The screening tool addresses specific problematic behaviors or behaviors that are preconditional to alcohol or other dependence or use disorder(s);
4. ***Appropriate Setting***. Screenings are provided in a public health, medical, or other treatment setting (e.g., Eds, primary care physicians' offices, or a public health clinic);

76. The amount of time varies by the clinical setting and the specific need of the older adult patient for assessment, education, motivational discussion, and referral for specialized treatment. The BI sessions can last for up to 60 minutes.

5. ***Comprehensiveness.*** The program includes a seamless transition between brief universal screening, a brief intervention (BI) and/or brief treatment (BT), and referral to specialized treatment (RT) for alcohol or other dependence or use disorder(s);
6. ***Supportive Evidence.*** Strong research, with substantial experimental evidence, supports the model. At a minimum, programmatic outcomes demonstrate a successful approach.

The universal "screening" component of SBIRT is used to identify current or developing alcohol and other abusable psychotropic-related problems among older adults. "Brief intervention," or "BI," provides behavioral intervention—generally motivational intervention—over a single, or several sessions, as deemed necessary for older adults who are at minimal to moderate risk for alcohol or other abusable psychotropic-related problems. The goals of brief intervention are to: (1) educate patients regarding alcohol, or other abusable psychotropic, use; and (2) provide brief intervention that attempts to accomplish the following:

- Decrease denial of alcohol or other abusable psychotropic-related problems;
- Increase readiness to change;
- Reduce related risky behavior.

"Referral to Treatment," or "RT," is used for older adults who are deemed to be at moderate to high risk for alcohol or other abusable psychotropic-related problems. Consequently, RT involves more intensive and prolonged treatment than that provided by BI.[77]

However, many clinicians have argued that screening older adults for minimal to high risk for alcohol or other psychotropic-related problems—particularly, when performed as a part of an annual physical examination or as part of a routine office visit—is both: (1) time consuming; and (2) an inefficient use of valuable clinical resources (see Table 1.4). Other clinicians have argued that screening older adults for problems related to the use of alcohol or other abusable psychotropics can result in both: (1) misdiagnoses; and (2) missed diagnoses. Thus, for screening to become recognized as more valuable for clinicians, it is essential that it can be quickly administered and can contribute to the development of accurate diagnoses.

In order to maximize the successful application of SBIRT, Nunes, Richmond, and Marzano (2017, p. 508), commenting on ten years of related clinical experience, recommend the following seven key components:

1. Strong clinical and management advocates;
2. Full integration of services into practices' workflows, utilizing technology whenever possible;
3. Interprofessional team approaches;
4. Appropriate options for the small proportion of patients screening positive for a possible [alcohol or other] substance use disorder;

77. N.B. Although brief intervention has been widely endorsed during the new millennium (e.g., by the CDC and WHO), it has been recognized for some time (e.g., CDC, 1999; Henry-Edwards, Humeniuk, & Ali, 2003) that brief intervention is not generally effective for the treatment of serious cases of alcohol or other abusable psychotropic use involving patterns of abusive or compulsive use (Pagliaro & Pagliaro, *Clinical Patient Data Files*). For related definitions, see the earlier subsection—"Nine Patterns of Older Adult Alcohol Use."

Table 1.4 Major Constraints Affecting Appropriate Use of SBIRT and Quick-Screen Psychometric Tests Among Older Adults

MAJOR CONSTRAINTS	DESCRIPTIONS & EXAMPLES
Personal & Professional Constraints	• Beliefs regarding professional role and responsibilities that do *not* include: ◦ Testing for drug and substance abuse; ◦ Treating drug and substance abuse; ◦ Referring patients for needed help for drug and substance abuse. • Perceived lack of the efficacy of quick-screen psychometric tests; • Lack of training in administering and interpreting quick-screen psychometric tests; • Negative attitudes toward older adults, particularly older adults who use drugs and substances of abuse: ◦ Lack of confidence in patient self-report/self-evaluation (e.g., that patients lie, particularly when they may perceive it to be to their advantage to do so); ◦ Worried about angering /insulting the patient; ◦ Belief regarding long-standing drug and substance use disorders that "you can't teach an old dog a new trick" (i.e., that the potential for a successful intervention is minimal). • Inadequate education/training or self-confidence regarding delivering optimal older adult care concerning the use of the drugs and substances of abuse: ◦ Poor interpersonal skills (e.g., uncomfortable with test administration procedures); ◦ Poor social skills (e.g., unable to comfortably discuss alcohol or other dependence or use disorders with older adults and their adult children, as indicated); ◦ Poor technical skills (e.g., unable to answer related questions from the older adult test-taker); ◦ Unable to effectively administer structured interviews; ◦ Unable to discuss positive results with older adults and their adult children, as indicated.
Environmental Constraints	• Lack of time (already overbooked and overburdened); • Difficulties scheduling and conducting necessary follow-up appointments; • Lack of space; • Limited resources, including staff turnover of those who would administer quick-screen psychometric tests; • Inflexible electronic medical records; • Lack of standardized, validated quick-screen psychometric tests for older adults.

Sources: Aspy et al., 2008; Crome et al., 2006; Palmer, Karakus, & Mark, 2019; Searight, 2009.

5. Cannabis screening that accounts for legalization, and interventions that acknowledge differences between alcohol and cannabis use;
6. Incorporating SBIRT into standard health care professionals' training;
7. Addressing the significant issues regarding reimbursement through private and public payers for SBIRT services.

Table 1.5 DMS-5 Criteria for Alcohol Use Disorder

A maladaptive pattern of substance use leading to clinically significant impairment or distress as manifested by two or more of the following occurring at any time in the same 12-month period:

- Alcohol is often taken in larger amounts or over a longer period than was intended;
- There is a persistent desire or unsuccessful efforts to cut down or control alcohol use;
- A great deal of time is spent in activities necessary to obtain alcohol, use alcohol, or recover from its effects;
- Craving, or a strong desire or urge to use alcohol;
- Recurrent alcohol use resulting in a failure to fulfill major role obligations at work, school, or home;
- Continued alcohol use despite having persistent or recurrent social or interpersonal problems caused or exacerbated by the effects of alcohol;
- Important social, occupational, or recreational activities are given up or reduced because of alcohol use;
- Recurrent alcohol use in situations in which it is physically hazardous;
- Alcohol use is continued despite knowledge of having a persistent or recurrent physical or psychological problem that is likely to have been caused or exacerbated by alcohol;
- Tolerance, as defined by either of the following:
  - A need for markedly increased amounts of alcohol to achieve intoxication or desired effect;
  - A markedly diminished effect with continued use of the same amount of alcohol.
- Withdrawal, as manifested by either of the following:
  - The characteristic withdrawal syndrome for alcohol;
  - Alcohol (or closely related substance, such as benzodiazepine) is taken to relieve or avoid withdrawal symptoms.

Source: APA, 2013.

DSM-5 Criteria for AUD

Rather than utilizing a quick-screen diagnostic test for detecting alcohol dependence or use disorder, many clinicians prefer to use the DSM-5 criteria (see Table 1.5). The major differences between the earlier DSM-IV and DSM-5 criteria are that:

1. DSM-IV described two distinct disorders (i.e., alcohol abuse and alcohol dependence) while DSM-5 integrated the two disorders into a single alcohol use disorder (i.e., AUD);
2. DSM-5 eliminated the legal test item from DSM-IV (i.e., "More than once gotten arrested, been held at a police station, or had other legal problems because of your drinking?");
3. DSM-5 added new criterium related to craving (i.e., "Wanted a drink so badly you couldn't think of anything else?").

(NIAAA, 2016, p. 1)

Scoring of the DSM-5 Criteria for AUD

The scoring of the DSM-5 criteria for AUD is quite simple, only requiring the presence of at least two of the AUD symptoms (see Table 1.10). The severity of the AUD is defined as:

- Mild: The presence of two or three symptoms;
- Moderate: The presence of four or five symptoms;
- Severe: The presence of six or more symptoms.

(NIAAA, 2016, p. 2)

Quick-Screen Psychometric Tests

Several specific psychometric tests are available for detecting alcohol dependence or use disorder among older adults.[78] These tests have been developed for use in clinical practice settings—both institutional and office settings—and are capable of:

1. Quick administration (i.e., efficient);
2. Easy scoring;
3. High levels of accuracy (i.e., valid and reliable) regarding the specific detection of alcohol or other abusable psychotropic dependence of use disorder(s) among older adults.

(Pagliaro & Pagliaro, 2020)

The following four tests are useful examples that have demonstrated statistical validity and reliability:

1. Alcohol Use Disorders Identification Test—Consumption (AUDIT-C);
2. CAGE;
3. Comorbidity-Alcohol Risk Evaluation Tool (CARET);
4. Short Michigan Alcoholism Screening Test—Geriatric Version (SMAST-G).

Each of these psychometric tests, which can be clinician-administered as part of a diagnostic interview or self-administered by an older adult patient, are presented in the following sub-sections that include a brief overview of the test, its scoring criteria, and recommendations for its use for older adults.

The AUDIT-C

The AUDIT-C, which was derived from the ten-item full AUDIT that was developed by the WHO, is a three-item psychometric test that is simple and quick to administer (see Table 1.6). It focuses on the amount and frequency of alcohol consumption and, consequently, has been widely recommended for use (USPSTF, 2019). However, the AUDIT-C does not provide information regarding the potential stressors and behaviors related to alcohol use.

Scoring the Audit-C Each item of the AUDIT-C is scored 0 to 4 resulting in a total possible scale score of 0 to 12 (scores of 0 reflect no alcohol use). In men, a score of 4 or more is

78. For a comprehensive review and analysis of all available psychometric tests used to detect alcohol or other abusable psychotropic dependence or use disorder(s)—as well as an explanation of related test statistics—see Pagliaro and Pagliaro (2020).

Table 1.6 The AUDIT-C

THE AUDIT-C: QUESTIONS, FORCED RESPONSES, AND POINT ALLOCATION FOR SCORING

Question 1 How often do you have a drink containing alcohol?

Forced Response & Point Allocation
Never—(0 points)
Monthly or less—(1 point)
2 to 4 times/month—(2 points)
2 to 3 times/week—(3 points)
4 or more times/week—(4 points)

Question 2 How many standard drinks containing alcohol do you have on a typical day when you are drinking?

Forced Response & Point Allocation
None, I don't drink—(0 points)
1 or 2—(0 points)
3 or 4—(1 point)
5 or 6—(2 points)
7 to 9—(3 points)
10 or more—(4 points)

Question 3 How often do you have six or more drinks on one occasion?

Forced Response & Point Allocation
Never—(0 points)
Less than monthly—(1 point)
Monthly—(2 points)
Weekly—(3 points)
Daily or almost daily—(4 points)

Source: Bush, Kivlahan, & McDonell, 1998.

considered positive; in women, a score of 3 or more is considered positive. Generally, the higher the AUDIT-C score, the more likely the older adult's drinking is affecting his/her health and safety.

The CAGE

The CAGE is a four-question, quick-screen psychometric test (Table 1.7) that was developed by Ewing in 1968 as part of a clinical study aimed at detecting alcoholism (Ewing, 1984). Overall, the CAGE performs significantly better for men, when compared to women, regarding detecting alcoholism (Dhalla & Kopec, 2007). However, because its major focus is on detecting "alcoholism," concerns have been raised that it: (1) may fail to detect "heavy drinkers," who may be in "denial," or who may "lack insight;" and (2) will miss a significant number of older adults who display less harmful or hazardous patterns of alcohol use or have significant related problems related to its use. Specifically, regarding these concerns, the AUDIT has demonstrated clinical superiority to the CAGE (McCusker, Basquille, & Khwaja, 2002).

Table 1.7 The CAGE

THE CAGE: QUESTIONS, ALTERNATE PHRASING, FORCED RESPONSES, AND POINT ALLOCATIONS FOR SCORING
Question 1 Have you ever felt you ought to **C**ut down on your drinking?
Forced Response & Point Allocation
No—(0 points); Yes—(1 point)
Alternate phrasing Have you ever felt the need to cut down your drinking?
Forced Response & Point Allocation
No—(0 points); Yes—(1 point)
Question 2 Have people **A**nnoyed you by criticizing your drinking?
Forced Response & Point Allocation
No—(0 points); Yes—(1 point)
Alternate phrasing Have you ever felt annoyed by criticism of your drinking?
Forced Response & Point Allocation
No—(0 points); Yes—(1 point)
Question 3 Have you ever felt bad or **G**uilty about your drinking?
Forced Response & Point Allocation
No—(0 points); Yes—(1 point)
Alternate phrasing Have you ever had guilty feelings about your drinking?
Forced Response & Point Allocation
No—(0 points); Yes—(1 point)
Question 4 Have you ever had a drink first thing in the morning to steady your nerves or to get rid of a hangover (i.e., as an **E**ye-opener)?
Forced Response & Point Allocation
No—(0 points); Yes—(1 point)
Alternate phrasing Have you ever taken a morning eye-opener?
Forced Response & Point Allocation
No—(0 points); Yes—(1 point)

Sources: Ewing, 1984; Mayfield, McLeod, & Hall, 1974.

Scoring the Cage When scoring the CAGE, each affirmative answer is given a score of 1. A total score of 2 or higher is indicative of "alcoholism" (Buchsbaum, Buchanan, & Centor, 1991; Kitchens, 1994; NIAAA, 1995b). However, several researchers (e.g., Aertgeerts, Buntinx, & Kester, 2004) found the CAGE to be of limited screening value at this cutoff score. For example, O'Brien (2008) recommends that a score of 2 or 3 is "highly indicative" of alcoholism and that a score of 4 is "diagnostic" of alcoholism.

The CARET

The CARET (Table 1.8) is a screening test based on the "Alcohol Related Problems Survey" (ARPS) (Fink, Morton, & Beck, 2002). Both the CARET and the ARPS screening tests identify harmful and hazardous drinking behavior in addition to alcohol dependence or use disorder. Additionally, both tests were specifically developed for, and tested with, older

Table 1.8 The CARET

ITEM	AMOUNT OF DRINKING CONSIDERED AT-RISK
[Alcohol use and behaviors in the last 12 months]	[5 drinks or more/day at any frequency; 4/day at least 2 times/month; 8/day at least 4 times/week]
Number of alcohol drinks and frequency of drinking:	
• 4 or more drinks on one occasion (binge drinking)	• At least 1 time/week
• Driving within 2 hours of drinking three or more drinks	• Any frequency
• Someone concerned about participant's alcohol use	• Any amount
• Someone concerned about participant's alcohol use more than 12 months ago	4 or more/day at any frequency; or 2 to 3/day at least 4 times/week
***Alcohol use and medications taken at least 3 to 4 times per week currently*:**	
• Medications that may cause bleeding, dizziness, or sedation	4 or more/day at any frequency; or 2 to 3/day at least 4 times/week
• Medications used for gastroesophageal reflux, ulcer disease, or depression	4 or more/day at any frequency; or 2 to 3/day at least 4 times/week
• Medications for hypertension	5 or more/day at any frequency; 4/day at least 2 times/week; or 3/day at least 4 times/week
Alcohol use and comorbidities in the past 12 months:	
• Liver disease or pancreatitis	Any amount
• Gout or depression	4 or more/day at any frequency; 3/day at least 2 times/week; or 2/day at least 4 times/week
• High blood pressure or diabetes	5 or more/day at any frequency; 4/day at least 2 times /month; or 3/day at least 4 times/week
• *Sometimes* have problems with sleeping, falling, memory, heartburn, stomach pain, nausea, vomiting, or feel sad/blue	5 or more/day at any frequency; 4/day at least 2 times/month; or 3/day at least 2 times per week
• *Often* have problems with sleeping, falling, memory, heartburn, stomach pain, nausea, vomiting, or feel sad/blue	4 or more/day at any frequency; or 2 to 3/day at least 2 times/week

Source: Barnes et al., 2010.

adults in the U.S. (e.g., Barnes, Moore, & Xu, 2010; Kuerbis, Yuan, & Borok, 2015). The CARET, as a self-report instrument, is often administered as a mailed survey, particularly in research contexts.

The CARET identifies older adults who are at risk for alcohol-related problems because of their:

1. Comorbid diseases;
2. Concurrent use of prescription drugs;

3. High-risk behaviors (e.g., drinking and driving);
4. Quantity and frequency of alcohol ingestion.

The CARET is more difficult to administer and more time consuming than the AUDIT-C, CAGE, and the SMAST-G. In addition, the scoring and interpretation of the results of the CARET are more difficult and significantly more subjective than what is generally encountered with most psychometric screening tests. However, it provides data regarding the amount and frequency of alcohol consumption as well as data concerning related diseases and concurrent use of prescription and non-prescription drugs. As such, the CARET addresses the following alcohol-related comorbid risk factors:

- Alcohol interacting drug use;
- Drinking and driving;
- Frequency and quantity of alcohol consumption;
- Mental and physical disorders;
- Physical functioning;
- Signs and symptoms of abuse/dependence;
- Symptoms of disease.

(Towers, Sheridan, & Newcombe, 2018)

The SMAST-G

The SMAST-G (Table 1.9) was designed specifically for older adults (Blow, Schulenberg, & Demo-Dananberg, 1992). It was derived from the 24-question, full MAST-G and primarily focuses on drinking-related behaviors within the past year. The 10-item SMAST-G is easy and quick to administer but lacks drinking information regarding the frequency and amount of alcohol consumed.

Scoring the SMAST-G Each positive (i.e., "yes") response is given a score of 1 for a maximum possible total score of 10. A score of 2 or higher is considered to be indicative of alcoholism/problem drinking.

> ***Related Professional Reminder:** Psychometric screening test results provide useful data, but do not constitute a diagnoses of alcohol dependence or use disorder per se because, in and of themselves, the results are not pathognomonic or diagnostic for several reasons including "faking bad" or "faking good."[79] Thus, the data provided should be combined with other relevant data (e.g., clinical interview, related laboratory test results, and physical examination) in order to formulate an accurate diagnosis of alcohol dependence or use disorder.*

79. See also the in-depth analysis of the strengths, weaknesses, and limitations associated with all of the various psychometric screening tests, including issues concerning validity and reliability, in Pagliaro and Pagliaro (2020).

Table 1.9 THE SMAST-G

ITEM #	QUESTION	SCORING CRITERIA (*POINT ALLOCATION*) YES (1) NO (0)
1.	When talking with others, do you ever underestimate how much you drink?	
2.	After a few drinks, have you sometimes not eaten or been able to skip a meal because you didn't feel hungry?	
3.	Does having a few drinks help decrease your shakiness or tremors?	
4.	Does alcohol sometimes make it hard for you to remember parts of the day or night?	
5.	Do you usually take a drink to relax or calm your nerves?	
6.	Do you drink to take your mind off your problems?	
7.	Have you ever increased your drinking after experiencing a loss in your life?	
8.	Has a doctor or nurse ever said they were worried or concerned about your drinking?	
9.	Have you ever made rules to manage your dinking?	
10.	When you feel lonely, does having a drink help?	
		Total SMAST-G Score (0–10)

Source: Naegle, 2018.

COMMON CONTEMPORANEOUS DIAGNOSES AMONG OLDER ADULTS

Over the years, several closely related terms have been commonly used to denote a "contemporaneous diagnosis," such as:

- "Dual addiction"—concomitant alcoholism and drug abuse (Kreek & Stimmel, 1984);
- "Dual disorder"—concurrent diagnosis of alcoholism plus a psychiatric diagnosis (Daley, Moss, & Campbell, 1987, p. 3);
- "Dual diagnosis"—the identification of two, or more, mental disorders at the same time (Pagliaro, 1990);
- "Comorbidity"—cases of two diagnosable disorders in the realm of substance abuse and mental illness (Belfer, 1993);
- "Dual diagnosis"—the concurrence of another disorder (psychiatric or medical) existing independent of an addictive disorder (Miller, Leukefeld, & Jefferson, 1994, p. 8);
- "Multiple diagnosis"—two or more mental health diagnoses in addition to a substance use diagnosis (Slesnick & Prestopnik, 2005, p. 179).

The diversity of these terms and definitions has contributed to much semantic confusion in the published literature and in clinical settings. Thus, for clarity, the term "contemporaneous diagnosis" is used in this reference text and is defined as:

The detection—in an older adult—of the simultaneous occurrence of:

1. *Alcohol dependence or use disorder, and/or;*
2. *One or more other abusable psychotropic dependences or use disorders;*
   One or more other mental disorders;[80]
   One or more physical medical disorders[81] *that may, or may not, be directly related.*

(Pagliaro & Pagliaro, 2018)

Contemporaneous Diagnoses Involving Other Mental Disorders

As originally recognized by Pagliaro (1990), the presence of more than one other mental disorder with alcohol dependence or use disorder, and/or one or more abusable psychotropic dependences or use disorders, is more common than once thought. In fact, among the patients we have encountered in our clinical practices, who had been diagnosed with an alcohol dependence or use disorder and/or one or more abusable psychotropic dependences or use disorders, almost three-quarters (74%) had two or more other mental disorders (Pagliaro & Pagliaro, *Clinical Patient Data Files*). In cases in which the alcohol dependence or use disorder, abusable psychotropic dependence or use disorder, and another mental disorder are "directly" related, the alcohol dependence or use disorder and/or the abusable psychotropic dependence or use disorder most commonly occur as an antecedent to, or as a consequence of, the other mental disorder (e.g., Lehman, Myers, & Corty, 1994; Pagliaro, 1995).[82]

As previously noted, older adults who present with a primary diagnosis of alcohol dependence or use disorder, another abusable psychotropic dependence or use disorder, and another mental disorder, can generally be expected to have a contemporaneous diagnosis.[83] A diagnosis of alcohol dependence or use disorder or other abusable psychotropic dependence

---

80. For the sake of parsimony, and to further reduce semantic confusion, we use the term, "other mental disorder," to include all related disorders, diseases, and conditions that are typically diagnosed and treated by psychiatrists and psychologists (i.e., all psychiatric disorders and all psychological disorders).
81. In addition, for the sake of parsimony, and to further reduce semantic confusion, we use the term, "physical medical disorder," to include all related disorders, diseases, and health conditions that are typically diagnosed and treated by physicians (i.e., all physical medical disorders, including neurological disorders).
82. Usually, the distinction as to whether or not a co-occurring mental disorder is an "antecedent" or a "consequence" to alcohol dependence or use disorder, is not particularly relevant in many clinical contexts. However, in cases where the co-occurring mental disorder is an "antecedent" to the alcohol dependence or use disorder and/or other abusable psychotropic dependence, intervention aimed at ameliorating the co-occurring mental disorder (e.g., major depressive disorder) will also ameliorate the related alcohol dependence or use disorder and/or the other abusable psychotropic dependence or use disorder—and vice versa.
83. In our clinical practice, which specializes in the treatment of patients who have contemporaneous diagnoses, we have found that most patients, themselves, are often unaware that they have a contemporaneous diagnosis (i.e., the contemporaneous diagnosis has not been previously identified or diagnosed). Generally, these patients are only consciously aware that they are "depressed" or that they have a "drinking problem" (i.e., the reason for their referral), or that they smoke cigarettes "more than they should." They are not aware that they have two, or generally more, active other mental disorders—all of which are generally highly interrelated (Pagliaro & Pagliaro, *Clinical Patient Data Files*).

or use disorder is commonly expected in approximately 10% to 20% of patients who have another mental disorder. However, the published literature (e.g., Drake, Essock, & Shaner, 2001) and our own clinical experiences suggest that the actual incidence of contemporaneous diagnoses is significantly higher (i.e., more than 50% and often closer to 100%) for older adults whose primary disorder is a clinically significant diagnosis of alcohol dependence or use disorder and/or another abusable psychotropic dependence or use disorder (Pagliaro & Pagliaro, *Clinical Patient Data Files*). Additionally, when compared to older adults who have a single diagnosis of alcohol dependence or use disorder, other abusable psychotropic dependence or use disorder, or a mental disorder, older adults who concurrently have alcohol dependence or use disorder, another abusable psychotropic dependence or use disorder(s), and other mental disorders, generally have:

1. A significantly more severe form of the related disorders;
2. A poorer prognosis regarding therapeutic outcomes;
3. Major physical medical disorders often associated with significant related health (e.g., hepatitis, HIV, or tuberculosis) and social care requirements (e.g., homelessness, reduction or lack of physical mobility, or social isolation).

Older adults, who concurrently have alcohol dependence or use disorder, other abusable psychotropic dependence or use disorder(s), and other mental disorder(s), are also more likely to present with increased rates/incidence of:

- Arrests and incarcerations;
- Homelessness and reliance on social assistance;
- Hospitalization or institutionalization;
- Job loss and unemployment;
- Little or no response to treatment interventions;
- Poor compliance with prescribed pharmacotherapy, psychotherapy (e.g., family, group, or individual), and other treatment interventions;
- Poor interpersonal relationships (i.e., difficulty making and keeping friends);
- Recidivism or relapse;
- Relationship difficulties (e.g., spousal separation or divorce);
- Suicide, attempted or completed;[84]
- Work difficulties (e.g., absenteeism or quitting jobs).

As identified three decades ago by Stowell (1991, p. 98):

> Dual diagnosis patients are [generally] heterogeneous as to their psychiatric diagnoses, as well as the various substances they abuse.

However, a review of the published literature suggests that the majority of cases of contemporaneous diagnoses detected among older adults involve: (1) one or more abusable psychotropic dependences or use disorders—related to the use of alcohol, amphetamines, cannabis,

84. See the related discussion in the earlier pharmacology subsection, Undesired, or Harmful, Effects and Toxicities—"Depression and Suicide."

cocaine, nicotine, opiate analgesics, or prescription sedative-hypnotics; and (2) one or more other mental disorders from the following seven categories:[85]

1. Anxiety disorders (e.g., panic disorder [PD] or PTSD);
2. Eating disorders (e.g., anorexia nervosa or bulimia nervosa);
3. Gender dysphoria;
4. Mood disorders (e.g., bipolar disorder [BD] or MDD);
5. Personality disorders (e.g., borderline personality disorder [BPD]);
6. Psychotic disorders (e.g., schizophrenia);
7. Sleep disorders (e.g., insomnia).

(Pagliaro & Pagliaro, 2018)

Of these mental disorders, the three that are the most frequently implicated with a contemporaneous diagnosis among older adults are:

1. Anxiety disorders;
2. MDD;
3. Sleep disorders (e.g., insomnia).

As noted by Anker and Kushner (2019, p. 1):

> Research has shown that up to 50% of individuals receiving treatment for problematic alcohol use also met diagnostic criteria for one or more anxiety disorders.

Appropriate pharmacotherapy and psychotherapy are a common and integral component of the management of the contemporaneous diagnoses commonly presented by older adults. The symptomatic management of alcohol dependence or use disorder, various abusable psychotropic dependences or use disorders, other mental disorders, and physical medical disorders may be adversely affected by the inadequate treatment of one or more of these disorders. The complexity of diagnosing, planning therapeutic intervention, and delivering appropriate pharmacotherapy, together with optimal psychotherapy/counseling and needed medical treatment, generally requires a significant degree of: (1) multidisciplinary expertise; (2) communication; and (3) coordination.

We now turn to the approaches for treating alcohol dependence or use disorder.

TREATING OLDER ADULT ALCOHOL DEPENDENCE OR USE DISORDER

More research is available on the treatment of alcohol dependence or use disorder than for all of the other abusable psychotropics combined. However, as emphasized by Reus, Fochtmann, and Bukstein (2018b, p. 4) in an AUD practice guideline for the APA:

> Despite its high prevalence and numerous negative consequences, AUD remains undertreated.

85. For example, over 90% of individuals with alcohol dependence or use disorder also have nicotine dependence or use disorder (e.g., Van Skike, Maggio, & Reynolds, 2015; Verplaetse & McKee, 2017).

The treatment of alcohol dependence or use disorder involves both pharmacotherapeutic and psychotherapeutic/counseling, including 12-step programs and other approaches. We have consistently found that the combination of both efficacious pharmacotherapy and psychotherapy/counseling provide optimal results in terms of achieving and maintaining abstinence (i.e., "resumed nonuse")[86] by: (1) dealing with the alcohol withdrawal syndrome; and (2) preventing patterns of "relapsed use," or "resumed compulsive use."[87] Each of these approaches are discussed separately in the following subsections, "Pharmacotherapeutic Approaches" and "Psychotherapeutic/Counseling Approaches."

Pharmacotherapeutic Approaches

There are no available pharmacotherapeutic approaches for "preventing" the development of alcohol dependence or use disorder among older adults. However, pharmacotherapeutic approaches have been developed, and found to be efficacious for older adults, regarding: (1) management of the "alcohol withdrawal syndrome;" and (2) abstinence maintenance facilitation. In the following subsections, we present and discuss these pharmacotherapeutic approaches.[88]

Before proceeding, we would like to briefly discuss a related, seriously flawed approach based exclusively on the concept of "harm reduction" and typically referred to as "managed alcohol programs" (MAPs). As emphasized by Alan Marlatt, one of the primary proponents of harm reduction, "harm reduction is an orientation and belief system" (Witkiewitz & Marlatt, 2006, p. 285) (i.e., it is not an empirical, or science-based, approach to treatment).

MAPs

Since the 1970s, MAPs have been primarily operationalized in Canada (Watts, 2018), where these programs were largely established on the concept of harm reduction proposed by the then Minister of Health, Marc Lalonde. Typically, MAPs provide participants with:

1. Shelter/housing (often motel/hotel rooms);
2. On average, 12 standard drinks of alcohol daily (usually wine) at 60- to 90-minute intervals;
3. Opportunity to access treatment.

In this context, MAPs can be compared to other harm reduction programs (e.g., methadone maintenance [see Chapter 5, *Prescription Opiate Analgesics and Heroin*]).

The primarily related social benefits of MAPs include: (1) decreased crime (e.g., theft); (2) fewer related hospital admissions; and (3) getting chronic "skid row drunks" off the

86. Although controlled use has been found to be successful in some cases, we have consistently argued, during the last 40 years of our clinical practice, that complete abstinence is the better goal for older adults who are diagnosed with alcohol dependence or use disorder.
87. See the related discussion of the cited patterns of drug and substance use in the earlier section, "Nine Patterns of Abusable Psychotropic Use."
88. It should be kept in mind that the approaches discussed in these subsections, particularly those related to "psychotherapeutic/counseling approaches," may also be applied in the context of treating other abusable psychotropic dependence or use disorders, including those discussed in the following chapters.

streets, and, thus, decreasing police contact and increasing local business activity (e.g., Vallance, Stockwell, & Pauly, 2016).

The major concerns related to the implementation of MAPs include:

- Attracting older adults with alcohol dependence or use disorder (i.e., "alcoholism") to areas (e.g., inner cities) where the programs provide free alcoholic drinks;
- Facilitating the occurrence, or exacerbation, of alcohol-related diseases (see the earlier pharmacology subsection—"Undesired, or Harmful, Effects and Toxicities");
- Forestalling attempts at more effective pharmacotherapeutic and psychotherapeutic/counseling approaches for alcohol dependence or use disorder.

(Pagliaro & Pagliaro, *Clinical Patient Data Files*)

Consequently, we have never recommended the use of MAPs for older adults with alcohol dependence or use disorder. However, MAPs have been increasingly used in selected cities across the U.S. For example, as part of the attempt to deal with the COVID-19 pandemic, MAPs were widely implemented in the city of San Francisco in 2020, particularly for older homeless people and those with underlying health conditions (Miles, 2020). As shared by a recovering "formerly homeless addict:"

> I just found out that homeless placed in hotels in SF are being delivered Alcohol, Weed and Methadone because they identified as an addict/alcoholic for FREE. You're supposed to be offering treatment. This is enabling and is wrong on many levels.

In response, the San Francisco Department of Public Health emphasized that:

> These harm reduction-based practices, which are not unique to San Francisco, and are not paid for with [city] taxpayer money, help guests successfully complete isolation and quarantine and have significant individual and public health benefits in the COVID-19 pandemic.
>
> (Miles, 2020, p. 1)

While we do not impugn the motives of the proponents of MAPs, we believe, with a great deal of generosity toward the proponents of MAPs, that consideration of the following aphorism is particularly appropriate and applicable in this context:

> The road to hell is paved with good intentions.
>
> (Samuel Johnson, 1709–1784)

***Related Professional Reminder*: As with all pharmacotherapies, before initiating the selected pharmacotherapeutic approach, ensure that the older adult:**

- ***Does not have any contraindications to the use of the selected pharmacotherapeutic approach;***
- ***Is not at risk for any clinically significant drug-drug interactions (i.e., the risk has been identified and has been appropriately dealt with);***
- ***Has been identified as having appropriate renal and hepatic function and that any other necessary related adjustments to the dosage or dosing interval of the associated pharmacotherapeutic approach has been carefully addressed.***

Alcohol Withdrawal Syndrome Management[89]

For over 50 years, the acute alcohol withdrawal syndrome has been managed quite successfully with a long-acting benzodiazepine—usually chlordiazepoxide (Librium®) or diazepam (Valium®). Benzodiazepine pharmacotherapy for the management of alcohol withdrawal generally requires a gradual reduction of dosage over a one to two-week period. When appropriately used, benzodiazepine therapy can make the alcohol withdrawal syndrome virtually "symptomless" (Pagliaro & Pagliaro, 1999). In their literature review of management for the alcohol withdrawal syndrome among hospitalized patients, Muzyk, Leung, and Nelson (2013) found that, "diazepam loading"[90] provided rapid symptom relief and reduced the incidence of seizures and the duration of delirium tremens, or "DTs" (p. 113). Currently, the benzodiazepines are considered to be the cornerstone for the management of the alcohol withdrawal syndrome (e.g., Long, Long, & Koyfman, 2017; Pagliaro & Pagliaro, 1999, 2009; Ricks, Replogle, & Cook, 2010).

For the treatment of cases that are resistant to benzodiazepine pharmacotherapy, the barbiturate, phenobarbital (Luminal®), and the general anesthetic, propofol (Diprivan®; "Milk of Amnesia"), have been recommended alone, or in combination with a benzodiazepine (e.g., Brotherton, Hamilton, & Kloss, 2016; Long et al., 2017; Mo, Thomas, & Karras, 2016; Schmidt et al., 2016).

Although pharmacologically not as efficacious as other pharmacotherapeutic approaches, the alpha-adrenergic agonist, clonidine (Catapres®), which is generally clinically used for its antihypertensive effects, has been used as an adjunct, in conjunction with benzodiazepines, for the management of moderate to severe alcohol withdrawal syndrome (Bayard, McIntyre, & Hill, 2004; Stanley, Worrall, & Lunsford, 2005). In this context, clonidine may help to reduce the signs and symptoms of withdrawal associated with the hyperadrenergic state (e.g., anxiety; diaphoresis, hypertension, tachycardia). In this context, the optimal dosage of clonidine has not been established, particularly for older adults. If used, we recommend to "start low" (i.e., 0.05 mg orally at bedtime) and "go slow" (i.e., increase the dosage gradually, as tolerated, based on individual patient clinical response and cardiovascular status). Alternatively, a clonidine patch has been recommended in lieu of oral dosing. The clonidine dosage is gradually decreased over a one- to two-week period.[91] However, generally, we do not recommend the use of clonidine for older adults in this clinical context.

The use of other pharmacotherapeutic approaches for managing the alcohol withdrawal syndrome, such as the: (1) muscle relaxant, baclofen (Lioresal®); and (2) anticonvulsant, topiramate (Topamax®), are limited and of questionable efficacy (e.g., Guglielmo,

89. See also the related discussion in the earlier pharmacology subsection, Physical and Psychological Dependence—"Alcohol Withdrawal Syndrome."

90. Diazepam loading (i.e., administration of fixed 20 mg oral doses every two hours) has long been demonstrated to be a generally safe and effective management for alcohol withdrawal. Use is predicated on the pharmacology of diazepam, as well as its pharmacokinetics—rapid achievement of peak concentrations following oral use and a relatively long half-life of elimination (Heinala, Piepponen, & Heikkinen, 1990; Muzyk et al., 2013; Sellers, Naranjo, & Harrison, 1983; Weintraub, 2017). See Chapter 6, *Prescription Sedative-Hypnotics*, for additional related discussion concerning diazepam (Valium®).

91. N.B. Rebound hypertension has been associated with the abrupt discontinuation of higher dosages of clonidine, particularly with long-term use. Although not expected in this context of use, the use of clonidine for older adults necessitates extra precautions.

Martinotti, & Quatrale, 2015). However, gabapentin (Neurontin®), another anticonvulsant, also has been utilized—"off-label"—to treat alcohol withdrawal.[92] Results, particularly at higher dosages, appear both promising and significantly superior to placebo (Hammond, Niciu, & Drew, 2015; Leung, Hall-Flavin, & Nelson, 2015; Mason, Quello, & Goodell, 2014; Wilming, Alford, & Klaus, 2018).[93] Regardless, for older adults, particularly those who also have a positive history of abusable psychotropic use, we do not recommend the use of gabapentin for the treatment of the alcohol withdrawal syndrome because of the significant potential for gabapentin: (1) abuse; (2) physical dependence; and (3) withdrawal syndrome.

Alcohol Abstinence Maintenance Facilitation

Pharmacotherapeutic approaches for facilitating alcohol abstinence maintenance helps to assure continued "resumed nonuse" of alcohol, by means of either:

1. Aversive stimulation (i.e., pairing unpleasant effects with the use of alcohol);
2. Prevention of rewarding effects (i.e., "blocking" the desired effects associated with alcohol use).[94]

Three drugs have been developed and approved by the FDA to help to assure continued resumed nonuse of alcohol among people who have discontinued their regular, long-term abusive or compulsive use of alcohol:

1. Acamprosate (Campral®);
2. Disulfiram (Antabuse®);
3. Naltrexone (ReVia®).

(Garbutt, 2009, 2010; Oural, Paris, & Sullivan, 2008; Swift, 2007)

In addition, topiramate (Topamax®), an anticonvulsant, has been clinically used, "off-label," for this indication and has demonstrated some noted clinical efficacy. Each of these drugs are presented and discussed (in alphabetical order) in the following sections.

However, before proceeding, it should be noted that pharmacotherapy for alcohol dependence or use disorder is infrequently prescribed for older adults in the U.S. by either family physicians or internists. As identified by Bernstein, Guo, and Goto (2021, p. 3):

> The top decile [of physicians in the study] prescribed [pharmacotherapy for alcohol dependence or use disorder] to 14.6% of their patients. The bottom 4 deciles [of physicians] had no prescriptions [for alcohol dependence or use disorder among older adults].

---

92. Although the APA has recommended the use of gabapentin for the treatment of alcohol dependence or use disorder (Reus et al., 2018a, 2018b), until significantly more data are available supporting its therapeutic efficacy, we do not recommend gabapentin pharmacotherapy for the management of the alcohol withdrawal syndrome, particularly for older adults.
93. It should be recognized that, because gabapentin is predominantly excreted in unchanged form in the urine, dosage reduction is required in the presence of mild to severe renal impairment (Raouf, Atkinson, & Crumb, 2017), which is commonly encountered among older adults (Pagliaro & Pagliaro, 1983).
94. Abstinence, in this context, is a form of relapse prevention (see the Psychotherapeutic/ Counseling Approaches subsection—"Relapse Prevention"—later in this chapter).

Acamprosate (Campral®) Pharmacotherapy

Acamprosate (Campral®), is a synthetic chemical compound that is a structural analog of both GABA and the amino acid neuromodulator, taurine. It received approval for use by the FDA in 2004 and has been demonstrated to be both safe and effective for the prevention of relapsed use of alcohol among abstinent drinkers (Jung & Namkoong, 2006; Kennedy, Leloux, & Kutscher, 2010; Rosner, Hackl-Herrwerth, & Leucht, 2010).

Acamprosate appears to have minimal psychotropic activity (e.g., it does not possess anxiolytic, anticonvulsant, or antidepressant effects) and its use is not associated with the development of physical dependence. The use of acamprosate is generally well-tolerated (Mason & Heyser, 2010b; Yahn, Watterson, & Olive, 2013) with diarrhea and insomnia being the most reported undesired effects (Boothby & Doering, 2005; Crowley, 2015; Diehl, Ulmer, & Mutschler, 2010).[95] Overall, the clinical efficacy of acamprosate has been found to be acceptable and similar to that obtained with naltrexone. Additionally, some researchers (e.g., Crowley, 2015; Plosker, 2015) have noted that acamprosate pharmacotherapy has a generally superior efficacy in comparison to that obtained with other pharmacotherapeutic approaches.

The exact neurochemical mechanism of action for the success of acamprosate pharmacotherapy has not yet been determined (Kiefer & Mann, 2010; Yahn et al., 2013; Witkiewitz, Litten, & Leggio, 2019). However, it has been identified that the regular long-term use of alcohol (i.e., alcohol dependence or use disorder) is associated with an increase in the numbers of NMDA receptors. Consequently, during alcohol withdrawal, the NMDA receptors are stimulated by a surge in the release of neurotransmitters, such as glutamate. Given these observations, it has been suggested that acamprosate may work as a neuromodulator by reducing the glutamate surge (i.e., glutamatergic neurotransmission is restored to normal) (De Witte, Littleton, & Parot, 2005; Mason & Heyser, 2010a; Swift, 2007). Thus, acamprosate may have a dual role as a neuromodulator (i.e., as a GABA agonist and as a NMDA glutamate antagonist).

Available from the manufacturer as a 333 mg, delayed-release, enteric coated oral tablet, acamprosate is ingested daily in three divided dosages (i.e., two tablets three times daily). To increase GI absorption due to its low oral bioavailability (i.e., ~ 11%), it should be ingested on an empty stomach. However, because the food-associated reduction is only approximately 20%, acamprosate is generally ingested without regard to meals (Mason & Heyser, 2010b; Wright & Myrick, 2006).

Acamprosate does not undergo hepatic metabolism and is primarily eliminated in unchanged form in the urine (Mason & Heyser, 2010b; Saivin, Hulot, & Chabac, 1998). Consequently, the use of acamprosate is contraindicated for older adults who have severe renal impairment (i.e., creatinine clearance less than 30 ml/minute). Although not generally recommended as the "drug of first choice" for older adults who have moderate renal impairment, acamprosate can be used with an appropriate reduction in dosage (i.e., one 333 mg tablet, three times daily) (Plosker, 2015; Reus, Fochtmann, & Bukstein, 2018a; Wright & Myrick, 2006). The half-life of elimination of acamprosate is 24 to 32 hours (Kalk & Lingford-Hughes, 2014; Wright & Myrick, 2006).

---

95. Diarrhea and insomnia each have a reported incidence of approximately 10%. Additionally, diarrhea has been associated with the discontinuation of acamprosate use in approximately 2% of patients.

Acamprosate combination pharmacotherapy for the facilitation of alcohol abstinence maintenance (e.g., acamprosate and naltrexone), along with adjunctive psychotherapy (e.g., acamprosate and cognitive behavioral therapy), have been found to significantly increase related therapeutic outcomes (Boothby & Doering, 2005; Kennedy et al., 2010; Mason, 2001, 2003).

Disulfiram (Antabuse®) Pharmacotherapy

In 1951, disulfiram (Antabuse®) became the first drug that was approved by the FDA for the management of "alcoholism" (Soghoian, Wiener, & Diaz-Alcala, 2016). It is well, but slowly, absorbed following oral ingestion and is highly protein bound. Disulfiram is highly lipid-soluble and, consequently, initially concentrated in adipose tissue. It is extensively metabolized in the liver to both toxic and nontoxic metabolites with 5% to 20% of disulfiram being excreted in unchanged form in the feces (Soghoian et al.f, 2016). Its half-life of elimination has been estimated to range from 50 to 120 hours.

Disulfiram blocks the metabolism of alcohol at the "acetaldehyde stage" by means of irreversible inhibition of the enzyme, acetaldehyde dehydrogenase (see Figure 1.3, "Alcohol Metabolism," and the related discussion in the earlier pharmacology subsection, "Pharmacokinetics—Metabolism"). Consequently, when alcohol is ingested, even in small amounts, acetaldehyde accumulates in the circulatory system and elicits many undesired, or harmful, effects and toxicities throughout the body, including:

- Anxiety;
- Blurred vision;
- Chest pain;
- Confusion;
- Copious vomiting;
- Diaphoresis;
- Dyspnea;
- Facial flushing;
- Hyperventilation;
- Hypotension;
- Nausea;
- Palpitations;
- Respiratory distress;
- Syncope;
- Tachycardia;
- Thirst;
- Throbbing headache;
- Vertigo;
- Weakness.

(AHFS, 2017; Pagliaro & Pagliaro, 2004, 2009; Stokes, 2020)

The intensity of this reaction—known as the "disulfiram-alcohol (-ethanol) reaction," or more commonly, "Antabuse® reaction," "Asian Flush," or "disulfiram flush"—is generally proportional to both the amount of:

1. Disulfiram used as a component of the alcohol abstinence maintenance facilitation approach;
2. Alcohol ingested during a drinking session.

(Pagliaro & Pagliaro, 1999)

Disulfiram pharmacotherapy is initiated following at least one day of abstinence from alcohol use to avoid inadvertently precipitating the disulfiram reaction.[96] Subsequently, disulfiram is orally ingested in doses of 500 mg, on a daily basis each morning, for a period of months to years until abstinence can be maintained without the aid of the drug.[97] Daytime drowsiness/tiredness and nighttime sleep disturbances are the most commonly reported undesired effects (Diehl et al., 2010). Regarding contraindications to the use of disulfiram, several have been identified, including coronary occlusion, heart failure, hypersensitivity, metronidazole pharmacotherapy, myocardial disease (severe), and psychosis (Pagliaro & Pagliaro, 1999; Rundio, 2010).

***<u>Related Professional Reminder</u>:* Older adult disulfiram pharmacotherapy for alcohol abstinence maintenance facilitation requires health and social care professionals to clearly explain and discuss with older adults the following factors that are associated with this pharmacotherapeutic approach:**

1. ***Before initiating disulfiram pharmacotherapy, the mechanism of disulfiram action as a means for maintaining alcohol abstinence;***
2. ***When receiving disulfiram pharmacotherapy, the need to avoid alcohol and alcohol-containing items that may precipitate a disulfiram reaction, such as:***
   - ***Alcohol-containing cough syrups;***
   - ***Alcohol-containing aftershave products;***
   - ***Alcohol-containing hand sanitizers;***
   - ***Alcohol-containing mouthwashes;***
   - ***Candies that contain liqueurs;***
   - ***Chinese cooking wine;***
   - ***Cosmetics that contain alcohol;***
   - ***Pure vanilla extract.***
3. ***When discontinuing disulfiram pharmacotherapy, because of its long-lasting effects that are related to its half-life of elimination, it is imperative to discuss***

96. Although, the FDA-approved drug monograph for disulfiram states that its use is contraindicated during alcohol intoxication and within "12 hours of alcohol ingestion," we recommend, with an abundance of caution, that its use be contraindicated within "24 hours of alcohol abstinence," particularly for older adults.
97. Systematic reviews (e.g., Skinner, Lahmek, & Pham, 2014) generally have not supported significant efficacy for disulfiram pharmacotherapy when used alone—particularly in the context of double-blind controlled studies. Both acamprosate and naltrexone are safer to use and more efficacious in this clinical context (see related discussion in this chapter).

> ***the need to avoid the use of alcohol for two weeks following the last dose of disulfiram in order to avoid the precipitation of a disulfiram reaction.***

Based on the potential for undesired, or harmful, effects and toxicities, which can be serious, particularly for older adults 60 years of age or older, we do not generally recommend the use of disulfiram pharmacotherapy for this age group.[98] Overall, we consider disulfiram to be a second-line option when compared to acamprosate or naltrexone pharmacotherapy for alcohol dependence or use disorder.

Naltrexone (ReVia®) Pharmacotherapy

Another approach for promoting alcohol abstinence maintenance facilitation is naltrexone (ReVia®) pharmacotherapy, which received FDA approval in 1994. Naltrexone is a long-acting oral opiate analgesic antagonist (see Chapter 5, *Prescription Opiate Analgesics and Heroin*) that was originally developed and marketed under the brand name, "Trexan®," for the treatment of opiate analgesic dependence or use disorder (Kirchmayer, Davoli, & Verster, 2000). However—by serendipity—naltrexone was also found to block the disinhibitory euphoria associated with alcohol use.[99] Naltrexone is usually ingested once daily (i.e., 50 mg/day) without regard to meals. Overall, the clinical efficacy of naltrexone is acceptable and similar to that obtained for acamprosate. Naltrexone combination therapy with appropriate psychotherapeutic/counseling approaches increases efficacious outcomes.

An injectable form of naltrexone (Vivitrol®) also is available and is considered a major pharmaceutical advancement regarding alcohol abstinence maintenance facilitation (Garbutt, Kranzler, & O'Malley, 2005). The naltrexone injectable form is an extended-release, microsphere injectable suspension formulation (380 mg). It is injected intramuscularly (IM), generally once a month, in a major gluteal muscle by a health care provider or trained family member. The IM injection of naltrexone significantly increases compliance with alcohol abstinence maintenance facilitation pharmacotherapy (Swift, 2007).

The endogenous opiate system plays a significant role in the mediation of the disinhibitory euphoria and other desired effects associated with alcohol use, particularly those related to the modulation of dopaminergic neurotransmission in the mesolimbic area of the brain (Jung & Namkoong, 2006; Soyka & Rosner, 2010).[100] Consequently, when the receptors are blocked by naltrexone, the associated "urge" to drink is reduced, thus, strengthening the ability to abstain from drinking. Although additional research is required, it appears that carriers of a variant of the mu-opiate receptor gene may be particularly receptive to the

98. N.B. When we do recommend the use of disulfiram, we attempt to ensure that the older adult is, and remains, well-motivated. Low motivation—and, consequently, low compliance—has been a perennial problem related to disulfiram pharmacotherapy. For example, some 40 years ago when we were both working at a county hospital in California with a large ward for women and men who were "alcoholics," we noted that the containers of disulfiram and multiple vitamins, which were dispensed to them upon discharge, were commonly found unopened and discarded in the bushes near the front entrance of the hospital by the groundskeeping staff (Pagliaro & Pagliaro, *Clinical Patient Data Files*).
99. N.B. The CNS depressant effects, including those related to the effects on cognition, do not appear to be significantly affected by naltrexone. Thus, it is not a "sobriety pill."
100. This current theory is based upon the observation originally expressed in the Walsh-Davis hypothesis. The Walsh-Davis hypothesis, first posited in the 1970s, proposed that a common molecular biochemical mechanism may be responsible for, or at least contribute to, addiction to both alcohol and the opiate analgesics (Davis & Walsh, 1970a, 1970b).

efficacious effects of naltrexone abstinence maintenance pharmacotherapy for promoting self-restraint among regular, continuous long-term users of alcohol—including, for example, those who are identified as: addicted to alcohol, physically and psychologically dependent on alcohol, having alcoholism, or having been diagnosed with AUD (Mann & Hermann, 2010; Pagliaro & Pagliaro, 2018). As a result of these actions, the use of naltrexone can be of particular benefit for those older adults who have a contemporaneous diagnosis involving the abuse of both alcohol and opiate analgesics.

As an adjunct to effective psychotherapeutic approaches, naltrexone pharmacotherapy demonstrates:

1. A significant clinical utility with reports of less craving for alcohol;
2. A lower rate of relapse;
3. When drinking, the ingestion of fewer drinks per drinking episode.

(Liang & Olsen, 2014; Volpicelli, Clay, & Watson, 1995)

Nausea is the most common adverse effect associated with naltrexone pharmacotherapy. However, dizziness, headaches, and sleep disturbances have also been commonly reported. The long-term safety and efficacy of naltrexone have not yet been clearly established. Additionally, the FDA has added a "boxed warning" to its official monograph stating that: "Naltrexone may cause liver damage when taken in large doses."[101]

Naltrexone, as a potent opiate analgesic antagonist, can precipitate the opiate analgesic withdrawal syndrome among regular, long-term users of the opiate analgesics, including those who are being medically managed for pain (e.g., acute, severe pain; chronic cancer; or other malignant, pain). Thus, caution must be exercised when naltrexone pharmacotherapy is implemented for these users, who also would require alternative pain relief measures until naltrexone is no longer required and its effects have dissipated (Pagliaro & Pagliaro, 1999; Volpicelli et al., 1995).[102] Of note, because of both naltrexone's primary hepatic metabolism and its propensity for hepatotoxicity, the use of naltrexone pharmacotherapy is contraindicated for older adults who have acute hepatitis or hepatic failure.

Topiramate (Topamax®) Pharmacotherapy

Topiramate (Topamax®) is an anticonvulsant that has been used to symptomatically manage various seizure disorders in the U.S. for over 30 years (Maryanoff, Nortey, & Gardocki, 1987). While not FDA approved for alcohol abstinence maintenance, its "off-label" use for this indication has been reported for well over a decade (Johnson, Ait-Daoud, & Bowden, 2003; Johnson, Rosenthal, & Capece, 2007). Several published studies and reviews (e.g., De Sousa, 2010; Florez, Saiz, & Garcia-Portilla, 2010; Jefee-Bahloul, Jorandby, & Arias, 2019;

101. In the absence of other pre-existing liver damage or disease (e.g., hepatitis or hepatic carcinoma), the risk for naltrexone-induced liver disease appears to be extremely low—particularly, at the recommended dosage of 50 mg per day.
102. Alternatively, if the use of opiate analgesic pharmacotherapy for the treatment of severe pain is clinically indicated, the naltrexone should be discontinued and appropriately replaced with alternative pharmacotherapeutic approaches (e.g., acamprosate).

Johnson & Ait-Daoud, 2010; Kenna, Lomastro, & Schiesl, 2009) have indicated that, when compared to either placebo or naltrexone pharmacotherapy for alcohol abstinence maintenance, topiramate pharmacotherapy resulted in:

1. Fewer drinks per day;
2. Fewer drinks per drinking day;
3. Fewer heavy drinking days;
4. Greater reduction in reports of craving;
5. More days abstinent.

Regarding alcohol abstinence maintenance facilitation, the mechanism of action for topiramate has not yet been determined. However, topiramate appears to modulate dopaminergic neurotransmission in the mesolimbic area of the brain by decreasing the changes in NMDA receptor activity associated with the damage caused by regular, long-term alcohol use—or "heavy drinking." Consequently, dopamine release is inhibited, and GABA function is enhanced (Johnson et al., 2003; Olmsted & Kockler, 2008).

Topiramate is ingested orally in dosages of 200 to 300 mg daily. It is rapidly and well-absorbed from the GI tract with approximately 70% excreted in unchanged form in the urine. Thus, dosage adjustment may be required for older adults who have renal impairment. The most common reported undesired, or harmful, effects and toxicities associated with the use of topiramate, include:

- Cognitive impairment (e.g., short-term memory impairment);
- Dizziness;
- GI distress;
- Paresthesia;
- Psychomotor slowing;
- Sedation;
- Weight loss.

These undesired effects and toxicities may significantly limit the use of topiramate for alcohol abstinence maintenance facilitation for some older adults (Arbaizar, Diersen-Sotos, & Gomez-Acebo, 2010; Shinn & Greenfield, 2010).

Kranzler, Armeli, and Tennen (2014) and Kranzler, Covault, and Feinn (2014) reported an interesting observation regarding the influence of glutamate receptor, ionotropic, kainate 1 genotype on the efficacy of topiramate moderated by a functional single nucleotide polymorphism. Specifically, with topiramate pharmacotherapy, they found that rs2832407*C-allele homozygotes were associated with significantly higher reductions in "heavy drinking."

> ***Related Professional Reminder:*** ***While pharmacogenetics has been a topic of discussion in the context of clinical drug use for over 40 years, it was not until the beginning of the new millennium that the sequencing of the human genome was completed and related research began in earnest. However, 20 years later, the associated results remain limited, particularly in the field of drug and substance abuse—except in relation to the genetic polymorphism of the cytochrome P450 isoenzymes, as discussed in this text.***

Psychotherapeutic/Counseling Approaches

Armstrong-Moore, Haighton, and Davinson (2018) conducted a systematic review of studies of various cognitive-behavioral interventions (e.g., brief intervention, diaries, motivational enhancement, telephone counseling) that have been utilized to reduce the negative effects of alcohol consumption among older adults. Although the data were limited to six studies in the U.S., results tend to indicate that older adults, 55 years of age and older, respond well to the various interventions. In fact, both individual and group psychotherapeutic and counseling approaches can be used effectively for older adults, alone, or as adjuncts to pharmacotherapy (e.g., Azorin, Bowden, & Garay, 2010; Pagliaro & Pagliaro, *Clinical Patient Data Files*). These approaches include the following seven major approaches that have been utilized for older adults who have been diagnosed with alcohol or other dependence or use disorder(s):

1. Alcoholics Anonymous (AA);
2. Brief Intervention (BI);
3. Cognitive Therapy (CT) and Cognitive Behavioral Therapy (CBT);
4. Group Therapy;
5. Motivational Interviewing (MI);
6. Short-Term Residential Treatment Programs;
7. 12-Step Facilitation.

Each of these approaches are highlighted in the following subsections, beginning with brief intervention, and concluding with AA and 12-step facilitation.[103] However, before proceeding, we would like to briefly discuss the biological/biochemical basis of psychotherapy/counseling.

From the mid-19th century, psychotherapy was largely visualized as a "mental process" with no regard to any associated biological/biochemical underpinnings.[104] This situation began to change during the early 21st century as research in psychology began to focus on the neurotransmitters, particularly dopamine, glutamate, and serotonin. As identified by Kelley (2004, p. 161):

> neurotransmitter systems, widely distributed in many regions of [the] cortex, limbic system, and basal ganglia, appear to play a key integrative role in motivation, learning, and memory, thus modulating adaptive behavior.

The noted effects on "adaptive behavior" appear to play a particularly significant role regarding addictive behaviors, including the desire to re-achieve the pleasurable effects experienced when an abusable psychotropic was first used—a desire that is also apparent later during withdrawal. These contextual experiences of "desire," which are related to underlying changes in neurotransmitter function, significantly contribute to both continued use and relapsed use following a period of resumed nonuse of an abusable psychotropic. The noted "drug desire" can be conceptualized as a largely unconsciously learned association between

103. Although pharmacotherapy and psychotherapy/counseling approaches are discussed separately, optimal therapeutic outcomes for older adults—as clearly and consistently demonstrated by many researchers (e.g., Hudmon, Corelli, & Prokhorov, 2010; McCaul & Petry, 2003; Swift, 2007)—generally involve various combinations of these approaches.
104. This notion was a result of the long-standing dichotomy between mind and brain that dates back to René Descartes (1596–1650) and his concept of "mind-body dualism."

abusable psychotropic cues and rewards. This "drug desire" has been theorized to primarily involve episodic (biographical) memory (Boning, 2009; Bornstein & Pickard, 2020).

Consequently, psychotherapy/counseling—which attempts, for example, to either break the learned associations between the use of an abusable psychotropic and its rewards or create new associations between abusable psychotropic use and adverse consequences—may be eliciting their therapeutic effect at the biochemical level, by means of neurotransmitter-facilitated modulation of adaptive behavior.

> ***Related Professional Reminder:* The success of psychotherapy/counseling depends on many factors—the most important of which are the professional commitment, capabilities, and experiences (i.e., competence) of the individual psychotherapist/counselor[105] in relation to the specific form of psychotherapy/ counseling individually selected for a specific older adult or group of older adults.**

Brief Intervention (BI)[106]

Brief interventions are short in duration and are directed at helping older adults reduce their risk for the harmful effects associated with alcohol or other dependence or use disorder, particularly those who: (1) have relatively minor related mental or physical problems (e.g., display minor symptoms or are in the early stages of alcohol or other abusable psychotropic dependence or use disorder—as well as those who appear to be at risk for the future development of alcohol or other abusable psychotropic dependence or use disorder); and (2) are highly motivated to change.[107] Brief intervention often occurs in primary care settings and can range in length/format from a single five- to 30-minute session to a short series of five one-hour sessions. Generally, these sessions:

- Utilize an empathetic clinical style;
- Utilize aspects of motivational interviewing/therapy (see the related discussion in the later subsection, "Motivational Interviewing");
- Utilize a self-efficacy approach to build confidence;
- Provide nonconfrontational education/support;
- Provide normative feedback (e.g., comparison of the older adult's drinking behavior with that of other older adults);
- Provide specific advice and examples on how to change;

---

105. An equally important implicit factor is the neuropsychological status of older adults. Although not consistently taken into consideration, we have found it to be a truism that the greater the neurocognitive impairment, the less likely that psychotherapy/counseling (e.g., cognitive therapy), will be of therapeutic benefit. Consequently, if, during our initial therapeutic assessment, we determine that significant neuropsychological impairment is present, or likely, we first conduct necessary neuropsychological testing (e.g., Mini-Mental State Examination [MMSE]; California Verbal Learning Test-II [CVLT-II])—prior to the commencement of psychotherapy/counseling. See also the related discussion in the earlier subsection, Effects of Alcohol on Body Systems—"Regarding Executive Processes."
106. See also the related discussion in the earlier section Diagnosis and Treatment of Alcohol Dependence or Use Disorder Among Older Adults, Assessment and Diagnosis of Alcohol Dependence or Use Disorder—"Screening, Brief Intervention, and Referral to Treatment (SBIRT) Model." This model utilizes BI, but also includes assessment, brief treatment for high-risk use (i.e., education, problem solving, coping mechanisms, and building a supportive social environment), and referral to treatment (SAMHSA, 2011).
107. N.B. Brief intervention, generally, is not effective as the sole "treatment" of alcohol or other abusable psychotropic dependence or use disorder among older adults.

- Emphasize that the older adult is responsible for change (i.e., alcohol or other abusable psychotropic dependence or use disorder is a personal choice, as is nonuse of alcohol or other abusable psychotropics).

(CDC, 1999; Henry-Edwards et al., 2003; Kuerbis et al., 2014)

As emphasized by the CDC (1999), the use of brief intervention by health and social care professionals can provide several benefits for older adults, who are admitted—or not yet admitted—to treatment, including:

- Providing the opportunity to address noncompliance with residential treatment rules (e.g., smoking in undesignated places or unauthorized visits or telephone calls);
- Increasing compliance for doing treatment-related homework (e.g., completing lists or diary entries or bibliotherapy);
- Increasing compliance with outpatient mental health referrals;
- Increasing compliance with pharmacotherapeutic and psychotherapeutic treatment approaches;
- Increasing participation in treatment groups;
- Increasing attendance in mutual-help groups;
- Encouraging engagement in treatment activities after intake assessment;
- Obtaining a sponsor, if involved with a 12-step program;
- Reducing aggressive and hostile behavior (e.g., verbal and physical violence toward staff and other patients);
- Reducing no-show rates for the start of treatment;
- Reducing dropout rates after the first session of treatment;
- Serving as an interim intervention for older adults who are on treatment program waiting lists.

Cognitive Therapy & Cognitive Behavioral Therapy

"Cognitive therapy" (CT) is explicitly based on the original cognitive model of depression proposed by Aaron T. Beck (1961, 1967) in the context of the treatment for mental depression. Breaking from his initial psychoanalytical focus, Beck proposed that behavior change could be best accomplished by altering three levels of cognition:

1. "Core Beliefs," which are learned early in life and are deeply held;
2. "Dysfunctional Assumptions," which are rules for living that are generally maladaptive;
3. "Negative Automatic Thoughts," which are irrational, but accepted as plausible by the patient.

Cognitive therapy is often referred to, in the broader context, as "cognitive-behavioral therapy" (CBT). Cognitive Behavioral Therapy is "problem focused" and emphasizes the present-day situation with specific attention to:

- Identifying problem behaviors or relationships, including those associated with alcohol or other abusable psychotropic dependence or use disorder and/or other mental disorder(s);

- Developing—in both individual and group treatment settings—"action-oriented" or "personal coping" strategies that can later be used by older adults to effectively deal with, or manage, their problem behavior.

Cognitive behavioral therapy guides health and social care professionals to teach older adults to "be their own therapist."

Cognitive behavioral therapy is a "psychosocial" intervention that empirically has clearly and consistently demonstrated efficacy (e.g., Carroll, 2014; McHugh, Hearon, & Otto, 2010). As previously noted, although originally used for the treatment of major depressive disorder, CBT has been used for alcohol dependence or use disorder and virtually every other type of abusable psychotropic dependence or use disorder (e.g., cannabis, cocaine, nicotine, and opiate analgesic dependence or use disorders). It also has been used for the treatment of several other mental disorders that are commonly identified among older adults (e.g., eating disorders, generalized anxiety disorder (GAD), major depressive disorder (MDD), obsessive compulsive disorder (OCD), and post-traumatic stress disorder (PTSD). Additionally, CBT has been used with older adults in the context of both individual and group therapy, as well as couples and family therapy.

Cognitive behavioral therapy, often the first choice in terms of the form of psychotherapeutic/counseling approaches selected for older adults, generally follows ten specific steps:

1. Establishing and maintaining rapport with the older adult and the family/group;
2. Assessing:
    - Presenting "problems;"
    - Problem-related behavior;
    - Behavior "deficits;"
    - Incidence and severity of related behaviors, or lack thereof.
3. Re-conceptualizing the "problem(s):"
    - Helping the older adult to recognize the problem, including its duration and extent.
4. Teaching and developing needed skills, including skills to cope with "craving" and to assertively resist offers for abusable psychotropics;
5. Applying needed skills and monitoring results;
6. Re-assessing and adjusting the therapy plan, as needed;
7. Generalizing and continuing the maintenance of needed skills;
8. Assessing or evaluating post-treatment outcomes;
9. Terminating therapy, which begins during the first session with the older adult, with clarification of treatment approach, goals, objectives, and expected general time frame for needed CBT;
10. After termination, following up, as deemed necessary and appropriate for the older adult, in terms of both form and duration.[108]

108. In the context of CBT for older adults with alcohol or other abusable psychotropic dependence or use disorder, intervention terminates at the end of the formal scheduled treatment as the older adult successfully meets his or her goals and expectations. However, this involves the realization that reinforcement may be needed during the long-term because of the general nature and characteristics of alcohol or other abusable psychotropic dependence or use disorder that may result in a need for help to maintain patterns of nonuse and prevent the occurrence of relapsed use.

Cognitive behavioral therapy assumes that harmful patterns of alcohol and/or other abusable psychotropic use, are indicative of maladaptive coping in which "learning processes" play a major role (i.e., the older adult has not learned effective ways to cope with problems or to meet certain individual needs, particularly developmental needs).[109] Integral to this theory is the acceptance that "feelings/emotions," "thoughts," and "behaviors" all influence each other (see Figure 1.9). As illustrated, the triangle in the center represents the CBT tenet that the "core beliefs" of all humans can be divided into three categories: (1) "view of self;" (2) "view of others/world;" and (3) "view of future."

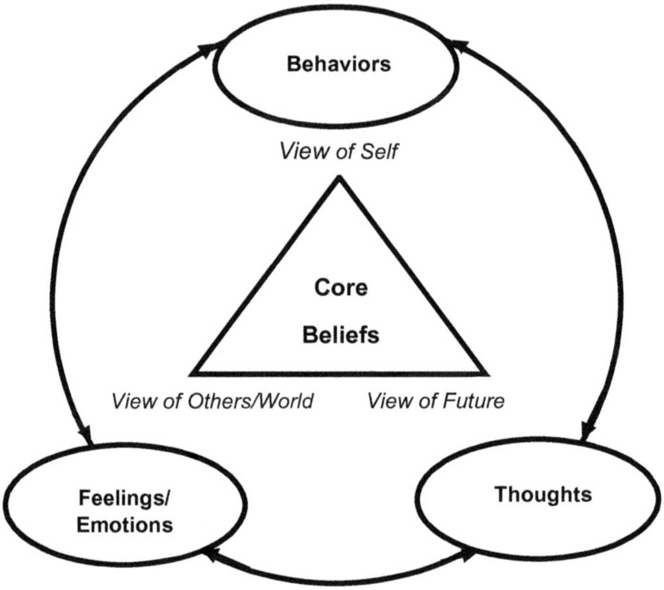

Figure 1.9 Basic Tenets of CBT

Consequently, successful intervention is predicated upon helping an older adult to both: (1) recognize or admit specific problems; and (2) learn to correct these problems by applying a range of different effective strategies, including:

- Changing maladaptive/dysfunctional core beliefs (e.g., "no one likes me;" "people can't be trusted");[110]
- Learning and developing new and effective coping mechanisms (e.g., distraction, imagery, minimizing negative thoughts, motivational self-talk) to deal with related anticipated problems;
- Learning and developing better information processing skills.

109. In comparison to, for example, treatment using traditional psychoanalysis, during which the therapist, utilizing observed/reported behaviors, dreams, or memories, looks for "unconscious" meaning, which, subsequently results in the formulation of a diagnosis.

110. These dysfunctional core beliefs, or identified "errors" in patient thinking, can often be non-exclusively categorized as: catastrophizing, dichotomous reasoning, emotional reasoning, magnification, minimization, mind reading, overgeneralizing, personalization, and selective abstraction.

Thus, CBT is directed at the correction, or modification, of:

1. Faulty thinking patterns or styles;
2. Irrational belief systems;
3. Maladaptive or deficient coping skills.

Sharing of thoughts and feelings/emotions with a therapist is attempted as part of the training process of CBT. This training in self-observation involves the systematic analysis of the validity of negative and irrational self-statements, and the gradual substitution of positive, logical thinking patterns based on rational belief systems.[111] Through this training process, older adults are gradually made more aware of their problems associated with their use of alcohol or other abusable psychotropics, which may have been denied or avoided. Through CBT, they are helped to develop the coping strategies, skills, and abilities that they need to effectively deal with these problems.

An integral component of cognitive therapy is the development, or strengthening, of specific intrapersonal and interpersonal skills, including anger control, leisure time management, problem solving, and resistance training. Cognitive behavioral therapy is often used, in the context of alcohol dependence or use disorder, to help older adults to both achieve resumed nonuse of alcohol and prevent the occurrence of relapsed use. Thus, attention is focused on the positive gains achieved during early abstinence and how these gains can be maintained in order to prevent relapse. A central component in the achievement of this goal involves teaching older adults to: (1) identify and anticipate high-risk situations that may lead to relapsed use; and (2) apply previously learned and rehearsed techniques to effectively avoid or deal with them.

> ***Related Professional Reminder:*** ***When a behavior changes, the new behavior does not completely erase the old behavior. Consequently, appropriate follow-up strategies must be planned and implemented in order to maintain/sustain the therapeutic gains/successes associated with behavior change.***

Unfortunately, behavioral change—even when successfully achieved with CBT or other forms of psychotherapy—is often temporary. As explained by Bouton (2014, p. 29), many factors contribute to this situation:

> The research suggests that methods used to create behavior change (including extinction, counterconditioning, punishment, reinforcement of alternative behavior, and abstinence reinforcement) tend to inhibit, rather than erase, the original behavior.

Hence, older adults, who have developed patterns of "compulsive use" of alcohol or other abusable psychotropics, may require periodic reinforcement following successful intervention. This periodic reinforcement, in many cases, may be required over their lifetime.

Cognitive behavioral therapy, primarily delivered by direct face-to-face interaction between the older adult and the therapist, also can be effectively delivered to small groups of similarly aged older adults. In addition, CBT can be delivered with the use of a

---

111. For example, the health and social care professional, or other clinician, can help patients to self-identify irrational "automatic" thoughts (also referred to as: "cognitive distortions" or "negative automatic thoughts") by asking questions such as, "What was going through your mind at that time?" or "What are you thinking right now?" The irrational thoughts generally occur spontaneously and, thus, are not immediately self-evident to the patient, who, consequently, generally accepts them as plausible.

(1) computerized, or Internet-based delivery system;[112] or (2) a self-help guide. We generally recommend that the latter be used only in conjunction with direct face-to-face interaction with the therapist.

> ***Related Professional Reminder:*** ***Indirect methods of CBT delivery generally are associated with lower rates of compliance to, and completion of, planned therapy. They also are associated with a higher incidence of negative effects associated with uncorrected self-rumination.***

Group Psychotherapy

It has been well established for over 30 years that group psychotherapy for older adults can be extremely effective (e.g., for the treatment of mental depression [Arean, Perri, & Nezu, 1993]). Stead and Lancaster (2005), in their meta-analysis of group behavioral therapy programs for smoking cessation, found that group participants were able to:

1. Learn behavioral techniques for smoking cessation;
2. Provide each other with mutual support.

In terms of smoking cessation, they also found that outcomes were:

3. Superior to those achieved with self-help;
4. Similar to those achieved with individual counseling.

However, not all psychotherapists are equally adept at effectively practicing group psychotherapy. For additional details and discussion of group therapy, see also the Psychotherapy/ Counseling subsection: "Short-Term Residential Treatment Programs."

Motivational Interviewing

Motivational interviewing (MI) was largely extended from the humanistic approach developed by Carl Rogers (1902–1987). It attempts to motivate change by activating an individual's capacity to achieve beneficial positive change. As such, MI is recommended to encourage older adults to weigh the risks and benefits of, as indicated, either continuing or modifying their current pattern of alcohol use. Typically, a number of interviewing, coaching, and feedback techniques are employed by the health or social care clinician or counselor, including:

- Asking open-ended questions;
- Encouraging and supporting positive statements regarding discontinuing harmful drinking behaviors (i.e., support self-efficacy and optimism);

---

112. Several researchers (e.g., Kiluk, Nich, & Buck, 2018) have found computer-delivered CBT to be equally efficacious as clinician-delivered CBT. Sarlin (2018), in a report for the NIDA, noted that:

  - Patients, who self-administer cognitive behavioral therapy (CBT) using computerized training modules reduced their drug use as much as patients who received clinician-delivered CBT, and they maintained this advantage through a 6-month follow-up;
  - By reducing the time that clinicians need to spend with individual patients, computer-based CBT training may enable treatment programs to accommodate larger caseloads and increase access to treatment (p. 1).

- Handling resistance without direct confrontation;
- Listening reflectively;
- Reframing patient statements of resistance to change drinking behavior (e.g., "So you don't think that your behavior is hurting your relationship with your spouse?");
- Using summary statements to pull together the views expressed by the older adult patient.

Overall, MI can be conceptualized as a directive counseling style that is empathic, non-argumentative, noncoercive, nonconfrontational, nonjudgmental, and nonthreatening.

The concept of MI and its techniques were largely developed by Miller and colleagues (e.g., Miller, 1999; Miller & Mount, 2001; Miller & Rollnick, 1991; Miller, Yahne, & Moyers, 2004). However, results have tended to be disappointing. For example, Miller, Yahne, and Tonigan (2003, p. 754), in a study that focused on individuals who had alcohol dependence or use disorder (i.e., AUD) and were receiving inpatient or outpatient treatment, found significant effects in terms of program retention, but not in terms of modifying alcohol use during follow-up:

> MI showed no effect on drug use outcomes when added to inpatient or outpatient treatment, although both groups showed substantial increases in abstinence from illicit drugs and alcohol.

Similarly, Carroll, Ball, and Nich (2006) conducted a study of individuals seeking treatment for abusable psychotropic use in five community-based treatment settings. The participants were assigned to one of two groups: (1) those who received a standard intake assessment; or (2) those who received a standard intake assessment that was modified to integrate MI techniques and strategies. Although those who received the integrated MI intake assessment had significantly greater retention rates, in terms of substance use outcomes, they did not differ from the control group at either the 28-day or 84-day follow-up.

Based on these outcomes, we recommend that motivational interviewing only be used for older adults who have early, moderate, or relatively isolated issues/problems with alcohol use (e.g., alcohol misuse; "risky drinking"). We do not recommend the use of motivational interviewing for older adults with alcohol dependence or use disorder (i.e., AUD). Consequently, this psychotherapeutic/counseling approach is not further discussed in this chapter.

Short-Term Residential Treatment Programs

In comparison to Therapeutic Communities, short-term residential treatment programs (e.g., Hazelden) began to be developed during the early 1970s in response to several identified issues, including the:

- Lack of adequate treatment services for those who had problems related to cocaine use;
- Desire for treatment services other than those that "institutionalize" for months;
- Limitations placed by third party insurance carriers for the reimbursement of fees paid for provided treatment services (i.e., often with a 30-day limit). (Pagliaro & Pagliaro, *Clinical Patient Data Files*)

For an overview of the program objectives and elements employed by a "typical" short-term residential treatment program, see Table 1.10.

Table 1.10 Short-term Residential Treatment Program Objectives and Key Elements

PROGRAM OBJECTIVES AND KEY ELEMENTS
Program Objectives:
1. Maintain "sobriety" or nonuse;
2. Learn about alcohol or other dependence or use disorder(s) and the process of recovery;
3. Recognize the effects of alcohol or other dependence or use disorder(s) on self and others (e.g., family, friends, or co-workers);
4. Develop strategies to "maintain sobriety" or nonuse;
5. Share thoughts and feelings with others (e.g., group therapy sessions);
6. Utilize the basics of the AA program.
Program Key Elements:
1. Personal inventory and plan;
2. Daily schedule of program activities;
3. Educational component;
4. Group therapy sessions;
5. Provision of a safe and supportive environment.

Modified from: Laundergan & Williams, 1993; Pagliaro & Pagliaro, 2018.

The major problem with residential treatment programs is the risk for resumed use of alcohol or other abusable psychotropics following discharge. Recidivism is extremely high and significantly increases as soon as the older adult is released, "clean and sober," from supervised residential treatment.

Alcoholics Anonymous[113]

Alcoholics Anonymous (AA) was started in 1935 in Akron, Ohio by Bill W. (a stockbroker) and Bob S. (a physician), who were its first two members. Alcoholics Anonymous has since spread across North America and now holds meetings worldwide. AA has become, particularly in North America, the most frequently used form of alcohol treatment with

113. Alcoholics Anonymous (AA) is the prototypical 12-step program for many other programs, including:

- Cocaine Anonymous (CA);
- Emotions Anonymous (EA);
- Gamblers Anonymous (GA);
- Marijuana Anonymous (MA);
- Men's Way through the 12-Steps;
- Narcotics Anonymous (NA);
- Overeaters Anonymous (OA);
- Sixteen Steps to Empowerment;
- Women for Sobriety;
- Women's Way through the 12-Steps.(See also the related discussion in the following subsection, "Twelve-Step Facilitation.")

over one million recovering members. According to several researchers and therapists (e.g., Room & Greenfield, 1993; Weisner, Greenfield, & Room, 1995), the popularity of AA is due in large part to its American themes of individualism, equality, and spirituality, which are embodied in the Twelve Steps (see later in this subsection).[114] The organizational structure of AA also supports these themes in that there is no central authority or hierarchy, the only officer in AA groups is a secretary, and members avoid the use of last names.

The key distinguishing principles of AA include that:

1. There is no cure for alcoholism;
2. Abstinence is the only viable goal;
3. Member support is vital to maintain recovery;
4. Recidivism, or resumed use (i.e., "slips" or "falling off the wagon"), is less important than what one does in response;
5. Progress is more important than perfection.

These principles are actualized by active participation in the 12-step program that includes:

- Avoiding the first drink;
- Focusing on each day;
- Actively dealing with "slips."

Alcoholics Anonymous is regarded as neither a medical nor a psychological approach for the treatment of alcoholism (Borkman, 2008). As such, the organization maintains that alcoholism is a disease without cure and that treatment is social[115] or spiritual (McGee, 2000). Consequently, several slogans have been adopted and are frequently used by AA members, including:

- *Be part of the solution, not the problem;*
- *But for the grace of God;*
- *Don't quit before the miracle happens;*
- *Easy does it;*
- *Faith without works is dead;*

---

114. These same themes that account for much of the success attributed to AA, also make it an inappropriate treatment approach for some older adults. The spiritual characteristics of AA are reflected by the wording in the 12-Steps, and also in both the generally accepted moto, "Let Go and Let God," and the "Serenity Prayer," which is often used to conclude group meetings (AA, 1939):

> God grant me the serenity to accept the things I cannot change, the courage to change the things I can, and the wisdom to know the difference.
>
> Reinhold Niebuhr (1892–1971)

Our clinical experience indicates that regardless of gender, ethnicity, or sexual orientation, most older adults, who have alcohol dependence or use disorder (i.e., alcoholism) and other problems related to using abusable psychotropics, can generally derive significant benefit from AA as a component of their psychotherapy. However, we also have found over the last two decades that an increasing number of older adults, who identify themselves as agnostic, generally reject AA as a component of their therapy because they generally find the tenets of AA philosophically incompatible with their own personal views of the world (i.e., lack of a strong belief in God) (Pagliaro & Pagliaro, *Clinical Patient Data Files*).

115. For this reason, AA has often been labeled as a "social" form of treatment.

- *Feelings are not facts;*
- *First things first;*
- *I am an alcoholic;*
- *Keep it simple, stupid;*
- *Let go and let God;*
- *Nothing changes if nothing changes;*
- *One day at a time;*
- *Progress, not perfection;*
- *Sick and tired of being sick and tired;*
- *Sobriety is a journey . . . not a destination;*
- *When all else fails, follow instructions.*

As identified by Valliant (2005, p. 431):

> The suggested mechanism of action of AA is that it employs four factors widely shown to be effective in relapse prevention in addictions: (1) external supervision; (2) substitute dependency; (3) new caring relationships; and (4) increased spirituality.

Alcoholics Anonymous relies on a rather informal form of "group" therapy and social support (i.e., frequent meetings with other fellow recovering members who maintain total abstinence from alcohol use) and a "buddy" system (i.e., the use of sponsors who have remained sober for a period of time by "working" the 12 steps and who can, thus, show "newcomers" the way to sobriety)—as guided by the following 12-steps:

1. We admitted we were powerlessness over alcohol—that our lives had become unmanageable;
2. Came to believe that a Power greater than ourselves could restore us to sanity;
3. Made a decision to turn our will and our lives over to the care of our God as we understand Him;
4. Made a searching and fearless moral inventory of ourselves;
5. Admitted to God, to ourselves, and to another human being the exact nature of our wrongs;
6. Were entirely ready to have God remove all these defects of character;
7. Humbly asked Him to remove our shortcomings;
8. Made a list of all persons we had harmed, and became willing to make amends to them all;
9. Made direct amends to such people wherever possible, except when to do so would injure them or others;
10. Continued to take personal inventory and when we were wrong promptly admitted it;
11. Sought through prayer and meditation to improve our conscious contact with God, praying only for knowledge of His will for us and the power to carry that out;
12. Having had a spiritual awakening as the result of these steps, we tried to carry this message to alcoholics, and to practice these principles in all our affairs.

(AA, 1939)

As part of the "group therapy," members hear from other members that they are not alone and that they share common, painful experiences in relation to their alcohol use. In addition, in conjunction with Step 1, members learn to overcome their strong denial[116] of their own drinking problem. The confrontation of denial is both clearly and directly reflected in the members' introductions of themselves at AA group meetings, "Hello, my name is ____ and I'm an alcoholic."

"Denial," which is typically characterized by such statements as, "I don't have a drinking (or other abusable psychotropic) problem," or "I can stop drinking" (or using another abusable psychotropic) whenever I want to," is a hallmark of the development of compulsive use of alcohol (or other abusable psychotropics). Compulsive use of alcohol (or other abusable psychotropics), which follows the earlier patterns of habitual and abusive use: (1) prevents early therapeutic intervention; (2) after achieving "resumed nonuse," contributes to "relapsed use;" and (3) encourages the progressive development of increasingly undesired, or harmful, effects and toxicities (see Figure 1.6). (Also see, respectively, the section in each chapter, "Undesired, or Harmful, Effects and Toxicities.")

Consequently, to optimize assessment and subsequent treatment approaches, a major primary goal is to breakdown the defensive wall of denial. Commonly identified as simply a "weakness in character," traditionally, denial was also largely viewed psychoanalytically as a means to protect the ego.[117] More recently, denial is generally considered to be a psychological construct that can be best dealt with by using other psychological approaches (e.g., CBT).

> ***Related Professional Reminder:*** ***Regardless of the selected therapeutic intervention, denial is a prominent characteristic feature of alcohol or other abusable psychotropic dependence or use disorder that must be effectively addressed, as needed, for all older adults.***

Nowinski, Baker, and Carroll (1992/1999, pp. 39–40) identified several common forms of "denial:"

- Refusing to face facts: refusing to do a serious alcohol history, refusing to acknowledge negative consequences of use, rejecting clear evidence of tolerance, refusing to go to AA meetings;
- Minimizing the facts: Understating negative consequences, tolerance, and so forth;
- Avoiding: Sleeping a lot, becoming socially isolated, or becoming compulsive (addictive) in some other way, such as work or eating;
- Exaggerating others' use of alcohol to "normalize" one's own use;
- Blaming someone/something else for alcohol use (a "bad" marriage, family conflicts, or feeling depressed) as opposed to accepting the fact that cravings for alcohol are responsible for use;

---

116. Denial is, of course, a well and long recognized psychological component of abusable psychotropic dependences or use disorders. Various theories and related models have been proposed to help explain this behavior (e.g., Tarter, Alterman, & Edwards, 1984). Among the models, two have been widely adopted to help explain the concepts of denial: (1) the psychodynamic model (e.g., Kline, Becker, & Giese, 1992); and (2) the biopsychosocial model (e.g., Engel, 1977; Papadimitriou, 2017).
117. Anna Freud (1934) was the first person to formally propose "denial" as one of a number of specific ego defense mechanisms.

- Bargaining: Trying to limit or control either the amount or type of alcohol used or when it is used;
- Rationalizing: Making up "good" reasons (usually ones that will get sympathy) for drinking.

Members are encouraged to "work through" and "practice" the 12 steps daily. This encouragement is particularly important given that the AA model is based on the premise that there is no cure for alcoholism[118] and that the maintenance of lifelong abstinence is achieved by continued membership in the "fellowship" (i.e., AA) with regular attendance at meetings.

<u>Related Professional Reminder</u>: In the context of the philosophical underpinnings of AA, it is important for both health and social care professionals, as well as AA members, to keep in mind that while alcoholics are **not** ***responsible for their illness, they*** **are** ***responsible for their recovery.***

The number of AA meetings that an active member attends generally ranges from one daily to one weekly. The number of meetings attended on a regular basis is dictated, in large part, by such factors as the:

- Amount of time that a member has been sober (e.g., one day versus one year);
- Personality of the member (e.g., avoidant, dependent, or compulsive);
- Accessibility of scheduled meetings for a member (e.g., meetings are nearby or transportation, both to and from meetings, is readily available);
- Style of the meeting is compatible with the member's needs.

For many alcoholics, AA provides both the social support necessary to maintain abstinence and an effective surrogate for their previously patterned "drinking time" or "familiar bar scene" (i.e., AA meetings serve as a place to go on evenings, weekends, and holidays for socializing with "friends" who, in addition to other benefits, provide understanding and help to alleviate social isolation and loneliness).[119]

The overall effectiveness of AA is difficult to ascertain because:

- AA does not maintain formal records;
- Very few scientific studies have been conducted to formally measure the efficacy of AA;
- Available data are primarily observational;
- Lack of sufficient theories to explain the inherent mechanisms of AA;
- Research is not an AA mandate;

---

118. This AA belief would be consonant with what we describe as "compulsive use" (see Figure 1.4, "Nine Patterns of Abusable Psychotropic Use"). In this regard, we would concur with the AA philosophy that, once compulsive use has been achieved, treatment, in order to have optimal opportunity for success, must include a lifetime of "total" abstinence.
119. In some cases, however, an individual member will develop a "cult-like" relationship with AA (i.e., will become obsessive and compulsive regarding AA doctrine; will limit social interaction to AA meetings and members; will increasingly become estranged from other social groups such as family and colleagues) (Pagliaro & Pagliaro, *Clinical Patient Data Files*). These situations, although relatively infrequently encountered, should be appropriately monitored for, and dealt with as part of the patient's program of psychotherapy.

- The amount of time that members remain active in AA is extremely variable;
- Drop-out rates are high.

A qualitative analysis of the stories of 60 older women, who were members of AA, indicated that AA played a significant role in their recovery experiences (Sanders, 2021). Obviously, the approach used by AA will *not* be suitable for all older adults and we would not recommend it as the sole approach to therapy.[120] However, for patients who are willing to attend the AA meetings, we have found AA to be an effective and useful adjunct to individual psychotherapy—as have others (e.g., Ferri, Amato, & Davoli, 2006)—and we highly recommend it in this context.[121] In addition, the efficacy of AA programs appears to be substantiated de facto by the: (1) large number of members who speak positively about it; and (2) use of the AA approach by groups that have been based on, or extended from, it (e.g., Cocaine Anonymous [CA], Crystal Meth Anonymous [CMA], Gamblers Anonymous [GA], Marijuana Anonymous [MA], and Narcotics Anonymous [NA]). It also has been extended to other 12-Step self-help groups for families who have parents or members, respectively, who have harmful patterns of using drugs and substances of abuse (e.g., Al-ATEEN, Al-ANON, and Families of Alcoholics [FA]) (Laudet, 2008). (See also the related discussion in the following section, "Twelve-Step Facilitation.") In addition, AA has generally been rated highly by health and social care professionals.

Twelve-Step Facilitation

Twelve-step facilitation (TSF), as opposed to AA (or the "12-Steps"), is a specific method of therapeutic intervention for older adults, who have contemporaneous diagnoses involving alcohol and other abusable psychotropic dependence or use disorder(s), and/or other related mental disorder(s) (e.g., eating disorders). These programs are generally: (1) brief in duration (i.e., 12 to 15 sessions); (2) structured; and (3) manual-driven or guided. As explained by Nowinski et al. (1992/1999, pp. 1–4), it is a process guided by a written manual and delivered by a drug counselor or therapist. Usually, twelve sessions are used to accomplish three major goals:

1. To facilitate acceptance—acceptance by patients that they suffer from the chronic and progressive illness of alcoholism, that they have lost the ability to control their drinking, and since there is no effective cure for alcoholism, the only viable alternative is complete abstinence from the use of alcohol;
2. To facilitate surrender—acknowledgment on the part of the patient that there is hope for recovery (sustained sobriety), but only through accepting the reality of loss of control and by having faith that some Higher Power can help the individual whose own willpower has been defeated by alcoholism;
3. To facilitate active involvement or participation in 12-step meetings and related activities—maintenance of a personal journal that is reviewed with the therapist[122]

120. From a random survey, it has been estimated that approximately 40% of the membership of AA in the U.S. is over 51 years of age (Laudet, 2008).
121. As with most forms of psychotherapy or counseling, the efficacy of AA for older adults is highly correlated with the frequency and duration of their attendance at meetings (Pagliaro & Pagliaro, *Clinical Patient Data Files*).
122. In the context of 12-step facilitation, the major agent of change (i.e., the active therapeutic modality) is the fellowship of AA and not the individual therapist, who is seen more as a facilitator or coach.

at the beginning of each session; attendance at AA (or other 12-step) meetings; and bibliotherapy usually involving readings from the "AA Service Manual" or "Big Book."[123]

As identified by Nowinski et al. (1992/1999) in the introduction to the original "AA Service Manual" that they prepared on behalf of the National Institute on Alcohol Abuse and Alcoholism (NIAAA, p. 1):

> The [12-Step] facilitation program described in this manual is intended for use in brief individual outpatient treatment for persons who satisfy the criteria for a diagnosis of alcohol dependence and abuse.

Relapse Prevention

The rate of relapsed use, or recidivism, which often follows the "successful" treatment of alcohol or other dependence use disorder(s) among older adults, is quite high (see Figure 1.10). Although much research has examined treatment factors (e.g., family involvement in treatment, provision of special services, staff characteristics, and time in treatment) these factors have not been able to account for the majority of variance in post-treatment return to harmful patterns of alcohol and other abusable psychotropic use. Obviously, much more research is required in this area.

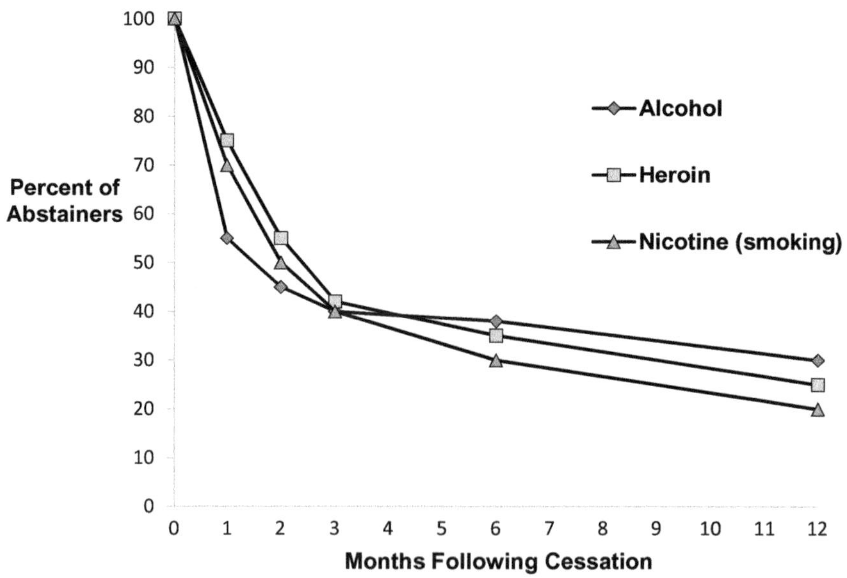

Figure 1.10 Typical Relapse Rates

123. A mobile Android app, "12 Step Guide-AA," is available to explain and facilitate each of the 12-steps of AA. Additionally, the "Big Book" (AA, 1939) is available as an electronic text.

Major contributory factors that have been implicated to the occurrence of relapsed use following treatment, include:

- Active (untreated) mental disorders;
- Boredom;
- Cognitive factors ("stinking-thinking");
- Complacency;
- Exposure to "triggers;"
- Increased desire for alcohol or other drugs and substances of abuse ("craving");
- Interpersonal problems;
- Lack of, or poor, coping abilities;
- Lack of support systems;
- Loneliness (social isolation);
- Negative affective states;
- Stress.

(Andersson, Wenaas, & Nordfjaern, 2019; Azmi, Hussin, & Ishak, 2018; McKay, 1999; Pagliaro & Pagliaro, *Clinical Patient Data Files*)

In addition, it has been noted that a complicated and dynamic interplay of "proximal" and "distal" factors plays a major role in the relapse process (e.g., Feingold, Capaldi, & Owen, 2015; McKay, Franklin, & Patapis, 2006). Examples of "proximal factors," include current drinking behavior and social influences. Examples of "distal factors," include genetic predisposition and inappropriate parenting (Pagliaro & Pagliaro, *Clinical Patient Data Files*).

Our own clinical experience and the currently available published research data suggest that the use of the following three recommendations would at least minimize the potential for the relapsed use of alcohol or other abusable psychotropics:

1. Individualize treatment to the specific needs and characteristics of the older adult (i.e., "cut the shoe to fit the foot");[124]
2. Employ specific indicators or performance goals to objectively evaluate the success of treatment outcomes and, subsequently, the degree of relapse or efficacy of relapse prevention;
3. Periodically, as individually indicated, and specifically defined (e.g., one week, one month, six months, or annually) prophylactically re-assess older adults and proactively intervene to prevent the occurrence of relapsed use.

Some of this periodic monitoring is addressed, for example, in "aftercare" programs and in continued attendance at AA meetings, which have both been positively correlated with significantly higher rates and duration of post-treatment abstinence, or "resumed nonuse" (Pagliaro & Pagliaro, *Clinical Patient Data Files*). We would suggest, particularly for older adults, who have engaged in abusive or compulsive use of alcohol or other abusable

124. The use of "patient-treatment matching" has been known and used for three decades (e.g., Mattson & Allen, 1991; Mattson, Allen, & Longabaugh, 1994; Project MATCH, 1993). However, usually due to economic and/or time constraints, patient-treatment matching is currently the "exception to the rule."

psychotropics, that the propensity for relapsed use and, thus, the return to compulsive use, be considered a "life-long" concern (i.e., we do not subscribe to, nor do we endorse, the often noted belief among many addiction counselors, health, social, and other care professionals, parents, and therapists that the harmful use of drugs and substances of abuse—at the compulsive level of use—can be "cured").

Whenever possible, once older adults are abstinent, we gradually decrease the frequency and length of their psychotherapy sessions (e.g., from bi-weekly, to weekly, to every other week, to monthly, to every other month, to phone contact every six months). This strategy helps to maintain a communication linkage and "help-line," or "safety line," for each patient. This strategy also demonstrates continued concern and support, while providing an opportunity for the early detection of problems by the health or social care professional and for patients to request needed assistance before problems get "out of control." In our practice, this strategy (i.e., if we can maintain patient contact), has resulted in a long-term (i.e., generally longer than five years) relapse rate of less than 20% (Pagliaro & Pagliaro, *Clinical Patient Data Files*).

Related Professional Reminder:

- ***Be willing to consider available and appropriate treatment approaches and strategies (e.g., AA, cognitive therapy, or pharmacotherapy) that may be efficacious for a particular older adult;***
- ***Individualize treatment approaches;***
- ***Remember that reasons for using alcohol or other abusable psychotropics may differ from one older adult to another and may also differ for the same older adult over time;***
- ***Be nonjudgmental in approaching treatment;***
- ***Break the denial of problems associated with the use of alcohol or other abusable psychotropics;***
- ***Respect older adults who have problems with the use of alcohol or other abusable psychotropics, including those with contemporaneous diagnoses—alcohol dependence or use disorder (i.e., AUD), and/or one or more other abusable psychotropic dependence or use disorder (i.e., SUDs), and/or one or more other mental disorder, and/or one or more physical medical disorders—and do not treat them in a condescending manner;***
- ***Provide education in a straightforward, nonbiased way that is appropriately tailored to the older adult—including her or his visual and hearing abilities, cognitive abilities, developmental level, and learning and social needs;***
- ***Work toward realistic and achievable goals that have been mutually agreed upon;***
- ***Appropriately address underlying problems (e.g., low self-esteem, poor coping skills, history of sexual abuse/assault);***
- ***Involve family, friends, and others, as appropriate, in confrontation, treatment planning, and program implementation (family members, particularly spouses /significant others, can play important related roles that can facilitate either positive or negative outcomes);***
- ***Use community social agencies designed for older adults, as appropriate;***
- ***Make referrals, as necessary, to other appropriate health and social care professionals and agencies;***

- ***Develop and use procedures and techniques that help to: (1) minimize treatment attrition, or drop-out; and (2) maximize treatment compliance and completion of treatment programs;***
- ***Anticipate, and provide, effective cognitive rehearsal strategies for high-risk situations that may be associated with relapse;***
- ***Provide appropriate follow-up or aftercare services;***
- ***Remember that success or failure is ultimately the older adult's responsibility (i.e., do not become co-dependent or over-responsible);***
- ***If for any reason, and at any time, you feel that you cannot provide optimal treatment for a specific older adult, then:***
    - ***Discuss your concerns with the older adult (and their spouse, adult children, or legal guardian, as necessary and appropriate) and, following this discussion, and with their concurrence and permission***
    - ***Make an appropriate referral to another therapist/program that you feel would be better able to provide optimal treatment;***
    - ***Ensure that contact is made, and that the older adult is accepted by the therapist/program that you referred her or him to;***
    - ***Provide "bridge" treatment/support services until the older adult begins her or his new program.***

The "Dry Drunk Syndrome"

The cessation of regular, long-term alcohol use following successful therapeutic treatment, does not assure a complete "cure for alcoholism" among older adults. As noted in the previous subsection, the first concern following resumed nonuse of alcohol is the prevention of recidivism, or relapsed use. Attention to another related concern is the residual treatment of older adults who are "dry drunks."[125]

Not restricted to older adults, dry drunks refer to men and women who are: (1) sober (i.e., BAC = 0); (2) have not ingested alcohol for some period of time (e.g., 1 week, 1 month, or 1 year); and (3) continue to think and act in the same manner as they did when they were drinking (i.e., display developed attitudes, pathological behaviors, and personalities reflective of [learned] over ten to 50 years, or more, of regular, long-term alcohol use). Having achieved sobriety, dry drunks generally share a number of commonly encountered signs and symptoms, including:

- Anger that they, unlike most others, cannot drink alcohol without exposing themselves to significant risk;
- Cross-addiction (e.g., problematic behavior related to food, gambling, sex, or the Internet);
- Denial that they still have significant issues to deal with;

125. This term has also been used by some practicing members of AA as a pejorative term for fellow members who they believe are not working had enough on their 12-steps (i.e., are "working the system," instead of "working the steps)." (See also the related discussion of AA in the earlier psychotherapeutic/counseling approaches subsection—"Alcoholics Anonymous.")

- Difficulty dealing with daily encountered problems that, previously, were "maladaptively" coped with by drinking;
- Difficulty with interpersonal relationships;
- Disengagement from recovery treatment program involvement;
- Disproportionate over-reaction to minor life events/inconveniences (e.g., someone taking their parking space at the local mall parking lot);
- Engaging in irresponsible and unsafe behavior;
- Dreaming about drinking;
- Fear of relapsing;
- Feelings of hopelessness;
- Insomnia;
- Irrational irritability toward others;
- Jealousy or resentment toward those who have not had to deal with alcohol dependence or use disorder;
- Low tolerance for stress;
- "Playing the victim;"
- Poor impulse control;
- Regret related to the cost that alcohol had for their personal dreams, goals, and potential;
- Resentment toward family and friends—particularly those who may have encouraged/pushed them to stop drinking;
- Romanticizing their previous history of alcohol use;
- Significant self-pity;
- Social isolation;
- Unresolved contemporaneous diagnoses (e.g., pain-producing disorders or MDD).

Although the term "dry drunk" has been circulating in the clinical literature for almost 75 years (e.g., Flaherty, McGuire, & Gatski, 1955), published research regarding this syndrome is extremely sparse. We first used this term in the context of our forensic work in the early 1980s (Pagliaro & Pagliaro, *Clinical Patient Data Files*).[126]

Treatment of the Dry Drunk Syndrome

There is no available pharmacotherapeutic approach for the treatment of dry drunk syndrome. Consequently, treatment consists exclusively of individually designed and implemented psychotherapeutic/counseling approaches. We have used CBT with excellent results and have found AA to be a valuable adjunct. Additionally, if the patients are willing and able to actively participate in AA, active involvement of a spouse or significant other is also a helpful approach to pursue. As well, in this context, couples therapy can be utilized in which the participating spouse or significant other:

126. Although we do not share this particular perspective, some clinicians consider the "dry drunk syndrome" as being subsumed under the phenomenon of the "post-acute withdrawal syndrome" (PAWS).

1. Must be fully informed regarding the nature of the dry drunk syndrome;
2. Can work on projects (e.g., exercise or hobbies) together with the patient to learn how to relate and work together in a sober state;
3. Needs to be empathetic and provide positive support and encouragement for positive behaviors.

REFERENCES[127,128,129]

AA, Alcoholics Anonymous. (1939). *Alcoholics Anonymous* (1st ed.). New York: Works Publishing Company.

Abbey, A., Zawacki, T., & Buck, P. O. (2001). Alcohol and sexual assault. *Alcohol Research & Health, 25*(1), 43–51.

Achenbach, J. (2018, April 1). Study show baby boomers are drinking alcohol at an alarming rate. *The Washington Post*, pp. 1–3.

Addolorato, G., Ancona, C., & Capristo, E. (2003, September–December). Metadoxine in the treatment of acute and chronic alcoholism: A review. *International Journal of Immunopathology and Pharmacology, 16*(3), 207–214.

Aertgeerts, B., Buntinx, F., & Kester, A. (2004). The value of the CAGE in screening for alcohol abuse and alcohol dependence in general clinical populations: A diagnostic meta-analysis. *Journal of Clinical Epidemiology, 57*(1), 30–39. doi:10.1016/S0895-4356(03)00254-3

Afifi, T. O., Henriksen, C. A., & Asmundson, G. J. (2012). Victimization and perpetration of intimate partner violence and substance use disorders in a nationally representative sample. *Journal of Nervous and Mental Disease, 200*(8), 684–691. doi:10.1097/NMD.0b013e3182613f64

Agrawal, A., Tillman, R., & Grucza, R. A. (2017, April 15). Reciprocal relationships between substance use and disorders and suicidal ideation and suicide attempts in the collaborative study of the genetics of alcoholism. *Journal of Affective Disorders, 213*, 96–104. doi:10.1016/j.jad.2016.12.060

AHFS, American Society of Health-System Pharmacists. (2017, August 15). Disulfiram. *MedlinePlus*, pp. 1–3. Bethesda, MD: AHFS.

Allampati, S., & Mullen, K. D. (2016, August). Long-term management of alcoholic liver disease. *Clinical Liver Disease, 20*(3), 551–562. doi:10.1016/j.cid.2016.02.011

127. As per publisher style, only the first three authors are listed for each reference.
128. Several times the number of references listed were found, obtained, and analyzed by the authors during the preparation of this chapter. However, only those references that were cited at least once in the body of the text are listed. Major reasons for not citing other references include that they: (1) did not provide any additional unique information or research findings; (2) were not well researched or written by their authors (i.e., were evaluated as not being valid or reliable); (3) were based predominately, or exclusively, on animal studies; (4) dealt exclusively with other population groups (e.g., children, adolescents, or young adults); (5) provided usage statistics from outside the U.S.; and/or (6) were redundant with, or not as recent as, the already cited references—unless the reference was of classical, historical, or seminal importance.
129. The reference citation, "Pagliaro & Pagliaro, *Clinical Patient Data Files*," refers to unpublished data collected, with permission, by the authors, in the formal course of their professional academic roles as clinician scientists and professors, from their patients, research subjects or participants, and students, from the 1970s to date. Most of the related data have been discussed and made public in a wide and large number of formal academic presentations, including graduate seminars, grand rounds, guest lectures, professional conferences, and undergraduate lectures.

Allen, N. E., Beral, V., & Casabonne, D. (2009, March 4). Moderate alcohol intake and cancer incidence in women. *Journal of the National Cancer Institute*, *101*(5), 296–305. doi:10.1093/jnci/djn514

Anantharaju, A., & Van Thiel, D. H. (2004, September 29). Liver transplantation for alcoholic liver disease. In *Understanding the impact of alcohol on human health and well-being*. Bethesda, MD: NIAAA.

Anderson, L. J., Flynn, A., & Pilgrim, J. L. (2017, April). A global epidemiological perspective on the toxicology of drug-facilitated sexual assault: A systematic review. *Journal of Forensic and Legal Medicine*, *47*, 46–54. doi:10.1016/j.jflm.2017.02.005

Andersson, H. W., Wenaas, M., & Nordfjaern, T. (2019, March). Relapse after inpatient substance use treatment: A prospective cohort study among users of illicit substances. *Addictive Behaviors*, *90*, 222–228. doi:10.1016/j.addbeh.2018.11.008

Anker, J. J., & Kushner, M. G. (2019, December 30). Co-occurring alcohol use disorder and anxiety: Bridging psychiatric, psychological, and neurological perspectives. *Alcohol Research: Current Reviews*, *40*(1), 1–7.

Anstee, Q. M., Daly, A., & Day, C. P. (2015, November). Genetics of alcoholic liver disease. *Seminars in Liver Disease*, *35*(4), 361–374. doi:10.1055/s-0035-1567832

AP, Associated Press. (2018, January 17). Science panel recommends lowering blood-alcohol threshold for drunken driving. *U.S. World & News Report*, pp. 1–7. Washington. Retrieved from http:///ww.syracuse.com/us-news/index.ssf/2018/01/science_panel_recommends_lowingh_blood-alcohol_threshold_for_drunken_driving.html

APA, American Psychiatric Association. (2013). *Diagnostic and Statistical Manual of Mental Disorders* (5th ed.). Arlington, Virginia: American Psychiatric Association.

Arbaizar, B., Diersen-Sotos, T., & Gomez-Acebo, I. (2010). Topiramate in the treatment of alcohol dependence: A meta-analysis. *Actas Espanolas de Psiquiatria*, *38*(1), 8–12.

Arean, P. A., Perri, M. G., & Nezu, A. M. (1993). Comparative effectiveness of social problem-solving therapy and reminiscence therapy as treatments for depression in older adults. *Journal of Consulting and Clinical Psychology*, *61*(6), 1003–1010.

Armstrong-Moore, R., Haighton, K., & Davinson, N. (2018). Interventions to reduce the negative effects of alcohol consumption in older adults: A systematic review. *BMC Public Health*, *18*, 302–315. doi:10.1186/s12889-018-5199-x

Aspy, C. B., Mold, J. W., & Thompson, D. M. (2008). Integrating screening and interventions for unhealthy behaviors into primary care practices. *American Journal of Preventive Medicine*, *53*(Suppl 5), S373–S380.

Atassi, W. A., Noghnogh, A. A., & Hariman, R. (1999). Hemodialysis as a treatment of severe ethanol poisoning. *The International Journal of Artificial Organs*, *22*(1), 18–20.

Azmi, A., Hussin, H., & Ishak, S. (2018). Drug addicts: Psychosocial factor contributing to relapse. *MATEC Web of Conferences*, *150*(05097), 1–6. doi:10.1051/matecconf/201815005097

Azorin, J. M., Bowden, C. L., & Garay, R. P. (2010). Possible new ways in the pharmacological treatment of bipolar disorder and comorbid alcoholism. *Neuropsychiatric Disease and Treatment*, *6*, 37–46.

Babor, T. F., McRee, B. G., & Kassebaum, P. A. (2007). Screening, brief intervention, and referral to treatment (SBIRT): Toward a public health approach to the management of substance abuse. *Substance Abuse*, *28*(3), 7–30. doi:10.1300/J465v28n03_03

Bailey, R. K., Patel, T. C., & Avenido, J. (2011). Suicide: Current trends. *Journal of the National Medical Association*, *103*(7), 614–617.

Bao, L., & Shi, H. (2010). Potential molecular mechanisms for combined toxicity of arsenic and alcohol. *Journal of Inorganic Biochemistry*, *104*(12), 1229–1233.

Barkla, X. M., McArdle, P. A., & Newbury-Birch, D. (2015, October 30). Are there any potentially dangerous pharmacological effects of combining ADHD medication with alcohol and drugs of abuse? A systematic review of the literature. *BMC Psychiatry, 125*, 270. doi:10.1186/sd12888-015-0657-9

Barnes, A. J., Moore, A. A., & Xu, H. (2010). Prevalence and correlates of at-risk drinking among older adults: The project SHARE study. *Journal of General Internal Medicine, 25*(8), 840–846. doi:10.1007/s11606-010-1341-x

Barry, K. L., & Blow, F. C. (2016). Drinking over the lifespan. *Alcohol Research, 38*(1), 115–120.

Bayard, M., McIntyre, J., & Hill, K. R. (2004, March 15). Alcohol withdrawal syndrome. *American Family Physician, 69*(5), 1443–1450.

Beck, A. T. (1961). A systematic investigation of depression. *Comprehensive Psychiatry, 2*, 163–170.

Beck, A. T. (1967). *Depression: Clinical, experimental and theoretical aspects*. New York: Harper & Row.

Belfer, M. L. (1993). Substance abuse with psychiatric illness in children and adolescents: Definitions and terminology. *American Journal of Orthopsychiatry, 63*(1), 70–79.

Bernstein, E., Guo, N., & Goto, T. (2021). Characterizing the variation of alcohol cessation pharmacotherapy in primary care. *Journal of General Internal Medicine, 53*(9), 1–3. doi:10.1007/s11606-020-06454-1

Bickel, W. K., Moody, L., & Mueller, E. T. (2013). Executive dysfunction among alcohol- and cocaine-dependent women. *American Psychological Association 2013 Convention Presentation.*

Blazer, D. G., & Wu, L.-T. (2009). The epidemiology of at-risk and binge drinking among middle-aged and elderly community adults: National survey on drug use and health. *American Journal of Psychiatry, 166*(10), 1162–1169. doi:10.1176/appi/ajp.2009.09010016

Blow, F. C., Schulenberg, J. E., & Demo-Dananberg, L. M. (1992). The Michigan alcoholism screening test—geriatric version (MAST-G): A new elderly-specific screening instrument. *Alcoholism: Clinical and Experimental Research, 16*, 372.

Boning, J. (2009, May). Addiction memory as a specific, individually learned memory imprint. *Pharmacopsychiatry, 42*(Suppl 1), S66–S68. doi:10.1055/s-0029-1216357

Boothby, L. A., & Doering, P. L. (2005). Acamprosate for the treatment of alcohol dependence. *Clinical Therapeutics, 27*(6), 695–714.

Borkman, T. (2008). The twelve-step recovery model of AA: A voluntary mutual help association. *Recent Developments in Alcoholism, 18*, 9–35.

Bornstein, A. M., & Pickard, H. (2020, May). "Chasing the first high": Memory sampling in drug choice. *Neuropsychopharmacology, 45*(6), 907–915. doi:10.1038/s41386-019-0594-2

Bosron, W. F., & Li, T. (1986, May–June). Genetic polymorphism of human liver alcohol and aldehyde dehydrogenases, and their relationship to alcohol metabolism and alcoholism. *Hepatology*. doi:10.1002/hep.1840060330

Bouton, M. E. (2014, November). Why behavior change is difficult to sustain. *Preventive Medicine*, 29–36. doi:10.1016/j.ypmed.2014.06.010

Bows, H., & Westmarland, N. (2017). Rape of older people in the United Kingdom: Challenging the 'real-rape' stereotype. *British Journal of Criminology, 57*, 1–17. doi:10.1093/bjc/azv116

Brady, J. E., & Guohua, L. (2013). Prevalence of alcohol and other drugs in fatally injured drivers. *Addiction, 108*(1), 104–114. doi:10.1111/j.1360-0443.2012.03993.x

Brotherton, A. L., Hamilton, E. P., & Kloss, H. G. (2016). Propofol for treatment of refractory alcohol withdrawal syndrome: A review of the literature. *Pharmacotherapy, 36*(4), 433–442. doi:10.1002/phar.1726

Brower, K. J. (2001). Alcohol's effects on sleep in alcoholics. *Alcohol Research & Health, 25*(2), 110–125.

Bryan, A., Kim, H., & Fredriksen-Goldsen, K. I. (2017). Factors associated with high-risk alcohol consumption among LGB older adults: The roles of gender, social support, perceived stress, discrimination, and stigma. *The Gerontologist, 57*(S1), S95–S104. doi:10.1093/geront/gnw100

Buchsbaum, D. G., Buchanan, R. G., & Centor, R. M. (1991). Screening for alcohol abuse using CAGE scores and likelihood ratios. *Annals of Internal Medicine, 115*(10), 774–777. doi:10.7326/0003-4819-115-10-774

Bush, K., Kivlahan, D. R., & McDonell, M. B. (1998). The AUDIT Alcohol Consumption Questions (AUDIT-C): An effective brief screening test for problem drinking. *Archives of Internal Medicine, 3*, 1789–1795.

Capasso, A., Jones, A. M., & Ali, S. H. (2021, April). Increased alcohol use during the COVID-19 pandemic: The effects of mental health and age in a cross-sectional sample of social media users in the U.S. *Preventive Medicine, 145*(106422), 1–26. doi:10.1016/j.ypmed.2021.106422

Carroll, K. M. (2014, October). Lost in translation? Moving contingency management and cognitive behavioral therapy into clinical practice. *Annals of the New York Academy of Sciences, 1327*(1), 94–111. doi:10.1111/nyas.12501

Carroll, K. M., Ball, S. A., & Nich, C. (2006). Motivational interviewing to improve treatment engagement and outcomes in individuals seeking treatment to substance abuse: A multisite effectiveness study. *Drug and Alcohol Dependence, 81*(3), 301–312. doi:10.1016/j.drugalcdep.2005.08.002

CDC, Centers for Disease Control and Prevention. (1999). *Brief interventions and brief therapies for substance abuse*. Rockville, MD: Substance Abuse and Mental Health Services Administration.

CDC, Centers for Disease Control and Prevention. (2004). Alcohol-attributable deaths and years of potential life lost—United States, 2001. *MMWR, Morbidity and Mortality Weekly Report, 53*(37), 866–870. Retrieved from MMWR, Morbidity and Mortality Weekly Report.

CDC, Centers for Disease Control and Prevention. (2010). Vital signs: Binge drinking among high school students and adults—United States 2009. *MMWR, Morbidity and Mortality Weekly Report, 59*(39), 1274–1279.

CDC, Centers for Disease Control and Prevention. (2012a). *Underlying cause of death, 1999–2008 results form* (pp. 1–9). Retrieved from CDC.gov http://wonder.cdc.gov/controller/datarequest/D67;jsessionid=B09E7BE6825E31EB884 . . .

CDC, Centers for Disease Control and Prevention. (2015, January). Alcohol poisoning deaths: A deadly consequence of binge drinking. In *CDC vital signs* (pp. 1–4). Atlanta, GA: CDC.

CDC, Centers for Disease Control and Prevention. (2017, November 30). Older adult drivers. In *Motor vehicle safety* (p. 1). Washington, DC: CDC.

CDC, Centers for Disease Control and Prevention. (2018, February). Prescribing guideline. In *Alcohol screening and brief intervention for people who consume alcohol and use opioids.* Atlanta, GA: U.S. Department of Health & Human Services.

CDC, Centers for Disease Control and Prevention. (2020, October 1). Deaths from excessive alcohol use in the U.S. In *Alcohol and public health* (pp. 1–2). Atlanta, GA: Centers for Disease Control and Prevention.

CDC, Centers for Disease Control and Prevention. (2021, February 17). Alcohol and substance use: Basics of excessive alcohol use. In *COVID-19: Act now* (pp. 1–4). Atlanta, GA: Centers for Disease Control and Prevention.

Cederbaum, A. I. (2012). Alcohol metabolism. *Clinical Liver Disease, 16*(4), 667–685. doi:10.1016/j.cld.2012.08.002

Center On Addiction. (2000, May). *Missed opportunity: National survey of primary care physicians and patients on substance abuse*. New York, NY: Center On Addiction.

Chan, L. N., & Anderson, G. D. (2014). Pharmacokinetics and pharmacodynamic drug interactions with ethanol (alcohol). *Clinical Pharmacokinetics, 53*(12), 1115–1136. doi:10.1007/s40262-014-0190-x

Chang, E. T., Canchola, A. J., & Lee, V. S. (2007). Wine and other alcohol consumption and risk of ovarian cancer in the California Teachers Study cohort. *Cancer Causes & Control, 18*(1), 91–103. doi:10.1007/s10552-006-0083-x

Chang-Mu, C., Jen-Kun, L., & Shing-Hwa, L. (2010). Characterization of neurotoxic effects of NMDA and the novel neuroprotection by phytopolyphenols in mice. *Behavioral Neuroscience, 124*(4), 541–553.

Charlton, M. E., Sweetnan, P. M., & Fitzgerald, L. W. (2002). Chronic ethanol administration regulates the expression of GABBA receptor alpha1 and alpha5 subunit in the ventral tegmental area and hippocampus. *Journal of Neurochemistry, 68*(1), 121–127.

Chartier, K. G., Vaeth, P. A., & Caetano, R. (2013). Focus on: Ethnicity and the social and health harms from drinking. *Alcoholism Research: Current Reviews, 35*(2), 229–237.

Cho, J., Bhimani, J., & Milapkumar, P. (2018, March). Substance abuse among older adults: A growing problem. *Current Psychiatry, 17*(3), 14–20.

Coltrain, I. M., Nicholas, C. L., & Baker, F. C. (2014). Alcohol and the sleeping brain. *Handbook of Clinical Neurology, 125*, 415–431. doi:10.1016/B978-0-444-62619-6.00024-0

Conner, K. R., & Bagge, C. L. (2019). Suicidal behavior: Links between alcohol use disorder and acute use of alcohol. *Alcohol Research: Current Reviews, 40*(1), 1–3. doi:10.35946/arcr.v40.1.02

Cook, J. M., Dinnen, S., & O'Donnell, C. (2011). Older women survivors of physical and sexual violence: A systematic review of the quantitative literature. *Journal of Womens Health, 20*(7), 1075–1081. doi:10.1089/jwh.2010.2279

Costin, B. N., & Miles, M. F. (2014). Molecular and neurologic responses to chronic alcohol use. *Handbook of Clinical Neurology (on-line version, ScienceDirect.com), 125*, 157–171. doi:10.1016/B978-0-444-62619-6.00010-0

Crome, I. B., Bloor, R., & Thom, B. (2006). Screening for illicit drug use in psychiatric hospitals: Whose job is it? *Advances in Psychiatric Treatment, 12*, 375–383.

Crowley, P. (2015). Long-term drug treatment of patients with alcohol dependence. *Australian Prescriber, 38*, 41–43. doi:10.18773/austprescr.2015.015

Daley, D. C., Moss, H., & Campbell, F. (1987). *Dual disorders: Counseling clients with chemical dependency and mental illness*. Center City, MN: Hazelden.

Darvishi, N., Farhadi, M., & Haghtalab, T. (2015). Alcohol-related risk of suicidal ideation, suicide attempt, and completed suicide: A meta-analysis. *PLoS One, 10*(5), e0126870. doi:10.1371/journal.pone.0126870

Davis, V. E., & Walsh, M. J. (1970a, February 13). Alcohol, amines, and alkaloids: A possible biochemical basis for alcohol addiction. *Science, 167*(3920), 1005–1007.

Davis, V. E., & Walsh, M. J. (1970b, September 11). Alcohol addiction and tetrahydropapaveroline. *Science, 169*(3950), 1105–1106.

De Sousa, A. (2010). The role of topiramate and other anticonvulsants in the treatment of alcohol dependence: A clinical review. *CNS Neurological Disorders—Drug Targets, 9*(1), 45–49.

De Witte, P., Littleton, J., & Parot, P. (2005). Neuroprotective and abstinence-promoting effects of acamprosate: Elucidating the mechanism of action. *CNS Drugs, 19*(6), 517–537.

Deitrich, R. A., Dunwiddie, T. V., & Harris, R. A. (1989). Mechanism of action of ethanol: Initial central nervous system actions. *Pharmacological Reviews*, *41*, 489–537.

Delker, E., Brown, Q., & Hasin, D. S. (2016). Alcohol consumption in demographic subpopulations: An epidemiologic overview. *Alcohol Research: Current Reviews*, *38*(1), 7–15.

Devries, K. M., Child, J. C., & Bacchus, L. J. (2014). Intimate partner violence victimization and alcohol consumption in women: A systematic review and meta-analysis. *Addiction*, *109*(3), 379–391. doi:10.1111/add.12393

Dhalla, S., & Kopec, J. A. (2007). The CAGE questionnaire for alcohol misuse: A review of reliability and validity studies. *Clinical and Investigative Medicine*, *30*(1), 33–41. doi:10.25011/cim.v30i1.447

Diaz Martinez, M. C., Diaz Martinez, A., & Villamil Salcedo, V. (2002, January–February). Efficacy of metadoxine in the management of acute alcohol intoxication. *The Journal of International Medical Research*, *30*(1), 44–51.

Diehl, A., Ulmer, L., & Mutschler, J. (2010). Why is disulfiram superior to acamprosate in the routine clinical setting? A retrospective long-term study in 353 alcohol-dependent patients. *Alcohol and Addiction*, *45*(3), 271–277.

Dixit, D., Endicott, J., & Burry, L. (2016). Management of acute alcohol withdrawal syndrome in critically ill patients. *Pharmacotherapy*, *36*(7), 797–822. doi:10.1002/phar.1770

Drake, R. E., Essock, S. M., & Shaner, A. (2001). Implementing dual diagnosis services for clients with severe mental illness. *Psychiatric Services*, *52*(4), 469–476.

Ducharme, J. (2019, July 31). Millennials may be drinking less, but binge drinking is on the rise among older adults. *Time Magazine*, pp. 1–3.

Eberhard, S., Nordstrom, G., & Hoglund, P. (2009). Secondary prevention of hazardous alcohol consumption in psychiatric out-patients: A randomized controlled study. *Social Psychiatry and Psychiatric Epidemiology*, *44*(12), 1013–1021. doi:10.1007/s00127-009-0023-7

Ebrahim, I. O., Shapiro, C. M., & Williams, A. J. (2013). Alcohol and sleep I: Effects on normal sleep. *Alcoholism: Clinical & Experimental Research*, *37*(4), 539–549. doi:10.1111/acer.12006

Ellin, A. (2014, October 3). More older adults are struggling with substance abuse. *The New York Times*, pp. 1–2.

Emiliussen, J., Sogaard Nielsen, A., & Andersen, K. (2017). Identifying risk factors for late-onset (50+) alcohol use disorder and heavy drinking: A systematic review. *Substance Use & Misuse*, *52*(12), 1575–1588. doi:10.1080/10826084.2017.1293102

Engel, G. L. (1977, April 8). The need for a new medical model: A challenge for biomedicine. *Science*, *196*(4286), 129–136. doi:10.1126/science.847460

Ewing, J. A. (1984, October 12). Detecting alcoholism: The CAGE questionnaire. *JAMA*, *252*(14), 1905–1907. doi:10.1001/jama.252.14.1905

Feingold, A., Capaldi, D. M., & Owen, L. D. (2015, May). Proximal vs. distal predictors of alcohol use disorders and treatment utilization in at-risk men in early middle age. *Comprehensive Psychiatry*, *61*, 64–71. doi:10.1016/j.comppsych.2015.05.010

Ferri, M., Amato, L., & Davoli, M. (2006, July 19). Alcoholics Anonymous and other 12-step programmes for alcohol dependence. *Cochrane Database of Systematic Reviews*, *3*, CD005032.

Fink, A., Morton, S. C., & Beck, J. C. (2002). The alcohol-related problems survey: Identifying hazardous and harmful drinking in older primary care patients. *Journal of the American Geriatrics Society*, *50*, 1717–1722.

Flaherty, J. A., McGuire, H. T., & Gatski, R. L. (1955, December). The psychodynamics of the dry drunk. *The American Journal of Psychiatry*, *112*(6), 460–464. doi:10.1176/ajp.112.6.460

Florez, G., Saiz, P. A., & Garcia-Portilla, P. (2010). Topiramate for the treatment of alcohol dependence: Comparison with naltrexone. *European Addiction Research, 17*(1), 29–36.

Flowers, N. T., Naimi, T. S., & Brewer, R. D. (2008). Patterns of alcohol consumption and alcohol-impaired driving in the United States. *Alcoholism: Clinical and Experimental Research, 32*(4), 639–644. doi:10.1111/j.1530-0277.2008.00622.x

Foran, C. (2020, January 15). Arizona congresswoman to seek treatment for 'alcohol dependence'. *CNN TV,* pp. 1–2. Washington, DC: Turner Broadcasting System.

Freud, A. (1934). *The ego and mechanisms of defense*. London: Hogarth Press.

Freud, S. (2005). *Civilization and its discontents*. London: Penquin.

Freudenheim, J. L. (2020). Alcohol's effects on breast cancer in women. *Alcohol Research: Current Reviews, 40*(2), 1–12. doi:10.35946/arcr.v40.2.11

Friedman, R. A. (2013, April 29). A rising tide of substance abuse. *The New York Times*, pp. 1–2.

Garbutt, J. C. (2009). The state of pharmacotherapy for the treatment of alcohol dependence. *Journal of Substance Abuse Treatment, 36*(1), S15–S23.

Garbutt, J. C. (2010). Efficacy and tolerability of naltrexone in the management of alcohol dependence. *Current Pharmaceutical Design, 16*(19), 2091–2097.

Garbutt, J. C., Kranzler, H. R., & O'Malley, S. S. (2005). Efficacy and tolerability of long-acting injectable naltrexone for alcohol dependence: A randomized controlled study. *JAMA, The Journal of the American Medical Association, 293*, 1617–1625.

GBD, Global Burden of Diseases. (2018, August 23). Alcohol use and burden for 195 countries and territories, 1990–2016: A systematic analysis for the global Burden of Disease Study 2016. *The Lancet*, 1–21. doi:10.1016/S0140-6736(18)31310-2

Gomi, I., Fukushima, H., & Shiraki, M. (2007). Relationship between serum albumin level and aging in community-dwelling self-supported elderly population. *Journal of Nutritional Science and Vitaminology, 53*, 37–42.

Gonzales, R. A., & Jaworski, J. N. (1997). Alcohol and glutamate. *Alcohol Health & Research World, 21*(2), 120–127.

Greene, M., Jackson, J. W., & Dean, L. T. (2020, July). Examining disparities in excessive alcohol use among black and hispanic lesbian and bisexual women in the United States: An intersectional analysis. *Journal of Studies on Alcohol and Drugs, 81*(4), 462–470. doi:10.15288/jsad.2020.81.462

Guglielmo, R., Martinotti, G., & Quatrale, M. (2015). Topiramate in alcohol use disorders: Review and update. *CNS Drugs, 29*(5), 383–395. doi:10.1007/s40263-015-0244-0

Gupta, S., & Warner, J. (2008). Alcohol-related dementia: A 21st-century silent epidemic? *The British Journal of Psychiatry, 193*, 351–353. doi:10.1192/bjp.bp.108.05.1425

Gutierrez Garcia, M. L., Blasco-Algora, S., & Fernandez-Rodriguez, C. M. (2015, July 28). Alcohol liver disease: A review of current therapeutic approaches to achieve long-term abstinence. *World Journal of Gastroenterology, 21*(28), 8516–8526. doi:10.3748/wjg.v21.i28.8516

Hamajima, N., Hirose, K., & Tajima, K. (2002). Alcohol, tobacco and breast cancer—collaborative reanalysis of individual data from 53 epidemiological studies, including 58,515 women with breast cancer and 95,067 without the disease. *British Journal of Cancer, 87*(11), 1234–1245.

Hammond, C. J., Niciu, M. J., & Drew, S. (2015). Anticonvulsants for the treatment of alcohol withdrawal syndrome and alcohol use disorders. *CNS Drugs, 29*(4), 293–311. doi:10.1007/s40263-015-0240-4

Han, B. H., Moore, A. A., & Ferris, R. (2019, July 31). Binge drinking among older adults in the United States, 2015 to 2017. *Journal of the American Geriatric Society*. doi:10.1111/jgs.16071

Han, B. H., Moore, A. A., & Sherman, S. E. (2017, January 1). Demographic trends of binge alcohol use and alcohol use disorders among older adults in the United States, 2005–2014. *Drug and Alcohol Dependence, 170*, 198–207. doi:10.1016/j.drugalcdep.2016.11.003

Han, B. H., Moore, A. A., & Sherman, S. E. (2018, June 1). Prevalence and correlates of binge drinking among older adults with multimorbidity. *Drug and Alcohol Dependence, 187*, 48–54. doi:10.1016/j.drugalcdep.2018.012.038

Harada, M. Y., Gangi, A., & Ko, A. (2015, December). Bicycle trauma and alcohol intoxication. *International Journal of Surgery, 24*(Part A), 14–19. doi:10.1016/j.ijsu.2015.10.013

Heinala, P., Piepponen, T., & Heikkinen, H. (1990). Diazepam loading in alcohol withdrawal: Clinical pharmacokinetics. *International Journal of Clinical Pharmacology, Therapy and Toxicology, 28*(5), 211–217.

Henry-Edwards, S., Humeniuk, R., & Ali, R. (2003). Brief intervention for substance use: A manual for use in primary care. In *Field testing manual*. Geneva: World Health Organization.

Hoffman, P. L. (1995, March). Glutamate receptors in alcohol withdrawal-induced neurotoxicity. *Metabolic Brain Disease, 10*(1), 73–79.

Hoffman, P. L., & Tabakoff, B. (1994). The role of the NMDA receptor in ethanol withdrawal. *EXS, 71*, 61–70.

Holtzman, J. L. (1983). Definition and implications of dose-dependent kinetics in clinical medicine. *Drug Metabolism Reviews, 14*(6), 1103–1117.

Hovda, K. E., & Jacobsen, D. (2016). Management of alcohol poisoning. In A. Webb, D. Angus, & S. Finfer (Eds.), *Oxford textbook of critical care* (2nd ed., pp. 1–11). Oxford: Oxford University Press.

Hudmon, K. S., Corelli, R. L., & Prokhorov, A. V. (2010, February). Current approaches to pharmacotherapy for smoking cessation. *Therapeutic Advances in Respiratory Disease, 4*(1), 35–47. doi:10.1177/1753465809353768

IIHS, Insurance Institute for Highway Safety. (2018, December). Older people. *Fatality Facts 2017*, 1–13.

Jackson, K. M., Barnett, N. P., & Colby, S. M. (2015). The prospective association between sipping alcohol by the sixth grade and later substance use. *Journal of Studies on Alcohol and Drugs, 76*(2), 212–221. doi:10.15288/jsad.2015.76.212

Jefee-Bahloul, H., Jorandby, L., & Arias, A. J. (2019). Topiramate treatment of alcohol use disorder in clinical practice. *Journal of Addiction Medicine, 13*(1), 23–27. doi:10.1097/ADM0000000000000444

Jiao, L., Silverman, D. T., & Schairer, C. (2009, May 1). Alcohol use and risk of pancreatic cancer: The NIH-AARP diet and health study. *American Journal of Epidemiology, 169*(9), 1043–1051. doi:10.1093/aje/kwp034

Johnson, B. A., & Ait-Daoud, N. (2010). Topiramate in the new generation of drugs: Efficacy in the treatment of alcoholic patients. *Current Pharmaceutical Design, 16*(19), 2103–2112.

Johnson, B. A., Ait-Daoud, N., & Bowden, C. L. (2003). Oral topiramate for treatment of alcohol dependence: A randomized controlled study. *The Lancet, 361*(9370), 1677–1685.

Johnson, B. A., Rosenthal, N., & Capece, J. A. (2007). Topiramate for treating alcohol dependence: A randomized controlled study. *JAMA, The Journal of the American Medical Association, 298*(14), 1641–1685.

Jones, C. M., Paulozzi, L. J., & Mack, K. A. (2014). Alcohol involvement in opioid pain reliever and benzodiazepine drug abuse-related emergency department visits and drug-related deaths—United States, 2010. *MMWR, Morbidity and Mortality Weekly Report, 63*(40), 881–885.

Jung, Y. C., & Namkoong, K. (2006). Pharmacotherapy for alcohol dependence: Anticraving medications for relapse prevention. *Yonsei Medical Journal, 47*(2), 167–178.

Kalk, N. J., & Lingford-Hughes, A. R. (2014). The clinical pharmacology of acamprosate. *British Journal of Clinical Pharmacology, 77*(2), 315–323. doi:10.1111/bcp.12070

Kanny, D., Naimi, T. S., & Liu, Y. (2018). Annual total binge drinks consumed by U.S. adults, 2015. *American Journal of Preventive Medicine, 54*(4), 486–496.

Kanny, D., Naimi, T. S., & Liu, Y. (2020, January 17). Trends in total binge drinks per adult who reported binge drinking—United States, 2011–2017. *MMWR, Morbidity and Mortality Weekly Report, 69*(2), 30–34.

Kaukonen, J. P., Nurmi-Luthje, I., & Luthje, P. (2006, May/June). Acute alcohol use among patients with acute hip fractures: A descriptive incidence study in southeastern Finland. *Alcohol and Alcoholism, 41*(3), 345–348. doi:10.1093/alcalc/agh259

Kaysen, D., Dillworth, T. M., & Simpson, T. (2007). Domestic violence and alcohol use: Trauma-related symptoms and motives for drinking. *Addictive Behaviors, 32*(6), 1272–1283. doi:10.1016/jaddbeh.2006.09.007

Kelley, A. E. (2004, September 30). Memory and addiction: Shared neural circuitry and molecular mechanisms. *Neuron, 44*(1), 161–179. doi:10.1016/j.neuron.2004.09.016

Kenna, G. A., Lomastro, T. L., & Schiesl, A. (2009). Review of topiramate: An antiepileptic for the treatment of alcohol dependence. *Current Drug Abuse Reviews, 2*(2), 135–142.

Kennedy, W. K., Leloux, M., & Kutscher, E. C. (2010). Acamprosate. *Expert Opinion on Drug Metabolism & Toxicology, 6*(3), 363–380.

Kiefer, F., & Mann, K. (2010). Acamprosate: How, when, and for whom does it work? Mechanisms of action, treatment targets, and individualized therapy. *Current Pharmaceutical Design, 16*(19), 2098–2102.

Kiluk, B. D., Nich, C., & Buck, M. B. (2018, May 24). Randomized clinical trial of computerized and clinician-delivered CBT in comparison with standard outpatient treatment for substance use disorders: Primary within-treatment and follow-up outcomes. *The American Journal of Psychiatry*. doi:10.1176/appi.ajp.2018.17090978

Kim, Y., Han, K., & Choi, J. (2019). Frequent drinking is a more important risk factor for new-onset atrial fibrillation than binge drinking: A nationwide population-based study. *Eurospace, 0*, 1–9. doi:10.1093/eurospace/euz256

Kirchmayer, U., Davoli, M., & Verster, A. (2000). Naltrexone maintenance treatment for opioid dependence. *The Cochrane Database of Systematic Reviews, 2*, CD0013333. doi:10.1002/14651858.CD001333

Kitchens, J. M. (1994). Does this patient have an alcohol problem? *JAMA, 272*(22), 1782–1787. doi:10.1001/jama.1994.03520220076034

Kivimaki, M., Singh-Manous, A., & Batty, G. D. (2020, September 1). Association of alcohol-induced loss of consciousness and overall alcohol consumption with risk for dementia. *JAMA Network Open, 3*(9), e2016084. doi:10.1001/jamanetworkopen.2020.16084

Kline, J., Becker, J., & Giese, C. (1992). Psychodynamic interventions revisited: Options for the treatment of schizophrenia. *Psychotherapy: Theory, Research, Practice, Training, 29*(3), 366–377. doi:10.1037/h008853

Kogawa, M., & Wada, S. (2005). Osteoporosis and alcohol intake. *Clinical Calcium, 15*(1), 102–105.

Kranzler, H. R., Armeli, S., & Tennen, H. (2014, December). GRIK1 genotype and daily expectations of alcohol's positive effects moderate the reduction of heavy drinking by topiramate. *Experimental and Clinical Psychopharmacology, 22*(6), 494–501. doi:10.1037/a0038350

Kranzler, H. R., Covault, J., & Feinn, R. (2014). Topiramate treatment for heavy drinkers: Moderation by a GRIK1 polymorphism. *American Journal of Psychiatry, 171*, 445–452. doi:10.1176/appi.ajp.2013.13081014

Kraut, J. A., & Mullins, M. E. (2018, January 18). Toxic alcohols. *The New England Journal of Medicine, 378*(3), 270–280. doi:10.1056/NEJMra1615295

Kreek, M. J., & Stimmel, B. (Eds.). (1984). *Dual addiction: Pharmacological issues in the treatment of concomitant alcoholism and drug abuse*. Binghamton, NY: Haworth.

Kuerbis, A. N., Sacco, P., & Blazer, D. G. (2014, August). Substance abuse among older adults. *Clinics in Geriatric Medicine, 30*(3), 629–654. doi:10.1016/j.cger.2014.04.008

Kuerbis, A. N., Yuan, S. E., & Borok, J. (2015, February). Testing the initial efficacy of a mailed screening and brief feedback intervention to reduce at-risk drinking in middle-aged and older adults: The Comorbidity Alcohol Risk Evaluation (CARE) Study. *Journal of the American Geriatrics Society, 63*(2), 321–326. doi:10.1111/jgs.13237

Kunzmann, A. T., Coleman, H. G., & Huang, W. Y. (2018). The association of lifetime alcohol use with mortality and cancer risk in older adults: A cohort study. *PLoS Medicine, 15*(6), e1002585. doi:10.1371/journal.pmed.1002585

Larsson, S. C., Drca, N., & Wolk, A. (2014, July 22). Alcohol consumption and risk of atrial fibrillation: A prospective study and dose-response meta-analysis. *Journal of the American College of Cardiology, 64*(3), 281–289. doi:10.1016/j.jacc.2014.03.048

Laudet, A. B. (2008). The impact of Alcoholics Anonymous on other substance abuse related twelve step programs. *Recent Developments in Alcoholism, 18*, 71–89.

Laundergan, J. C., & Williams, T. (1993). The Hazelden residential family program: A combined systems and disease model approach. In T. J. O'Farrell (Ed.), *Treating alcohol problems: Marital and family interventions* (pp. 145–169). New York: Guilford Press.

Lee, M. R., & Sher, K. J. (2018). "Maturing out" of binge and problem drinking. *Alcohol Research Current Reviews, 39*(1), e1–e12.

Lehman, A. F., Myers, C. P., & Corty, E. (1994, March-April). Prevalence and patterns of "dual diagnosis" among psychiatric inpatients. *Comprehensive Psychiatry, 35*(2), 106–112.

Leung, J. G., Hall-Flavin, D., & Nelson, S. (2015). The role of gabapentin in the management of alcohol withdrawal and dependence. *The Annals of Pharmacotherapy, 49*(8), 897–906. doi:10.1177/1060028015585849

Li, G., Brady, J. E., & Chen, Q. (2013, November). Drug use and fatal motor vehicle crashes: A case-control study. *Accident Analysis & Prevention, 60*, 205–210. doi:10.1016/j.aap.2013.09.001

Liang, J., & Olsen, R. W. (2014). Alcohol use disorders and current pharmacological therapies: The role of GABA(A) receptors. *Acta Pharmacologica Sinica, 35*(8), 981–993. doi:10.1038/aps.2014.50

Lieber, C. S. (1999). Microsomal ethanol-oxidizing system (MEOS): The first 30 years (1968–1998)—a review. *Alcoholism: Clinical & Experimental Research, 23*(6), 991–1007.

Ling, J., Stephens, R., & Heffernan, T. M. (2010). Cognitive and psychomotor performance during alcohol hangover. *Current Drug Abuse Reviews, 3*(2), 80–87.

Little, J., Barron, S., & Prendergast, M. (2007, May–June). Smoking kills (alcoholics)! Shouldn't we do something about it? *Alcohol and Alcoholism, 42*(3), 167–173. doi:10.1093/alcalc/agm019

LoConte, N. K., Brewster, A. M., & Kaur, J. S. (2018). Alcohol and cancer: A statement of the American Society of Clinical Oncology. *Journal of Clinical Oncology, 36*(1), 83–93. doi:10.1200/JCO.2017.76.1155

Long, D., Long, B., & Koyfman, A. (2017). The emergency medicine management of severe alcohol withdrawal. *The American Journal of Emergency Medicine, 35*(7), 1005–1011. doi:10.1016/j.ajem.2017.02.002

Lovinger, D. M. (1997). Serotonin's role in alcohol's effects on the brain. *Alcohol Health & Research World, 21*(2), 114–120.

Luo, Z., Liu, Y., & Liu, Y. (2017, December). Cellular and molecular mechanisms of alcohol-induced osteopenia. *Cellular and Molecular Life Sciences, 74*(24), 4443–4453. doi:10.1007/s00018-017-2585-y

Ma, K., Baloch, Z., & He, T.-T. (2017). Alcohol consumption and gastric cancer risk: A meta-analysis. *Medical Science Monitor, 23*, 238–246. doi:10.12659/MSM.899423

Maddur, H., & Shah, V. H. (2020). Alcohol and liver function in women. *Alcohol Research Current Reviews, 40*(2), 1–5. doi:10.35946/arcr.v40.2.10

Madea, B., & Musshoff, F. (2009, May). Knock-out drugs: Their prevalence, modes of action, and means of detection. *Deutsches Arzteblatt International, 106*(20), 341–347. doi:10.3238/arztebl.2009.0341

Madras, B. K., Compton, W. M., & Avula, D. (2009, January). Screening, brief interventions, referral to treatment (SBIRT) for illicit drug and alcohol use at multiple sites: Comparison at intake and 6 months later. *Drug and Alcohol Dependence, 99*(1–3), 280–295. doi:10.1016/j.drugalcdep.23008.08.003

Mann, K., & Hermann, D. (2010). Individualised treatment in alcohol-dependent patients. *European Archives of Psychiatry & Clinical Neuroscience, 260*(Suppl 2), S116–S120.

Mann, R. E., Smart, R. G., & Govoni, R. (2003). The epidemiology of alcoholic liver disease. *Alcohol Research & Health, 27*(3), 209–219.

Marcinkiewcz, C. A. (2015). Serotonergic systems in the pathophysiology of ethanol dependence: Relevance to clinical alcoholism. *ACS Chemical Neuroscience, 6*(7), 1026–1039. doi:10.1021/cn5003573

Maryanoff, B., Nortey, O., & Gardocki, J. (1987). Anticonvulsant O-alkyl sulfamates. 2,3:4,5-Bis-O-(1-methyethylidene)-beta-D-fructopyranose sulfamate and related compounds. *Journal of Medicinal Chemistry, 30*(5), 880–887.

Mason, B. J. (2001). Treatment of alcohol-dependent outpatients with acamprosate: A clinical review. *The Journal of Clinical Psychiatry, 62*(Suppl 20), 42–48.

Mason, B. J. (2003). Acamprosate. *Recent Developments in Alcoholism, 16*, 203–215.

Mason, B. J., & Heyser, C. J. (2010a). The neurobiology, clinical efficacy and safety of acamprosate in the treatment of alcohol dependence. *Expert Opinion on Drug Safety, 9*(1), 177–188.

Mason, B. J., & Heyser, C. J. (2010b, March). Acamprosate: A prototypic neuromodulator in the treatment of alcohol dependence. *CNS & Neurological Disorders Drug Targets, 9*(1), 23–32.

Mason, B. J., Quello, S., & Goodell, V. (2014). Gabapentin treatment for alcohol dependence: A randomized clinical trial. *JAMA Internal Medicine, 174*(1), 70–77. doi:10.1001/jamainternmed.2013.11950

Matejcic, M., Gunter, M. J., & Ferrari, P. (2017). Alcohol metabolism and oesophageal cancer: A systematic review of the evidence. *Carcinogenesis, 38*(9), 859–872. doi:10.1093/carcin/bgx067

Mattson, M. E., & Allen, J. P. (1991). Research on matching alcoholic patients to treatments: Findings, issues, and implications. *Journal of Addictive Diseases, 11*(2), 33–49.

Mattson, M. E., Allen, J. P., & Longabaugh, R. (1994, December). A chronological review of empirical studies matching alcoholic clients to treatment. *Journal of Studies on Alcohol Supplement, 12*, 16–29.

Mattson, M. E., Lipari, R. N., & Hays, C. (2017, May 11). A day in the life of older adults: Substance use facts. In *The CBHSQ report* (pp. 1–5). Rockville, MD: Substance Abuse and Mental Health Services Administration.

Maurel, D. B., Boisseau, N., & Benhamou, C. L. (2012). Alcohol and bone: Review of dose effects and mechanisms. *Osteoporosis International*, *23*(1), 1–16. doi:10.1007/s00198-011-1787-7

Mayfield, D., McLeod, G., & Hall, P. (1974). The CAGE questionnaire: Validation of a new alcoholism screening instrument. *American Journal of Psychiatry*, *131*(10), 1121–1123. doi:10.1176/ajp.131.10.1121

McCaul, M. E., & Petry, N. M. (2003). The role of psychosocial treatments in pharmacotherapy for alcoholism. *The American Journal on Addictions*, *12*(Suppl 1), S41–S52.

McCusker, M. T., Basquille, J., & Khwaja, M. (2002). Hazardous and harmful drinking: A comparison of the AUDIT and CAGE screening questionnaires. *QJM: An International Journal of Medicine*, *95*(9), 591–595. doi:10.1093/qjmed/95.9.591

McGee, E. M. (2000). Alcoholics Anonymous and nursing: Lessons in holism and spiritual care. *Journal of Holistic Nursing*, *18*(1), 11–26.

McGuinness, C. (2019, January 3). Aged and addicted: Senior drug and alcohol abuse on the Central Coast. *New Times*, pp. 1–4. San Luis Obispo.

McHugh, R. K., Hearon, B. A., & Otto, M. W. (2010). Cognitive behavioral therapy for substance use disorders. *Psychiatric Clinics of North America*, *33*(3), 511–525.

McHugh, R. K., & Weiss, R. D. (2019). Alcohol use disorder and depressive disorders. *Alcohol Research: Current Reviews*, *40*(1), e1–e8.

McKay, J. R. (1999). Studies of factors in relapse to alcohol, drug and nicotine use: A critical review of methodologies and findings. *Journal of Studies on Alcohol*, *60*(4), 566–576.

McKay, J. R., Franklin, T. R., & Patapis, N. (2006, March). Conceptual, methodological and analytical issues in the study of relapse. *Clinical Psychology Review*, *26*(2), 109–127. doi:10.1016/j.cpr.2005.11.002

McKetin, R., Coen, A., & Kaye, S. (2015, June 1). A comprehensive review of the effects of mixing caffeinated energy drinks with alcohol. *Drug and Alcohol Dependence*, *151*, 15–30. doi:10.1016/j.drugalcdep.20125.01.047

McKinney, A. (2010). A review of the next day effects of alcohol on subjective mood ratings. *Current Drug Abuse Reviews*, *3*(2), 88–91.

Meier, P., & Seitz, H. (2008). Age, alcohol metabolism and liver disease. *Current Opinion in Clinical Nutrition and Metabolic Care*, *11*(1), 21–26. doi:10.1097/MCO.0b013e3282f30564

Miles, F. (2020, May 6). San Francisco gives drugs, alcohol to homeless addicts in hotels during coronavirus, sparking debate. *Fox News,* pp. 1–2. San Francisco: FoxNews.com.

Miller, T. W., Leukefeld, C., & Jefferson, B. (1994, September). Dual diagnosis: Clinical issues in substance abuse treatment. *Journal of Contemporary Psychotherapy*, *24*(3), 169–177.

Miller, W. R. (1999). *Enhancing motivation for change in substance abuse treatment*. Rockville, MD: Center for Substance Abuse Treatment.

Miller, W. R., & Mount, K. A. (2001). A small study of training in motivational interviewing: Does one workshop change clinician and client behavior? *Behavior and Cognitive Psychotherapy*, *29*, 457–471.

Miller, W. R., & Rollnick, S. (1991). *Motivational interviewing: Preparing people to change addictive behavior*. New York, NY: Guilford.

Miller, W. R., Yahne, C. E., & Moyers, T. B. (2004, December). A randomized trial of methods to help clinicians learn motivational interviewing. *Journal of Consultant and Clinical Psychology*, *72*(6), 1050–1062. doi:10.1037/0022-006X.72.6.1050

Miller, W. R., Yahne, C. E., & Tonigan, J. S. (2003, August). Motivational interviewing in drug abuse services: A randomized trial. *Journal of Consultant and Clinical Psychology, 71*(4), 754–763. doi:10.1037/0022-006x.71.4.754

Mo, Y., Thomas, M. C., & Karras, G. E. (2016, April). Barbiturates for the treatment of alcohol withdrawal syndrome: A systematic review of clinical trials. *Journal of Critical Care, 32*, 101–107. doi:10.1016/j.jcrc.2015.11.022

Moore, A. A., Whiteman, E. J., & Ward, K. T. (2007, March). Risks of combined alcohol-medication use in older adults. *American Journal of Geriatric Pharmacotherapy, 5*(1), 64–67.

Moriyama, Y., Mimura, M., & Kato, M. (2006). Primary alcoholic dementia and alcohol-related dementia. *Psychogeriatrics, 6*, 114–118.

Moss, R. H., Schutte, K. K., & Brennan, P. L. (2010, April 1). Late-life and life history predictors of older adults of high risk alcohol consumption and drinking problems. *Drug and Alcohol Dependence, 108*(1–2), 13–20. doi:10.1016/j.drugalcdep.2009.11.005

Most, D., Ferguson, L., & Harris, A. (2014). Molecular basis of alcoholism. *Handbook of Clinical Neurology, 125*, 89–111. doi:10.1016/B987-0-444-62619-6.00006-9

Muller, C. P., & Homberg, J. R. (2015, January). The role of serotonin in drug use and addiction. *Behavioural Brain Research, 277*, 146–192.

Muzyk, A. J., Leung, J. G., & Nelson, S. (2013, March–April). The role of diazepam loading for the treatment of alcohol withdrawal syndrome in hospitalized patients. *The American Journal on Addictions, 22*(2), 113–118. doi:10.1111/j.1521-0391.2013.00307.x

Naegle, M. A. (2018). Alcohol use screening and assessment for older adults. In *Best practices in nursing care to older adults* (Vol. 17, pp. 1–2). New York, NY: New York University Rory Meyers College of Nursing.

Naimi, T. S., Nelson, D. E., & Brewer, R. D. (2009, October). Driving after binge drinking. *American Journal of Preventive Medicine, 37*(4), 314–320. doi:10.1016/j.amepre.2009.06.013

NCI, National Cancer Institute. (2018, September 13). *Alcohol and cancer risk* (pp. 1–7). Bethesda, MD: NIH.

Newman, T. (2017, December 8). What to know about alcohol poisoning. *Medical News Today*, pp. 1–5.

Newman, T. (2018, February 21). Alcohol use disorder is a 'major risk factor' for dementia. *Medical News Today*, pp. 1–2.

NHTSA, National Highway Traffick Safety Administration. (2018, November). Alcohol-Impaired Driving. *Traffic Safety Facts*, pp. 1–8.

NIA, National Institute on Aging. (2017, May 16). Facts about aging and alcohol. *National Institutes of Health.*

NIAAA, National Institute on Alcohol Abuse and Alcoholism. (1995a, April). Alcohol and tolerance. *Alcohol Alert* (No. 28 PH 356), 1–2.

NIAAA, National Institute on Alcohol Abuse and Alcoholism. (1995b). Screening tests. In *Understanding the impact of alcohol on human health and well-being*. Bethesda, MD: NIH.

NIAAA, National Institute on Alcohol Abuse and Alcoholism. (2005, April). The neurotoxicity of alcohol. In *Alcohol and the brain: Neuroscience and neurobehavior* (pp. 134–146). Bethesda, MD: National Institutes of Health.

NIAAA, National Institute on Alcohol Abuse and Alcoholism. (2016, July). Alcohol use disorder: A comparison between DSM-IV and DSM-5. In *Turning discovery into health* (pp. 1–2). Bethesda, MD: NIH, National Institutes of Health.

NIAAA, National Institute on Alcohol Abuse and Alcoholism. (2020a, January 10). Alcohol-related deaths increasing in the United States. In *News release* (pp. 1–2). Bethesda, MD: NIH, National Institutes of Health.

NIAAA, National Institute on Alcohol Abuse and Alcoholism. (2020b, February). *Alcohol facts and statistics* (pp. 1–7). Bethesda, MD: NIH, National Institutes of Health.

NIAAA, National Institute on Alcohol Abuse and Alcoholism. (2021, March). *Binge drinking* (pp. 1–5). Bethesda, MD: NIH.

NIDA, National Institute on Drug Abuse. (2020, July). Substance use in older adults. In *Drug facts* (pp. 1–9). Bethesda, MD: NIH, National Institutes of Health.

Nowinski, J., Baker, S., & Carroll, K. (1992/1999). *Twelve step facilitation therapy manual: A clinical research guide for therapists treating individuals with alcohol abuse and dependence*. Rockville, MD: National Institute on Alcohol Abuse and Alcoholism.

Nunes, A. P., Richmond, M. K., & Marzano, K. (2017, October–December). Ten years of implementing screening, brief intervention, and referral to treatment (SBIRT): Lessons learned. *Substance Abuse*, *38*(4), 508–512. doi:10.1080/08897077.2017.1362369

O'Brien, C. P. (2008). The Cage questionnaire for detection of alcoholism: A remarkable useful but simple tool. *JAMA*, *300*(17), 2054–2056. doi:10.1001/jama.2008.570

O'Keefe, J. H., Bhatti, S. K., & Bajwa, A. (2014). Alcohol and cardiovascular health: The dose makes the poison . . . or the remedy. *Mayo Clinic Proceedings*, *89*(3), 382–293. doi:10.1016/j.mayocp.2013.11.005

Olmsted, C. L., & Kockler, D. R. (2008). Topiramate for alcohol dependence. *Annals of Pharmacotherapy*, *42*(10), 1475–1480.

Orciari Herman, A. (2020, June 9). USPSTF: Screen adults for unhealthy drug use. In *Physician's first watch* (pp. 1–2). Waltham, MA: NEJM Journal Watch.

Osna, N. A., Donohue, T. M., & Kharbanda, K. K. (2017). Alcoholic liver disease: Pathogenesis and current management. *Alcohol Research: Current Reviews*, *38*(2), 147–161.

Ostroumov, A., Thomas, A. M., & Dani, J. A. (2015, October 15). Cigarettes and alcohol: The influence of nicotine on operant alcohol self-administration and the mesolimbic dopamine system. *Biochemical Pharmacology*, *97*(4), 550–557. doi:10.1016/j.bcp.2015.07.038

Oural, L., Paris, M. V., & Sullivan, O. (2008, January–February). Pharmacological review of alcoholic dependence treatment. *Vertex*, *19*(77), 512–521.

Paddock, C. (2019, October 18). Atrial fibrillation: Daily alcoholic drink risker than binge drinking. *Medical News Today*, pp. 1–4.

Pagliaro, A. M. (1986). Pharmacologic aspects of nursing: A historical overview. In A. M. Pagliaro & L. A. Pagliaro (Eds.), *Pharmacologic aspects of nursing* (pp. 3–29). St. Louis, MO: C. V. Mosby.

Pagliaro, A. M., & Pagliaro, L. A. (2003). An addictionologist's perspective on catastrophic injury. In K. N. Anchor, J. Shmerling, & J. M. Anchor (Eds.), *The catastrophic injury handbook* (pp. 213–0227). Dubuque, IA: Kendall/Hunt.

Pagliaro, A. M., & Pagliaro, L. A. (2018). *Women's drug and substance abuse: A comprehensive analysis and reflective synthesis*. New York, NY: Routledge.

Pagliaro, L. A. (1990). Dual diagnosis. *Alberta Psychology*, *19*(5), 23–24.

Pagliaro, L. A. (1995, Spring). The straight dope: A consideration of substance-induced disorders. *Psynopsis*, *17*, 14.

Pagliaro, L. A., & Benet, L. Z. (1975). Critical compilation of terminal half-lives, percent excreted unchanged, and changes of half-life in renal and hepatic dysfunction for studies in humans with references. *Journal of Pharmacokinetics and Biopharmaceutics*, *3*, 333–383.

Pagliaro, L. A., & Pagliaro, A. M. (1983). *Pharmacologic aspects of aging*. St. Louis, MO: C. V. Mosby.

Pagliaro, L. A., & Pagliaro, A. M. (1990, Spring). Alcoholism in the elderly: Relationship to accidents and suicide. In *Newsletter* (pp. 2–3). Edmonton, Alberta: Centre for Gerontology.

Pagliaro, L. A., & Pagliaro, A. M. (1992a). Alcohol metabolism. *CMAJ: Canadian Medical Association Journal, 146*(12), 2141.

Pagliaro, L. A., & Pagliaro, A. M. (1992b). Phenomenon of drug and substance abuse among the elderly: Part 1. *Journal of Pharmacy Technology, 8*, 65–73. doi:10.1177/875512259200800206

Pagliaro, L. A., & Pagliaro, A. M. (1998). *The pharmacologic basis of psychotherapeutics: An introduction for psychologists*. Washington, DC: Brunner/Mazel.

Pagliaro, L. A., & Pagliaro, A. M. (1999). *PNDR: Psychologists' neuropsychotropic drug reference*. Philadelphia, PA: Brunner/Mazel.

Pagliaro, L. A., & Pagliaro, A. M. (2004). *Pagliaro's comprehensive guide to drugs and substances of abuse* (1st, ed.) Washington, DC: American Pharmacists Association.

Pagliaro, L. A., & Pagliaro, A. M. (2009). *Pagliaros' comprehensive guide to drugs and substances of abuse* (2nd ed.). Washington, DC: American Pharmacists Association.

Pagliaro, L. A., & Pagliaro, A. M. (2020). *Child and adolescent drug and substance abuse*. New York: Routledge.

Palmer, A., Karakus, M., & Mark, T. (2019). Barriers faced by physicians in screening for substance use disorders among adolescents. *Psychiatric Services, 70*(5), 409–412.

Papadimitriou, G. (2017, April–June). The 'biopsychosocial model': 40 years of application in psychiatry. *Psychiatriki, 28*(2), 107–110. doi:10.22365/jpsych.2017.282.107

Peoples, R. W., Li, C., & Weight, F. F. (1996). Lipid versus protein theories of alcohol action in the nervous system. *Annual Review of Pharmacology and Toxicology, 36*, 185–201.

Piano, M. R. (2017). Alcohol's effects on the cardiovascular system. *Alcohol Research: Current Reviews, 38*(2), e1–e24.

Piasecki, T. M., Robertson, B. M., & Epler, A. (2010). Hangover and risk for alcohol use disorders: Existing evidence and potential mechanisms. *Current Drug Abuse Reviews, 3*(2), 92–102.

Pietrzykowski, A. Z., & Treistman, S. N. (2008). The molecular basis of tolerance. *Alcohol Research & Health, 31*(4), 298–309.

Plosker, G. L. (2015, July). Acamprosate: A review of its use in alcohol dependence. *Drugs, 75*(11), 1255–1268. doi:10.1007/s40265-015-0423-9

Prat, G., Adan, A., & Perez-Pamies, M. (2008). Neurocognitive effects of alcohol hangover. *Addictive Behaviors, 33*(1), 15–23. doi:10.1016/jaddbeh.2007.05.002

Project MATCH. (1993, December). Project MATCH (Matching Alcoholism Treatment to Client Heterogeneity): Rationale and methods for a multisite clinical trial matching patients to alcoholism treatment. *Alcoholism: Clinical & Experimental Research, 17*(6), 1130–1145.

Qato, D. M., Manzoor, B. S., & Lee, T. (2015, November). Drug-alcohol interactions among older adults in the United States. *Journal of the American Geriatrics Society, 63*(11), 2324–2331. doi:10.1111/jgs.13787

Quispe Gonzales, J. O., Gomez Giralda, B., & Ruiz-Zorrilla Lopez, C. (2011). Severe ethanol poisoning treated by haemodialysis. *Nefrologia, 31*(2), 226–227.

Raouf, M., Atkinson, T. J., & Crumb, M. W. (2017). Rational dosing of gabapentin and pregabalin in chronic kidney disease. *Journal of Pain Research, 10*, 275–278. doi:10.2147/JPR.S130942

Rehm, J., & Roerecke, M. (2017, November). Cardiovascular effects of alcohol consumption. *Trends in Cardiovascular Medicine, 27*(8), 534–538. doi:10.1016/j.tcm.2017.06.002

Reinberg, S. (2019, July 31). More and more seniors are binge drinking. *WebMD*, pp. 1–3. HealthDay.

Reus, V. I., Fochtmann, L. J., & Bukstein, O. (2018a). The American psychiatric association practice guidelines for the pharmacological treatment of patients with alcohol use disorder. *American Journal of Psychiatry, 175*(1), 86–90.

Reus, V. I., Fochtmann, L. J., & Bukstein, O. (2018b). *The American psychiatric association practice guidelines for the pharmacological treatment of patients with alcohol use disorder*. Washington, DC: American Psychiatric Association.

Reyes, L., Treitier, P., & Peterson, A. (2021). Testing relationships between racial-ethnic identity, racial-ethnic discrimination, and substance misuse among black and latinx older adults in a nationally representative sample. *Research on Aging*, 1–8. doi:10.1177/0164027520986952

Ricks, J., Replogle, W. H., & Cook, N. J. (2010, August 15). FPIN's clinical inquiries. Management of alcohol withdrawal syndrome. *American Family Physician, 82*(4), 344–347.

Ridley, N. J., Draper, B., & Withall, A. (2013). Alcohol-related dementia: An update of the evidence. *Alzheimer's Research & Therapy, 5*(3), 1–8.

Rigler, S. K. (2000, March 15). Alcoholism in the elderly. *American Family Physician, 61*(6), 1710–1716.

Roeggla, G., Roeggla, H., & Roeggla, M. (1995). Effect of alcohol on acute ventilatory adaptation to mild hypoxia at moderate altitude. *Annals of Internal Medicine, 122*(12), 925–927.

Roerecke, M., & Rehm, J. (2014, October 21). Alcohol consumption, drinking patterns, and ischemic heart disease: A narrative review of meta-analyses and a systematic review and meta-analysis of the impact of heavy drinking occasions on risk for moderate drinkers. *BMC Medicine, 12*, 182. doi:10.1186/s12916-014-0182-6

Room, R., & Greenfield, T. (1993). Alcoholics Anonymous, other 12-step movements and psychotherapy in the US population, 1990. *Addiction, 88*, 555–562.

Rosner, S., Hackl-Herrwerth, A., & Leucht, S. (2010). Acamprosate for alcohol dependence. *Cochrane Database of Systematic Reviews, 9*, CD004332.

Ross, S. (2005, January). Alcohol use disorders in the elderly. *Primary Psychiatry*, pp. 32–40.

Rossi, M., Anwar, M., & Usman, A. (2018). Colorectal cancer and alcohol consumption—populations to molecules. *Cancers, 10*(2), 38–45. doi:10.3390/cancers10020038

Rundio, A. (2010, March). Disulfiram (Antabuse). *Journal of Addictions Nursing, 21*(1), 54–55.

Rusyn, I., & Bataller, R. (2013, August). Alcohol and toxicity. *Journal of Hepatology, 59*(2), 387–388. doi:10.1016/j.jhep.2013.01.035

Sacks, J. J., Gonzales, K. R., & Bouchery, E. E. (2015). 2010 National and state costs of excessive alcohol consumption. *AJPM, American Journal of Preventive Medicine, 49*(5), e73-e79.

Sahirazi, F., Singal, A. K., & Wong, R. J. (2021). Alcohol-associated cirrhosis and alcoholic hepatitis hospitalization trends in the United States. *Journal of Clinical Gastroenterology, 55*(2), 174–179. doi:10.1097/MCG.0000000000001378

Sahn, S. A., Lakshminarayan, S., & Pierson, D. J. (1975). Effect of ethanol on the ventilatory responses to oxygen and carbon dioxide in man. *Clinical Science and Molecular Medicine, 49*(1), 33–38.

Saivin, S., Hulot, T., & Chabac, S. (1998, November). Clinical pharmacokinetics of acamprosate. *Clinical Pharmacokinetics, 35*(5), 331–345.

SAMHSA, Substance Abuse and Mental Health Services Administration. (2011, April). *Screening, brief intervention, and referral to treatment (SBIRT) in behavioral healthcare*. Rockville, MD: SAMHSA.

SAMHSA, Substance Abuse and Mental Health Services Administration. (2013). *Systems-level implementation of screening, brief intervention, and referral to treatment*. Technical Assistance Publication (TAP) Series 33. Rockville, MD: Substances Abuse and Mental Health Services Administration.

Sampson, H. W. (2002). Alcohol and other factors affecting osteoporosis risk in women. *Alcohol Research & Health, 26*(4), 292–298.

Sanders, J. (2021). A continuum of older women's experiences as members of Alcoholics Anonymous (AA): A qualitative study. *Alcoholism Treatment Quarterly, 39*(1), 30–46. doi:10.1080/07347324.2020.1824598

Sari, Y., Johnson, V. R., & Weedman, J. M. (2011). Role of the serotonergic system in alcohol dependence: From animal models to clinics. *Progress in Molecular Biology and Translational Science, 98*, 401–443. doi:10.1016/B978-0-12-385506-0.00010-7

Sarlin, E. (2018, June 25). Outcomes of computerized CBT rival those of clinician-delivered CBT. In *NIDA notes* (pp. 1–2). Bethesda, MD: National Institute on Drug Abuse.

Schmidt, K., Doshi, M. R., & Holzhausen, J. M. (2016). Treatment of severe alcohol withdrawal. *Annals of Pharmacotherapy, 50*(5), 389–401. doi:10.1177/1060028016269161

Schonfeld, L., Hazlett, R. W., & Hedgecock, D. K. (2015, January). Screening, brief intervention, and referral to treatment for older adults with substance misuse. *American Journal of Public Health, 105*(1), 205–211. doi:10.2105/AJPH.2013.301859

Schutte, K. K., Moos, R. H., & Brennan, P. L. (2006, May). Predictors of untreated remission from late-life drinking problems. *Journal of Studies on Alcohol, 66*, 354–362.

Schweighofer, N., Bertin, M., & Shishida, K. (2008). Low-serotonin levels increase delayed reward discounting in humans. *The Journal of Neuroscience, 28*(17), 4528–4532.

Searight, R. (2009). Realistic approaches to counseling in the office setting. *American Family Physician, 79*(4), 277–284.

Seitz, H. K., & Stickel, F. (2007, August). Molecular mechanisms of alcohol-mediated carcinogenesis. *Nature Reviews: Cancer, 7*, 599–612.

Sellers, E. M., Naranjo, C. A., & Harrison, M. (1983, December). Diazepam loading: Simplified treatment of alcohol withdrawal. *Clinical Pharmacology and Therapeutics, 34*(6), 822–826.

Sher, L., Stanley, B. H., & Harkavy-Friedman, J. M. (2008). Depressed patients with co-occurring alcohol use disorders: A unique patient population. *The Journal of Clinical Psychiatry, 69*(6), 907–915.

Shinn, A. K., & Greenfield, S. F. (2010). Topiramate in the treatment of substance-related disorders: A critical review of the literature. *The Journal of Clinical Psychiatry, 71*(5), 634–648.

Shpilenya, L. S., Muzychenko, A. P., & Gasbarrini, G. (2002). Metadoxine in acute alcohol intoxication: A double-blind, randomized, placebo-controlled study. *Alcoholism, Clinical and Experimental Research, 26*(3), 340–346.

Skinner, M. D., Lahmek, P., & Pham, H. (2014, February 10). Disulfiram efficacy in the treatment of alcohol dependence: A meta-analysis. *PLoS One, 9*(2), e87366. doi:10.1371/journal.pone.0087366

Slaughter, L. (2000). Involvement of drugs in sexual assault. *Journal of Reproductive Medicine, 45*(5), 425–430.

Slesnick, N., & Prestopnik, J. (2005). Dual and multiple diagnosis among substance using runaway youth. *The American Journal of Drug and Alcohol Abuse, 31*(1), 179–201.

Smith, P. H., Homish, G. G., & Leonard, K. E. (2012). Intimate partner violence and specific substance use disorders: Findings from the national epidemiologic survey on alcohol and related conditions. *Psychology of Addictive Behaviors, 26*(2), 236–245. doi:10.1037/a0024855

Soghoian, S., Wiener, S. W., & Diaz-Alcala, J. E. (2016, January 6). Disulfiram toxicity. *Medscape*.

Solomon, C. A., Laditka, S. B., & Forthofer, M. (2021). Alcohol consumption among older women in the United States. *Journal of Women & Aging*, *33*(1), 100–117. doi:10.1080/08952841.2019.1684176

Soyka, M., & Rosner, S. (2010). Nalmefene for treatment of alcohol dependence. *Expert Opinion on Investigational Drugs*, *19*(11), 1451–1459.

Span, P. (2017, September 14). Alcohol abuse is rising among older adults. *NYT Health*, pp. 1–2. New York Times.

Stanley, K. M., Worrall, C. L., & Lunsford, S. L. (2005). Experience with an adult alcohol withdrawal syndrome practice guideline in internal medicine patients. *Pharmacotherapy*, *25*(8), 1073–1083. doi:10.1592/phco.2005.25.8.1073

Stead, L. F., & Lancaster, T. (2005, April 18). Group behavior therapy programmes for smoking cessation. *Cochrane Database of Systematic Reviews*, *2*, CD001007.

Stokes, M. (2020, April 21). Disulfiram. *StatPearls*, pp. 1–5. StatPearls.com.

Stowell, R. J. (1991). Dual diagnosis issues. *Psychiatric Annals*, *21*(2), 98–104. doi:10.3928/0048-5713-19910201-09

Stuart, G. L., Meehan, J. C., & Moore, T. M. (2006). Examining a conceptual framework of intimate partner violence in men and women arrested for domestic violence. *Journal of Studies on Alcohol*, *67*(1), 102–112.

Stuart, G. L., Moore, T. M., & Ramsey, S. E. (2004). Hazardous drinking and relationship violence perpetration and victimization in women arrested for domestic violence. *Journal of Studies on Alcohol*, *65*(1), 46–53.

Stuart, G. L., Temple, J. R., & Follansbee, K. W. (2008). The role of drug use in a conceptual model of intimate partner violence in men and women arrested for domestic violence. *Psychology of Addictive Behaviors*, *22*(1), 12–24. doi:10.1037/0893-164X.22.1.12

Swift, R. (2007). Emerging approaches to managing alcohol dependence. *AJHP, American Journal of Health-System Pharmacy*, *64*(5, Suppl 3), S12–S22.

Tam, C. C., Lui, C. K., & Karriker-Jaffe, K. J. (2021). Intersections of neighborhood co-ethnic density and nativity status on heavy drinking in a general population sample of US Latinos and Asians. *Alcohol and Alcoholism*, *56*(1), 74–81. doi:10.1093/alcalc/agaa108

Tanaka, F., Yamamoto, K., & Suzuki, S. (2010). Strong interaction between the effects of alcohol consumption and smoking on oesophageal squamous cell carcinoma among individuals with ADH1B and/or ALDH2 risk alleles. *Gut*, *59*(11), 14578–1464. doi:10.1136/gut.2009.205724

Tarter, R. E., Alterman, A. I., & Edwards, K. L. (1984). Alcoholic denial: A biopsychologic interpretation. *Journal of Studies on Alcohol*, *45*(3), 214–218. doi:10.15288/jsa.1984.45.214

Teutsch, S. M., Baldwin, J. A., & Degutis, L. C. (2018, January 17). New report calls for lowering blood alcohol concentration levels for driving, increasing federal and state alcohol taxes, increasing enforcement, among other recommendations. *News, The National Academies of Sciences, Engineering, and Medicine*, pp. 1–6. Washington, DC.

Timko, C., Moos, B. S., & Moos, R. H. (2009). Gender differences in 16-year trends in assault- and police-related problems due to drinking. *Addictive Behaviors*, *34*(9), 744–750. doi:10.1016/j.addbeh.2009.04.013

Tollefson, G. D. (1989). Serotonin and alcohol: Interrelationships. *Psychophathology*, *22* (Suppl 1), 37–48.

Towers, A., Sheridan, J., & Newcombe, D. (2018). *The prevalence of hazardous drinking in older New Zealanders*. Wellington, New Zealand: Health Promotion Agency.

USDHHS, U.S. Department of Health and Human Services, Office of the Surgeon General. (2016). *Facing addiction in America: The surgeon general's report on alcohol, drugs, and health, executive summary*. Washington, DC: Health and Human Services. Retrieved December 14, 2016

USPSTF, U.S. Preventive Services Task Force. (2019, June 15). Screening and behavioral counseling interventions to reduce unhealthy alcohol use in adolescents and adults: Recommendation statement. *American Family Physician*, *99*(12), 770a–770g.

USPSTF, U.S. Preventive Services Task Force. (2020). Screening for unhealthy drug use: U.S. Preventive services task force recommendation statement. *JAMA*, *323*(22), 2301–2309. doi:10.1001/jama.2020.8020

Valenzuela, C. F. (1997). Alcohol and neurotransmitter interactions. *Alcohol Health & Research World*, *21*(2), 144–148.

Vallance, K., Stockwell, T., & Pauly, B. (2016). Do managed alcohol programs change patterns of alcohol consumption and reduce related harm? A pilot study. *Harm Reduction Journal*, *13*(13), 1–11. doi:10.1186/s12954-016-0103-4

Valliant, G. E. (2005). Alcoholics anonymous: Cult or cure? *Australian & New Zealand Journal of Psychiatry*, *39*(6), 431–436. doi:10.1080/j.1440-1614.2005.01600.x

Van Skike, C. E., Maggio, S. E., & Reynolds, A. R. (2015, February 4). Critical needs in drug discovery for cessation of alcohol and nicotine polysubstance abuse. *Progress in Neuropsychopharmacology & Biological Psychiatry*, *65*, 269–287. doi:10.1016/j.pnpbp.2015.11.004

Verplaetse, T. L., & McKee, S. A. (2017, March). An overview of alcohol and tobacco/nicotine interactions in the human laboratory. *The American Journal of Drug and Alcohol Abuse*, *43*(2), 186–196. doi:10.1080/00952990.2016.1189927

Verplaetse, T. L., Peltier, M. R., & Roberts, W. (2021, May). Gender and past year serious psychological distress are associated with past year AUD: Time-varying results from the National Survey on Drug Use and Health (NSDUH; 2008–2017). *Addictive Behaviors*, *116*(106815), 1–3. doi:10.1016/j.addbeh.2020.106815

Vessell, E. S. (1986). Pharmacogenetics. In A. M. Pagliaro, & L. A. Pagliaro (Eds.), *Pharmacologic aspects of nursing*. St. Louis, MO: C. V. Mosby.

Vezali Costardi, J. V., Teruaki Nampo, R. A., & Lourenco Silva, G. (2015). A review on alcohol: From the central action mechanism to chemical dependency. *Revista da Associacao Medica Brasileira*, *61*(4), 381–387.

Villalonga-Olives, E., Almansa, J., & Shaya, F. (2020, September 1). Perceived social capital and binge drinking in older adults: The health and retirement study, US data from 2006–2014. *Journal of Drug and Alcohol Dependence*, *214*, 108099. doi:10.1016/j.drugalcdep.2020.108099

Volpicelli, J. R., Clay, K. L., & Watson, N. T. (1995). Naltrexone in the treatment of alcoholism: Predicting response to naltrexone. *The Journal of Clinical Psychiatry*, *56*(Suppl 7), 39–44.

Vonghia, L., Leggio, L., & Ferrulli, A. (2008). Acute alcohol intoxication. *European Journal of Internal Medicine*, *19*, 561–567. doi:10.1016/j.ejim.2007.06.033

Wakabayahi, I., & Araki, Y. (2010). Influences of gender and age on relationships between alcohol drinking and atherosclerotic risk factors. *Alcoholism: Clinical and Experimental Research*, *34*(S1). doi:10.1111/j.1530-0277.2008.00758.x

Watts, R. (2018, March 11). Harm-reduction programs help alcoholics one drink at a time. *Times Colonist*, pp. 1–2. Times Colonist.

Weaving, G., Batstone, G. F., & Jones, R. G. (2016). Age and sex variation in serum albumin concentration: An observational study. *Annals of Clinical Biochemistry*, *53*(1), 106–111. doi:10.1177/0004563215593561

Weintraub, S. J. (2017). Diazepam in the treatment of moderate to severe alcohol withdrawal. *CNS Drugs*, *31*(2), 87–92. doi:10.1007/s40263-016-0403-y

Weisner, C., Greenfield, T., & Room, R. (1995). Trends in the treatment of alcohol problems in the US general population: 1979 through 1990. *AJPH, American Journal of Public Health*, *85*, 55–60.

White, A., Castle, I., & Hingson, R. (2020). Using death certificates to explore changes in alcohol-related mortality in the United States, 1999 to 2017. *Alcoholism Clinical and Experimental Research*, *44*(1), 178–187. doi:10.1111/acer.14239

White, M. C., Holman, D. M., & Goodman, R. A. (2019). Cancer risk among older adults: Time for cancer prevention to go silver. *The Gerontologist*, *59*(S1), S1–S6. doi:10.1093/geront/gnz038

White, M. C., Lindsey, S., & Vincente, C. (1981). Alcohol increases sleep apnea and oxygen desaturation in asymptomatic men. *The American Journal of Medicine*, *71*(2), 240–245.

WHO, World Health Organization. (2006). Intimate partner violence and alcohol. In *WHO facts on . . .* (pp. 1–12). Geneva, Switzerland: World Health Organization.

Wilming, C., Alford, M., & Klaus, L. (2018, March). Gabapentin use in acute alcohol withdrawal management. *Federal Practitioner*, pp. 40–46.

Wilson, F. A., Stimpson, J. P., & Tibbits, M. K. (2013, November). The role of alcohol use on recent trends in distracted driving. *Accident Analysis & Prevention*, *60*, 189–192. doi:10.1016/j.aap.2013.08.025

Winek, C. L., & Murphy, K. L. (1984, July). The rate and kinetic order of ethanol elimination. *Forensic Science International*, *25*(3), 159–166.

Witkiewitz, K., Litten, R. Z., & Leggio, L. (2019, September 25). Advances in the science and treatment of alcohol use disorder. *Science Advances*, *5*(9), eaax4043. doi:10.1126/sciadv.aax4043

Witkiewitz, K., & Marlatt, G. A. (2006). Overview of harm reduction treatments for alcohol problems. *The International Journal of Drug Policy*, *17*, 285–294. doi:10.1016/j.drugpo.2006.03.005

Wood, A. M., Kaptoge, S., & Butterworth, A. S. (2018, April 14). Risk thresholds for alcohol consumption: Combined analysis of individual-participant data for 599,912 current drinkers in 83 prospective studies. *The Lancet*, *391*, 1513–1523.

Wood, E., Samet, J. H., & Volkow, N. D. (2013, October 23). Physician education in addiction medicine. *JAMA*, *310*(16), 1673–1674. doi:10.1001/jama.2013.280377

Wright, T. M., & Myrick, H. (2006, December). Acamprosate: A new tool in the battle against alcohol dependence. *Neuropsychiatric Disease and Management*, *2*(4), 445–453.

Yahn, S. L., Watterson, L. R., & Olive, M. F. (2013). Safety and efficacy of acamprosate for the treatment of alcohol dependence. *Substance Abuse*, *7*, 1–12. doi:10.4137/SART.S9345

Yan-Hong, H., Jing, L., & Hong, L. (2015). Association between alcohol consumption and the risk of ovarian cancer: A meta-analysis of prospective observational studies. *BMC Public Health*, *15*(223), 1–28. doi:10.1186/s12889-015-1355-8

Yarnell, S., Li, L., & MacGrory, B. (2020). Substance use disorders in later life: A review and synthesis of the literature of an emerging public health concern. *The American Journal of Geriatric Psychiatry*, *28*(2), 226–236. doi:10.1016/j.jagp.2019.06.005

Yonker, J. E., Nilsson, L. G., & Herlitz, A. (2005). Sex differences in spatial visualization and episodic memory as a function of alcohol consumption. *Alcohol and Alcoholism*, *40*(3), 201–207. Retrieved June 30, 2014

Yuan, Z., Dawson, N., & Cooper, G. S. (2001, July). Effects of alcohol-related disease on hip fracture and mortality: A retrospective cohort study of hospitalized medicare beneficiaries. *American Journal of Public Health*, *91*(7), 1089–1093.

Zahr, N. M., & Pfefferbaum, A. (2017). Alcohol's effects on the brain: Neuroimaging results in humans and animal models. *Alcohol Research & Health, 38*(2), 183–206.

Zakhari, S. (2006). Overview: How is alcohol metabolized by the body? *Alcohol Research & Health, 29*(4), 245–254.

Zanjani, F., Allen, H. K., & Schoenberg, N. (2018). Immediate effects of a brief intervention to prevent alcohol and medication interactions among older adults. *Health Education Research, 33*(4), 261–270. doi:10.1093/her/cyy021

Zhang, C., & Zhong, M. (2015). Consumption of beer and colorectal cancer incidence: A meta-analysis of observational studies. *Cancer Causes & Control, 26*(4), 549–560. doi:10.1007/s10552-015-9532-5

Zhu, J., Jiang, X., & Niu, Z. (2020, July). Alcohol consumption and risk of breast and ovarian cancer: A Mendelian randomization study. *Cancer Genetics, 245*, 35–41. doi:10.1016/j.cancergen.2020.06.001

Zinberg, N. E. (1986). Drug, set, and setting: The basis for controlled intoxicant use. New Haven, CT: Yale University Press.

CHAPTER 2

AMPHETAMINES AND COCAINE

In order to provide health and social care professionals with a comprehensive understanding of the use of the amphetamines and cocaine by older adults, these two major psychostimulants are separately presented and discussed in their own individual sections of this chapter.

We begin with the "Amphetamines."

AMPHETAMINES

The amphetamines (see Table 2.1) include the:

1. Licit, prescription amphetamines (e.g., amphetamine [Evekeo®], dextroamphetamine [Dexedrine®], and mixed amphetamines [Adderall®]);
2. Illicitly produced and illicitly obtained amphetamines (e.g., "Speed" or "Uppers"), particularly methamphetamine (i.e., "Crank," "Crystal Meth," "Glass," "Meth," or "Tweak").

Particular attention is given to the following topics:

1. Amphetamine history;
2. Pharmacology—pharmacodynamics; pharmacokinetics; drug-drug interactions; and undesired, or harmful, effects and toxicities;
3. Physical and psychological dependence;
4. Overdosage/unintentional poisoning—occurrence and management;
5. Illicit methamphetamine production;
6. Older adult involvement in amphetamine trafficking and dealing;
7. New millennial trends in older adult amphetamine use;
8. Assessment and diagnosis of amphetamine dependence or use disorder;
9. Treating older adult amphetamine dependence or use disorder;
10. Common contemporaneous diagnoses.

Amphetamine History

The amphetamines are chemically related to ephedrine—the active ingredient of the ancient herb, Ephedra,[1] that was first medically used more than 5,000 years ago in China (Pagliaro &

---

1. Ephedrine is found in many of the over 50 species of Ephedra, including *Ephedra equisetina*, *Ephedra Sinica*, and *Ephedra vulgaris*. These species of Ephedra are native to specific countries and regions worldwide including Central America, China, India, the Mediterranean, Mongolia, and North America (Blumenthal & King, 1995).

DOI: 10.4324/9781003010333-2

Table 2.1 The Amphetamines

GENERIC NAME	BRAND/TRADE NAMES[2]	COMMON STREET NAMES[3]
Amphetamine[4]	Adzenys XR-ODT®[5]	"Ace," "Amp," "Co-Pilot"
Dextroamphetamine	Dexedrine®	"Co-Pilots," "Dex," "Dexies," "Hearts"
Lisdexamfetamine[6]	Vyvanse®	"Lizzies," "Vicky"
Methamphetamine[7]	Desoxyn®	"Crank," "Crystal Meth," "Glass," "Hillbilly Crack," "Ice," "Jib," "Meth," "Speed," "Stove Top," "Tina"
Mixed amphetamines[8]	Adderall®	"Addies," "Blueberries," "Oranges," "Tic-Tac"

Pagliaro, 2004; Schaneberg, Crockett, & Bedir, 2003).[9] Ephedrine was chemically isolated from the plant form, *Ephedra vulgaris*, in 1885, by the Japanese organic chemist, Nagai Nagayoshi.[10] However, the sympathomimetic actions of ephedrine were not generally recognized in the U.S. until the early 1920s when its use—as an alternative to epinephrine (i.e., adrenaline) for the treatment of nasal congestion and bronchoconstriction—was explored (Lee, 2011).[11] Ephedrine was soon touted as being superior to epinephrine because it:

1. Could be ingested or inhaled;
2. Had a longer duration of action;
3. Displayed predictable actions with fewer related harmful effects and toxicities.

As medical use began to significantly increase, concerns about depleting the natural supplies of ephedrine also began to rise. These concerns encouraged researchers in Europe, Japan, and the U.S. to search for a synthetic substitute. The divergent research directions taken by these scientists led to the subsequent synthesis of the amphetamines—amphetamine sulfate, dextroamphetamine, and methamphetamine.

2. Examples of common brand/trade names of related prescription drugs.
3. Partial list. Examples of the most common street names are provided. See Pagliaro and Pagliaro (2009) for a comprehensive listing of the drugs and substances of abuse and their common street names.
4. Amphetamine, in its salt forms (i.e., amphetamine aspartate and amphetamine sulfate) is only legally available in the U.S. in the combination, mixed amphetamine product, Adderall®.
5. Adzenys XR-ODT® is an extended-release (XR), orally disintegrating tablet (ODT) approved for the medical treatment of ADHD. However, as noted in the product labeling, "Adzenys XR-ODT® has not been studied in the geriatric population."
6. Lisdexamfetamine is an amphetamine pro-drug. It is composed of the amino acid L-lysine attached to dextroamphetamine.
7. Methamphetamine is a commonly used contraction for N-methylamphetamine.
8. This product contains the amphetamine salt forms—amphetamine aspartate and amphetamine sulfate. It also contains dextroamphetamine.
9. Ephedrine, the primary constituent of the medicinal herb *Ma huang*, was brewed and ingested as a tea in ancient China and continues to be widely used in Traditional Chinese Medicine. Today, China is the major pharmaceutical source for ephedrine in the entire world.
10. Pseudoephedrine (Sudafed®), a diastereomer (i.e., a non-mirror image stereoisomer) of ephedrine, was isolated from the *Ephedra vulgaris* plant a few years later in 1889 by German chemists.
11. Ephedrine is currently approved by the FDA as a bronchodilator and nasal decongestant.

The psychostimulant action of amphetamine was discovered in Los Angeles by Gordon Alles, who, at that time, was a young research chemist. Having reviewed ephedrine research, he concluded that phenylisopropylamine, a volatile base synthesized during the late 1800s, provided the best direction for further research.[12] In 1932, performing animal experiments, as well as experimenting on himself, he discovered that Benzedrine® (i.e., racemic or dextro-levo-amphetamine) and Dexedrine® (i.e., the "right-handed" isomer of Benzedrine®) had powerful psychostimulant actions, in addition to, the peripheral alpha-adrenergic and beta-adrenergic actions characteristic of the indirectly acting sympathomimetics.[13] During the early 1930s, the Benzedrine® inhaler was introduced for use in the U.S. by the pharmaceutical company, Smith, Kline, and French, as an over-the-counter product. It quickly became a "huge" success.[14]

Commonly injected intravenously, the amphetamines also could be ingested or inhaled with the latter surpassing the former in alleviating fatigue, enhancing alertness, and creating "euphoric confidence" (Grinspoon & Hedblom, 1975). Methamphetamine (Desoxyn®), the N-methyl analogue of dextro rotatory amphetamine—also known as methedrine—was synthesized by Japanese scientists in 1919. This form of amphetamine has remained the most potent member of this class of psychostimulants.

Since their synthesis, amphetamines, commonly known on the street as "Bennies," "Bombers," "Cartwheels," "Crystal," "Dexies," "Ice," and "Pep Pills," have been, and continue to be, widely used in the U.S. and other countries for their dose-dependent psychostimulant actions that include enhanced alertness; increased psychomotor abilities; and suppression of feelings of drowsiness, fatigue, or hunger. These actions have also made the amphetamines attractive as "performance enhancers" for aircraft pilots, athletes, entertainers, parents and grandparents, soldiers, surgeons, teachers, truck drivers, and others. The initial pleasurable mental states of elation and euphoria associated with amphetamines also make them particularly attractive to many users.

Pharmacology

The amphetamines are synthetic drugs that produce dose-dependent actions on both the central and peripheral (i.e., sympathetic) nervous systems (Pagliaro & Pagliaro, 2009). As psychostimulants, their actions are similar to those produced by the endogenous catecholamine excitatory neurotransmitters:

- Dopamine;
- Epinephrine;
- Norepinephrine;
- Serotonin.

Peripherally, they promote the actions of the sympathetic nervous system that, consequently, increase heart rate and constrict blood vessels, thus elevating blood pressure. However, the

12. Phenylisopropylamine (i.e., amphetamine [1-methyl-2-phenethylamine]) was initially synthesized in Germany in 1887 by the Romanian chemist, Lazar Edeleanu.
13. Amphetamine is also chemically known as, alpha-methyl-phenethylamine (AMPH).
14. By the late 1930s, adults—young and old—were commonly removing the amphetamine impregnated paper or cotton strips from the Benzedrine® inhalers and placing them into a cup of coffee, or simply chewing and swallowing the strips, to get "high" (Pagliaro & Pagliaro, 2004).

amphetamines, being more potent than natural ephedrine (see also the related discussion in the earlier Amphetamine subsection—"Amphetamine History") achieve higher levels of central and peripheral nervous system stimulation resulting in significantly: (1) heightened alertness; (2) heightened psychomotor abilities; and (3) diminished feelings of drowsiness and fatigue. It is mainly these actions that make the amphetamines attractive as "performance enhancers."

Pharmacodynamics: Mechanism of Action

The amphetamines are "non-catecholamine" sympathomimetics—drugs that mimic the actions of the sympathetic nervous system, which is involved with the homeostatic regulation of:

- Blood pressure;
- Bronchial airway tone;
- Carbohydrate and fatty acid metabolism, particularly during periods of physical activity or psychological stress;
- Force of cardiac contraction;
- Heart rate;
- Vasomotor tone.

These responses are usually endogenously mediated by circulating levels of the hormones—epinephrine (adrenaline) and norepinephrine (noradrenaline)—which act at five adrenergic receptors:

1. Alpha one (α_1);
2. Alpha two (α_2);
3. Beta one (β_1);
4. Beta two (β_2);
5. Beta three (β_3).

Agonist action at alpha adrenergic receptors includes decreased gut motility, glycogenolysis, mydriasis, piloerection, sweating, urinary retention, and vasoconstriction. Agonist action at β_1-receptors, which are predominant in the heart, is associated with: decreased gut motility and secretions, increased heart rate, increased lipolysis, and increased renin release.[15] Agonist action at β_2-receptors, which are predominant in the lungs, includes: bronchodilation, fine skeletal muscle tremor, glycogenolysis, mast cell stabilization, and vasodilation.[16] Agonist action at β_3-receptors, which are predominant in adipose tissues and which appear to upregulate during cardiovascular diseases, includes (1) lipolysis; and (2) potential cardiodepressant effects on human ventricles (Dessy & Balligand, 2010; Skeberdis, 2004).

15. The agonist actions at the β_1-receptors are primarily mediated by the stimulation of adenyl cyclase enzyme activity which, in turn, facilitates the conversion of ATP to cAMP with resultant "opening" of calcium channels.
16. The agonists actions at the β_2-receptors also are primarily mediated by stimulation of adenyl cyclase enzyme activity in association with the resultant "closing" of calcium channels.

The amphetamines are indirect-acting psychostimulants. As such, they stimulate the release of the biogenic amines (i.e., dopamine, norepinephrine, and serotonin) from the presynaptic nerve terminal storage vesicles that are primarily located in the midbrain and mesolimbic dopamine pathway (Pagliaro & Pagliaro, 2004; Rothman, Baumann, & Dersch, 2001). They also inhibit the reuptake of the biogenic amines, primarily by blocking the: (1) neuronal dopamine transporter (dopamine active transporter [DAT]) (i.e., the normal ability of DAT—to clear dopamine from the synapse—is blocked); and (2) vesicular monoamine transporter-2[17] (Faraone, 2018; Fleckenstein, Volz, & Riddle, 2007). These actions result in an increase in synaptic extracellular neurotransmitters, particularly dopamine and norepinephrine.[18] Figure 2.1 provides a simplified, stylized representation of the principal sites and mechanisms of these psychostimulant actions.[19]

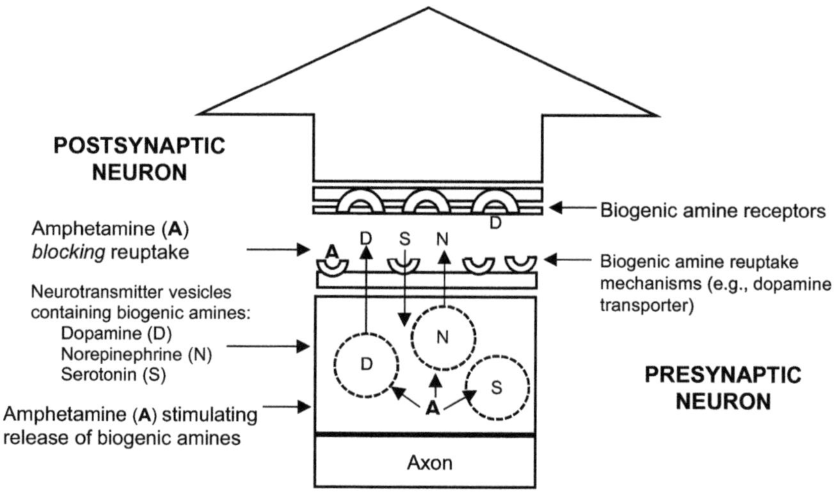

Figure 2.1 Amphetamines: Mechanism of Psychostimulant Action

Pharmacokinetics: Absorption, Distribution, Metabolism, and Excretion

This subsection discusses the pharmacokinetics of the amphetamines. We begin with absorption.

17. Also referred to as the norepinephrine transporter (NET).
18. This effect is enhanced by amphetamine inhibition of the degradative enzymes monoamine oxidase A (MAO-A) and monoamine oxidase B (MAO-B).
19. Interestingly, as noted by Berman, Kuczenski, and McCracken (2009, p. 123):

> Amphetamine exists as two stereoisomers that differ in effects. The L-enantiomer (levoamphetamine) produces more cardiovascular and peripheral effects than the D-enantiomer (dextroamphetamine). At low does, levoamphetamine produces greater arousal than dextroamphetamine, acting primarily on norepinephrine. At higher doses, dextroamphetamine has stimulant properties that are three to four times as strong as those of levoamphetamine and acts primarily on dopamine.

Absorption

The amphetamines are licitly available in several ingestible formulations including capsules, chewable tablets, and liquid products. However, they are commonly illicitly self-administered by means of: (1) intravenous (IV) injection; (2) nasal insufflation, or "snorting;" and (3) pulmonary inhalation (i.e., "smoking," "vaporizing," or "vaping").

Regardless of the route of administration, the amphetamines are well-absorbed. For example, like all other drugs, the amphetamines are immediately and completely absorbed following IV injection. They are also well-absorbed following ingestion. In addition, because of their high lipid solubility, they are well-absorbed following nasal insufflation and pulmonary inhalation.[20] Transmucosal absorption, after rectal or vaginal insertion, is also high.

Distribution

Following absorption, the amphetamines are widely distributed throughout body tissues, and, due to their lipid solubility, readily cross the blood-brain barrier (BBB).[21] Plasma protein binding of the various amphetamines is low.

> ***Related Professional Reminder:*** ***When considering plasma protein binding, it is important to keep in mind that only "free," or unbound, drugs—including abusable psychotropics—can readily cross biological membranes, including, the "BBB." Consequently, and of clinical significance, plasma protein binding is—in the vast majority of clinical contexts—only of concern for abusable psychotropics or other drugs that are highly protein bound (i.e., in excess of 98%). This is of concern because, at this level of protein binding, seemingly small changes in the concentration of unbound drugs can have profound therapeutic or toxic consequences. For example, in this context, a 1% change in plasma protein binding (i.e., from 98% to 97%) would result in a 50% increase in free drug, including abusable psychotropics, plasma concentrations.***

Elimination

Urinary excretion of amphetamines is pH-dependent with acidic urine (i.e., pH lower than 7) increasing excretion and alkaline urine (i.e., pH higher than 7) decreasing excretion. These differences in urinary pH and associated changes in excretion rates explain why regular, long-term amphetamine users commonly ingest antacids (e.g., calcium carbonate, Tums®) to alkalinize their urine (Pagliaro & Pagliaro, *Clinical Patient Data Files*). This action both enhances and prolongs the desired pharmacologic actions of the amphetamines. The half-life of elimination of the various amphetamines is approximately ten hours, with

20. Interestingly, when methamphetamine is smoked, it is significantly degraded to amphetamine due to pyrolysis by means of N-demethylation (Sato, Hida, & Nagase, 2004).
21. Because of the addition of a methyl (-CH_3) chemical group to the amphetamine molecule, methamphetamine has greater lipophilicity and, consequently, crosses the BBB more rapidly than the other amphetamines.

Table 2.2 Comparative Pharmacokinetic Processes and Values Following Ingestion of Dextroamphetamine and Methamphetamine

PROCESSES FOLLOWING INGESTION	VALUES FOLLOWING INGESTION	
	Dextroamphetamine	**Methamphetamine**
Absorption		
Bioavailability	Good, ~ 85% (100% intravenous)	Good, ~ 65% (~ 75% pulmonary) (~ 80% intranasal) (100% intravenous)
Time to peak blood concentration	~ 3.5 hours[22]	~ 4 hours (~ 3 hours pulmonary) (~ 2.5 hours intranasal) (< 10 minutes intravenous)
Distribution		
Volume of distribution	5.4 L/kg	4.2 L/kg
Plasma protein binding	Low, ~ 25%	Low, ~ 15%
Metabolism		
	Hepatic (primarily involves CYP2D6)	Hepatic (primarily involves CYP2D6)[23]
Total body clearance	0.7 L/kg/hour	~ 270 L/kg/hour
Mean half-life of elimination	~ 12 hours	~ 10 hours
Excretion		
Urinary excretion	pH dependent	pH dependent[24]

Sources: Cruickshank & Dyer, 2009; Pagliaro & Benet, 1975; Pagliaro & Pagliaro, 2009; Roberts, Cook, & Stockman, 2015; Schepers, Oyler, & Joseph, 2003.

slight variations among amphetamine sulfate, dextroamphetamine, and methamphetamine (Pagliaro & Pagliaro, 2009) (see Table 2.2).[25]

> Old Misbelief: The half-life of elimination of a specific amphetamine (e.g., methamphetamine) depends on its method of use (i.e., route of administration).

False. In fact, this old misbelief is simply not true. While the method of use may affect the rate of absorption and, consequently, the onset of action, it does not affect the half-life of elimination.

22. Increased to ~ 8 hours with the ingestion of a sustained-release capsule.
23. At least seven different metabolites of methamphetamine have been identified in urine. Amphetamine is the major active metabolite of methamphetamine.
24. Approximately 40% of an ingested dose is excreted in unchanged form in the urine together with ~ 20% as amphetamine. The urinary excretion is enhanced with acidic urine.
25. An exception is "lisdexamfetamine." Lisdexamfetamine is a prodrug that is rapidly converted to dextroamphetamine by an aminopeptidase present within erythrocytes. Consequently, the mean half-life of elimination of lisdexamfetamine is approximately 30 minutes (Ermer, Pennick, & Frick, 2016).

Drug-Drug Interactions

Amphetamines have been involved in several drug-drug interactions. The major clinically significant drug-drug interactions involving these psychostimulants are presented and briefly discussed in Table 2.3.

Undesired, or Harmful, Effects and Toxicities

Amphetamine use is associated with several undesired, or harmful, effects and toxicities that can be acute[26] or chronic, direct or indirect, minor or major, and physical or mental. These "adverse effects" involve virtually every major body system (Pagliaro & Pagliaro, 2009). The incidence and severity of these effects are not generally given the attention that they deserve in the published medical literature. However, the following quote from the SAMHSA (2020, p. 6) review illustrates the seriousness and extent of this issue:

> Between 2008 and 2015, amphetamine-related hospitalizations more than tripled, increasing from 55,447 instances to 206,180. As of 2019, methamphetamine has surpassed opioids as the leading cause of overdose death in many western U.S. states.

The frequency and severity of these effects are generally related to:

1. Dosage used (e.g., 40 mg versus 1,000 mg);
2. Method of use (e.g., ingestion versus IV injection—see later discussion);
3. Frequency of use (e.g., every hour over one or two days versus twice a week);
4. Pattern of use (e.g., occasional use versus regular, long-term use);
5. Mental health status at the time of use (e.g., an older adult who has a contemporaneous mental disorder versus one who does not);
6. Physical health status at the time of use (e.g., an older adult who has a significant cerebral aneurysm versus one who does not);
7. Specific personality characteristics (e.g., an older adult who has a risk-taking personality trait versus one who does not);
8. Interactions associated with the concurrent use of licit or illicit prescription and nonprescription abusable psychotropics (see also the related discussion in the previous subsection, "Drug-Drug Interactions" and Table 2.3).

> The increased use of amphetamines as maintenance medications in adults, the longer elimination half-life in adults compared with children or adolescents, the larger dosages and treatment durations applied to adults, and the increased prevalence of problematic use in adults all underscore the need for careful evaluation of the potential for adverse effects of cumulative amphetamine administration in adulthood.
>
> (Berman et al., 2009, p. 128)

26. Following ingestion, the acute toxicities associated with the use of amphetamines generally begin within 20 to 60 minutes. However, following IV injection or pulmonary inhalation (e.g., methamphetamine), toxicities can begin within 30 to 60 seconds.

Table 2.3 Amphetamines: Major Potential Drug-Drug Interactions[27]

DRUGS THAT INTERACT WITH AMPHETAMINES	COMMENTS
Adrenergic Blockers (e.g., atenolol, prazosin, propranolol)	Amphetamines inhibit the actions of the adrenergic blockers, both alpha and beta (see the earlier amphetamines pharmacology subsection, "Pharmacodynamics: Mechanism of Action").
Antidepressants	
Monoamine Oxidase Inhibitors (MAOIs) (e.g., phenelzine, tranylcypromine)	MAOIs, when used with amphetamines, increase the possibility of a hypertensive crisis (i.e., noradrenergic syndrome).
Selective Serotonin Reuptake Inhibitors (SSRIs) (e.g., fluoxetine, paroxetine, sertraline)	SSRIs, when used with amphetamines, increase the possibility of the occurrence of the serotonergic syndrome.
Tricyclic Antidepressants (TCAs) (e.g., amitriptyline, nortriptyline)	Tricyclic antidepressants, when used with amphetamines, can potentially enhance the actions of both drugs (see the earlier amphetamine pharmacology subsection, "Pharmacodynamics: Mechanism of Action").
Antipsychotics (e.g., chlorpromazine, haloperidol)	Antipsychotics inhibit the psychostimulant actions of the amphetamines (see the earlier amphetamine pharmacology subsections, "Pharmacodynamics: Mechanism of Action" and "Overdosage/Unintentional Poisoning").
Proton Pump Inhibitors (e.g., omeprazole, rabeprazole)	Proton pump inhibitors decrease gastric acid production and, consequently, may facilitate a shortened time to maximal amphetamine serum concentration resulting in a more rapid onset of amphetamine action.
Psychodepressants (e.g., opiate analgesics, sedative-hypnotics)	Psychodepressants, when used with amphetamines, antagonize the psychostimulant actions of the amphetamines.
Psychostimulants (e.g., caffeine, cocaine, nicotine)	Psychostimulants, when used with amphetamines, cause additive psychostimulant actions.
Urinary Acidifiers (e.g., ammonium chloride)	Urinary acidifiers, when used with amphetamines, increase the urinary excretion of amphetamines (see the earlier related discussion in the amphetamines pharmacology subsections, "Pharmacodynamics: Mechanism of Action" and "Pharmacokinetics").
Urinary Alkalinizers (e.g., sodium bicarbonate)	Urinary alkalinizers, when used with amphetamines, decrease the urinary excretion of amphetamines (see the related discussion in the earlier amphetamines pharmacology subsection, Pharmacokinetics—"Excretion").

27. The clinical significance of these potential drug-drug interactions depends upon several factors, including the: (1) dosage of each drug; (2) characteristics of the older adult (e.g., gender and genetics); (3) concomitant physical health status (e.g., hepatic and renal function); and (4) concomitant mental health status.

The "acute" toxicities that are related to amphetamine use are more likely to occur among older adults, who are novice or occasional amphetamine users,[28] rather than regular, long-term users—even though the latter, being more tolerant to the amphetamines, typically use higher dosages (see also the later Amphetamine subsection, "Overdosage"). The "chronic" toxicities are usually related to the regular, long-term use of amphetamines. These undesired, or harmful, effects and toxicities are presented and discussed, in alphabetical order, in the following subsections:

- Amphetamine Psychosis;
- Cardiotoxicities;
- Diminished Executive Function;
- Excessive Dosage;
- Fatalities;
- Human Immunodeficiency Virus Infection and Acquired Immune Deficiency Syndrome (HIV/AIDS);
- Intravenous Toxicities;
- "Meth Mouth;"
- Other Toxicities.

We begin with "Amphetamine Psychosis."

Amphetamine Psychosis

Amphetamine-induced psychosis is usually associated with the continuous use of amphetamines over several weeks or months (Curran, Byrappa, & McBride, 2004; Pagliaro & Pagliaro, 2009). However, it also may occur within 24 hours of amphetamine use or within two days following the ingestion of a single, large dose of amphetamine by a sensitive user (Pagliaro & Pagliaro, *Clinical Patient Data Files*).[29] As observed by Berman et al. (2009, p. 131):

> High doses of amphetamines can produce psychotic behavior indistinguishable from schizophrenia in asymptomatic schizophrenics and in some healthy human subjects.

Of note, once amphetamine psychosis has occurred, it can re-occur with:

1. Oral ingestion of a moderate dose (e.g., 30 mg) of amphetamine (Pagliaro & Pagliaro, *Clinical Patient Data Files*);
2. Severe psychosocial stress (Berman et al., 2009).[30]

---

28. For example, older adults, who may feel "a bit down," "depressed," "rundown," or "tired"—having "heard" that amphetamines provided additional energy to various presidents (e.g., John F. Kennedy and Joseph R. Biden)—accept a "hit" of amphetamine offered to them from a friend or relative (e.g., adult child or grandchild) to help to alleviate their symptoms or to "give them a boost."
29. N.B. Older adults with genetic histories of schizophrenia and those with pre-existing psychosis are particularly at risk.
30. This apparent "sensitization" may be mediated by a process of catecholamine supersensitivity related to enhanced dopamine release.

As identified by Wearne and Cornish (2018, p. 2) in their review of comparisons between methamphetamine-induced psychosis and schizophrenia:

> Research has shown that METH psychosis is a prevalent health concern among recreational users.

In their systematic review and meta-analysis of mental health outcomes associated with the use of amphetamines, McKetin, Leung, and Stockings (2019) found that, regarding psychosis:

1. Any use of amphetamines was associated with double the odds of psychosis;
2. Amphetamine use disorder was associated with three times the odds of psychosis;
3. Longitudinal cohort studies confirmed a dose-related increase in psychotic symptoms during periods of amphetamine use.

Older adults with amphetamine-induced psychosis display behaviors that resemble the signs and symptoms of paranoid schizophrenia. Although relatively more common during an acute "amphetamine run," aggressive and violent behavior may also occur in the context of amphetamine psychosis, when, for example, users—experiencing acute paranoia—often can be found holding a loaded handgun or rifle, peeking from behind closed curtains for the "enemy"—perhaps a "narc" (i.e., police or Drug Enforcement Administration [DEA] officer). This behavior is well-documented and has been recognized for some time in medical, psychological, and legal contexts of practice (Pagliaro & Pagliaro, *Clinical Patient Data Files*).

Efforts have been made to differentiate the clinical similarities and differences between amphetamine psychosis and schizophrenia (e.g., Bramness & Rognli, 2016; Wearne & Cornish, 2018). Although both conditions may be associated with delusional thinking, a flattened affect, hallucinations, mental depression, and paranoia, they generally differ in etiology and duration.

Generally, older adults, who develop mild forms of psychotic-like behavior associated with their amphetamine use, can be treated by "talking them down." However, acute or severe forms of psychosis usually require medical management with a sedative-hypnotic (i.e., diazepam, Valium®) in combination with an antipsychotic (e.g., chlorpromazine, Thorazine®; haloperidol, Haldol®). Efficacious treatment can promptly reverse many of the signs and symptoms of the psychosis (Buxton & Dove, 2008). Untreated, the psychosis generally resolves within two to 14 days. (See also the later amphetamine subsection, "Other Toxicities.")

Cardiotoxicities

Amphetamine use, in general, and methamphetamine use, in particular, have long been associated with cardiotoxicity, including sudden death, which may occur as a direct result of the mechanism of action of the amphetamines (Kevil, Goeders, & Woolard, 2019). (See the related discussion in the earlier amphetamines pharmacology subsection—"Pharmacodynamics: Mechanism of Action.")

As found by Kaye, McKetin, and Duflou (2007, p. 1204), in their review of methamphetamine and cardiovascular pathology:

1. Methamphetamine users are at higher risk of cardiac pathology.
2. Risk is unlikely to be limited to the duration of their methamphetamine use because of its associated chronic pathology.
3. Risk of cardiac pathology is highest among regular, long-term methamphetamine users.
4. Pre-existing cardiac pathology, due to methamphetamine use or other factors, increases the risk of an acute cardiac event.
5. Methamphetamine use is likely to exacerbate the risk of cardiac pathology associated with other factors and may, therefore, lead to premature mortality.

A decade later, Darke, Duflou, and Kaye (2017) noted that methamphetamine-related cardiovascular pathology includes a significant incidence of cardiomegaly, cardiomyopathy, left ventricular hypertrophy, replacement fibrosis, and severe coronary artery disease.

Other cardiac and related physical toxicities that have been associated with the use of amphetamines, include:

- Atherosclerotic coronary artery disease;
- Cardiac dysrhythmias;
- Chest pain;
- Coronary vasospasm;
- Dilated cardiomyopathies;
- Heart failure;
- Heart palpitations;
- Hypertension;
- Myocardial infarction;
- Pulmonary hypertension;
- Tachycardia.

Diminished Executive Function

Higher order, cognitive performance is controlled by executive function—mental processes associated with integration, synthesis, and problem solving—which are typically required for goal- or task-oriented behaviors, including consciously planning, implementing, monitoring, and ceasing goal-directed behaviors. Minor and temporary deficits and fluctuations in executive function are largely situational. For example, while occurring among most people at some time in their lives, these deficits and fluctuations are more likely to occur when a person is: (1) extremely tired; (2) under extreme psychological stress; (3) experiencing reactive depression following a significant loss; or (4) acutely intoxicated with alcohol or another abusable psychotropic psychodepressant (Pagliaro & Pagliaro, *Clinical Patient Data Files*).

Significant deficits in executive function among older adults are associated with several mental and neurological disorders, including:

- AUD;
- MDD;
- OCD;

- Psychotic disorder;
- Tourette's syndrome.

In addition, diminished executive function has been identified as both a "cause" and "result" of abusable psychotropic use (e.g., Goldstein & Volkow, 2011; Pagliaro & Pagliaro, 2012, 2018). As found by Ersche, Clark, and London (2006, p. 1036), in their study of both regular, long-term amphetamine and opiate analgesic users:

> Chronic drug users display pronounced neurophysiological impairment in the domains of executive and memory function. Impairment persists after several years of drug abstinence and may reflect neuropathology in frontal and temporal cortices. . . . Compared to opiate users, amphetamine users showed more pronounced deficits on tasks of executive function.

(Also see the related discussion of executive function in Chapter 1, *Alcohol*, Chapter 4, *Cannabis*, and Chapter 5, *Prescription Opiate Analgesics and Heroin*.)

Methamphetamine-related diminished cognitive and executive function also includes deficits in abstract thinking, learning, memory, and psychomotor speed (Dean, Kohno, & Morales, 2015). These deficits appear to be related to neurotoxicity associated with the dopamine terminals. Specifically, this neurotoxicity has long been associated with methamphetamine-induced damage to: (1) dopaminergic neurons[31] in the basal ganglia; and (2) reduced dopamine transporter density in the caudate/putamen, nucleus accumbens, and prefrontal cortex (see Figure 2.2). Among older adults, this neurotoxicity is related to normal aging, in which the:

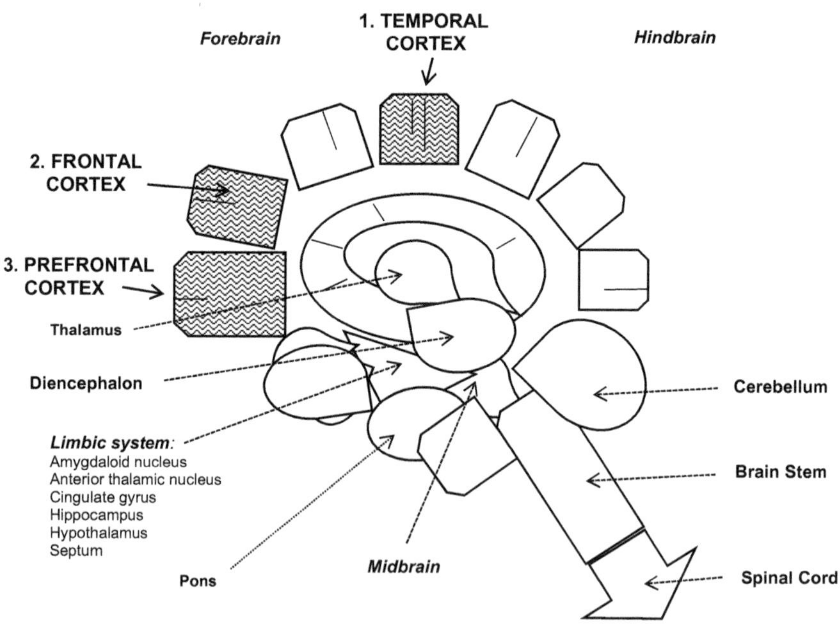

Figure 2.2 Three Major Sites of Amphetamine CNS Toxicity

31. Several researchers (e.g., Shin, Tran, & Nguyen, 2017) have suggested that the damage to dopaminergic neurons may be mediated by impairment of mitochondrial function.

1. Availability of DAT in the striatum declines at an average rate of 6% per decade;
2. Nigrostriatal neurons in the putamen decline by up to 70% after approximately 55 years of age;
3. Age-related loss of dopamine appears to accelerate after approximately 60 years of age (Erixon-Lindroth, Farde, & Robins Wahlin, 2005; Karrer, Josef, & Mata, 2017; Martin, Palmer, & Patlak, 1989; Shumay, Chen, & Fowler, 2011).

Although not as well characterized, methamphetamine-induced damage to serotonergic neurons, which may be mediated by the formation of reactive oxygen species (ROS) (e.g., peroxides or superoxide), also has been identified (Hanson, Rau, & Fleckenstein, 2004). In addition, methamphetamine neurotoxicity may be mediated by downregulation (i.e., temporary neuroadaptive changes of some dopaminergic and serotonergic systems). Consequently, in this context, the associated neurotoxicity may be reversible with long-term abstinence from methamphetamine use.

The etiology of the neurotoxicity associated with amphetamine use appears to be both complex and multifactorial. For example, Yu, Zhu, and Shen (2015) identified eight specific possible mechanisms for amphetamine-related neurotoxicity:[32]

1. D_3 receptors—by means of alteration of the immune response and the induction of hyperthermia;
2. Endoplasmic reticulum stress—linked to the process of neuronal apoptosis;
3. Excessive dopamine—linked to both the increased production of reactive oxygen species and the activation of D_1 receptors;
4. Expression of apoptosis-inducing transcription factor p53—methamphetamine mediated oxidative stress-induced p53 binding activated downstream of apoptotic pathways and death of monoaminergic neuronal cells;
5. Inflammatory cytokine—involvement of neuroinflammatory processes in methamphetamine-induced neurotoxicity;
6. Microtubule deacetylation—and related increased permeability of the blood-brain barrier and resultant release of inflammatory mediators and astrogliosis;
7. Protein nitration—radical nitric oxide plays an essential role in the pathogenesis associated with oxidative stress;
8. Ubiquitin-Proteasome system dysfunction—and related impaired degradation of short-lived and cytosolic proteins.

Of particular concern is the observation that some of the neurotoxic effects appear to be permanent. For example, research findings indicate that regular, long-term, high dosage methamphetamine use can selectively damage the striatal dopaminergic axons in the substantia nigra. This methamphetamine neurotoxicity has been associated with permanent parkinsonian-like signs (e.g., pill-rolling tremor; shuffling gait) (Ares-Santos, Granado, & Espadas, 2014; Ares-Santos, Granado, & Moratalla, 2013; Matthew & Gedzior, 2015; Todd, Noyes, & Flavel, 2013).[33]

32. N.B. These possible mechanisms are: (1) not mutually exclusive; and (2) may interact with each other.
33. This affected area of the substantia nigra, when visualized by transcranial sonography, assumes an abnormally enlarged and bright appearance. This change in appearance is referred to as "hyperechogenicity" (Todd et al., 2013).

Excessive Dosage

As the dosage of amphetamine is increased, abdominal pain (severe); anorexia, with loss of body weight; blurred vision; chest pain; dizziness; emotional lability; headache; nausea; palpitations; punding; tremor; and urinary retention may be experienced. A further increase in amphetamine dosage may culminate in amphetamine psychosis (see the related discussion in the earlier subsection—"Amphetamine Psychosis").

Fatalities

Although relatively uncommon, the use of amphetamines can "directly" or "indirectly" result in death. For example, amphetamine use has been "directly" related to death due to myocardial infarctions (Kaye et al., 2007); cerebrovascular accidents (Zhu, Osman, & Stradling, 2020 [see the earlier subsection—"Cardiotoxicities"]); and overdosages (see the later amphetamine pharmacology subsection—"Amphetamine Overdosage"). The most severe, and potentially fatal, acute physical toxicities associated with amphetamine use are:

1. "Hypertensive crisis," which is characterized by a drastic increase in blood pressure;
2. "Hyperpyretic crisis," which is characterized by a sustained elevated body temperature exceeding 106° F (41° C). (Matsuomoto, Seminerio, & Turner, 2014; Richards & Laurin, 2019; Wako, LeDoux, & Mitsumori, 2007)

These two acute physical toxicities require emergency medical support, including appropriate medical intervention and monitoring of body systems.

"Indirectly," amphetamine use has been related to deaths due to: (1) fatal hepatitis C infection or HIV/AIDS—usually contracted through the use of contaminated needles and syringes; (2) fatal IV injection of an adulterated or contaminated form of amphetamine, or an unknown toxic substance thought to be amphetamine; (3) fatal injuries due to amphetamine induced psychotic episodes and homicidal rages; and (4) fatal accidents related to amphetamine use (Pagliaro & Pagliaro, *Clinical Patient Data Files*). (See also the related discussion in the later amphetamine subsection, "Overdosage/Unintentional Poisoning.")

Additionally, McKetin et al. (2019), in their systematic review and meta-analysis of mental health outcomes associated with the use of amphetamines, found that:

1. Any amphetamine use was associated with 4.4 times the odds of suicidality;
2. Amphetamine use disorder was associated with 2.5 times the odds of suicidality;
3. Amphetamine use was associated with 3.6 times the odds of suicide attempts.

Human Immunodeficiency Virus (HIV) Infection and Acquired Immune Deficiency Syndrome (AIDS)

More recently, the use of abusable psychotropics—psychostimulants (i.e., amphetamine and methamphetamine),[34] psychodepressants (e.g., alcohol), and psychedelics

34. For example, it has been estimated that men who have sex with men are over 12 times more likely to use amphetamines, including methamphetamine, than men who do not have sex with men (Hunt, 2012; Santos, Miller, & Jain, 2020–2021).

(e.g., methylenedioxymethamphetamine [Ecstasy or MDMA])—before and during bisexual, homosexual, and transgender sex among men who have sex with men (MSM), including older men, has become inculcated among these subcultures (Santos et al., 2020–2021). This sexualized use of abusable psychotropics has become colloquially known as "party and play," or more commonly, "chemsex" (Melendez-Torres & Bourne, 2016; Pakianathan, Lee, & Kelly, 2016).

Of increasing concern, chemsex, in addition to being associated with related abusable psychotropic dependencies or use disorders, also is associated with other undesired effects including a documented higher incidence of:

1. Acute bacterial sexually transmitted diseases (STDs);
2. Hepatitis C;
3. HIV infection;
4. Rectal STDs. (e.g., Bourne, Reid, & Hickson, 2015; Hegazi, Lee, & Whittaker, 2017; Sewell, Miltz, & Lampe, 2017)

As found by SAMHSA (2020, p. 7), in a comprehensive review of psychostimulant dependence or use disorders:

People who use stimulants are more likely to engage in unprotected sex and sex with multiple partners. In addition, intravenous administration of stimulants may result in reusing or sharing needles, syringes, and other paraphernalia. These behaviors place people who misuse stimulants at higher risk for HIV and other blood-borne pathogens, such as hepatitis B and hepatitis C. This is of concern because chronic stimulant use is linked to weakened immune response, increased susceptibility to infection, and accelerated retroviral replication.

Perhaps surprising to some, all of the aforementioned effects, which are addressed in this subsection, have particular relevance for older adults in the U.S. This relevance is due to several related observations including that:

1. Older adults living with HIV/AIDs have significantly higher rates of abusable psychotropic use, including use of the amphetamines, than do their age-matched HIV-negative cohorts;
2. Over 50% of all cases of HIV/AIDS in the U.S. reportedly occur among those 50 years of age and older;
3. The significant rates of HIV/AIDS and associated use of abusable psychotropics are expected to continue to increase through the third decade of the new millennium as the baby boomer generation ages—and because Americans, in general, are living longer. (CDC, 2019; Deren, Cortes, & Vaughan Dickson, 2019; Edelman, Tetrault, & Fiellin, 2014; Heath, Lanoye, & Maisto, 2019; Pilowsky & Wu, 2015)

An additional concern is the potential additive effects of HIV infection and methamphetamine use on neurotoxicity. As explained by Yu et al. (2015, p. 2):

> Neurotoxic outcomes of METH abuse and HIV-1 CNS infection include, but are not limited to, brain hyperthermia, release of inflammatory mediators and reactive oxygen species (ROS), excitotoxicity, and astrogliosis.

(See also the related discussion in the earlier subsection, "Diminished Executive Function.")

Intravenous Toxicities

Direct acute toxicities have been related to both the early and late phases of intravenous amphetamine use. Commonly, during the "early phase," which generally occurs following the IV injection of 20 to 40 mg of amphetamine, a desired "flash," or "rush," is experienced that is reportedly characterized by:

1. Extreme euphoria—a sense of increased physical energy, mental capacity, and self-confidence;
2. Heightened sexual orgasm.

During the "later phase," or "run," users frequently inject increasingly higher dosages of amphetamine in an effort to achieve the desired actions that they experienced during the early phase. Unable to achieve these actions, primarily due to the development of tolerance (see the related discussion in the later amphetamine subsection, "Physical and Psychological Dependence—Tolerance"), they typically remain awake and, while generally eating little, if at all, continue to inject their amphetamine every one to three hours, for several days—around the clock—until their run ends, typically when they:

1. Deplete their amphetamine supplies (e.g., the total available supply is used);
2. Are unable to obtain additional amphetamine because their funds are exhausted;
3. Become so mentally disorganized, or paranoid, that they cannot continue their amphetamine use.

Finally, incapable of continuing their amphetamine use, they usually fall into a deep, but restless, sleep that lasts for 12 to 18 hours, or more. Upon awakening, they typically feel tired, weak, depressed, and hungry (Pagliaro & Pagliaro, *Clinical Patient Data Files*).

Also of concern, the IV injection (i.e., "mainlining") of amphetamines, or any other abusable psychotropic, is associated with several well-identified toxicities, including:

- Abscesses at the injection site;
- Aneurysms;
- Bacteremia;
- Cellulitis;
- Cotton fever;[35]
- Cutaneous venous ulcers;
- Endocarditis;
- Gangrene;
- Hepatitis B;

35. "Cotton fever" is associated with using a cotton ball, or a small piece of cotton, to filter illicit solutions of dissolved crushed tablets, capsule contents, or powdered drug formulations, prior to IV injection. It has been reported to be associated with the endotoxin, *Pantoea agglomerans*, a Gram-negative bacterium that lives in various plants, including cotton plants. In addition to fever, associated signs and symptoms can include abdominal pain, chills, headache, leukocytosis, myalgia, nausea, shortness of breath, tachycardia, and vomiting. Signs and symptoms generally: (1) have their onset within 20 minutes of IV injection; (2) follow a benign course; and (3) resolve within 12 hours of onset (Pagliaro & Pagliaro, *Clinical Patient Data Files*; Xie, Pope, & Hunter, 2016; Zerr, Ku, & Kara, 2016).

- Hepatitis C;
- HIV infection;[36]
- Myonecrosis;
- Myositis;
- Necrotizing fasciitis;
- Neuropathy (as a direct result of physical needle trauma);
- Scarring of skin (i.e., "railroad tracks");
- Septicemia;
- Tetanus;
- Thrombophlebitis;
- Thrombosis;
- Venous sclerosis;
- Wound botulism.

It is important to note that these serious toxicities do not occur "directly" because of the pharmacology of the amphetamines, but rather occur "indirectly" as a result of: (1) adulterants added to the amphetamine product; (2) improper/poor IV injection techniques; and (3) using/sharing contaminated needles and syringes. Thus, they do not occur when the amphetamines are administered by other routes, such as: ingestion, nasal insufflation, or pulmonary inhalation (Pagliaro & Pagliaro, 2004, 2009).

Related Professional Reminder:* *The use of "safe injection sites" are associated with harm reduction,* not *harm prevention. Consequently, many of the toxicities that are associated with IV injection will* not *be prevented or reduced by the use of "safe injection sites"—even with the provision of sterile needles and syringes.[37]

"Meth Mouth"

The condition of meth mouth is associated with the regular, long-term use of methamphetamine and prolonged neglect of oral hygiene, both of which contribute to the loss of teeth and the associated distinctive appearance commonly referred to as "meth mouth" (e.g., Brown, Morisky, & Silverstein, 2013; Pagliaro & Pagliaro, *Clinical Patient Data Files*; Rommel, Rohleder, & Koerdt, 2016). This condition also is characterized by "rampant caries, periodontal diseases, and excessive tooth wear" (Rommel, Rohleder, & Wagenpfeil, 2016, p. 469). In addition, several researchers, such as Boyer, Thompson, and Hill (2015, p. 119),[38] have noted that:

36. See the related discussion in the previous subsection—"Human Immunodeficiency Virus (HIV) Infection and Acquired Immune Deficiency Syndrome (AIDS)."
37. In addition, an unanticipated consequence of "safe injection sites" is that they often promote, or at least "enable," abusable psychotropic use, which, consequently, can result in the continuation of regular, long-term use with associated harmful effects and toxicities—both to the user and others (Pagliaro & Pagliaro, *Clinical Patient Data Files*). As a matter of record (e.g., making this belief explicit upon a specific request for our related professional opinion from the White House Office of National Drug Control Policy [ONDCP]), it should be noted that we do not now, nor have we ever, endorsed the use of "safe injection sites." See the *Index* for entries and discussion regarding the related topic of "harm reduction."
38. It should be kept in mind that this observation may be influenced by the fact that, in the U.S., the highest percentage of methamphetamine users are of European continental descent.

> For missing teeth, there was a significant methamphetamine race/ethnicity interaction ($p = 0.028$) among Whites, who used methamphetamine, compared to Whites, who did *not* use methamphetamine.

In their study of 100 chronic methamphetamine users and 100 matched-pair controls, Rommel et al. (2016) found that total saliva production among the methamphetamine users was significantly lower and had a lower pH than that found for controls. These findings led Rommel and colleagues to posit that the noted differences in saliva production and pH contribute to the increased risk for dental caries and erosions that are seen among regular, long-term methamphetamine users.[39]

Other Toxicities

Other toxicities associated with amphetamine use include both mental and physical toxicities. Other "mental" toxicities, include:

- Aggression;
- Agitation;
- Anxiety;
- Compulsive behavior;
- Confusion;
- Delirium;
- Emotional lability;
- Euphoric grandiosity;
- Formication;[40]
- Hallucinations;
- Hyperactivity;
- Hypervigilance;
- Impaired judgment;
- Insomnia;
- Irritability;
- Loquacity extending to pressured speech;
- Mania;
- Nervousness;
- Obsessive behavior;
- Panic attacks;

---

39. "Meth mouth" has also been suggested to be possibly related to deficiencies in vitamins and minerals associated with the "meth" using lifestyle (e.g., Thomas & Mirowski, 2010). Additionally, we have noted that the condition appears to be exacerbated among older methamphetamine users, particularly among those who smoke tobacco cigarettes (Pagliaro & Pagliaro, *Clinical Patient Data Files*).
40. Formication is the delusional sensation of something (e.g., "bugs") crawling under the skin. Usually characterized by touching, scratching, and picking of the arms and face, which, over time, often results in extensive disfiguration due to associated infections and scarring. The typical facial appearance resembles severe acne—with open sores, or lesions (Mullin, 2016; Pagliaro & Pagliaro, *Clinical Patient Data Files*).

- Paranoia;
- Preoccupation with thinking processes and philosophical concerns about meaning;
- Punding;
- Restlessness;
- Suicidal ideation.

Other "physical" toxicities, include:

- Acute renal failure;
- Anorexia;
- Bruxism, which usually occurs during sleep and is associated with involuntary contraction, or spasm, of the jaw muscles;
- Cerebrovascular accident;
- Coma;
- Cramps;
- Diaphoresis;
- Dizziness;
- Dysuria;
- Headache;
- Hyperglycemia;
- Hyperthermia;
- Local skin burns, which are often associated with methamphetamine production;
- Metabolic acidosis;
- Rhabdomyolysis;
- Seizures;
- Tachypnea;
- Tremor;
- Urinary retention;
- Vomiting;
- Weight loss.

Physical and Psychological Dependence

In the U.S., the inability to discontinue the use of amphetamines, particularly methamphetamine, has led over a million people—across the lifespan—to seek professional assistance from physicians, psychiatrists, psychologists, and other health and social care professionals, for the management of amphetamine dependence or use disorder, and related tolerance and withdrawal.

Over the new millennium, many research studies, which have addressed amphetamine, or other dependence or use disorders, have focused on the genetic basis (i.e., contribution of specific genes) regarding desired or undesired drug effects (e.g., Ducci & Goldman, 2012; Hart, de Wit, & Palmer, 2012). These gene-focused studies reflect various research approaches (i.e., in vitro studies, in vivo laboratory animal studies, clinical case studies, and experimental, controlled human research studies). Although many hypotheses and avenues for additional future research have been generated, clinically useful, definitive data are scarce. As noted by Ducci and Goldman (2012, p. 495):

> The identification of specific genes and functional loci moderating vulnerability has been challenging because of the genetic complexity of addictive disorders. This complexity derives from multiple sources, including incomplete penetrance, phenocopies, variable expressivity, gene-environment interactions, genetic heterogeneity, polygenicity, and epistasis.

However, some related findings have shown promise for future clinical directions. For example, Lott, Kim, and Cook (2005, p. 602), conducting a double-blind, crossover design, placebo-controlled study, reported:

> Subjects were genotyped for the DAT1 3'-untranslated region VNTR [variable number tandem repeats] polymorphism and divided into groups based on genotype: homozygous for 9 repeats (9/9, N=8); heterozygous (9/10, N=36); and homozygous for 10 repeats (10/10, N=52). The effects of amphetamine on ratings of Feel Drug, Anxiety, and Euphoria were examined with ANCOVA, in 9/10 and 10/10 subjects, amphetamine produced its expected effects of increased Euphoria, Anxiety, and Feel Drug ($p < 0.01$). However, in 9/9 subjects, the effects of amphetamine were indistinguishable from placebo, suggesting that 9/9 genotype has diminished subjective response to acute amphetamine [administration].

Additionally, Hart, Engelhardt, and Wardle (2012, p. e42646), in their genome-wide association study of amphetamine response in healthy adult volunteers, reported the following:

> Responses to amphetamine were measured using a double-blind, placebo-controlled, within-subjects design. We used sparse factor analysis to reduce the dimensionality of the data to ten factors. We identified several putative associations; the strongest was between a positive subjective drug-response factor and a SNP (rs3784943) in the 8th intron of cadherin 13 (*CDH13*; $P=4.58 \times 10^{-8}$), a gene previously associated with a number of psychiatric traits including methamphetamine dependence.

Tolerance

Regular, long-term use of amphetamines results in a tolerance to their desired psychostimulant actions. Thus, in an effort to achieve desired effects, including associated euphoria, users often increase their dosages to several grams per day (Pagliaro & Pagliaro, *Clinical Patient Data Files*). Tolerance also affects other related actions, particularly those that are centrally mediated, including cardiovascular effects and hyperthermia. However, tolerance to the occurrence of chronic toxicities, such as amphetamine psychosis, does not generally occur. Thus, regular, long-term users of the amphetamines, particularly among those users who are tolerant and increase their dosages in an effort to achieve desired effects, inevitably increase their risk for experiencing amphetamine psychosis (see the related discussion in the earlier pharmacology subsection—"Amphetamine Psychosis").

Withdrawal Syndrome

A true or classic withdrawal syndrome—such as that which occurs following the abrupt discontinuation of the regular, long-term use of alcohol, opiate analgesics, or nicotine, and which can be immediately relieved with the resumed use of the abusable psychotropic—has not been documented for any of the amphetamines, including methamphetamine (Pagliaro &

Pagliaro, 2004, 2009). However, the abrupt discontinuation of regular, long-term patterns of high dosage amphetamine or methamphetamine use may result in the signs and symptoms of "early-phase" amphetamine or methamphetamine withdrawal, which include:

- Anxiety;
- Apathy;
- Cognitive impairment;
- Depressed mood (which may be severe);
- Drug craving (often quite intense);
- Fatigue;
- Increased appetite;
- Loss of interest in usually pleasurable activities;
- Sleep disturbance (i.e., hypersomnia);
- Vivid unpleasant dreams.

The early phase of amphetamine or methamphetamine withdrawal largely resolves within one week of the discontinuation of amphetamine or methamphetamine use. Of note, it is during early-phase amphetamine or methamphetamine withdrawal, that most users perpetrate acts of violence against others, including other family members (Hamilton & Goeders, 2010; Pagliaro & Pagliaro, *Clinical Patient Data Files*). A "later-phase" amphetamine withdrawal follows, characterized by similar, but significantly less severe signs and symptoms, which may last for two additional weeks (McGregor, Srisurapanont, & Jittiwutikarn, 2005). During both phases, older adults remain at high risk for resumed use. There is no specific pharmacotherapy for the management of the signs and symptoms associated with amphetamine or methamphetamine withdrawal (Shoptaw, Kao, & Heinzerling, 2009). Medical management remains symptomatic (Pagliaro & Pagliaro, 2009, 2018).

Illicit Methamphetamine Production

Generally, illicit methamphetamine (i.e., "Crystal Meth") is chemically synthesized in sophisticated, large scale clandestine "super labs" for subsequent sale "on the street." The so-called "super labs," which are primarily controlled and directed by Mexican criminal organizations in Mexico and in Los Angeles, California, can generally produce ten or more pounds of methamphetamine per day (Kasper, 2019; Pagliaro & Pagliaro, *Clinical Patient Data Files*). Other super labs are operated by major Asian and other criminal organizations, including outlaw motorcycle gangs (e.g., the Hells Angels Motorcycle Club) (Pagliaro & Pagliaro, 2009; Shukla, Crump, & Chrisco, 2012).

In large parts of the U.S., illicit methamphetamine—produced in Mexico (i.e., "Mexican Meth")—significantly replaced that produced in illicit home laboratories (i.e., "home-cooked meth"). This change became established by 2007 and since that time, the average purity of "Mexican Meth" has increased from approximately 37% to approximately 100% (Berkes, 2007; Buie & Tamburin, 2014), while the street price has significantly decreased (Pagliaro & Pagliaro, *Clinical Patient Data Files*). As identified by Shukla et al. (2012, p. 426):

> Transnational [criminal] organizations now control much of the methamphetamine supply in the U.S. and methamphetamine remains widely available.

And as later identified by Mammoser (2017, p. 1):

> Super-strength methamphetamine from Mexico super labs is flooding streets in the United States.

By 2019 the Mexican illicit drug cartels began producing methamphetamine in increasingly larger amounts (i.e., up to 100 pounds per day) and with consistently high purity (i.e., ~ 97%). This increase in production became commonly known by the lay press as "Meth 2.0" and was widely, and incorrectly, touted as a new, stronger version of methamphetamine. China is the major source country for the precursor chemicals (i.e., ephedrine and pseudoephedrine) that are utilized by the Mexican cartels to produce the methamphetamine destined for the U.S. As noted by the U.S.-China Economic and Security Review Commission:

> While Mexican cartels produce the majority (around 90%) of meth used in the United States, around 80% of precursor chemicals used in Mexican meth come from China.
>
> (USCC, 2016, p. 1)

During the second decade of the new millennium, Mexican drug smugglers increasingly turned to shipping "liquid meth" into the U.S. Liquid meth is simply methamphetamine crystals that have been dissolved in water (note that methamphetamine base is a colorless, volatile oil that is insoluble in water) resulting in a dark yellow, syrupy fluid that can be stored in sealed liquor bottles (or other larger containers) in order to avoid detection at U.S. ports of entry along the U.S.-Mexico border (e.g., Cheromcha, 2018; D'Angelo, 2018; Eldridge, 2016). Once successfully transported across the border to its intended destination, which is often several states away from the border crossing point, the liquid meth is converted back to methamphetamine crystals prior to sale to users (Pagliaro & Pagliaro, *Clinical Patient Data Files*).

> South Florida federal prosecutors have charged the leader of a notorious Mexican drug cartel and five others for their alleged roles in importing into the United States over 500 kilograms of Mexican methamphetamine. In the largest methamphetamine seizure in Miami-Dade County history, law enforcement agents seized the over 1,200 pounds of crystal meth before it ever hit the streets.
>
> The rest of the meth (over 300 kilograms) arrived in Miami on March 26, 2021, say the court documents. This time, it was dissolved within five-gallon buckets of house paint. According to the allegations, Comparan-Bedolla and two chemists (Gonzalez-Aguilar and Valdez) worked for days inside a warehouse, extracting pure crystal methamphetamine from the paint.
>
> (Hibbert, 2021, p. 1)

Old Misbelief: Only a little chemistry knowledge and experience are needed to illicitly produce methamphetamine.

False. In fact, actually, no chemistry knowledge or experience is needed. Methamphetamine is relatively easy to illicitly synthesize—in "cookbook" fashion—from inexpensive, over-the-counter ingredients and commonly available supplies.[41] It can, and continues to be, synthesized in small, unsophisticated, clandestine labs across the U.S., which range from small

41. These ingredients and supplies include acetone, anhydrous ammonia, common cold and allergy tablets that contain pseudoephedrine, coffee filters, drain cleaner, isopropyl (rubbing) alcohol, lithium batteries,

basement laboratories (e.g., so-called "mom and pop labs") to larger, more sophisticated laboratories on college/university campuses. Methamphetamine also is synthesized in kitchens, bathrooms, and other places in the family home.

The "easiest" methods of methamphetamine production (i.e., the "anhydrous ammonia method" or the "red phosphorus method") frequently utilize precursor drugs, such as amphetamine, phenylalanine, phenylpropanolamine, or pseudoephedrine.[42,43,44,45] To prevent, or at least significantly diminish, the wide-spread diversion of these precursor drugs for the illicit production of methamphetamine, the *Comprehensive Methamphetamine Control Act* of 1996 was passed. In 2005, Congress passed a related law, the *Combat Methamphetamine Epidemic Act* (CMEA), that was followed by the *Methamphetamine Production Prevention Act of 2008*, which was implemented in 2011 (DEA, 2011).[46]

Shake and Bake Method

The increasing adoption of the "shake and bake" method of methamphetamine production from 2000 through 2010 largely nullified the past regulatory efforts aimed at controlling methamphetamine production (Hamilton, 2010; Pagliaro & Pagliaro, *Clinical Patient Data Files*). The "shake and bake" method only requires: a few packages of "common cold pills;"

---

lye, Mason® jars, pillowcases, and toluene. (Also see later list of supplies in text associated with "shake and bake" method of production.)

42. Alterations to the licit pharmaceutical formulations of pseudoephedrine have been used in an attempt to impede the illicit production of methamphetamine from pseudoephedrine. For example, the Nexafed® pseudoephedrine tablet maintains bioequivalence with Sudafed® pseudoephedrine tablets, while utilizing the Impede® technology to limit the extraction of pseudoephedrine and its subsequent conversion to methamphetamine (Brzeczko, Leech, & Stark, 2013).
43. Also, commonly referred to as either the "Birch Method" or the "Nazi Method" because this method of production was used during World War II to supply German soldiers with methamphetamine to increase their alertness (Pagliaro & Pagliaro, 2004).
44. N.B. Amphetamine (i.e., dextroamphetamine) is legally available only by prescription while, generally, phenylalanine and pseudoephedrine, which are commonly found in common cold products, are legally available without a prescription (i.e., over the counter ["OTC"]).
45. The anhydrous ammonia method is more often used in the production of large quantities of methamphetamine because of the ready, and unregulated, availability of nitrogen farm fertilizer (i.e., the source of anhydrous ammonia).
46. In this context, various state and federal regulations have been enacted, including: (1) prior to sale, keeping these and other related products (e.g., ephedrine and pseudoephedrine) "behind the counter" in pharmacies; (2) limiting the amount of related product sold; and (3) for several states, such as Oregon and Mississippi, requiring a prescription for the purchase of related products. As identified by Messina, Marinelli-Casey, and West (2014, p. 1874):

    > A review of state bills and regulations on over-the-counter purchases of these products reveals that as of 2005, 34 of the 50 states have passed bills to restrict access to and/or purchase of "cold medications" that include pseudoephedrine.

    As noted by the National Drug Intelligence Center (2006, p. 1), these changes had an unanticipated consequence:

    > Law enforcement pressure and strong precursor chemical sales restrictions have achieved marked success in decreasing domestic methamphetamine production. Mexican DTOs, however, have exploited the vacuum created by rapidly expanding their control over methamphetamine distribution—even to eastern states—as users and distributors, who previously produced the drug, have sought new, consistent sources.

    (See the related discussion in the previous amphetamine section, "Illicit Methamphetamine Production.")

several corrosive, or flammable chemicals, which can be readily purchased at most hardware, farm supply, Walmart®, and similar stores; water; and an empty, 32- or 64-ounce plastic soda bottle to quickly and easily produce enough methamphetamine for personal use or sale on a very small scale (Carnevale Associates, 2011; Hall & Dunham, 2013; ONDCP, 2010; Pagliaro & Pagliaro, 2009).

Various detailed lists of the typical supplies needed for the "shake and bake method" of illicit methamphetamine production can be found on the Internet. For example, the following list is from "Some Chick's Blog" (Shake and bake, no date, p. 2):

- Two 32 oz. Gatorade® bottles;
- Two Mason® jars;
- Three to four ft. of aquarium tubing;
- Aquarium air pump (optional);
- Fine coffee filters;
- Funnel;
- 75g 100% lye;
- 130g 15–0–15 fertilizer (no weed killers);
- Two 96 ct. pseudoephedrine capsules or tablets (emptied and crushed into fine powder);
- Coleman® lantern fuel;
- 1.5g ice;
- Two AA lithium batteries;
- Iodized salt;
- Liquid Lightning® (drain cleaner);
- Needle nose pliers;
- Pipe cutter;
- Xacto® knife/Scissors.

Illicit methamphetamine producers generally identify three benefits of the "shake and bake method," when compared to other methods of illicit methamphetamine production (Pagliaro & Pagliaro, *Clinical Patient Data Files*):

1. Ease of preparation (i.e., no need for basic knowledge, skills, or techniques in chemistry);
2. Less expenditure (i.e., no need for costly, specialized chemical laboratory equipment);
3. Quick "cooking time" (i.e., using this method, a "batch" of methamphetamine can be easily produced in as little as 30 minutes).

The identification of illicit "meth labs" is crucial for law enforcement, as well as for mental health care professionals, public health nurses, and social workers.[47] Thus, various

47. During the first two decades of the new millennium, the state of Missouri was generally considered to be the "meth production capital of the U.S."

lists of related signs[48] of the presence of a possible meth lab have been compiled (e.g., Bartos, 2005). From these lists, we have provided three main areas for inspection: (1) inside; (2) outside; and (3) around meth labs and drug houses.

Positive "inside meth lab" inspections include the presence of:

- Basic laboratory equipment (e.g., clear glass jugs, glassware, and rubber tubing);
- Camp stoves, heat plates, or other heat sources;
- Coolers or thermos bottles;
- Cookware that contains powdery substances;
- Empty cold/allergy medication packaging;
- Strong odor of urine or unusual chemical odors such as acetone, ammonia, or ether;
- Used coffee filters that have a white or red pasty or powdery coating;
- Various drugs or chemicals in plain sight (e.g., cold/allergy medications or ether).

Positive "outside meth lab" inspections include the presence of:

- Empty containers of acetone, antifreeze, drain cleaners (e.g., Draino®), Freon®, Heet®, lye, starting fluids, or paint thinner;
- Empty propane tanks;
- Strong chemical odors.

Positive "around meth lab" and "drug house" inspections include the presence of:

- Heavily covered windows;
- Little or no pedestrian or vehicle traffic during the day, but a large amount of traffic at night;
- Never putting out the trash;
- Reinforced doors;
- Renters who pay landlords in cash;
- Renters who are unfriendly, paranoid, or secretive;
- Unemployed people who seem to have plenty of cash.

Overdosage/Unintentional Poisoning

Overdosages involving amphetamines commonly occur among older adults, particularly when they are illicitly obtained "on the street" for either IV injection (i.e., injecting methamphetamine) or pulmonary inhalation (i.e., vaping "Crystal Meth").[49]

48. It should be kept in mind that the signs included in these listings are indicative of, but not definitive for, methamphetamine production activity.
49. Illicit street purchase of the amphetamines is particularly problematic in terms of overdosage because, what is purchased, generally cannot be verified as: (1) actually being an amphetamine (e.g., methamphetamine); (2) not containing adulterants or other illicit drugs; and (3) being the actual dosage, or strength, claimed by the dealer.

In the U.S., psychostimulant-related deaths increased three-fold during the first decade of the new millennium from 0.2 per 100,000 person-years in 2000, to 0.6 per 100,000 person-years in 2009 (Calcaterra & Binswanger, 2013, p. 11). The rates of psychostimulant deaths were highest among individuals of European continental descent, American Indian descent, and those who resided in the western states (Calcaterra & Binswanger, 2013; Kerley, Leban, & Copes, 2014). As identified by Calcaterra and Binswanger (2013), who utilized the *CDC Wonder Database* for their comprehensive review of all deaths in the U.S. from 1999 to 2009:

> Accidental poisoning, was the most frequently listed cause of death among those who died with psychostimulants.
>
> (p. 1)

Overdosages involving the amphetamines continued to significantly increase during the second decade of the new millennium with the NIH reporting a significant surge in methamphetamine overdose deaths from 2011 to 2018. During this period, related deaths more than quadrupled in the United States—from 1.3 per 100,000 population to 7.3 per 100,000 population. The highest rates remained among individuals of America Indian and Alaska Native descent followed by those of European descent (NIDA, 2021). In 2016, the overall death rate associated with psychostimulant use in the U.S. increased, overall, by 33% (Orciari Herman, 2018).

Amphetamine poisoning can be unintentional (i.e., accidental) or intentional (i.e., attempted or completed suicide).[50] Most cases of amphetamine poisoning are associated with the ingestion of oral amphetamine formulations (i.e., capsules; tablets) that are easily ingested. These poisonings are generally treated with slurries of activated charcoal that, when appropriately administered, can prevent the further absorption of the ingested amphetamines from the stomach (see also the related discussion in the following subsection). In these cases, the use of emetics to induce vomiting are contraindicated because of the risk for: (1) precipitating seizures; and (2) aspirating the vomitus that may subsequently result in the development of aspiration pneumonia, or death.

Signs and symptoms of acute amphetamine overdosage, include:

- Agitation;
- Constipation;
- Hallucinations;

---

50. Several studies of methamphetamine users in outpatient treatment (e.g., Glasner-Edwards, Mooney, & Marinelli-Casey, 2008; Zweben, Cohen, & Christian, 2004) provide strong evidence to support a significant association with suicide attempts. For example, in their related review and study of a "large sample of treatment-seeking methamphetamine users," Durell, Kroutil, and Crits-Christoph (2008), identified that "27% reported a previous suicide attempt, and 43% reported violent behavior problems" (p. 2). In addition, as found by Kaland and Klein-Schwartz (2015), regarding amphetamine exposures reported to U.S. poison centers, for "both adolescents and adults, the most common reasons were suicide attempts" (p. 477). More recently, McKetin et al. (2019) conducted a systematic review and meta-analysis of the published data concerning amphetamine toxicity and found that "suicidality" was significantly associated with both:

    1. Any use of amphetamine;
    2. Amphetamine dependence or use disorder. We, too, have recognized this relationship in our own clinical practice (Pagliaro & Pagliaro, *Clinical Patient Data Files*). However, based on other available data, we would suggest that the relationship between methamphetamine use and suicide is more complex—being related, for example, to an underling intervening variable such as MDD.

- Irrational behavior/thought;
- Panic;
- Paranoia;
- Restlessness;
- Seizures;
- Tachycardia;
- Tachypnea;
- Tremor.

Depression and fatigue usually follow the initial phase of psychostimulation (see earlier related discussion). Other signs and symptoms, include:

- Abdominal cramps;
- Anxiety;
- Chest pain;
- Circulatory collapse;
- Combativeness;
- Diaphoresis;
- Diarrhea;
- Dysrhythmias;
- Flushing;
- Headache;
- Hostility;
- Hyperreflexia;
- Hypertension;
- Hyperthermia;
- Hypovolemia;
- Mydriasis;
- Nausea;
- Palpitations;
- Vomiting;
- Xerostomia.

In addition, as noted by Vallersnes, Dines, and Wood (2016), amphetamine psychosis is commonly observed among cases of amphetamine poisoning (see also the earlier related discussion in the amphetamines pharmacology subsection, Undesired, or Harmful, Effects and Toxicities—"Amphetamine Psychosis"). Hyperthermia, renal damage, rhabdomyolysis, and death also can occur. (See the earlier discussion in this subsection.)

Treatment of Overdosage/Unintentional Poisoning

Generally, most older adults with non-life-threatening amphetamine overdosage fully recover without significant sequelae when treated with appropriate sedation and monitoring (Handy, 2017; Pagliaro & Pagliaro, 2009; Van Loggerenberg, 2007; Vasan & Olango,

2020). However, in some situations, amphetamine overdosage may require appropriate: (1) supportive medical treatment with close monitoring to maintain vital organ functions; and (2) pharmacotherapy to manage troublesome signs and symptoms. For example, many of the toxic effects associated with amphetamine overdosage can be effectively managed with the use of antipsychotic drugs, including:

- Chlorpromazine (Thorazine®), a phenothiazine antipsychotic;
- Haloperidol (Haldol®), a butyrophenone antipsychotic;
- Olanzapine (Zyprexa®), an atypical antipsychotic. (Pagliaro & Pagliaro, 1999, 2009, 2020)

These antipsychotics can also be used, if necessary, for the management of amphetamine-induced aggressive paranoid behavior and to prevent associated self-harm or harm to others (i.e., to provide effective "chemical restraint"). (See also the earlier amphetamine pharmacology subsection, Undesired or Harmful Effects and Toxicities—"Amphetamine Psychosis.")

Diazepam (Valium®), a benzodiazepine sedative-hypnotic/anticonvulsant, is generally effective for managing associated agitation and seizures. Ammonium chloride also may be used to acidify the urine to increase amphetamine renal excretion (see the related discussion in the earlier amphetamines pharmacology subsection, Pharmacokinetics—"Excretion"). However, it is not generally recommended because urinary acidification can exacerbate renal failure due to rhabdomyolysis.

Additionally, further appropriate diagnostic examination and tests may be required to further characterize the etiology of the observed signs and symptoms and, subsequently, assist in the selection and delivery of necessary therapeutic interventions. For example:

- Chest x-rays and/or electrocardiogram (EKG) when patients complain of chest pain or palpitations;
- Computed tomography (CT) scans of the head when altered mental status or seizures are observed in order to rule out intracranial hemorrhage or amphetamine-induced stroke.

There is no known antidote for amphetamine overdosage (Pagliaro & Pagliaro, 2009; Van Loggerenberg, 2007).

Older Adult Involvement in Amphetamine Trafficking and Dealing

In addition to being involved in illicit amphetamine production generally utilizing a version of the "shake and bake" method (see the related discussion in the previous subsection), older adults are increasingly becoming involved in amphetamine trafficking and dealing.

Involvement in Drug Trafficking

The trafficking of amphetamines by older adults often occurs in the context of international travel (e.g., in relation to a vacation or foreign sight-seeing tour) (Harris, 2018; Nixon, 2016; Pagliaro & Pagliaro, *Clinical Patient Data Files*).

> Floridian Ralph Soles, 74, said he was caught transporting methamphetamine into New Zealand two years ago. He was arrested and spent the next 18 months in custody.
>
> (Sands, 2016, p. 1)

> According to DHS, the scam begins with a criminal organization building relationships with seniors, usually online. The drug traffickers trick them into traveling overseas to claim lottery winnings, deliver important documents to their new online friend, or another seemingly believable reason. The scammers usually back up their story with fake documents like forged bank statements or government letters, convincing seniors they're telling the truth.
>
> (Corrigan, 2016, p. 1)

The lay press is replete with articles detailing methamphetamine trafficking by older adults across the U.S.—from the southern border to the Midwest, and throughout Appalachia. For example, as reported by Osbourne (2020, p. 1):

> Authorities [in Austin, Texas] over the past two weeks arrested 21 people linked to an Austin-area cocaine and methamphetamine trafficking operation, according to the U.S. Department of Justice . . . seized about 50 kilograms of meth. . . . Those arrested included Jose Miquel Campuzano-Gonzalez, 52, of Austin; Jose Ramiro Castellan-Ortiz, 50, of Austin; Edward Keane, 55, of Perryopolis; Elvis Jackson, 59, of Taylor; and Angela Eans, 59, of Bastrop.

Numerous other examples exist, as represented by the following.

As reported on behalf of the DEA by Williamson and Briano (2021, p. 1):

> Gelaldo Paz [53 years-of-age, El Paso, Texas] pleaded guilty to conspiracy with intent to distribute . . . federal agents witnessed Paz transport and deliver approximately eight kilograms of methamphetamine [from Mexico] to an El Paso residence.

Or, as reported by Shannon (2020, p. 2):

> Multiple kilos of meth were trafficked from Atlanta [Georgia] up into Central Pennsylvania. . . . [Those charged with] bringing kilo quantities of meth from Atlanta for distribution throughout north central PA included: Ronald Bean, 55, Winburne, Pennsylvania; Alex Brolin, Jr., 51, Allport, Pennsylvania; Tammie Brolin, 52, Allport Pennsylvania; John Cyphert, 59, Centre Hall, Pennsylvania; John McKinney, 51, Hyde, Pennsylvania; Robert Morgret, 56, Avis, Pennsylvania; Robert Nyman, 58 Mill Hall, Pennsylvania; and Jeffrey Swanson, 50, Houtzdale, Pennsylvania.
>
> Felix Franz Forjan, 71, pleaded guilty before U.S. District Judge Stephen R. Bough to one count of possessing methamphetamine with the intent to distribute.
>
> . . .
>
> The deputy searched Forjan's vehicle and found six bags of methamphetamine, wrapped in black electrical tape, in a laundry basket in the back seat of the vehicle. The bundles of methamphetamine weighed a total of approximately six pounds.
>
> (Swanson, 2021, p. 1)

> Garland Beardsley aka Charlie Beardsley, 53, of Jamestown NY, pleaded guilty before U.S. Magistrate Judge Michael J. Roemer to conspiring to possess with intent to distribute, and distributing, 50 grams or more of methamphetamine. . . .
>
> The defendant was an associate in a drug trafficking ring led by his nephew, co-defendant Rocco Beardsley, which sold methamphetamine, heroin, fentanyl, crack cocaine, cocaine, and hydrocodone in the Jamestown area. Garland Beardsley distributed methamphetamine to Rocco Beardsley's customers.
>
> (Donovan & Mulvey, 2021, p. 1)

A joint taskforce of U.S. Immigration and Customs Enforcement (ICE) and Homeland Security, as part of "Operation Cocoon," which was investigating illicit transnational transport of cocaine, heroin, and methamphetamine by individual adults, found that:

1. Over 30 older adults, who are U.S. citizens, are incarcerated overseas as a consequence of "Operation Cocoon;"
2. The average age of the couriers was 59 years of age, with the oldest involved individual being 97 years old and the oldest, who was taken into custody (i.e., arrested) being 87 years old. (Nixon, 2016; Sands, 2016)

Involvement in Drug Dealing

Older adults across the U.S. are actively involved in the sale of methamphetamine. For example, as reported by Pinarski (2020, p. 1):

> 58-year-old Carolyn Sue Evans was arrested [in Walker County, Alabama] and charged with trafficking methamphetamine [103 grams] . . . 53-year-old Ricky Lynn Naramore is wanted for conspiracy to traffic methamphetamine.

Other examples of drug dealing include the following:

> Deputies found 8 people trafficking methamphetamine at the residence [in London Kentucky]. Among those arrested included: Stevie Westerfield, 62; Jesse Westerfield, 56; Edward Belt, 50; and Judy Westerfield, 63.
>
> (Staff, 2018, p. 1)

> A Providence [Rhode Island] woman pleaded guilty Wednesday to trafficking methamphetamine . . . Alexa Samoiloff, 51, admitted to a federal court that she facilitated drug deals from her apartment.
>
> (Gammans, 2020, p. 1)

> A Coffee County man [Israel Moreno, 56, of Wray, Georgia] has been sentenced to nearly six years in federal prison after admitting to trafficking methamphetamine [50 grams].
>
> (Murphy & Truesdell, 2021, p. 1)

> Carlton Cash [49, Fort Lauderdale, Florida] was sentenced to ten years in prison for distributing crystal methamphetamine. Cash holds an active Florida medical license.
>
> (DEA, 2021, p. 1)

Additionally, although less commonly encountered, older adults are also involved in major drug dealings, particularly, those involving methamphetamine sales. For example:

> An elderly farmer claims he sold crystal meth to save his son from vengeful Mexican cartel members tied to Louisville. James Ronald Muse, a grandfather known as "Ronnie," gained a reputation as a hardworking corn and soybean farmer in south-central Kentucky who sometimes made extra money driving semitrucks. Now he's a 72-year-old federal prisoner, notorious in his hometown of Monticello as one of the area's largest drug dealers.
>
> (Warren, 2019, p. 1)

New Millennial Trends in Older Adult Amphetamine Use

With attention to new millennial trends, we begin with older adult use of medical prescription amphetamines. We then present and discuss older adult use of nonmedical/illicit amphetamines.

Medical Prescription Amphetamine Use

The amphetamines are approved by the FDA for the treatment of ADHD among children, 3 years of age or older and adults.[51] The amphetamines are also approved by the FDA for the treatment of narcolepsy among children, 6 years of age or older and adults.[52] Although the use of the amphetamines for the short-term treatment of obesity among older adults has been long practiced, we do not recommend this use because the:

1. Amphetamines are only FDA approved for short-term use, whereas obesity tends to be a chronic, long-term, condition that requires long-term treatment;
2. Benefits (i.e., rapid weight loss) are apt to quickly disappear upon discontinuation of amphetamine use (i.e., lost weight is quickly regained);
3. Risk of undesired, or harmful, effects and toxicities, including psychological dependence.

Additionally, amphetamines have been medically used "off-label" for a variety of mental and neurological disorders among older adults (e.g., Alzheimer's disease and other dementias, cognitive decline, and depression) (Moreira Sassi, Pessoa Rocha, & Delevati Colpo, 2020; Pagliaro & Pagliaro, *Clinical Patient Data Files*). Safer (2016, p. 471), in a review of trends in stimulant use, found that:

> Stimulant medication treatment—particularly of amphetamines—is rapidly expanding in the United States. Off-label use is reported to be at least 40% of total use and appears to be more common in adults.

Unfortunately, we have not found adequate published empirical support for significant clinical efficacy associated with the use of amphetamines for the treatment of any of these conditions. Consequently—and mindful of the significant risk of amphetamine use (see the earlier related discussion in the amphetamine subsection, "Undesired, or Harmful, Effects and Toxicities")—we do not recommend these "off-label" medical uses of amphetamines for older adults.

Nonmedical/Illicit Amphetamine Use

During the 1980s, the illicit use of amphetamines was largely replaced by the use of cocaine (see the "Cocaine" section of this chapter). However, by the mid-1990s, there was a renewed interest in amphetamine use, particularly the use of illicit methamphetamine, as an economic alternative to the significantly more expensive cocaine.

This renewed interest in the use of amphetamines was further encouraged by the increased availability of both its "powdered" form (e.g., "chalk") and "crystalline" form (i.e., "Crystal Meth," "Glass," or "Ice"). The use of Crystal Meth—the "smokable" form—had its origin in Hawaii from where it quickly spread to California (hence, one of its common street names, "West Coast"). Subsequently, it quickly spread across the U.S. (Pagliaro & Pagliaro, 2009, 2012, 2018), where its use became particularly widespread across urban and rural areas in the

---

51. Attention-deficit hyperactivity disorder may occur among older adults—commonly in the context of having been undiagnosed at an earlier age (Inserro, 2018; Michielsen, Semejin, & Comijs, 2012; Semeijn, Michielsen, & Comijs, 2013). As identified by Safer (2016, p. 471), "Total stimulant prescription sales to adults have surpassed those for youth."
52. Among older adults, narcolepsy is often diagnosed in the context of co-occurring cataplexy (Chakravorty & Rye, 2003; Suzuki, Uehara, & Ohira, 2015). Typically, it is initially diagnosed during the second or third decade of life and requires lifelong treatment because of the absence of a cure.

Table 2.4 General Comparison Between Methamphetamine and Cocaine

METHAMPHETAMINE	COCAINE
Classification: Psychostimulant, (amphetamine), synthetic	**Classification:** Psychostimulant, natural
Available Form: Powdered crystal	**Available Forms:** Cocaine base (crack[53] or rocks) and cocaine hydrochloride (powdered crystal)
Desired Effects: Produces long-lasting euphoria, sexual inhibition, and other desired effects due to its relatively long half-life of elimination.	**Desired Effects:** Produces a brief euphoria and other desired effects due to its relatively short half-life of elimination.
Medical Use: Not legally available in the U.S.	**Medical Use:** Limited dental and medical use as a local anesthetic for brief surgical and other procedures.
Methods of Use: Methamphetamine is ingested, dissolved and IV injected, or nasally insufflated ("snorted"). It is also heated and the fumes are inhaled from a glass pipe, the top of a discarded soda pop can, or on a piece of tin foil.	**Methods of Use:** Cocaine HCl powder can be dissolved and IV injected or nasally insufflated ("snorted"). Cocaine base is heated, and the fumes are inhaled from a crack pipe, the top of a discarded soda pop can, or on a piece of tin foil.
Mechanism of Action: Acts by increasing dopamine release and blocking its re-uptake.	**Mechanism of Action:** Acts by blocking dopamine re-uptake.
Metabolism/Elimination: 50% is excreted in unchanged form in the urine over approximately 12 hours (pH dependent).	**Metabolism/Elimination:** 50% is excreted in unchanged form in the urine over approximately one hour (pH dependent).
Abuse Potential: High abuse potential with a characteristic methamphetamine withdrawal syndrome that is not relieved with resumed use. However, does not display a true, or classical, withdrawal syndrome such as that which, for example, occurs with the abrupt discontinuation of abusive or compulsive alcohol or opiate analgesic use and is immediately relieved with resumed use.	**Abuse Potential:** High abuse potential with extreme psychological craving and a characteristic cocaine withdrawal syndrome that cannot be relieved with the resumed use of cocaine. However, does not display a true or classical withdrawal syndrome such as that which, for example, occurs with the abrupt discontinuation of abusive or compulsive alcohol or opiate analgesic use and is immediately relieved with resumed use.
Street Names: "Crank," "Crystal," "Glass," "Ice," "Meth," "Speed," "Tina," "Tweak"	**Street Names:** Cocaine Hydrochloride—"Blow," "C," "Coke," "Nose Candy," "Powder," "Snow," "Toot" Cocaine base—"Crack," "Freebase," "Rock"

53. "Crack" is cocaine base that has been prepared from the salt form of cocaine (i.e., cocaine hydrochloride) utilizing the addition of sodium bicarbonate. The associated chemical reaction is:

Cocaine HCl + NaHCO3 —> Cocaine + H_2O + CO_2 + NaCl

(i.e., cocaine hydrochloride + sodium bicarbonate produce cocaine base + water + carbon dioxide + sodium chloride).

midwestern and southern states (e.g., Kentucky; Tennessee; West Virginia)—hence, another common street name, "Hillbilly Crack" (Gonzales, Mooney, & Rawson, 2010; Hauer, 2010; McWilliams, 2019; Winslow, Voorhees, & Pehl, 2007).

The use of methamphetamine, primarily the use of the crystalline form (i.e., "Crystal Meth"), soared from 2000 to 2010 because of its ready availability, relatively low cost, and rapid achievement of high methamphetamine blood concentrations (along with desired psychostimulant effects)—without IV injection. Crystal Meth, smoked in much the same way as crack cocaine,[54] also could produce a longer duration of desired psychostimulant effects than crack cocaine (i.e., four to eight hours versus 15 to 60 minutes).

By 2010, the use of methamphetamine again began to be slowly replaced with cocaine (e.g., Johnston, O'Malley, & Bachman, 2013).[55] (See the next major section of this chapter, "Cocaine.") It may seem ironic, or even surprising, to some readers that the same attributes that made methamphetamine so popular—its widespread availability, cheaper price, and longer duration of action in comparison to cocaine—subsequently contributed to its decline in popularity as it increasingly became known as, the "Poor Man's Drug" or the "White Trash Drug" (Pagliaro & Pagliaro, *Clinical Patient Data Files*) (see Table 2.4).

Lifetime prevalence of methamphetamine use among men and women in the U.S. is approximately 8% (Durell et al., 2008). The CDC (Jones, Compton, & Mustaquim, 2020, pp. 317–318) reported that:

> During 2015–2018, an estimated 1.6 million U.S. adults aged ≥ 18 years, on average [approximately 25% of these adults were ≥ 50 years of age], reported past-year methamphetamine use; 52.9% had methamphetamine use disorder, and 22.3% reported injecting methamphetamine within the past year. . . . During 2015–2018, the estimated annual average rate of lifetime methamphetamine use was 59.7 per 1,000 adults [i.e., 6%].

However, as noted previously in this chapter subsection, the use of methamphetamine, waxes and wanes over time. As identified by Calcaterra and Binswanger (2013), "methamphetamine use declined significantly [in the U.S.] from 2002 to 2008, but rose again in 2009" (p. 2). Additionally, as noted in a 2019 DEA report, the use of methamphetamine is resurging and "several large swaths of the U.S. see meth as their primary drug threat" (McWilliams, 2019, p. 1). Consequently, treatment statistics vary from year to year and from location to location—and, obviously, fall behind use statistics. While related amphetamine data are generally lacking for older adults, it is generally accepted that approximately 0.5% of those 50 years of age or older in the U.S. abuse amphetamines.

Assessment and Diagnosis of Amphetamine Dependence or Use Disorder

During the past two decades of the new millennium, in the U.S., the illicit use of amphetamines by rural adults across the country—particularly, those of European descent—significantly

54. "Crystal Meth" is most often smoked with a small glass pipe that is commonly referred to as a "bubble," "crack pipe," "pizzo," or "tweak pipe" (Pagliaro & Pagliaro, *Clinical Patient Data Files*).
55. N.B. When discussing methamphetamine—or any other abusable psychotropic—related usage statistics often appear inconsistent, or even contradictory. However, all these statistics may actually be "factually correct." Apparently different, even contradictory, statistics are most often the result of differences in: (1) sampling (e.g., all older adults versus only those currently retired, or those over 50 years of age versus those over 65 years of age); and (2) definitions (e.g., is "current use" defined by use within the previous day, week, month, or year?).

increased. However, for this population group, little attention was given to related research and publication of findings regarding assessment, diagnosis, and treatment of amphetamine dependence or use disorder. Whereas several generic tools exist—such as the *Diagnostic and Statistical Manual of Mental Disorders-5* (DSM-5) criteria for identifying "stimulant use disorder"—no specific quick-screen psychometric tests have been developed with attention to detecting amphetamine dependence or use disorder among older adults.

However, one general psychometric test—"The Severity of Dependence Scale" (SDS)—has been used and provides related research regarding amphetamine dependence or use disorder (e.g., Topp & Mattick, 2006) that is applicable for older adults. This psychometric test is presented and discussed in the following subsection.

Severity of Dependence Scale (SDS)

The SDS was developed by Gossup, Dark, and Griffiths (1995) to detect the degree of dependence experienced by users of different abusable psychotropics. It is a five-item quick-screen psychometric test (Table 2.5) that can be completed in less than one minute. The items comprising the SDS are explicitly concerned with psychological components of dependence and—using principal components analysis—load significantly on a single factor.

The SDS was originally tested with attention to the use of amphetamine, cocaine, and heroin in Australia and England. Woody, Cottler, and Cacciola (1993, p. 1)—utilizing data from the DSM-IV field trials—evaluated "the applicability and clinical utility of the dependence syndrome across a wide range of substances" and determined that:

> Across all drug classes, severity correlated reasonably well with measures of quantity and frequence of use with associated problems.

The SDS has been recommended for use by the World Health Organization (WHO) and has been produced in several different language versions, including Chinese (Chen, Chen, &

Table 2.5 The Severity of Dependence Scale (SDS)

ITEM/QUESTION	SCORING CRITERIA [Point Allocation]
Over the last 3 months:	
1. Did you ever think your use of [insert drug name] was out of control?	Never or almost never [0]; Sometimes [1]; Often [2]; Always or nearly always [3]
2. Did the prospect of missing the use of [insert drug name] make you very anxious or worried?	Never or almost never [0]; Sometimes [1]; Often [2]; Always or nearly always [3]
3. Did you worry about your use of [insert drug name]?	Never or almost never [0]; Sometimes [1]; Often [2]; Always or nearly always [3]
4. Did you wish you could stop using [insert drug name]?	Never or almost never [0]; Sometimes [1]; Often [2]; Always or nearly always [3]
5. How difficult would you find it to stop or go without [insert drug name]?	Not difficult [0]; Quite difficult [1]; Very difficult [2]; Impossible [3]
	Total SDS Score: __/15

Modified from: Gossup et al., 1995.

Lin, 2008) and Portuguese (Ferri, Marsden, & de Araujo, 2000). Additionally, the SDS has been found to be both valid and reliable in a sample of older adults, 65 to 90 years of age (Cheng, Siddiqui, & Gossop, 2019).

Scoring the SDS

Each item of the SDS is scored on a 4-point scale (i.e., "0," "1," "2," or "3"). See Table 2.5 for scoring criteria. The scores are summed for a possible maximal total score of 15. For older adults, a total score of 4 or higher indicates the likelihood of a significant degree of "psychological" dependence.

Treating Older Adult Amphetamine Dependence or Use Disorder

Once a professional assessment is completed and a diagnosis of amphetamine dependence or use disorder is made for an older adult, the development of an individualized intervention plan is required. This plan requires the involvement of the older adult with attention to the selection and implementation of generally two major categories of appropriate treatment that can be used individually or together: (1) pharmacotherapeutic approaches; and (2) psychotherapeutic/counseling approaches. Appropriately combined therapeutic approaches have been generally associated with more efficacious outcomes for older adults (see the related discussion in Chapter 1, *Alcohol*).[56]

Unfortunately, to date, no published research studies have been identified that offer empirically determined effective treatment interventions, or "best practices," for older adults with amphetamine dependence or use disorder (Harada, Tsutomi, & Mori, 2014). However, we begin with an overview of what is known regarding related pharmacotherapeutic approaches for the treatment of amphetamine dependence or use disorder.

Pharmacotherapeutic Approaches

Currently, no prescription drugs have been approved by the FDA for the treatment or management of amphetamine or methamphetamine dependence or use disorder, including relapse prevention (e.g., Ballester, Valentine, & Sofuoglu, 2017; Cao, Shi, & Hao, 2016; Chan, Kondo, & Ayers, 2018; Lee, Jenner, & Nielsen, 2014; Morley, Cornish, & Faingold, 2017). As identified by Ballester et al. (2017, p. 305):

> Clinical trials examining the potential for pharmacotherapies of methamphetamine use disorder have largely been negative.

Similarly, as further identified by Morley et al. (2017, p. 563):

> Effective management for methamphetamine dependence remains elusive and the large majority of methamphetamine users relapse following treatment.

56. Researchers have generally reported that, when an AUD and/or SUD is responsive to both an appropriate pharmacotherapeutic approach and a psychotherapeutic/counseling approach, an optimal outcome can be obtained by combining and utilizing both approaches.

Additionally, Siefried, Acheson, and Lintzeris (2020, p. 361), in their systematic review of pharmacotherapies for amphetamine dependence or use disorder, concluded that:

> No pharmacotherapy for the treatment of amphetamine/methamphetamine dependence/use disorder has provided convincing results.

This conclusion was supported by SAMHSA (2020, p. 2) in their "Evidence-Based Resource Guide Series" that specifically addressed the treatment of amphetamine use disorders:

> There is no FDA-approved medication currently available for stimulant use disorders.

However, several prescription drugs have been used in an "off-label" context to treat amphetamine use disorder. While several research studies have been published regarding the efficacy of many of these prescription drugs, most report a lack of efficacy for treating amphetamine dependence or use disorders, particularly those for managing methamphetamine use or withdrawal. Nevertheless, some show potential promise for some patients (see Table 2.6).

Our own re-analysis of the data available from these studies revealed several "reasons" for the lack of reported efficacy. Thus, even when the "results" (i.e., the authors' conclusions) suggest some therapeutic promise, these "reasons"—examples of which are presented in the following bullet list—negatively affect the reliability of the research findings presented in Table 2.6 and consequently, severely limit their generalizability:

- Conflation of correlation and causation in data analyses;
- High rate of subject/participant attrition;
- Inadequate or inconsistent identification of amphetamine use among study participants;
- Inadequate sample size;
- Lack of consideration of potential confounding variables;
- Lack of control group;
- Lack of long-term follow-up;
- Lack of objective outcome criteria;
- Lack of placebo control;
- Non-blinded study;
- Nonrandom sample selection (e.g., use of convenience sampling);
- Nonrandom assignment of subject/participant to "treatment" groups;
- Reliance on self-report;
- Short duration of research study.

Additionally, little or no attention has been given to the study of the prevention and treatment of "relapsed use," which often occurs subsequently to "successful" treatment of amphetamine dependence or use disorder (e.g., Brackins, Brahm, & Kissack, 2011; Lee et al., 2014; Morley, Cornish, & Faingold, 2017; Pagliaro & Pagliaro, 2018).

We now turn to the psychotherapeutic/counseling approaches used for amphetamine dependence or use disorder.

Table 2.6 Examples of the Efficacy of Pharmacotherapeutic Approaches for Amphetamine Dependence or Use Disorder, Program Retention, and/or Withdrawal Syndrome

PHARMACOTHERAPEUTIC APPROACH UTILIZED	EFFICACY	SOURCES
Amlodipine (Norvasc®) *Calcium channel blocker*	Ineffective	Karila, Weinstein, & Aubin, 2010
Aripiprazole (Abilify®) *Antipsychotic, atypical*	Increased amphetamine use	Elkashef, Vocci, & Hanson, 2008
	Ineffective; may increase methamphetamine use	Karila et al., 2010
Baclofen (Lioresal®) *Antispastic,* *GABA receptor agonist*	Ineffective	Elkashef et al., 2008
	Ineffective for reducing methamphetamine use	Karila et al., 2010
Benzodiazepines (e.g., Ativan®, Valium®) *Sedative-hypnotics*	Ineffective for treating amphetamine "withdrawal"	Lee et al., 2014
Bupropion (Wellbutrin®) *Antidepressant*	Limited efficacy for limited populations	Brensilver, Heinzerling, & Shoptaw, 2013
	Limited efficacy for "light" methamphetamine users May reduce signs and symptoms of methamphetamine withdrawal	Karila et al., 2010
	Limited efficacy for treating amphetamine dependence among "low frequency" users (less than 18 days/month	Lee et al., 2014
	Ineffective	Perez-Mana, Castells, & Torrens, 2013
Bupropion (Wellbutrin®) *Antidepressant* **AND** **Naltrexone** (ReVia®) *Opiate analgesic receptor antagonist*	"Low, but higher than that among participants who received placebo"	Trivedi, Walker, & Ling, 2021
Dextroamphetamine (Dexedrine®) *Psychostimulant, amphetamine*	Limited efficacy Potential for addiction to dextroamphetamine	Elkashef et al., 2008
	Increased retention in treatment group/program; limited efficacy in reducing methamphetamine use and potential for addiction to dextroamphetamine	Karila et al., 2010

(Continued)

Table 2.6 (Continued)

PHARMACOTHERAPEUTIC APPROACH UTILIZED	EFFICACY	SOURCES
	May be effective for reducing signs and symptoms of methamphetamine "withdrawal" Limited efficacy for increasing retention in treatment for amphetamine dependence or use disorder	Lee et al., 2014
	Effective for increasing treatment program retention and decreasing methamphetamine use	Longo, Wickes, & Smout, 2010
	Ineffective	Perez-Mana et al., 2013
Fluoxetine (Prozac®) *Antidepressant, selective serotonin reuptake inhibitor (SSRI)*	Ineffective	Karila et al., 2010
Gabapentin (Neurontin®) *Non-Selective GABA agonist*	Ineffective for reducing methamphetamine use	Karila et al., 2010
Imipramine (Tofranil®) *Antidepressant, tricyclic*	Ineffective	Elkashef et al., 2008
Lobeline *Naturally occurring alkaloid, partial nicotinic receptor antagonist*	Possibly effective	Karila et al., 2010
Methylphenidate (Ritalin®) *Psychostimulant, amphetamine-like*	Limited efficacy in limited populations	Brensilver et al., 2013
	Limited efficacy in reducing methamphetamine use Potential for addiction to methylphenidate	Elkashef et al., 2008
	Limited efficacy among IV amphetamine users Potential for addiction to methylphenidate	Karila et al., 2010
	Limited efficacy for treatment of amphetamine dependence	Lee et al., 2014
	Ineffective	Perez-Mana et al., 2013
Mirtazapine (Remeron®) *Antidepressant, atypical*	Limited efficacy in limited populations	Brensilver et al., 2013
	Ineffective	Karila et al., 2010
	Possibly effective in reducing signs and symptoms of methamphetamine "withdrawal"	Lee et al., 2014

PHARMACOTHERAPEUTIC APPROACH UTILIZED	EFFICACY	SOURCES
Modafinil (Provigil®) *Psychostimulant, nonamphetamine*	Limited efficacy in decreasing methamphetamine use and the severity of the methamphetamine withdrawal syndrome	Karila et al., 2010
	May be effective in reducing the signs and symptoms of the methamphetamine withdrawal syndrome	Lee et al., 2014
	Ineffective	Perez-Mana et al., 2013
Naltrexone (ReVia®) *Opiate analgesic receptor antagonist*	Limited efficacy in limited populations	Brensilver et al., 2013
	Possibly effective in decreasing both the craving for amphetamines and using amphetamines	Karila et al., 2010
	Limited efficacy for amphetamine treatment program retention and reducing craving for amphetamines	Lee et al., 2014
Ondansetron (Zofran®) *Antiemetic, serotonin receptor antagonist*	Ineffective	Elkashef et al., 2008
	Ineffective	Johnson, Ait-Daoud, & Elkashef, 2008
	Ineffective	Karila et al., 2010
Paroxetine (Paxil®) *Antidepressant, selective serotonin reuptake inhibiter (SSRI)*	Ineffective	Karila et al., 2010
Risperidone (Risperdal®) *Antipsychotic, atypical*	Possibly effective in reducing methamphetamine use	Karila et al., 2010
Rivastigmine (Exclon®) *Parasympathomimetic cholinesterase inhibitor*	Possibly effective	Karila et al., 2010
Sertraline (Zoloft®) *Antidepressant, selective serotonin reuptake inhibitor (SSRI)*	Ineffective	Elkashef et al., 2008
	Ineffective	Karila et al., 2010
Topiramate (Topamax®) *Anticonvulsant, sulfamate substituted monosaccharide*	Ineffective May increase methamphetamine plasma concentrations	Karila et al., 2010

(Continued)

Table 2.6 (Continued)

PHARMACOTHERAPEUTIC APPROACH UTILIZED	EFFICACY	SOURCES
Tyrosine *Amino acid*	Ineffective	Elkashef et al., 2008
Vigabatrin (Sabril®) *GABA agonist, inhibitor of GABA-aminotransferase*	Possibly effective for reducing methamphetamine use	Karila et al., 2010

Psychotherapeutic/Counseling Approaches

Fifteen years ago, the NIDA/NIH noted the following:

> At this time, the most effective treatments for methamphetamine addiction are behavioral interventions. These approaches are designed to help to modify the patient's expectancies and behaviors related to drug use, and to increase skills in coping with various life stressors.
> (NIDA/NIH, 2005, p. 8)

This situation has not changed over the ensuing 15 years of the new millennium. Psychotherapeutic/counseling approaches continue to be the mainstay for the treatment of amphetamine dependence or use disorder, including the management of the amphetamine withdrawal syndrome. However, overall success has been limited and, consequently, a significant number of patients with amphetamine dependence or use disorder fail to successfully respond to these interventions (i.e., recidivism rates are high).[57]

The most common psychotherapeutic/counseling approaches, which have been used for older adults with amphetamine dependence or use disorder, include:[58]

- Brief cognitive behavioral therapy (BCBT);
- Cognitive behavioral therapy (CBT);
- Contingency management (CM);[59]
- Interpersonal therapy (IT);
- Motivational interviewing (MI);
- Twelve-step/facilitation programs (12-Step).

57. Although long-term (i.e., longitudinal) studies of recidivism among amphetamine users in the U.S. are scarce, one related study was found. In this study, Brecht and Herbeck (2014), utilizing "self-report data from natural history interviews" of methamphetamine users that were conducted three to five years post-discharge from a large country substance abuse treatment program, found that: (1) 61% of subjects relapsed within one year following treatment; and (2) an additional 14% relapsed during years two though five following treatment. Additionally, in a ten-year longitudinal study from Japan, Hazama and Katsuta (2020), who were investigating "drug-related recidivism among paroled amphetamine-type stimulant users," found a recidivism rate of approximately 50%.
58. For an additional, general overview and discussion of each of these approaches, see the subsection in Chapter 1, Alcohol—"Psychotherapeutic/Counseling Approaches."
59. Although listed, all of the studies of CM in the context of treatment for amphetamine dependence or use disorder have involved adolescents and young adults. We have only used CM with older adults when they have been residing in a treatment care center (e.g., halfway house, for example, after release from prison; community homeless center; or treatment center that utilizes day passes into the community).

Virtually, all of the research studies, which have focused upon the treatment of amphetamine dependence or use disorder, have involved the application of either CBT and/or CM (e.g., Harada et al., 2014; Lee & Rawson, 2008). Related randomized controlled studies have consistently, at least for adults, resulted in several positive outcomes that include:

- Increased abstinence at follow-up;
- Increased treatment retention;
- Longer periods of abstinence;
- More amphetamine-free urine samples;
- Reduced amphetamine use.

It also has been found that positive outcomes are more likely to persist post-CBT treatment rather than post-CM treatment.

Brief Cognitive Behavioral Therapy (BCBT)

Among adults, the results of several empirical studies (e.g., Baker, Boggs, & Lewin, 2001; Baker, Lee, & Claire, 2005; Yen, Wu, & Yen, 2004) indicated that BCBT (i.e., two to five sessions) was associated with a significant increase in abstinence at six months among regular amphetamine users in comparison to either "placebo" or a control approach consisting of structured assessment and use of a self-help booklet. However, longer term efficacy and prevention of related relapsed use of methamphetamine have not been established with BCBT (Lee & Rawson, 2008).

Cognitive Behavioral Therapy (CBT)

Cognitive behavioral therapy does not have a "good track record" of documented use and associated success in the treatment of amphetamine related disorders (e.g., Harada et al., 2014, 2018). In one of the few empirical studies of CBT for methamphetamine dependence, Keoleian, Stalcup, and Poicin (2013)—noting that "psychosocial treatments for methamphetamine dependence are of limited effectiveness" (p. 434)—developed and tested a "CBT-based text messaging intervention" that was used in conjunction with standard CBT group therapy. Although concluding that the texted messages were rated as useful by the participants, a re-analysis of their data indicated a lack of clinical significance and a reported increase in "craving" following the receipt of the text messages.

A considerable amount of the related research involving CBT and methamphetamine use has focused on adult gay men as the subjects (e.g., McElhiney, Rabkin, & Rabkin, 2009; Reback & Shoptaw, 2014; Shoptaw, Reback, & Peck, 2005). From these studies, findings generally indicate significant reductions in the number of male sexual partners, but only modest, short-term reductions in methamphetamine use.

> ***Related Professional Reminder:** Although therapeutic success for amphetamine dependence or use disorder is limited, when successful, it almost always involves the combination of pharmacotherapeutic and psychotherapeutic/counseling approaches.*

Additionally, we, and others (e.g., Minozzi & Saulle, 2016; Pagliaro & Pagliaro, 2018), have generally recommended the combination of two or more of the psychotherapeutic/counseling approaches (e.g., "CBT" and "12-step program"). In addition, as deemed appropriate for specific older adults and their amphetamine dependence or use disorder, we often add pharmacotherapy to this combination (see related discussion of in the preceding subsection of this chapter—"Pharmacotherapeutic Approaches").

Common Contemporaneous Diagnoses[60]

Older adults are susceptible to, and may experience, virtually every form of contemporaneous diagnoses. However, the most often reported contemporaneous diagnosis, particularly in the context of older adult amphetamine dependence or use disorder, is MDD (Pagliaro & Pagliaro, 2018; Pagliaro & Pagliaro, *Clinical Patient Data Files*).

Amphetamine dependence or use disorder among older adults also has been associated with several other mental disorders:

- Anxiety Disorders;
- AUD;
- Cannabis Use Disorder;
- Eating Disorders;
- Psychotic Disorders (e.g., schizophrenia);
- PTSD;
- Substance dependence or use disorder(s) (SUDs), particularly opioid use disorder (OUD). (Jones, Underwood, & Compton, 2020; Kolodny, 2006; McKetin et al., 2019; Mullen, Richards, & Crawford, 2020; Pagliaro & Pagliaro, 2018; Salo, Flower, & Kielstein, 2011)

As reported by the CDC (Jones et al., 2020, p. 317):

> Co-occurring substance use and mental illness were common among those [adults] who used methamphetamine within the past year.

Although various prescription antidepressants have been used in an attempt to simultaneously treat both the MDD and the methamphetamine use disorder, these attempts have been largely unsuccessful. For example, as found by Hellem, Lundberg, and Renshaw (2015, p. 1) in their detailed integrative review of related studies:

> Psychological approaches and [the] combination of psychological with pharmacological approaches have not been shown to be effective in treating these co-occurring conditions [i.e., MDD and methamphetamine use disorder].

We now turn to "Cocaine."

COCAINE

Widely available across the U.S. for the last 60 years, cocaine—"Blow," "C," "Coke," "Crack," "Rock," or "Snow"—is commonly used by older adults for such desired psychostim-

60. See also the related overview and discussion in Chapter 1, Alcohol—"Common Contemporaneous Diagnoses Among Older Adults."

ulant effects as euphoria and heightened sexual experiences. For a significant number of older adults who use cocaine, the cocaine "high" can become the only, or at least primary, reason for living (e.g., cocaine use is preferred to personal likes, desires, or needs, family, food, friends, recreation, or future retirement goals—including lifelong plans, such as going on a world cruise or traveling extensively "to see the grandkids"). This pattern of cocaine use results in significant adverse social consequences for these older adults and their families and friends.

In the second major section of Chapter 2, we begin with the botany of cocaine, followed by its pharmacology, cocaine overdosage, and physical and psychological dependence. We then present and discuss new millennial trends in older adult cocaine use in the U.S. during the first two decades of the new millennium and involvement in illicit drug dealing and trafficking. The cocaine section concludes with an overview of the assessment, diagnosis, and treatment of older adult cocaine dependence or use disorder, and contemporaneous diagnoses that are commonly detected among older adults who use cocaine.

Botany

Cocaine[61] (benzoylmethylecgonine) is a natural liquid alkaloid that is extracted from the leaves of two cultivated species of the coca plant—from the family Erythroxylaceae—that are indigenous to South America: (1) *Erythroxylum coca*; and (2) *Erythroxylum novogranatense*. Each if these species are discussed in the following two subsections.

Erythroxylum Coca

Erythroxylum coca has two varieties:

1. *Coca variety* (i.e., Bolivian or Huánuco coca), which is found primarily in the moist, tropical mountainous forest regions of the eastern Andes with cultivation extending from Ecuador south to Bolivia. It is a large shrub, typically three to nine feet in height, and grows primarily at elevations between 1,500 and 4,500 feet.
2. *Ipadu variety* (i.e., Amazonian coca), which is found primarily in the lowland Amazon Basin regions of Brazil, Colombia, and Peru, where it has been cultivated for many centuries.

Erythroxylum Novogranatense

Erythroxylum novogranatense also has two varieties:

1. *Novogranatense variety* (i.e., Colombian coca), which is primarily found in the drier regions throughout Colombia. An adaptable plant, it is also grown in both high- and low-land areas. In comparison to *E. coca*, *E. novogranatense* has several distinct differences, including, for example, that *E. novogranatense*: (1) grows well in arid regions in which *E. coca* generally would not survive; and (2) leaves also contain methyl salicylate, whereas *E. coca* leaves do not.

61. The name, cocaine, was derived from the plant's name, "coca," and the alkaloid suffix, "ine."

2. *Truxillense* variety (i.e., Trujillo coca) is a drought-resistant shrub, that is tall and bushy and grown primarily in Columbia and Peru. (DEA, 1991; Pagliaro & Pagliaro, 2004; Plowman, 1985)

Coca plants have been cultivated in South America since the pre-Columbian era. During the 20th and 21st centuries, coca leaves were, and continue to be, the major cash crop for the South American countries of Argentina, Bolivia, Colombia, Ecuador, and Peru. The green leaves ("matu") are harvested by hand and are initially spread in thin layers to dry in the sun. The dried leaves are then packed into burlap sacks, which are kept dry, until ready for sale and transport. The Native Indigenous Peoples of South America traditionally chew the cocaine leaves, much like tobacco is chewed, or grind the leaves into a powder to make tea. Coca tea, or "mate de coca," is also made by brewing raw or dried leaves much like other herbal teas. Mate de coca also is made with commercially available mate de coca teabags. Drug traffickers typically purchase the sacks of dried cocaine leaves and then chemically extract the cocaine alkaloid utilizing a variety of organic solvents—a process that typically occurs in unsophisticated "jungle laboratories" (Pagliaro & Pagliaro, 2004).

Leaves from coca plants typically contain, by weight, about 1% cocaine. However, reported concentrations have ranged from 0.25% to 1.5%. Other natural alkaloids found in these leaves include benzoylecgonine and ecgonine. Concentrations are primarily dependent on the: (1) species and variety of the coca plant; (2) region of cultivation; and (3) growing conditions. The presence of cocaine in coca leaves purportedly serves as a natural insecticide for the plant (Lewis, 1994; Nathanson, Hunnicutt, & Kantham, 1993).

Pharmacology

Cocaine is generally produced for illicit distribution and sale in two forms: (1) cocaine hydrochloride (HCl), a white powder; and (2) "crack cocaine," small white or light tan to brownish "rocks." Each of these forms has its own distinct pharmacologic characteristics and patterns of use. The pharmacology of both of these forms of cocaine—pharmacodynamics; pharmacokinetics; undesired, or harmful, effects and toxicities; drug-drug interactions; and overdosage—is presented and discussed.

Cocaine Hydrochloride

Cocaine hydrochloride, the salt form of cocaine, is a white crystalline powder that is highly water soluble (i.e., 1 gram in 0.5 ml). This high solubility of the cocaine powder in water allows it to be readily dissolved for IV injection. It also allows it to be rapidly absorbed from the moist mucous membranes that line the oral,[62] nasal, rectal, and vaginal cavities. For these reasons, cocaine hydrochloride is commonly intranasally "snorted" or inserted rectally or vaginally.

62. Cocaine hydrochloride, because of its high-water solubility, also is used for selected medical and dental purposes, such as local anesthesia of the membranes of the oral, laryngeal, and nasal cavities. In illicit drug deals, it also is commonly rubbed on the gums, numbing them—thus, serving as "proof" that the product actually is cocaine hydrochloride (although any "caine"-based local anesthetic would produce the same numbing effect).

Crack Cocaine

Crack Cocaine (i.e., cocaine base), is produced from the natural form of cocaine that is directly extracted from the coca leaves (see Figure 2.3). Only slightly soluble in water (i.e., 1 gram in 1,300 ml), crack cocaine readily dissolves in ethanol (i.e., 1 gram in 7 ml), ether (i.e., 1 gram in 4 ml), and chloroform (i.e., 1 gram in 0.5 ml).[63] The melting point of crack cocaine is significantly lower than that for cocaine hydrochloride (i.e., 98° Celsius versus 195° Celsius). Thus, when heated, crack cocaine, as compared to cocaine hydrochloride, vaporizes much more readily and, consequently, is involved in less pyrolysis (i.e., heat-related chemical destruction).[64] Accordingly, pulmonary inhalation of the vaporized crack cocaine can achieve blood cocaine concentrations that are equal to those achieved by the IV injection of cocaine hydrochloride.

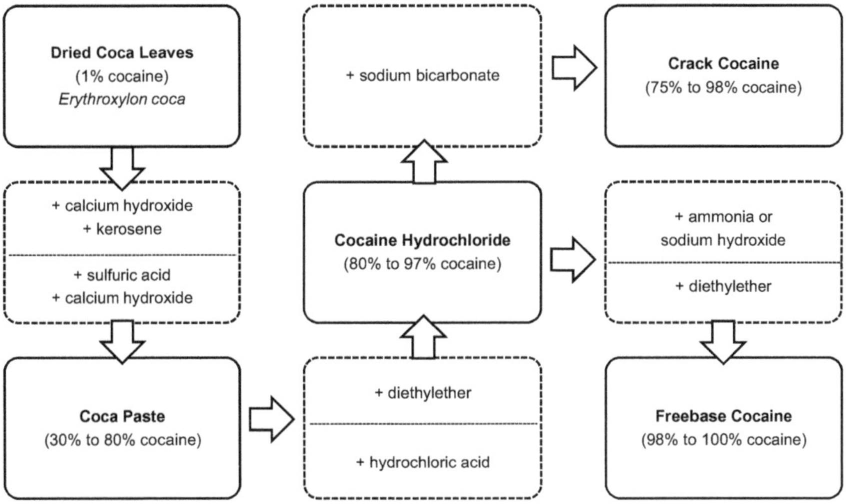

Figure 2.3 Production of Cocaine

Additionally—because of the mechanisms inherent in pulmonary absorption (i.e., extremely large surface area provided by approximately 500 million alveoli)—the onset of action for pulmonary inhalation is more rapid than that for IV injection. It also produces a more intense desired action—at least as subjectively reported by crack cocaine users (Pagliaro & Pagliaro, *Clinical Patient Data Files*). For these and other reasons (e.g., convenience, lower cost, avoidance of infections—such as HIV infection associated with IV injection), older adults generally prefer the pulmonary inhalation of vaporized crack cocaine to any other method of cocaine use.

63. Thus, the requisite use of organic solvents (e.g., acetone, gasoline, or kerosene) in South American "jungle" laboratories to extract the cocaine from harvested cocaine leaves.
64. The common street name, "Crack," originates from the "crackling" sound produced when "crack rocks" are heated and vaporized by holding a cigarette lighter under a crack pipe, a piece of aluminum foil, or the lid of a soft drink can upon which a piece of crack cocaine (a "rock") has been placed.

Pharmacodynamics: Mechanism of Action

Cocaine appears to produce its psychostimulant effects primarily within the mesolimbic dopamine system—the major "reward" pathway in the CNS (NIDA, 2016).[65] After absorption into the systemic circulation, cocaine can be found in virtually all areas of the brain. However, it appears to preferentially accumulate in the: (1) caudate nucleus of the basal ganglia; (2) nucleus accumbens in the forebrain; and (3) ventral tegmental area in the midbrain.

Cocaine decreases the dopamine transporter (DAT) clearance of dopamine from the synaptic cleft by blocking its reuptake into the presynaptic cells. It also appears to block the reuptake of other monoamines, including serotonin and norepinephrine. Consequently, cocaine increases the accumulation and activity of neurotransmitters in the synaptic cleft. A simplified representation of the proposed principal site and mechanism of the psychostimulant action of cocaine is shown in Figure 2.4.

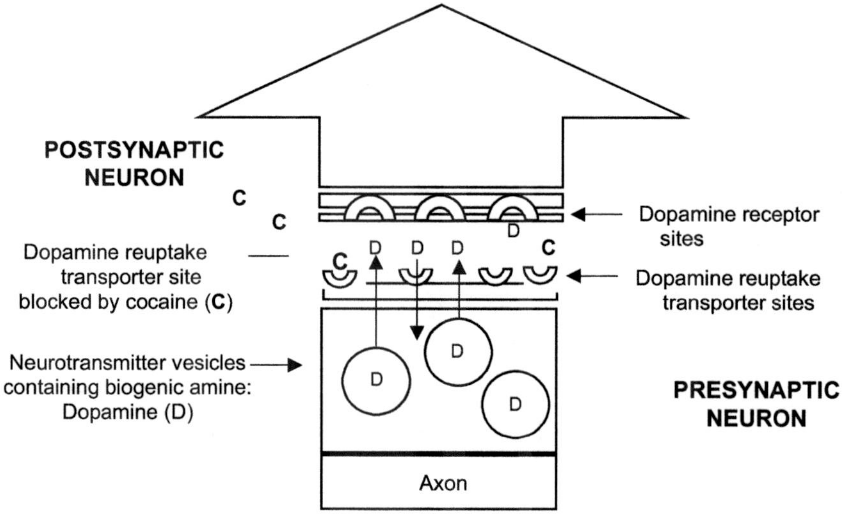

Figure 2.4 Cocaine: Mechanism of Psychostimulant Action

> Old Misbelief: Acting at different brain centers, the actions of crack cocaine are much stronger than those of cocaine hydrochloride.

False. In fact, once absorbed into the systemic circulation, both crack cocaine and cocaine hydrochloride share exactly the same mechanism of action and, at equivalent dosages, produce exactly the same effects. As reported by Grabus (2017), NIH-funded research has demonstrated that in addition to increasing dopamine concentration in the synaptic cleft by blocking the dopamine transporter, cocaine stimulates the production of the endocannabinoid molecule, 2-arachidonoylglycerol (2-AG). In turn, 2-AG is reportedly associated with

65. N.B. The local anesthetic action of cocaine is produced by reversibly binding to and inactivating sodium channels. Consequently, sodium dependent depolarization and related propagation of impulses along the course of the nerve are impeded. Cocaine is the only local anesthetic that also possesses vasoconstrictive properties (Pagliaro & Pagliaro, 1986, 2004).

a significant increase in dopamine concentration within the nucleus accumbens (see related discussion in Chapter 4, *Cannabis*).

The ability of cocaine to increase neurotransmitter activity in the brain causes several desired effects that contribute to its continued use. These effects, include:

1. Diminished feelings of fatigue and hunger;
2. Feelings of increased energy and competence;
3. Heightened sociability and sexual desire;
4. Increased mental alertness;
5. Indifference to pain and discomfort;
6. Intense euphoria/happiness. (NIDA, 2018; Pagliaro & Pagliaro, 1999, 2004)

Over thirty years ago, Dackis and Gold (1990) identified that, during cocaine use episodes, the CNS actions of cocaine and associated effects could be divided into three phases: Phase 1: "Mild Stimulation;" Phase 2: "Excitation;" and Phase 3: "Depression."

Phase 1

During "Phase 1," cocaine stimulates the CNS, beginning with the cerebral cortex, by decreasing the re-uptake of neurotransmitters (e.g., dopamine and serotonin). These actions can generally result in agitation, bruxism, emotional lability, euphoria, excitation, headache, nausea, pseudohallucinations (e.g., of cocaine bugs), tics, tremor, and vertigo. As the amount of cocaine is increased, for example, by continued inhalation of vaporized crack cocaine, IV injection of dissolved cocaine hydrochloride, or nasal insufflation of more lines of cocaine powder, "Phase 2"—the excitation phase—begins.

Phase 2

During Phase 2, CNS stimulation becomes more pronounced with various associated effects (e.g., dyspnea, hypertension, hyperthermia, pressured speech, seizures, tachycardia, tachypnea, and vomiting). However, as cocaine use continues, the endogenous neurotransmitters in the CNS (i.e., dopamine and serotonin) become depleted and "Phase 3"—the depression phase—begins.

Phase 3

Phase 3 is characterized by a depression of the cortical areas of the CNS, which may progress to medullary depression and associated respiratory failure. Associated signs and symptoms may include areflexia, cardiac arrest, circulatory failure, coma, cyanosis, flaccid paralysis, and respiratory failure. Medical intervention is directed at providing life support and maintaining major organ functioning—according to the individual signs and symptoms noted and the associated severity. For example, hyperthermia can be treated by an ice bath or convection cooling. Rhabdomyolysis, if it occurs, should be managed preferably in an intensive care unit with the infusion of IV fluids, correction of electrolyte abnormalities, and close monitoring of hourly urine output and pH.[66]

66. We recommend that moderate to severe cases of acute rhabdomyolysis, which is associated with cocaine use, be treated, at least initially, in the ICU because of the significant potential for death related to the

This phase spontaneously resolves, but not until after the depleted endogenous neurotransmitters have had sufficient time to be naturally replenished.[67] The associated mental depression experienced during this phase is commonly referred to as the "cocaine blues" (Pagliaro & Pagliaro, 2009). (Also see the later cocaine pharmacology subsection, "Physical and Psychological Dependence.")

Pharmacokinetics: Absorption, Distribution, Metabolism, and Excretion

The absorption, distribution, metabolism, and excretion of cocaine is affected by its: (1) formulation—cocaine hydrochloride versus crack cocaine; (2) purity; and (3) method of use, or route of administration (see Table 2.7).

Absorption

Peak serum cocaine concentrations occur approximately: 45 minutes after ingestion, 10 minutes after intranasal insufflation (i.e., "snorting"), and one to two minutes after IV injection (i.e., "mainlining") and pulmonary inhalation (e.g., inhaling vapors from a crack pipe, piece of aluminum foil, or the surface of a soft drink can) (Fattinger, Benowitz, & Jones, 2000; Pagliaro & Pagliaro, 2004).[68]

Because cocaine is a weak base with a pKa of 8.6, it is poorly absorbed from the stomach, but relatively well-absorbed from the small intestine. Consequently, after oral ingestion the mean bioavailability of cocaine hydrochloride is low, approximately only 33% (Coe, Jufer Phipps, & Cone, 2018). Thus, older adults rarely use this method of administration. Likewise, following intranasal insufflation, or "snorting," the bioavailability of cocaine is reduced, approximately 50% to 60%, because the rate of intranasal absorption is constrained by: (1) the limited surface area of the nasal mucosa; and (2) local nasal vasoconstriction due to the actions of cocaine.[69]

In comparison, when crack cocaine is vaporized and inhaled into the lungs, pulmonary bioavailability is high (i.e., over 90%). However, the use of a glass crack pipe[70] may affect overall bioavailability because: (1) a small portion of the dose can be destroyed by

---

associated occurrence of acute renal failure, disseminated intravascular coagulation, and severe hepatic impairment (Pagliaro & Pagliaro, *Clinical Patient Data Files*).

67. Because of this mechanism, cocaine withdrawal cannot be effectively treated or "self- managed" by simply administering additional cocaine. Consequently, the use of cocaine does not meet the classic criteria for physical dependence. See the related discussion in the later cocaine pharmacology subsection, "Physical and Psychological Dependence."
68. Interestingly, and contrary to the passive "side-stream" exposure to nicotine that has been associated with e-cigarette vapor (e.g., Czogala, Goniewicz, & Fidelus, 2014), passive "side-stream" exposure to freebase cocaine vapors does not generally result in the absorption of clinically significant amounts of cocaine (Cone, Yousefnejad, & Hillsgrove, 1995). (See Chapter 3, *Caffeine and Nicotine*.)
69. N.B. With IV injection, the bioavailability of cocaine hydrochloride is 100%.
70. A crack cocaine pipe, which is also known as a "pizzie," typically utilizes a fine mesh screen (e.g., brass gauze mesh) to hold the crack cocaine rock so that it can be heated, vaporized, and inhaled through the opposite end of the pipe to which a mouthpiece has been attached. Crack pipes are not durable (i.e., develop cracks or chips) and, consequently, must be frequently replaced. The simplest form of a crack pipe, commonly known as a "stem," is generally comprised of a small tube of glass, two to four inches long, with the diameter of a ballpoint pen. Some "upscale" glass pipes or stems are commercially manufactured from Pyrex® or tempered glass in order to increase durability.

Table 2.7 Cocaine Pharmacokinetics

COCAINE PHARMACOKINETICS	
Absorption	
• Bioavailability	33% oral 70% intranasal ≥ 90% pulmonary 100% intravenous
• Time to peak blood concentration	~ 45 minutes, oral ~ 10 minutes, intranasal 1 minute, intravenous or pulmonary
Distribution	
• Volume of distribution	~ 3 L/kg
• Plasma protein binding	Moderate (~90%)
Metabolism	
(Hydrolysis and metabolism primarily occur in the liver by CYP3A4[71])	
• Total body clearance	~ 1 L/minute
• Mean half-life of elimination	1.25 hours
Excretion	
• Urinary excretion	~ 1% to 5% in unchanged form. Influenced by urinary pH with slower excretion with alkaline urine and more rapid excretion with acidic urine.

Sources: Laizure, Mandrell, & Gades, 2003; Pagliaro & Benet, 1975; Pagliaro & Pagliaro, 2009.

pyrolysis;[72] and (2) a relatively larger portion of the dose often remains adhered to the inner surfaces of the crack pipe.[73] Interestingly, as first experimentally demonstrated by Cone (1995, p. 459):

> Cocaine [i.e., crack cocaine] administered by the smoked route produced substantially higher behavioral responses [e.g., "good effects;" "high;" "liking"] than an equivalent dose of cocaine administered by the intravenous route.

71. Carboxylesterases, present in several tissues, including the liver, catalyze the hydrolysis of cocaine to its two major metabolites: (1) benzoylecgonine; and (2) ecgonine methyl ester.
72. The major product of the pyrolysis of crack cocaine is "methylecgonidine." The amount of methylecgonidine that is produced generally ranges from 1% to 5%, depending upon the temperature and the rate of air flow in the crack pipe. The presence of methylecgonidine (i.e., anhydroecgonine methyl ester) has been used as a biological marker to differentiate (e.g., in forensic biological samples) crack cocaine smoking from other methods of cocaine use.
73. This build-up of cocaine within the pipe is referred to as "residual" or "push" and can be "harvested" by cleaning (i.e., pushing the gauze filter through the glass pipe stem with the use of a "push stick") and heating the gauze (Pagliaro & Pagliaro, *Clinical Patient Data Files*).

Distribution

Following absorption, cocaine is widely distributed throughout the body. It readily crosses biological membranes and is found in virtually all areas of the CNS. Cocaine is moderately bound (i.e., 70% to 90%) to serum proteins, particularly alpha-1-acid glycoprotein and albumin. The volume of distribution is ~ 1.5–3 L/kg (Chow, Ambre, & Rue, 1985; Coe et al., 2018; Edwards & Bowles, 1988; Heard, Palmer, & Zahniser, 2008; Pagliaro & Pagliaro, 2004).

Metabolism

Cocaine (i.e., benzoylmethylecgonine) is hydrolyzed and metabolized primarily in the liver by CYP3A4 to several metabolites, including benzoylecgonine, ecgonine, ecgonine methyl ester, hydroxycocaine, hydroxybenzoylecgonine, and norcocaine.[74] Esterases found in the plasma are predominately responsible for the formation of the major metabolite, benzoylecgonine. Esterases also are found in many other body tissues, including the brain, liver, lungs, and pancreas. When ingested, cocaine undergoes significant (i.e., ~ 50%) dose-limited (i.e., saturable) first-pass hepatic metabolism. Total body clearance is ~ 2 L/minute. The mean half-life of elimination for cocaine is ~ 1.25 hours (Pagliaro & Benet, 1975; Pagliaro & Pagliaro, 2004).

Excretion

Generally, approximately 1% to 5% of the cocaine that is absorbed into the systemic circulation is excreted, in unchanged form, in the urine. The urinary elimination of cocaine is influenced by urinary pH (as observed with the amphetamines—see earlier related discussion in the Amphetamine section of this chapter). Consequently, cocaine elimination is increased in acidic urine (i.e., pH below 7) and decreased in alkaline urine (i.e., pH above 7). In addition, the total body clearance of cocaine may be significantly reduced with the concurrent use of alcohol (see also the related discussion of cocaethylene in the later subsection, "Cocaine Drug-Drug Interactions").

> Old Misbelief: The half-life of elimination of crack cocaine is significantly shorter than that of cocaine hydrochloride.

False. In fact, the half-life of elimination of cocaine is exactly the same regardless of the form of cocaine that is used or its route of administration.

Drug-Drug Interactions

A metabolic interaction exclusively involving the concomitant use of cocaine and alcohol may result in approximately 23% of the systemically available cocaine being converted to "cocaethylene," a psychoactive ethyl homologue of cocaine (Harris, Everhart, &

74. In the presence of alcohol in the blood stream, cocaine is also hepatically metabolized to cocaethylene (i.e., ethylbenzoylecgonine) (Andrews, 1997).

Table 2.8 Cocaine: Major Potential Drug-Drug Interactions[75, 76]

DRUGS THAT INTERACT WITH COCAINE	COMMENTS
CYP3A4 Inhibitors (e.g., clarithromycin, erythromycin, ketoconazole, and nefazodone)	CYP3A4 inhibitors, when used with cocaine, may increase risk for, or severity of, cocaine toxicity.
Monoamine Oxidase Inhibitors (MAOIs) (e.g., phenelzine [Nardil®] and tranylcypromine [Parnate®])	MAOIs, when used with cocaine, increase the possibility of a hypertensive crisis (noradrenergic syndrome).
Psychodepressants (e.g., opiate analgesics and sedative-hypnotics)	Psychodepressants, when used with cocaine, ameliorate the psychostimulant effects of cocaine.
Psychostimulants (e.g., caffeine, cocaine, and nicotine)	Psychostimulants, when used with cocaine, cause additive psychostimulant effects.

Mendelson, 2003; Herbst, Harris, & Everhart, 2011). Older adults who concomitantly use alcohol and cocaine, often share that their use of alcohol and cocaine appears to: (1) enhance, or prolong, the euphoria they experience with cocaine alone; and (2) mitigate the undesired effects associated with the use of alcohol (e.g., sedation) (Pagliaro & Pagliaro, *Clinical Patient Data Files*). These effects may be explained, at least in part, by the formation of cocaethylene.

Several other drugs—including other abusable psychotropics—have been involved in clinically significant cocaine drug-drug interactions. These major related drug-drug interactions are presented and briefly discussed in Table 2.8.

Undesired, or Harmful, Effects and Toxicities

> Cocaine use is associated with multiple medical consequences in older individuals, including higher rates of hypertension, pulmonary issues, myocardial infarctions or spasms, cerebrovascular accidents, and cognitive impairment.
>
> (Yarnell, 2015, p. 1)

The use of cocaine has been commonly associated with several "acute" toxicities that are directly related to its specific pharmacologic actions on various body systems. The regular, long-term use of cocaine also has been implicated with the development of "chronic" toxicities, including physical and psychological dependence or use disorder. Other toxicities have been specifically related to its adulteration and methods of use—intranasal "snorting," pulmonary inhalation of the vaporized form, and IV injection (i.e., "mainlining" or "shooting-up"). These common toxicities are presented and discussed in the following subsections.

75. The clinical significance of these drug-drug interactions depends upon several factors, including the: (1) dosage of each drug; (2) characteristics of the older adult (e.g., age, genetics, and sex); (3) concomitant physical health (e.g., hepatic and renal function); and (4) concomitant mental health status.
76. Topical drug interactions for cocaine are not included.

Acute Toxicities

The use of cocaine has been associated with several acute toxicities, which are primarily related to its psychostimulant action, including:

- Agitation;
- Angina;
- Anorexia;
- Anxiety;
- Apathy;
- Cerebral vascular accident;
- Difficulty concentrating;
- Dizziness;
- Hallucinations;
- Headache;
- Hyperpnea;
- Hypersensitivity to sight, sound, and touch;
- Hyperthermia;
- Hypertension;
- Insomnia;
- Irritability;
- Loss of sexual desire;
- Memory impairment;
- Muscle twitching/tics;
- Mydriasis and associated sensitivity to light;
- Myocardial infarction;
- Nausea;
- Panic attacks;
- Premature ventricular contractions;
- Pressured speech;
- Restlessness;
- Rhabdomyolysis;
- Seizures;
- Suicide attempts;
- Tachycardia;
- Tachypnea;
- Tremors;
- Violent behavior;
- Vomiting;
- Xerostomia.

The acute toxicities of cocaine, which are directly related to its pharmacologic actions, primarily depend upon the dosage used (i.e., the larger the dosage, the larger the associated effect—in this context, toxicity).[77] However, because cocaine is predominantly used in an illicit context and, consequently, predominantly illicitly produced without stringent quality control standards (i.e., as used with pharmaceutical-grade cocaine), the dose used depends upon the purity of the cocaine. Studying the apparent correlation between cocaine purity and trends in emergency department (ED) visits (i.e., as a measure of toxicity), Zhu, Wilson, and Stimpson (2014, p. 1015) found that:

> Cocaine purity is positively correlated with cocaine-related ED visits, and our findings suggest decreases in powder cocaine purity were associated with significant declines in ED visits.[78]

Chronic Toxicities

Regular, long-term use of cocaine has been associated with the development of additional toxicities, including decreased libido, male impotence, mental depression, paranoia, psychological dependence, severe chest pain, and severe respiratory distress (e.g., Pagliaro & Pagliaro, *Clinical Patient Data Files*; Pagliaro, Jaglalsingh, & Pagliaro, 1992). Increasing attention also is being given to data that suggest an association between regular, long-term use of cocaine with cognitive impairment—particularly, deficits in executive, or high-level, cognitive function that involves decision-making and problem-solving abilities (Bickel, Franck, & Moody, 2013; Moody, Franck, & Jarmolowicz, 2014). Cocaine psychosis and intimate partner violence (IPV) are two other troubling undesired, or harmful, effects that are commonly associated with cocaine abuse (see the following subsections for further discussion).

Cocaine Psychosis Cocaine psychosis is virtually indistinguishable from amphetamine psychosis, although it is usually of shorter duration (see the related discussion in the major "Amphetamines" section of this chapter). Cocaine psychosis also shares, together with amphetamine psychosis, a similarity to paranoid schizophrenia. Both cocaine psychosis and amphetamine psychosis are often characterized by hypervigilance and paranoia and have been associated with an increased incidence of violent behavior, including homicide (Pagliaro & Pagliaro, *Clinical Patient Data Files*).

Intimate Partner Violence (IPV) In a retrospective analysis of data from 96 related studies, Moore, Stuart, and Meehan (2008) found that, of all the abusable psychotropics, cocaine had the strongest relationship with IPV. Although associated factors (e.g., personality traits, concurrent mental disorders, and concomitant use of alcohol or other abusable psychotropics) are likely major contributing factors (Pagliaro & Pagliaro, *Clinical Patient Data Files*), IPV has been consistently found to be strongly associated with cocaine use (e.g., Ernst, Weiss, & Enright-Smith, 2008; Gilchrist, Dennis, & Radcliffe, 2019; Smith, Homish, & Leonard, 2012; Stuart, Moore, & Elkins, 2013; Winhusen & Lewis, 2013).

77. The health status of the user, age, and concomitant use of other abusable psychotropics, both illicit and licit, also can significantly affect the nature, extent, and consequential impact of acute cocaine toxicity.
78. The researchers' findings were based on, or supported by, available data that indicated that the average purity for cocaine powder in the greater Chicago area/market, fell from 65.2% in 2004 to 37% in 2010 (Zhu et al., 2014, p. 1013).

Potentially Fatal Toxicities

Cocaine use has been directly related to four potentially fatal toxicities that can occur regardless of the method of use:

1. Cardiotoxicity;
2. Cerebrovascular accidents (CVA);
3. Hyperthermia;
4. Seizures.

It also has been indirectly associated with potentially fatal toxicities related to the: (1) inadvertent contamination, or deliberate adulteration, of street supplies of cocaine prior to their distribution, sale, and use; and (2) cocaine drug-drug interactions involving concomitant use of other drugs, particularly alcohol and heroin (Bernstein, Bucciarelli, & Piper, 2007; Pagliaro & Pagliaro, 2009). (See the earlier subsection, "Cocaine Drug-Drug Interactions" and the later subsection, "Adulterants.") We begin with cardiotoxicity.

Cardiotoxicity The actions of cocaine on the cardiovascular system have been associated with both increases in heart rate and blood pressure. In addition, Diercks, Kirk, and Turnipseed (2007) reported a significantly high rate of coronary artery disease (CAD) among cocaine-using patients. These actions, in turn, may lead to increased risk for dysrhythmias, end-stage renal disease, myocardial infarction (MI), and CVA, or stroke (e.g., Kim & Park, 2019; Norris, Thornhill-Joynes, & Robinson, 2001; Phillips, Luk, & Soor, 2009; Pilgrim, Woodford, & Drummer, 2013; Schwartz, Rezkalla, & Kloner, 2010).

> Recently, a 75-year-old man was admitted with an acute ST elevation MI secondary to smoking crack cocaine.
>
> (Chait, Fahmy, & Caceres, 2010, p. 1)

These severe, and potentially fatal, cardiotoxicities (Phillips et al., 2009) appear to occur, in part, because of the decrease in blood pH that is associated with cocaine use. The acidemia has been reported to cause scarring and disruption of the cardiac electrical conduction system with prolongation of the QRS complex and QTc (i.e., corrected QT interval) duration on the electrocardiogram (Wang, 1999). However, others have suggested molecular mechanisms of action for the cardiovascular effects associated with cocaine use, including: (1) interaction with cardiac calcium, potassium, and sodium (i.e., cation) channels (Turillazzi, Bello, & Neri, 2012); and (2) oxidative stress and resultant antioxidant cellular system injuries (Cerretani, Fineschi, & Bello, 2012).

***Related Professional Reminder:* Different purported mechanisms of cocaine-induced cardiotoxicity are not mutually exclusive.**

***Related Professional Reminder:* When evaluating, or caring for, older adults who are sudden cardiac arrest survivors, always inquire about their illicit use of abusable psychotropics, particularly the psychostimulants—amphetamines and cocaine—and, if necessary, recommend appropriate follow-up care regarding identified dependence or use disorder(s) prior to discharge.**

Cerebrovascular Accidents (CVAs) CNS hemorrhage, or stroke, results from the combined effects of the vasoconstriction and increased cardiac output (i.e., expected pharmacological effects) associated with cocaine use (Sordo, Iciar Indave, & Barrio, 2014). As noted by Martin-Schild, Albright, and Hallevi (2010, p. 680):

> Recent cocaine ingestion is associated with hemorrhages that occur more frequently in subcortical locations, have a higher risk of intraventricular hemorrhage, and have a poor prognosis compared to patients with cocaine-negative, spontaneous ICH [intracerebral hemorrhage].

Additionally, ischemic stroke—since the early 1970s—has long been documented in the context of cocaine use. More recently, histological findings support vasospasm, either of large cranial arteries or within the cortical microvasculature, as the principal mechanism for cocaine-induced ischemic stroke (Johnson, Devous, & Ruiz, 2001; Rice-Mesa, Rice-Mesa, & Berrouet, 2017; Treadwell & Robinson, 2007).

The risk for CVAs associated with cocaine use, although generally considered to be low (e.g., Merenda, Muir, & Koch, 2016), reportedly increases with age, irrespective of the previous length of time that cocaine was used.[79] Cerebrovascular accidents also occur more often among older adults who have cerebral aneurysms. Although it is estimated that approximately one in 20 people have a cerebral aneurysm (e.g., Rinkel, Djibuti, & Algra, 1998), most older adults who use cocaine are personally unaware of this risk.

Hyperthermia Cocaine-induced hyperthermia—a body temperature exceeding 104° Fahrenheit (41° Celsius)—is usually caused by the combined effects of: (1) excessively stimulated body metabolism; and (2) vasoconstriction, which significantly impairs the ability of the body to cool itself (i.e., thermoregulation) (Barkley Burnett, 2018b; Callaway & Clark, 1994).[80] A body temperature of this magnitude can cause renal failure, seizures, and coma, and may be fatal in up to 20% of cases—more, if left untreated. In non-fatal cases, irreversible brain damage may occur. Hyperpyrexia also is an associated sign that is observed in both: (1) cocaine-induced fatal excited (agitated) delirium; and (2) cocaine-induced rhabdomyolysis (Bauwens, Boggs, & Hartwell, 1989; Crandall et al., 2002; Madera, Cabrejas, & Holguin, 2016).

Seizures Cocaine seizures, colloquially referred to as "doing the chicken," are commonly experienced (Pagliaro & Pagliaro, *Clinical Patient Data Files*). "The DEA also has noted a bump in cocaine seizures" (Leonard, 2017, p. 1). The isolated, tonic-clonic seizures, which are associated with cocaine use, usually resolve quickly on their own and, generally, do not require professional intervention. If the seizures do not completely resolve within a couple of minutes, or if there is an indication of neurological impairment, then a formal clinical work-up, evaluation, and possible treatment (e.g., diazepam) are indicated (Chen, Albertson, & Olson, 2015; Majlesi, Shih, & Fiesseler, 2010).

Status epilepticus, associated with cocaine use, occurs relatively infrequently and may terminate in cardiovascular collapse. Several actions of cocaine have been linked with the

---

79. In a large retrospective analysis of patients admitted to a stroke service from 2004 to 2007, Martin-Schild et al. (2010, p. 680) found that:

> Patients with cocaine-associated intracerebral hemorrhage were nearly three times more likely to die during their acute hospitalization when compared to cocaine-negative patients.

Similarly, Chang, Kowalski, and Caserta (2013) found that among hospitalized patients with aneurysmal subarachnoid hemorrhage, cocaine users are three times more likely to die than are nonusers.

80. Impaired heat dissipation (i.e., cocaine-induced impairment of both sweating and cutaneous vasodilation) is believed to be the primary mechanism underlying the development of cocaine-induced hyperthermia (Crandall, Vongpatanasin, & Victor, 2002).

occurrence of status epilepticus, including: (1) anoxia; (2) heightened psychostimulation; and (3) hyperthermia.

On a molecular level, it has been proposed that the seizures associated with cocaine use are mediated by the enhancement of monoamine—particularly, dopamine and serotonin—activity (Lason, 2001). This cocaine-induced seizure activity appears to be modulated by the stimulation of dopamine D_1 receptors and the inhibition of gamma-aminobutyric acid ($GABA_A$) receptors. Rolland, Karila, and Geoffroy (2011) extended this hypothesis by suggesting that the activation of the D_1 receptor produces a neurological kindling process involving the NMDA receptor phosphorylation state.

Adulterants

Due to the lack of stringent quality control that is normally associated with good manufacturing practices (GMP),[81] the potential risk for unique and unexpected toxicities can occur whenever an illicitly manufactured abusable psychotropic is prepared, sold, bought, or used (Pagliaro & Pagliaro, *Clinical Patient Data Files*). Adulterants (e.g., arsenic, benzocaine [and other related local anesthetics, such as lidocaine, procaine, and tetracaine], boric acid, caffeine, corn starch, lactose, mannitol, quinine, sodium bicarbonate, strychnine, and talc) are often purposely used by illicit drug dealers to "cut" various abusable psychotropics, including cocaine, prior to their sale—most often to increase their bulk/volume and, consequently, to increase dealer profits. Several unique toxicities, which can be even more serious than those directly associated with the particular abusable psychotropic that is adulterated, have been associated with the use of many of these adulterants—including those used to adulterate cocaine. (See also, for example, the related discussions in Chapter 5, *Prescription Opiate Analgesics and Heroin.*)

For example, during 2008–2009, a specific adulterant, "levamisole" (Ergamisol®),[82] was found in approximately two-thirds of all of the cocaine samples that were seized and analyzed by the U.S. government (Kudlacek, Hofmaier, & Luf, 2017; Pagliaro & Pagliaro, 2009). Added to illicit cocaine to boost its effects or to increase its weight and, consequently, the related profits for the distributor/seller, it resulted in significant toxicity among users. For example, as reported by Lee, Ladizinski, and Federman (2012, p. 1033):

> Complications associated with the use of levamisole-laced cocaine include neutropenia, agranulocytosis, arthralgias, retiform purpura, and skin necrosis.

Toxicities Associated with Method of Use

Several toxicities have been commonly associated with four specific methods of cocaine use:

1. Intranasal insufflation, or "snorting;"
2. IV injection, or "mainlining;"

---

81. These practices present a set of principles and procedures that guide licit pharmaceutical production in the U.S. in order to help ensure quality control.
82. Levamisole (Ergamisol®), a veterinary anthelminthic, which also has psychostimulant action, was experimentally used for the treatment of some types of human cancers (Larocque & Hoffman, 2012). It was withdrawn from U.S. markets in 2005 because of reports of agranulocytosis (Buxton, Omura, & Kuo, 2015).

3. Pulmonary inhalation, or "vaping" (i.e., inhaling crack cocaine vapor);
4. Subcutaneous injection.

The toxicities associated with each of these methods of use are presented and discussed in the following subsections.

Intranasal Insufflation or "Snorting" Intranasal "snorting" of cocaine hydrochloride is associated with minor, local irritation to nasal mucosal membranes; eczema, in and around the nostrils; loss of smell, or anosmia; epistaxis; and rhinitis (Alexandrakis, Tse, & Rosa, 1999; Villa, 1999). Particularly, with regular, long-term intranasal use of cocaine, it is also associated with more serious effects, including nasal erosion and perforation of the nasal septum (Vilela, Langford, & McCullagh, 2002).

> Repeated snorting [of cocaine] sets up a cascade of ischemia, inflammation, micronecrosis, infection, and then macronecrosis leading to perforation. Nasal septum perforations of both the cartilaginous and bony tissues have been well documented. With larger defects, support of the nose is compromised resulting in the typical saddlenose deformity. Some patients have been known to use various narrow instruments to debride intranasal crusting, increasing the potential for perforations. In extreme cases, adjacent bony structures may become eroded and vital tissues damaged.
>
> (Villa, 1999, p. 220)

Several other documented effects associated with regular, long-term snorting of cocaine, include:[83]

- Cerebrospinal fluid leak through the ethmoid sinuses;
- Diplopia;
- Erosion of the cribriform plate, ethmoids, medial sinus walls, orbital walls, and turbinates;
- Ethmoid sinusitis;
- Halitosis;
- Loss of visual acuity;
- Nasolacrimal duct obstruction;
- Nasal crusting;
- Nasal hair loss;
- Nasal septal defect;
- Orbital cellulitis;
- Osteolytic sinusitis;
- Palatal perforation;
- Pneumomediastinum;
- Saddlenose deformity;
- Sinusitis.

83. Additionally, intranasal warts, commonly referred to as, "snorter warts" (Pagliaro & Pagliaro, *Clinical Patient Data Files*) are generally caused by human papillomavirus (HPV) transmitted by sharing drug paraphernalia (e.g., glass straws or rolled-up currency) with others, in order to facilitate intranasal cocaine use.

The minor irritation, as well as the more serious injuries to the nose, are caused by the:

1. Direct action of cocaine (i.e., vasoconstriction) on the surrounding skin and mucous membranes;
2. Direct irritation caused by the hydrochloride salt-form of cocaine, which, when it encounters nasal secretions, forms a dilute, but irritating, solution of hydrochloric acid.

The occurrence of these local effects, together with the relatively small surface area of the nasal mucosa—which effectively restricts absorption rates to begin with—have contributed to the increase in the popularity of pulmonary inhalation, or "smoking" cocaine in its freebase, or crack, form. This form of cocaine use is currently the most popular method of use in the U.S.[84] Unfortunately, "smoking" or "vaping" cocaine is associated with its own toxicities, particularly those associated with the pulmonary system. (See the later subsection—"Pulmonary Inhalation, or Vaping.")

Intravenous Injection, or "Mainlining"[85] The IV injection of cocaine solution has been related to the development of abscesses at injection sites, local skin and soft tissue infections, and phlebitis. Generally, these undesired, or harmful, effects occur when injected veins become irritated and inflamed as a response to being pierced with the syringe needle and injected with the irritating cocaine solution. The IV injection of cocaine also is associated with thrombosis development, which may be fatal.

For example, in their retrospective cohort analysis of hospitalizations in the state of Oregon from 2008 to 2018, Capizzi, Leahy, and Wheelock (2020, p. e0242165) found that:

1. During the study period, hospitalizations for injection drug use-related serious bacterial infection increased from 980 to 6,265 per year;
2. Hospitalizations for bacteremia/sepsis rose most rapidly with an 18-fold increase;
3. Hospitalizations for amphetamine-type stimulant-related serious bacterial infections rose most rapidly with a 15-fold increase.

---

84. Freebase and crack cocaine are essentially the same forms of cocaine—at least in terms of their purity and method of use. However, freebase is more difficult and dangerous to produce because of the need to "heat-off" a flammable solvent prior to its use (see Figure 2.3)—with the resultant risk of fire (Feaver, 1986; People Staff, 1980).
85. Although seldomly done, crack cocaine "rocks" can be made into a solution "suitable" for IV or subcutaneous (SC) injection by dissolving them in an organic acid (e.g., lemon juice, lime juice, or white vinegar). The process is generally encountered in a particular neighborhood or city, when the availability of powdered cocaine HCl is severely curtailed and, consequently, its price increases significantly (Albini, Sun, & Holz, 2007; Harris, Scott, & Wright, 2019; Lankenau, Clatts, & Goldsamt, 2004; Waninger, Gotsch, & Watts, 2007).

> When you're doing snowballs (heroin and crack) you have to have a bit more citric . . . like the white won't dissolve if you don't have enough citric in it.
>
> (Harris et al., 2019, p. 6)

Although at least one published case report in the clinical literature involved an older adult, in our clinical experience, the few individuals who use this method to dilute crack cocaine rocks for IV or SC injection, are most likely to: (1) be middle-aged men of European continental descent; (2) be homeless or residing in inner city neighborhoods; and (3) experience significantly more adverse effects related to this method of use (Pagliaro & Pagliaro, *Clinical Patient Data Files*).

It is important to note that these effects commonly occur with the IV use of any abusable psychotropic (see also the related discussion in the earlier amphetamines pharmacology subsection, Undesired, or Harmful, Effects and Toxicities—"Intravenous Toxicities"). It also is important to note that the IV injection of cocaine was a major contributing factor to the spread of the HIV infection during the late 1980s and through the 1990s (Pagliaro, Pagliaro, & Thauberger, 1990, 1993). Currently, IV drug use continues to be a major factor in the spread of HIV and hepatitis C infections (Loguidice, 2020). (See also the related discussion in Chapter 5, *Prescription Opiate Analgesics and Heroin.*)

Pulmonary Inhalation, or "Vaping" The toxicities associated with inhaling cocaine vapor result in both irritation and damage to the lungs, including pneumomediastinum, pneumonia, and pulmonary infiltrates. Acute exacerbation of asthma and bronchitis also may occur among older adults who already have chronic obstructive pulmonary diseases (Ali, Krugar, & Houghton, 2002; Gatof & Albert, 2002). In addition, the regular, long-term smoking of crack cocaine has been associated with alveolar and microvascular lung damage at the microscopic level—a condition that has been commonly referred to as "crack lung" (e.g., Bulbena-Cabre, Ramos Dunn, & Gorman Swift, 2015; Giacomi & Srivali, 2019; Shah, Patel, & Mousa, 2015).[86] Signs and symptoms associated with "crack lung," include diffuse alveolar infiltrates, fever, "ground glass" opacifications (revealed by enhanced CT), hemoptysis, hypoxemia, and respiratory failure (Giacomi & Srivali, 2019; Restrepo, Carrillo, & Martinez, 2007). Interestingly, Alvarez and van der Jagt (2008) present the case of a 65-year-old man in whom "crack lung" preceded the diagnosis of "crack heart."

Additionally, the smoking of crack cocaine has been associated with several harmful ocular effects and toxicities, including:

- Bilateral amblyopia (i.e., "lazy eye");
- Corneal anesthesia;
- Corneal ulceration (i.e., "crack cornea" or "crack eye syndrome");
- Glaucoma exacerbation;
- Keratitis;
- Mydriasis;
- Orbital disease;
- Retinal emboli;
- Retinal venous occlusion. (Colatrella & Daniel, 1999; Hoffman & Reimer, 1993; Peragallo, Blousse, & Newman, 2013; Pilon & Scheiffle, 2006; Sachs, Zagelbaum, & Hersh, 1993; Stuard, Gallerson, & Robertson, 2017)

Subcutaneous Injection "Coke burns" are associated with the repeated inadvertent subcutaneous (SC) injection of cocaine by intravenous cocaine users who "miss the vein." In much the same way as intranasal irritation and damage occurs with "snorting cocaine" (see the discussion in the earlier undesired or harmful effects and toxicities subsection, Toxicities Associated

86. We have posited that the prolonged contact of the alveolar tissue with the hot vaporized gases produced in association with this method of crack cocaine use is a major contributory factor to the noted toxicity (Pagliaro & Pagliaro, *Clinical Patient Data Files*). In this regard, a similar mechanism of action may contribute to the pulmonary toxicity associated with vaping (see Chapter 4, *Cannabis*).

with Method of Use—"Intranasal Insufflation or 'Snorting'"), coke burns are associated with the formation of dilute hydrochloric acid when the dissolved cocaine hydrochloride interacts with the subcutaneous body fluids (Pagliaro & Pagliaro, *Clinical Patient Data Files*).

Additionally, inadvertent SC administration of cocaine has reportedly resulted in various related, and "expected," complications at the injection site, including:

- Abscesses;
- Cellulitis;
- Edema;
- Lesions;
- Open wounds/sores;
- Pain;
- Scar tissue formation;
- Tenderness;
- Tissue necrosis;
- Viral infections (e.g., hepatitis C or HIV). (Harris et al., 2019; Hope, Parry, & Ncube, 2016; Pagliaro & Pagliaro, *Clinical Patient Data Files*; Raiker, Aouthmany, & Ezra, 2016)

Overdosage/Unintentional Poisoning

During the second decade of the new millennium, cocaine, after the opiate analgesics (see Chapter 5, *Prescription Opiate Analgesics and Heroin*), was involved in most of the overdosage deaths in the U.S. (Cano, Oh, & Salas-Wright, 2020; Pagliaro & Pagliaro, 2020).

A significant contributor to these deaths was the growing use of "speedballs"—the use of cocaine in combination with an opiate analgesic (e.g., fentanyl, heroin, or morphine).[87] For example, as noted by Leonard (2017, p. 1):

> An examination of CDC data shows that 6,784 people died of a cocaine-involved overdose in 2015. Of these 2,565 also had heroin as a contributing cause of death and 1,077 had a prescription pain reliever. In 1,542 cases, fentanyl contributed to the cause of death, and some of these drugs overlapped, meaning that about 63 percent of cases involved an opioid.

In 2017, the CDC reported 14,556 overdosage deaths in the U.S. related to cocaine use (NIH, 2018, p. 1). This was the highest reported number of cocaine overdosage deaths at any time during the preceding years of the new millennium. Additionally, utilizing data concerning cocaine use and overdosage available from both the *Multiple Cause of Death* database of the National Center for Health Statistics and the *National Survey on Drug Use and Health* (combined N of approximately 16,000 U.S. adults), Cano et al. (2020, p. 108148) found that:

> Cocaine-involved overdose mortality is disproportionately affecting individuals who are Black, older, or with lower educational attainment.

Cocaine overdosage may be fatal with death being generally a result of cardiac dysrhythmias, hyperthermia, intracranial hemorrhage, respiratory arrest, or status epilepticus

87. This pattern of use appears to continue a trend that became significant three decades earlier (Pagliaro & Pagliaro, *Clinical Patient Data Files*).

(NIDA, 2018). (See the related discussion in the earlier amphetamine subsection, Undesired, or Harmful, Effects and Toxicities—"Potentially Fatal Toxicities.") Acute cocaine overdosage requires emergency medical support of body systems, with attention to increasing cocaine elimination (see related discussion of urinary pH in the earlier cocaine pharmacology subsection, Pharmacokinetics—"Excretion.") Activated charcoal can be used for gastrointestinal decontamination, particularly for "body packers" (Van Loggerenberg, 2007).

Medical management is primarily directed at preventing related body organ damage and ameliorating associated signs and symptoms. For example:

- Cardiac arrest has been treated with standard basic life support and advanced cardiac life support algorithms (The American Heart Association [AHA] notes that no specific/unique validated interventions currently exist in relation to cardiac arrest due to cocaine overdosage);
- Chest pain has been treated with aspirin and intravenous benzodiazepines. If not adequately relieved, chest pain can be treated with intravenous nitroglycerin;
- Excited delirium has been treated with a combination of diazepam and an antipsychotic (e.g., haloperidol or olanzapine);
- Hyperthermia has been treated with cooling measures (e.g., cooling blankets or tepid water misting with convection fan cooling);
- Hypertension and tachycardia have been treated with diazepam and/or labetalol[88] (without contributing to unopposed alpha-stimulation related adverse reactions). Persisting hypertension has been treated with intravenous nitroglycerin;
- Unstable angina/non-ST-elevation myocardial infarction has been treated with labetalol;
- Ventricular tachydysrhythmias, particularly those that occur immediately after cocaine use and likely result from local anesthetic effects on the myocardium, have been treated by the intravenous administration of sodium bicarbonate. (Barkley Burnett, 2018a, b; McCord, Jneid, & Hollander, 2008); Pagliaro & Pagliaro, 2009; Richards, Garber, & Laurin, 2016; Richards & Le, 2019; Van Loggerenberg, 2007)

Many of the associated signs and symptoms (e.g., agitation, aggressive behavior, anxiety, insomnia, irritability, panic attacks, seizures, and tremors) respond well to benzodiazepine (e.g., diazepam [Valium®]) pharmacotherapy.[89] There is no known antidote for cocaine overdosage (Pagliaro & Pagliaro, 2009).

Physical and Psychological Dependence

> The number of geriatric and older individuals with a substance abuse disorder, especially abuse of cocaine and heroin, is on the rise; despite this known trend, substance abuse remains underestimated, underidentified, underdiagnosed, and undertreated in this population.
>
> (Yarnell, 2015, p. 1)

It has been estimated that, of a group of 100 people who try cocaine, 30 will become "abusive users" and ten will become "compulsive users" (Pagliaro & Pagliaro, *Clinical Patient*

88. The use of propranolol, a beta-adrenergic blocker, in this clinical situation may exacerbate coronary artery constriction and increase blood pressure because of unopposed alpha-adrenergic effects. Consequently, the use of propranolol in the acute treatment of cocaine overdosage is contraindicated.
89. N.B. Patient must be closely monitored for possible exacerbation of respiratory depression.

Data Files). However, over the last two decades, the consensus has been that there is no true physical dependence associated with the regular, long-term use of cocaine as classically defined by the existence of both: (1) the development of tolerance with regular, long-term use; and (2) when regular long-term use is abruptly discontinued, a withdrawal syndrome occurs that is immediately relieved when the use of the abusable psychotropic is resumed.

Similar to the amphetamines, cocaine does not fit this classic definition of physical dependence because the endogenous neurotransmitters—which become depleted with continued cocaine use—must be naturally replenished before desired effects can, once again, be achieved or undesired effects be relieved. (See also the discussion in the earlier Amphetamines pharmacology subsection—"Pharmacodynamics: Mechanism of Action.")

Although based largely on data obtained from animal studies, as reported by the NIDA (2016), females appear to be more likely to develop cocaine dependence than males, as demonstrated by: (1) reportedly more intense "highs;" and (2) a proclivity for developing cocaine dependence more rapidly (i.e., "telescoping effect"). Based on these findings, the NIH posited that these effects are due to the female hormone estradiol and are mediated by activation of the mGluR5 receptor on neurons that, in turn, stimulate the release of endocannabinoid neurotransmitters (see also the earlier cocaine pharmacology subsection—"Pharmacodynamics: Mechanism of Action"). Interestingly, older women are more likely than older men to report craving for cocaine within one hour of discontinuing its use (Kennedy, Epstein, & Phillips, 2013; Pagliaro & Pagliaro, 2018). Additionally, as identified by Ducci and Goldman (2012, p. 496), in their comprehensive review of the genetic basis of addictive disorders:

> Addictive disorders are etiologically complex conditions that result from multiple genetic and environmental risk factors. Heritability estimates for addiction range between 0.4 (hallucinogens) to 0.7 (cocaine).

Cocaine Withdrawal Syndrome

Although, cocaine does not fit the classic definition of "physical" dependence, the abrupt discontinuation of cocaine—following regular, long-term use—may result in "psychological" dependence, or a "cocaine withdrawal syndrome." This syndrome is characterized by several undesired effects, including:

- Anhedonia;
- Anxiety;
- Apathy;
- Dysphoria;
- Fatigue, both mental and physical;
- Headaches;
- Increased appetite (hunger);
- Irritability;
- Mental depression;
- Muscle cramps;
- Somnolence;
- Violent behavior;
- Vivid and unpleasant dreams.

These signs and symptoms may begin within a few hours of discontinuing cocaine use and generally resolve within 24 hours (Walsh, Stoops, & Moody, 2009). However, as previously noted, they cannot be immediately relieved by resuming cocaine use (Pagliaro & Pagliaro, 2009).

The underlying cellular mechanism involved regarding cocaine withdrawal syndrome appears to be related to a decrease in mesolimbic dopamine activity (Hu, 2007; Kuhar & Pilotte, 1996). Dopamine modulates neuronal activity in the prefrontal cortex, which is necessary for optimal cognitive functioning (Nogueira, Kalivas, & Lavin, 2006). The decrease in dopamine activity, associated with the cocaine withdrawal syndrome, has been related to severe psychological dependence with intense craving for cocaine, and, consequently, resumed cocaine use (Kuhar & Pilotte, 1996; Pagliaro & Pagliaro, *Clinical Patient Data Files*; Walsh et al., 2009).

New Millennial Trends in Older Adult Cocaine Use

We begin this subsection with the prescription medical use of cocaine and conclude with attention to the nonmedical/illicit use of cocaine by older adults.

Medical Prescription Cocaine Use

In the U.S., the only currently approved medical use for cocaine is its use as a local anesthetic. A topical solution of cocaine (4% or 10%) is applied to accessible mucous membranes of the oral, laryngeal, or nasal cavities, where it blocks the initiation and conduction of nerve impulses and, thus, elicits local anesthetic action. As noted in the position statement of the American Academy of Otolaryngology—Head and Neck Surgery, "No other single drug combines the anesthetic and vasoconstriction properties of cocaine" (2013, p. 1). The cocaine solution is not generally prescribed, nor is it particularly attractive to users who prefer the use and effects of cocaine hydrochloride—crystalline powder—and crack cocaine.[90]

Nonmedical/Illicit Cocaine Use[91,92]

> With a crack hit, five minutes later you're running and chasing that feeling, that high.
>
> (Ryder & Brisgone, 2013, p. 48)

90. An exception that we found in our clinical practice involved several dentists, of whom all were men and several were older adults, who were abusing pharmaceutical grade cocaine topical solution administered through empty, disposable nasal spray containers (e.g., empty Dristan® nasal spray containers). The containers were "refilled" with the solution and kept readily available in their dental jacket pockets or from a chain or cord hanging from their necks—reportedly, "to treat nasal congestion." Additionally, we have encountered pharmacists, including students and older pharmacists, who diverted the cocaine solution from the pharmacies where they were employed and subsequently, sold, "shared with friends," or self-injected the cocaine solution intravenously (Pagliaro & Pagliaro, *Clinical Patient Data Files*).
91. N.B. Variance in the rates of cocaine use reported in this subsection reflect several significant variables including: (1) subject age; (2) subject gender and gender orientation; (3) subject continental descent and ethnicity; (4) subject sampling procedures; (5) month/year sampled; (6) city/state/region sampled; and (7) period of use sampled (e.g., past month, past year, or lifetime). Thus, while of interest in a global sense and informative in relation to trends in cocaine use, none of the reported statistics can be validly and reliably generalized across the U.S.—or to specific individual practice sites.
92. Of historical interest, it should be recognized that illicit use of cocaine began in the U.S. in 1914 with the enactment of the *Harrison Narcotics Act*, which banned the nonprescription use of cocaine-containing

Various U.S. studies and reports estimate that the annual rate of illicit/recreational use of cocaine by adults, generally, is approximately 2%. (e.g., University of Michigan, 2008). For older adults, 50 to 64 years of age, use is generally estimated at 1.5%, while for those 65 years of age and older, it is 0.5% (e.g., Blazer & Wu, 2009). Importantly, as emphasized by Yarnell (2015, p. 2):

> The number of geriatric and older individuals with a substance abuse disorder, especially abuse of cocaine and heroin, is on the rise, despite this known trend, substance abuse remains underestimated, underidentified, underdiagnosed, and undertreated in this population.

Related Professional Reminder: ***Reported general trends in the use of various abusable psychotropics may not accurately reflect those found for individual clinics or private practices because of local "biases," particularly regarding: (1) demographic factors; and (2) availability and cost of specific abusable psychotropics.***

Demographic Factors

Throughout the U.S. during the new millennium, the reported incidence of older adult cocaine use was found to be related to several demographic factors, including:

- Continental or other descent;
- Family history of alcoholism;
- Homelessness;
- Socioeconomic status. (e.g., John & Wu, 2017; Pagliaro & Pagliaro, *Clinical Patient Data Files*; Pope, Falck, & Carlson, 2011)

Related research findings for each of these factors are highlighted in the following subsections.

Continental or Other Descent A preference for cocaine or amphetamine (i.e., methamphetamine) appears to be generally divided in the U.S. largely by continental descent. As found by several researchers, older adults who abuse "crack cocaine," are predominantly of African continental descent. While those who abuse "methamphetamine," are predominantly of European continental descent (e.g., Pagliaro & Pagliaro, 2009, 2018). Additionally, a secondary analysis of data from the *National Survey on Drug Use and Health, 2009–2012*, also identified that, in the U.S.:

1. Cocaine hydrochloride was primarily used by Americans of European continental descent;
2. Crack cocaine (i.e., cocaine base) was primarily used by Americans of African continental descent.

Although available data appear to support arguments that preferences for cocaine (or amphetamines) among older adults of different continental descents may be primarily

products. Until that time, cocaine was widely available in a number of proprietary products including "Coca-Cola®" and "Vin Mariani®" (Pagliaro & Pagliaro, 2004).

related to genetic differences, the noted preferences are much more likely to be related to demographic, socioeconomic, and sociocultural differences, including, for example, drug availability and cost. In addition, older adults, regardless of any of these factors, may use cocaine to self-medicate their depression, as reported by Pagliaro et al. (1992) and, more recently, by Hammond, Lai, and Wright (2016), who concluded that the use of cocaine in their study was associated with a "nearly twofold increased odds of depression" (p. 345). See also the related discussion in the earlier cocaine pharmacology subsection, Pharmacodynamics: Mechanism of Action—"Phase 3," the depression phase.

Family History of Alcoholism During the early part of the new millennium, a positive history of alcoholism in an immediate family member was noted to be associated with a risk for initiating cocaine use and subsequent psychological dependence (e.g., Bierut, Dinwiddle, & Begleiter, 1998; Numberger, Wiegand, & Bucholz, 2004).[93] However, the full nature of the genetic and/or sociocultural relationship is quite complex and has not yet been clearly determined (Compton, Cottler, & Ridenour, 2002)—even now, 20 years later.

Sinha (2008, p. 3) posited that the relationship between alcoholism and cocaine abuse is indirect, being mediated by the covariable, "stress."

> Many of the major theories of addiction also identify an important role of stress in addiction processes. These range from psychological models of addiction that view drug use and abuse as a coping strategy to deal with stress. To reduce tension, to self medicate, and to decrease withdrawal-related distress to neurobiological models that propose incentive sensitization and stress allostasis concepts to explain how neuroadaptations in reward, learning, and stress pathways may enhance craving, loss of control, and compulsion, the key components in the transition from casual use of substances to the inability to stop chronic use despite adverse consequences, a key feature of addiction.

Additionally, he noted that other researchers (e.g., Fox, Hong, & Siedlarz, 2008) found that, in comparison to social drinkers, both stress and drug cues were significantly higher (and of a similar magnitude) among both those who were "alcoholics" and those who used cocaine. As explained by Fox, Hong, and Siedlarz (2009, p. 575):

> Chronic alcohol and drug dependence leads to neuroadaptations in hypothalamic-pituitary-adrenal (HAP) and sympathetic adrenal medullary (SAM) stress symptoms, which impact response sensitivity to stress and alcohol [and cocaine] cues and facilitate risk of relapse.

Regarding possible related gender variations in these processes, their research results indicated that in comparison to healthy control [HC] volunteers and substance-abusing [SA] subjects:

> SA males showed a generalized suppression of HPA, SAM system and cardiovascular markers following both stress and cue, SA women demonstrated a selective sympatho-adrenal suppression to stress only and an enhanced HPA response to both stress and cue.[94]

---

93. N.B. Some four decades ago (in the mid-1980s), we noted that approximately 10% of several samples of our forensic (incarcerated) patients, who had abused cocaine, reported positive family histories for "alcoholism" (Pagliaro & Pagliaro, *Clinical Patient Data Files*).
94. N.B. This result may help to explain the finding that women, in general, experience more craving for cocaine sooner after discontinuation than men (see the related discussion in the earlier cocaine

In a more recent study, Marks, Pike, and Stoops (2015, p. 1823) identified an interesting relationship between alcohol and cocaine use—although the mechanism has not yet been discerned. Recognizing that "alcohol consumption is a known antecedent to cocaine relapse," they conducted a double-blind, placebo-controlled, within-subjects study with 20 current cocaine users. The purpose of their study was to evaluate the effect of three different doses of alcohol on cocaine cue attentional bias. The result was that "alcohol administration increased craving for cocaine in a dose-dependent manner." (See also the related discussion of cocaethylene in the earlier cocaine pharmacology subsection, Pharmacokinetics—"Metabolism.")

Homelessness and Socioeconomic Status As noted by Spinelli, Ponath, and Tieu (2017, p. 88):

> The median age of the single adult homeless population [in the U.S.] is 50 and rising.

Older adults, who are homeless or otherwise socioeconomically disadvantaged, concurrently use multiple abusable psychotropics and, when compared to older adults who are not homeless, use significantly more, and higher dosages of, individual abusable psychotropics (Spinelli et al., 2017).[95] They also are more likely to be involved in drug dealing and trafficking (Pagliaro & Pagliaro, 2018; Pagliaro & Pagliaro, *Clinical Patient Data Files*).

Involvement In Illicit Drug Dealing and Trafficking

During the new millennium, older adults became increasingly involved in drug dealing and trafficking. Typical characteristics of these older adults include that they:

- Are poorly educated;
- Are socioeconomically disadvantaged;
- Deal from their homes or apartments;
- Have relatives who use cocaine;
- Have previously been incarcerated;
- Live in an ethnic "ghetto" or enclave;
- Receive social assistance;
- Use cocaine themselves.

Recognized exceptions to these characteristics are the cases of Leo Earl Sharp and Pastor Andy Martin. Leo Earl Sharp became known as El Tata ("the grandfather"). Using his Lincoln Mark LT pickup truck, he would regularly transport 100 to 300 kg of cocaine from the southern U.S. border to Detroit, Michigan. Sharp continued his work as a courier for the Mexican Sinaloa drug cartel for over a decade until his arrest (at age 87 years) in 2011 (Dolnick, 2014).

Regarding Pastor Martin:

> "I cannot emphasize enough how important it is that seniors and their families become aware of their techniques, and take action to protect themselves and their loved-ones from these

---

subsection, "Physical and Psychological Dependence"). It also helps to explain the higher recidivism rates observed among women.

95. N.B. In their study of 350 homeless adults aged 50 years and older in Oakland, California, they found that cocaine was the single most problematic abusable psychotropic followed by alcohol.

> heartless criminals," said Susan Collins, R-Maine, who chairs the committee (on aging). . . . At the hearing, Andy Martin of Henderson, Nevada, spoke on behalf of his father, a retired pastor who was duped into taking 2 kg of cocaine to Europe by a woman he met online. Martin's father, 77, is serving a six-year sentence in a Spanish jail. "He just wants to come home" and "not die in prison," Martin said.
>
> (Corrigan, 2016, pp. 1–2)

Examples of the "typical" older adults involved in cocaine distribution and sale—across the U.S.—abound in both the lay and forensic literature. For example:

> Pierre Riley, 52, Macon, Georgia was sentenced for his role in a large trafficking ring . . . [which obtained and shipped] large quantities of methamphetamine and cocaine [from Atlanta, Georgia, to Kokomo, Indiana, for distribution and sale].
>
> (Bell & Smith, 2020, pp. 1–3)

> Melvin Felix, 54, of Englewood Cliffs, New Jersey, pleaded guilty to possession with the intent to distribute [20 kilograms of cocaine transported from California to New Jersey]. . . . His wife, Keila Ravelo, 55, also of Englewood Cliffs, New Jersey, worked as a partner [in two involved law firms].
>
> (Gibson & McMahon, 2020, pp. 1–2)

> Wayne Jordan, 62, of Douglas, Georgia, was sentenced for . . . conspiracy to possess with intent to distribute cocaine and crack cocaine. . . . Jordan who had served multiple stints in state and federal prison on drug trafficking charges since his first arrest and conviction more than 30 years ago.
>
> (Murphy & Truesdell, 2020, pp. 1, 3)

Assessment and Diagnosis of Older Adult Cocaine Dependence or Use Disorder[96]

As emphasized by Yarnell (2015, p. 1):

> As trends in use change, clinicians need to better recognize cocaine use in older individuals and adjust screening protocols accordingly.

Unfortunately, and similar to the situation with amphetamines, during the past two decades of the new millennium, little formal research has been directed to the assessment and diagnosis of cocaine dependence or use disorder among older adults in the U.S. Generic evaluations of substance use disorders (SUDs), such as the DSM-5 criteria, exist, but specific criteria for cocaine use disorder and specific related psychometric tests have not been formally developed and tested for use with older adults.

However, one general psychometric test, the Severity of Dependence Scale (SDS) has been used to detect cocaine use disorder by Kaye and Darke (2002), who determined that utilizing a cut-off score of 3 or greater: (1) was consistent with a DSM-IV diagnosis of cocaine use disorder; and (2) yielded an optimal sensitivity of 67% and specificity of 93%. Overall, however, related published research data are scarce. See additional discussion and a copy of the SDS (Table 2.5) in the earlier Amphetamine subsection—"Psychometric Tests."

96. For a general overview and discussion of the assessment and diagnosis of dependence or use disorders among older adults, see the "Assessment and Diagnosis" section of Chapter 1, *Alcohol*.

Treating Older Adult Cocaine Dependence or Use Disorder

> Mr. A, a 60-year-old man with history of post-traumatic stress disorder and chronic back, neck, and knee pain, presented to urgent care requesting admission for detoxification from cocaine and alcohol. He had been admitted for 1 week of acute detoxification 1month earlier for a similar presentation; however, he relapsed 1 week post-discharge. He attributed his relapse as an attempt to dull his chronic pain. He presented to urgent care after he had spent $3,000 on cocaine in 3 weeks.
>
> (Yarnell, 2015, p. 2)

Similar to the amphetamines,[97] the treatment of cocaine dependence or use disorder among older adults during the new millennium has mainly involved: (1) pharmacotherapeutic approaches;[98] and (2) psychotherapeutic/counseling approaches. These approaches are discussed in the following subsections. We begin with the pharmacotherapeutic approaches.

Pharmacotherapeutic Approaches

Although a number of different classes of prescription drugs—anticonvulsants, antidepressants, antihypertensives, and antipsychotics—have been used in an attempt to successfully treat cocaine dependence or use disorder, antipsychotic pharmacotherapy has been the major focus of research and treatment during the last decade (see Table 2.9). Various antidepressants have also received considerable clinical attention regarding the treatment of cocaine use disorder. Unfortunately, as noted in a review by Chan, Kondo, and Freeman (2019, p. 2858):

> Antidepressants were the most widely studied drug class, but appear to have no effect on cocaine use or treatment retention.

Others have come to similar conclusions. For example, as noted in a systematic review prepared by Chan et al. (2018, p. 22) for the Department of Veterans Affairs:

> There is moderate strength evidence that antidepressants as a class are no better than placebo for sustained abstinence. . . . Data from 30 RCTs [randomized controlled trials] provide high strength evidence that antidepressants are no better than placebo for study retention, and we identified no difference between antidepressants and placebo on severe adverse effects or the number of study withdrawals due to adverse events.

Unfortunately, the results of all of the pharmacotherapy studies for cocaine dependence or use disorder have been generally disappointing. For example, as identified by Howell and Cunningham (2015, p. 192):

> Although cocaine abuse is a significant public health problem, no effective pharmacotherapeutics are available to treat this disorder.

---

97. See the earlier Amphetamine subsection—“Treating Amphetamine Dependence or Use Disorder.”
98. For over a decade, researchers (e.g., Haile, Kosten, & Kosten, 2009), have examined the application of pharmacogenetically based treatments for cocaine dependence or use disorder. Unfortunately, although several promising avenues of research have been explored, to date, none have yielded significant, and applicable, clinical results.

Table 2.9 Representative Studies of the Efficacy of Pharmacotherapeutic Approaches for Treating Cocaine Dependence or Use Disorder[99]

GENERIC NAME (BRAND NAME®)	SUBJECT SAMPLE,[100] STUDY DESIGN, & PHARMACOTHERAPEUTIC EFFICACY FINDINGS	SOURCE
Acamprosate (Campral®)		
Acamprosate	60 subjects with cocaine dependence—double-blind, placebo-controlled study. Findings: Lack of efficacy,[101] "no more efficacious than placebo."	Kampman, Dackis, & Pettinati, 2011
Amantadine (Symmetrel®)		
Amantadine	69 subjects with cocaine dependence—double-blind, placebo-controlled study. Findings: Lack of efficacy.	Shoptaw, Kintaudi, & Charuvastra, 2002
Amantadine	10 "cocaine smokers"—in-patient, double-blind, cross-over study. Findings: Lack of efficacy, "Amantadine maintenance did *not* modify the choice to self-administer smoked cocaine."	Collins, Vosburg, & Hart, 2003
Amantadine	199 cocaine-dependent subjects—random, placebo-controlled study. Findings: Lack of efficacy.	Kampman, Dackis, & Lynch, 2006
ANTICONVULSANTS		
Anticonvulsants selected for study:		
Carbamazepine *Gabapentin* *Lamotrigine* *Phenytoin*		

(*Continued*)

99. See also Table 2.10, " Representative Studies of the Efficacy of Psychotherapeutic Approaches for Treating Cocaine Dependence or Use Disorder," for a discussion of the efficacy of related combinations of pharmacotherapy and psychotherapy/counseling.
100. Only human studies are included in this table.
101. "Lack of efficacy" indicates that, according to our assessment and interpretation of the presented data, results in terms of cocaine use fail to demonstrate statistical significance in comparison to no pharmacotherapy or placebo intervention. Note that our assessment is generally more critical/stringent than that of the study authors, who in many cases have equivocated on the results with descriptors such as "moderate support," "may reduce," "possibly helpful," and "further study is needed."

Table 2.9 (Continued)

GENERIC NAME (BRAND NAME®)	SUBJECT SAMPLE,[100] STUDY DESIGN, & PHARMACOTHERAPEUTIC EFFICACY FINDINGS	SOURCE
Tiagabine *Topiramate* *Vigabatrin*		
Gabapentin (Neurontin®)		
Gabapentin	Double-blind, crossover design study. Findings: Lack of efficacy.	Hart, Ward, & Collins, 2004
Gabapentin	12 nontreatment-seeking" cocaine abusers—inpatient/outpatient study. Findings: Lack of efficacy.	Hart, Haney, & Vosburg, 2008
Gabapentin	6 "nontreatment seeking" cocaine-dependent subjects—double-blind, crossover design study. Findings: Lack of efficacy.	Hart, Haney, & Collins, 2007
Tiagabine (Gabitril®)		
Gabitril®	141 cocaine-dependent subjects—double-blind, placebo-controlled, outpatient trial. Findings: Lack of efficacy "in changing cocaine use."	Winhusen, Somoza, & Ciraulo, 2007
Topiramate (Topamax®)		
Topiramate	170 cocaine and alcohol dependent subjects—double-blind, placebo-controlled study. Findings: Lack of efficacy, "topiramate was no better than placebo in reducing cocaine use."	Kampman, Pettinati, & Lynch, 2013
Topiramate	171 cocaine-dependent methadone maintenance patients—double-blind, placebo-controlled clinical study. Findings: Lack of efficacy, "no significant difference in cocaine abstinence between topiramate and placebo conditions."	Umbricht, DeFulio, & Winstanley, 2014

ANTIDEPRESSANTS		
Bupropion (Wellbutrin®)		
Bupropion	70 chronic cocaine users—randomized, double-blind, placebo-controlled, outpatient study. Findings: Lack of efficacy.	Shoptaw, Heinzerling, & Rotheram-Fuller, 2008
Bupropion	Systematic review of 5 studies. Findings: Lack of efficacy, "Efficacy of bupropion appears to be limited to when it is combined with robust behavioral treatments or administered to *lighter users*."	Stoops & Rush, 2013
Citalopram (Celexa®)		
Citalopram	76 cocaine-dependent patients—double-blind, placebo-controlled study. Findings: Possibly effective, "Citalopram-treated subjects showed a significant reduction in cocaine-positive urines during treatment."	Moeller, Schmitz, & Steinberg, 2007
ANTIHYPERTENSIVES		
Reserpine (Serpasil®)		
Reserpine (Serpasil®)	119 cocaine dependent subjects—double-blind, placebo-controlled, outpatient trial. Findings: Lack of efficacy.	Winhusen, Somoza, Sarid-Segal, 2007
ANTIPSYCHOTICS		
Antipsychotics identified in study: Aripiprazole (Abilify®), Haloperidol (Haldol®), Olanzapine (Zyprexa®), Quetiapine (Seroquel®),	719 total participants—systematic review of 14 studies comparing antipsychotic drugs to placebo. Findings: Lack of efficacy, "comparing any antipsychotic drug versus placebo, we found that antipsychotics reduced dropout." "We found no other significant differences."	Indave et al., 2016

(Continued)

Table 2.9 (Continued)

GENERIC NAME (BRAND NAME®)	SUBJECT SAMPLE,[100] STUDY DESIGN, & PHARMACOTHERAPEUTIC EFFICACY FINDINGS	SOURCE
Risperidone (Risperdal®), and the antihypertensive, *Reserpine* (*Serpasil®*)		
Olanzapine (*Zyprexa®*), *Risperidone* (*Risperdal®*), and the anti-hypertensive, *Reserpine* (*Serpasil®*)	562 subjects with "primary cocaine dependence"—meta-analysis of 10 studies comparing selected antipsychotics to placebo. Findings: "Antipsychotics did not differ from placebo regarding cocaine use days, abstinence, or craving."	Kishi, Matsuda, & Iwata, 2013
Baclofen (Lioresal®)		
Baclofen	7 nontreatment-seeking, recent, cocaine users—double-blind, placebo-controlled study. Findings: Lack of efficacy, "pretreatment with baclofen had no effect on any cocaine-related measure."	Lile, Stoops, & Allen, 2004
Baclofen	160 subjects with "severe cocaine dependence"—multi-site, double-blind study. Findings: Lack of efficacy, (no significant differences between baclofen-treated and placebo groups).	Kahn, Biswas, & Childress, 2009
Buspirone (Buspar®)		
Buspirone	9 current cocaine users—repeated measures, inpatient study. Findings: Lack of efficacy.	Bolin, Lile, & Marks, 2016
Citicoline (Ceraxon®)		
Citicoline	130 with bipolar disorder and cocaine dependence—randomized, double-blind, placebo-controlled outpatient study Findings: Lack of efficacy.	Brown, Todd, & Schmitz, 2015

Disulfiram (Antabuse®)		
Disulfiram	121 cocaine-dependent subjects—randomized double-blind, placebo-controlled, factorial study. Findings: Possibly effective, "participants assigned to disulfiram reduced their cocaine use significantly more than those assigned to placebo."	Carroll, Fenton, & Ball, 2004
Disulfiram	492 total participants—systematic review of 7 studies. Findings: Lack of efficacy.	Pani, Trogu, & Vacca, 2010
Disulfiram	112 cocaine dependent subjects—randomized, double-blind, placebo-controlled study. Findings: Lack of efficacy, "no significant main effects for disulfiram versus placebo."	Carroll, Nich, & Shi, 2012
Modafinil (Provigil®)		
Modafinil	62 cocaine dependent patients, predominately of African continental descent—randomized, double-blind, placebo-controlled study. Findings: "Modafinil improves clinical outcome when combined with psychosocial treatment for cocaine dependence."	Dackis, Kampman, & Lynch, 2005
Modafinil	8 "nontreatment-seeking," cocaine-dependent subjects—double-blind, crossover design study. Findings: Modafinil attenuated the "subject-effect ratings" associated with cocaine self-administration.	Hart, Haney, & Vosburg, 2008
Modafinil	210 cocaine dependent "treatment-seekers"—double-blind, placebo-controlled study. Findings: "Modafinil, in combination with individual behavioral therapy," demonstrated an *increase* in the maximum number of consecutive nonuse days for cocaine and a reduction in craving. However, there was *no* significant difference between modafinil and placebo "in average weekly percent of cocaine non-use days."	Anderson, Reid, & Li, 2009

(Continued)

Table 2.9 (Continued)

GENERIC NAME (BRAND NAME®)	SUBJECT SAMPLE,[100] STUDY DESIGN, & PHARMACOTHERAPEUTIC EFFICACY FINDINGS	SOURCE
Modafinil	210 subjects, "who were actively using cocaine"—randomized, double-blind, placebo-controlled study. Findings: Lack of efficacy, "No significant difference between modafinil and placebo."	Dackis, Kampman, & Lynch, 2012.
Modafinil	Systematic review of 3 studies. Findings: Lack of efficacy, "Analysis showed little difference between placebo and modafinil."	Stoops & Rush, 2013
Modafinil	94 cocaine- dependent subjects—double-blind, placebo-controlled, clinical trial. Findings: In comparison to placebo, modafinil significantly increased abstinence and reduced self-reported "levels of cocaine craving."	Kampman, Lynch, & Pettinati, 2015
Naltrexone (ReVia®)		
Naltrexone	164 patients "with co-occurring cocaine and alcohol dependence"—randomized, double-blind, placebo-controlled study. Findings: Lack of efficacy (when added to psychosocial treatment—possibly effective for men, but *not* for women).	Pettinati, Kampman, & Lynch, 2008b
Naltrexone	208 patients "with co-occurring cocaine and alcohol dependence"—randomized, double-blind, placebo-controlled study. Findings: Lack of efficacy.	Pettinati, Kampman, & Lynch, 2008a
Naltrexone	87 subjects "with both cocaine and alcohol dependence"—randomized, double-blind, placebo-controlled study. Findings: Lack of efficacy.	Schmitz, Lindsay, & Green, 2009
Progesterone		
Progesterone	45 male methadone-stabilized cocaine users—randomized, double-blind, placebo-controlled study. Findings: Lack of efficacy.	Sofuoglu, Poling, & Gonzalez, 2007

Progesterone	25 cocaine-dependent women "recruited from obstetrical clinics"—randomized, double-blind, placebo-controlled study. Findings: Lack of efficacy.	Yonkers, Forray, & Nich, 2014
PSYCHOSTIMULANTS		
Methylphenidate (Ritalin®)		
Methylphenidate	4 studies—systematic review. Findings. Lack of efficacy, "Generally, does not reduce cocaine use."	Stoops & Rush, 2013
Psychostimulants (6 selected for study) & Dopamine reuptake inhibitor	2366 total participants—systematic review of 26 studies with attention to: (1) Six selected psychostimulants: Dexamphetamine (Dexedrine®); Lisdexamfetamine (Vyvanse®); Mazindol (Sanorex®); Methamphetamine; Methylphenidate (Ritalin®); Mixed-Amphetamines (Adderall®); and (2) One dopamine reuptake inhibitor: Modafinil (Provigil®). Findings: Lack of efficacy.	Castells, Cunill, & Perez-Mana, 2016

As summarized by Indave, Minozzi, and Pani (2016, p. 1), based on their review of 14 studies representing a combined total of 719 participants and seven different drugs—five antipsychotics (i.e., aripiprazole, haloperidol, olanzapine, quetiapine, and risperidone); one antihypertensive (i.e., reserpine); and one anticonvulsant (i.e., lamotrigine):

> At present, there is no evidence supporting the clinical use of antipsychotic medications in the treatment of cocaine dependence.

As observed by Davidson (2016, p. 52):

> Despite many years of research, there are no approved medications for stimulant dependence, and treatment is focused on psychotherapy and abstinence.

And, as noted by the NIDA (2016, p. 1):

> Presently, there are no medications approved by the U.S. Food and Drug Administration to treat cocaine addiction.

And again, as more recently identified by Chan et al. (2019, p. 2858), in their relatively recent systematic review and meta-analysis:

> Currently, there are no accepted FDA-approved pharmacotherapies for cocaine use disorder, though numerous medications have been tested in clinical trials.

In addition, as we, and others (e.g., Tobin, 2017) have noted, preventing "relapsed use" of cocaine is another major concern related to successful treatment that, unfortunately, has proven to be equally resistant to efficacious pharmacotherapeutic approaches (see Table 2.9).[102]

We now turn to the psychotherapeutic/counseling approaches for cocaine dependence or use disorder.

Psychotherapeutic/Counseling Approaches

Various psychotherapeutic/counseling approaches have been utilized in an attempt to treat cocaine dependence or use disorder. However, although some approaches have shown potential, or partial success (e.g., increasing the number of days in treatment versus "non-intervention" control), the overall results have been disappointing. Currently, there are no established "best practices" (i.e., empirically validated and reliable psychotherapeutic approaches) for treating cocaine use disorder among older adults. However, as identified by Vocci and Montoya (2009), "psychosocial and behavioral treatments, notably CBT and contingency management, of cocaine and methamphetamine users are moderately effective." An overview of the findings from related published research studies is presented in Table 2.10 in order to highlight the nature and extent of past attempted interventions and to identify, for the reader, potentially efficacious psychotherapeutic approaches.

---

102. Interestingly, and of clinical relevance, is the observation by Parvaz, Moeller, and Goldstein (2016) that both subjective measures of craving (e.g., self-reports of "liking cocaine" and "wanting cocaine") and findings from measures of EEG cue reactivity demonstrated a linear decline from two days of abstinence (rated lowest at a rating of 1 on a scale of 0 to 5)—this rating persisted among those abstinent formerly "cocaine dependent" adults sampled at one year of abstinence.

Table 2.10 Representative Studies of the Efficacy of Psychotherapeutic Approaches for Treating Cocaine Dependence or Use Disorder[103]

APPROACH	STUDY SAMPLE, DESIGN, & FINDINGS	SOURCE
Cognitive-Behavioral Therapy (CBT)		
CBT; CM; CBT & CM	93 cocaine-dependent, methadone-maintained outpatients—randomized treatment study. Findings: CBT "showed no main effects on any of the cocaine-related outcome measures." CM "had robust main effects on all cocaine-related outcome measures." Combined CBT & CM was more effective than CBT alone, although initial therapeutic effects were "briefly [initially] dampened if CM was augmented with CBT."	Epstein, Hawkins, & Covi, 2003
CBT & Disulfiram; CBT & Placebo; Interpersonal Therapy (IPT) & Disulfiram; IPT & Placebo	121 cocaine dependent subjects (non-alcoholics)—randomized placebo-controlled, double-masked, factorial trial. Findings: Possibly effective—CBT reduced cocaine use more than IPT; and disulfiram reduced cocaine use more than placebo.	Carroll et al., 2004
CBT	Literature review. Findings: Lack of efficacy "in longitudinal studies, where long-term abstinence is the primary outcome of interest."	Penberthy, Ait-Daoud, & Vaughan, 2010
CBT; CM	5 studies—literature review examining CBT and CM effects on cocaine dependence. Findings: Possibly effective, with CBT being less effective than CM in the acute treatment phase but having a more lasting effect in the post-treatment phase.	Farronato, Dursteler-Macfarland, & Wiesbeck, 2013
CBT; Disulfiram	434 total cocaine-dependent subjects—literature review of clinical trials for treating cocaine dependence. Findings: Possibly effective. CBT is possibly effective for both men and women. Disulfiram is possibly effective, but less so for women.	DeVito, Babuscio, & Nich, 2014

(Continued)

103. Behavioral treatment approaches that include pharmacotherapeutic approaches also are presented in this table.

Table 2.10 (Continued)

APPROACH	STUDY SAMPLE, DESIGN, & FINDINGS	SOURCE
Contingency Management (CM)		
CM; CBT; CM & CBT; Methadone maintenance, alone	120 cocaine-dependent patients who were receiving methadone maintenance therapy—randomized treatment study. Findings: Possibly effective. Those in the CM and CM & CBT groups, "had significantly superior in-treatment urinalysis results." CBT "in-treatment urinalysis results" were not significantly different than those obtained with methadone alone.	Rawson, Huber, & McCann, 2002
CM; "Day Treatment;" CM & "Day Treatment"	127 "homeless persons with crack/cocaine disorders"—randomized treatment study. Findings: Possibly effective. "CM & day treatment was 2.1 times more likely to have a positive treatment outcome than day treatment [alone]."	Schumacher, Milby, & Wallace, 2003
CM; Group Therapy (GT); CM & GT	77 cocaine-dependent methadone patients—randomized treatment study. Findings: Possibly effective. "Patients in the CM condition submitted more cocaine-negative [urine] samples and attended more groups than patients in standard treatment [i.e., group therapy]."	Petry, Martin, & Simcic, 2005
CM; CM & bupropion; CM & placebo; Voucher control & bupropion; Voucher control & placebo	106 cocaine abusing, methadone-maintained outpatients—randomized double-blind, placebo-controlled trial. Findings: Possibly effective. The CM & bupropion "proportion of cocaine-positive samples significantly decreased during weeks 3 to 13." CM & placebo, "significantly increased cocaine use during weeks 3 to 13." Voucher control & bupropion or placebo "showed no significant improvement in cocaine use."	Poling, Oliveto, & Petry, 2006
CM; CRA & 12-Step facilitation (TSF); Voucher control	145 cocaine-dependent women (with children or pregnant)—randomized 2X2 study. Findings: Possibly effective. "CM was associated with significantly greater duration of cocaine abstinence;" and "CRA and TSF "were *not* significant for any measures."	Schottenfeld, Moore, & Pantalon, 2011
CM; GT; CM & GT (abstinence, negative urine); CM & GT (attendance)	333 cocaine-negative patients—randomized treatment study. Findings: Possibly effective, "both attendance and abstinence-based CM resulted in improvements in some measures."	Petry, Barry, & Alessi, 2012

CM	1664 total subjects—literature review of 19 studies. Findings: Possibly effective. CM appears to: (1) increase cocaine abstinence; (2) improve treatment retention; and (3) "may act synergistically with pharmacotherapy."	Schierenberg, van Amsterdam, & van den Brink, 2012
Community Reinforcement Approach (CRA)		
CRA; CRA & Vouchers	70 cocaine-dependent outpatients—randomized treatment study. Findings: Possibly effective, "Abstinence-contingent incentives [i.e., vouchers] significantly increased cocaine abstinence during treatment and at 1 year of follow-up compared with noncontingent incentives."	Higgins, Wong, & Badger, 2000
CRA; CRA & Vouchers; Vouchers only	100 cocaine-dependent outpatients—randomized treatment study. Findings: Possibly effective, "patients treated with CRA & vouchers were retained better in treatment, used cocaine at a lower frequency during treatment, but not follow-up."	Higgins, Sigmon, & Wong, 2003
CRA	11 studies with 812 total subjects—systematic review of 4 studies focusing on "cocaine treatment." Findings: Possibly effective. "CRA with incentives is more effective than usual care or CRA without incentives in the treatment of cocaine abuse or dependence."	Roozen, Boulogne, & van Tulder, 2004

Regardless of the limited success associated with the psychotherapeutic/counseling approaches of cocaine use disorder, over the first two decades of the new millennium, as noted by Kampman (2019, p. eaax1532):

> Psychological treatments remain the treatments of choice for cocaine use disorder.

<u>Related Professional Reminder</u>: The lack of an identifiable "best practice" does **not** ***mean that: (1) older adults should*** **not** ***be treated; nor (2) some older adults will*** **not** ***respond well to some psychotherapeutic interventions.***

Also, see the earlier related discussion of the psychotherapeutic approaches, which can be utilized for the treatment of amphetamine-related disorders, because, as identified by Vocci and Montoya (2009, p. 6):

> There is currently no evidence for a differential treatment effect of any psychosocial treatment in the management of cocaine and methamphetamine users in treatment.

CONTEMPORANEOUS DIAGNOSES INVOLVING COCAINE[104]

Older adults are susceptible to, and may experience, virtually every form of contemporaneous diagnosis. However, the most often reported contemporaneous diagnosis, particularly associated with older adult cocaine dependence or use disorder, is major depressive disorder (MDD) (Pagliaro et al., 1992; Pagliaro & Pagliaro, *Clinical Patient Data Files*). Additionally, cocaine dependence or use disorder among older adults also has been commonly associated with several other mental disorders, particularly:

- AUD;
- BD;
- Eating disorders;
- OCD;
- PTSD;
- Schizophrenia;
- SUDs (Addy, Rodhakrishnan, & Cortes, 2012; Brown, Gorman, & Hynan, 2007; Brown, Monti, & Myers, 1998; Conner, Pinquart, & Holbrook, 2008; Haasen, Prinzleve, & Gossop, 2005; Holstege, 2016; Liu, Ball, & Elliot, 2019).

Cocaine dependence or use disorder also has been associated with numerous medical physical disorders, including: AIDS; hypertension; seizures; and stroke. (See the related discussion in the earlier cocaine pharmacology subsection—"Undesired, or Harmful, Effects and Toxicities").

104. See also the related overview and discussion in Chapter 1, *Alcohol*—"Common Contemporaneous Diagnoses Among Older Adults."

REFERENCES[105,106,107]

Addy, P. H., Radhakrishnan, R., & Cortes, J. A. (2012, Spring). Comorbid alcohol, cannabis, and cocaine use disorders in schizophrenia: Epidemiology, consequences, mechanisms, and treatment. *Focus, 10*(2), 140–153. doi:10.1176/appi.focus.10.1.140

Albini, T. A., Sun, R. L., & Holz, E. R. (2007). Lemon juice and Candida endophthalmitis in crack-cocaine misuse. *British Journal of Ophthalmology, 91*(5), 702–703. doi:10.1136/bjo.2006.0108365

Alexandrakis, G., Tse, D. T., & Rosa, R. H. (1999). Nasolacrimal duct obstruction and orbital cellulitis associated with chronic intranasal cocaine abuse. *Archives of Opththalmology, 117*(12), 1617–1622. doi:10.1001/archopht.117.12.1617

Ali, S. R., Krugar, M., & Houghton, J. (2002). Upper airway obstruction and acute lung injury associated with cocaine abuse. *International Journal of Clinical Practice, 56*(6), 484–485.

Alvarez, G. G., & van der Jagt, R. (2008, January). "Crack lung and heart" presenting after chemotherapy in a 65-year-old man with non-Hodgkin lymphoma. *Current Oncology, 15*(1), 63-65. doi:10.3747/co.2008.202

American Academy of Otolaryngology-Head and Neck Surgery. (2013, May 6). *Position statement: Medical use of cocaine* (pp. 1–3). Retrieved March 11, 2016, from entnet.org http://www.entnet.org/content/medical-use-cocaine

Anderson, A. L., Reid, M. S., & Li, S. H. (2009, September 1). Modafinil for the treatment of cocaine dependence. *Drug and Alcohol Dependence, 104*(1–2), 133–139. doi:10.1016/j.drugalcdep.2009.04.015

Andrews, P. (1997). Cocaethylene toxicity. *Journal of Addictive Diseases, 165*(3), 75–84. doi:10.1300/J069v16n03_08

Ares-Santos, S., Granado, N., & Espadas, I. (2014). Methamphetamine causes degeneration of dopamine cell bodies and terminals of the nigrostriatal pathway evidenced by silver staining. *Neuropsychopharmacology, 39*(5), 1066–1080. doi:10.1038/npp.2013.307

Ares-Santos, S., Granado, N., & Moratalla, R. (2013). The role of dopamine receptors in the neurotoxicity of methamphetamine. *Journal of Internal Medicine, 273*(5), 437–453. doi:10.1111/joim.12049

Baker, A., Boggs, T. G., & Lewin, T. J. (2001). Randomized controlled trial of brief cognitive-behavioural interventions among regular users of amphetamine. *Addiction, 96*, 1279–1287.

105. As per publisher style, only the first three authors are listed for each reference.
106. Several times the number of references listed were found, obtained, and analyzed by the authors during the preparation of this chapter. However, only those references that were cited at least once in the body of the text are listed. Major reasons for not citing other references include that they: (1) did not provide any additional unique information or research findings; (2) were not well researched or written by their authors (i.e., were evaluated as not being valid or reliable); (3) were based predominately, or exclusively, on animal studies; (4) dealt exclusively with other population groups (e.g., children, adolescents, or young adults); (5) provided usage statistics from outside the U.S.; and/or (6) were redundant with, or not as recent as, the already cited references—unless the reference was of classical, historical, or seminal importance.
107. The reference citation, "Pagliaro & Pagliaro, *Clinical Patient Data Files*," refers to unpublished data collected, with permission, by the authors, in the formal course of their professional academic roles as clinician scientists and professors, from their patients, research subjects or participants, and students, from the 1970s to date. Most of the related data have been discussed and made public in a wide and large number of formal academic presentations, including graduate seminars, grand rounds, guest lectures, professional conferences, and undergraduate lectures.

Baker, A., Lee, N. K., & Claire, M. (2005). Brief cognitive behavioural interventions for regular amphetamine users: A step in the right direction. *Addiction, 100*, 367–378. doi:10.1111/j.1360-0443.2005.001002.x

Ballester, J., Valentine, G., & Sofuoglu, M. (2017). Pharmacological treatments for methamphetamine addiction: Current status and future directions. *Expert Review of Clinical Pharmacology, 10*(3), 305–314. doi:10.1080/17512433.2017.1268916

Barkley Burnett, L. (2018a, September 1). How is cardiac arrest treated in cocaine toxicity? *Medscape*, pp. 1–3.

Barkley Burnett, L. (2018b, September). What is the pathophysiology of hyperthermia in cocaine toxicity? *Medscape*, pp. 1–2.

Bartos, L. (2005, July). *Meth production is toxic to communities (methtoxic)*. NEBLINE Newsletter (pp. 1–4). Lincoln, NE: University of Nebraska-Lincoln. Retrieved November 2, 2016, from http://lancaster.uni.edu/family/methtoxic.shtml

Bauwens, J. E., Boggs, J. M., & Hartwell, P. S. (1989). Fatal hyperthermia associated with cocaine use. *WJM, Western Journal of Medicine, 150*(2), 210–212.

Bell, R. J., & Smith, T. (2020, November 9). Drug trafficking source sentenced to 490 months in federal prison. *DEA Press Release, Chicago Division*, pp. 1–3. Washington, DC: U.S. Department of Justice.

Berkes, H. (2007, April 4). *Mexican "ice" replaces home-cooked meth in U. S* (pp. 1–15). National Public Radio (NPR). Retrieved from http://www.npr.org/templates/story/story.php?storyld=9193186

Berman, S. M., Kuczenski, R., & McCracken, J. T. (2009). Potential adverse effects of amphetamine treatment on brain and behavior: A review. *Molecular Psychiatry, 14*(2), 123–142. doi:10.1038/mp.2008.90

Bernstein, K. T., Bucciarelli, A., & Piper, T. M. (2007, March 9). Cocaine- and opiate-related fatal overdose in New York City, 1990-2000. *BMC Public Health, 7*, 31. doi:10.1186/1471-2458-7-31

Bickel, W. K., Franck, C. T., & Moody, L. (2013). *Executive dysfunction among alcohol- and cocaine-dependent women: 2013*. APA 121st Annual Convention Proceedings (p. NP). Honolulu, Hawai'i: American Psychological Association. doi:10.1037/e612522013-001

Bierut, L. J., Dinwiddle, S. H., & Begleiter, H. (1998, November). Familial transmission of substance dependence: Alcohol marijuana, cocaine, and habitual smoking: A report from the collaborative study on the genetics of alcoholism. *Archives of General Psychiatry, 55*(11), 982–988. doi:10.1001/archpsyc.55.11.982

Blazer, D. G., & Wu, L.-T. (2009). The epidemiology of substance use and disorders among middle aged and elderly community adults: National survey on drug use and health (NSDUH). *The American Journal of Geriatric Psychiatry, 17*(3), 237–245. doi:10.1097/JGP.0b01.3e318190b8ef

Blumenthal, M., & King, P. (1995). Ma huang: Anient herb, modern medicine, regulatory dilemma: A review of the botany, chemistry, medicinal uses, safety concerns, and legal satus of ephredra and its alkaloids. *HerbalGram, 34*, 22–30.

Bolin, B. L., Lile, J. A., & Marks, K. R. (2016, June). Buspirone reduces sexual risk-taking intent but not cocaine self-administration. *Experimental and Clinical Psychopharmacology, 24*(3), 162–173. doi:10.1037/pha0000076

Bourne, A., Reid, D., & Hickson, F. (2015). Illicit drug use in sexual settings (chemsex) and HIV/STI transmission risk behaviour among gay men in South London: Findings from a qualitative study. *Sexually Transmitted Infections, 91*(8), 564–568. doi:10.1136/sextrans-2015-052052

Boyer, E. M., Thompson, N., & Hill, T. (2015). The relationship between methamphetamine use and dental caries and missing teeth. *Journal of Dental Hygiene, 89*(2), 119–131.

Brackins, T., Brahm, N. C., & Kissack, J. C. (2011, December). Treatments for methamphetamine abuse: A literature review for the clinician. *Journal of Pharmacy Practice, 24*(6), 541–550. doi:10.1177/0897190011426557

Bramness, J. G., & Rognli, E. B. (2016). Psychosis induced by amphetamines. *Current Opinion in Psychiatry, 29*(4), 236–241. doi:10.1097/YCO.0000000000000254

Brecht, M.-L., & Herbeck, D. (2014, June). Time to relapse following treatment for methamphetamine use: A long-term perspective on patterns and predictors. *Drug and Alcohol Dependence, 139*, 18–25. doi:10.1016/j.drugalcdep.2014.02.702

Brensilver, M., Heinzerling, K. G., & Shoptaw, S. (2013, September). Pharmacotherapy of amphetamine-type stimulant dependence: An update. *Drug and Alcohol Review, 32*(5), 449–460. doi:10.1111/dar.12048

Brown, E. S., Gorman, A. R., & Hynan, L. S. (2007, October). A randomized, placebo-controlled trial of citicoline add-on therapy in outpatients with bipolar disorder and cocaine dependence. *Journal of Clinical Pharmacolgy, 27*(5), 498–502. doi:10.1097/JCP.0b013e31814db4c4

Brown, E. S., Todd, J. P., & Schmitz, J. M. (2015). A randomized, double-blind, placebo-controlled trial of citicoline for cocaine dependence in bipolar I disorder. *The American Journal of Psychiatry, 172*(10), 1014–1021. doi:10.1176/appi.ajp.2015.14070857

Brown, R. A., Monti, P. M., & Myers, M. G. (1998, February 1). Depression among cocaine abusers in treatment: Relation to cocaine and alcohol use and treatment outcome. *Psychiatry Online*, pp. 1–10.

Brown, R. E., Morisky, D. E., & Silverstein, S. J. (2013). Meth mouth severity in response to drug-use patterns and dental access in methamphetamine users. *Journal of the California Dental Association, 41*(6), 421–428.

Brzeczko, A. W., Leech, R., & Stark, J. G. (2013, September). The advent of a new pseudoephedrine product to combat methamphetamine abuse. *American Journal of Drug and Alcohol Abuse, 39*(5), 284–290. doi:10.3109/00952990.2013.821476

Buie, J., & Tamburin, A. (2014, November 17). Meth-lab busts down; dealers getting drug from Mexico. *The Tennessean.* Retrieved from http://www.story/news/crime/2014/11/16/meth-labs-tn-dealers-turning-mexico/19141893/

Bulbena-Cabre, A., Ramos Dunn, N., & Gorman Swift, R. (2015). "Crack Lung": A pulmonary complication of crack cocaine case. *Journal of Addiction Medicine*, 164–165. doi:10.1097/ADM.0000000000000172

Buxton, H. A., & Dove, N. A. (2008). The burden and management of crystal meth use. *CMAJ, Canadian Medical Association Journal, 178*(12), 1537–1539. doi:10.1503/cmaj.071234

Buxton, J. A., Omura, J., & Kuo, M. (2015, June 13). Genetic determinants of cocaine-associated agranulocytosis. *BMC Research Notes, 8*, 240. doi:10.1186/s13104-015-1219-4

Calcaterra, S., & Binswanger, I. A. (2013). Psychostimulant-related deaths as reported by a large national database. *Substance Abuse, 34*(2), 1–17. doi:10.1080/08897077.2012.726959

Callaway, C. W., & Clark, R. F. (1994, July). Hyperthermia in psychostimulant overdose. *Annals of Emergency Medicine, 24*(1), 68–76. doi:10.1016/s0196-0644(94)70165-2

Cano, M., Oh, S., & Salas-Wright, C. (2020, September 1). Cocaine use and overdose mortality in the United States: Evidence from two national data sources, 2002-2018. *Drug and Alcohol Dependence, 214*, 108148. doi:10.1016/j.drugalcdep.2020.108148

Cao, D. N., Shi, J. J., & Hao, W. (2016, June 5). Advances and challenges in pharmacotherapeutics for amphetamine-type stimulants addiction. *European Journal of Pharmacology, 780*, 129–135. doi:10.1016/j.ejphar.2016.03.040

Capizzi, J., Leahy, J., & Wheelock, H. (2020). Population-based trends in hospitalizations due to injection drug use-related serious bacterial infections, Oregon, 2008-2018. *PLoS One, 15*(11), e0242166. doi:10.1371/journal.pone.0242165

Carnevale Associates. (2011, March). *Update: The changing landscape of the methamphetamine epidemic*. Policy Brief. Gaithersburg, MD: Carnevale Associates.

Carroll, K. M., Fenton, L. R., & Ball, S. A. (2004). Efficacy of disulfiram and cognitive behavioral therapy in cocaine-dependent outpatients: A randomized placebo-controlled trial. *Archives of General Psychiatry, 61*(3), 264–272. doi:10.1001/archpsyc.61.3.264

Carroll, K. M., Nich, C., & Shi, J. M. (2012, November 1). Efficacy of disulfiram and Twelve Step Facilitation in cocaine-dependent individuals maintained on methadone: A randomized placebo-controlled trial. *Drug and Alcohol Dependence, 126*(1–2), 224–231. doi:10.1016/j.drugalcdep.2012.05.019

Castells, X., Cunill, R., & Perez-Mana, C. (2016, September 27). Psychostimulant drugs for cocaine dependence. *The Cochrane Database of Systematic Reviews, 9*, CD007380. doi:10.1002/14651858.CD007380.pub4

CDC, Centers for Disease Control and Prevention. (2019, September 18). *HIV and older Americans*. Centers for Disease Control and Prevention, Division of HIV/AIDS Prevention. Bethesda: National Center for HIV/AIDS.

Cerretani, D., Fineschi, V., & Bello, S. (2012). Role of oxidative stress in cocaine-induced cardiotoxicity and cocaine-related death. *Current Medicinal Chemistry, 19*(33), 5619–5623.

Chait, R., Fahmy, S., & Caceres, J. (2010). Cocaine abuse in older adults: An underscreened cohort. *Journal of the American Geriatrics Society, 58*(2), 1–3. doi:10.1111/j.1532-5415.2009.02697.x

Chakravorty, S. S., & Rye, D. B. (2003). Narcolepsy in the older adult: Epidemiology, diagnosis and management. *Drugs & Aging, 20*(5), 361–376. doi:10.2165/00002512-200320050-00005

Chan, B., Kondo, K., & Ayers, C. (2018). *Pharmacotherapy for stimulant use disorders: A systematic review of the evidence*. Washington, DC: Department of Veterans Affairs.

Chan, B., Kondo, K., & Freeman, M. (2019, December). Pharmacotherapy for cocaine use disorder – a systematic review and meta-analysis. *Journal of General Internal Medicine, 34*(12), 2858–2873. doi:10.1007/s11606-019-05075-8

Chang, T. R., Kowalski, R. G., & Caserta, F. (2013). Impact of acute cocaine use on aneurysmal subarachnoid hemorrhage. *Stroke, 44*(7), 1825–1829. doi:10.1161/STROKEAHA.111.000749

Chen, V., Chen, H., & Lin, T-Y. (2008). Severity of heroin dependence in Taiwan: Reliability and validity of the Chinese version of the Severity of Dependence Scale. *Addictive Behavior, 33*(12), 1590–1593. DOI: 10.1016/j.addbeh.2008.06.001

Chen, H.-Y., Albertson, T. E., & Olson, K. R. (2015). Treatment of drug-induced seizures. *British Journal of Clinical Pharmacology, 81*(3), 412–419. doi:10.1111/bcp.12720

Cheng, S., Siddiqui, T., & Gossop, M. (2019, June). The severity of dependence scale detects medication misuse and dependence among hospitalized older patients. *BMC Geriatrics, 174*, 1–5. doi:10.1186/s128677-019-1182-3

Cheromcha, K. (2018, October 29). Cops find 1,200 pounds of liquid meth worth $4.4M hidden in semi-truck fuel tank. *Time Magazine*.

Chow, M. J., Ambre, J. J., & Rue, T. I. (1985, September). Kinetics of cocaine distribution, elimination, and chronotropic effects. *Clinical Pharmacology and Therapeutics, 38*(3), 318–324. doi:10.1038/clpt.1985.179

Coe, M. A., Jufer Phipps, R. A., & Cone, E. J. (2018, June). Bioavailability and pharmacokinetics of oral cocaine in humans. *Journal of Analytical Toxicology, 42*(5), 285–292. doi:10.1093/jat/bky007

Colatrella, N., & Daniel, T. E. (1999). Crack eye syndrome. *Journal of the American Optometric Association, 70*(3), 193–197.

Collins, E. D., Vosburg, S. K., & Hart, C. L. (2003, December). Amantadine does not modulate reinforcing, subjective, or cardiovascular effects of cocaine in humans. *Pharmacology, Biochemistry, and Behavior, 76*(3–4), 401–407.

Compton, W. M., Cottler, L. B., & Ridenour, T. (2002). The specificity of family history of alcohol and drug abuse in cocaine abusers. *The American Journal on Addictions, 11*(2), 85–94.

Cone, E. J. (1995, October). Pharmacokinetics and pharmacodynamics of cocaine. *Journal of Analytical Toxicology, 19*(6), 459–478. doi:10.1093/jat/19.6.459

Cone, E. J., Yousefnejad, D., & Hillsgrove, M. J. (1995, October). Passive inhalation of cocaine. *Journal of Analytical Toxicology, 19*(6), 399–411.

Conner, K. R., Pinquart, M., & Holbrook, A. P. (2008, November). Meta-analysis of depression and substance use and impairment among cocaine users. *Drug and Alcohol Dependence, 98*(1–2), 13–23. doi:10.1016/j.alcdep.2008.05.005

Corrigan, J. (2016, February 10). Drug mules. *USA Today*, pp. 1–2. Washington, DC.

Crandall, C. G., Vongpatanasin, W., & Victor, R. G. (2002). Mechanism of cocaine-induced hyperthermia in humans. *Annals of Internal Medicine, 136*(11), 785–791.

Cruickshank, C. C., & Dyer, K. R. (2009). A review of the clinical pharmacology of methamphetamine. *Addiction, 104*, 1085–1099. doi:10.1111/j.1360-0443.2009.02564.x

Curran, C., Byrappa, N., & McBride, A. (2004, September). Stimulant psychosis: Systematic review. *British Journal of Psychiatry, 185*, 196–204. doi:10.1192/bjp.185.3.196

Czogala, J., Goniewicz, M. L., & Fidelus, B. (2014, June). Secondhand exposure to vapors from electronic cigarettes. *Nicotine & Tobacco Research, 16*(6), 655–662. doi:10.1093/ntr/ntt203

Dackis, C. A., & Gold, M. S. (1990). Addictiveness of central stimulants. *Advances in Alcohol & Substance Abuse, 9*(1–2), 9–26. doi:10.1300/J251v09n01_02

Dackis, C. A., Kampman, K. M., & Lynch, K. G. (2005). A double-blind, placebo-controlled trial of modafinil for cocaine dependence. *Neuropsychopharmacology, 30*(1), 205–211. doi:10.1038/sj.npp.1300600

Dackis, C. A., Kampman, K. M., & Lynch, K. G. (2012, October). A double-blind, placebo-controlled trial of modafinil for cocaine dependence. *Journal of Substance Abuse Treatment, 43*(3), 303–312. doi:10.1016/j.jsat.2011.12.014

D'Angelo, B. (2018, May 20). North Carolina deputies find nearly $91 million of liquid meth on truck. *Dayton Daily News*. Cox Media Group.

Darke, S., Duflou, J., & Kaye, S. (2017, October 1). Prevalence and nature of cardiovascular disease in methamphetamine-related death: A national study. *Drug and Alcohol Dependence, 179*, 174–179. doi:10.1016/j.drugalcdep.2017.07.001

Davidson, C. (2016, June). Developing treatments for stimulant abuse: A brief overview. *East Asian Archives of Psychiatry, 26*(2), 52–59.

DEA, Drug Enforcement Administration. (2011, December 1). Implementation of the methamphetamine production prevention act of 2008. Final rule. *Federal Register, 76*(231), 74696–74699.

DEA, Drug Enforcement Administration. (2021, March 22). Medical doctor turned crystal meth dealer sentenced to ten years in federal prison. *Press Release*, p. 1. Washington, DC: U.S. Department of Justice.

DEA, Drug Enforcement Agency. (1991, February). *Coca cultivation and cocaine processing: An overview* (pp. 1–15). Washington, DC: U.S. Department of Justice.

Dean, A., Kohno, M., & Morales, A. M. (2015, June 1). Denial in methamphetamine users: Associations with cognition and functional connectivity in brain. *Drug and Alcohol Dependence, 151*, 84–91. doi:10.1016/j.drugalcdep.2015.03.004

Deren, S., Cortes, T., & Vaughan Dickson, V. (2019, April 24). Substance use among older people living with HIV: Challenges for health care providers. *Frontiers in Public Health, 7*(94), 1–9. doi:10.3389/fpubh.2019.00094

Dessy, C., & Balligand, J. L. (2010). Beta3-adrenergic receptors in cardiac and vascular tissues emerging concepts and therapeutic perspectives. *Advances in Pharmacology, 59*, 135–163. doi:10.1016/S1054-3589(10)59005-7

DeVito, E. E., Babuscio, T. A., & Nich, C. (2014, December 1). Gender differences in clinical outcomes for cocaine dependence: Randomized clinical trials of behavioral therapy and disulfiram. *Drug and Alcohol Dependence*, 156–167. doi:10.1016/j.drugalcdep.2014.10.007

Diercks, D. B., Kirk, J. D., & Turnipseed, S. D. (2007, December). Evaluation of patients with methamphetamine- and cocaine-related chest pain in a chest pain observation unit. *Critical Pathways in Cardiology, 6*(4), 161–164.

Dolnick, S. (2014, June 11). There's a true story behind 'the mule': The Sinaloa cartel's 90-year-old mule. *The New York Times*, pp. 1–15.

Donovan, R. P., & Mulvey, E. (2021, April 14). Uncle of drug trafficking ring leader pleads guilty for his role in narcotics conspiracy operating in the Jamestown, NY area. *DEA Press Release, New York Region*, p. 1. Buffalo, NY: U.S. Department of Justice.

Ducci, F., & Goldman, D. (2012, June). The genetic basis of addictive disorders. *Psychiatric Clinics of North America, 35*(2), 495–519. doi:10.1016/j.psc.2012.03.010

Durell, T. M., Kroutil, L. A., & Crits-Christoph, P. (2008). Prevalence of nonmedical methamphetamine use in the United States. *Substance Abuse Treatment, Prevention, and Policy, 3*, 1–10. doi:10.1186/1747-597X-3-19

Edelman, E. J., Tetrault, J. M., & Fiellin, D. A. (2014, July). Substance use in older HIV-infected patients. *Current Opinion in HIV and AIDS, 9*(4), 317–324. doi:10.1097/COH.0000000000000069

Edwards, D. J., & Bowles, S. K. (1988). Protein binding of cocaine in human serum. *Pharmaceutical Research, 5*(7), 440–442. doi:10.1023/a:1015992502509

Eldridge, E. (2016, Masrch 3). Cops: Drug smugglers disguise liquid meth as beer, use tour buses. *The Atlantic Journal-Constitution*. Cox Media Group.

Elkashef, A., Vocci, F., & Hanson, G. (2008). Pharmacotherapy of methamphetamine addiction: An update. *Substance Abuse, 29*(3), 31–49. doi:10.1080/08897070802218554

Epstein, D. H., Hawkins, W. E., & Covi, L. (2003, March). Cognitive-behavioral therapy plus contingency management for cocaine use: Findings during treatment and across 12-month follow-up. *Psychology of Addictive Behaviors, 17*(1), 73–82.

Erixon-Lindroth, N., Farde, L., & Robins Wahlin, T.-B. (2005). The role of the striatal dopamine transporter in cognitive aging. *Psychiatry Research: Neuroimaging, 138*, 1–12. doi:10.1016/j.psychresns.2004.09.005

Ermer, J. C., Pennick, M., & Frick, G. (2016, May). Lisdexamfetamine dimesylate: Prodrug delivery, amphetamine exposure and duration of efficacy. *Clinical Drug Investigation, 36*(5), 341–356. doi:10.1007/s40261-015-0354-y

Ernst, A. A., Weiss, S. J., & Enright-Smith, S. (2008). Perpetrators of intimate partner violence use significantly more methamphetamine, cocaine, and alcohol than victims: A report by victims. *The American Journal of Emergency Medicine, 26*(5), 592–596. doi:10.1016/j.ajem.2007.09.015

Ersche, K. D., Clark, L., & London, M. (2006). Profile of executive and memory function associated with amphetamine and opiate dependence. *Neuropsychopharmacology, 31*(5), 1036–1047. doi:10.1038/sj.npp.1300889

Faraone, S. V. (2018). The pharmacology of amphetamine and methylphenidate: Relevance to the neurobiology of attention-deficit/hyperactivity disorder and other psychiatric comorbidities. *Neuroscience and Biobehavioral Reviews, 87*, 255–270. doi:10.1016/j.neubiorev.2018.02.001

Farronato, N. S., Dursteler-Macfarland, K. M., & Wiesbeck, G. A. (2013). A systematic review comparing cognitive-behavioral therapy and contingency management for cocaine dependence. *Journal of Addictive Diseases, 32*(3), 274–287. doi:10.1080/10550887.2013.824328

Fattinger, K., Benowitz, N. L., & Jones, R. T. (2000, July). Nasal mucosal versus gastrointestinal absorption of nasally administered cocaine. *European Journal of Clinical Pharmacology, 56*(4), 305–310. doi:10.1007/s002280000147

Feaver, D. B. (1986, January 15). Drug-related fire suspected in Rick Nelson plane crash. *The Washington Post*.

Ferri, C., Marsden, J., de Araujo, M. (2000). Validity and reliability of the Severity of Dependence Scale (SDS) in a Brazilian sample of drug users. *Drug and Alcohol Review, 19*(4), 451–455.

Fleckenstein, A. E., Volz, T. J., & Riddle, E. L. (2007). New insights into the mechanism of action of amphetamines. *Annual Review of Pharmacology & Toxicology, 47*, 681–698. doi:10.1146/annurev.pharmtox.47.120505.105140

Fox, H. C., Hong, K. A., & Siedlarz, K. M. (2008). Enhanced sensitivity to stress and drug/alcohol craving in abstinent cocaine-dependent individuals compared to social drinkers. *Neuropsychopharmacology, 33*, 796–805. doi:10.1038/sj.npp.1301470

Fox, H. C., Hong, K. A., & Siedlarz, K. M. (2009, November-December). Sex-specific dissociations in autonomic and HPA responses to stress and cues in alcohol-dependent patients with cocaine abuse. *Alcohol and Alcoholism, 44*(6), 575–585. doi:10.1093/alcalc/agp060

Gammans, B. (2020, September 9). Providence woman pleads guilty to trafficking meth. *WPRI, Channel 12 News*, p. 1. Providence, Rhode Island: WPRI.

Gatof, D., & Albert, R. K. (2002). Bilateral thumb burns leading to the diagnosis of crack lung. *Chest, 121*(1), 289–291.

Giacomi, F. D., & Srivali, N. (2019). Cocaine use and crack lung syndrome. *QJM: An International Journal of Medicine, 112*(2), 125–126. doi:10.1093/qjmed/hcy255

Gibson, S. A., & McMahon, T. P. (2020, November 6). Bergen county man sentenced to 14 years in prison for role in $7 million fraud scheme and cross-country drug distribution scheme. *DEA Press Release, New Jersey Division*, pp. 1–2. Washington, DC: U.S. Department of Justice.

Gilchrist, G., Dennis, F., & Radcliffe, P. (2019). The interplay between substance use and intimate partner violence perpetration: A meta-ethnography. *International Journal of Drug Policy, 65*, 8–23.

Glasner-Edwards, S., Mooney, L. J., & Marinelli-Casey, P. (2008). Risk factors for suicide attempts in methamphetamine-dependent patients. *The American Journal on Addictions, 17*(1), 24–27. doi:10.1080/10550490701756070

Goldstein, R. Z., & Volkow, N. D. (2011, November). Dysfunction of the prefrontal cortex in addiction: Neuroimaging findings and clinical implications. *Nature Reviews | Neuroscience, 12*, 652–669. Retrieved from www.nature.com/reviews/neuro

Gonzales, R., Mooney, L., & Rawson, R. A. (2010). The methamphetamine problem in the United States. *Annual Review of Public Health, 31*, 385–398. doi:10.1146/annurev.publhealth.012809.103600

Gossup, M., Darke, S., & Griffiths, P. (1995). The severity of dependence scale (SDS): Psychometric properties of the SDS in English and Australian samples of heroin, cocaine and amphetamine users. *Addiction, 90*(5), 607–614. doi:10.1046/j.1360-0443.1995.9056072.x

Grabus, S. (2017, March 22). *Endocanabinoid regulates cocaine reward*. National Institute on Drug Abuse (NIDA). Retrieved December 13, 2017, from https://www.drugabuse.gov/news-events/nida-notes/2017/03/endocannabinoid-regulates-cocaine-reward

Grinspoon, L., & Hedblom, P. (1975). *The speed culture: Amphetamine use and abuse in America*. Cambridge, MA: Harvard University.

Haasen, C., Prinzleve, M., & Gossop, M. (2005, October). Relationship between cocaine use and mental health problems in a sample of European cocaine powder or crack users. *World Psychiatry, 4*(3), 173–176.

Haile, C. N., Kosten, T. R., & Kosten, T. A. (2009). Pharmacogenetic treatments for drug addiction: Cocaine, amphetamine and methamphetamine. *The American Journal of Drug and Alcohol Abuse, 35*(3), 161–177. doi:10.1080/00952990902825447

Hall, K., & Dunham, T. (2013, November 11). The methiest states in the U. S. (Infographic). *Hoffpost Crime*. Retrieved from http://www.huffingtonpost.com/2013/10/07/meth-states_n_4057372.html

Hamilton, A. B., & Goeders, N. E. (2010). Violence perpetrated by women who use methamphetamine. *Journal of Substance Use, 15*(5), 313–329. doi:10.3109/14659890903431611

Hamilton, K. (2010, May 19). Methology 101: Old-school meth labs give way to "shake and bake". *St Lewis News and Events | Riverfront Times*. Retrieved November 2, 2016, from http://www.riverfronttimes.com/stlouis/methology-101-old-school-mth-labs-give-way-to-shake-and-bake/Cont?mode=print&old=2483461

Hammond, E. R., Lai, S., & Wright, C. M. (2016). Cocaine use may be associated with increased depression in persons infected with HIV. *AIDS and Behavior, 20*(2), 345–352. doi:10.1007/s10461-015-1187-7

Handy, M. (2017, December 19). Amphetamine toxicity treatment & management. *Medscape*, pp. 1–6. emedicine.

Hanson, G. R., Rau, K. S., & Fleckenstein, A. E. (2004). The methamphetamine experience: A NIDA partnership. *Neuropharmacology, 47*(Suppl. 1), 92–100. doi:10.1016/j.neuropharm.2004.06.004

Harada, T., Tsutomi, H., & Mori, R. (2014). Cognitive-behavioural treatments for amphetamine-type stimulants (ATS) use disorders (Protocol). *Cochrane Database of Systematic Reviews, 10*(CD011315), 1–9. doi:10.1002/14651858.CD011315

Harada, T., Tsutomi, H., & Mori, R. (2018). Cognitive-behavioural treatment for amphetamine-type stimulants (ATS)-use disorders. *Cochrane Database of Systematic Reviews, 12*. doi:10.1002/14651858.CD011315.pub2

Harris, D. S., Everhart, E. T., & Mendelson, J. (2003, November). The pharmacology of cocaethylene in humans following cocaine and ethanol administration. *Drug and Alcohol Dependence, 72*(2), 169–182.

Harris, K. (2018, November 18). Scammed senior citizens being recruited as drug mules: CBSA. *CBC News*, pp. 1–2.

Harris, M., Scott, J., & Wright, T. (2019). Injecting-related health harms and overuse of acidifiers among people who inject heroin and crack cocaine in London: A mixed-methods study. *Harm Reduction Journal, 16*(6), 1–16. doi:10.1186/s12954-019-0330-6

Hart, A. B., de Wit, H., & Palmer, A. A. (2012). Genetic factors modulating the response to stimulant drugs in humans. *Current Topics in Behavioral Neurosciences, 12*, 537–577. doi:10.1007/7854_2011_187

Hart, A. B., Engelhardt, B. E., & Wardle, M. C. (2012). Genome-wide association study of amphetamine response in healthy volunteers identifies putative associations, including Cadherin 13 (CDH13). *PLoS One, 7*(8), e42646. doi:10.1371/journal.pone.0042646

Hart, C. L., Haney, M., & Collins, E. D. (2007, January). Smoked cocaine self-administration by humans is not reduced by large gabapentin maintenance doses. *Drug and Alcohol Dependence, 86*(2–3), 274–277. doi:10.1016/j.drugalcdep.2006.05.028

Hart, C. L., Haney, M., & Vosburg, S. K. (2008, March). Smoked cocaine self-administration is decreased by modafinil. *Neuropsychopharmacology, 33*(4), 761–768. doi:10.1038/sj.npp.1301472

Hart, C. L., Ward, A. S., & Collins, E. D. (2004, March 8). Gabapentin maintenance decreases smoked cocaine-related subjective effects, but not self-administration by humans. *Drug and Alcohol Dependence, 73*(3), 279–287. doi:10.1016/j.drugalcdep.2003.10.015

Hauer, P. (2010). Systemic affects of methamphetamine use. *South Dakota Medicine, 63*(8), 285–287.

Hazama, K., & Katsuta, S. (2020). Factors associated with drug-related recidivism among paroled amphetamine-type stimulant users in Japan. *Asian Journal of Criminology, 15*(5), 1–14. doi:10.1007/s11417-019-09299-8

Heard, K., Palmer, R. I., & Zahniser, N. R. (2008). Mechanisms of acute cocaine toxicity. *Open Pharmacology Journal, 2*(9), 70–78. doi:10.2174/1874143600802010070

Heath, J., Lanoye, A., & Maisto, S. A. (2019). The role of alcohol and substance use in risky sexual behavior among older men who have sex with men. *Medscape*, pp. 1–2.

Hegazi, A., Lee, M. J., & Whittaker, W. (2017, March). Chemsex and the city: Sexualised substance use in gay bisexual and other men who have sex with men attending sexual health clinics. *International Journal of STD & AIDS, 28*(4), 362–366. doi:10.1177/0956462416651229

Hellem, T. L., Lundberg, K. J., & Renshaw, P. F. (2015). A review of treatment options for co-occurring methamphetamine use disorders and depression. *Journal of Addictions Nursing, 26*(1), 14–23. doi:10.1097/JAN.0000000000000058

Herbst, E. D., Harris, D. S., & Everhart, E. T. (2011, April). Cocaethylene formation following ethanol and cocaine administration by different routes. *Experimental and Clinical Psychopharmacology, 19*(2), 95–104. doi:10.1037/a0022950

Hibbert, L. J. (2021, April 1). Leader of Mexico's united cartels and others charged in South Florida federal court with importing over 1200 pounds of crystal methamphetamine. *DEA Press Release, Miami Division*, pp. 1–3. Miami, FL: U.S. Department of Justice.

Higgins, S. T., Sigmon, S. C., & Wong, C. J. (2003). Community reinforcement therapy for cocaine-dependent outpatients. *Archives of General Psychiatry, 60*(10), 1043–1052. doi:10.1001/archpsych.60.9.1043

Higgins, S. T., Wong, C. J., & Badger, G. J. (2000, February). Contingent reinforcement increases cocaine abstinence during outpatient treatment and 1 year of follow-up. *Journal of Consulting and Clinical Psychology, 68*(1), 64–72.

Hoffman, R. S., & Reimer, B. I. (1993). "Crack" cocaine-induced bilateral amblyopia. *The American Journal of Emergency Medicine, 11*(1), 35–37. doi:10.1016/0735-6757(93)90055-G

Holstege, C. P. (2016, April 14). Cocaine-related psychiatric disorders. *Medscape*, pp. 1–2.

Hope, V. D., Parry, J. V., & Ncube, F. (2016, February). Not in the vein: 'Missed hits', subcutaneous and intramuscular injections and associated harms among people who inject psychoactive drugs in Bristol, United Kingdom. *International Journal of Drug Policy, 28*, 83–90. doi:10.1016/j.drugpo.2015.11.003

Howell, L. L., & Cunningham, K. A. (2015, January). Serotinin 5-HT2 receptor interactions with dopamine function: Implications for therapeutics in cocaine use disorder. *Pharmacological Reviews, 67*, 176–197. Retrieved from http://DX.DOI.ORG/10.1124/PR.114.009514

Hu, X. T. (2007). Cocaine withdrawal and neuro-adaptations in ion channel function. *Molecular Neurobiology, 35*(1), 95–112.

Hunt, J. (2012, March 9). *Why the gay and transgender population experiences higher rates of substance use*. Issue Brief (pp. 1–5). Washington, DC: Center for American Progress.

Indave, B. I., Minozzi, S., & Pani, P. P. (2016, March 19). Antipsychotic medications for cocaine dependence. *Cochrane Database of Systematic Reviews, 3*, CD006306. doi:10.1002/14651858.CD006306.pub3

Inserro, A. (2018, January 19). 5 things about ADHD in older adults you may not know. *American Journal of Managed Care*, 1–2.

John, W. S., & Wu, L.-T. (2017, November 1). Trends and correlates of cocaine use and cocaine use disorder in the United States from 2011 to 2015. *Drug and Alcohol Dependence, 180*, 376–384. doi:10.1016/j.drugalcdep.2017.08.031

Johnson, B. A., Ait-Daoud, N., & Elkashef, A. M. (2008, February). A preliminary randomized, double-blind, placebo-controlled study of the safety and efficacy of ondansetron in the treatment of methamphetamine dependence. *International Journal of Neuropsychopharmacology, 11*(1), 1–14. doi:10.1017/S1461145707007778

Johnson, B. A., Devous, M. D., & Ruiz, P. (2001). Treatment advances for cocaine-induced ischemic stroke: Focus on dihydropyridine-class calcium channel antagonists. *American Journal of Psychiatry, 158*(8), 1191–1198. doi:10.1176/appi.ajp.158.8.1191

Johnston, L. D., O'Malley, P. M., & Bachman, J. G. (2013). *Monitoring the future: National survey results on drug use 1975-2012*. Institute for Social Research. Ann Arbor, MI: The University of Michigan.

Jones, C. M., Compton, W. M., & Mustaquim, D. (2020, March 27). Patterns and characteristics of methamphetamine use among adults—United States, 2015-2018. *MMWR, Morbidity and Mortality Weekly Report, 69*(12), 317–323.

Jones, C. M., Underwood, N., & Compton, W. M. (2020). Increases in methamphetamine use among heroin treatment admissions in the United States, 2008-17. *Addiction, 115*(2), 347–353. doi:10.1111/add.14812

Kahn, R., Biswas, K., & Childress, A. R. (2009, July 1). Multi-center trial of baclofen for abstinence initiation in severe cocaine-dependent individuals. *Drug and Alcohol Dependence, 103*(1–2), 59–64. doi:10.1016/j.drugalcdep.2009.03.011

Kaland, M. E., & Klein-Schwartz, W. (2015, June). Comparison of lisdexamfetamine and dextroamphetamine exposures reported to U.S. poison centers. *Clinical Toxicology (Phila), 53*(5), 477–485. doi:10.3109/15563650.2015.1027903

Kampman, K. M. (2019, October 16). The treatment of cocaine use disorder. *Science Advances, 5*(10), eaax1532. doi:10.1126/sciadv.aax1532

Kampman, K. M., Dackis, C., & Lynch, K. G. (2006, November 8). A double-brind, placebo-controlled trial of amantadine, propranolol, and their combination for the treatment of cocaine dependence in patients with severe cocaine withdrawal symptoms. *Drug and Alcohol Dependence, 85*(2), 129–137. doi:10.1016/j.drugalcdep.2006.04.002

Kampman, K. M., Dackis, C., & Pettinati, H. M. (2011). A double-blind, placebo-controlled pilot trial of acamprosate for the treatment of cocaine dependence. *Addictive Behaviors, 36*(3), 217–221. doi:10.1016/j.addbeh.20210.11.003

Kampman, K. M., Lynch, K. G., & Pettinati, H. M. (2015, October 1). A double-blind, placebo controlled trial of modafinil for the treatment of cocaine dependence without co-morbid alcohol dependence. *Drug and Alcohol Dependence, 155*, 105–110. doi:10.1016/j.drug alcdep.20215.08.005

Kampman, K. M., Pettinati, H. M., & Lynch, K. G. (2013, November 1). A double-blind, placebo-controlled trial of topiramate for the treatment of comorbid cocaine and alcohol dependence. *Drug and Alcohol Dependence, 133*(1), 94–99. doi:10.1016/j.drugalcdep.2013.05.026

Karila, L., Weinstein, A., & Aubin, H.-J. (2010). Pharmacological approaches to methamphetamine dependence: A focused review. *British Journal of Clinical Pharmacology, 69*(6), 578–592. doi:10.1111/j.1365-2125.2010.03639.x

Karrer, T. M., Josef, A. K., & Mata, R. (2017, September). Reduced dopamine receptors and transporters but not synthesis capacity in normal aging adults: A meta-analysis. *Neurobiology of Aging, 57*, 36–46. doi:10.1016/j.neurobiolaging.2017.05.006

Kasper, K. (2019, August 21). *DEA warns of national methamphetamine comeback* (p. 1). Washington, DC: kbtx.com.

Kaye, S., & Darke, S. (2002). Determining a diagnostic cut-off on the Severity of Dependence Scale (SDS) for cocaine dependence. *Addiction, 97*(6). doi:10.1046/j.1360-0443.2002.00121.x

Kaye, S., McKetin, R., & Duflou, J. (2007). Methamphetamine and cardiovascular pathology: A review of the evidence. *Addiction, 102*(8), 1204–1211. doi:10.1111/j.1360-0443.2007.01874.x

Kennedy, A. P., Epstein, D. H., & Phillips, K. A. (2013). Sex differences in cocaine/heroin users: Drug-use triggers and craving in daily life. *Drug and Alcohol Dependence, 132*(1–2), 29–37. doi:10.1016/j.drugalcdep.2012.12.025

Keoleian, V., Stalcup, A., & Poicin, D. (2013). A cognitive behavioral therapy-based text messaging intervention for methamphetamine dependence. *Journal of Psychoactive Drugs, 45*(5), 434–442.

Kerley, K. R., Leban, L., & Copes, H. (2014). Methamphetamine using careers of White and Black women. *Deviant Behavior, 35*(6), 477–495. doi:10.1080/01639625.2013.859046

Kevil, C. G., Goeders, N. E., & Woolard, M. D. (2019, August). Methamphetamine use and cardiovascular disease. *Arteriosclerosis, Thrombosis, and Vascular Biology, 39*, 1739–1746. doi:10.1161/ATVBAHA.119.312461

Kim, S. T., & Park, T. (2019, February). Acute and chronic effects of cocaine on cardiovascular health. *International Journal of Molecular Sciences, 20*(3), 584–590. doi:10.3390/ijms20030584

Kishi, T., Matsuda, Y., & Iwata, N. (2013, December). Antipsychotics for cocaine or psychostimulant dependence: Systematic review and meta-analysis of randomized placebo-controlled trials. *Journal of Clinical Psychiatry, 74*(12), e1169–e1180. doi:10.4088/JCP.13r08525

Kolodny, A. J. (2006). Psychiatric consequences of methamphetamine use. *Journal of Gay & Lesbian Psychotherapy, 10*(3–4), 67–72. doi:10.1300/j236v10n03-06

Kudlacek, O., Hofmaier, T., & Luf, A. (2017, October). Cocaine adulteration. *Journal of Chemical Neuroanatomy, 83–84*, 75–81. doi:10.1016/j.chemneu.2017.06.001

Kuhar, M. J., & Pilotte, N. S. (1996). Neurochemical changes in cocaine withdrawal. *Trends in Pharmacological Sciences, 17*(7), 260–264.

Laizure, S. C., Mandrell, T., & Gades, N. M. (2003). Cocaethylene metabolism and interation with cocaine and ethanol: Role of carboxylesterases. *Drug Metabolism and Disposition, 31*(1), 16–20.

Lankenau, S. E., Clatts, M. C., & Goldsamt, L. A. (2004). Crack cocaine injection practices and HIV risk: Findings from New York and Bridgeport. *Journal of Drug Issues, 34*(2), 319–332.

Larocque, A., & Hoffman, R. S. (2012). Levamisole in cocaine: Unexpected news from an old acquaintance. *Clinical Toxicology, 50*(4), 231–241. doi:10.3109/15563650.2012.665455

Lason, W. (2001). Neurochemical and pharmacological aspects of cocaine-induced seizures. *Polish Journal of Pharmacology, 53*(1), 57–60.

Lee, K. C., Ladizinski, B., & Federman, D. G. (2012). Complications associated with use of levamisole-contaminated cocaine: An emerging public health challenge. *Mayo Clinic Proceedings, 87*(6), 581–586.

Lee, M. R. (2011). The history of Ephredra (ma-huang). *The Journal of the Royal College of Physicians of Edinburgh, 41*, 78–84. doi:10.4997/JRCPE.2011.116

Lee, N. K., & Rawson, R. A. (2008, May). A systematic review of cognitive and behavioural therapies for methamphetamine dependence. *Drug and Alcohol Reviews, 27*, 309–317. doi:10.1080/09595230801919494

Lee, N., Jenner, L., & Nielsen, S. (2014). *Medication treatment: Options for amphetamine-type stimulant users*. Canberra: Australian National Council on Drugs. Retrieved October 24, 2017

Leonard, K. (2017, January 3). What's behind the rise in cocaine-linked deaths? *US News & World Report*, pp. 1–5. Retrieved from https://www.usnews.com/topics/subjects/cocaine

Lewis, D. (1994, January 12). Cocaine and other botanical insecticides. *Horticulture and Home Pest News*. Iowa State University.

Lile, J. A., Stoops, W. W., & Allen, T. S. (2004, February). Baclofen does not alter the reinforcing, subject-rated or cardiovascular effects of intranasal cocaine in humans. *Psychopharmacology (Berlin), 171*(4), 441–449. doi:10.1007/s00213-003-1598-4

Liu, Y., Ball, J., & Elliot, A. L. (2019, March 25). Diagnostic sequence of cocaine use disorder in relation to other mental health conditions among college students. *Journal of American College Health*. doi:10.1080/07448481.2019.1583657

Loguidice, C. (2020, February 5). Cocaine use and hepatitis C infection: What's the link? *Infectious Disease Advisor*, pp. 1–7. Haymarket Media.

Longo, M., Wickes, W., & Smout, M. (2010). Randomized controlled trial of dexamphetamine maintenance for the treatment of methamphetamine dependence. *Addiction, 105*(1), 146–154. doi:10.111/j.1360-0443.2009.02727.x

Lott, D. C., Kim, S.-J., & Cook, E. H. (2005). Dopamine trasporter gene associated with diminished subjective response to amphetamine. *Neuropsychopharmacology, 30*(3), 602–609. doi:10.1038/sj.npp.1300637

Madera, G., Cabrejas, M., & Holguin, P. (2016). Acute rhabdomyolysis and acute cocaine intoxication. *Journal of Family Medicine and Disease Prevention, 2*(1), 24.

Majlesi, N., Shih, R., & Fiesseler, F. W. (2010, May). Cocaine-associated seizures and incidence of status epilepticus. *Western Journal of Emergency Medicine, 11*(2), 157–160.

Mammoser, G. (2017, December 12). Latest 'street meth' coming from labs in Mexico. *Healthline*, pp. 1–3. Healthline Media.

Marks, K. R., Pike, E., & Stoops, W. W. (2015). Alcohol administration increases cocaine craving but not cocaine cue attentional bias. *Alcoholism: Clinical & Experimental Research, 39*(9), 1823–1831. doi:10.111/acer.12824

Martin, W. R., Palmer, M. R., & Patlak, C. S. (1989). Nigrostrial function in humans studied with positron emission tomography. *Annals of Neurology, 26*(4), 1–5. doi:10.1002/ana.410260407

Martin-Schild, S., Albright, K. C., & Hallevi, H. (2010). Intracerebral hemorrhage in cocaine users. *Stroke, 41*(4), 680–684. doi:10.1161/STROKEAHA.109.573147

Matthew, B. J., & Gedzior, J. S. (2015). Drug-induced parkinsonism following chronic methamphetamine use by a patient on haloperidol decanoate. *The International Journal of Psychiatry in Medicine, 50*(4), 405–411. doi:10.1177/0091217415612736

McCord, J., Jneid, H., & Hollander, J. E. (2008). Management of cocaine-associated chest pain and myocardial infarction. *Circulation, 117*, 1897–1907. doi:10.1161/CIRCULA TIONAHA.107.188950

McElhiney, M. C., Rabkin, J. G., & Rabkin, R. (2009). Provigil (Modafinil) plus cognitive behavioral therapy for methamphetamine use in HIV+ gay men: A pilot study. *The American Journal of Drug and Alcohol Abuse, 35*(1), 34–37. doi:10.1080/00952990802342907

McGregor, C., Srisurapanont, M., & Jittiwutikarn, J. (2005). The nature, time course, and severity of methamphetamine withdrawal. *Addiction, 100*(9), 1320–1329. doi:10.1111/j.1360-0443.2005.01160.x

McKetin, R., Leung, J., & Stockings, E. (2019). Mental health outcomes associated with the use of amphetamines: A systematic review and meta-analysis. *EClinicalMedicine, 16*, 81–97. doi:10.1016/j.eclinm.2019.09.014

McWilliams, K. (2019, August 19). DEA targets methamphetamine in three states with operation crystal mountain. *Press Release*, p. 1. Louisville, KY: Drug Enforcement Administration.

Melendez-Torres, G. J., & Bourne, A. (2016, February). Illicit drug use and its assciation with sexual risk behavior among MSM: More questions than answers? *Current Opinion In Infectious Diseases, 29*(1), 58–63. doi:10.1097/QCO.0000000000000234

Merenda, A., Muir, K. W., & Koch, S. (2016). Cracking the role of cocaine in stroke. *Stroke, 47*, 909–910. doi:10.1161/STROKEAHA.116.012681

Messina, N., Marinelli-Casey, P., & West, K. (2014). Children exposed to methamphetamine use and manufacture. *Child Abuse & Neglect, 38*(11), 1872–1883. doi:10.1016/j.chiabu.2006.06.009

Michielsen, M., Semejin, E., & Comijs, H. C. (2012). Prevalence of attention-deficit hyperactivity disorder in older adults in the Netherlands. *The British Journal of Psychiatry, 201*, 298–305. doi:10.1192/bjp.bp.111.101196

Minozzi, S., Cinquini, M., & Amato, L. (2015, April 17). Anticonvulsants for cocaine dependence. *Cochrane Database of Systematic Reviews, 4*, CD006754. doi:10.1002/146451858.CD006754.pub4

Minozzi, S., & Saulle, R. D. (2016, Septembert 29). Psychosocial interventions for psychostimulant misuse. *Cochrane Database of Systematic Reviews, 9*, CD011866. doi:10.1002/14651858.CD011866.pub2

Moeller, F. G., Schmitz, J. M., & Steinberg, J. L. (2007). Citalopram combined with behavioral therapy reduces cocaine use: A double-blind, placebo-controlled trial. *The American Journal of Drug and Alcohol Abuse, 33*(3), 367–378. doi:10.1080/00952907013113686

Moody, L., Franck, C., & Jarmolowicz, D. P. (2014). Executive functioning deficits in cocaine-dependent individuals. *Drug and Alcohol Dependence, 140*, e155.

Moore, T. M., Stuart, G. L., & Meehan, J. C. (2008). Drug abuse and aggression between intimate partners: A meta-analytic review. *Clinical Psychology Review, 28*(2), 247–274.

Moreira Sassi, K. L., Pessoa Rocha, N., & Delevati Colpo, G. (2020). Amphetamine use in the elderly: A systematic review of the literature. *Current Neuropharmacology, 18*(2), 126–135. doi:10.2174/1570159X17666191010093021

Morley, K. C., Cornish, J. L., & Faingold, A. (2017). Pharmacotherapeutic agents in the treatment of methamphetamine dependence. *Expert Opinion on Investigational Drugs, 26*(5), 563–578. doi:10.1080/13543784.2017.1313229

Mullen, J. M., Richards, J. R., & Crawford, A. T. (2020). *Amphetamine related psychiatric disorders*. Treasure Island, FL: StatPearls Publishing.

Mullin, G. (2016, January 28). Faces of crystal meth: Shocking before and after pictures reveal damage of prolonged drug use. *World News*.

Murphy, R. J., & Truesdell, C. (2020, October 13). Major South Georgia drug trafficker sentenced to nearly two decades in federal prison. *DEA Press Release, Atlanta Division*, pp. 1–3. Washington, DC: U.S. Department of Justice.

Murphy, R. J., & Truesdell, C. (2021, March 11). Coffee county man sentenced to federal prison for trafficking methamphetamine. *DEA Press Release, Atlanta Division*, pp. 1–2. Washington, DC: U.S. Department of Justice.

Nathanson, J. A., Hunnicutt, E. J., & Kantham, L. (1993, October 15). Cocaine as a naturally occurring insecticide. *Proceedings of the National Academy of Science of the United States of America, 90*(20), 9645–9648.

National Drug Intelligence Center. (2006). *National methamphetamine threat assessment 2007*. Johnstown: U.S. Department of Justice. Retrieved June 30, 2018

NIDA, National Institute of Drug Abuse. (2016, May 6). *Cocaine. Research reports*. Bethesda, MD: NIH. Retrieved January 18, 2020, from https://www.drugabuse.gov/publications/research-reports/cocaine

NIDA, National Institute on Drug Abuse. (2018, July). *Cocaine. Drug Facts* (pp. 1–6). NIH, National Institutes of Health.

NIDA, National Institute on Drug Abuse. (2021, January 20). Methamphetamine overdose deaths rise sharply nationwide. *News Release*, pp. 1–4. Bethesda, MD: NIH.

NIDA/NIH, National Institute on Drug Abuse/National Institutes of Health. (2005). *Medications development research for treatment of amphetamine and methamphetamine addiction*. Bethesda, MD: Department of Health and Human Services. Retrieved October 24, 2017

NIH, National Institutes on Health. (2018, August). Overdose death rates. *National Overdose Deaths*, pp. 1–7. NIH.

Nixon, R. (2016, February 10). Drug traffickers turn to new type of courier: Seniors. *The New York Times*, pp. 1–2.

Nogueira, L., Kalivas, P. W., & Lavin, A. (2006). Long-term neuroadaptations produced by withdrawal from repeated cocaine treatment: Role of dopaminergic receptors in modulating cortical excitability. *The Journal of Neuroscience, 26*(47), 12308–12313. doi:10.1523/JNEUROSCI.3206-06.2006

Norris, K. C., Thornhill-Joynes, M., & Robinson, C. (2001). Cocaine use, hypertension, and end-stage renal disease. *American Journal of Kidney Diseases, 38*(3), 523–528. doi:10.1053/ajkd.2001.26845

Numberger, J. I., Wiegand, R., & Bucholz, K. (2004). A family study of alcohol dependence: Coaggregation of multiple disorders in relatives of alcohol-dependent probands. *Archives of General Psychiatry, 61*(12), 1246–1256. doi:10.1001/archpsyc.61.12.1246

ONDCP, Office of National Drug Control Policy. (2010, July). *Fact sheet: Methamphetamine trends in the United States*. Retrieved April 5, 2016, from www.WhiteHouseDrugPolicy.gov

Orciari Herman, A. (2018, March 30). Drug overdose deaths still increasing, opioids largely to blame. *NEJM Journal Watch*.

Osbourne, H. (2020, August 28). Authorities arrest 21 in Austin area drug bust, feds say. In *Austin American-statesman* (pp. 1–2). Austin, Texas: Austin American-Statesman.

Pagliaro, A. M., & Pagliaro, L. A. (Eds.). (1986). *Pharmacologic aspects of nursing*. St. Louis: C. V. Mosby.

Pagliaro, A. M., & Pagliaro, L. A. (2018). *Women's drug and substance abuse: A comprehensive analysis and reflective synthesis*. New York: Routledge.

Pagliaro, A. M., Pagliaro, L. A., & Thauberger, P. C. (1990). AIDS and injection drug use: Changing dimensions of the epidemic. *Alberta Psychology, 19*(5), 5–7.

Pagliaro, A. M., Pagliaro, L. A., & Thauberger, P. C. (1993). Knowledge, behaviours, and risk perception of intravenous drug users in relation to HIV infection and AIDS: The PIARG projects. *Advances in Medical Psychotherapy, 6*, 1–28.

Pagliaro, L. A., & Benet, L. Z. (1975). Critical compilation of terminal half-lives, percent excreted unchanged, and changes in renal and hepatic dysfunction for studies in adults with references. *Journal of Pharmacokinetics and Biopharmaceutics, 3*, 333–383.

Pagliaro, L. A., Jaglalsingh, L. H., & Pagliaro, A. M. (1992). Cocaine use and depression. *Canadian Medical Association Journal, 147*, 1636–1637.

Pagliaro, L. A., & Pagliaro, A. M. (1999). *PPDR: Psychologists' Psychotropic drug reference*. Philadelphia, PA: Brunner/Mazel.

Pagliaro, L. A., & Pagliaro, A. M. (2004). *Pagliaros' comprehensive guide to drugs and substances of abuse* (1st ed.). Washington, DC: American Pharmacists Association.

Pagliaro, L. A., & Pagliaro, A. M. (2009). *Pagliaros' comprehensive guide to drugs and substances of abuse* (2nd ed.). Washington, DC: American Pharmacists Association.

Pagliaro, L. A., & Pagliaro, A. M. (2012). *Handbook of child and adolescent drug and substance abuse*. Hoboken, NJ: Wiley & Sons.

Pagliaro, L. A., & Pagliaro, A. M. (2020). *Child and adolescent drug and substance abuse*. New York: Routledge.

Pakianathan, M. R., Lee, M. J., & Kelly, B. (2016, December). How to assess gay, bisexual and other men who have sex with men for chemsex. *Sexually Transmitted Infections, 92*(8), 568–570. doi:10.10365/sextrans-2015-052405

Pani, P. P., Trogu, E., & Vacca, R. (2010, January 20). Disulfiram for the treatment of cocaine dependence. *Cochrane Database of Systematic Reviews, 1*, CD007024. doi:10.1002/146541858.CD007024.pub2

Parvaz, M. A., Moeller, S. J., & Goldstein, R. Z. (2016). Incubation of cue-induced craving in adults addicted to cocaine measured by electroencephalography. *JAMA Psychiatry, 673*(11), 1127–1134.

Penberthy, J. K., Ait-Daoud, N., & Vaughan, M. (2010, March). Review of treatment for cocaine dependence. *Current Drug Abuse Reviews, 3*(1), 49–62.

People Staff. (1980, June 30). Richard Pryor's tragic accident spotlights a dangerous drug craze: Freebasing. *People*, 1–4.

Peragallo, J., Blousse, V., & Newman, N. J. (2013, November). Ocular manifestations of drug and alcohol abuse. *Current Opinion in Ophthalmology, 24*(6), 566–573. doi:10.1097/ICU.0b013e3283654db2

Perez-Mana, C., Castells, X., & Torrens, M. (2013, September 2). Efficacy of psychostimulant drugs for amphetamine abuse or dependence. *Cochrane Database of Systematic Reviews, 9*, CD009695. doi:10.1002/14651858.CD009695.pub2

Petry, N. M., Barry, D., & Alessi, S. M. (2012, April). A randomized trial adapting contingency management targets based on initial abstinence status of cocaine-dependent patients. *Journal of Consulting and Clinical Psychology, 80*(2), 276–285. doi:10.1037/a0026883

Petry, N. M., Martin, B., & Simcic, F. (2005). Prize reinforcement contingency management for cocaine dependence: Integration with group therapy in a methadone clinic. *Journal of Consulting and Clinical Psychology, 73*(2), 354–359. doi:10.1037/0022-006X.73.2.354

Pettinati, H. M., Kampman, K. M., & Lynch, K. G. (2008a). A double-blind, placebo-controlled trial that combines disulfiram and naltrexone for treating co-occurring cocaine and alcohol dependence. *Addictive Behaviors, 33*(3), 651–667. doi:10.1016/j.addbeh.2007.11.011

Pettinati, H. M., Kampman, K. M., & Lynch, K. G. (2008b, June). Gender differences with high-dose naltrexone in patients with co-occurring cocaine and alcohol dependence. *Journal of Substance Abuse Treatment, 34*(4), 378–390. doi:10.1016/j.jsat6.2007.05.011

Phillips, K., Luk, A., & Soor, G. S. (2009). Cocaine cardiotoxicity: A review of the pathophysiology, pathology, and treatment options. *American Journal of Cardiovascular Drugs, 9*(3), 177–196. doi:10.2165/00129784-200909030-00005

Pilgrim, J. L., Woodford, N., & Drummer, O. H. (2013). Cocaine in sudden and unexpected death: A review of 49 post-mortem cases. *Forensic Science International, 227*(1–3), 52–59. doi:10.1016/j.forsciint.2012.08.037

Pilon, A. F., & Scheiffle, J. (2006). Ulcerative keratitis associated with crack-cocaine abuse. *Contact Lens & Anterior Eye, 29*(5), 263–267. doi:10.1016/j.clae.2006.09.002

Pilowsky, D., & Wu, L. (2015, April 21). Sexual risk behaviors and HIV risk among Americans aged 50 years or older: A review. *Dovepress, 6*, 51–60. doi:10.2147/SAR.S78808

Pinarski, P. (2020, December 3). Significant drug bust in Walker County seizes 103 grams of meth, 1 suspect still on the loose. *CBS 42 News*, p. 1.

Plowman, T. (1985). Coca chewing and the botanical origins of coca (Erythroxylum spp.) in South America. In D. Pacini & C. Franquemont (Eds.), *Coca and cocaine: Effects on people and policy in Latin America* (pp. 1–31). Peterborough: Transcript Printing.

Poling, J., Oliveto, A., & Petry, N. (2006). Six-month trial of bupropion with contingency management for cocaine dependence in a methadone-maintained population. *Archives of General Psychiatry, 63*(2), 219–228. doi:10.1001/archpsyc.63.2.219

Pope, S. K., Falck, R. S., & Carlson, R. G. (2011, November). Characteristics of rural crack and powder cocaine use: Gender and other correlates. *American Journal of Drug and Alcohol Abuse, 37*(6), 491–496. doi:10.3109/00952990.2011.600380

Raiker, N., Aouthmany, M., & Ezra, N. (2016). Dermatologic signs and symptoms of substance abuse. *Journal of Clinical & Experimental Dermatology Research, 7*(2), 1–7. doi:10.4172/2155-9554.1000337

Rawson, R. A., Huber, A., & McCann, M. (2002). A comparison of contingency management and cognitive-behavioral approaches during methadone maintenance treatment for cocaine dependence. *Archives of General Psychiatry, 59*(9), 817–824.

Reback, C. J., & Shoptaw, S. (2014, August). Development of an evidence-based gay-specific cognitive behavioral therapy intervention for methamphetamine-abusing gay and bisexual men. *Addictive Behaviors, 39*(8), 1286–1291. doi:10.1016/j.addbeh.2011.11.029

Restrepo, C. S., Carrillo, J. A., & Martinez, S. (2007, July–August). Pulmonary complications from cocaine and cocaine-based substances: Imaging manifestations. *RadioGraphics, 27*(4), 941–956. doi:10.1148/rg274065144

Rice-Mesa, J. S., Rice-Mesa, M. A., & Berrouet, M. C. (2017). Ischemic stroke related to acute consumption of cocaine. *CES Medicine, 31*(2), 207–214. doi:10.21615/cesmedicina.31.2.10

Richards, J. R., & Le, J. K. (2019). *Cocaine toxicity*. Treasure Island, FL: StatPearls.

Richards, J. R., Garber, D., & Laurin, E. G. (2016, June). Treatment of cocaine cardiovascular toxicity: A systematic review. *Clinical Toxicology (Philadelphia), 54*(5), 345–364.

Rinkel, G. J., Djibuti, M., & Algra, A. (1998). Prevalence and risk of rupture of intracranial aneurysms: A systematic review. *Stroke, 29*, 251–256.

Roberts, J. K., Cook, S. F., & Stockmann, C. (2015, October). A population pharmacokinetic analysis of dextroamphetamine in the plasma and hair of healthy adults. *Clinical Drug Investigation, 35*(10), 633–643. doi:10.1007/s40261-015-0323-5

Rolland, B., Karila, L., & Geoffroy, P. A. (2011). Shared vulnerability between seizures and psychosis in cocaine addiction? *Epilepsy & Behavior, 22*(3), 596–598. doi:10.1016/j.yebeh.2011.08.004

Rommel, N., Rohleder, N. H., & Koerdt, S. (2016, May 26). Sympathomimetic effects of chronic methamphetamine abuse on oral health: A cross-sectional study. *BMC Oral Health, 16*(1), 59. doi:10.1186/s12903-016-0218-8

Rommel, N., Rohleder, N. H., & Wagenpfeil, S. (2016, April). The impact of the new scene drug "crystal meth" on oral health: A case-control study. *Clinical Oral Investigations, 20*(3), 469–475. doi:10.1007/s00784-015-1527-z

Roozen, H. G., Boulogne, J. J., & van Tulder, M. W. (2004). A systematic review of the effectiveness of the community reinforcement approach in alcohol, cocaine and opioid addiction. *Drug and Alcohol Dependence, 74*(1), 1–13.

Rothman, R. B., Baumann, M. H., & Dersch, C. M. (2001). Amphetamine-type central nervous system stimulants release norepinephrine more potently than they release dopamine and serotonin. *Synapse, 39*(1), 32–41. doi:10.1002/1098-2396(20010101)39:1<32::AID-SYN5>3.0.CO:2-3

Ryder, J. A., & Brisgone, R. E. (2013). Cracked perspectives: Reflections of women and girls in the aftermath of the crack cocaine era. *Feminist Criminology, 8*(1), 40–62. doi:10.1177/1557085112444899

Sachs, R., Zagelbaum, B. M., & Hersh, P. S. (1993). Corneal complications associated with the use of crack cocaine. *Ophthalmology, 100*(2), 187–191.

Safer, D. J. (2016, June). Recent trends in stimulant usage. *Journal of Attention Disorders, 20*(6), 471–477. doi:10.1177/1087054715605915

Salo, R., Flower, K., & Kielstein, A. (2011, April 30). Psychiatric comorbidity in methamphetamine dependence. *Psychiatry Research, 186*(2–3), 356–361. doi:10.1016/j.psychres.2010.09.014

SAMHSA, Substance Abuse and Mental Health Services Administration. (2020). *Treatment of stimulant use disorders*. Rockville, MD: National Mental Health and Substance Use Policy Laboratory, Substance Abuse and Mental Health Services Administration.

Sands, G. (2016, February 10). The elderly being conned into trafficking drugs. *ABC News*, pp. 1–4.

Santos, G. M., Miller, D., & Jain, J. (2020–2021, Winter). Prevalence and correlates of methamphetamine use among older men who have sex with men in San Francisco. *Generations*, pp. 1–14.

Sato, M., Hida, M., & Nagase, H. (2004, November–December). Analysis of pyrolysis products of methamphetamine. *Journal of Analytical Toxicology, 28*(8), 638–643.

Schaneberg, B. T., Crockett, S., & Bedir, E. (2003, March). The role of chemical fingerprinting: Application to Ephedra. *Phytochemistry, 62*(6), 911–918.

Schepers, J. F., Oyler, J. M., & Joseph, R. E. (2003). Methamphetamine and amphetamine pharmacokinetics in oral fluid and plasma after controlled oral methamphetamine administration to human volunteers. *Clinical Chemistry, 49*(1), 121–132. doi:10.1373/49.1.121

Schierenberg, A., van Amsterdam, J., & van den Brink, W. (2012, December). Efficacy of contingency management for cocaine dependence treatment: A review of the evidence. *Current Drug Abuse Reviews, 5*(4), 320–331.

Schmitz, J. M., Lindsay, J. A., & Green, C. E. (2009, September–October). High-dose naltrexone therapy for cocaine-alcohol dependence. *The American Journal on Addictions, 18*(5), 356–362. doi:10.3109/10550490903077929

Schottenfeld, R. S., Moore, B., & Pantalon, M. V. (2011, October 1). Contingency management with community reinforcement approach or twelve-step facilitation drug counseling for cocaine dependent pregnant women or women with young children. *Drug and Alcohol Dependence, 118*(1), 48–55. doi:10.1016/j.drugalcdep.2011.02.019

Schumacher, J. E., Milby, J. B., & Wallace, D. (2003, May). Diagnostic compared with abstinence outcomes of day treatment and contingency management among cocaine-dependent homeless persons. *Experimental and Clinical Psychopharmacology, 11*(2), 146–157.

Schwartz, B. G., Rezkalla, S., & Kloner, R. A. (2010). Cardiovascular effects of cocaine. *Circulation, 122*(24), 2558–2569. doi:10.1161/CIRCULATIONAHA.110.940569

Semeijn, E. J., Michielsen, M., & Comijs, H. C. (2013, July). Criterion validity of an attention deficit hyperactivity disorder (ADHD) screening list for screening ADHD in older adults aged 60-94 years. *The American Journal of Geriatric Psychiatry, 21*(7), 631–635. doi:10.1016/j.jagp.2012.08.003

Sewell, J., Miltz, A., & Lampe, F. C. (2017, May). Poly drug use, chemsex drug use, and associations with sexual risk behaviour in HIV-negative men who have sex with men attending sexual health clinics. *The International Journal of Drug Policy, 43*, 33–43. doi:10.1016/j.drugpo.2017.01.001

Shah, R., Patel, A., & Mousa, O. (2015). Crack lung: Cocaine-induced lung injury. *QJM: An International Journal of Medicine, 108*(9), 749. doi:10.1093/qjmed/hcv064

Shake and bake or one pot meth making. (n.d.). Some chick's blog all about meth (pp. 1–11). Retrieved November 2, 2016, from http://somechicksblog.com/make-meth/shake-and-bake-or-one-pot-meth-making

Shannon, B. (2020, July 15). *38 Arrested in massive meth bust crossing multiple counties*. Johnstown, PA: WETM.

Shin, E. J., Tran, H. Q., & Nguyen, P. T. (2017, June 7). Role of mitochondria in methamphetamine-induced dopaminergic neurotoxicity: Involvement in oxidative stress, neuroinflammation, and pro-apoptosis—A review. *Neurochemical Research*. doi:10.1007/s11064-017-2318-5

Shoptaw, S. J., Heinzerling, K. G., & Rotheram-Fuller, E. (2008). Bupropion hydrochloride versus placebo, in combination with cognitive behavioral therapy, for the treatment of cocaine abuse/dependence. *Journal of Addictive Diseases, 27*(1), 13–23. doi:10.1300/J069v27n01_02

Shoptaw, S. J., Kao, U., & Heinzerling, K. (2009, April 15). Treatment for amphetamine withdrawal. *Cochrane Database of Sytematic Reviews, 2009*(2), CD003021. doi:10.1002/14651858.CD003021.pub2

Shoptaw, S. J., Kintaudi, P. C., & Charuvastra, C. (2002, May 1). A screening trial of amanatadine as a medication for cocaine dependence. *Drug and Alcohol Dependence, 66*(3), 217–224.

Shoptaw, S. J., Reback, C. J., & Peck, J. A. (2005). Behavioral treatment approaches for methamphetamine dependence and HIV-related sexual risk behaviors among urban gay and bisexual men. *Drug and Alcohol Dependence, 78*, 125–134. doi:10.1016/j.drugalcdep.2004.10.004

Shukla, R. K., Crump, J. L., & Chrisco, E. S. (2012, November). An evolving problem: Methamphetamine production and trafficking in the United States. *The International Journal on Drug Policy, 23*(6), 426–435. doi:10.1016/_drugpo.2012.07.004

Shumay, E., Chen, J., & Fowler, J. S. (2011). Genotype and ancestry modulate brain's DAT availability in healthy humans. *PloS One, 6*(8), e22754. doi:10.1371/journal.pone.0022754

Siefried, K. J., Acheson, L. S., & Lintzeris, N. (2020, April). Pharmacological treatment of methamphetamine/amphetamine dependence: A systematic review. *CNS Drugs*, 337–365. doi:10.1007/s40263-020-00711-x

Sinha, R. (2008, October). Chronic stress, drug use, and vulnerability to addiction. *Annals of the New York Academy of Sciences, 1141*, 105–130. doi:10.1196/annals.1441.030

Skeberdis, V. A. (2004). Structure and function of beta3-adrenergic receptors. *Medicina, 40*(5), 407–413.

Smith, P. H., Homish, G. G., & Leonard, K. E. (2012). Intimate partner violence and specific substance use disorders: Findings from the national epidemiologic survey on alcohol and related conditions. *Psychology of Addictive Behaviors, 26*(2), 236–245. doi:10.1037/a0024855

Sofuoglu, M., Poling, J., & Gonzalez, G. (2007, October). Progesterone effects on cocaine use in male cocaine users maintained on methadone: A randomized, double-blind, pilot study. *Experimental and Clinical Psychopharmacology, 15*(5), 454–460. doi:10.1037/1064-1297.15.5.453

Sordo, L., Iciar Indave, B., & Barrio, G. A. (2014, August). Cocaine use and risk of stroke: A systematic review. *Drug and Alcohol Dependence*, 1–5. doi:10.1016/j.drugalcdep.2014.06.041

Spinelli, M. A., Ponath, C., & Tieu, L. (2017, January–March). Factors associated with substance use in older homeless adults: Results from the HOPE HOME Study. *Substance Abuse, 38*(1), 88–94. doi:10.1080/08897077.2016.1264534

Staff. (2018, May 8). 8 Arrested in Laurel County drug bust involving methamphetamine. *WDKY, Fox News 56*, pp. 1–2. WDKY.

Stoops, W. W., & Rush, C. R. (2013). Agonist replacement for stimulant dependence: A review of clinical research. *Current Pharmaceutical Design, 19*(40), 7026–7035.

Stuard, W. L., Gallerson, B. K., & Robertson, D. M. (2017). Alterations in corneal nerves following crack cocaine use mimic diabetes-induced nerve damage. *Endocrinology, Diabetes & Metabolism Case Reports, 2017*(1), 1–6. doi:10.1530/EDM-16-0131

Stuart, G. L., Moore, T. M., & Elkins, S. R. (2013, August). The temporal association between substance use and intimate partner violence among women arrested for domestic violence. *Journal of Consulting and Clinical Psychology, 81*(4), 1–18. doi:10.1037/a0032876

Suzuki, S., Uehara, T., & Ohira, Y. (2015). Narcolepsy with cataplexy in an elderly woman. *Journal of General Internal Medicine, 30*(8), 1222–1224. doi:10.1007/s11606-015-3277-7

Swanson, A. (2021, May 4). Union man pleads guilty to meth trafficking on day of trial. *DEA Report, St. Louis Division*, p. 1. Springfield, MO: U.S. Department of Justice.

Thomas, D. M., & Mirowski, G. W. (2010, July–August). Nutritional and oral mucosal diseases. *Clinics in Dermatology, 28*(4), 426–431. doi:10.1016/j.clindermatol.2010.03.025

Tobin, S. C. (2017). *EEG indicates that cocaine relapse vulnerability peaks 1 to 6 months into abstinence*. National Intitute on Drug Abuse. Retrieved November 5, 2017

Todd, G., Noyes, C., & Flavel, S. C. (2013). Illicit stimulant use is associated with abnormal substantia nigra morphology in humans. *PLoS One, 8*(2), e56438. doi:10.1371/journal.pone.0056438

Topp, L., & Mattick, R. P. (2006, January 24). Choosing a cut-off on the Severity of Dependence Scale (SDS) for amphetamine users. *Addiction, 92*(7). doi:10.1111/j.1360-0443.1997.tb02953.x

Treadwell, S. D., & Robinson, T. G. (2007, June). Cocaine use and stroke. *Postgraduate Medical Journal, 83*(980), 389–394. doi:10.1136/pgmj.2006.055970

Trivedi, M. H., Walker, R., & Ling, W. (2021, January 14). Bupropion and naltrexone in methamphetamine use disorder. *New England Journal of Medicine, 384*, 140–153. doi:10.1056/NEJMoa2020214

Turillazzi, E., Bello, S., & Neri, M. (2012). Cardiovascular effects of cocaine: Cellular, ionic and molecular mechanisms. *Current Medicinal Chemistry, 19*(33), 5664–5676.

Umbricht, A., DeFulio, A., & Winstanley, E. L. (2014, July 1). Topiramate for cocaine dependence during methadone maintenance treatment: A randomized controlled trial. *Drug and Alcohol Dependence, 140*, 92–100. doi:10.1016/j.drugalcdep.20124.03.033

University of Michigan. (2008, October). *Monitoring the future: National survey results on drug use, 1975-2007: Volume II: College students and adults ages 19–45, 2007*. Ann Arbor, MI: University of Michigan.

USCC, U.S.-China Economic and Security Review Commission. (2016, July 18). Meth precursor chemicals from China: Implications for the United States. *Press Release*, pp. 1–3.

Vallersnes, O. M., Dines, A. M., & Wood, D. M. (2016, August 18). Psychosis associated with acute recreational drug toxicity: A European case series. *BMC Psychiatry, 16*, 293. doi:10.1186/s12888-016-1002-7

Van Loggerenberg, C. J. (2007, March). Management of stimulant drug overdose. *CME, 25*(3), 128–133.

Vasan, S., & Olango, G. J. (2020). *Amphetamine toxicity* (pp. 1–10). Treasure Island, FL: StatPearls Publishing.

Vilela, R. J., Langford, C., & McCullagh, L. (2002). Cocaine-induced oronasal fistulas with external nasal erosion but without palate involvement. *Ear, Nose, & Throat Journal, 81*(8), 562–563.

Villa, P. D. (1999). Midfacial complications of prolonged cocaine snorting. *Journal of the Canadian Dental Association, 65*(4), 218–223.

Vocci, F. J., & Montoya, I. D. (2009, May). Psychological treatments for stimulant misuse, comparing and contrasting those for amphetamine dependence and those for cocaine dependence. *Current Opinion in Psychiatry, 22*(3), 263–268. doi:10.1097/YCO.0b013e32832a3b44

Wako, E., LeDoux, D., & Mitsumori, L. (2007, July). The emerging epidemic of methamphetamine-induced aortic dissections. *Journal of Cardiac Surgery, 22*(5). doi:10.1111/j.1540-8191.2007.00432.x

Walsh, S. L., Stoops, W. W., & Moody, D. E. (2009). Repeated dosing with oral cocaine in humans: Assessment of direct effects, withdrawal, and pharmacokinetics. *Experimental and Clinical Psychopharmacology, 17*(4), 205–216. doi:10.1037/a0016469

Wang, R. Y. (1999). pH-dependent cocaine-induced cardiotoxicity. *The American Journal of Emergency Medicine, 17*(4), 364–369.

Waninger, K. M., Gotsch, P. B., & Watts, D. (2007). Use of lemon juice to increase crack cocaine solubility for intravenous use. *The Journal of Emergency Medicine, 34*(2), 207–209. doi:10.1016/jemermed.2007.05.015

Warren, B. (2019, January 25). Deal drugs or die: Grandpa says he sold meth to save son from cartel. *Louisville Courier Journal*, 1–3. Louisville Courier Journal.

Wearne, T. A., & Cornish, J. L. (2018, October 10). A comparison of methamphetamine-induced psychosis and schizophrenia: A review of positive, negative, and cognitive symptomatology. *Frontiers in Psychiatry, 9*, 1–20. doi:10.3389/fpsyt.2018.00491

Williamson, K., & Briano, C. A. (2021, March 16). El Paso man sentenced to federal prison for trafficking meth and assaulting co-defendant. *DEA Press Release, El Paso Division*, pp. 1–2. Washington, DC: U.S. Department of Justice.

Winhusen, T., & Lewis, D. (2013). Sex differences in disinhibition and its relationship to physical abuse in a sample of stimulant-dependent patients. *Drug and Alcohol Dependence, 129*(1–2), 158–162. doi:10.1016/j.drugalcdep.2012.09.014

Winhusen, T., Somoza, E., & Ciraulo, D. A. (2007, December 1). A double-blind, placebo-controlled trial of tiagabine for the treatment of cocaine dependence. *Drug and Alcohol Dependence, 91*(2–3), 141–148. doi:10.210216/j.drugalcdep.2007.05.028

Winhusen, T., Somoza, E., & Sarid-Segal, O. (2007, December 1). A double-blind, placebo-controlled trial of reserpine for the treatment of cocaine dependence. *Drug and Alcohol Dependence, 91*(2–3), 205–212. doi:10.1016/j.drugalcdep.2007.05.021

Winslow, B. T., Voorhees, K. I., & Pehl, K. A. (2007). Methamphetamine abuse. *American Family Physician, 76*(8), 1169–1174.

Woody, G. E., Cottler, L. B., & Cacciola, J. (1993, November). Severity of dependence: Data from DSM-IV field trials. *Addiction, 88*(11), 1–5. doi:10.1111/j.1360-0443.1993.tb3144.x

Xie, Y., Pope, B. A., & Hunter, A. J. (2016). Cotton fever: Does the patient know best? *Journal of General Internal Medicine, 31*(4), 442–444. doi:10.1007/s.11606-015-3424-1

Yarnell, S. C. (2015). Cocaine abuse in later life: A case series and review of the literature. *The Primary Care Companion for CNS Disorders, 17*(2), 1–9. doi:10.4088/PCC.14r01727

Yen, C.-F., Wu, H.-Y., & Yen, J.-Y. (2004). Effects of brief cognitive-behavioral interventions on confidence to resist the urges to use heroin and methamphetamine in relapse-related situations. *The Journal of Nervous and Mental Disease, 192*(11), 788–791. doi:10.1097/01.nmd.0000144699.80765.7f

Yonkers, K. A., Forray, A., & Nich, C. (2014, October 1). Progesterone reduces cocaine use in postpartum women with a cocaine use disorder: A randomized, double-blind study. *Lancet Psychiatry, 1*(5), 360–367. doi:10.1016/S2215-0366(14)70333-5

Yu, S., Zhu, L., & Shen, Q. (2015). Recent advances in methamphetamine neurotoxicity mechanisms and its molecular pathophysiology. *Behavioural Neurology, Article ID 103969*, 1–11. doi:10.1155/2015/103969

Zerr, A. M., Ku, K., & Kara, A. (2016, March–April). Cotton fever: A condition self-diagnosed by IV drug users. *Journal of the American Board of Family Medicine, 29*(2), 276–279. doi:10.31212/jabfm.2016.02.150267

Zhu, H., Wilson, F. A., & Stimpson, J. P. (2014). Correlation between cocaine prices and purity with trends in emergency department visits in a major metropolitan area. *Journal of Urban Health: Bulletin of the New York Academy of Medicine, 91*(5), 1009–1018. doi:10.1007/s11524-014-9899-y

Zhu, Z., Osman, S., & Stradling, D. (2020). Clinical characteristics and outcomes of methamphetamine-associated verus non-methamphetamine intracerebral hemorrhage. *Scientific Reports, 10*(6375), 1–20. doi:10.1038/s41598-020-633480-z

Zweben, J. E., Cohen, J. B., & Christian, D. (2004). Psychiatric symptoms in methamphetamine users. *The American Journal on Addictions, 13*(2), 181–190.

CHAPTER 3

CAFFEINE AND NICOTINE

Caffeine and nicotine—the most widely used psychostimulants in the world—are "natural" psychostimulants that are commonly used by older adults in the U.S.[1] to:

- Achieve a sense of well-being;
- "Fit in," or conform, with friends/peers;
- Improve golf, tennis, or other sport performance;
- Improve memory;
- Increase attention/concentration;
- "Just relax;"
- "Keep going" during a long day at work or during a day with the grandchildren;
- Lose or maintain body weight;
- Prevent or self-manage caffeine and/or nicotine withdrawal syndromes;
- Stay awake to socialize with family and friends at birthday and holiday parties;
- Wake-up, or "get going," in the morning. (e.g., Fulgoni, Keast, & Lieberman, 2015; Pagliaro & Pagliaro, 2018; Pagliaro & Pagliaro, *Clinical Patient Data Files*)

In fact, older adults often use these two psychostimulants together. For example, drinking a cup of coffee and smoking a cigarette: (1) after a meal; (2) before a new bingo game begins in the smoking section; (3) during a coffee break at work; and (4) while chatting with friends. Both caffeine and nicotine have interesting histories, botany, pharmacology, and patterns of use.

We begin with "Caffeine."

CAFFEINE

Caffeine, primarily in the forms of coffee (e.g., "Brew," "Java," or "Joe")[2] or tea (e.g., "Boston Water," "T-Bag," "Tea Pee"), is ingested worldwide by billions of people every morning upon awakening to "get them going," and during work breaks, throughout the day, to "keep them going." For many older adults, coffee also is ingested during the early evening—to complete an enjoyable dinner or to relax from a hectic day with friends and family. In fact, over 97% of the daily caffeine intake among older adults is attributed to the ingestion of caffeine-containing beverages (Mitchell, Knight, & Hockenberry, 2014; Somogyi, 2010).[3]

---

1. For an overview and discussion of two other psychostimulants, which are also commonly used by older adults in the U.S., see Chapter 2, *Amphetamines and Cocaine*.
2. N.B. While caffeine is the major psychoactive compound found in coffee, it should be kept in mind that approximately 1,500 different chemical compounds—including those produced or added during the coffee bean roasting process—are found in coffee.
3. Less than 3% of daily caffeine intake among older adults in the U.S. is associated with the ingestion of foods, including chocolate candies and desserts, and other food products to which caffeine has been added.

DOI: 10.4324/9781003010333-3

Table 3.1 Average Caffeine Content for Selected Caffeinated Beverages Used by Older Adults

CAFFEINATED BEVERAGE	AVERAGE CAFFEINE CONTENT
Brewed coffee[4]	65 to 200 mg per 8 oz
Carbonated sodas	25 to 40 mg per 12 oz
Chocolate milk	2 to 8 mg per 8 oz
Cocoa	11 to 15 mg per 8 oz[5]
Energy drinks	200 mg per 12 oz
Energy shots	200 mg 2 oz
Tea	20 to 80 mg per 8 oz

These beverages include coffee, tea, cocoa, and carbonated drinks, including colas (see the later related discussion in the "Caffeine" subsection, "Caffeinated Beverages"). (See Table 3.1.)

During the second decade of the new millennium, several researchers reported the following facts and statistics regarding caffeine use among older adults in the U.S.:

- Caffeine is the most commonly used drug or substance of abuse;
- Nearly 100% of adults over 65 years of age ingest caffeinated beverages;
- Daily caffeine consumption is approximately 20% higher for men than for women;
- Average daily consumption of caffeine by older adults, 50 to 64 years of age, is 203 mg;
- The highest daily intake of caffeine in the U.S. is found among older adults;
- Approximately 70% of older adults, 60 years of age or older, consume coffee daily;
- "Baby-Boomers" are twice as likely as "millennials" to consume regular, traditional (i.e., "non-gourmet") coffees;
- Approximately 80% of the caffeine ingested is in the form of coffee;
- Usual mean daily intake of coffee is highest among older adults of European continental descent;
- Usual mean daily intake of coffee is significantly higher among tobacco smokers, both former and current, in comparison to those who have never smoked;
- Usual mean daily intake of coffee is significantly higher among daily alcohol drinkers in comparison to abstainers;
- In the U.S., approximately 50% of the coffee, which is ingested outside the home or office, is usually obtained from a favorite drive-through branded "coffee shop chain" such as:
  - Starbucks® (~ 40%);
  - Dunkin' Donuts® (~ 26%);
  - "Others" (e.g., McDonald's®, Tim Hortons®) (~ 21%);
  - Caribou Coffee® (~ 13%).

4. Decaffeinated coffee contains 2.5 to 10 mg of caffeine per 8 ounce serving.
5. Made with 2 tablespoons of cocoa powder.

- Among older adults, energy drinks account for less than 1% of the caffeine that is ingested;
- Most coffee consumption (~ 70%) occurs before noon—commonly with breakfast—while the least amounts are consumed after 9 pm;
- Approximately 90% of older coffee drinkers ingest coffee with breakfast;
- Total daily caffeine consumption has remained stable over the second decade of the new millennium. (Brown, 2020; Lieberman, Agarwal, & Fulgoni, 2019; Loftfield, Freedman, & Dodd, 2016; Meredith, Juliano, & Hughes, 2013; Mitchell et al., 2014; Pagliaro & Pagliaro, 2018; Verster & Koenig, 2018)

The FDA has designated caffeine as being "generally regarded as safe," or "GRAS" (Wikoff, Welsh, & Henderson, 2017). Additionally, both the European Food Safety Authority and Health Canada determined that the consumption of up to 400 mg of caffeine daily is safe for adults (Verster & Koenig, 2018). However, caffeine, like other drugs and substances of abuse, is associated with several undesired, or harmful, effects and toxicities, including physical and psychological dependence (see the later discussion in the Caffeine subsection—"Undesired, or Harmful, Effects and Toxicities"). Although most mental health care professionals seldom encounter older adults whose major presenting problem is caffeine dependence,[6] they often encounter older adults who—in addition to using other drugs and substances of abuse—socially, habitually, abusively, or compulsively, use caffeine.

Caffeine Plant Botany and Naturally Caffeinated Beverages—Coffee, Tea, and Cocoa

Although caffeine is found in over 60 different plants from around the world, including guarana berries, guayusa leaves, kola nuts, yaupon, holly leaves, yerba mate leaves, and yoco bark sap (Hu, 2018), the major natural sources of the caffeine that is used in the U.S. are generally obtained from the:

- Beans of two species of coffee, *Coffea arabica* and *Coffea robusta;*
- Leaves of one species of tea, *Camellia sinensis* (*Thea sinensis*);
- Beans of *Theobroma cocoa*, from which cocoa is obtained and chocolate is made.

Coffea arabica, which is native to Ethiopia,[7] is now widely grown in Brazil and Colombia. *Coffea robusta*, which is native to Saudi Arabia, also is currently widely grown in Brazil, as well as Africa and Indonesia. The caffeine content in a cup of coffee (generally, 65 to 150 mg) primarily depends on: (1) the type of coffee bean selected; and (2) its method of roasting. For example, *Arabica* coffee generally contains less caffeine than the *Robusta*

6. For various reasons, which are discussed later in this chapter, "caffeine use disorder" is not included in the DSM-5. However, both "caffeine intoxication disorder" and "caffeine withdrawal disorder" are included (APA, 2013a). (For further related discussion, see the later caffeine pharmacology subsection, Undesired, or Harmful, Effects and Toxicities—"Physical and Psychological Dependence.")
7. The use of coffee, as a beverage, is thought to have originated—over 1,000 years ago—in Kaffa, an ancient kingdom, and currently a region of Ethiopia. The etymology of Kaffa is from the Arabic and translates as "a drink from berries." (For additional details, see Pagliaro & Pagliaro, [2004].)

variety and "dark roast" coffee generally contains less caffeine than "light-roast" coffee (Pagliaro & Pagliaro, 2004).[8,9]

Camellia sinensis, a tea bush native to China and India, continues to be grown primarily in these two countries. Black tea, green tea, oolong tea, white tea, and yellow tea all come from the leaves of the *Camellia sinensis* plant. Fresh tea leaves contain approximately 4% caffeine and the average cup of tea contains approximately 20 to 80 mg per cup. The differences in color and flavor of these teas are due to their methods of processing and the associated chemical reaction (i.e., oxidation). Indian tea ("Assam" and "Darjeeling"—named after the regions in which they are produced) also are made from *Camellia sinensis*, but from a different variety of the plant (e.g., *Camellia sinensis assamica*) (Pagliaro & Pagliaro, 2004). Although tea is the most widely consumed prepared beverage in the world, significantly more older adults in the U.S. drink coffee (Martyn, Lau, & Richardson, 2018).

Coffee and tea grow best in the "coffee bean belt," the area within 1,000 miles of the equator, or the band that encircles the earth between the Tropic of Capricorn and the Tropic of Cancer. The well-known "Kona" coffee, grown on coffee plantations in the Hawaiian Islands, particularly the big island of Oahu, is the only coffee grown in the U.S. Most teas, sold in cans of loose tea leaves or packages of tea bags, are composed of various tea blends. Scents and flavorings also may be added to improve taste and to distinguish one brand or type of tea from another. For example, "Earl Grey" tea contains oil of bergamot, while "Jasmine" tea contains jasmine flowers or jasmine oil (Pagliaro & Pagliaro, 2004).

Theobroma cocoa, which is native to South America, now grows in several parts of the world, although South America continues to be the primary source of cocoa beans. Cocoa is commonly ingested by many older adults in chocolate candy, cakes, and ice cream, as well as hot chocolate.[10,11]

Artificially Caffeinated Beverages

There are two major types of artificially caffeinated beverage products that are commercially produced and consumed in the U.S.: (1) caffeinated carbonated colas; and (2) caffeinated

8. The roasting process reduces caffeine content (Somogyi, 2010). Thus, light roast coffee beans typically have 10% to 20% more caffeine per bean than do dark roast coffee beans. On average, roasted coffee beans contain between 1% and 3% caffeine (Pagliaro & Pagliaro, 2004).
9. N.B. Additional caffeine is often added to augment the caffeine content found in coffee. For example, Starbucks® significantly increases the natural caffeine content of several of their coffees. Solo Shot® of espresso contains 75 mg of caffeine, while a Caffe Americano® has 225 mg of caffeine, and a Pikes Place® drip coffee has 310 mg of caffeine (Appelbaum, 2017). Other coffee producers also commonly add caffeine to their products. For example, Maxwell House adds 1.5 times more caffeine to produce their MAX Boost® coffee blend.
10. The generally mild psychostimulant effects associated with the ingestion of cocoa is primarily due to its generally low-level amount of caffeine (i.e., 11 to 15 mg in a typical 1-ounce chocolate bar). Other methylxanthines (i.e., theobromine and theophylline) found in cocoa also may contribute to the observed psychostimulation associated with the ingestion of chocolate.
11. N.B. White chocolate, which is made using cocoa butter—not cocoa solids—contains no caffeine. As the concentration of coca solids increases in chocolate, so does the caffeine content. Consequently, milk chocolate bars contain approximately 6 mg of caffeine per ounce of chocolate, while dark chocolate bars contain approximately 12 mg of caffeine per ounce of chocolate (Olsen, 2018).

energy drinks and shots.[12] These artificially caffeinated sources contain considerable amounts of caffeine because they are made with:

- Caffeine-containing extracts of the nuts of the *Cola acuminata* (i.e., guru nuts that are traditionally chewed by indigenous peoples of the Sudan for their psychostimulant effects);
- Guarana, which naturally contains higher concentrations of caffeine than found in cocoa, coffee, kola, or tea;
- Additional caffeine that is added during their production.

Caffeinated Carbonated Colas

Caffeinated carbonated colas are non-alcoholic, naturally, or artificially, sweetened beverages to which caffeine has been added or included as a natural derivative of the ingredients used in the preparation of the cola beverage. Carbonated colas typically contain approximately 40 mg of caffeine per 12 ounces of beverage.[13]

Caffeine Pharmacology

Caffeine, 1,3,7-trimethylxanthine, is a mild, natural psychostimulant. It was identified by the German analytical chemist, Friedrich Ferdinand Runge (1795–1867), who first isolated caffeine from the coffee bean in 1819. The dose-dependent psychostimulant actions of caffeine first affect the cerebral cortex, the most sensitive part of the CNS, followed by the medulla oblongata. The spinal cord is affected last, and only after extremely high amounts of caffeine are ingested (see the later caffeine subsection—"Undesired, or Harmful, Effects and Toxicities"). In addition to the CNS, caffeine also affects other body systems, particularly the cardiovascular and pulmonary systems.

Desired Psychostimulant and Other Effects

The ingestion of caffeine produces such desired psychostimulant effects as:

- A faster, and clearer, flow of thoughts;
- Enhanced mental attentiveness;
- Heightened wakefulness, without disrupting coordinated intellectual or psychomotor performance. (Hindmarch, Rigney, & Stanley, 2000; McLellan, Caldwell, & Lieberman, 2016; van Duinen, Lorist, & Zijdewind, 2005).

---

12. At present, adolescents and young adults are the primary consumers of caffeinated energy drinks (e.g., Coca-Cola Energy® or Red Bull®). Consequently, these beverages are not further discussed in this text. (For further information regarding these beverages, see Pagliaro & Pagliaro, 2020.)
13. Carbonated cola drinks were initially referred to as "soft drinks" to differentiate them from those that contained high percentages of alcohol (i.e., "hard liquor"). During the late 19th and early 20th centuries, one of the earliest carbonated cola "soft drinks" produced in the U.S., Coca-Cola®, contained cocaine as its active psychostimulant until it was replaced by caffeine in 1903 (Pagliaro & Pagliaro, 2004). (See for related discussion, Chapter 2, *Amphetamines and Cocaine*.)

Subsequently, unlike most psychodepressants and psychodelics, the use of caffeine (as well as nicotine and other psychostimulants)—under specific conditions of use—can improve dose-dependent performance on vigilance tasks.

For example, in one of the few studies of its kind, Sharwood, Elkington, and Meuleners (2013, p. 1) evaluated the use of caffeine by over 1,000 long-distance commercial truck drivers (both men and women) and its relationship to crashes that were attended by police. They found that 43% of the commercial drivers consumed caffeine products "for the express purpose of staying awake." When compared to drivers who did not use caffeine to stay awake, the caffeine consuming drivers "had a 63% reduced likelihood of crashing."

The use of caffeine can also affect attention, learning, and memory in various ways. For example, the ingestion of as little as 100 to 200 mg of caffeine, or one to two cups of coffee, can sustain intellectual effort.[14] This effect is mediated primarily by improving attention, particularly among users who are tired, sleepy, or otherwise in a less than optimal state of attentiveness (Lorist & Tops, 2003; Nehlig, 2010; Pagliaro & Pagliaro, 2012). Caffeine may also enhance memory (Pagliaro & Pagliaro, 2012) and as found by Borota, Murray, and Keceli (2014), memory consolidation that consequently enhances performance for up to 24 hours after use.

In addition to its desired psychostimulant actions, caffeine also:

1. "Directly" affects the cardiovascular system;
2. "Directly" affects the pulmonary system;
3. "Indirectly" affects other body systems.

Cardiovascular System

Cardiovascular effects include: (1) a marginal increase in heart rate; (2) increased cardiac contractility; and (3) increased blood pressure, particularly diastolic blood pressure. Cumulatively, these three effects increase cardiac output. Caffeine also produces dilation of the coronary arteries and, thus, increases the amount of oxygen that is delivered to the myocardium. These effects result in an increase in cardiac work capacity or performance (Echeverri, Montes, & Cabrera, 2010, 2019).

By increasing cardiac performance, caffeine increases renal blood flow causing a mild diuretic effect (Maughan & Griffin, 2003). Overall, the cardiovascular effects of caffeine are generally mild and short-term in nature without any significant lasting cardiovascular toxicity (Gluckman, 2010). (See also the related discussion in the later caffeine pharmacology subsection, Undesired, or Harmful, Effects and Toxicities—"Caffeine and Cardiovascular Disease.") In addition, caffeine decreases blood flow to the brain by constricting cerebral blood vessels, providing some relief for both hypertensive and certain migraine headaches—conditions for which caffeine has been medically used for over a century.

Pulmonary System

Pulmonary system effects associated with caffeine use include the stimulation of the respiratory center in the lower brain stem, or medulla oblongata—particularly, in response to

14. Hence, the rationale for the development and use of traditional nonprescription, solid oral dosage forms of caffeine (e.g., 200 mg NoDoz® caplets; Stay Awake® tablets) that have been available and used for over 50 years as aids to increase alertness and forestall sleep.

functional body changes associated with disease or injury (e.g., respiratory depression related to opiate analgesic overdosage). Caffeine also appears to increase the sensitivity of the respiratory center to the stimulant action of carbon dioxide. This action, in turn, increases the volume of air that is inhaled or exhaled in one minute. In addition, caffeine affects the smooth muscles of the bronchi that results in mild bronchodilation making breathing easier and facilitating air exchange. Consequently, it is not surprising that Welsh, Bara, and Barley (2010, p. 3), in their systematic review of the use of "caffeine for asthma" found that, "even small amounts of caffeine can improve lung function for up to four hours."

Other Body Systems

In a review of over 200 published meta-analyses, Herman (2017, p. 1) found several positive benefits associated with coffee consumption:[15]

- Daily consumption of three cups of coffee—regular or decaffeinated—was associated with a 17% lower risk for all-cause mortality, relative to no coffee consumption;
- Caffeinated coffee was linked to lower risks for cardiovascular disease, coronary heart disease, and stroke with benefits highest at three to five cups daily;
- Caffeinated coffee was associated with lower risks for cancer and hepatic disorders;
- Both regular and decaffeinated coffee appeared to lower risk for type 2 diabetes.

***Related Professional Reminder:* Generally, meta-analyses, because of their very nature, "collapse" data across subgroups. Consequently, although the overall reported finding(s) may be factually correct—the possible occurrence of an "interaction effect" or of a "selective effect" within a particular subgroup, is left unaddressed and unanswered (e.g., "Would a different result have occurred if analyses included only older adults 50 to 65 years of age, 65 to 80 years of age, or over 85 years of age?").**

Old Misbelief: Caffeine is primarily used as a nutrient.

False. In fact, caffeine—although commonly found in several popular beverages, foods, candies, gums, and other edible products—is not a nutrient and does not provide the body with any elements (e.g., minerals or vitamins) that are necessary for growth and the maintenance of life. Additionally, caffeine, even as consumed in coffee or tea, does not provide any significant amount of calorie producing macronutrients (e.g., carbohydrate, fat, or protein). Consequently, caffeine is most appropriately considered to be an abusable psychostimulant that is used predominantly for its psychostimulant effects (Pagliaro & Pagliaro, 2004, 2009).[16]

Pharmacodynamics: Mechanism of Action

Caffeine is a naturally occurring xanthine plant alkaloid. Being similar to adenosine in chemical structure and having no receptor sites of its own, caffeine elicits its psychostimulant

15. Several researchers (e.g., Butt & Sultan, 2011) attribute these potential positive effects to components of coffee (e.g., cafestol, caffeic acid, chlorogenic acid, hydroxyhydroquinone, and kahweol) other than caffeine.
16. In contrast, the whole roasted coffee bean contains approximately 40% carbohydrates and 20% lipids (Echeverri, Montes, & Cabrera, 2010).

actions by competitively binding to adenosine receptor subtypes in the CNS—specifically subtypes A_1 and A_{2A}—where adenosine functions as an inhibitory neurotransmitter that promotes sedation (Fisone, Borgkvist, & Usiello, 2004; Pagliaro & Pagliaro, 2009).[17] Acting as an antagonist, caffeine blocks endogenous adenosine and, consequently, the inhibitory effects of adenosine (see Figure 3.1).[18] Several adenosine receptor subtypes have been identified.[19]

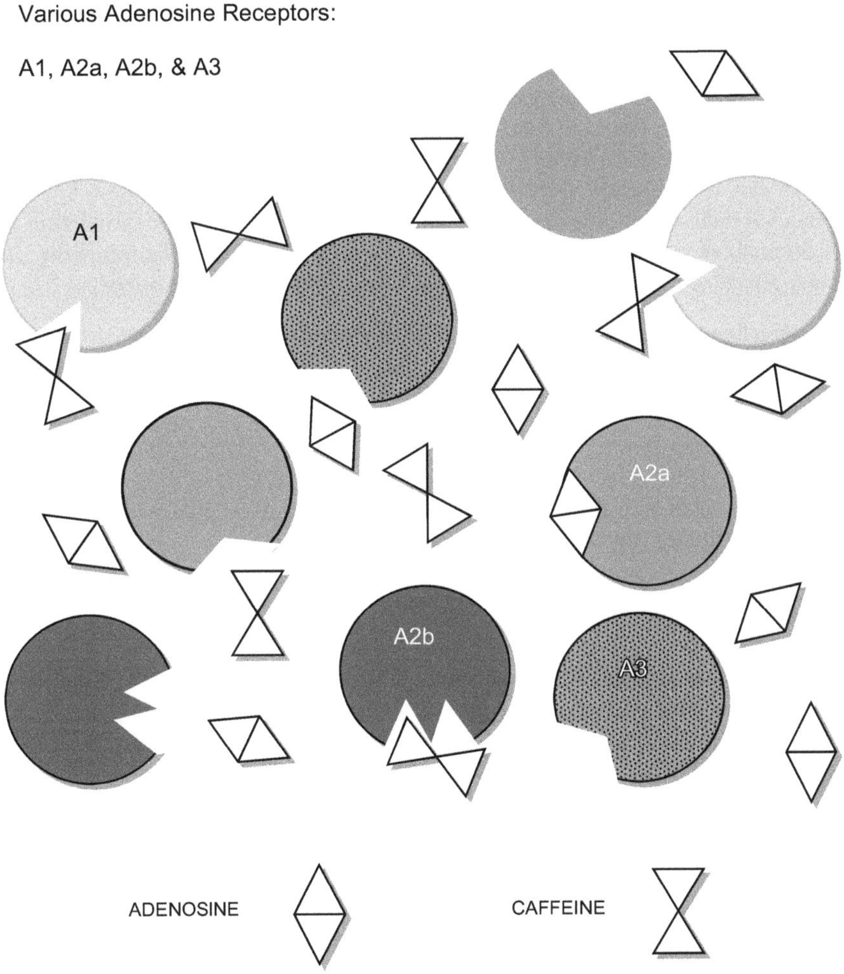

Figure 3.1 Caffeine: Mechanism of Action

17. Additionally, caffeine—as a xanthine—inhibits tissue phosphodiesterase, which, consequently, increases cyclic AMP levels by means of inhibition of its metabolism (Echeverri et al., 2010; NIDDK, 2020).
18. N.B. Paraxanthine (i.e., the major metabolite of caffeine) is a more potent blocker of adenosine receptors than is caffeine.
19. The major identified adenosine receptor subtypes include A_1, A_{2A}, A_{2B}, and A_3.

A1 and A2A Adenosine Receptor Subtypes

The A_1 adenosine receptor subtypes are present throughout the brain with the highest density found in the cerebellum, cortex, hippocampus, and hypothalamus. The A_1 subtype is also found in the adrenal gland, eyes, heart, and spinal cord (Willson, 2018).[20] The highest density of A_{2A} receptor subtypes are found within the amygdala, nucleus accumbens, olfactory tubercles, and the striatum (McLellan et al., 2016). The A_1 adenosine receptor subtype is coupled to "inhibitory" G proteins while the A_{2A} adenosine receptor subtype is coupled to "stimulatory" G proteins.

The adenosine A_{2A} receptors are colocalized with the dopamine D1 and D2 receptors. "Presynaptically," adenosine inhibits dopamine and glutamate release by actions on adenosine A_1 receptors that are localized in nerve terminals. "Postsynaptically," adenosine causes an antagonistic interaction between adenosine and dopamine receptors that results in decreased dopaminergic activity (Solinas, Ferre, & You, 2002). Caffeine, as an adenosine antagonist, can, consequently, directly potentiate dopamine neurotransmission by stimulating dopamine release and potentiating the effects of dopamine receptor stimulation. Thus, within 30 minutes of ingesting a low to moderate dose of caffeine, the following desired excitatory effects are produced, which can last for approximately three hours:

1. Heightened alertness, because of increased CNS neuron activity;
2. A sense of well-being, or mild euphoria, because of the increased release of dopamine.

Pharmacokinetics

This section presents and discusses the pharmacokinetics of caffeine with attention to its absorption, distribution, metabolism, and excretion.

Absorption

Following ingestion, caffeine is well-absorbed (i.e., 80% to 95%), primarily from the small intestine. Peak plasma concentrations generally occur within 30 to 45 minutes in a fasting state and may be delayed by the ingestion of food (Echeverri et al., 2010; Liguori, Hughes, & Grass, 1997).

Distribution

Following absorption, caffeine is distributed to all body tissues. However, caffeine distribution is preferential to lean body tissues. Consequently, a dose of caffeine based on mg/kg may result in higher plasma concentrations for older versus younger adults (Massey, 1998) due to their higher percentage of body fat (Pagliaro & Pagliaro, 1983). The apparent volume of distribution is 0.5 to 0.7 L/kg (Amaud, 2011). Plasma protein binding is low (i.e., less than 30%) for caffeine and it readily crosses the blood-brain barrier.

---

20. A significantly lower density of the A_1 receptor subtype is found in adipose tissue and skeletal muscle (Fredholm, Arsian, & Halldner, 2000; Fredholm, IJzerman, & Jacobson, 2001).

Metabolism

Caffeine is extensively metabolized (i.e., greater than 90%) in the liver by the cytochrome P450 oxidase enzyme system, particularly the CYP1A2 isoenzyme, to three major active metabolites (i.e., paraxanthine [~84%], theobromine [~11%], and theophylline [~5%]) (Alsabri, Mari, & Younes, 2018; Amaud, 2011).[21] First pass hepatic metabolism does not occur (Blanchard & Sawers, 1983).

The mean half-life of elimination for caffeine is approximately five to six hours (Pagliaro & Pagliaro, 2004; Teekachunhatean, Tosri, & Rojanasthien, 2013).[22] Thus, for example, if an older adult drinks a Starbucks® Grande brewed coffee containing 320 mg of caffeine in the morning on the way to work, half of the caffeine ingested from that beverage (in this case, ~ 160 mg of caffeine) will still be acting in the body at the end of the normal workday. This half-life of elimination is the reason why consuming caffeine in the evening (i.e., up to five hours before retiring to bed) can result in one of the most common undesired pharmacological effects of caffeine—"insomnia."

The half-life of elimination of caffeine may be increased by several factors including age-related changes in liver function. Regarding older adults, severe liver diseases (e.g., cirrhosis or hepatitis C) can increase the half-life of elimination for caffeine to up to 100 hours. The half-life of elimination for caffeine can be significantly decreased for older adults who smoke tobacco cigarettes, which can induce the production of the hepatic isoenzyme CYP1A2 (Zevin & Benowitz, 1999).

Excretion

Less than 2% of ingested caffeine is excreted in unchanged form in the urine (Amaud, 2011). The active metabolites of caffeine are further metabolized and are also excreted (~ 85%) in the urine (Pagliaro & Pagliaro, 2009; Trang, Blanchard, & Conrad, 1982; Willson, 2018).

Drug-Drug Interactions[23]

Literally hundreds of caffeine drug-drug interactions can be found in the published literature. Fortunately, the actions associated with these drug-drug interactions can be reduced to:

1. "Pharmacodynamic" drug-drug interactions;
2. "Pharmacokinetic" drug-drug interactions.

---

21. Older adults, who possess a variant genotype for the CYP1A2 isoenzyme, have a slower rate of caffeine metabolism. Consequently, they may be at increased risk for caffeine-induced toxicities such as hypertension and myocardial infarction (Meredith et al., 2013). (See also the later caffeine subsection—"Undesired, or Harmful, Effects and Toxicities.")
22. In a small sample of older men, 66 to 86 years of age, Trang et al. (1982) found that the average half-life of elimination was 4.6 hours.
23. N.B. In addition to caffeine, other chemicals that are found in coffee or tea may also be involved in clinically significant drug interactions. For example:

> Polyphenols in coffee can bind nonheme iron and inhibit its intestinal absorption. Drinking 150–250 ml of coffee with a test meal has been found to inhibit the absorption of iron by 24–73%.
> (Higdon & Frei, 2006, p. 113)

Pharmacodynamic Drug-Drug Interactions

Caffeine, as a psychostimulant, can interact with: (1) other psychostimulants (e.g., amphetamines, cocaine, and nicotine) resulting in "additive" psychostimulation; and (2) psychodepressants (e.g., alcohol, opiate analgesics, and prescription sedative-hypnotics) resulting in the moderation of psychostimulant effects.

Pharmacokinetic Drug-Drug Interactions

Caffeine is primarily metabolized by the hepatic microsomal enzyme system, particularly CYP1A2. Drugs that induce or inhibit the production of CYP1A2 enzymes can significantly affect caffeine metabolism and, consequently, its effects. Primary "inducers" of CYP1A2 include carbamazepine (Tegretol®), rifampin (Rifadin®), and tobacco smoking. Primary "inhibitors" of CYP1A2 include cimetidine (Tagamet®), ciprofloxacin (Cipro®), ethinylestradiol, and fluvoxamine (Luvox®) (Horn & Hansten, 2007). (See also the related discussion of older adult CYP1A2 activity in the earlier Pharmacokinetics subsection—"Metabolism.")

> ***Related Professional Reminder:*** ***When compared to younger adults, drug-drug interactions among older adults, are:***
>
> - ***More common because of their generally significant age-related need for, and use of, more prescription and non-prescription (over-the-counter) drugs due to multiple active acute and chronic medical conditions;***
> - ***More likely to result in multiple serious clinical effects because of their significant age-related reduction in the reserve capacity of major body organ systems (e.g., cardiac, hepatic, pulmonary, and renal).***

Undesired, or Harmful, Effects and Toxicities

Undesired, or harmful, effects and toxicities have been reported by approximately one-third of caffeinated beverage drinkers. These dose-related effects and toxicities are "directly" associated with blood caffeine concentrations, and include:[24]

- Abdominal pain;
- Agitation;
- Anorexia;
- Anxiety;
- Chest pain;
- Dehydration;
- Diuresis;
- Dizziness;
- Dyspepsia;

24. N.B. Interestingly, and rather unusually, several of the signs and symptoms of caffeine toxicity (e.g., agitation, headache, irritability, nausea, restlessness, and tremors) are also displayed during the caffeine withdrawal syndrome. (See also the later subsection—"Withdrawal Syndrome.")

- Excitation;
- Fever;
- Flushed face;
- Headache;
- Heart palpitations;
- Hypertension;
- Hyperventilation;
- Insomnia;
- Irritability;
- Nausea;
- Nervousness;
- Restlessness;
- Seizures;
- Tachycardia;
- Tinnitus;
- Tremors;
- Vomiting. (Felman, 2019; Pagliaro & Pagliaro, 2004, 2009; Willson, 2018)

***Related Professional Reminder:* Undesired, or harmful, effects and toxicities associated with caffeine use generally have a significantly greater impact on older adults because of:**

1. ***Underlying physiological changes (e.g., dehydration);***
2. ***Contemporaneous medical conditions (e.g., cardiovascular disease or insomnia secondary to other conditions, such as severe pain related to osteoarthritis).***

Low to moderate daily caffeine use (i.e., the ingestion of less than 400 mg per day) is usually not associated with significant harmful effects or toxicities among healthy older adults (Nawrot, Jordan, & Eastwood, 2003). However, more serious toxicities are associated with high to extremely high daily caffeine use.[25] Caffeine use also has been associated with cancer and cardiovascular disease.

Low to Moderate Caffeine Use[26]

Undesired effects associated with low to moderate caffeine use are relatively minor psychostimulant effects, and include:

- Anxiety;
- Diuresis;

25. N.B. An older term (i.e., "caffeinism") is sometimes used to refer to a constellation of various signs and symptoms (e.g., diuresis, excitement, facial flushing, GI disturbance, insomnia, nervousness, and tachycardia) associated with the chronic daily ingestion of greater than 1 gram of caffeine.
26. As recognized by Wikoff et al. (2017, p. 585):

> Consumption of up to 400 mg of caffeine per day in healthy adults in not associated with overt, adverse cardiovascular effects, behavioral effects, reproductive and developmental effects, or bone status.

- Excitement;
- Facial flushing;
- GI disturbances (e.g., abdominal pain or dyspepsia);
- Insomnia, particularly when caffeine beverages are ingested later in the day or prior to retiring for bed in the evening;
- Nervousness or restlessness, particularly at the end of a busy workday during which caffeine beverages or other caffeinated products were ingested throughout the day.

High to Extremely High Caffeine Use

High to extremely high daily doses of caffeine are usually associated with more serious toxicities, including severe caffeine-induced stimulation, than those that are associated with low to moderate caffeine use. For example, the ingestion of:

- 12 or more cups of coffee per day (1.5 gm of caffeine) can cause intense psychostimulation characterized by anxiety, cardiac dysrhythmias, headache, heart palpitations, hyperventilation, insomnia, irritability, tachycardia, and tremors.
- 20 to 50 cups of coffee per day (i.e., 2 to 5 gm) can excite the spinal cord causing increased stimulation of the spinal reflexes.
- 100 cups of coffee per day, or more (i.e., over 10 gm), can cause seizures and death. However, fatalities are relatively rare because of the large amounts of coffee, or other common caffeine-containing beverages (e.g., colas or teas), that would need to be ingested.

Caffeine and Cancer

Concerns and related proposed theories regarding the possible relationships among caffeine use and various cancers (e.g., breast, colon, endometrial, or rectal) have been widely studied for several decades. Currently, the preponderance of available published research data and reported findings (e.g., Dik, Bueno-de-Mesquita, & Van Oijen, 2014; Gierach, Freedman, & Andaya, 2012; Kennedy & Abraham, 2017; Phelps & Phelps, 1988; Yang, Crowe, & Cairns, 2015) indicate that these relationships, if they do exist, are tenuous at best, and that any relationships found are probably best accounted for by individual genetic and/or environmental variables. As noted by Higdon and Frei (2006, p. 101), "At present, there is little evidence that coffee consumption increases the risk of cancer."

Additionally, as noted on behalf of the American Cancer Society by Mendes (2018, p. 1):

> Numerous studies have shown that coffee drinking is associated with a lower risk of dying from all causes of death. However, associations with cancer overall or with specific types of cancer are unclear. In 2016, an expert working group convened for the International Agency for Research on Cancer Monographs Program, [found that the] reviewed evidence of carcinogenicity of coffee drinking to be "unclassifiable. They also found that coffee drinking is not a cause of female breast, pancreas, and prostate cancers, but may reduce the risk of uterine endometrium and liver cancers.[27] The evidence was judged to be inadequate for other

27. Zhao, Li, and Feng (2020), in their comprehensive meta-analysis of related observational studies, came to the same conclusion.

cancer types. Reasons for the lack of convincing evidence included inconsistent results across studies and issues with data quality.

Caffeine and Cardiovascular Disease

The ingestion of low to moderate amounts of caffeine has not been associated with the increased risk for cardiac toxicities—even among older adults who have pre-existing heart disease (Klatsky, Hasan, & Armstrong, 2011; O'Keefe, Bhatti, & Patil, 2013; Pelchovitz & Goldberger, 2011; Turnbull, Rodricks, & Mariano, 2017; Wilson & Bloom, 2016). However, high daily amounts of caffeine—usually in the form of the ingestion of coffee—may cause various cardiac toxicities, including cardiac dysrhythmias (e.g., tachycardia) and heart palpitations.

Atrial or supraventricular tachycardia has been associated with the concurrent ingestion of various amounts of caffeine-containing products, including candies, coffee, cola drinks, and teas. For older adults who are at risk (i.e., those who have a pre-existing heart disease, including dysrhythmias), low dosages of caffeine may be enough to cause these effects. However, in most reported cases, the caffeine doses are high (e.g., more than one pot of coffee daily) (Kinugawa, Kurita, & Nohara, 2011; Pagliaro & Pagliaro, *Clinical Patient Data Files*).[28]

In addition, the oily lipid components of coffee contain both "cafestol" and "kahweol." These components appear to raise serum cholesterol levels, which increase the risk for myocardial infarction and cerebral vascular accidents (Butt & Sultan, 2011). This risk would be particularly significant among older adults, who both:

1. Have familial hypercholesterolemia;
2. Regularly consume large amounts of coffee daily.

As also noted by Higdon and Frei (2006, p, 116):

> Unfiltered coffee is a significant source of cafestol and kahweol, which are diterpenes that have been implicated in the cholesterol-raising effects of coffee.

Related Professional Reminder: ***Generally, no significant undesired, or harmful, effects and toxicities have been associated with the ingestion of up to 200 mg/day of caffeine—approximately one cup of coffee (8 to 12 ounces)—by older adults.***[29] ***Consequently, according to the FDA, caffeine use is "generally recognized as safe" ("GRAS").***[30,31]

---

28. See also the related discussion of the increased risk for cardiotoxicity associated with variation of the CYP1A2 gene, which is primarily responsible for the metabolism of caffeine (see the earlier caffeine pharmacology subsection, Pharmacokinetics—"Metabolism").
29. Others, including ourselves (Pagliaro & Pagliaro, 2018), have suggested that up to 400 mg/day of caffeine, in the form of brewed coffee, is generally safe for healthy adults (e.g., FDA, 2018; Health Canada, 2017; Mayo Clinic Staff, 2020).
30. N.B. GRAS does not imply an inherent quality of a drug or substance, but rather that it has been "generally recognized by qualified experts to be safe [for human use] under the conditions of its intended use" (Mattia, 2013, p. 6). Consequently, for caffeine, the FDA requires beverage alcohol companies to list caffeine in the ingredients list on product labels but does not require specification of the precise amount of caffeine present in a product—although soda manufacturers in the U.S. generally voluntarily label the amount of caffeine contained in their beverages in compliance with adopted American Beverage Association guidelines.
31. However, we would caution that, due to the possible stimulation of gastric acid secretion, any amount of caffeine use (e.g., ingesting as little as 8 ounces of a caffeinated cola drink) can be distressing—if not risky—for older adults, who have severe, untreated active stomach ulcers.

Caffeine Physical and Psychological Dependence

Old Misbelief: Caffeine has little, or no, abuse liability.

False. However, the American Psychiatric Association has formally contributed to, endorsed, and perpetuated this false belief:

> DSM-5 will not include caffeine use disorder, although research shows that as little as two to three cups of coffee can trigger a withdrawal effect marked by tiredness or sleepiness. There is sufficient evidence to support this as a condition, however it is not yet clear to what extent it is a clinically significant disorder.
>
> (APA, 2013b, p. 2)

In fact, the regular, long-term use of caffeine is associated with both physical and psychological dependence (Pagliaro & Pagliaro, 1999, 2004, 2018, 2020). Regarding physical dependence, both the development of: (1) tolerance to the desired effects of caffeine; and (2) a caffeine withdrawal syndrome—which occurs when: (a) regular, long-term caffeine use is abruptly discontinued; and (b) is immediately relieved with the resumed use of caffeine—have been identified.

The development of physical dependence, as well as its associated undesired signs and symptoms of caffeine withdrawal, promotes both continued and resumed caffeine use. Regarding psychological dependence, the development of craving becomes another primary reason for the continued use of caffeine. In fact, for caffeine users who want to quit caffeine use, craving is the major reason given for the prevention of quitting, as well as for the return to resumed use (Pagliaro & Pagliaro, 2009).

Several specific terms have been used as diagnostic labels to denote the occurrence of caffeine physical and psychological dependence. These terms include:

- Caffeine dependence syndrome (ICD-10);
- Caffeine use disorder (DSM-5);[32]
- Substance use disorder (DSM-IV).

Although, "caffeine use disorder," is not listed in the DSM-5, "Caffeine Intoxication" and "Caffeine Withdrawal" are included in the taxonomy.

***Related Professional Reminder*: Caffeine, like other abusable psychotropic drugs, meets the general criteria required for classification as an abusable psychotropic:**

- ***Caffeine is primarily used for its major psychotropic actions, in this case—psychostimulation;***
- ***Regular, long-term use of caffeine is associated with both physical dependence (i.e., tolerance and caffeine withdrawal syndrome) and psychological dependence (i.e., craving).***

Tolerance

The regular, long-term use of small amounts of caffeine is associated with the development of a low degree of tolerance, particularly regarding the psychostimulant actions of

32. N.B. Caffeine use disorder is not formally recognized as a mental disorder in the DSM-5. Rather, it is identified as, "a condition for further study" (APA, 2013a).

caffeine (Watson, Deary, & Kerr, 2002). Correspondingly, the regular, long-term use of large amounts of caffeine is associated with a high degree of tolerance.

Withdrawal Syndrome

The regular, long-term use of moderate amounts of caffeine (e.g., approximately five or more cups of caffeinated coffee daily) may result in caffeine withdrawal syndrome when caffeine use is abruptly discontinued (Addicott, 2014; Juliano & Griffiths, 2004). Up-regulation of the adenosine receptor system is suggested as the primary mechanism underlying the caffeine withdrawal syndrome (Meredith et al., 2013). As noted by Echeverri et al. (2010, p. 6):

> When you abruptly stop the consumption of caffeine in a habitual consumer, there is a greater number of available adenosine receptors, which potentiates the vasodilation produced by adenosine, causing the symptoms.

(See also the related discussion in the earlier caffeine pharmacology subsection, "Pharmacodynamics: Mechanism of Action.")

The caffeine withdrawal syndrome is characterized by:

- Agitation;
- Anxiety;
- Depression;
- Drowsiness;
- Dysphoria;
- Fatigue (marked);
- Headache;
- Impaired concentration;
- Increased appetite;
- Irritability;
- Muscle pain and stiffness;
- Nausea;
- Restlessness;
- Tremors;
- Weakness. (Addicott, 2014; Dews, O'Brien, & Bergman, 2002; Felman, 2019; Meredith et al., 2013; Pagliaro & Pagliaro, 2004)

These signs and symptoms are:

1. Generally mild and begin within 12 to 24 hours after the last use of caffeine;
2. Peak between 24 and 48 hours after onset;
3. Short-lived, but may last for up to one week.

The caffeine withdrawal syndrome is immediately relieved by the resumed ingestion of caffeine (Pagliaro & Pagliaro, 2009). In the past, those who had relatively mild dose-related signs and symptoms of caffeine withdrawal, tended to manage their withdrawal signs and symptoms with a cup of coffee—"first thing in the morning," and "periodically throughout the day." However, the amounts of caffeine now available in many beverages, foods, and other products contain several times the amount of caffeine that was available at the beginning of the new millennium.

In fact, in the past, these blood caffeine concentrations would require drinking approximately 50 cups of coffee a day. Thus, mental health care professionals may be confronted with a new population that requires assistance with the prevention and management of harmful patterns of caffeine use. They also need to be aware that, like other drugs and substances of abuse, genetic and other factors may significantly affect both the incidence and severity of the caffeine withdrawal syndrome experienced by older adults. Mental health care professionals also are reminded that when helping older adults who are trying to "cut down" or "quit" their use of caffeine, individual and novel treatment approaches may be required because of the following factors:

- Different signs and symptoms of caffeine withdrawal (e.g., dose-related moderate to severe effects or prolonged withdrawal period) that are primarily mediated by genetic factors;
- Multiple-drug and substance abuse withdrawal syndromes (e.g., alcohol and nicotine withdrawal syndromes) that may be concomitant with caffeine withdrawal or otherwise related in ways that could affect positive treatment outcomes. For example, older adults who have specific mental disorders, such as eating disorders (i.e., anorexia nervosa), anxiety disorders (i.e., panic disorder), and MDD have a significant correlation with caffeine tolerance and withdrawal (i.e., they possess shared environmental or genetic factors with caffeine use phenotypes—see earlier related discussion) (Bergin & Kendler, 2012);
- Several unsuccessful attempts to decrease or totally discontinue caffeine use (i.e., several attempts to maintain resumed nonuse with several returns to relapsed use) (Juliano, Evatt, & Richards, 2012);
- Expense associated with the daily/weekly purchase of caffeinated beverages, foods, or other caffeine products;
- Persistent dyspepsia or gastric ulcer disease that are aggravated by the continued use of caffeine (Juliano et al., 2012; Pagliaro & Pagliaro, *Clinical Patient Data Files*).

Caffeine Overdosage/Unintentional Poisoning

Fatalities associated with caffeine overdosage are relatively rare (Temple, Bernard, & Lipshultz, 2017). When reported—generally in the context of "case reports"—the following features are noted:

- Most victims are middle-aged adults;
- An overwhelming majority of cases of fatal caffeine overdosage are associated with deliberate suicide attempts, usually involving the powder and tablet forms of caffeine rather than caffeinated beverages;
- The median lethal dose of caffeine is approximately 10 grams for an adult;
- The minimum fatal blood caffeine concentration is approximately 80 mg/L;
- The median fatal blood caffeine concentration is approximately 100 mg/L;
- The typical cause of death is ventricular fibrillation.

(Banerjee, Ali, & Levine, 2014; Bonsignore, Sblano, & Pozzi, 2014; Jabbar & Hanly, 2013; Jones, 2017; Marengo & Sissons, 2019)

Associated signs and symptoms of caffeine overdosage can include:

- Agitation;
- Anxiety;
- Chest pain;
- Confusion;
- Diaphoresis;
- Diarrhea;
- Dizziness;
- Fever;
- Headache;
- Hyperreflexia;
- Hypertension;
- Insomnia;
- Irritability;
- Mydriasis;
- Nausea;
- Nervousness;
- Panic;
- Restlessness;
- Seizures;
- Tachycardia;
- Thirst;
- Vomiting.

The management of caffeine overdosage depends on its severity. Mild signs and symptoms of caffeine overdosage, such as anxiety, diaphoresis, dizziness, fever, headache, hyperreflexia, insomnia, irritability, heart palpitations (mild), mydriasis, nausea, restlessness, tachycardia, tremor, and vomiting are generally self-managed until the signs and symptoms resolve. The management is facilitated by:

1. Discontinuing caffeine use;
2. Drinking adequate amounts of water to rehydrate;
3. Initiating mild exercise (e.g., walking a short distance).

More severe signs and symptoms (e.g., cardiac dysrhythmias, chest pain, confusion, hallucinations, hypertension followed by hypotension, or seizures) require medical assessment (e.g., electrocardiogram monitoring) and appropriate treatment (e.g., hemodialysis, or respiratory support) in a hospital emergency department setting. There is no specific antidote for the treatment of caffeine overdosage. Adjunctive pharmacotherapy may include, for example, the use of:

1. Activated charcoal to bind caffeine in the GI tract (if ingestion is recent);[33]
2. Cardioselective beta-blocker (e.g., esmolol [Brevibloc®]) for associated tachycardia;

33. This can also help to diminish serum levels related to the enterohepatic circulation of caffeine.

3. Benzodiazepine sedative-hypnotic (e.g., diazepam [Valium®] for associated anxiety and seizures);
4. Intravenous isotonic fluids to rehydrate and manage hypotension. (Fabrizio, Desiderio, & Coyne, 2016; Murray & Traylor, 2020; Pagliaro & Pagliaro, 2004).[34]

New Millennial Trends in Older Adult Caffeine Use

Over the first two decades of the new millennium, several new trends developed regarding the medical prescription and nonmedical/recreational use of caffeine among older adults. These trends are presented and discussed in the following subsections. We begin with the medical prescription use of caffeine.

Medical Prescription Use

Since the last century, caffeine has been medically used as a respiratory stimulant to treat apnea in premature neonates (Pagliaro & Pagliaro, 1987). Classic pharmacologic studies of caffeine published during the first half of the 20th century confirmed the CNS stimulant actions that were associated with caffeine use, including an elevated mood, decreased fatigue, and increased capacity for work that had been recognized since the "dawn of history" (Pagliaro & Pagliaro, 2004). These studies also revealed that methylxanthines, such as caffeine, theobromine, and theophylline possess other important pharmacologic properties. These properties were exploited for many years in a variety of therapeutic applications (e.g., headaches) that are now, in the 21st century, being generally treated with more specific and efficacious pharmacotherapeutic approaches. However, as discussed earlier in this chapter, caffeine is still widely used by older adults—both in "pill" (e.g., NoDoz®; Stay Awake®; Vivarin®) and beverage forms (e.g., coffee)—to counteract drowsiness or fatigue.

Nonmedical/Recreational Use

As identified and listed in the introduction to this chapter, caffeine is nonmedically/recreationally used by older adults for a variety of reasons. The *National Health and Nutrition Examination Survey* (NHANES) presents one of the most comprehensive analyses of caffeine use among adults in the U.S. Data involving older adults were extracted from that survey and are presented in Table 3.2.

These data from NHANES support the general finding—from the earlier research of Mitchell et al. (2014)—that the highest daily intake of caffeine in the U.S., from caffeinated beverages among all age cohorts, is among older adults, 50 years of age and older. Among this age cohort:

- Mitchell et al. (2014) found an average daily caffeine intake of 216 mg;
- Lieberman et al. (2019) found an average daily caffeine intake of 190 mg.

In their study of 94 regular caffeine users seeking treatment for caffeine dependence, Juliano et al. (2012) found that daily caffeine consumption ranged from 120 mg to 2,667 mg, with a mean of 548 mg and a median of 388 mg.

---

34. Other additional related therapeutic interventions, such as the use of IV lipid emulsion (Intralipid®), have been suggested in isolated clinical case studies—particularly in the context of concern for imminent cardiac arrest (e.g., Muraro, Longo, & Geraldini, 2016; Schmidt, Farna, & Kurcova, 2015).

Table 3.2 Average Daily Caffeine Intake Among Older Adults in the U.S.

OLDER ADULT AGE RANGE (Years)	AVERAGE DAILY CAFFEINE INTAKE (Mg/Day +/– SEM)
50–54	211 +/– 6
55–59	196 +/– 5
60–64	199 +/– 4
65–69	202 +/– 9
70–74	177 +/– 6
75–79	153 +/– 4

Source: Lieberman et al., 2019.

Assessment and Diagnosis of Older Adult Caffeine Dependence or Use Disorder

The assessment and diagnosis of caffeine dependence or use disorder among older adults is limited in clinical practice because of several factors, including:

- Social normalization of caffeine use in the U.S. (and other countries);
- Inconsistent clinical criteria for detection;
- Absence of available valid and reliable diagnostic criteria or quick-screen psychometric tests for detecting caffeine dependence or use disorder among older adults.

For example, caffeine use disorder is not listed in the DSM-5 (APA, 2013a, 2013b)[35]—although "Caffeine Intoxication,"[36] and "Caffeine Withdrawal" are listed.[37]

---

35. The DSM-5 does, however, formally recognize a "Caffeine Use Disorder" as a "research diagnosis" that may be considered for inclusion in a future revision of the DSM. Similarly, the ICD does not include a category for "Caffeine Dependence."
36. The DSM-5 (APA, 2013a, 2013b) criteria for the diagnosis of "caffeine intoxication" requires the identification of five, or more, of the following signs and symptoms in an older adult who has recently ingested a "large amount of caffeine:"

    - Diuresis;
    - Excitement;
    - Flushed face;
    - GI disturbance;
    - Insomnia;
    - Muscle twitching;
    - Nervousness;
    - Periods of inexhaustibility;
    - Psychomotor agitation;
    - Rambling flow of thought and speech;
    - Restlessness;
    - Tachycardia.

    Additionally, the signs and symptoms must be associated with significant physical and social distress (Meredith et al., 2013).
37. According to DSM-5 (APA, 2013a), common signs and symptoms of caffeine withdrawal include anxiety, depression, difficulty concentrating, fatigue, flu-like symptoms, headache, low energy, and nausea.

Given this current diagnostic dilemma, we recommend a comprehensive clinical assessment that includes the older adult's interview/history with attention to patterns of caffeine use, related physical examination, appropriate laboratory tests (e.g., toxicology analysis for caffeine blood concentrations), and the following three basic criteria for detecting caffeine dependence or use disorder:

1. Unsuccessful attempts to restrict or discontinue caffeine use—often related to signs and symptoms of caffeine withdrawal (see following item);
2. Continued caffeine use despite the risk for, or experiencing of, undesired or harmful effects and toxicities associated with its use (e.g., cardiovascular effects or nervousness);
3. Presence of signs and symptoms of caffeine tolerance or caffeine withdrawal syndrome (see the earlier caffeine subsection, "Caffeine Physical and Psychological Dependence").

Additionally, as with other drugs and substances of abuse, it should be noted that individual "expectancies" play a major role in the initiation and continuation of caffeine use. For example, Huntley and Juliano (2012, p. 592), who developed the "Caffeine Expectancy Questionnaire" (Table 3.3), found that:

> The frequency and quantity of caffeine use were associated with greater expectancies for withdrawal/dependence, energy/work enhancement, appetite suppression, social/mood enhancement, and physical performance enhancement and lower expectancies for anxiety/negative physical effects and sleep disturbance. Caffeine expectancies predicted various caffeine-associated features of substance dependence (e.g., use despite harm, withdrawal incidence and severity, perceived difficulty stopping use, tolerance). Expectancies for caffeine consumed via coffee were stronger than for caffeine consumed via soft drinks or tea.

Treating Older Adult Caffeine Dependence or Use Disorder

Empirically based treatment approaches for caffeine dependence or use disorder are extremely limited because of the general "lack" of:

1. Formal, official recognition of caffeine dependence or use disorder (see the related discussion in the previous subsection);
2. Concern for the clinical significance of caffeine dependence or use disorder.

No pharmacotherapeutic approaches have been developed, demonstrated to be efficacious, or approved by the FDA for the treatment of caffeine dependence or use disorder. Consequently, therapeutic intervention—with little empirical validation—has focused on psychotherapeutic/counseling approaches (e.g., Evatt, Juliano, & Griffiths, 2016). In our own practice, we have found the use of cognitive therapy to be successful for older adults who are well motivated to actively address their caffeine dependence or use disorder. We also embed the following auxiliary therapeutic behavioral techniques as individually required:

- Using a diary to track the date, time, and price of each caffeine purchase/use;
- Avoiding coffee bars and espresso shops (e.g., Starbucks®);
- Limiting caffeine (i.e., coffee, tea) use to specific locations and times (e.g., first thing in the morning at home); (*continued p. 239*)

Table 3.3 Caffeine Expectancy Questionnaire

Instructions: We are interested in your beliefs about the effects that caffeine has on you. Below is a list of possible effects of caffeine. Using the scale below as a guide, please rate each statement in terms of how Likely or Unlikely you believe each consequence is for you when you use caffeine.
Base your responses on your caffeinated product of choice. If you use many types of caffeinated products, choose just one to base your responses on, or you may choose to base your responses on "caffeine in general." (You can change your choice after responding to the questions.)

Even if you very rarely consume caffeine, please rate how you would expect caffeine to affect you, if you consumed it. My responses below are based on: (please check one)

- □ **Coffee**
- □ **Soft drinks**
- □ **Tea**
- □ **Caffeine-containing medications (e.g., Excedrin; No-Doz)**
- □ **Caffeine in general**
- □ **Other (please specify):**

Item	**Very Unlikely**	**Unlikely**	**A Little Unlikely**	**A Little Likely**	**Likely**	**Very Likely**
1. Caffeine picks me up when I am feeling tired.	□	□	□	□	□	□
2. Conversations are better when using caffeine.	□	□	□	□	□	□
3. Caffeine helps me avoid eating more than I should.	□	□	□	□	□	□
4. I am easily stressed after having caffeine.	□	□	□	□	□	□
5. Caffeine improves my athletic performance.	□	□	□	□	□	□
6. I feel less sleepy after having caffeine.	□	□	□	□	□	□
7. Caffeine suppresses feelings of hunger.	□	□	□	□	□	□
8. I feel miserable when I do not have my usual caffeine.	□	□	□	□	□	□
9. Caffeine improves my mood.	□	□	□	□	□	□
10. I would get anxious if I abstained from caffeine.	□	□	□	□	□	□
11. Caffeine makes me jittery.	□	□	□	□	□	□
12. Workouts are better after having caffeine.	□	□	□	□	□	□
13. I would experience caffeine withdrawal if I went without caffeine.	□	□	□	□	□	□
14. I don't like the way caffeine makes me feel.	□	□	□	□	□	□

(*Continued*)

Table 3.3 (Continued)

Item	Very Unlikely	Unlikely	A Little Unlikely	A Little Likely	Likely	Very Likely
15. I would feel sick if I went without caffeine.	☐	☐	☐	☐	☐	☐
16. Caffeine increases my motivation to work.	☐	☐	☐	☐	☐	☐
17. I feel more confident after having caffeine.	☐	☐	☐	☐	☐	☐
18. Caffeine at any time-of-day throws off my sleep.	☐	☐	☐	☐	☐	☐
19. Caffeine makes me feel nervous.	☐	☐	☐	☐	☐	☐
20. Caffeine makes me feel more alert.	☐	☐	☐	☐	☐	☐
21. Even a small amount of caffeine makes me anxious.	☐	☐	☐	☐	☐	☐
22. Caffeine improves my concentration.	☐	☐	☐	☐	☐	☐
23. Caffeine makes me friendlier.	☐	☐	☐	☐	☐	☐
24. I need to have caffeine every day.	☐	☐	☐	☐	☐	☐
25. Caffeine makes me sweat.	☐	☐	☐	☐	☐	☐
26. Caffeine allows me to skip meals.	☐	☐	☐	☐	☐	☐
27. I have a strong desire for caffeine if I do not have my usual amount.	☐	☐	☐	☐	☐	☐
28. I have difficulty sleeping after having caffeine.	☐	☐	☐	☐	☐	☐
29. Caffeine makes me irritable.	☐	☐	☐	☐	☐	☐
30. I often crave caffeine.	☐	☐	☐	☐	☐	☐
31. Caffeine helps me to work over long periods of time.	☐	☐	☐	☐	☐	☐
32. Caffeine makes me feel happy.	☐	☐	☐	☐	☐	☐
33. I would be unable to function without caffeine.	☐	☐	☐	☐	☐	☐
34. Caffeine makes my heart beat irregularly.	☐	☐	☐	☐	☐	☐

Item	Very Unlikely	Unlikely	A Little Unlikely	A Little Likely	Likely	Very Likely
35. I would have difficulty starting my day without caffeine.	☐	☐	☐	☐	☐	☐
36. Caffeine upsets my stomach.	☐	☐	☐	☐	☐	☐
37. I would have trouble giving up caffeine.	☐	☐	☐	☐	☐	☐
38. Using caffeine late in the day disrupts my sleep.	☐	☐	☐	☐	☐	☐
39. Caffeine helps me to control my weight.	☐	☐	☐	☐	☐	☐
40. I would get a headache if I went without caffeine.	☐	☐	☐	☐	☐	☐
41. Caffeine improves my attention.	☐	☐	☐	☐	☐	☐
42. I feel more social after having caffeine.	☐	☐	☐	☐	☐	☐
43. I can exercise longer if I have caffeine.	☐	☐	☐	☐	☐	☐
44. Caffeine helps get me through the day.	☐	☐	☐	☐	☐	☐
45. Caffeine makes me feel more energetic.	☐	☐	☐	☐	☐	☐
46. Caffeine decreases my appetite.	☐	☐	☐	☐	☐	☐
47. Caffeine late in the day gives me insomnia.	☐	☐	☐	☐	☐	☐

Modified from: Huntley & Juliano, 2012.

- Substituting decaffeinated coffee (approximately 5 mg of caffeine per 8 ounces) for caffeinated coffee (approximately 100+ mg caffeine per 8 ounces);
- Substituting caffeine-free carbonated soda beverages (0 mg per 12 ounces) for caffeinated soda beverages (e.g., approximately 30 mg per 12 ounces);
- Substituting milk chocolate (20 mg caffeine per 100 gm milk chocolate) for dark chocolate (40 mg caffeine per 100 gm dark chocolate).

Rather than obtaining complete abstinence from caffeine, our therapeutic goal is generally to reduce caffeine consumption to controlled levels and, consequently, significantly decrease problems[38] related to caffeine use.

38. In our clinical experience, the major reasons patients with caffeine use disorder seek therapeutic intervention has been because of associated physical medical disorders (e.g., aggravation of gastric ulcers or cardiac tachydysrhythmias)—treatment is rarely, if ever, sought specifically for the treatment of

Common Contemporaneous Diagnoses Among Older Adults with Caffeine Dependence or Use Disorder

In addition to caffeine dependence or use disorder, older adults are also susceptible to concurrent alcohol and other dependence or use disorders, as well as one or more other mental disorders and physical medical disorders. Together these disorders comprise more serious and complicated contemporaneous diagnoses that often require more complex interdisciplinary health care planning, implementation, and management (Pagliaro & Pagliaro, 2018; Pagliaro & Pagliaro, *Clinical Patient Data Files*). For older adults, who are diagnosed with caffeine dependence or use disorder, other mental disorders that are commonly involved or significantly correlated—include:

- Anxiety disorders;
- Alcohol Dependence or Use Disorder (AUD);
- MDD;
- Nicotine [Tobacco] Dependence or Use Disorder (NUD);
- Psychotic Disorders (Schizophrenia).

We now turn to "Nicotine."

NICOTINE

Nicotine is a widely available, and relatively safe, psychostimulant that is enjoyed by older adults across the U.S. However, the general method of nicotine use—"tobacco cigarette smoking"—is identified as the highest single cause of premature death worldwide and is estimated to kill more than 5 million people each year. As reported by the U.S. Preventive Services Task Force:

> Tobacco use is the leading preventable cause of disease, disability, and death in the United States.
>
> (Patnode, Henderson, & Thompson, 2015a, p. 1)

Nicotine is only one of approximately 5,000 chemicals found in tobacco smoke—including over 60 known human carcinogens (Graves, Johnson, & Nishida, 2020; Pagliaro & Pagliaro, 2004; Streller & Roth, 2014a; Streller & Roth, 2015a). Although it is less toxic than many of the other chemicals, it is the only chemical in tobacco smoke that is associated with physical and psychological dependence (Pagliaro & Pagliaro, 2004). We begin with the primary natural source of nicotine, the tobacco plant.

Related Professional Reminder: ***Tobacco cigarette smoke and, consequently, its chemical constituents, display significant variability due to several factors including, additives, filter materials, mixtures of various tobacco species and varieties, processing techniques, and wrapping papers.***

"caffeine use disorder" (Pagliaro & Pagliaro, *Clinical Patient Data Files*). (See also the following caffeine subsection—"Common Contemporaneous Diagnoses Among Older Adults with Caffeine Dependence or Use Disorder.")

Tobacco Plant Botany

The tobacco plant, the primary source of nicotine,[39] is a member of the family *Solanaceae*, or Nightshade, which is indigenous in both North and South America—but is currently cultivated worldwide.[40] The principal alkaloid found in tobacco plants is nicotine—approximately 95%—with significantly lower concentrations of other alkaloids including anabasine, anatabine, and nornicotine (Streller & Roth, 2014a).[41] Nicotine serves a significant defensive function in protecting the tobacco plant (i.e., as both an insect repellant and as an insecticide). Interestingly, chemicals (e.g., glutamine), which are present in the saliva of insects eating tobacco leaves, trigger an increase in the production of nicotine by tobacco plants (Streller & Roth, 2014b).

Nicotine is produced in the roots of the tobacco plant from where it is transported throughout the plant by the xylem, particularly to the leaves (i.e., approximately 5% in the flowers, 13% in the root, 18% in the stem, and 64% in the leaves).[42] Depending on the type and brand of tobacco, the concentration of nicotine varies from 15 to 20 mg of nicotine per gram of tobacco leaf (Malson, Sims, & Murty, 2001).

Nicotine, a natural occurring liquid alkaloid,[43] was first isolated from the leaves of the tobacco plant (*Nicotiana tabacum*) by two German students at the university of Heidelberg—Wilhelm Heinrich Posselt (1806–1877) and Karl Ludwig Reimann (1804–1872).[44] Finding the pure chemical salt form of nicotine bitter to the taste, they considered it to be a poison (Pagliaro & Pagliaro, 2004).[45] Later, nicotine was more correctly identified/characterized as a psychostimulant and neurotoxin.

Nicotine tabacum, which does not grow wild in nature, is an annual herbaceous plant that requires cultivation. After the tobacco leaves are harvested, usually by hand, they are cured/dried by air, fire, flue, or sun methods for several days to several weeks. The dried crude tobacco is then moistened with steam and sprayed with flavoring agents (Streller & Roth, 2014a). The leaves are then aged for up to three years to enhance their flavor and aroma.[46] Tobacco cigarettes contain a mixture of different

39. Nicotine is also found in significantly lower concentrations in related plants from the family, *Solanaceae*. These plants include cauliflower, eggplant, green pepper, potato, and tomato (Domino, Hornbach, & Demana, 1993; Sheen, 1988).
40. There are over 70 species of tobacco plants. *Nicotiana rustica* (i.e., Aztec tobacco or wild tobacco) has a higher nicotine content than *Nicotiana tobacum* and was used primarily by ancient (e.g., Mayan) and rural, isolated peoples (e.g., Russian farmers/peasants). Current use is generally limited to ethnobotanical shamanism (Pagliaro & Pagliaro, 2004).
41. In addition to nicotine, the tobacco plant contains another psychotropic, "harmine," a harmala alkaloid (Streller & Roth, 2014a).
42. N.B. The nicotine content of tobacco decreases by 30% to 50% during the drying and fermentation process (Streller & Roth, 2014a).
43. The nicotine naturally found in the tobacco plant is, primarily (i.e., ~ 99%), in the form of the levorotary-isomer.
44. The plant and its alkaloid were named in honor of the French diplomat, Jean Nicot de Villemain, who brought the seeds and leaves of the plant to France from Brazil in 1556.
45. Nicotine can be harmful to humans (e.g., Rogers, Denk, & Wax, 2004) (see also the later nicotine subsection, "Pharmacology—Undesired, or Harmful, Effects and Toxicities"). Although, nicotine has been used as an insecticide, it has now been largely replaced by a related, and more potent class of insecticides—the "neonicotinoids" (Tomizawa & Casida, 2005).
46. During the aging period, the process of fermentation occurs resulting in the degradation of some proteins and the reduction in nicotine concentration. Additionally, numerous new chemicals are produced (Streller & Roth, 2014a).

varieties of tobacco—as well as various additives—that vary by the brand name of the finished cigarette (Streller & Roth, 2015b).

During the first decade of the new millennium, tobacco smoking, particularly cigarette smoking, continued to be the most common method of nicotine use. However, during the second decade of the new millennium, another method of use became popular—"e-cigarette vaping." The pharmacology of nicotine is discussed in the following subsections, with attention to these and other methods of use.

Nicotine Pharmacology

Although the nicotine content of dry tobacco can be as high as 9% (Streller & Roth, 2014a), a tobacco cigarette usually contains 1% to 2% nicotine by weight (Taghavi, Khashyarmanesh, & Moalemzadeh-Haghighi, 2012). After smoking one to two cigarettes, the plasma concentration of neurotransmitters—particularly, noradrenaline, dopamine, and the amino acid, glutamate—increase significantly in specific areas of the central nervous, cardiovascular, and pulmonary systems. In the CNS, nicotine stimulates the cerebral cortex, where it causes increased cognitive activity with observed attention-enhancing effects (Hahn, 2015), followed by CNS depression.[47] It also stimulates the ventral tegmental area, where it causes the release of dopamine and further stimulates the release of glutamate. These actions trigger additional dopamine release in the limbic system causing feelings of euphoria (Zickler, 2003). The well-recognized anorexiant effect of nicotine appears to be regulated within the CNS, specifically in the arcuate nucleus of the hypothalamus. Here nicotine binds to the $\alpha_3\beta_4$ nicotine acetylcholine receptors resulting in the release of an endogenous peptide hormone, alpha-melanocyte-stimulating hormone (α-MSH). The α-MSH binds to the melanocortin 4 receptor (MC4R) producing a neuronal signal that is interpreted as satiation (Mineur, Abizaid, & Rao, 2011; Streller & Roth, 2015b).

Cardiovascular effects associated with nicotine use include tachycardia, vasoconstriction, and, consequently, hypertension associated with the action of nicotine on the sympathetic ganglia, adrenal medulla, and aortic and carotid chemoreceptors. The actions of nicotine on motor neurons in the muscular-skeletal system lead to a marked reduction in muscle tone, associated feelings of relaxation, and a decrease in the muscle tone of some skeletal muscles (e.g., rectus femoris muscles of the thighs)—actions that are often reported by tobacco smokers. In addition to decreasing deep-tendon reflexes, nicotine also typically causes an increase in hand tremor and an alerting pattern on the electroencephalogram. These effects are thought to involve Renshaw cell stimulation in the spinal cord (Curtis & Eccles, 1958).

Pharmacodynamics: Mechanism of Action

The psychostimulant action of nicotine is dose dependent. At lower dosages, nicotine acts as an agonist and stimulates the autonomic ganglia. At higher dosages, it acts as an antagonist and blocks the autonomic ganglia (Heeschen, Weis, & Aicher, 2002; Kimura, Ushiyama, & Fujii, 2003). Interestingly, for regular, long-term nicotine users, agonistic actions may vary

---

47. The associated CNS depression appears to be related to nicotine-induced changes in nAChR function. However, the exact cause and relationship between nicotine use and CNS depression is variable and not yet fully explained (e.g., Fluharty, Taylor, & Grabski, 2017; Mineur & Picciotto, 2010).

according to the degree of their nicotine tolerance. (For related discussion, including signs and symptoms, see the later nicotine subsection—"Overdosage/Unintentional Poisoning.")

Nicotine exerts its psychostimulant actions by stimulating nicotinic acetylcholine (cholinergic) receptors (nAChRs) (Figure 3.2). The nAChRs are ligand-gated ion channels, or "pores" in cell plasma membranes, which open and close when stimulated.[48] Nicotine rapidly increases the cellular permeability of nAChRs to sodium (Na^+) and calcium (Ca^{++}) ions, which results in their depolarization and resultant excitation. There are five types of structurally diverse subunits of nAChRs: (1) alpha (α); (2) beta (β); (3) delta (δ); (4) epsilon (ε); and (5) gamma (γ). These subunits are found in six different combinations. For nAChR subunit combinations located at skeletal neuromuscular junctions (e.g., α1-ε-α1-β1-δ), depolarization primarily affects muscle tone by producing muscular contraction.

For nAChR combinations located at synapses between neurons in the CNS (e.g., α4-β2-α4-β2-β2), associated depolarization and associated excitation primarily produce: (1) arousal; (2) enhanced cognitive functioning—including learning and memory; and (3) reward (Pagliaro &

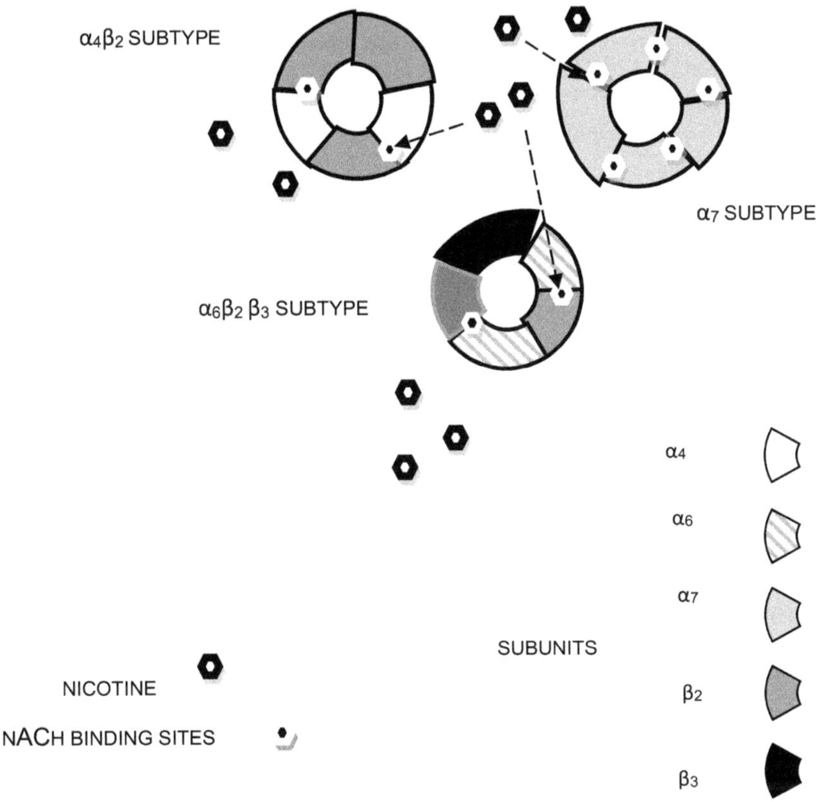

Figure 3.2 Nicotine Mechanism of Action

48. To elicit an action, a ligand binds to a chemical—in this case, acetylcholine, or nicotine.

Pagliaro, 2009). In the CNS, combinations of α subunits and β subunits appear to be particularly relevant to the achievement of both the desired and undesired actions of nicotine. For example, the α4 and β2 subunits appear to contribute to the euphoria associated with nicotine use, whereas the α3, α5, and β3 subunits appear to be responsible for determining both the risk for and severity of nicotine use disorder, or nicotine physical dependence (Whitten, 2009).

Subunits in autonomic ganglia also affect depolarization and firing of postganglionic neurons. In the adrenal medulla, they also affect the secretion of catecholamines, because of the opening of cation channels and the influx of calcium ions through the depolarized membrane pores of the nAChRs (Araki, Suemaru, & Gomita, 2002).

Thought to be genetically influenced, the response of the nAChRs to nicotine helps to explain various patterns of nicotine use among older adults, including the development of nicotine dependence or use disorder (NUD) (see the related discussion in the later nicotine subsection, "Nicotine Physical and Psychological Dependence"). It also helps to explain the signs and symptoms of nicotine withdrawal syndrome, which occurs as blood nicotine concentrations (BNCs) decline when regular, long-term nicotine use is abruptly discontinued.[49] Additionally, whereas individually, women "inherit different forms of half a dozen genes that dictate the features of the brain receptor to which nicotine binds" (Whitten, 2009, p. 1), collectively, "the protective effects of progesterone on craving in nicotine-dependent women may be mediated through its inhibitory effect on β2-nAChR function" (Moran-Santa Maria, Flanagan, & Brady, 2014, p. 5).

Pharmacokinetics

The pharmacokinetics of nicotine—absorption, distribution, metabolism, and excretion—are presented and discussed in the following subsections.

Absorption

The absorption of nicotine, like most other drugs and substances of abuse, is dependent upon the route of administration, or method of use, and the formulation (e.g., gum, leaf tobacco, or transdermal patch) in which it is contained. Chemically, nicotine is a weak base (pka = 8.0).[50] Consequently, its transfer across biological membranes is pH dependent.[51] Thus, the buccal and sublingual absorption of nicotine can significantly vary because of pH differences in tobacco products. For example, American cigarettes, which are usually produced using "flue cured" tobacco, have an "acidic" pH. The acidic pH results in the nicotine being predominantly in an ionized form that does not readily cross biological membranes. As a result, buccal or sublingual absorption is minimal.

49. Some more recent research (e.g., Gamaleddin, Trigo, & Gueye, 2015; Merritt, Martin, & Walters, 2008) suggests a significant role for the endocannabinoids and the associated CB_1 receptors in modulating the effects of nicotine—both the reinforcing effects and those involved with nicotine withdrawal. A noted significant limitation is that most of these studies have been conducted with experimental laboratory animals (e.g., genetically modified mice). (For additional related discussion of the endocannabinoids and their receptors, see Chapter 4, *Cannabis*.)
50. For example: at a tobacco smoke pH of 6.0, 1% of nicotine is in the neutral (i.e., non-ionized form); at pH 7.0, 9% of nicotine is in the non-ionized form; at pH 8.0, 50% of nicotine is in the non-ionized form; and at pH 9.0, 91% of nicotine is in the non-ionized form (Streller & Roth, 2015b).
51. For additional related discussion of the effects of pH on absorption and excretion, see Chapter 2, *Amphetamines and Cocaine,* amphetamine pharmacology subsection—"Pharmacokinetics."

Conversely, some European cigarettes, as well as cigar and pipe tobacco, which are usually produced using "air cured" tobacco, have an "alkaline" pH (i.e., ~ 8.5). The alkaline pH, in turn, results in "maximal" buccal and sublingual absorption of nicotine (Hukkanen, Jacob, & Benowitz, 2005).

An average American tobacco cigarette, when smoked, delivers only about 1 mg of nicotine because approximately 90% of the nicotine is destroyed by pyrolysis. However, older adults who smoke tobacco cigarettes can achieve relatively high BNCs due to the relatively large surface area of their lungs and excellent blood supply that results in the high pulmonary absorption of nicotine (i.e., F = 0.9).[52]

When nicotine is inadvertently ingested, its absorption into the circulatory system is low (i.e., F = 0.3, or approximately 30%). It also undergoes significant "first-pass" hepatic metabolism (see the later subsection—"Metabolism") that results in its rapid and extensive inactivation. In comparison, the nicotine in buccal absorption spray products (e.g., Nicorette Quick Mist®) and lozenges (e.g., Thrive® lozenges), is rapidly absorbed from the inner cheeks of the mouth and, consequently, avoids first-pass hepatic metabolism.

Buccally absorbed chewing tobacco and nicotine chewing gum formulations (e.g., Nicorette®)—when chewed and the juices held in the mouth before being spat out—achieve BNCs that approximate those obtained by smoking a regular tobacco cigarette (i.e., F = 0.9). Interestingly, the nicotine in chewing gum products, which is bound to an ion-exchange resin, is only released by chewing. Thus, the amount of nicotine released from the chewing gum, and the resultant BNCs that are achieved, are related to the rate and vigor of chewing.

Nasal absorption of nicotine from nicotine nasal spray or snuff products is more rapid and complete than absorption from the oral mucosa. Nasal tobacco products, such as sprays and snuff, are formulated to have an alkaline pH that facilitates absorption. In comparison, after topical application, transdermal delivery systems (TDSs)—or "patches"—are well-absorbed (i.e., ~ 80%) through intact skin sites. However, the absorption rate is significantly slower than that associated with pulmonary inhalation or other methods of use. Additionally, it should be recognized that significant interindividual variability occurs in the absorption (i.e., bioavailability) of nicotine. This variability is highest (i.e., up to fivefold) with nicotine nasal spray and lowest (i.e., up to twofold) with nicotine TDSs (Benowitz, Zevin, & Jacob, 1997; Herman & Sofuoglu, 2013; Pagliaro & Pagliaro, 2009).

> ***Related Professional Reminder*: Regarding the absorption processes involved in the use of TDSs, or "nicotine patches," it should be kept in mind that: (1) there is an initial time lag of approximately one hour between the application of a nicotine patch and the onset of nicotine absorption into the bloodstream; and (2) following removal of the nicotine patch, a residual amount of nicotine (approximately 10% of the total dose) continues to be absorbed from the placement site.**

---

52. N.B. Bioavailability can be increased significantly by the smoking techniques used, for example:

    1. Increasing the number of puffs per tobacco cigarette (e.g., 30 to 60 seconds can elapse between puffs);
    2. Inhaling the smoke more deeply into the lungs;
    3. Holding the inhaled smoke in the lungs for a longer period before exhaling.

Distribution

Regardless of the method of use, once nicotine is absorbed, it is only negligibly bound to plasma proteins (i.e., less than 5%). Having a low affinity for adipose tissue, it is distributed to, and preferentially binds to brain,[53] hepatic, pulmonary, and renal tissues (Benowitz, Hukkanen, & Jacob, 2009). The volume of distribution of nicotine is approximately 2 to 3 L/kg (Tutka, Mosiewicz, & Wielosz, 2005). However, the volume of distribution has been identified to be lower in older adults because of a general age-related decrease in lean body mass (Molander, Hansson, & Lunell, 2001).

Metabolism

Nicotine is primarily metabolized (i.e., ~ 90%) by the hepatic microsomal enzyme CYP2A6[54] to several metabolites—the most important being the "inactive" metabolite, cotinine (Benowitz et al., 2009).[55,56,57] Cotinine accounts for 70% to 80% of nicotine metabolism. Cotinine, itself, is subsequently metabolized into four metabolites, including 3-hydroxycotinine—the major nicotine metabolite that is detected in the urine of tobacco smokers (i.e., accounting for ~ 40% to 50% of the administered nicotine dose) (Benowitz & Jacob, 2001).

> ***Related Professional Reminder:* Large individual differences in the metabolism of nicotine—resulting from developmental, environmental, and genetic influences—have been widely documented.**

The hepatic clearance rate of nicotine is approximately 1.2 L/minute, which means that the liver is extremely efficient at clearing and, hence, removing nicotine from the circulatory system.[58] However, nicotine clearance displays large interindividual variability being highly correlated with age, continental or other descent, diet, and gender (e.g., Hukkanen et al., 2005; Johnstone, Benowitz, & Cargill, 2006; Tricker, 2003). For example:

1. In comparison to older adults of European continental descent, older adults of African or Asian continental descent generally display a slower metabolism of nicotine—primarily because of their slower metabolism (i.e., conjugation) of cotinine (e.g., Benowitz et al., 2009; Hukkanen et al., 2005; Schoedel, Hoffmann, & Rao, 2004);
2. Women generally metabolize nicotine faster than men (e.g., Benowitz, Lessov-Schlaggar, & Swan, 2006; Piper, Cook, & Schlam, 2010; Streller & Roth, 2015a);

---

53. Nicotine is rapidly distributed to the brain and readily crosses the blood-brain barrier. Thus, for example, CNS effects can be detected within 10 seconds after the first puff of a tobacco cigarette (i.e., as rapidly as that achieved by IV injection).
54. Differences in the observed rates of nicotine metabolism have been directly related to identified variations in the CYP2A6 gene (St Helen, Dempsey, & Wilson, 2013).
55. Hepatic flavin-containing monooxygenases also contribute to the metabolism of nicotine (Perez-Paramo, Watson, & Chen, 2017).
56. Nicotine also is metabolized, although to a significantly lesser extent, in the brain, kidneys, and lungs (Sobkowiak & Lesicki, 2013).
57. Over 20 different metabolites of nicotine have been identified. These metabolites are not as pharmacologically active as their parent drug, nicotine.
58. In addition to hepatic clearance, nicotine also undergoes renal clearance, but at a significantly lower rate (i.e., ~ 75 ml/minute).

3. Nicotine clearance is significantly deceased in older adults, 65 years of age and older, primarily because of reduced hepatic blood flow (e.g., Molander et al., 2001; Pagliaro & Pagliaro, 1983);
4. The increased blood flow in the liver following a meal may accelerate nicotine metabolism (e.g., Lee, Jacob, & Jarvik, 1989; Streller & Roth, 2015a).

In addition, genetic variation in the multiple alleles of the CYP2A6 gene has been associated with the slow, intermediate, and normal metabolism of nicotine (e.g., Nakajima, Kuroiwa, & Yokoi, 2002; Nakajima & Yokoi, 2005). Interestingly, slow metabolizers have generally demonstrated: (1) lower rates of smoking; (2) decreased risk for developing NUD; and (3) greater success in smoking cessation (Ho & Tyndale, 2007; Malaiyandi, Sellers, & Tyndale, 2005; Mwenifumbo & Tyndale, 2007; Tanner, Chenoweth, & Tyndale, 2015).

The mean half-life of elimination for nicotine is two hours (Pagliaro & Pagliaro, 2004; Streller & Roth, 2015a).[59] Thus, regular, long-term smokers of tobacco cigarettes will need to "light-up," on average, at least every two hours to maintain BNCs that are needed to avoid the occurrence of the signs and symptoms of the nicotine withdrawal syndrome (see the related discussion in the later nicotine subsection, Nicotine Physical and Psychological Dependence—"Withdrawal Syndrome").

Excretion

Nicotine and its metabolites are rapidly excreted in the urine (approximately 5% to 10% in unchanged form). Affected by urinary pH, nicotine excretion is decreased in alkaline urine (i.e., urine pH above 7.4), and increased in acidic urine (i.e., urine pH below 7.4). In fact, the acidification of the urine to below a pH of 5 can result in up to 30% of a dosage of nicotine being excreted in the urine in unchanged form. Renal clearance of nicotine is significantly reduced in mild renal failure.[60] A small percentage of nicotine (i.e., ~ 1%) and its metabolites are excreted in the feces and sweat (Hukkanen et al., 2005).

Nicotine and Tobacco Smoke Drug-Drug Interactions

Nicotine—primarily, in the form of nicotine E-cigarettes, tobacco cigarettes, and nicotine replacement products (e.g., buccal/mouth sprays, chewing gums, and TDSs)—is often concurrently used with over-the-counter drugs ("OTCs") (e.g., acetaminophen, Tylenol®), and prescription drugs (e.g., insulins, theophylline, Theolair-SR®). Nicotine also is concurrently used with other drugs and substances of abuse—alcohol, benzodiazepines, caffeine, and opiate analgesics (Cross, Lotfipour, & Leslie, 2017; Pagliaro & Pagliaro, 2009, 2018; Verplaetse & McKee, 2017).

---

59. By comparison, the mean half-life of elimination for cotinine, nicotine's first and principal metabolite, is approximately 18 hours (Tutka et al., 2005). Cotinine concentrations can be readily measured in biological samples (e.g., hair, saliva, serum, and urine) to determine tobacco exposure/use (Pagliaro & Pagliaro, 2004).
60. Additionally, it has been suggested that the accumulation of uremic toxins may inhibit the metabolic activity of CYP2A6 (Benowitz et al., 2009). (See the related discussion in the previous nicotine pharmacology subsection, Pharmacokinetics—"Metabolism.")

Drug interactions involving nicotine can be generally classified as being either pharmacodynamic or pharmacokinetic interactions. Those involving nicotine and tobacco smoke are a special case.

Nicotine Pharmacodynamic Interactions

Pharmacodynamic drug-drug interactions are mediated by actions at the sites of drug action. Typically, they involve the synergistic actions of other concurrently used psychostimulants (e.g., amphetamines, cocaine, or caffeine) or the antagonistic actions of concurrently used psychodepressants (e.g., alcohol, benzodiazepines, or opiate analgesics).

Nicotine Pharmacokinetic Interactions

Pharmacokinetic drug-drug interactions are mediated by effects on the pharmacokinetic processes of absorption,[61] distribution, metabolism, and excretion. In the context of pharmacokinetic drug-drug interactions involving nicotine, the principal process that is affected is metabolism. Specifically, drugs that induce the CYP2A6 enzyme (e.g., dexamethasone, phenobarbital, or rifampicin)—when used concurrently with nicotine—reduce blood nicotine concentrations (BNCs). In comparison, drugs that inhibit the CYP2A6 enzyme (e.g., coumarin, methoxsalen, or tranylcypromine)—when used concurrently with nicotine—increase BNCs. Additionally, some foods (e.g., grapefruit) and some tobacco "additives" (e.g., menthol) inhibit CYP2A6 and, consequently, decrease the rate of nicotine metabolism (Streller & Roth, 2015a).

Special Cases: Tobacco Smoke—Nicotine and Other Constituent Interactions

The clinical significance of potential drug-drug interactions involving tobacco smoke is generally both more subtle and complex than generally expected or recognized. Being predicated on several factors related to tobacco smoking (e.g., product type—filter or nonfilter tobacco cigarettes; cigars versus cigarillos; or pipe tobacco), tobacco smoke drug-drug interactions may also be affected by the specific pattern of use at a particular period of time. For example, when:

1. Initiating and gradually increasing use;
2. Maintaining regular, long-term use;
3. Decreasing or ceasing use, including use of nicotine replacement therapy.

Drug-drug interactions involving tobacco smoke present a special case because they involve both nicotine and other constituents found in tobacco smoke, including polycyclic

61. As discussed in the earlier Nicotine pharmacology subsection, "Pharmacokinetics—Excretion," the process of nicotine urinary excretion is significantly affected by the pH of the urine. Consequently, drugs that either acidify the urine (e.g., ammonium chloride or vitamin C) or alkalinize the urine (e.g., calcium carbonate or sodium bicarbonate) can interact with nicotine and significantly affect its rate of urinary excretion.

aromatic hydrocarbons that induce the production of the hepatic microsomal enzyme CYP1A2 and, consequently, affect the metabolism of many other drugs (Anderson & Chan, 2016; Schaffer, Yoon, & Zadezensky, 2009; Zevin & Benowitz, 1999). An overview of other major potentially clinically significant drug-drug interactions involving nicotine and other constituents in tobacco smoke—and for which more published data are available—is presented in Table 3.4. (Also see the following nicotine pharmacology subsection, Undesired, or Harmful, Effects and Toxicities—"Nicotine and Other Constituents in Tobacco Smoke.")

Table 3.4 Drug-Drug Interactions Involving Nicotine and Other Constituents in Tobacco Smoke[62]

DRUGS AND SUBSTANCES THAT INTERACT WITH NICOTINE	COMMENTS
Acetaminophen (e.g., Tylenol®)	Concurrent acetaminophen use with tobacco smoking may require an increase in the acetaminophen dosage due to the: (1) induction of hepatic microsomal enzymes (e.g., CYP1A2) associated with tobacco smoking; and (2) resultant increased metabolic clearance of acetaminophen.
Alcohol[63]	Concurrent alcohol use with tobacco smoking appears to have a reciprocal effect resulting in increased craving for and increased use of alcohol and tobacco smoking.
Benzodiazepines (e.g., oxazepam, Serax®)	Concurrent benzodiazepine use with tobacco smoking may require an increase in the benzodiazepine dosage due to the: (1) induction of hepatic microsomal enzymes (e.g., CYP1A2) associated with tobacco smoking; and (2) resultant increase in the metabolic clearance[64] of the benzodiazepine.
Caffeine	Concurrent caffeine use with tobacco smoking may increase the usual amount of caffeine ingested due to the: (1) induction of hepatic microsomal enzymes (e.g., CYP1A2) associated with tobacco smoking; and (2) resultant increased metabolic clearance of caffeine.
Estrogens	Estrogens can induce the production of CYP2A6—of which nicotine is a substrate—resulting in lower nicotine concentrations.

(Continued)

62. The clinical significance of these potential nicotine drug-drug interactions depends upon several factors, including the: (1) dosage of each drug; (2) characteristics of the adolescent or young adult (e.g., age, gender, and genetics); (3) concomitant physical health status (e.g., hepatic and renal function); and (4) concomitant mental health status.
63. As identified by Yardley, Mirbaba, and Ray (2015, p. 834):

> The link between heavy drinking and smoking is thought to be driven by many factors including genetics, neurobiological mechanisms, conditioning processes, and psychosocial influences.

64. N.B. Nicotine-related tobacco exposure/use is a special case that requires consideration. Polycyclic aromatic hydrocarbons that are present in tobacco smoke reduce the production of the hepatic microsomal for the metabolism of many drugs (Anderson & Chan, 2016; Schaffer et al., 2009; Zevin & Benowitz, 1999).

Table 3.4 (Continued)

DRUGS AND SUBSTANCES THAT INTERACT WITH NICOTINE	COMMENTS
Insulin	Nicotine related cutaneous vasoconstriction may slow the rate of insulin absorption when injected subcutaneously. Conversely, with smoking cessation, a decrease in insulin dosage may be required due to the associated increase in insulin subcutaneous absorption.
Opiate Analgesics[65] (e.g., pentazocine, Talwin®; propoxyphene, Darvon®)	Concurrent pentazocine use and tobacco smoking may require an increase in the opiate analgesic dosage due to the: (1) induction of hepatic microsomal enzymes (e.g., CYP1A2) associated with tobacco smoking; and (2) resultant increase in metabolic clearance of the opiate analgesic.
	Concurrent propoxyphene use during tobacco smoking cessation, may require a decrease in the propoxyphene dosage due to the reduction of first-pass hepatic metabolism associated with smoking cessation.
Theophylline (e.g., Theolair®)	Concurrent theophylline use with tobacco smoking may require an increase in the theophylline dosage due to the: (1) induction of the hepatic microsomal enzymes (e.g., CYP1A2) associated with tobacco smoking; and (2) resultant increased metabolic clearance of theophylline.

Undesired, or Harmful, Effects and Toxicities

The major undesired, or harmful, effects and toxicities associated with nicotine and other constituents in tobacco smoke are presented and discussed in the following subsections. We begin with an overview of the "direct" effects of nicotine on the CNS and other body systems—acute or chronic, mild or severe, and, rarely, fatal.

Direct Acute Effects of Nicotine

Several acute psychostimulant effects related to nicotine use are often identified as desired effects, such as euphoria, increased cognitive abilities, and vigilance. Nicotine use is also associated with many undesired effects, which include anorexia,[66] diarrhea, dizziness, edema, flushing, GI cramps, headache, heart palpitations, hypertension, hypoglycemia (in insulin-dependent diabetics), hyperventilation, increased salivation, insomnia,[67] irrita-

65. Most opiate analgesic users, including those participating in methadone maintenance programs, smoke tobacco cigarettes. Smoking cessation is particularly difficult to achieve for these nicotine users regardless of pharmacological, psychological/counseling, or other treatment approaches (e.g., Stein, Weinstock, & Herman, 2006; Zirakazdeh, Shuman, & Stauter, 2013).
66. Anorexia can be a "desired" effect of nicotine use for older adults, most often women, who want to lose, or maintain, body weight.
67. Insomnia can be a "desired" effect of nicotine use for older adults who want to stay awake in order to, for example, watch a favorite television program or movie.

bility, lightheadedness, nausea, tachycardia, tinnitus, tremors, and vomiting (e.g., Mishra, Chaturvedi, & Datta, 2015; Pagliaro & Pagliaro, 2004).

Direct Long-Term Effects of Nicotine and Other Constituents in Tobacco Smoke

> Tobacco use is the leading preventable cause of disease, disability, and death in the United States. According to the Centers for Disease Control and Prevention (CDC), cigarette smoking results in more than 480,000 premature deaths in the United States each year—about 1 in every 5 U.S. deaths—and . . . for every one person who dies from smoking, about 30 more suffer from at least one serious tobacco-related illness.
>
> (NIDA, 2016, p. 1)

We analyzed the data provided by the U.S. Surgeon General (USDHHS, 2014) and determined that the reported annual deaths attributed to tobacco smoking in the U.S. fell into the following categories, presented in order of percentage:

- Lung cancer (27%);
- COPD (21%);
- Coronary heart disease (21%);
- Other diagnoses (12%);
- Other cancers (7%);
- Other heart disease (5%);
- Cerebrovascular disease (3%);
- Other vascular diseases (2%).

(See the related discussion in the following subsections.)

As emphasized by Carter, Abnet, and Feskanich (2015), "mortality among current smokers is 2 to 3 times as high as that among persons who never smoked" (p. 631).

The chemical constituents that are present in tobacco smoke include:

1. Chemicals naturally found in tobacco leaves (e.g., heavy metals, such as arsenic, chromium, and lead);
2. Chemicals added during the farming (e.g., insecticides) and curing processes (e.g., menthol flavoring);
3. Chemicals (i.e., combustion products) produced by pyrolysis (e.g., carbon dioxide and tar). For example, carbon dioxide can be found in concentrations 200 to 300 times that found in normal room air.[68]

Graves et al. (2020, p. 1), in their comprehensive characterization of the chemical components of mainstream tobacco smoke found that:

- Over 97% of the mass and volume of the tobacco smoke particles are semi-volatile;
- A total of 4,350 different compounds were detected;

68. The high concentrations of carbon dioxide (i.e., approximately 13%) have been associated with an inflammatory response in pulmonary tissues (Guais, Brand, & Jacquot, 2011; Schwartz, Guais, & Chaumet-Riffaud, 2010).

- 173 of the detected compounds are known to cause adverse health effects by means of established carcinogenic, mutagenic, teratogenic, or other toxic mechanisms.

The three major classes of carcinogens present in tobacco smoke are: (1) "polycyclic aromatic hydrocarbons" (PAHs), including benzo(a)pyrene, chrysene, and naphthalene;[69] (2) "nicotine-derived nitrosamines" (NDNs);[70] and (3) other known carcinogens, including acetaldehyde, arsenic, benzene, cadmium, formaldehyde, and vinyl chloride (American Cancer Society, 2017; CDC, 2010b; Health Canada, 2011; Talhout, Schulz, & Florek, 2011). These chemicals are present in various physical forms (i.e., gases, liquids, and solids) in tobacco smoke. In addition, their concentrations can vary significantly as a result of several factors, including the:

- Type of tobacco used in the preparation of cigarettes, cigars, pipe tobacco, and other tobacco products;
- Conditions under which tobacco plants are grown (e.g., soil content);
- Process of fermentation;
- Additives used in the preparation of the tobacco leaves (e.g., menthol);
- Processing of the tobacco leaf after harvesting;
- Type of paper/wrap used for preparing tobacco cigarettes and cigars;
- Type of filter used, if any, in association with tobacco cigarettes;
- Smoking techniques used by the smoker.

All types of smoke, regardless of the source, are comprised of colorless gases (e.g., carbon dioxide, carbon monoxide, nitrogen, and oxygen), which contain particulate, or solid, matter. The generally warm gases and particulate matter dispersed in tobacco smoke, irritate, and dry the pulmonary system leading, particularly over a period of regular, long-term use, to a characteristic dry, non-productive cough (i.e., "smokers cough"). Regular, long-term exposure to tobacco smoke also leads to the loss of respiratory muscle mass and the development of related respiratory dysfunction even before the development of overt, symptomatic pulmonary toxicity (Degens, Gayan-Ramirez, & van Hees, 2015). In addition, particulate matter that makes its way into the alveolar sacs can get "trapped" and compromise alveolar function.

In addition to aging of the skin and other undesired effects (e.g., tobacco stains on fingers and yellow teeth) tobacco smoke has been associated with increased occurrence of coronary heart and pulmonary diseases, as well as several cancers involving numerous body systems (see the following subsections). In fact, as previously noted, during the first decade of the new millennium, tobacco smoking was identified as the major single preventable cause of illness and disease in the U.S., where it contributes to an estimated 1,500 deaths every day[71] (USDHHS, 2010, 2014).

---

69. Several studies (e.g., Ding, Yan, & Jain, 2006) have found that "flue-cured" tobacco, typically, can deliver more PAHs than other tobacco types.
70. In the published literature, NDNs are also referred to as "tobacco-specific nitrosamines" (TSNAs) (Wu, Zhang, & Jain, 2005). Two major TSNAs that are present in tobacco and tobacco smoke are 4-(methylnitrosamino)-1-(3-pyridyl)-1-butanone (NNB) and N-nitrosonornicotine (NNN) (Hecht, 2014; Pfeifer, Denissenko, & Olivier, 2002; Vu, Taylor, & Holman, 2015; Wang, Li, & Guo, 2016).
71. N.B. The specific contributions of tobacco cigarette smoking to illness and death are often difficult to properly identify. Consequently, the actual rate of illness and death may be higher than what is presented.

Cardiovascular Diseases

As identified in an expert consensus statement from the American College of Cardiology regarding cardiovascular diseases (CVDs):

> Tobacco is the leading cause of premature deaths before age 70 years due to CVD.
> (Roth, Forouzanfar, & Barber, 2015, p. 1333)

As also identified by Mons, Muezzinler, and Gellert (2015, p. 1):

> Smoking is a strong independent risk factor for cardiovascular events and mortality among older adults.

And, as identified by Barua, Rigotti, and Benowitz (2018, p. 3332):

> Tobacco use, especially cigarette smoking, is a major risk factor for cardiovascular disease and mortality.

And, a final example, as shared in "Suzy's Story:"

> Suzy, age 62. . . began sneaking cigarettes at age 15. . . at age 57, suffered a stroke, which her doctors linked to her many years of smoking.
> (CDC, 2018b, 2020)

Whereas the effects of nicotine and other constituents in tobacco smoke on coronary heart disease were identified over 80 years ago by English, Willius, and Berkson (1940), it is now generally recognized that tobacco smoke is associated with a two- to four-fold increased risk for coronary heart disease among regular, long-term tobacco smokers. Several interrelated factors contribute to this complex cardiovascular toxicity. As explained by D'Allessandro, Boeckelmann, and Hammwhoner (2012, p. 297), regarding cardiac dysrhythmias, the:

> Profibrotic effect of nicotine on myocardial tissue with consequent increased susceptibility to catecholamine might play a role. In addition, other constituents of tobacco smoke, such as carbon monoxide and oxidative stress, are likely to contribute to the generation of cardiac dysrhythmias. Finally, tobacco smoke may induce coronary artery disease and chronic obstructive pulmonary disease, which may cause dysrhythmias independently.

Interestingly, Hackshaw, Morris, and Boniface (2018), in their large-scale meta-analysis of 141 cohort studies, identified that among adults, both men and women, the pooled relative

---

For example, O'Cleirigh, Valentine, and Pinkston (2015), in their study of people living in the U.S. with HIV, found that the tobacco smoking rate among participants in the study was triple that reported for the general population (i.e., 57% versus 19%). They also found several confounding variables when they compared smokers to non-smokers, who were identified as having:

1. Lower adherence to anti-AIDS medication regimens;
2. Higher detectable viral loads;
3. Fewer routine medical visits;
4. More recent hospitalizations;
5. More concurrent use of drugs and substances of abuse, particularly "alcohol, cocaine, heroin, and/or marijuana" (p. 178).

Thus, for example, the total impact of tobacco cigarette smoking on the health of those with HIV is significant, but complex, and, consequently, extremely difficult to directly quantify.

risk for coronary heart disease was estimated to be 50% higher for those who smoked as little as "one cigarette per day" (p. 1).

Pulmonary Diseases Pulmonary diseases associated with tobacco smoke (e.g., cancer of the lungs, bronchi, and trachea and chronic obstructive pulmonary disease [COPD]) are associated with three major factors: (1) the direct irritant and damaging effects of tobacco smoke; (2) carcinogens present in tobacco and/or produced by the pyrolysis of tobacco leaves and wrapping paper; and (3) other chemicals that are present in tobacco smoke.[72] In addition, nicotine itself "induces" the formation of oxygen radicals and "reduces" the anti-oxidant capacity of the lungs (Henley, Thomas, & Sharapova, 2016; Maritz, 2008).

Chronic Obstructive Pulmonary Disease As shared in "Becky's Story:"

> Becky started smoking cigarettes in 1976 as an exchange student when she was living with a host family in Germany. . . . At age 45, Becky was diagnosed with chronic obstructive pulmonary disease. . . . Today, Becky needs continuous oxygen to help her breathe.
>
> (CDC, 2016a, p. 1)

As shared in "Michael F.'s Story:"

> Michael, age 58, started smoking when he was 12 years old because he wanted his friends to think he was cool. . . . Then at 47 years old, Michael was diagnosed with smoking-related chronic obstructive pulmonary disease (COPD). He had part of his right lung removed because of an infection. A few years later, Michael had more surgery, on his left lung this time.
>
> (CDC, 2018b, 2020)

As shared in "Leonard's Story:"

> Leonard, an American actor best known for his role as Spock on the popular television and film series *Star Trek*, started smoking as a teenager. He finally quit for good after 37 years, but his lungs were badly damaged. Leonard was diagnosed with chronic obstructive pulmonary disease (COPD), which led to his death in February 2015.
>
> (CDC, 2019a, p. 1)

Additionally, as identified by the CDC (2019a, p. 1):

> Smoking accounts for as many as 8 out of 10 COPD-related deaths and 38% of the nearly 16 million U.S. adults, who are diagnosed with COPD, report being current smokers.

Lung Cancer Tobacco smoke is clearly associated with an increased risk for lung cancer (e.g., CDC, 2019c) and this association has been recognized for decades (e.g., Doll & Hill, 1950). In most of these cases, the risk for developing lung cancer is directly related to the number of cigarettes smoked per day—with due consideration of genetic contributions. However, in the U.S., for cigarette smokers of African continental descent, when compared to those of European continental descent:

1. The incidence of lung cancer is higher;
2. Lung cancer occurs in association with a significantly lower rate of daily tobacco cigarette smoking.

72. See the related discussion in the earlier nicotine subsection, "Tobacco Plant Botany."

Several researchers (e.g., Benowitz, Dains, & Dempsey, 2011; St Helen et al., 2013) suggest that the associated increased risk for lung cancer may be due to the noticeable, significant differences in cigarette smoking techniques between smokers of African and European continental descents (i.e., related to the former's inhalation of larger amounts of carcinogens per tobacco cigarette smoked). Others suggest differences in environmental, physiological, and socioeconomic factors. For example, regarding physiological factors, Etzel, Kachroo, and Liu (2008, p. 255) noted that:

> African Americans have lower forced vital capacity, low forced expiratory volume, and higher percentage of forced expiratory capacity expired in 1 second compared to whites.

In comparison to matched cohorts of European continental descent, these differences in pulmonary function may contribute to differences in lung cancer risk associated with tobacco smoking.

As shared in "Rose's Story:"

> Rose started smoking at age 13 and continued for many years, smoking two packs a day. Rose developed lung cancer from smoking cigarettes and . . . had chemotherapy, surgery, radiation, and a painful drainage tube in her left chest. . . . She died in January 2015, at age 60 from cancer caused by smoking.
>
> (CDC, 2016b, p. 1)

As shared in Annette's Story:

> Annette experimented with cigarettes as a teenager, smoking occasionally. But by the time she turned 20, Annette was a regular smoker. . . . At age 52, Annette went to the doctor because she was having difficulty breathing and was diagnosed with lung cancer.
>
> (CDC, 2018b, 2020)

Other Cancers Tobacco smoke also has been associated with cancers of the breast, cervix, colon, esophagus, head, kidneys and renal pelvises, larynx, liver, neck, mouth and oropharynx, ovaries, pancreas, rectum, stomach, and urinary bladder (e.g., Beral, Gaitskell, & Hermon, 2012; Gallaway, Henley, & Steele, 2018; Kuper, Boffetta, & Adami, 2002; Thun, Henley, & Calle, 2002), and acute myeloid leukemia (AML) (Fircanis, Merriam, & Khan, 2014). However, for many of these cancers, a direct cause-and-effect relationship with tobacco smoke remains tentative.

Research findings increasingly suggest a significant genetic contribution to the relationship between tobacco smoke and cancer. However, this putative relationship is complex, and findings are not always consistent (Fagan, Moolchan, & Pokhrel, 2015). For example, tobacco smokers with higher CYP2A6 activity have higher rates of nicotine metabolism (see the related discussion in the earlier nicotine pharmacology subsection—"Pharmacokinetics"). Thus, they smoke more extensively and, consequently, are exposed to more carcinogens in tobacco smoke that, consequently, place them at higher related risk for developing cancer (Derby, Cuthrell, & Caberto, 2008).

We have consistently emphasized, for over four decades, that the nicotine, which is a constituent of tobacco, has a relatively low level of toxicity in comparison to tobacco "smoke," which is unsafe at any level of exposure due to the chemical/physical constitution of "smoke" (Pagliaro & Pagliaro, *Clinical Patient Data Files*). Consequently, the therapeutic index for tobacco smoke is "zero."

Effects of Passive Smoke

As emphasized by the World Health Organization (WHO, 2009, p. 14):

> There is no safe level of exposure to tobacco smoke. All people should be protected from such exposure.

As further emphasized by the CDC:

> There is no risk-free level of exposure to tobacco smoke, and there are no safe tobacco products.
>
> (USDHHS, 2010, p. 1)

As such, tobacco smoke is identified as the leading cause of preventable and unnecessary deaths adding up to over 500,000 deaths annually with approximately 50,000 of these indirect deaths due to passive exposure to second-hand, or side-stream, smoke (Carter et al., 2015; CDC, 2010a; Danaei, Ding, & Mozaffarian, 2009; USDHHS, 2014).

Unfortunately, cigarette, cigar, and pipe smoking continues to be widespread in the U.S. and appears to be increasing in certain population groups (e.g., members of the military and individuals who have mental disorders) despite cautions and wide publicity of the harmful effects and toxicities associated with use.[73] (See also the later discussion in the following nicotine subsection, "E-Cigarettes.")

E-Cigarettes

The increased public awareness of the serious toxicities associated with tobacco smoking—in addition to the successful outcomes of major lawsuits for previous tobacco cigarette smokers and their families (e.g., CBC News, 2015; Reuters, 2015)—has been associated with decreased rates of tobacco smoking in the U.S. It also has been the basis for a significant refocusing by cigarette manufacturers and marketers, during the new millennium, regarding the research and development of "smoke-free" nicotine products. This attention has involved research with various concentrations and flavors of liquid nicotine products along with convenient delivery systems, which, in general, are both attractive and similar in shape and style to traditional cigarettes (i.e., electronic cigarettes or e-cigarettes) (Pagliaro & Pagliaro, 2009).

The result was the development and introduction of a major new and innovative product—the e-cigarette (e.g., "SmokeStik®"). The prototype for the current e-cigarette was developed by the Chinese pharmacist, Hon Lik, in 2003 and was first introduced into the U.S. in 2006/2007. Currently, over 500 different brands of e-cigarettes are available. E-Cigarettes, which are also known as "electronic nicotine delivery systems"

---

73. In a government sponsored attempt to reduce the toxicity associated with tobacco cigarette smoking, the composition of cigarettes was significantly changed in the U.S. during the last half of the 20th century. As identified by Hoffmann and Hoffmann (1997, p. 307):

> In the United States the sales-weighted average "tar" and nicotine yields have declined from a high of 38 mg tar and 2.7 mg nicotine in 1954 to 12 mg and 0.95 mg in 1992, respectively.

However, as previously discussed, nicotine and tar are not the sole—nor even the principal—toxic agents that are found in tobacco smoke. Consequently, the changes made by the U.S. government to cigarette content did not result in significantly improved health among cigarette-smoking Americans.

(ENDS),[74] generally resemble common tobacco cigarettes,[75] which makes them attractive to traditional cigarette smokers and to older adults who have not yet begun to smoke. (See also the related discussion in the later subsection, New Millennial Trends in Older Adult Nicotine Use—"Older Adult Recreational Nicotine Use.")

E-cigarette delivery systems of produce an inhalable liquid nicotine vapor[76] rather than the smoke produced by "lighting-up" and burning the leaf tobacco of a typical tobacco cigarette, cigar, or pipe—which in addition to nicotine—delivers significantly more harmful and toxic chemicals to the pulmonary system (Czogala, Goniewicz, & Fidelus, 2014; Oh & Kacker, 2014; Rom, Pecorelli, & Valacchi, 2015; Schroeder & Hoffman, 2014). (Also see the discussion of nicotine toxicity related to tobacco smoking earlier in this nicotine pharmacology subsection—"Undesired, or Harmful, Effects and Toxicities.")

Typically, e-cigarettes have several basic components (Brown & Cheng, 2014; Pagliaro & Pagliaro, 2009) (see also Figure 4.2, p. 359):[77]

- An LED light cover to resemble a burning cigarette and to also indicate that the product is activated;
- A rechargeable battery (and external battery charger) in portable models, to provide an energy source so that it can be conveniently used almost anywhere;
- A storage unit/space to contain a solution of nicotine (i.e., a refill cartridge);
- An atomizer, or heating element, to vaporize the liquid nicotine;[78]
- A flow sensor that controls the amount of nicotine delivered to the atomizer;
- A cartridge mouthpiece that is placed between the lips (like a traditional cigarette) to provide a familiar and convenient means for inhaling the vaporized nicotine into the lungs.

Related Professional Reminder: ***Nicotine concentrations vary among the different brands of tobacco cigarettes. However, this variance is significantly more pronounced among the different brands of e-liquid solutions available for use***

---

74. ENDS broadly encompass several related products variously known as "cigalikes," "e-cigars," "e-cigs," "e-cigarettes," "e-hookahs," "electronic cigarettes," "e-Pods," "mods," "pod mods," "tank systems," "vape pens," and "vapes."
75. A noted exception to the typical look of e-cigarettes is the JUUL®, which is shaped like a USB flash drive (i.e., 9.45 cm x 1.50 cm x 0.69 cm; weight 100 gm) (McKeganey, Russell, & Haseen, 2020). A single JUUL® pod can contain as much nicotine (i.e., 42 mg) as a package of 20 regular tobacco cigarettes. JUUL® became available for sale in the U.S. in 2015 and by 2017 it became the top-selling e-cigarette brand among adolescents and young adults—capturing ~ 50% of the e-cigarette market by 2018. The use of the JUUL® is commonly referred to as "Juuling" (Kavuluru, Han, & Hahn, 2018).
76. Consequently, the use of e-cigarettes is commonly referred to as "vaping." See the related discussion of "vaping" in the cannabis subsection of Chapter 4, *Cannabis*.
77. Most of these systems are "open systems" (i.e., various components can be replaced, and the nicotine solution can be refilled). They are generically referred to as "atomizers," "cartomizers," "clearomizers," and differ in tank appearance and size/capacity, type of wire/coil utilized (e.g., Kanthal®, nickel, stainless steel, or titanium); and type of wick (i.e., usually cotton, but can be silica-based).

    An example of an exception is the "Vype ePod®," which is a "closed system" resembling a small insulin pen. It consists of two components—a central sealed unit and a sealed e-Pen cartridge. The closed system minimizes the leakage and mess that are associated with open-systems. The previously discussed JUUL® is also an example of a closed system. Its pods are prefilled and are not designed to be refilled.
78. Propylene glycol, glycerol (glycerin), and water are generally the major pharmaceutical vehicles for most e-liquid nicotine solutions (Grana, Benowitz, & Glantz, 2014). Consequently, e-cigarettes typically aerosolize and deliver to the smoker a chemical mixture consisting primarily of: (1) nicotine; (2) propylene glycol; and (3) various flavoring agents (Chun, Moazed, & Calfee, 2017).

with e-cigarettes—particularly because of the significantly greater variance in nicotine concentrations.

The liquid nicotine refill cartridges (i.e., "e-liquid" or "e-juice") are available in several strengths generally ranging from 0.3 mg to 25 mg of nicotine per refill cartridge (Goniewicz, Kuma, & Gawron, 2013).[79] The cartridges typically last for as long as a standard package of 20 tobacco cigarettes. Further increasing the attractiveness of e-cigarettes to older adults, e-cigarette refill cartridges come in a vast variety of flavors, including, for example: apple, Boston cream pie, caramel, cherry, chocolate, clove, coffee, crème brûlée, menthol, pear, peppermint, spearmint, strawberry daiquiri, tobacco, and vanilla. In fact, well over 5,000 different e-cigarette flavors are currently available (Zhu, Sun, & Bonnevie, 2014). In response to the increasing use of flavored tobacco products during the first decade of the new millennium, the FDA banned their use in 2009.[80] However, these bans were not as effective as anticipated because the e-cigarettes, as well as their liquid nicotine cartridges, are widely available for purchase over the Internet.

Interestingly, as identified by Zhu et al. (2014, p. iii3):

> Older brands [of e-cigarettes] tend to highlight their advantages over conventional cigarettes while newer brands emphasize consumer choice in multiple flavors and product versatility.

E-Cigarettes and EVALI

With vaping, there is no tobacco or cigarette wrap to burn, there is no odor, and, more importantly, there is little, or no, production of cancer-producing chemicals—carbon monoxide, tars, and other carcinogens—to inhale.[81] However, in 2019, a new pulmonary disease, "electronic-cigarette or vaping associated lung injury" (i.e., "EVALI"),[82] was formally recognized by the CDC. Through 2019, approximately 2,000 cases of EVALI, including 50 fatalities, were reported across the U.S. (Moritz, Zapata, & LeKiachvili, 2019). The reported EVALI injuries and deaths were reported in the context of vaping nicotine and/or THC. (For further related discussion, also see the Chapter 4, *Cannabis*, subsection—"Vaping.")

---

79. More than 500 different brands of e-cigarettes are available in smoke/vapor shops, over the Internet, and every major commercial tobacco manufacturer actively markets these products (Shields, Berman, & Brasky, 2017; Zhu et al., 2014). Whereas several e-cigarette components, including nicotine solution containing cartridges, are interchangeable among similar products, others are not. Unapproved and inappropriate use of components made for one e-cigarette product for another product may subject users to potential harm, including improper delivery of nicotine (i.e., too much or too little) and fires/explosions.
80. In 2009, Congress passed the *Family Smoking Prevention and Tobacco Control Act of 2009* that extended the regulatory authority of the FDA to include the manufacturing, distribution, and marketing of e-cigarettes. The final related rule was published in the Federal Register by the FDA in May 2016 (FDA, 2016a). On August 8, 2016, all e-cigarettes and other ENDS products became subject to the FDA's tobacco authorities and required FDA authorization in order to be legally marketed in the U.S. (FDA, 2020).
81. Even when concerns are raised, and some issues remain unresolved (e.g., the risk posed by products that are high in nitrosamines), the consensus is that "smokeless" tobacco products cause less than 10% of the toxicity associated with equivalent tobacco cigarette smoking (e.g., National Academies, 2018; Varlet, 2016).
82. "Electronic-cigarette or vaping associated lung injury" is also known by other titles, such as:
    - E-cigarette or vaping product use associated lung injury;
    - Pulmonary electronic cigarette associated lung injury;
    - Vaping associated lung injury.

Of the EVALI cases reported in 2019 by the CDC, 1,139 were discharged on or before October 31, 2019. The CDC conducted a secondary analysis of the data obtained from those patients who further met the study inclusion criteria (n=768), and found that:

1. 31 patients required rehospitalization;
2. Seven deaths occurred after hospital discharge.

Of those patients 51 years of age or older:

3. Two patients required rehospitalization;
4. Five deaths occurred after hospital discharge. (Mikosz, Danielson, & Anderson, 2019)

On behalf of the CDC, Mikosz et al. (2019, p. 1) further found that the:

> Characteristics of EVALI patients, who were re-hospitalized or died after hospital discharge, suggest that chronic medical conditions, including cardiac disease, chronic pulmonary disease (e.g., chronic obstructive pulmonary disease [COPD] and obstructive sleep apnea), and diabetes, are risk factors leading to higher morbidity and mortality among some EVALI patients.

As noted by the AARP in their update on vaping for their members:

> Reports of severe breathing problems and deaths related to vaping began to surface in late summer and have now soared to 1,299 confirmed cases of vaping-related illness. There have been 33 confirmed deaths as of Oct. 17—roughly half of them in people over age 50, according to the CDC.
>
> (Harrar, 2019, p. 1)

> A 76-year-old San Diego woman who died on May 24 has become San Diego County's first EVALI death, according to a Thursday news release from the County of San Diego.
>
> (Farber, 2020, p. 1)

***Related Professional Reminder:* Tobacco smoking and/or any form of vaping (e.g., use of e-cigarettes) is never recommended for older adults with COPD. If assistance with smoking cessation is required, always recommend non-smoking /non vaping approaches. (See the later nicotine subsection—"Treating Nicotine Dependence or Use Disorder Among Older Adults"—for examples of specific approaches that can be used.)**

Other Toxicities Associated with E-Cigarettes

Since their initial development and marketing, we have consistently emphasized that because of the absence of tobacco smoke and particulate matter—which is associated with burning tobacco products (e.g., cigarettes, cigars, and pipe tobacco)—vaping produces significantly less pulmonary toxicity (e.g., COPD, lung cancer, and lung irritation) than that produced by tobacco smoking (e.g., Pagliaro & Pagliaro, *Clinical Patient Data Files*). Oh and Kacker (2014, p. 2702) found that:

> Studies show that EC vapors contain far less carcinogenic particles than TC [tobacco cigarette] smoke.

This finding has since been repeatedly supported by numerous groups. For example:

> E-cigarette aerosol contains fewer and lower levels of most toxicants than smoke from combustible tobacco cigarettes do.
>
> (National Academies, 2018, p. S1)

> After switching from tobacco to e-cigarettes, nicotine exposure remains unchanged, while exposure to selected carcinogens and toxicants is substantially reduced.
>
> (Goniewicz, Gawron, & Smith, 2017, p. 160)

However, it should be kept in mind that, as identified by the U.S. Surgeon General:

> Although e-cigarettes generally emit fewer toxicants than combustible tobacco products, we know that aerosol from e-cigarettes is not harmless.
>
> (USDHHS, 2016, p. vii)[83]

This observation and caution has also been emphasized by others. For example:

> E-cigarette use increases airborne concentrations of particulate matter, nicotine and other toxicants [e.g., carbonyls, glycerol, heavy metals, propylene glycol, volatile organic compounds] in indoor environments compared with background levels.
>
> (Public Health Ontario, 2018, p. 1)

E-Cigarettes and Tobacco Smoking Cessation[84]

Although not approved for smoking cessation by the FDA, many older adults report using e-cigarettes to help them decrease, or quit, their tobacco smoking (Foulds, Veldheer, & Berg, 2011; Pagliaro & Pagliaro, *Clinical Patient Data Files*). In addition, as identified by several researchers (e.g., Benowitz & Goniewicz, 2013; Pacifici, Pichini, & Graziano, 2015; Perkins, Karelitz, & Michael, 2017), when compared to "placebo e-cigarettes," nicotine-containing e-cigarettes (i.e., "regular" e-cigarettes) can relieve abstinence symptoms (i.e., the nicotine withdrawal syndrome) in a manner similar to the FDA-approved nicotine replacement therapy products. (See the related discussion in the later nicotine subsection, Treating Nicotine Dependence or Use Disorder—"Nicotine Replacement Therapy.") As found by Cataldo, Berit Petersen, and Hunter (2015) regarding older smokers and e-cigarettes:

> Older adults are using e-cigarettes for cessation and as a way to circumvent no-smoking policies.
>
> (p. 361)

Utilizing data from a nationally representative, longitudinal, online survey of approximately 16,000 U.S. adult tobacco cigarette smokers, Caraballo, Shafer, and Patel (2017, p. 2) further noted that:

---

83. The aerosol "vapor" from e-cigarettes contains nicotine, carbonyl compounds, glycerol (i.e., glycerin), heavy metals (e.g., lead, nickel, and tin), propylene glycol, and volatile organic compounds. When heated, glycerol and propylene glycol can be converted to acrolein, acetaldehyde, and formaldehyde—compounds that are both irritating to the respiratory system and possible carcinogens (Shields et al., 2017; USDHHS, 2016a).
84. See also the related discussion in the later section "Treating Older Adult Nicotine Dependence or Use Disorder—"Pharmacotherapeutic Approaches."

> Substituting some cigarettes with e-cigarettes or switching completely from cigarettes to e-cigarettes was each used by 1.1% of smokers.

However, available data concerning the efficacy of e-cigarettes as an aid to cease tobacco smoking, although limited, indicate extremely variable results. For example, as found by Zhuang, Cummins, and Sun (2016, p. i90):

> Short-term e-cigarette use was not associated with a lower rate of smoking cessation. Long-term use of e-cigarettes was associated with a higher rate of quitting smoking.

Similarly, Rigotti, Chang, and Tindle (2018, p. 8) found that:

> In conclusion, this large prospective study of recently-hospitalized smokers who planned to quit found a negative association between the use of any e-cigarettes after discharge and subsequent tobacco abstinence.

More recently, Grabovac, Oberndorfer, and Fischer, in their systematic review and meta-analysis of the efficacy of e-cigarettes (ECs) in tobacco smoking cessation, found positive results (i.e., e-cigarettes were approximately twice as effective as counseling, non-nicotine cigarettes, or nicotine replacement therapy [NRT] in achieving abstinence). Nevertheless, in summary, they concluded that:

> Our results suggest that nicotine ECs may be more effective in smoking cessation when compared with placebo ECs or NRT. However, when compared with counseling alone, nicotine ECs are more effective short term, but their effectiveness appears to diminish with later follow-ups . . . [However, overall,] it is not possible to offer clear recommendations. The results of this study do not allow for a conclusive argument.
>
> (2021, p. 625)

Based on our review of the data, and our related clinical experiences with older adults,[85] we have generally identified that:

1. Many older adults (i.e., ~ 25% to 33%), who want to cease tobacco smoking, are amenable to using e-cigarettes;
2. Some older adults (i.e., ~ 10% to 20%), who start e-cigarette use, continue use with or without ceasing tobacco smoking;
3. A small number of older adults (i.e., ~ 10% to 20%) successfully cease tobacco smoking with the use of e-cigarettes.[86]

<u>Related Professional Reminder</u>: Health and social care professionals need to be fully aware that e-cigarettes can deliver as much, or more, nicotine as traditional

---

85. N.B. These observations are presented to provide the reader with a general appreciation of the interactions between older adult e-cigarettes use and tobacco smoking cessation. Data have been broadly collapsed to fit the presentation and it is highly likely that associated confounding variables (e.g., use of an additional supplement NRT product, such as nicotine chewing gum; attendance at nicotine anonymous meetings; or adjunctive psychotherapy) may have significantly influenced outcomes.
86. In their study, Wagener, Avery, and Leavens (2021, p. 761), found that:

    > Among smokers switching to an e-cigarette, greater increases in e-cigarette puff duration was associated with greater reductions in cigarette smoking.

    This finding is interesting, however, the generalizability of this research finding is significantly limited because of the small sample size utilized in the study (i.e., n = 6).

tobacco cigarettes. Thus, older adults are at risk for the development, or continuation, of nicotine dependence—both physical and psychological dependence—or use disorder.

This concern becomes increasingly significant when considering that the sale and use of e-cigarettes is projected to increase by over ten-fold (i.e., 1,000%) by 2030 (Electronic nicotine delivery systems, 2014). In this regard, we fully expect that by mid-century (i.e., 2050) conventional tobacco cigarettes will become virtually "extinct" (i.e., reduced to the same extent that chewing tobacco and pipe smoking currently are) and that the recreational, self-administration of nicotine will be virtually, exclusively performed by means of vaping e-cigarettes.

Nicotine Physical and Psychological Dependence[87]

Prior to the 1970s, the medical and scientific communities generally, and erroneously, agreed that the regular, long-term use of nicotine, as a component of tobacco smoke, was *not* associated with "physical" dependence. However, they generally, and correctly, agreed that tobacco smoking was associated with "psychological" dependence (i.e., "craving" and "habitual use"). These views were strongly supported by the large tobacco companies and the research—including much university-based research—that they financially supported.[88] However, during the 1970s and 1980s, scientific data accumulated that increasingly supported a change to the view that the regular, long-term use of nicotine caused both physical and psychological dependence. A decade later, Collins (1990, p. 84) summarized the 20th Report of the Surgeon General on the health consequences of tobacco smoking, which was entitled, "Nicotine Addiction." The summary, a 500-page comprehensive review of over 1,000 published studies, led to the conclusions that:

1. Tobacco products are associated with the development of physical dependence;
2. The nicotine in tobacco products is the substance identified as causing physical dependence;
3. Nicotine physical dependence is like that observed for "classic" alcohol, opiate analgesic, and sedative-hypnotic physical dependence;
4. Nicotine physical dependence also occurs with the use of all smokeless tobacco products (e.g., snuff or snus) because they can achieve the same BNCs as tobacco smoking.

87. The previous DSM categories of "nicotine abuse" and "nicotine dependence" were replaced in the DSM-5 with the category, "Tobacco Use Disorder." This terminology reflects other related DSM-5 categories, including "alcohol use disorder" (AUD) and the more general "substance use disorder" (SUD). However, in response to the identification that nicotine is the addictive component of tobacco smoke and the increased use by older adults of "tobacco-free," smokeless products—such as e-cigarettes—which quickly developed during the second decade of the new millennium (see the related discussion in the previous nicotine subsection, "E-Cigarettes"), we suggest the use of the term, "nicotine use disorder (NUD)." Reflecting the fact that nicotine is associated with both physical and psychological dependence, we use the preferred terminology, "nicotine dependence or use disorder."
88. Prior to, and during this period of time, it was common to observe patients and health care professionals—particularly, nurses, pharmacists, and physicians—smoking cigarettes in health care facilities, including medical offices and hospital settings (e.g., cafeteria or the nursing desk) during working breaks and when providing medical and other health services to patients (Pagliaro & Pagliaro, *Clinical Patient Data Files*).

Since the publication of this pivotal report over 30 years ago in 1990, it has been agreed upon that nicotine is, in fact, the component of tobacco smoke that is responsible for the development of the physical dependence related to the use of tobacco smoking products (Benowitz, 1999; Dani & De Biasi, 2001; Pagliaro & Pagliaro, 2004, 2009). Based on a sample of over 30,000 adults drawn from the 2001–2002 *National Epidemiological Survey of Alcoholism and Related Conditions* (NESARC), Goodwin, Keyes, and Hasin (2009) found that, although the overall rate of tobacco cigarette use declined significantly between 1964 and 2002, the rate of nicotine dependence did not decline.

In addition, most researchers, in this area of study (e.g., Benowitz, 2010; De Biasi & Dani, 2011; Vetulani, 2001), agree that the development of nicotine physical dependence is predominately related to the release of dopamine. The dopamine, subsequently, interacts at neural reward centers in the brain that are primarily located in the mesolimbic system, which connects the ventral tegmental area in the midbrain to the ventral stratum in the basal forebrain—predominately involving the amygdala and the nucleus accumbens (Benowitz, 2010; Sutherland, Carroll, & Salmeron, 2013). However, other researchers have suggested that any, or all, of the following four proposed mechanisms of action also could play a major role in the development of nicotine physical dependence:[89]

1. Nicotine-induced alteration in nAChR synaptic plasticity (e.g., Dani & De Biasi, 2001; Dani, Ji, & Zhou, 2001);
2. Nicotine-induced release of other neurotransmitters and neuromodulators (e.g., Kenny & Markou, 2001);
3. Up-regulation of nAChRs following prolonged exposure to nicotine (e.g., Buisson & Bertrand, 2002);
4. Interaction with, or modification by, the activation of the endogenous cannabinoid receptor, CB_1 (e.g., Gamaleddin et al., 2015).

Regardless of the actual mechanism(s) involved, physical dependence is characterized by: (1) the development of "tolerance" with the regular, long-term nicotine use by any method of use; and (2) a classic "nicotine withdrawal syndrome" that: (a) occurs when the regular, long-term use of nicotine is abruptly discontinued; and (b) immediately resolves when the use of nicotine is resumed.

Tolerance

The regular, long-term use of nicotine—in the form of tobacco smoking (e.g., smoking tobacco cigarettes, cigars, or pipes), e-cigarette vaping, or using other smokeless tobacco products (e.g., chewing tobacco, pharmaceutical nicotine replacement products, or snuff or snus tobacco[90])—can result in the development of tolerance to nicotine as respectively occurs with other drugs and substances of abuse (e.g., alcohol, opiate analgesics, or prescription sedative-hypnotics). The principal mechanism by which nicotine use mediates the

89. For additional details, see also the earlier nicotine pharmacology subsection, "Pharmacodynamics: Mechanism of Action."
90. "Snuff" is dry tobacco powder that is typically snuffed (i.e., "snorted") into the nasal cavity to obtain a quick "hit" of nicotine. "Snus," unlike snuff, is moist tobacco powder that is usually placed under the upper lip for extended periods of time to allow slow absorption (Pagliaro & Pagliaro, 2004).

development of tolerance is by means of neuroadaptation. For example, Streller and Roth (2015a, p. 5) noted that:

> Chronic smoking also reduces the number of dopamine receptors in the mesolimbic system, such that the stimulus threshold rises for activation of the reward system.

Additionally, the associated desensitization (i.e., ligand-induced closure and related unresponsiveness) of the nicotine acetylcholine receptors (nAChRs), particularly the $\alpha_4\beta_2$ subtype, facilitates craving for additional nicotine (e.g., Benowitz, 2010; Watkins, Koob, & Markon, 2000). (See also the related discussion in the earlier nicotine pharmacology subsection—"Pharmacodynamics: Mechanism of Action.")

With the regular, long-term use of nicotine, older adults characteristically utilize several techniques to counteract/mitigate this tolerance, including:

- Increasing the number of tobacco cigarettes that they smoke;
- Changing the brand of the nicotine product that they use to another that contains higher levels of nicotine;
- Changing their tobacco smoking or e-cigarette vaping techniques (e.g., increasing the number of puffs per tobacco cigarette or more rapidly inhaling e-cigarette vapor);
- Inhaling the tobacco smoke or e-cigarette vapor more deeply and holding it in the lungs for a longer period of time.

The adoption of these techniques associated with nicotine use, generally, are unconsciously made in an effort to increase the amount of nicotine absorbed from the lungs and into the systemic circulation for distribution to nicotinic receptors in the brain—consequently, achieving, once again (or almost) the original desired nicotine experience or effects (Pagliaro & Pagliaro, *Clinical Patient Data Files*).

Tolerance also develops to most of the undesired effects associated with nicotine use (e.g., dizziness, nausea, vomiting), but not all. For example, after one or two cigarettes, even a regular, long-term cigarette smoker exhibits an increase in blood pressure, pulse rate, and hand tremor. Tobacco cigarette smokers and e-cigarette vapers metabolize nicotine more rapidly than nonsmokers or non-vapers, respectively. Thus, tolerance to nicotine may be due to either: (1) "pharmacodynamic" changes (e.g., neuroadaptation of nicotine receptors); or (2) "pharmacokinetic" changes (e.g., changes in metabolism).

There also are conflicting reports on the duration of tolerance. In human smokers, some aspects of tolerance wax and wane repeatedly with the first tobacco cigarette or e-cigarette of the day producing a much greater cardiovascular and subjective response than subsequent tobacco cigarettes or e-cigarettes subsequently smoked or vaped later in the day. This response may also be due, at least in part, to the need to manage the signs and symptoms of nicotine withdrawal associated with the reduced blood nicotine concentrations that occur overnight when smokers are generally sleeping.

Withdrawal Syndrome

A classic nicotine withdrawal syndrome has been clearly identified and appears to be influenced by both genetic and environmental factors (McLaughlin, Dani, & De Biasi, 2015). For example, older adults, who are fast metabolizers of nicotine, report more frequent and serious signs and symptoms of nicotine withdrawal (Hartz, Short, & Saccone, 2012). Consequently, they are more likely to subconsciously "self-medicate"—immediately smoke a tobacco cigarette or vape an e-cigarette to relieve the undesired signs and symptoms of withdrawal (Mathew, Wahlquist, & Garrett-Mayer, 2014; Piper, McCarthy, & Baker, 2008). Both central and peripheral groups of nAChRs are involved in mediating the affective and somatic signs and symptoms of nicotine withdrawal.

Common signs and symptoms of the nicotine withdrawal syndrome, include:

- Anticipatory anhedonia;[91]
- Anxiety;
- Bradycardia;
- Dizziness;
- Fatigue;
- Headache;
- Hunger;
- Inability to concentrate;
- Insomnia;
- Irritability;
- Lack of energy;
- Mental depression;
- Memory impairment;
- Nightmares;
- Restlessness;
- Weight gain.

These signs and symptoms generally begin within four to 24 hours of discontinuing regular, long-term tobacco cigarette smoking, or other nicotine use,[92] because of nicotine's relatively short half-life of elimination (i.e., approximately two hours). To forestall or ameliorate nicotine withdrawal, older adult smokers, who are physically dependent on nicotine, will generally display various behaviors associated with boosting their BNCs, including the following (see also the earlier nicotine pharmacology subsection, "Pharmacokinetics"):

- Smoking first thing in the morning;
- Going out in a stormy night to buy a pack of cigarettes when they find they have none in the house;
- Taking a "break" during the workday as soon as possible to "have a smoke."

---

91. Anticipatory anhedonia, as reported by Hughes, Klemperer, and Peasley-Miklus (2020), is characterized by reduced anticipatory pleasure, or wanting. Generally recognized in laboratory animals undergoing experimental nicotine deprivation, it is less well-characterized or recognized among human subjects.
92. Other nicotine use includes e-cigarette use. While most should/would find this statement to be clearly self-evident (i.e., based on our related knowledge of e-cigarettes as presented earlier in this chapter), it has been empirically demonstrated in several related studies (e.g., Hughes, Peters, & Callas, 2020; Kalkhoran, Chang, & Rigotti, 2020) that the abrupt discontinuation of regular, long-term e-cigarette use is clearly associated with the onset of the nicotine withdrawal syndrome.

The nicotine withdrawal syndrome may intensify over two to four days and then gradually dissipate over one to three weeks. The aversive aspects of nicotine withdrawal often contribute to resumed nicotine use. Many older adults attempt to manage nicotine withdrawal by gradually decreasing nicotine use by cutting down the number of cigarettes smoked daily and while some may be successful, many others are not. To aid nicotine withdrawal, several pharmacotherapeutic approaches have been developed and approved, including nicotine-containing products, such as NicoDerm® TDSs ("patches") and Nicorette® chewing gum and buccal/mouth spray products (e.g., Nicorette Quick Mist®). Non-nicotine containing products, such as bupropion (Zyban®) and varenicline (Chantix®) also are available. (See the related discussion in the later nicotine subsection, "Pharmacotherapy—Nicotine Replacement Therapy.")

The argument that nicotine is the active substance in tobacco smoke that is responsible for continued regular use, also is supported by several studies of both the use of low-yield nicotine cigarettes and high-yield nicotine cigarettes (Benowitz & Jacob, 1984; Nakazawa, Shigeta, & Ozasa, 2004). For example, low-yield cigarette smokers have been found to smoke more cigarettes per day than high-yield cigarette smokers (i.e., smoke in a manner that satisfies their internal individual nicotine cravings) (CDC, 2018a; Pagliaro & Pagliaro, 2004). In addition, "brand-switching" studies have reported that when smokers are changed from high- to low-yield cigarettes, they may unconsciously change their smoking behavior to maintain their blood nicotine concentration by increasing the:

1. Number of cigarettes smoked;
2. Depth of puffs or rate of puffing;
3. Duration of inhalation.

For example, although light smokers are traditionally considered to be less dependent on nicotine, the findings of Krebs, Chen, and Zhu (2016) suggest that light smokers "are exposed to more nicotine per cigarette than are heavy smokers due to more frequent, intensive puffing" (p. 48). Additionally, Benowitz and colleagues (e.g., Benowitz et al., 2011; Perez-Stable, Herrera, & Jacob, 1998) identified that U.S. tobacco cigarette smokers of African continental descent "smoke cigarettes differently" than those of European continental descent, inhaling "on average" 30% more nicotine per individual cigarette smoked (St Helen et al., 2013, p. 2)

Consequently, in response to the observations that low-yield tobacco cigarettes: (1) are not generally safer to use than high-yield cigarettes; and (2) were deliberately being labeled as "light," "low," or "mild," by their manufacturer to make their product more marketable—related regulatory changes were enacted in the U.S.:

> The Family Smoking Prevention and Tobacco Control Act of 2009 now prohibits manufacturers from selling or distributing any tobacco products that have "light," "low," or "mild" on their labels.
>
> (FDA, 2010, p. 1)

An area that requires more study is the individual differences reported regarding the nicotine withdrawal experience. These experiences have been largely ignored. The assumption is generally made that, for example, a regular, long-term tobacco smoker is physically dependent on tobacco. This assumption may be as incorrect as is the assumption that all those who drink alcohol daily are physically dependent on alcohol. It may be that some older adults who smoke tobacco can regularly use nicotine for longer periods of time without becoming physically dependent on nicotine (Pagliaro & Pagliaro, *Clinical Patient Data Files*). In addition to the contribution of such factors as personality and the co-occurrence of other mental disorders, genetic variability appears to explain most of the variance noted in this context (e.g., De Biasi & Dani, 2011; Paolini & De Biasi, 2011). Because smokers often use other drugs and substances of abuse (e.g., alcohol, caffeine, or marijuana), the synergistic effects of concurrent drug and substance use, also may play a significant role in the experience of the nicotine withdrawal syndrome.

Nicotine Overdosage/Unintentional Poisoning

The regular, long-term use of tobacco cigarettes or that of other tobacco products, has not been associated with the occurrence of overdosage. However, it has been associated with unintentional nicotine poisoning. In fact, for older adults, ingestion of 50 mg to 60 mg (i.e., 0.5 to 1 mg/kg) of nicotine may be fatal.[93] Fortunately, nicotine overdosage and related deaths rarely occur because:

1. When tobacco leaf is smoked, ~ 90% of the nicotine in the tobacco product is destroyed by pyrolysis (see the earlier discussion in the nicotine pharmacology subsection, Pharmacokinetics—"Absorption and Distribution");
2. Oral bioavailability of nicotine from tobacco products is low (i.e., F = 0.3) when tobacco is ingested;
3. Nicotine stimulates vomiting as BNCs increase. Thus, tobacco products that are ingested often are vomited—offering some protection against fatal nicotine poisoning.

Signs and symptoms of nicotine overdosages/unintentional poisonings associated with the ingestion or use of e-cigarette solution, nicotine gums, TDSs, and other tobacco products are characterized by a biphasic pattern with an initial phase of psychostimulation ("Phase 1") followed by a second phase of psychodepression ("Phase 2"). (See also the related discussion in the earlier nicotine pharmacology subsection—"Pharmacodynamics: Mechanisms of Action.")

- Phase 1 signs and symptoms of "psychostimulation" include abdominal cramping/pain, agitation, anxiety, bronchial secretions (increased), cold sweat, confusion, diarrhea,

93. Several researchers (e.g., Maessen et al., 2020; Mayer, 2014) have questioned this generally accepted LD_{50} for nicotine arguing that it is erroneously based on unreliable data that are:

    - Outdated, being 50 to100 years old;
    - Inconsistent with the findings of documented cases of nicotine overdosages and unintentional poisonings (i.e., reported cases of survival after consumption of significantly higher amounts).

    While, agreeing that nicotine is a toxic substance that is potentially lethal, they argue that the LD_{50} for humans is five-fold to ten-fold higher (i.e., 500+ mg) than the current estimate (i.e., 50 to 60 mg)—an argument that is interesting and plausible, but not yet empirically substantiated. We would emphasize that because the bioavailability of nicotine is significantly affected by the route of administration, this factor should be taken into consideration when evaluating the LD_{50} (see the related discussion in the earlier Nicotine pharmacology subsection, Pharmacokinetics—"Absorption").

diaphoresis, dizziness, headache, hearing and vision disturbances, hypertension, nausea, pallor, salivation (excessive), seizures, tachycardia, tremor, and vomiting;

- Phase 2 signs and symptoms of "psychodepression" include bradycardia; circulatory collapse; coma; confusion; drowsiness; dyspnea; faintness and prostration; fatigue; hypotension; lethargy; muscle weakness; rapid, weak, irregular pulse; and respiratory failure due to paralysis of the muscles of respiration, which, within minutes, can result in death. (Falck, 2017; Maessen, Wijnhoven, & Neijzen, 2020; Safer Care Victoria, 2019)

Suspected, or actual, nicotine overdosage/unintentional poisoning requires immediate discontinuation of the use of the involved nicotine product and emergency medical support of body systems, with particular attention to maintaining adequate respiratory function and increasing nicotine elimination. For example, a slurry of activated charcoal may be administered to decrease GI absorption of nicotine or, for TDSs, removing the TDS[94] and flushing the skin with water—soap should *not* be used, because it may increase nicotine absorption from the skin site. Additionally, for example, a benzodiazepine (e.g., diazepam, Valium®) can be used to prevent or manage associated phase 1 seizures, while atropine can be used to manage phase 2 bradycardia. Severe respiratory failure may necessitate the use of mechanical ventilation. There is no known specific antidote for nicotine overdosage/unintentional poisoning (Pagliaro & Pagliaro, 2004).

New Millennial Trends in Older Adult Nicotine Use

New millennial trends in relation to: (1) medical use of nicotine for older adults; and (2) older adult recreational use of nicotine are presented and discussed in the following nicotine subsections. We begin with trends in the medical use of nicotine for older adults.

Older Adult Medical Use

For most of its history, the pharmacotherapeutic use of nicotine received little medical attention because of its early—and correct—identification as a poison. However, during the late 1970s, amidst the accumulation of research data supporting a relationship between tobacco smoking and lung cancer, nicotine replacement therapy (NRT) was medically initiated as an aid to facilitate the cessation of tobacco smoking among those who wanted to "kick-the-habit" (Hyde, Paxton, & Carr, 1982). NRT is currently available to older adults in the U.S., both by prescription and OTC. (See the later nicotine subsection, Treating Nicotine Dependence or Use Disorder Among Older Adults, Pharmacotherapeutic Approaches—"Nicotine Replacement Therapy [NRT].")

Older Adult Licit/ Recreational Nicotine Use

This subsection reviews and discusses the current recreational use of tobacco products (primarily cigarettes) and non-tobacco e-cigarettes among older adults in the U.S.

94. N.B. Because of the depot of nicotine that is formed in the skin, as part of the mechanism of action designed for TDSs, nicotine will continue to be delivered into the bloodstream for several hours after the removal of the TDS.

Old Misbelief: When compared to other older adults in the U.S., older adults of American Indian descent generally have lower rates of tobacco use because they primarily respect and smoke tobacco as a part of their traditional American Indian ceremonies.

False. In fact, as identified by the CDC (2019b, p. 1):

> American Indians/Alaska Natives (AIs/ANs) have a higher prevalence of current smoking than most other racial/ethnic groups in the United States.

A summary of tobacco use by all older adults in the U.S. is presented in Table 3.5.

It is somewhat both unexpected and ironic that:

1. People who began smoking tobacco cigarettes during their teen years and developed chronic patterns of tobacco use are significantly more likely to die a premature death (e.g., Nash, Liao, & Harris, 2017); (*continued, p. 270*)

Table 3.5 Summary of Tobacco Use by Older Adults in the U.S.

AGE RANGE IN YEARS	TYPE, FREQUENCY, AND METHOD OF USE	PERCENT OF USERS	SOURCE
45–64	Current any tobacco use	21.3%	Creamer, Wang, & Babb, 2019
45–64	Current any tobacco use	24.0%	King, Dube, & Tynan, 2012
45–64	Current any tobacco use	21.3%	Wang, Asman, & Gentzke, 2018
45–64	Current chew, dip, snuff use	2.4%	King et al., 2012
45–64	Current cigar use	4.9%	King et al., 2012
45–64	Current cigarette use	19.7%	King et al., 2012
45–64	Use of cigarettes every day or some days	16.5%	CDC, 2019b
45–64	Current pipe use	0.8%	King et al., 2012
45–64	Current snus use	0.7%	King et al., 2012
45–64	Current water pipe use	0.3%	King et al., 2012
65 or older	Current chew, dip, snuff use	1.7%	King et al., 2012
65 or older	Current cigar use	1.8%	King et al., 2012
65 or older	Current cigarette use	8.6%	King et al., 2012
65 or older	Current cigarette use	10.5%	Kulak & LaValley, 2018
65 or older	Use of cigarettes every day or some days	8.2%	CDC, 2019b
65 or older	Current pipe use	0.7%	King et al., 2012
65 or older	Current snus use	0.4%	King et al., 2012
65 or older	Current water pipe use	0%	King et al., 2012
65 or older	Current any tobacco use	11.9%	Creamer et al., 2019
65 or older	Current any tobacco use	11.8%	King et al., 2012
65 or older	Current any tobacco use	11.0%	Wang et al., 2018

2. However, the percentage of tobacco smokers in the U.S. has declined less over the past 50 years among those over 65 years of age in comparison to any other younger age cohort (Cataldo et al., 2015; Span, 2017).

For example, Henley, Asman, and Momin (2019, pp. 5, 7), in their analysis of data from the 2015 *National Health Interview Survey* for U.S. adults, 65 years of age or older, stated that:

> We also found that about half of older adults who currently smoked had been diagnosed with a smoking-related chronic disease and that a quarter have been diagnosed with a smoking-related cancer, suggesting that an opportunity exists for healthcare providers and others to motivate these persons to quit smoking.

Currently, approximately 10% of these older people continue to smoke tobacco products—primarily cigarettes (see Table 3.5).

Recreational E-Cigarette Use (See also the earlier subsection, "E-Cigarettes")

It is equally unexpected by many—particularly younger, health and social care professionals—that "baby boomers," who are old enough to be their parents or grandparents, are now a growing demographic of e-cigarette users. As noted by Delnevo, Giovenco, and Steinberg (2016, p. 715), in their analysis of patterns of e-cigarette use among adults in the U.S.:

> Daily use is highest among former smokers who quit in the past year and older adults.

The increased attraction to and use of e-cigarettes by older adults has been accompanied by an increase in related "public interest" articles in the lay press (e.g., Bodkin, 2018; Harrar, 2019; Span, 2017).

The use of e-cigarettes among older adults appears to be significantly influenced by age. For example, among older adults who are 45 to 64 years of age, approximately:

1. 11% have used e-cigarettes;
2. 2.4% are current ("daily or almost daily") users.

Among those 65 years of age and older, approximately:

1. 4.7% have used e-cigarettes;
2. 0.7% are current (i.e., "daily or almost daily") users. (Bao, Liu, & Du, 2020; McKeganey et al., 2020; Villarroel, Cha, & Vahratian, 2020; Wang et al., 2018).[95]

Assessment and Diagnosis of Older Adult Nicotine Dependence or Use Disorder

As recommended by the U.S. Department of Health and Human Services (USDHHS):

> It is essential that clinicians and health care delivery systems consistently identify, and document tobacco use status and treat every tobacco user seen in a health care setting.
>
> (Fiore, Jaen, & Baker, 2008, p. 10)

95. N.B. These percentages are expected to significantly increase in the U.S. as: (1) "baby boomers" continue to age; and (2) tobacco cigarette use is increasingly replaced by e-cigarette use.

The assessment and diagnosis of nicotine dependence or use disorder among older adults requires a detailed clinical interview and examination of presenting signs and symptoms that address both the extent and duration of nicotine use—with attention to patterns of using tobacco smoking products and e-cigarettes. Additionally, clinical sequelae that are commonly associated with nicotine use, particularly the regular, long-term use of tobacco cigarettes, cigars, and little cigars and cigarillos (LCCs), include COPD, oral cancers, and smoker's cough. Those associated with the use of e-cigarettes include irritation of the mouth and throat, and a dry cough, associated with the glycerol and the propylene glycol present in the e-cigarette aerosol or vapor.

The use of DSM-5 criteria for detecting "tobacco use disorder" or the use of specific quick-screen psychometric tests (e.g., the Fagerström Test for Nicotine Dependence) can assist with the determination of the nature and extent of nicotine use among tobacco-smoking older adults. However, to date, there are no available specific psychometric tests to assist with the determination of nicotine dependence or use disorder (NUD) associated with the use of e-cigarettes. Recent trends in preferred smoking methods for both tobacco and cannabis suggest a consistent and dominant change, particularly among older adults to the use of vaping devices—e-cigarettes and e-hookahs (see the related discussion in the earlier nicotine subsections, "E-cigarettes/Vaping" and "Recreational E-Cigarette Use").

Although the use of the "Screening, Brief Intervention, and Referral to Treatment" (SBIRT) model has been recommended, supportive empirical data—particularly, regarding older adult tobacco smokers—is conspicuously absent. (For related discussion of the SBIRT, see Chapter 1, *Alcohol*, Assessment and Diagnosis of Older Adult Alcohol Dependence or Use Disorder—"Screening, Brief Intervention, and Referral to Treatment.")

Quick-Screen Psychometric Tests

Two specific quick-screen psychometric tests are predominantly used to assess the nature and extent of nicotine dependence associated with tobacco smoking:

1. "Autonomy Over Tobacco Scale" (AUTOS);
2. "Fagerström Test for Nicotine Dependence" (FTND).

Autonomy Over Tobacco Scale (AUTOS)

The AUTOS, a 12-item, quick-screen psychometric test (Table 3.6), is comprised of 12 possible signs and symptoms of nicotine dependence. It was developed by DiFranza, Wellman, and Ursprung (2009) to provide a more reliable screening test for detecting nicotine dependence than the FTND (see the following nicotine subsection, "Fagerström Test for Nicotine Dependence"). Based on confirmatory factor analysis, the AUTOS appears to be unidimensional in adult smokers (Wellman, DiFranza, & O'Loughlin, 2015).

DiFranza et al. (2009, p. 656) claim 16 specific advantages, or "attractive features," associated with the AUTOS. As follows, it:

1. Is theory-based;
2. Has excellent internal reliability, retest reliability, and concurrent validity;
3. Is tested and recommended for all ages;
4. Is tested and recommended for tobacco smokers and buccal tobacco users;

Table 3.6 The AUTOS

ITEM #	QUESTION	THIS STATEMENT DESCRIBES ME . . .			
1.	When I go too long without a cigarette or a dip, I get impatient.	Not at all	A little	Pretty well	Very well
2.	When I see other people smoking or using dip, I want a cigarette or a dip.	Not at all	A little	Pretty well	Very well
3.	I rely on smoking or dipping to focus my attention.	Not at all	A little	Pretty well	Very well
4.	When I smell cigarette smoke or dip, I want a cigarette or dip.	Not at all	A little	Pretty well	Very well
5.	I rely on smoking or dipping to take my mind off being bored.	Not at all	A little	Pretty well	Very well
6.	When I go too long without a cigarette or a dip, I get strong urges to smoke or dip that are hard to get rid of.	Not at all	A little	Pretty well	Very well
7.	After eating I want a cigarette or dip.	Not at all	A little	Pretty well	Very well
8.	I would go crazy if I couldn't smoke or use dip.	Not at all	A little	Pretty well	Very well
9.	When I go too long without a cigarette or a dip, I lose my temper more easily.	Not at all	A little	Pretty well	Very well
10.	When I feel stressed, I want a cigarette or a dip.	Not at all	A little	Pretty well	Very well
11.	I rely on smoking or dipping to deal with stress.	Not at all	A little	Pretty well	Very well
12.	When I go too long without a cigarette or a dip, I feel nervous or anxious.	Not at all	A little	Pretty well	Very well

Source: DiFranza et al., 2009.

5. Can be used with daily and non-daily tobacco users;
6. Is invulnerable to cultural measurement bias caused by differences in the affordability of tobacco, or racial measurement bias caused by differences in nicotine metabolism;
7. Can be used before and after cessation (i.e., during active tobacco use as well as during abstinence);
8. Can be used in longitudinal analysis studies to track the development of nicotine dependence;
9. Can be used in cessation studies to track the persistence or resolution of signs and symptoms;
10. Measures nicotine withdrawal (i.e., nicotine physical dependence);
11. Measures psychological dependence;
12. Measures cue-induced urges, or craving, to use tobacco;
13. Can be used in cessation settings to guide anticipatory counseling and relapse prevention;
14. Can be easily scored;

15. Can be self-administered in less than three minutes;
16. Is currently available for use in Dutch, English, French, German, and Spanish.

Scoring the AUTOS Each of the 12 questions is scored per response from 0 to 3[96] and summed to provide a total AUTOS score. The potential total score can range from 0 to 36. Additionally, outcomes regarding the three, correlated, lower-order symptom domains are determined as follows:

1. "Withdrawal score"—sum of the total score for questions one through four;
2. "Psychological dependence"—sum of the total score for questions five through eight;
3. "Cue-induced urges to use tobacco"—sum of the total score for questions nine through twelve.

The potential "total score" from each of the three domains can range from 0 to 12.

Fagerström Test for Nicotine Dependence (FTND)

The FTND is a six-item psychometric test (Table 3.7) that was developed by Heatherton, Kozlowski, and Frecker (1991) as an improved version of the original "Fagerström Tolerance Questionnaire" (FTQ). The FTQ was originally developed by Kari Fagerström in 1978 to determine if nicotine replacement therapy (NRT) was required for the management of nicotine withdrawal. It was later found to be a useful test for measuring nicotine dependence. However, as determined by DiFranza et al. (2013), and others, the FTND correlated significantly greater with nicotine withdrawal than with nicotine dependence. The FTND should only be used for older adults who are current, active tobacco smokers.

Scoring the FTND Each of the six questions of the FTND is assigned 0 to 3 points depending on the selected response (see Table 3.7). All the scores are summed for a possible maximal score of 10. Total scores are generally evaluated as: 0 to 2, "very low" dependence; 3 or 4, "low" dependence;[97] 5, "medium" dependence; 6 or 7, "high" dependence; and 8 to 10, "very high" dependence.

Regarding the assessment, diagnosis, and treatment of "tobacco-dependent" adults, the American Thoracic Society recommends that:

1. All patients should be screened for tobacco use, and the potential diagnosis of tobacco dependence should be assessed;
2. The diagnosis of tobacco dependence, as well as the toxic effects of tobacco exposure, should be incorporated into the patient's problem list;
3. Simply encouraging patients to stop smoking is insufficient. All patients who use tobacco should be provided with evidence-based treatment, including pharmacotherapy, to help them stop smoking; (*continued, p. 274*)

96. "Scoring criteria" and "point allocations" are as follows: "not at all,"=0; "a little,"=1; "pretty well,"=2; and "very well,"=3.
97. Generally, patients with a total score of 0 to 4 are considered to be unlikely to require the use of selective therapeutic approaches for smoking cessation.

Table 3.7 The FTND

ITEM/QUESTION	SCORING CRITERIA [Point Allocation]
1. How soon after you wake-up do you have your first cigarette?	Within five minutes, [3]; six to 30 minutes, [2]; 31 to 60 minutes, [1]; after 60 minutes, [0]
2. Do you find it difficult to refrain from smoking in places where it is forbidden such as church, the library, or movie theaters?	Yes, [1]; No, [0]
3. Which cigarette would you hate most to give up?	The first one in the morning, [1]; all others, [0]
4. How many cigarettes do you smoke? (20 cigarettes per pack)	10 or less, [0]; 11 to 20, [1]; 21 to 30, [2]; 31 or more, [3]
5. Do you smoke more frequently during the first hours after wakening than the rest of the day?	Yes [1]; No [0]
6. Do you smoke if you are so ill that you are in bed most of the day?	Yes [1]; No [0]

Source: Heatherton et al., 1991.

4. Tobacco-dependence interventions require longitudinal follow-up, akin to the longitudinal evaluation and management of other chronic illnesses. (Leone, Zhang, & Evers-Casey, 2020, p. e8)

Treating Older Adult Nicotine Dependence or Use Disorder

The WHO, cited by RNAO (2017, p. 6), noted that:

> Through implementation of tobacco interventions, health-care providers can contribute to reducing tobacco use, which is the single greatest preventable cause of death in the world today.

The treatment of nicotine dependence or use disorder primarily involves two approaches—pharmacotherapy and psychotherapy/counseling. Each of these treatment approaches, alone or in combination, has demonstrated efficacy in the: (1) cessation of nicotine tobacco smoking; and, once achieved; (2) prevention of "resumed" tobacco smoking. We begin with an overview of factors that may affect treatment approaches for nicotine dependence or use disorder. We then present and discuss current approved pharmacotherapeutic approaches for older adults followed by approved psychotherapy/counseling approaches.

It is important to keep in mind that several extensive research studies and reviews (e.g., Cawkwell, Blaum, & Sherman, 2015; Mons et al., 2015) have demonstrated that tobacco smoking cessation, even at older ages, can significantly reduce cardiovascular events and mortality. For example, in their retrospective analysis of data from over 160,000 older adults (i.e., over 70 years of age), Nash et al. (2017, p. 280) found that:

> Former smokers were at substantially reduced risk of mortality after age 70 years relative to current smokers, even those who quit in their 60s. Therefore, smoking cessation should be emphasized to all smokers, regardless of age.

The timeline of benefits, which are associated with tobacco smoking cessation, are presented in Table 3.8.

The noted benefits and associated timeline are based on population data. Therefore, individual variability is to be expected. The basis of this variability is primarily related to the: (1) genetics of individual tobacco smokers; and (2) characteristics of their smoking

Table 3.8 Tobacco Smoking Cessation: A Timeline of Benefits

TIMELINE	POSSIBLE ASSOCIATED BENEFITS
Within 20 minutes of last cigarette:	• Blood pressure may drop to normal level; • Pulse rate drops to normal rate; • Body temperature of hands and feet increases to normal.
Within 8 hours:	• Nicotine level in blood is reduced by over 50%.
Within 12 hours:	• Carbon monoxide level in blood drops to normal; • Oxygen level in blood increases.
Within 24 hours:	• Chance of heart attack may reduce.
Within 48 hours:	• Nicotine is absent from the blood; • Nerve endings may regrow; • Ability to smell and taste is enhanced.
Within 72 hours:	• Bronchial tubes relax, if undamaged, making breathing easier; • Energy levels increase; • Lung capacity increases.
2 weeks to 3 months:	• Circulation improves; • Walking and running become easier; • Lung function may increase up to 20%.
1 month to 9 months:	• Coughing, sinus congestion, fatigue, and shortness of breath may decrease markedly over a number of weeks; • Potential for cilia to regrow in lungs, increasing ability to handle mucus, clean the lungs, and reduce infection; • Lung function increases by up to 10%.
1 year:	• The risk for heart disease is reduced by one half.
2 years:	• Cervical cancer risk is reduced compared to continuing smokers; • Bladder cancer risk is halved compared to continuing smokers.
5 years:	• Lung cancer death rate for average smoker (one pack a day) decreases from 137 per 100,000 to 72 per 100,000; • 5 to 15 years after quitting, stroke risk is reduced to that of someone who has never smoked.
10 years and longer:	• Precancerous cells are replaced; • Lung cancer risk falls to half that of a smoker; • Risk of other cancers—such as those of the cervix, bladder, esophagus, kidney, larynx, mouth, and pancreas—decreases; • After long-term quitting, the risk of death from COPD is reduced compared to someone who continues to smoke.
15 years:	• Risk of coronary heart disease decreases to that of a nonsmoker.

Modified from: Health Canada, 2016; RNAO, 2017; USDHHS, 2014; WHO, 2020.

histories (e.g., duration of tobacco cigarette use or number of cigarettes smoked during a typical smoking episode).

Pharmacotherapeutic Approaches

Two major areas of focus for the treatment of older adult nicotine dependence or use disorder are: (1) tobacco smoking cessation; and (2) nicotine maintenance, or nicotine replacement therapy (NRT). Each of these approaches are presented and discussed in the following subsections.

Tobacco Smoking Cessation

Various pharmacological approaches have been used to achieve tobacco smoking cessation (i.e., achieving abstinence)—bupropion (Wellbutrin SR® or Zyban®), varenicline (Chantix®), nicotine replacement therapy (NRT), and combination pharmacotherapy. Bupropion and varenicline are the principal components of pharmacotherapy approved by the FDA for facilitating smoking cessation and achieving tobacco smoking abstinence (Patnode, Henderson, & Thompson, 2015a, 2015b). The pharmacotherapeutic approaches to tobacco smoking cessation focus on the: (1) cessation to tobacco smoking; and (2) management of the signs and symptoms associated with the nicotine withdrawal syndrome.

Bupropion Two decades ago, bupropion, an antidepressant of the aminoketone class, was approved for the management of the nicotine withdrawal syndrome associated with cessation of tobacco smoking (Corelli & Hudmon, 2006; Pagliaro & Pagliaro, 1999). Since its approval, bupropion pharmacotherapy has been associated with several benefits, including:

- Decreasing the reward associated with smoking;
- Relieving the signs and symptoms of nicotine withdrawal;
- Decreasing post-cessation weight gain. (Barua et al., 2018)

The mechanism by which bupropion facilitates tobacco smoking cessation has not yet been clearly identified. Bupropion pharmacotherapy generally is initiated approximately one week before the patient's identified "quit date" in order to allow enough time to achieve steady-state blood concentrations. Bupropion pharmacotherapy is continued for two to three months while monitoring patient response and progress in terms of smoking cessation.[98] The sustained-release tablets should be swallowed whole and not crushed, divided, or chewed.

Bupropion has also been used in combination with NRT, including the use of nicotine transdermal systems (see the later subsection, "Nicotine Replacement Therapy [NRT]," for additional related discussion). Published research findings and reviews of tobacco smoking cessation approaches and the management of the signs and symptoms of nicotine withdrawal (e.g., Anthenelli, Benowitz, & West, 2016; Cahill, Stevens, & Perera, 2013) generally indicate that bupropion pharmacotherapy and NRT are equally efficacious—with each being significantly superior to placebo in regard to facilitating and maintaining tobacco smoking

98. N.B. Older adults who have been unable to quit smoking after 12 weeks of bupropion pharmacotherapy are unlikely to respond positively to further continued bupropion pharmacotherapy.

cessation. In addition, it is recommended that patients receive related counseling support throughout treatment.

However, it should be noted that several studies (e.g., Cox, Nollen, & Mayo, 2012; Robles, Singh-Franco, & Ghin, 2008) have failed to demonstrate long-term smoking cessation with bupropion use among smokers of African continental descent, particularly those who smoke: (1) menthol cigarettes; (2) fewer than 10 cigarettes per day; and/or (3) within 30 minutes of waking. These observations may have more to do with the menthol in the cigarettes than to continental or other descent (Ahijevych & Garrett, 2010). For example, Wickham (2015, p. 279) suggests four distinct biological mechanisms by which menthol can possibly affect smoking behavior and, consequently, the response to smoking cessation interventions:

1. Menthol acts to reduce the initially aversive experiences associated with tobacco smoking;
2. Menthol can serve as a highly reinforcing sensory cue when associated with nicotine, thus promoting smoking behavior;
3. Menthol's actions on nicotinic acetylcholine receptors may change the reinforcing value of nicotine;
4. Menthol can alter nicotine metabolism, thus increasing nicotine serum concentrations.

Associated undesired, or harmful, effects and toxicities, which have been identified in over 10% of patients treated with bupropion, include anxiety disorders, insomnia, and nausea. The most undesired, or harmful, effects and toxicities associated with bupropion pharmacotherapy for smoking cessation, include:

- Activation of mania/hypomania;
- Angle closure glaucoma;
- Hypersensitivity;
- Hypertension;
- Psychosis;
- Seizures;[99]
- Suicidal thoughts and behaviors.[100]

Long-term efficacy of bupropion for the facilitation of cigarette smoking cessation among older adults has generally not been formally evaluated because:

1. Pharmacotherapy is not recommended beyond 12 weeks;
2. It is generally agreed that, if smoking cessation is not achieved by 12 weeks, it is highly unlikely to be achieved with further continued use.

99. The risk of seizure appears to be dose related. Seizure disorders—as well as conditions that significantly increase the risk of seizures (e.g., CNS infection, CNS tumors, or severe stroke)—are contraindications to the use of bupropion. Additionally, bupropion is contraindicated for patients undergoing abrupt discontinuation (i.e., withdrawal) of sedative-hypnotics, including alcohol, barbiturates, and benzodiazepines.

100. As denoted in the FDA "black box" warning:

> Antidepressants increase the risk of suicidal thoughts and behaviors [particularly among patients with an additional mental disorder (e.g., MDD; OCD)].
>
> (FDA, 2009, p. 1)

Varenicline Varenicline (Chantix®) was approved by the FDA in 2006 as first-line pharmacotherapy aimed at facilitating smoking cessation. An alternative to NRT (Fant, Buchhalter, & Buchman, 2009; Frishman, 2007), varenicline use is associated with, on average, a 1.5 times greater efficacy in smoking cessation success (Cahill et al., 2013).

A partial nicotine antagonist, varenicline competitively binds to the nicotinic acetylcholine receptors (nAChRs), particularly the $\alpha_4\beta_2$ subtype where it helps to stop smoking by its actions as a:

1. Partial "agonist"—reducing the signs and symptoms of nicotine withdrawal by maintaining moderate levels of dopamine;
2. Partial "antagonist"—blocking nicotine from binding to the receptor sites and, consequently, reducing its desired actions, including smoking satisfaction.

Overall, the ability of nicotine to stimulate the mesolimbic dopamine system is significantly reduced by the use of varenicline.

Varenicline is available as an oral tablet that is ingested once or twice daily,[101] after meals, for generally three to six months (FDA, 2016b). Varenicline pharmacotherapy is generally initiated one to four weeks prior to the identified "quit date." The most common undesired effect associated with varenicline pharmacotherapy is nausea, which is usually mild to moderate and subsides over time (Cahill, Stead, & Lancaster, 2012; Faessel, Obach, & Rollema, 2010; Garrison & Dugan, 2009; Hays, Croghan, & Schroeder, 2010). Varenicline also can lower the seizure threshold.

Initially, the FDA required a "black box" warning for the official labeling of Chantix® that included the statement, "Some people have had changes in behavior, hostility, agitation, depressed mood, and suicidal thoughts" (FDA, 2009). The risk for these less common undesired, or harmful, effects and toxicities is reportedly greater for those who have a positive history of mental disorders (Ahmed, Ali, & Kramer, 2013). However, in late 2016, the FDA officially removed this "black box" warning from varenicline's official labeling (FDA, 2016b).

Older adults are generally cautioned to limit their ingestion of alcohol until they have monitored and evaluated the effects associated with their varenicline use (and the associated level of decreased tobacco smoking) on their drinking patterns. However, the results from a large scale, double-blind, triple-dummy, placebo-controlled study indicate that varenicline's associated risk for undesired neuropsychiatric effects and toxicities was not significantly greater than that associated with the use of a placebo (Anthenelli et al., 2016).

Serious cardiovascular events also have been reported to be related to varenicline pharmacotherapy, including congestive heart failure, dysrhythmias, and myocardial infarction (Singh, Loke, & Spangler, 2011). However, a comprehensive meta-analysis failed to substantiate either the clinical or statistical significance of these concerns (Prochaska & Hilton, 2012).

---

101. Optimal therapeutic response generally appears to be associated with a dosage of 1 mg twice daily. However—based on pharmacokinetic data (i.e., varenicline is primarily eliminated in unchanged form by renal excretion)—for older adults with significant renal impairment (i.e., creatinine clearance [CrCl] less than 50 ml/min), it has been recommended that the dosage be reduced to 0.5 mg twice daily (Faessel et al., 2010).

Although generally associated with nausea and a need for cautious use, varenicline pharmacotherapy for tobacco smoking cessation is well established as a suitable alternative to NRT, particularly for older adults who smoke tobacco and who have been unsuccessful in achieving smoking cessation with NRT. Several studies (e.g., Baker, Piper, & Stein, 2016; Gonzales, Rennard, & Nides, 2006; Nides, Oncken, & Gonzales, 2006; Tonstad, Tonnesen, & Hajek, 2006) have demonstrated significant increases in the achievement of smoking cessation with the use of varenicline when compared to placebo and/or bupropion pharmacotherapy.

For example, Jorenby, Hays, and Rigotti (2006) found that, after one year, the rate of continuous abstinence for varenicline was 23% in comparison to 15% for bupropion and 10% for placebo. Cahill, Lindson-Hawley, and Thomas (2016, p. 1), in their meta-analysis of 39 trials that tested varenicline, found that:

> Varenicline at standard dose increased the chances of successful long-term smoking cessation between two- and three-fold compared with pharmacologically unassisted quit attempts.

Additionally, Aubin, Bobak, and Britton (2008, p. 717), reported that:

> The outcomes of this trial established that abstinence from smoking was greater and craving, withdrawal symptoms and smoking satisfaction were less at the end of treatment with varenicline than with transdermal NRT.

Chang, Huang, and You (2019, p. 3462), in their retrospective cohort study of smoking cessation success among older adults (i.e., 60 years of age and older), found that:

> the patients who received varenicline were 3.22 times more likely to quit smoking than those who received NRT.

In a systematic review of approximately 20 random, controlled studies that compared varenicline pharmacotherapy with placebo, bupropion, nicotine replacement therapy, or counseling, Cahill et al. (2012) found varenicline to increase the overall chances of long-term smoking cessation by two- to three-fold. Zhu, Cummins, and Gamst (2016) reported similar findings. However, they cautioned that, after three months of varenicline pharmacotherapy, the relapse rate did not significantly differ from that associated with other related pharmacotherapies.

Most recently, a panel of experts from the American Thoracic Society conducted systematic reviews of related published research involving varenicline. These reviews resulted in the following published six recommendations for varenicline pharmacotherapy:

1. For tobacco-dependent adults in whom treatment is being initiated, we recommend varenicline over a nicotine patch;
2. For tobacco-dependent adults in whom treatment is being initiated, we recommend varenicline over bupropion;
3. For tobacco-dependent adults in whom treatment is being initiated, we suggest varenicline plus a nicotine patch over varenicline alone;
4. For tobacco-dependent adults in whom treatment is being initiated, we suggest varenicline over electronic cigarettes;
5. In tobacco-dependent adults who are not ready to discontinue tobacco use, we recommend that clinicians begin treatment with varenicline rather than waiting until patients are ready to stop tobacco use;

6. For tobacco-dependent adults with comorbid psychiatric conditions, including substance-use disorder, depression, anxiety, schizophrenia, and/or bipolar disorder, for whom retreatment is being initiated, we recommend varenicline over a nicotine patch.

(Leone et al., 2020, p. e 6)

Combination Varenicline Pharmacotherapy Chang, Chiang, and Ho (2015), in their systematic review and meta-analysis of randomized controlled trials of varenicline pharmacotherapy and NRT, found that combined varenicline and NRT generally has been recommended and touted as being more efficacious than varenicline alone.[102] In addition, others (e.g., Ebbert, Wyatt, & Hays, 2010; Ebbert, Wyatt, & Zirakzadeh, 2009; Hays et al., 2010) have found that the efficacy of varenicline can be increased significantly with combination varenicline pharmacotherapy and appropriate cognitive-behavioral psychotherapy.

Nicotine Replacement Therapy (NRT)/Maintenance[103]

Nicotine replacement therapy (i.e., maintenance), in its various formulations (e.g., buccal/mouth sprays, chewing gums, intranasal sprays, oral inhalers, oral lozenges, and TDSs—see Table 3.9),[104] has become the medical mainstay of tobacco smoking cessation because of its:

1. Safety and efficacy in regard to reducing the undesired signs and symptoms associated with nicotine withdrawal;
2. Enhancement of associated successful outcomes regarding "quitting" nicotine use (see the related discussion in the earlier nicotine subsection, Treating Nicotine Dependence or Use Disorder Among Older Adults—"Pharmacotherapeutic Approaches"). (*continued, p. 287*)

102. N.B. We do not generally recommend varenicline and NRT combination pharmacotherapy for older adults because of the increased risk for associated undesired, or harmful, effects and toxicities.
103. See also the related discussion in the earlier nicotine pharmacology subsection—"E-Cigarettes and Tobacco Smoking Cessation."
104. Supportive research for the buccal/mouth spray product includes a randomized double-blind, placebo-controlled parallel-group, 26-week study by Nides, Danielsson, and Saunders (2020). Promising results of their study of the nicotine mouth spray formulation tested, which delivered 1 mg of nicotine per spray, include:

- Had a more rapid nicotine absorption time in comparison to existing NRT formulations;
- Achieved a maximal plasma nicotine concentration more rapidly (i.e., ~ 10 minutes) than other existing NRT formulations;
- Using a naturalistic study design, was well-accepted by participating subjects;
- Resulted in a significantly higher continuous abstinence rates than did the placebo control.

The nicotine buccal/mouth spray preparation, "Nicorette Quick Mist®," is currently available as an over-the-counter (OTC) product in both the U.S. and Canada. It is available in "fresh mint" and "cool berry" flavors in a 150-spray dispenser. Relief from nicotine craving and withdrawal signs and symptoms generally occurs within 60 seconds of the administration of an oral spray dose.

Table 3.9 Nicotine Replacement Therapy (NRT) Formulations[105]

FORMULATION	USUAL ADULT DOSAGE	ADMINISTRATION	*ADVANTAGES/DISADVANTAGES*[106]
Buccal Spray[107] Nicorette Quick-Mist® Each buccal spray delivers 1 mg (i.e., approximately the same amount as 1 tobacco cigarette). Each spray pump bottle delivers 150 sprays. OTC	Weeks 1 to 6: 1 to 2 sprays every half hour. Generally, wait approximately 1 minute between sprays. Weeks 7 to 9: Reduce number of sprays per day by half. Weeks 10 to 12: 2 to 4 sprays per day. After 12 weeks: Stop using Quick-Mist®. Maximum: 2 sprays at a time; 4 sprays per hour; 64 sprays per day.	No food or drink 15 minutes prior to use and during use. Directions: 1. Push the black button down until you can push it lightly inwards. 2. While pushing the button in, slide upwards and continue until the top of the dispenser locks into place. 3. Before using for the first time, prime the pump by pressing the top firmly into a tissue until a fine mist appears. If you don't use the spray for a couple of days, you may need to repeat this step. 4. Place the dispenser as close as possible to your open mouth, avoiding the lips. 5. Press the top of the dispenser firmly to release one spray into your mouth. For best results, wait a few seconds before swallowing. Do not inhale the spray. Avoid spraying directly onto your lips or throat.	• Onset of action is generally within 1 minute. • If inadvertently sprayed into the eye, immediately flush with copious amounts of plain water. • Available in berry and mint flavors. • Use is discreet with most observers thinking that it is a breath freshener. • In terms of future cessation of use, it is important and helpful to keep track of/record the number of sprays used per day. • Significant risk of nicotine dependence, particularly if user does not consciously keep track of, and reduce, the number of daily sprays. • Relatively expensive. • Particularly upon initiation of use, some users may complain of a

(*Continued*)

105. These NRT formulations can be used together in various combinations or sequentially.
106. Every one of the NRT formulations is capable of causing nicotine dependence.
107. Referred to as "oral mouth spray" in Canada.

Table 3.9 (Continued)

FORMULATION	USUAL ADULT DOSAGE	ADMINISTRATION	*ADVANTAGES/DISADVANTAGES*[106]
		6. Repeat dose (i.e., step #5) once if craving is still present after 1 minute. 7. To close the dispenser, slide the button down until it can be pushed lightly inwards. Then, while pushing in, slide down to lock. Store at room temperature. Use for 3–6 months, as needed.	"burning" or "stinging" sensation and the need to "gasp for air." • Some formulations contain a small amount of alcohol as a vehicle—generally less than 100 mg/spray. • See "Oral Mouth Spray."
Chewing Gum (nicotine polacrilex) Nicorette Gum® Thrive Gum® 2 & 4 mg per piece OTC	If first cigarette is smoked ≤ 30 minutes after waking OR if smoking more than 1 package of cigarettes/day: 4 mg. Use 1 piece per hour. If first cigarette is smoked > 30 minutes after waking OR if smoking less than 1 package of cigarettes/day: 2 mg. Use one piece per hour. Average: 9 pieces per day. Maximum: 24 pieces per day. General guide: 1st 2 weeks, 9–24 pieces/day; 2nd two weeks, 8–15 pieces/day; Month 2, 4–10 pieces /day; Month 3, 2–5 pieces/day; Months 4–6, 1 piece as needed..	No food or drink 15 minutes prior to use and during use. Do not chew more than 1 piece of gum at a time (i.e., do not use 2 pieces to make-up for a missed dose). Directions: 1. Chew briefly until mouth tingles (or taste becomes strong), then "park" (i.e., rest) gum inside cheek until tingle fades. 2. Repeat chew-and-park each time tingle fades. Discard gum after 30 minutes of use. 3. Repeat use when craving to smoke returns. Use for 3–6 months, as needed.	• Oral substitute for cigarettes. • User controls nicotine dose. • Not chewed in same way as regular gum; requires careful instruction. • Can damage dental work and be difficult to use with dentures. • Vigorous chewing may strain jaw and neck muscles resulting in jaw/neck pain and migraine headaches. • Available in a variety of flavors from manufacturer (e.g., cinnamon, fruit, mint, and spearmint). • Unflavored gum often reported to taste like "cigarettes."

Intranasal Spray Nicorette Nasal Spray® Nicotrol NS® 10 mg/ml Each intranasal spray delivers 0.5 mg; each intranasal spray bottle delivers 200 sprays. Rx	Use 1 spray in each nostril, every 1–2 hours. <u>Maximum</u>: 2 sprays in each nostril per hour; 64 sprays per day.	<u>Directions</u>: 1. Wash your hands. 2. Gently blow your nose to clear your nasal passages. 3. Remove the cap of the nasal spray by pressing in the circles on the side of the bottle. 4. To prime the pump before the first use, hold the bottle in front of a tissue or paper towel. Pump the spray bottle 6 to 8 times until a fine spray appears. Throw away the tissue or towel. 5. Tilt your head back slightly. 6. Insert the tip of the bottle as far as you comfortably can into one nostril, pointing the tip toward the back of your nose. 7. Breathe through your mouth. 8. Pump the spray firmly and quickly one time. Do <u>not</u> sniff, swallow, or inhale while spraying. 9. If your nose runs, gently sniff to keep the nasal spray in your nose. Wait 2 to 3 minutes before blowing your nose. 10. Repeat steps 6 to 8 for the second nostril. 11. Replace the cover on the spray bottle. 12. Any time you have not used the nasal spray for 24 hours, prime the pump in a tissue one or two times. However, do not prime too much as it will decrease the amount of medication in the container. Store at room temperature. Use for 3–6 months, as needed.	• Of all NRT products, has most rapid delivery of nicotine with peak plasma levels within 5–10 minutes. • User controls nicotine dose. • Some users cannot tolerate local irritation to nasal mucosa, and this adversely affects compliance. • Significant risk of nicotine dependence has been associated with use.

(Continued)

Table 3.9 (Continued)

FORMULATION	USUAL ADULT DOSAGE	ADMINISTRATION	*ADVANTAGES/DISADVANTAGES*[106]
Oral Inhaler Nicorette Inhaler® Nicotrol Inhaler® 4 & 10 mg per cartridge; each cartridge delivers ~ 80 puffs. Rx	<u>Up to 12 weeks</u>: A minimum of 6 cartridges to a maximum of 12 cartridges per day. <u>12 to 24 weeks</u>: Gradually reduce the number of cartridges. <u>Maximum</u>: 16 puffs per day.	Do <u>not</u> inhale into the lungs. Puff into mouth or back of throat until cravings subside. Use 1 cartridge every 1–2 hours. Change cartridge when nicotine taste disappears. <u>Directions</u>: 1. Line up the markers and pull each end in the opposite direction. 2. Insert the cartridge into the mouthpiece and twist to close securely. 3. Bring the mouthpiece to your mouth. 4. Inhale deeply into the back of your throat, or puff in short breaths. Store at room temperature. Use for 3 to 6 months, as needed.	• Frequent puffing required for over 20 minutes. • Each cartridge lasts for approximately 20 minutes of frequent puffing. • User controls nicotine dose. • Nicotine cartridge and mouthpiece look similar to a tobacco cigarette. • Mimics hand-to-mouth ritual of smoking cigarettes. • Underdosing is common. • Relatively expensive.
Oral Lozenge (nicotine bitartrate) (nicotine polacrilex) Commit Lozenge® Nicorette Lozenge® Nicorette Mini Lozenge® Thrive Lozenge® 2 & 4 mg per lozenge OTC	<u>If first cigarette is smoked ≤ 30 minutes after waking</u>: 4 mg. <u>If first cigarette is smoked ≥ 30 minutes after waking</u>: 2 mg. <u>Weeks 1 to 6</u>: 1 lozenge every 1–2 hours. Minimally, use 9 lozenges/day for weeks 1–6. <u>Weeks 7 to 9</u>: 1 lozenge every 2–4 hours. <u>Weeks 10 to 12</u>: 1 lozenge every 4–8 hours.	<u>No</u> food or drink 15 minutes prior to use and during use. Do <u>not</u> chew, crush, or swallow lozenge. Do <u>not</u> use more than 1 lozenge at a time <u>Directions</u>: 1. Place lozenge between gum and cheek, let it dissolve slowly (i.e., over 20–30 minutes). Use for 3 to 6 months, as needed.	• User controls nicotine dose. • Easier to use than gum for those with dental work or dentures. • Underdosing is common. • In comparison to nicotine oral buccal/mouth sprays, the oral lozenge is generally considered by patients to have a much slower onset and lower efficacy in reducing nicotine craving.

	Use should be discontinued after 12 weeks if solely managed by patient. Maximum: 5 lozenges per 6 hours; 20 lozenges per 24 hours.		
Oral Mouth Spray (See "Buccal Spray")			
Transdermal Delivery System Nicoderm CQ Patch® Nicotrol Patch® 5, 7, 10, 14, 15, 21, & 25 mg per patch OTC or Rx	Usual Initial Dose: For ≥ 10 cigarettes per day: 21 or 25 mg. For < 10 cigarettes per day: 14 or 15 mg. After 6 weeks: Option to taper to lower doses (i.e., 5, 7, or 10 mg patch) for 2–6 weeks; or to continue original dose (either option is acceptable). Patch should be worn continuously for 16 to 24 hours depending upon the brand and product selected for use.	Directions: 1. Apply a new patch at the same time each morning to a clean, dry, hairless skin site on the chest, shoulder, upper arm, or hip as instructed by the package insert. 2. Avoid placing patch over areas of broken, irritated, oily, or scarred skin. 3. Do not shave the application site. If necessary, clip hair from the site before applying patch. 4. Do not cut patch 5. Never wear 2 patches at the same time. 6. To avoid skin irritation, rotate application sites daily—may reuse previous site in 3–7 days. 7. Can wear patch while bathing or showering, but avoid exposure of applied patch to a direct heat source (e.g., heated water bed, hot tub, or sauna) that may increase drug release from the patch.	• Easiest nicotine product to use. • Provides a steady nicotine level for 16–24 hours, depending on brand. • User cannot alter dose if cravings occur during the day (i.e., "fixed dose"). • If use of a 24-hour patch causes vivid dreams or interferes with sleep, then a 16-hour patch may be indicated. • If user of a 16-hour patch wakes up craving cigarettes, then a 24-hour patch may be indicated. • User may display an allergy to the adhesive tape used in the patch. • Fixed dose. • Not effective/suitable for addressing acute cravings. • Used patches may pose a risk to children and pets and should be appropriately disposed of.

(*Continued*)

Table 3.9 (Continued)

FORMULATION	USUAL ADULT DOSAGE	ADMINISTRATION	*ADVANTAGES/DISADVANTAGES*[106]
		8. If using a 16-hour patch, remove patch before going to sleep (see comments in "Advantages/Disadvantages" column). 9. Remove new patch from package, peel off protective strip, and apply "sticky side" to skin surface. 10. Press patch down with palm of hand for about 10 seconds to assure firm attachment, particularly around edges. 11. Wash your hands with plain water after applying patch—do not use soap because it can increase nicotine absorption from the skin. 12. Do not wear the same patch for longer than 24 hours. 13. Always remove old patch prior to application of a new/replacement patch. 14. If patch loosens, or falls off, replace it with a new one. Store at room temperature. Use for 3 to 6 months, as needed.	

Modified from:,[108, 109] FDA-approved prescription drug monographs; official manufacturer package inserts; Pagliaro & Pagliaro, 2004, 2020; Pagliaro & Pagliaro, *Clinical Patient Data Files*; and web sites for the products listed.

108. N.B. The data in this table are current and accurate. However, different manufacturers of similar products, particularly those that are OTC, may vary in their exact package directions. When disagreement is encountered, always follow the directions on the current package insert for the specific brand product that is being used.
109. Whether the use of e-cigarettes is efficacious as a means for NRT has not yet been demonstrated. However, we generally recommend the use of e-cigarettes (i.e., vaping) as an efficacious harm reduction strategy for those who would not—or cannot with repeated attempts—otherwise quit tobacco smoking (for related discussion, see earlier nicotine subsection, "E-Cigarettes"). E-Cigarette use as a mode of NRT has not been FDA approved.

The noted success and comparative safety of these products have encouraged their conversion from prescription to nonprescription status (e.g., Cawkwell et al., 2015; Crain & Bhat, 2010; Fant et al., 2009; Pagliaro & Pagliaro, 2018).[110]

Whereas methadone maintenance, in the context of opiate analgesic dependence or use disorder, is just that, maintenance, it is generally expected that nicotine replacement products, or substitutes, be used for short periods of time (e.g., up to 12 weeks).[111] The nicotine substitutes help older adults to slowly discontinue their regular, long-term nicotine use while experiencing diminished signs and symptoms of the nicotine withdrawal syndrome (Cahill et al., 2013; Frishman, 2007). The transdermal nicotine delivery systems (e.g., Habitrol®; NicoDerm®), nicotine nasal sprays (Nicotrol NS®), and other products have become important adjuncts to smoking cessation programs and have demonstrated positive results in relation to decreasing or ceasing tobacco smoking. In this context, the use of e-cigarettes (see earlier Nicotine subsection, "E-Cigarettes") has been suggested as another possible intervention to facilitate tobacco smoking cessation and the management of nicotine withdrawal. However, sufficient published research regarding e-cigarette NRT is not currently available to formally support the efficacy of this potential intervention (Shields et al., 2017; USDHHS, 2016b).[112]

Although NRT was neither intended nor approved by the FDA for long-term use (i.e., maintenance pharmacotherapy) several clinicians and researchers have suggested that this approach may secure a significant degree of "harm reduction" for those who cannot obtain complete abstinence. In their comprehensive systematic review of this topic, including consideration of the use of e-cigarettes, Lindsdon-Hawley, Hartmann-Boyce, and Fanshawe (2016) found that people who do not wish to [or cannot] quit tobacco cigarette smoking, in the long-term, can be helped to cut down on the: (1) number of tobacco cigarettes smoked daily; and (2) exposure to toxic tobacco smoke—with the aid of long-term NRT and/or e-cigarettes.

While NRT is of potential benefit, studies over the last 30 years have repeatedly demonstrated that the use of nicotine substitutes is, in most cases, only significantly effective when combined with appropriate counseling or other psychotherapeutic approaches.[113] For example, as noted over 30 years ago by Covey and Glassman (1991, p. 69):

> Evidence of the addictive nature of chronic tobacco use suggests that pharmacologic interventions, in conjunction with behaviorally oriented therapy, may present the best hope for achieving smoking cessation in refractory smokers.

---

110. N.B. None of the various dosage forms available for NRT have consistently provided superior results (Yardley et al., 2015). Consequently, we recommend the use of the nicotine replacement product that is most preferred by the patient (i.e., that the patient finds most affordable, comfortable, convenient, or "user friendly").
111. N.B. While this is the current, and probably ideal, recommendation regarding the length of nicotine pharmacotherapy, it should be noted that a significant number of (former) tobacco smokers continue the use of nicotine pharmacotherapy well beyond this recommended time frame. While we welcome the associated health benefits, which are related to the cessation of tobacco smoking (see the earlier discussion in this chapter, particularly the nicotine pharmacology subsection, "Nicotine Physical and Psychological Dependence"), we recognize and note that physical dependence to nicotine—as well as other nicotine-related toxicities—are maintained in this context of use (i.e., the "prolonged" use of NRT).
112. Interestingly, in our practice experience we have noted significantly more older adults, in comparison to younger adults, self-selecting e-cigarettes as their preferred mode of NRT (Pagliaro & Pagliaro, *Clinical Patient Data Files*). This observation appears to be supported by several current foreign studies. For example, Hajel, Phillips-Waller, and Przulj (2019), in their study of U.K. adults, found that: (1) e-cigarettes were commonly used to stop tobacco smoking; and (2) e-cigarettes were significantly more effective at promoting tobacco smoking abstinence in comparison to NRT (i.e., at one year, 18% abstinence for e-cigarette users and 9.9% for those who used traditional NRT).
113. Combination pharmacotherapeutic and psychotherapeutic/counseling approaches have also been consistently demonstrated to provide superior therapeutic outcomes in the treatment of contemporaneous diagnoses among older adults (e.g., Carroll, Mathew, & Leone, 2020; Pagliaro & Pagliaro, 2018).

Or, as identified by Generali (1992, p. 34):

> Smoking cessation rates associated with nicotine transdermal patch therapy have varied in clinical trials. However, appropriate patient instruction and an extensive behavioral modification program ensure optimal response to transdermal nicotine therapy.

In addition, as noted by Laniado-Laborin (2010, p. 74):

> The rate of successful smoking cessation at 1 year is 3% to 5% when the patient simply tries to stop, 7% to 16% if the smoker undergoes behavioral intervention, and up to 25% when receiving pharmacologic treatment and behavioral support.

And, finally, as noted by Stead, Koilpillai, and Fanshawe (2016, p. 1), in their retrospective meta-analysis of 53 studies including a total of over 25,000 participants:

> Interventions that combine pharmacotherapy and behavioral support increase smoking cessation success.

Psychotherapeutic/Counseling Approaches

Several psychotherapeutic/counseling approaches have been successfully used to treat older adults who have been diagnosed with nicotine dependence or use disorder. For example, CBT has demonstrated success (for further related discussion of CBT, see Chapter 1, *Alcohol*, Treating Older Adult Alcohol Dependence or Use Disorder, Pharmacotherapeutic and Psychotherapeutic Approaches—"Psychotherapy/Counseling").

Additionally, motivational interviewing (MI) has been used to support the patient's desire to quit tobacco smoking and/or to encourage the use of NRT (see the previous subsection). MI is a person-centered counseling style, which utilizes guided collaborated conversation, in an attempt to address patient ambivalence to change—while supporting their inherent potential and worth as an individual (i.e., to elicit and strengthen motivation to change). In comparison to most other related psychotherapeutic/counseling approaches, MI utilizes less confrontational methods regarding the issues of denial and resistance. Typical MI methods include:

- Avoiding arguments;
- Avoiding direct confrontation;
- Eliciting and affirming patient self-motivational statements;
- Expressing empathy;
- Supporting individual self-efficacy;
- Utilizing open-ended questioning;
- Utilizing reflective-listening;
- Utilizing summary statements.

Earlier published research (e.g., Heckman, Egleston, & Hofmann, 2010; Hettema & Hendricks, 2010; Lindson-Hawley, Thompson, & Begh, 2015) suggested that MI is effective in increasing smoking cessation rates in comparison to both no intervention and brief advice. However, as demonstrated in a Cochrane systematic literature review, data supporting the efficacy of motivational interviewing in this context has been found to be insufficient (Lindson-Hawley, Thompson, & Ferrey, 2019).

Community-Based Support-Service Programs

Community-based support-service programs can also be used to augment the psychotherapeutic approaches selected for the management of nicotine dependence or use disorder. Because of their ubiquitous availability to users, regardless of geographical location, use has quickly spread across the U.S. For example, the use of:

- Telephone quit lines (e.g., 1–800-QUIT-NOW [1–8OO-784–8669]; 1-800-227-2345 [The American Cancer Society Quitline]; 1-877-448-7848 [the National Cancer Institute's Quitline]);
- Text messaging programs for use with cell phones or personal computers (e.g., Smokefree TXT, which is available from the National Cancer Institute website);
- Web-based programs (e.g., BecomeAnEx.org that was developed by the Truth Initiative in collaboration with the Mayo Clinic).

The telephone quit lines offer several varied avenues/techniques to facilitate smoking cessations, including coaching, counseling, free provision of NRT, mailed education/self-help materials, training for health care professionals, and referral to related web-based services. The initial quit line call generally lasts approximately 30 minutes, during which a specific quit date is agreed upon. Typically, follow-up calls, which last for approximately 15 minutes each, are scheduled for the quit date, and at 3, 7, 14, and 30 days after quitting (Lichtenstein, Zhu, & Tedeschi, 2010).

Since the advent of the COVID-19 pandemic and the associated increased use of telemedicine for routine physician appointments, we have noted, not surprisingly, a significant increase in the acceptance of, and comfortability with the use of telephone quit lines and web-based assistance by older adults, who have nicotine dependence or use disorder.

Related 12-Step Programs[114]

Smokers Anonymous, which is also commonly referred to as Nicotine Anonymous (NicA)—in deference to the increasing use of e-cigarettes and the desire to cease all nicotine use—is a 12-step, non-profit recovery program that is predicated on the traditional 12-steps of alcoholic anonymous (Lichtenstein, 1999). One of the basic premises of Nicotine Anonymous is that the use of nicotine—in all forms—ceases.

Nicotine users, who have other dependence or use disorders (see following subsection, "Common Contemporaneous Diagnoses among Older Adults with Nicotine Dependence or Use Disorder") and/or who have participated in other 12-step programs, may find NicA to be particularly beneficial. As with AA, we tend to use the 12-step programs as a voluntary complimentary adjunct to other selected treatment modalities.

The only requirement to join NicA is the desire to cease all nicotine use. The group members meet on a regularly scheduled basis to openly share difficulties related to nicotine use and cessation—and to receive supportive feedback from other "fellowship" members.

114. For additional related discussion, see Chapter 1, *Alcohol,* Treating Older Adult Alcohol Dependence or Use Disorder, Pharmacotherapeutic and Psychotherapeutic/Counseling Approaches, "Psychotherapy/Counseling—"12-Step Programs").

This process usually occurs during face-to-face meetings. However, increasingly, online and social media platforms are used to "host" meetings—particularly, post-COVID-19.

The tools incorporated in the NicA 12-step process and group meetings, include:

1. Attendance at support group meetings;
2. A telephone/email list of other members, who are willing to offer advice and support;
3. Informational books and pamphlets;
4. Help from other members (i.e., "sponsors,"), who are able and willing to act as a personal coach for newcomers.

Related Professional Reminder: ***Regardless of which therapeutic intervention(s) are selected for a specific older adult who wants to quit smoking, it should be generally recognized that:***

1. ***Combination therapeutic interventions, as those previously discussed, usually provide the most favorable results;***
2. ***Although the optimal duration of therapy must be individually determined for each smoker, based on clinical experience, therapy should be maintained, for most smokers, for a minimal period of three to six months. Additionally, the potential for recidivism is significant and should be openly addressed with the patient and planned for.***

Preventing and Treating Relapsed Nicotine Use

Many older adults who use nicotine for its psychostimulant effects, find that after a period of continued use, they are unable to completely cease, or control, their nicotine use without the occurrence of undesired effects (i.e., craving and withdrawal signs and symptoms). Consequently, they often seek professional help (e.g., from a nurse, pharmacist, physician, or psychologist). However, even with professional help, 33% of these older adults are unable to cease nicotine use for more than a few days and only 20% to 30% remain "nicotine free" 12 months later.

The high rate of failure of the therapeutic approaches, which are utilized, for achieving tobacco smoking cessation (see the related discussion in the previous subsections), is a troubling reality. In fact, not only is it commonly encountered, but a vast majority of older adults, who are initially able to "stop smoking," subsequently resume tobacco smoking or other forms of nicotine use. As noted by Henley et al. (2019, p. 1):

> We also found that only 1 in 20 older adults successfully quit smoking in the past year.

Thus, relapsed nicotine use should be anticipated, planned for, and, if it occurs—treated.

The following list of relapse-related factors may assist health and social care professionals in the identification of both high-risk older adults with specific factors that: (1) may predispose older adults to relapse; and (2) if amenable, could be corrected/modified in order to diminish relapse rates.

- Alcohol use;
- Anxiety disorders;

- AUD;
- Dietary restrictions;
- Exposures to high-risk situations (e.g., arguments with others, financial pressures, uncomfortable social situations, other sources of stress);
- Friends or co-workers who smoke;
- Homelessness;
- Job employment that allows tobacco smoking (e.g., working outdoors);
- Lack of post-secondary education;
- Lack of cessation support;
- Living alone;
- Lower socioeconomic status;
- Mental depression;
- Negative self-talk;
- Nicotine withdrawal syndrome signs and symptoms;
- Obesity;
- Other smokers in the household;
- Perception that smoking is the major, perhaps the only, source of pleasure;
- Problems with pharmacotherapy (e.g., compliance challenges, premature discontinuation, undesired side-effects, under-dosing);
- Prolonged signs and symptoms of the nicotine withdrawal syndrome;
- Psychosis;
- Racial minority status;
- Recreational abuse of other drugs and substances of abuse;
- Smoking one or more packages of cigarettes daily;
- Smoking the first cigarette of the day within 30 minutes of awakening in the morning;
- SUDs;
- Use of low-tar/low-nicotine cigarettes. (Alboksmaty, Agaku, & Odani, 2019; Commonwealth of Australia, 2013; Gomes, Ladeira, & Guimaraes, 2012; Lee & Kahende, 2007; Pagliaro & Pagliaro, *Clinical Patient Data Files*; RNAO, 2017)

Once identified, relapsed nicotine use is treated in the same manners generally used for nicotine dependence (see the related discussion in the earlier subsection, "Treating Older Adult Nicotine Dependence or Use Disorder").

Common Contemporaneous Diagnoses Among Older Adults with NUD

Older adults are susceptible to, and often experience nicotine and other dependence or use disorders at the same time as one or more other mental and physical medical disorders. Together, these disorders comprise more serious and complicated contemporaneous diagnoses that often require more complex interdisciplinary professional health and social care treatment planning and management (Pagliaro & Pagliaro, 2018; Pagliaro & Pagliaro, *Clinical Patient Data Files*). For older adults diagnosed with nicotine dependence or use disorder, the most common mental disorders that are significantly correlated with the formulation of a contemporaneous diagnosis involve:

- Anxiety disorders;
- AUD;
- Bipolar disorder;
- Eating disorders;
- Major Depressive Disorder (MDD);
- Other Abusable Psychotropic Dependence or Use Disorders (i.e., SUDs);
- Psychotic Disorder.

REFERENCES[115, 116, 117]

Addicott, M. A. (2014). Caffeine use disorder: A review of the evidence and future implications. *Current Addiction Reports, 1*(3), 186–192. doi:10.1007/s40429-014-0024-9

Ahijevych, K., & Garrett, B. E. (2010, December). The role of menthol in cigarettes as a reinforcer of smoking behavior. *Nicotine & Tobacco Research, 12*(Suppl 2), S110–S116. doi:10.1093/ntr/ntq203

Ahmed, A., Ali, A., & Kramer, C. (2013). Neuropsychiatric adverse events of varenicline: A systematic review of published reports. *Journal of Clinical Psychopharmacology, 33*(1), 55–62.

Alboksmaty, A., Agaku, I., & Odani, S. (2019). Prevalence and determinants of cigarette smoking relapse among US adult smokers: A longitudinal study. *BMJ Open, 9*(e031676), 1–8. doi:10.1136/bmjopen-2019-031676

Alsabri, S. G., Mari, W. O., & Younes, S. (2018). Kinetic and dynamic description of caffeine. *Journal of Caffeine and Adenosine Research, 8*(1), 1–10. doi:10.1089/caff.2017.0011

Amaud, M. J. (2011). Pharmacokinetics and metabolism of natural methylxanthines in animal and man. *Handbook of Experimental Pharmacology, 2000*, 33–91. doi:10.1007/978-3-642-13443-2_3

American Cancer Society. (2017, April 5). Harmful chemicals in tobacco products. *Tobacco and Cancer*, pp. 1–2.

Anderson, G. D., & Chan, L. N. (2016). Pharmacokinetic drug interactions with tobacco, cannabinoids and smoking cessation products. *Clinical Pharmacokinetics, 55*(11), 1353–1368. doi:10.1007/s40262-016-0400-9

115. As per publisher style, only the first three authors are listed for each reference.
116. Several times the number of references listed were found, obtained, and analyzed by the authors during the preparation of this chapter. However, only those references that were cited at least once in the body of the text are listed. Major reasons for not citing other references include that they: (1) did not provide any additional unique information or research findings; (2) were not well researched or written by their authors (i.e., were evaluated as not being valid or reliable); (3) were based predominately, or exclusively, on animal studies; (4) dealt exclusively with other population groups (e.g., children, adolescents, or young adults); (5) provided usage statistics from outside the U.S.; and/or (6) were redundant with, or not as recent as, the already cited references—unless the reference was of classical, historical, or seminal importance.
117. The reference citation, "Pagliaro & Pagliaro, *Clinical Patient Data Files*," refers to unpublished data collected, with permission, by the authors, in the formal course of their professional academic roles as clinician scientists and professors, from their patients, research subjects or participants, and students, from the 1970s to date. Most of the related data have been discussed and made public in a wide and large number of formal academic presentations, including graduate seminars, grand rounds, guest lectures, professional conferences, and undergraduate lectures.

Anthenelli, R. M., Benowitz, N. L., & West, R. (2016). Neuropsychiatric safety and efficacy of varenicline, bupropion, and nicotine patch in smokers with and without psychiatric disorders (EAGLES): A double-blind, randomised, placebo-controlled clinical trial. *The Lancet*. doi:PIISO140-6736(16)30272-0

APA, American Psychiatric Association. (2013a). *Diagnostic and statistical manual of mental disorders, DSM-5*. Washington, DC: American Psychiatric Association.

APA, American Psychiatric Association. (2013b). Substance-related and addictive disorders. In *Press release* (pp. 1–2). Washington, DC: American Psychiatric Association.

Appelbaum, C. (2017, November 15). 10 popular Starbucks coffees, ranked by how much caffeine they have. *Business Insider*, pp. 1–6.

Araki, H., Suemaru, K., & Gomita, Y. (2002). Neuronal nicotinic receptor and psychiatric disorders: Functional and behavioral effects of nicotine. *The Japanese Journal of Pharmacology*, *88*(2), 133–138.

Aubin, H. J., Bobak, A., & Britton, J. R. (2008). Varenicline versus transdermal nicotine patch for smoking cessation: Results from a randomized open-label study. *Thorax*, *63*(8), 717–724. doi:10.1136/thx2007.090647

Baker, T. B., Piper, M. E., & Stein, J. H. (2016). Effects of nicotine patch vs varenicline vs combination nicotine replacement therapy on smoking cessation at 26 weeks: A randomized clinical trial. *JAMA, Journal of the American Medical Association*, *315*(4), 371–379. doi:10.1001/jama.2015.19284

Banerjee, P., Ali, Z., & Levine, B. (2014, May). Fatal caffeine intoxication: A series of eight cases from 1999 to 2009. *Journal of Forensic Sciences*, *59*(3), 865–868. doi:10.1111/1556-4029.12387

Bao, W., Liu, B., & Du, Y. (2020). Electronic cigarette use among young, middle-aged, and older adults in the United States. *JAMA Internal Medicine*, *180*(2), 313–314.

Barua, R. S., Rigotti, N. A., & Benowitz, N. L. (2018). 2018 ACC expert consensus decision pathway on tobacco cessation treatment. *Journal of the American College of Cardiology*, *72*(25), 3332–3365. doi:10.1016/j.jacc.2018.10.027

Benowitz, N. L. (1999). Biomarkers of environmental tobacco smoke exposure. *Environmental Health Perspectives*, *107*(Suppl 2), 349–355.

Benowitz, N. L. (2010). Nicotine addiction. *New England Journal of Medicine*, *362*(24), 2295–2303. doi:10.1056/NEJMra0809890

Benowitz, N. L., & Goniewicz, M. L. (2013). The regulatory challenge of electronic cigarettes. *JAMA*, *310*(7), 685–686. doi:10.1001/jama.2013.109501

Benowitz, N. L., & Jacob, P. (1984). Daily intake of nicotine during cigarette smoking. *Clinical Pharmacology and Therapeutics*, *35*(4), 499–504.

Benowitz, N. L., & Jacob, P. (2001). Trans-3'-hydroxycotinine: Disposition kinetics, effects and plasma levels during cigarette smoking. *British Journal of Clinical Pharmacology*, *51*(1), 53–59. doi:10.1046/j.1365-2125.2001.01309.x

Benowitz, N. L., Dains, K. M., & Dempsey, D. (2011, September). Racial differences in the relationship between number of cigarettes smoked and nicotine and carcinogen exposure. *Nicotine & Tobacco Research*, *13*(9), 772–783. doi:10.1093/ntr/ntr072

Benowitz, N. L., Hukkanen, J., & Jacob, P. (2009). Nicotine chemistry, metabolism, kinetics, and biomarkers. *Handbook of Experimental Pharmacology*, *192*, 29–60. doi:10.1007/978-3-540-69248-5_2

Benowitz, N. L., Lessov-Schlaggar, C. N., & Swan, G. E. (2006). Female sex and oral contraceptive use accelerate nicotine metabolism. *Clinical Pharmacology and Therapeutics*, *79*(5), 480–488. doi:10.1016/j.clpt.2006.01.008

Benowitz, N. L., Zevin, S., & Jacob, P. (1997). Sources of variability in nicotine and cotinine levels with use of nicotine nasal spray, transdermal nicotine, and cigarette smoking. *British Journal of Clinical Pharmacology*, *43*(3), 259–267.

Beral, V., Gaitskell, K., & Hermon, C. (2012). Ovarian cancer and smoking: Individual participant meta-analysis including 28,114 women with ovarian cancer from 51 epidemiological studies. *The Lancet Oncology*, *13*(9), 946–956. doi:10.1016/S1470-2045(12)70322-4

Bergin, J. E., & Kendler, K. S. (2012). Common psychiatric disorders and caffeine use, tolerance, and withdrawal: An examination of shared genetic and environmental effects. *Twin Research and Human Genetics*, *15*(4), 473–482. doi:10.1017/thg.2012.25

Blanchard, S., & Sawers, J. (1983, April). Comparative pharmacokinetics of caffeine in young and elderly men. *Journal of Pharmacokinetics and Biopharmaceutics*, *11*(2), 109–126. doi:10.1007/bf01061844

Bodkin, H. (2018, September 8). Vaping risk for elderly as pneumonia link revealed. *The Telegraph*, pp. 1–2. Telegraph Media.

Bonsignore, A., Sblano, S., & Pozzi, F. (2014, September). A case of suicide by ingestion of caffeine. *Forensic Science, Medicine, and Pathology*, *10*(3), 448–451. doi:10.1007/s120254-014-9571-6

Borota, D., Murray, E., & Keceli, G. (2014). Post-study caffeine administration enhances memory consolidation in humans. *Nature Neuroscience*, *17*(2), 201–203. doi:10.1038/nn.3623

Brown, C. J., & Cheng, J. M. (2014). Electronic cigarettes: Product characterisation and considerations. *Tobacco Control*, *23*(Suppl 2), 4–10. doi:10.1136/tobaccocontrol-2013-051476

Brown, N. (2020, March 26). 2020 coffee and beverage trends: Inside the NCA's annual report. *Daily Coffee News*, pp. 1–2. Daily Coffee News.

Buisson, B., & Bertrand, D. (2002). Nicotine addiction: The possible role of functional upregulation. *Trends in Pharmacological Sciences*, *23*(3), 130–136. doi:10.1016/S0165-6147(00)01979-9

Butt, M. S., & Sultan, M. T. (2011). Coffee and its consumption: Benefits and risks. *Critical Reviews in Science and Nutrition*, *51*(4), 363–373. doi:10.1080/10408390903586412

Cahill, K., Lindson-Hawley, N., & Thomas, K. H. (2016, May 9). Nicotine receptor partial agonists for smoking cessation. *Cochrane Database of Systematic Reviews* (5), CD006103. doi:10.1002/14651858.CD006103.pub7

Cahill, K., Stead, L. F., & Lancaster, T. (2012, April 18). Nicotine receptor partial agonists for smoking cessation. *Cochrane Database of Systematic Reviews* (4), CD006103. doi:10.1002/14651858.CD006103. . .

Cahill, K., Stevens, S., & Perera, R. (2013, May 31). Pharmacological interventions for smoking cessation: An overview and network meta-analysis. *Cochrane Database of Systematic Reviews* (5), CD009329. doi:10.1002/14651858.CD009329. . .

Caraballo, R. S., Shafer, P. R., & Patel, D. (2017, April). Quit methods used by US adult cigarette smokers, 2014–2016. *Preventing Chronic Disease*, *14*(E32), 1–5. doi:10.5888/ped14.160600

Carroll, A. J., Mathew, A. R., & Leone, F. T. (2020). Extended nicotine patch treatment among smokers with and without comorbid psychopathology. *Nicotine & Tobacco Research*, *22*(1), 24–31. doi:10.1093/ntr/nty191

Carter, B. D., Abnet, C. C., & Feskanich, D. (2015). Smoking and mortality—Beyond established causes. *The New England Journal of Medicine*, *372*(7), 631–640. doi:10.1056/NEJMsa1407211

Cataldo, J. K., Berit Petersen, A., & Hunter, M. (2015, May). E-cigarette marketing and older smokers: Road to renormalization. *American Journal of Health Behaviors*, *39*(3), 361–371. doi:10.5993/AJHB.39.3.9

Cawkwell, P. B., Blaum, C., & Sherman, S. E. (2015, May). Pharmacological smoking cessation therapies in older adults: A review of the evidence. *Drugs & Aging*, *32*, 443–451.

CBC News. (2015, June 1). Tobacco companies ordered to pay $15B in damages. *CBC News*.

CDC, Centers for Disease Control and Prevention. (2010a). Vital signs: Nonsmokers' exposure to secondhand smoke—United States, 1999–2008. *MMWR, Morbidity and Mortality Weekly Report*, *59*(35), 1141–1146. Retrieved October 7, 2016, from www.cdc.gov/mmwr/preview/mmwrhtml/mm5935a4.htm

CDC, Centers for Disease Control and Prevention. (2010b). *How tobacco smoke causes disease: The biology and behavioral basis for smoking-attributable disease*. Atlanta: National Center for Chronic Disease Prevention and Health Promotion, Office on Smoking and Health.

CDC, Centers for Disease Control and Prevention. (2016a, September 28). *Becky's story* (p. 1). Centers for Disease Control and Prevention. Retrieved November 11, 2016, from www.cdc.gov/tobacco/campaign/tips/quit-smoking/index.html?s_cid=OSH_tips_D9317

CDC, Centers for Disease Control and Prevention. (2016b, October 22). *Rose's story* (p. 1). Retrieved November 11, 2016, from www.cdc.gov/tobacco/campaign/tips/quit-smoking/index.html?s_cid=OSH_tips_D9317

CDC, Centers for Disease Control and Prevention. (2018a, January 17). *Low-yield cigarettes*. Office on Smoking and Health, National Center for Chronic Disease Prevention and Health Promotion.

CDC, Centers for Disease Control and Prevention. (2018b, April 20). CDC's tips from former smokers: Anti-smoking campaign launches seventh year. *Media Advisory*, p. 1. CDC.

CDC, Centers for Disease Control and Prevention. (2019a, April 1). Smoking and COPD. *Tips From Former Smokers*, pp. 1–2. Centers for Disease Control and Prevention.

CDC, Centers for Disease Control and Prevention. (2019b, February 25). Burden of tobacco use in the U.S.: Current cigarette smoking among U.S. adults aged 18 years and older. In *Tips from former smokers* (pp. 1–5). Atlanta, GA: Centers for Disease Control and Prevention.

CDC, Centers for Disease Control and Prevention. (2019c, September 18). What are the risk factors for lung cancer? In *Lung cancer* (pp. 1–2). Bethesda, MD: U.S. Department of Health and Human Services.

CDC, Centers for Disease Control and Prevention. (2020, March 23). CDC's 2020 tips from former smokers features all-new stories & ads. In *Tips* (p. 1). Atlanta, GA: CDC.

Chang, C. P., Huang, W. H., & You, C. H. (2019). Factors correlated with smoking cessation success in older adults: A retrospective cohort study in Taiwan. *International Journal of Environmental Research and Public Health*, *16*(18), 3462–3469. doi:10.3390/ijerph16183462

Chang, P. H., Chiang, C. H., & Ho, W. C. (2015). Combination therapy of varenicline with nicotine replacement therapy is better than varenicline alone: A systematic review and meta-analysis of randomized controlled trials. *BMC Public Health*, *15*, 689. doi:10.1186/s12889-015-2055-2055-0

Chun, L. F., Moazed, F., & Calfee, C. S. (2017, August 1). Pulmonary toxicity of e-cigarettes. *American Journal of Physiology, Lung Cellular and Molecular Physiology*, *13*(2), L193–L206. doi:10.1152/ajplung.00071.2017

Collins, A. C. (1990). An analysis of the addiction liability of nicotine. *Advances in Alcohol & Substance Abuse*, *9*(1–2), 83–101. Retrieved from www.tandfonline.com/doi/abs/10.1300/J251v09n01_06

Commonwealth of Australia. (2013). *Smoking and disadvantage*. Canberra, ACT: Australian National Preventive Health Agency.

Corelli, R. L., & Hudmon, K. S. (2006). Pharmacologic interventions for smoking cessation. *Critical Care Nursing Clinics of North America, 18*(1), 39–51.

Covey, L. S., & Glassman, A. H. (1991). New approaches to smoking cessation. *Physician Assistant, 15*, 69, 70, 73, 74, 77.

Cox, L. S., Nollen, N. L., & Mayo, M. S. (2012). Bupropion for smoking cessation in African American light smokers: A randomized controlled study. *Journal of the National Cancer Institute, 104*(4), 290–298. doi:10.1093/jnci/djr513

Crain, D., & Bhat, A. (2010). Current treatment options in smoking cessation. *Hospital Practice (Minneapolis), 38*(1), 53–61.

Creamer, M. R., Wang, T. W., & Babb, S. (2019, November 15). Tobacco product use and cessation indicators among adults—United States, 2018. *MMWR, Morbidity and Mortality Weekly Report, 68*(45), 1013–1019.

Cross, S. J., Lotfipour, S., & Leslie, F. M. (2017, March). Mechanisms and genetic factors underlying co-use of nicotine and alcohol or other drugs of abuse. *The American Journal of Drug and Alcohol Abuse, 43*(2), 171–185. doi:10.1080/00952990.2016.1209512

Curtis, D. R., & Eccles, R. M. (1958). The excitation of Renshaw cells by pharmacological agents applied electrophoretically. *The Journal of Physiology, 141*, 435–445.

Czogala, J., Goniewicz, M. L., & Fidelus, B. (2014, June). Secondhand exposure to vapors from electronic cigarettes. *Nicotine & Tobacco Research, 16*(6), 655–662. doi:10.1093/ntr/ntt203

D'Allessandro, A., Boeckelmann, I., & Hammwhoner, M. (2012). Nicotine, cigarette smoking and cardiac arrhythmia: An overview. *European Journal of Preventive Cardiology, 19*(3), 297–305.

Danaei, G., Ding, E. L., & Mozaffarian, D. (2009). The preventable causes of death in the United States: Comparative risk assessment of dietary, lifestyle, and metabolic risk factors. *PLoS Medicine, 6*(4), e1000058. doi:10.1371/journal.pmed.1000058

Dani, J. A., & De Biasi, M. (2001). Cellular mechanisms of nicotine addiction. *Pharmacology Biochemistry and Behavior, 70*(4), 439–446.

Dani, J. A., Ji, D., & Zhou, F. M. (2001). Synaptic plasticity and nicotine addiction. *Neuron, 31*(3), 349–352.

De Biasi, M., & Dani, J. A. (2011). Reward, addiction, withdrawal to nicotine. *Annual Review of Neuroscience, 34*, 105–130. doi:10.1146//annurev-neuro-061010-113734

Degens, H., Gayan-Ramirez, G., & van Hees, H. W. (2015). Smoking-induced skeletal muscle dysfunction: From evidence to mechanisms. *American Journal of Respiratory and Critical Care Medicine, 191*(6), 620–625. doi:10.1164/rccm.201410-1830PP

Delnevo, C. D., Giovenco, D. P., & Steinberg, M. B. (2016). Patterns of electronic cigarette use among adults in the United States. *Nicotine & Tobacco Research, 18*(5), 715–719. doi:10.1093/ntr/ntv237

Derby, K. S., Cuthrell, K., & Caberto, C. (2008). Nicotine metabolism in three ethnic/racial groups with different risks of lung cancer. *Cancer Epidemiology, Biomarkers & Prevention, 17*(12), 3526–3535. doi:10.1158/1055-9965.EP1-08-0424

Dews, P. B., O'Brien, C. P., & Bergman, J. (2002). Caffeine: Behavioral effects of withdrawal and related issues. *Food and Chemical Toxicology, 40*(9), 1257–1261.

DiFranza, J. R., Wellman, R. J., & Savageau, J. A. (2013). What aspect of dependence does the fagerstrom test for nicotine dependence measure? *Addiction, Article ID 906276*, 1–8.

DiFranza, J. R., Wellman, R. J., & Ursprung, S. (2009). The autonomy over smoking scale. *Psychology of Addictive Behaviors, 23*, 656–665.

Dik, V. K., Bueno-de-Mesquita, H. B., & Van Oijen, M. G. (2014). Coffee and tea consumption, genotype-based CYP1A2 and NAT2 activity and colorectal cancer risk-results from the EPIC cohort study. *International Journal of Cancer, 135*(2), 401–412. doi:10.1002/ijc.28655

Ding, Y. S., Yan, X. J., & Jain, R. B. (2006). Determination of 14 polycyclic aromatic hydrocarbons in mainstream smoke from U. S. brand and non-U. S. brand cigarettes. *Environmental Science & Technology, 40*(4), 1133–1138.

Doll, R., & Hill, A. B. (1950, September 30). Smoking and carcinoma of the lung. *British Medical Journal, 2*(4682), 739–748. doi:10.1136/bmj.2.4682.739

Domino, E. F., Hornbach, E., & Demana, T. (1993). The nicotine content of common vegetables. *The New England Journal of Medicine, 329*, 437. doi:10.1056/NEJM199308053290619

Ebbert, J. O., Wyatt, K. D., & Hays, J. T. (2010). Varenicline for smoking cessation: Efficacy, safety, and treatment recommendations. *Patient Preference and Adherence, 4*, 355–362.

Ebbert, J. O., Wyatt, K. D., & Zirakzadeh, A. (2009). Clinical utility of varenicline for smokers with medical and psychiatric comorbidities. *International Journal of Chronic Obstructive Pulmonary Disease, 4*, 421–430. doi:10.2147/cvopd.s6300

Echeverri, D., Montes, F. R., & Cabrera, M. (2010). Caffeine's vascular mechanisms of action. *International Journal of Vascular Medicine, 2010*(834060), 1–10. doi:10.1155/2010/834060

Echeverri, D., Montes, F. R., & Cabrera, M. (2019). Corrigendum to "caffeine's vascular mechanisms of action". *International Journal of Vascular Medicine, 2019*(7480780), 1. doi:10.1155/2019/7480780

Electronic nicotine delivery systems. (2014, July 21). *World health organization to 6th session of the conference of the parties to the WHO framework convention on tobacco control* (pp. 2–3). doi:fctc/PDF/cop6/fctc_COP6_10-en.pdf?ua=1

English, J. P., Willius, F. A., & Berkson, J. (1940, October 19). Tobacco and coronary disease. *JAMA, 115*(16), 1327–1329. doi:10.1001/jama.1940.02810420013004

Etzel, C. J., Kachroo, S., & Liu, M. (2008, September). Development and validation of a lung cancer risk prediction model for African-Americans. *Cancer Prevention Research, 1*(4), 255–265. doi:10.1158/1940-6207.CAPR-08-0082

Evatt, D. P., Juliano, L. M., & Griffiths, R. R. (2016). A brief manualized treatment for problematic caffeine use: A randomized control trial. *Journal of Consulting and Clinical Psychology, 84*(2), 113–121. doi:10.1037/ccp0000064

Fabrizio, C., Desiderio, M., & Coyne, R. F. (2016). Electrocardiogram abnormalities of caffeine overdose. *Circulation: Arrhythmia and Electrophysiology, 9*, 1–4. doi:10.1161/CIRCEP.115.003088

Faessel, H. M., Obach, R. S., & Rollema, H. (2010). A review of the clinical pharmacokinetics and pharmacodynamics of varenicline for smoking cessation. *Clinical Pharmacokinetics, 49*(12), 799–816. doi:10.2165/11537850-00000000-00000

Fagan, P., Moolchan, E. T., & Pokhrel, P. (2015). Biomarkers of tobacco smoke exposure in racial/ethnic groups at high risk for lung cancer. *American Journal of Public Health, 105*(6), 1237–1245. doi:10.2105/AJPH.2014.302492

Falck, S. (2017, October 6). Can you overdose on too much nicotine? *Medical News Today*, pp. 1–4. Healthline Media.

Fant, R. V., Buchhalter, A. R., & Buchman, A. C. (2009). Pharmacotherapy for tobacco dependence. *Handbook of Experimental Pharmacology, 192*, 487–510.

Farber, M. (2020, June 12). California woman dies of vaping-related lung injury, officials say. *Fox News*. Fox News Corporation.

FDA, U.S. Food and Drug Administration. (2010). *Guidance for industry and FDA staff: Use of "light," "mild," "low," or similar descriptors in the labeling or advertising of tobacco products*. Rockville, MD: USFDA, Center for Tobacco Products. Retrieved January 17, 2018, from www.fda.gov/TobaccoProducts/GuidanceComplianceRegulatoryInformation/ucm214597.htm

FDA, U.S. Food and Drug Administration. (2016a, August 8). *Extending authorities to all tobacco products, including e-cigarettes, cigars, and hookah*. Retrieved July 16, 2017, from www.fda.gov/TobaccoProducts/Labeling/RulesRegulationsGuidance/ucm388395.htm

FDA, U.S. Food and Drug Administration. (2016b, December 16). Chantix (varenicline) and Zyban (bupropion): Drug safety communication—Mental health side effects revised. In *Safety alerts for human medical products* (pp. 1–12). Silver Spring, MD: U.S. Food and Drug Administration.

FDA, U.S. Food and Drug Administration. (2018, December 12). Spilling the beans: How much caffeine is too much? In *E-Mail updates* (pp. 1–6). Silver Spring, MD: FDA.

FDA, U.S. Food and Drug Administration. (2020, January 2). FDA finalizes enforcement policy on unauthorized flavored cartridge-based e-cigarettes that appeal to children including fruit and mint. *FDA News Release*. FDA.

FDA, U.S. Food and Drug Administration. (2009, July 1). FDA requires new boxed warnings for the smoking cessation drugs Chantix and Zyban. *Public Health Advisory*. Retrieved from www.fda.gov/Drugs/DrugSafety/PostmarketDrugSafetyInformationforPatientsandP . . .

Felman, A. (2019, November 7). Is caffeine bad for you? *Medical News Today*, pp. 1–10. Healthline Media.

Fiore, M. C., Jaen, C. R., & Baker, T. B. (2008). *Treating tobacco use and dependence: 2008 update*. Bethesda, MD: U.S. Department of Health and Human Services.

Fircanis, S., Merriam, P., & Khan, N. (2014). The relation between cigarette smoking and risk of acute myeloid leukemia: An updated meta-analysis of epidemiological studies. *American Journal of Hematology*, *89*(8). doi:10.1002/ajh.23744

Fisone, G., Borgkvist, A., & Usiello, A. (2004, April). Caffeine as a psychomotor stimulant: Mechanism of action. *Cellular and Molecular Life Sciences*, *61*(7–8), 857–872. doi:10.1007/s00018-003-3269-3

Fluharty, M., Taylor, A. E., & Grabski, M. (2017). The association of cigarette smoking with depression and anxiety: A systematic review. *Nicotine & Tobacco Research*, 3–13.

Foulds, J., Veldheer, S., & Berg, A. (2011). Electronic cigarettes (e-cigs): Views of aficionados and clinical/public health perspectives. *International Journal of Clinical Practice*, *65*(10), 1037–1042. doi:10.1111/j.1742-1241.2011.02751.x

Fredholm, B. B., Arsian, G., & Halldner, L. (2000, November). Structure and function of adenosine receptors and their genes. *Naunyn Schmiedeberg's Archives of Pharmacology*, *362*(4–5), 364–374. doi:10.1007/s002100000313

Fredholm, B. B., IJzerman, A. P., & Jacobson, K. A. (2001). International Union of Pharmacology. XXV. Nomenclature and classification of adenosine receptors. *Pharmacological Reviews*, *53*, 527–552.

Frishman, W. H. (2007). Smoking cessation pharmacotherapy—Nicotine and non-nicotine preparations. *Preventive Cardiology*, *10*(2) (Suppl 1), 10–22.

Fulgoni, V. L., Keast, D. R., & Lieberman, H. R. (2015). Trends in intake and sources of caffeine in the diets of US adults: 2001–2010. *American Journal of Clinical Nutrition*, *101*(5), 1081–1087. doi:10.3945/ajcn.113.080077

Gallaway, M. S., Henley, S. J., & Steele, C. B. (2018, November 2). Surveillance for cancers associated with tobacco use—United States, 2010–2014. *MMWR, Morbidity and Mortality Weekly Report*, *67*(12), 1–42.

Gamaleddin, I. H., Trigo, J. M., & Gueye, A. B. (2015). Role of endogenous cannabinoid system in nicotine addiction: Novel insights. *Frontiers in Psychiatry*, *6*(Article 41), 1–2. doi:10.3389/psyt.2015.00041

Garrison, G. D., & Dugan, S. E. (2009). Varenicline: A first-line treatment option for smoking cessation. *Clinical Therapeutics*, *31*(3), 463–491.

Generali, J. A. (1992). Nicotine transdermal patches. *Facts and Comparisons Drug Newsletter*, *11*, 33–34.

Gierach, G. L., Freedman, N. D., & Andaya, A. (2012). Coffee intake and breast cancer risk in the NIH-AARP diet and health study cohort. *International Journal of Cancer*, *131*(2), 452–460. doi:10.1002/ijc.26372

Gluckman, T. (2010, July). *Ask an expert: How does caffeine affect the heart? Oregon and Southwest*. Washington: Providence Health & Services.

Gomes, T., Ladeira, I., & Guimaraes, M. (2012). Factors associated with relapse in smoking cessation. *European Respiratory Journal*, *40*(P4043).

Goniewicz, M. L., Gawron, M., & Smith, D. M. (2017, February). Exposure to nicotine and selected toxicants in cigarette smokers who switched to electronic cigarettes: A longitudinal within-subjects observational study. *Nicotine & Tobacco Research*, *19*(2), 160–167. doi:10.1093/ntr/ntw160

Goniewicz, M. L., Kuma, T., & Gawron, M. (2013). Nicotine levels in electronic cigarettes. *Nicotine & Tobacco Research*, *15*(1), 158–166.

Gonzales, D., Rennard, S. I., & Nides, M. (2006). Varenicline: An alpha4beta2 nicotine acetylcholine receptor partial agonist vs. sustained-release bupropion and placebo for smoking cessation. *JAMA, The Journal of the American Medical Association*, *296*(1), 47–55.

Goodwin, R. D., Keyes, K. M., & Hasin, D. S. (2009). Changes in cigarette use and nicotine dependence in the United States: Evidence from the 2001–2002 wave of the national epidemiologic survey of alcoholism and related conditions. *American Journal of Public Health*, *99*(8), 1471–1477.

Grabovac, I., Oberndorfer, M., & Fischer, J. (2021). Effectiveness of electronic cigarettes in smoking cessation: A systematic review and meta-analysis. *Nicotine & Tobacco Research*, *23*(4), 625–634. doi:10.1093/ntaa181

Grana, R., Benowitz, N., & Glantz, S. A. (2014, May 13). Contemporary reviews in cardiovascular medicine: E-Cigarettes: A scientific review. In *Circulation* (Vol. 129, pp. 1972–1986). Dallas, Texas: American Heart Association. doi:10.116/CIRCULATIONAHA.114007667, p. 1978

Graves, B. M., Johnson, T. J., & Nishida, R. T. (2020, April 20). Comprehensive characterization of mainstream marijuana and tobacco smoke. *Nature*, *10*(article 7160), 1–12. doi:10.1038/s41598-020-63120-6

Guais, A., Brand, G., & Jacquot, L. (2011). Toxicity of carbon dioxide: A review. *Chemical Research in Toxicology*, *24*(12), 2061–2070. doi:10.1021/tx200220r

Hackshaw, A., Morris, J. K., & Boniface, S. (2018). Low cigarette consumption and risk of coronary heart disease and stroke: Meta-analysis of 141 cohort studies in 55 study reports. *BMJ*, 1–15. doi:10.1136/bmj.j3984

Hahn, B. (2015). Nicotine receptors and attention. *Current Topics in Behavioral Neurosciences*, *23*, 103–135. doi:10.1007/978-3-319-13665-3_5

Hajel, P., Phillips-Waller, A., & Przulj, D. (2019). A randomized trial of e-cigarettes versus nicotine-replacement therapy. *New England Journal of Medicine, 380*, 629–637. doi:10.1056/NEJMoa1808779

Harrar, S. (2019, October 17). Vaping dangers for older adults. *AARP Interest Notes*, pp. 1–3. AARP, American Association of Retired People.

Hartz, S. M., Short, S. E., & Saccone, N. L. (2012). Increased genetic vulnerability to smoking at CHRNA5 in early-onset smokers. *Archives of General Psychiatry, 69*(8), 854–860. doi:10.1001/archgenpsychiatry.2012.124

Hays, J. T., Croghan, I. T., & Schroeder, D. R. (2010). Varenicline for tobacco dependence treatment in recovering alcohol-dependent smokers: An open-label pilot study. *Journal of Substance Abuse Treatment, 40*(1), 102–107.

Health Canada. (2011, March 29). Carcinogens in tobacco smoke. *Healthy Living*, pp. 1–4. Government of Canada.

Health Canada. (2016, May). *Benefits of quitting smoking*. Ottawa, ON: Government of Canada.

Health Canada. (2017, May 25). Health Canada is advising Canadians about safe levels of caffeine consumption. In *Information update*. Ottawa, ON: Government of Canada.

Heatherton, T. F., Kozlowski, L. T., & Frecker, R. C. (1991). The fagerstrom test for nicotine dependence: A revision of the fagerstrom tolerance questionnaire. *British Journal of Addiction, 86*(9), 1119–1127.

Hecht, S. S. (2014). It is time to regulate carcinogenic tobacco-specific nitrosamines in cigarette tobacco. *Cancer Prevention Research, 7*(7), 639–647. doi:10.1158/1940-6207???

Heckman, C. J., Egleston, B. L., & Hofmann, M. T. (2010, October). Efficacy of motivational interviewing for smoking cessation: A systematic review and meta-analysis. *Tobacco Control, 19*(5), 410–416. doi:10.1136/tc.2009.033175

Heeschen, C., Weis, M., & Aicher, A. (2002). A novel angiogenic pathway mediated by non-neuronal nicotinic acetylcholine receptors. *Journal of Clinical Investigation, 110*(4), 527–536. doi:10.1172/JCI14676

Henley, S. J., Asman, K., & Momin, B. (2019, August). Smoking cessation behaviors among older U.S. adults. *Preventive Medicine Reports, 16*(100978), 1–9. doi:10.1016/j.pmedr.2019.100978

Henley, S. J., Thomas, C. C., & Sharapova, S. R. (2016). Vital signs: Disparities in tobacco-related cancer incidence and mortality—United States, 2004–2013. *MMWR, Morbidity and Mortality Weekly Report, 65*, 1212–1218. Retrieved from http://dx.doi.org/10.15585/mmwr.mm6544a3

Herman, A. I., & Sofuoglu, M. (2013). Medications to treat addictions: Nicotine replacement. In *Interventions for addiction* (Vol. 3, pp. 337–343). West Haven, CT: Yale University.

Herman, A. O. (2017, November 27). Coffee's numerous health benefits detailed in new analysis. *NEJM, New England Journal of Medicine, 1*. Retrieved from www.jwatch.org/fw113569/2017/11/27/coffees-numerous-health-benefits-detailed-new-analysis?query=pfwTOC&jwd=0000200002443&jspc=

Hettema, J. E., & Hendricks, P. S. (2010). Motivational interviewing for smoking cessation: A meta-analytic review. *Journal of Consulting and Clinical Psychology, 78*(6), 868–884.

Higdon, J. V., & Frei, B. (2006). Coffee and health: A review of recent human research. *Critical Reviews in Food Science and Nutrition, 46*(2), 101–123. doi:10.1080/10408390500400009

Hindmarch, I., Rigney, U., & Stanley, N. (2000, April). A naturalistic investigation of the effects of day-long consumption of tea, coffee and water on alertness, sleep onset and sleep quality. *Psychopharmacology, 149*(3), 203–216.

Ho, M. K., & Tyndale, R. F. (2007). Overview of the pharmacogenomics of cigarette smoking. *Pharmacogenomics Journal, 7*(2), 81–98.

Hoffmann, D., & Hoffmann, I. (1997). The changing cigarette, 1950–1995. *Journal of Toxicology and Environmental Health, 50*(4), 307–364.

Horn, J. R., & Hansten, P. D. (2007, November 1). Get to know an enzyme: CYP1A2. *Pharmacy Times*.

Hu, D. (2018, September 13). Natural vs. added caffeine: What's the difference? *Food Insight*, pp. 1–2. International Food Information Council Foundation.

Hughes, J. R., Klemperer, E. M., & Peasley-Miklus, C. (2020). Possible new symptoms of tobacco withdrawal II: Anhedonia—A systematic review. *Nicotine & Tobacco Research, 22*(1), 11–17. doi:10.1093/ntr/nty171

Hughes, J. R., Peters, E. N., & Callas, P. W. (2020). Withdrawal symptoms from e-cigarette abstinence among former smokers: A pre-post clinical trial. *Nicotine & Tobacco Research, 22*(5), 734–739. doi:10.1093/ntr/ntz129

Hukkanen, J., Jacob, P., & Benowitz, N. L. (2005, April). Metabolism and disposition kinetics of nicotine. *Pharmacological Reviews, 57*(1), 79–115. doi:10.1124/pr.57.1.3

Huntley, E. D., & Juliano, L. M. (2012). Caffeine expectancy questionnaire (CaffEQ): Construction, psychometric properties, and associations with caffeine use, caffeine dependence, and other related variables. *Psychological Assessment, 24*(3), 592–607. doi:10.1037/a0026417

Hyde, R. F., Paxton, R., & Carr, T. E. (1982, September 18). Nicotine chewing-gum. *British Medical Journal (Clinical Research Edition), 285*(6344), 811–812.

Jabbar, S. B., & Hanly, M. G. (2013, December). Fatal caffeine overdose: A case report and review of literature. *The American Journal of Forensic Medicine and Pathology, 34*(4), 321–324. doi:10.1097/PAF.0000000000000058

Johnstone, E., Benowitz, N., & Cargill, A. (2006, October). Determinants of the rate of nicotine metabolism and effects on smoking behavior. *Clinical Pharmacology and Therapeutics, 80*(4), 319–330. doi:10.1016/j.cjpt.2006.06.011

Jones, A. W. (2017, April 1). Review of caffeine-related fatalities along with postmortem blood concentrations in 51 poisoning deaths. *Journal of Analytical Toxicology, 41*(3), 167–172. doi:10.1093/jat/bkx011

Jorenby, D. E., Hays, J. T., & Rigotti, N. A. (2006). Efficacy of varenicline, an alpha4beta2 nicotinic acetylcholine receptor partial agonist, vs. placebo or sustained-release bupropion for smoking cessation: A randomized controlled study. *JAMA, The Journal of the American Medical Association, 296*(1), 56–63.

Juliano, L. M., & Griffiths, R. R. (2004). A critical review of caffeine withdrawal: Empirical validation of symptoms and signs, incidence, severity, and associated features. *Psychopharmacology (Berlin), 176*, 1–29. doi:10.1007/s00213-004-2000-x

Juliano, L. M., Evatt, D. P., & Richards, P. D. (2012). Characterization of individuals seeking treatment for caffeine dependence. *Psychology of Addictive Behaviors, 26*(4), 948–954. doi:10.1037/a0027246

Kalkhoran, S., Chang, Y., & Rigotti, N. A. (2020). Electronic cigarette use and cigarette abstinence over 2 years among U.S. smokers in the population assessment of tobacco and health study. *Nicotine & Tobacco Research, 22*(5), 728–733. doi:10.1093/ntr/ntz114

Kavuluru, R., Han, S., & Hahn, E. J. (2018, April 13). On the popularity of the USB flash drive-shaped electronic cigarette Juul. *Tobacco Control*. doi:10.1136/tobaccocontrol-2018-054259

Kennedy, C. R., & Abraham, S. (2017). Association between coffee consumption and different types of cancers: A review of meta-analysis. *Cogent Psychology*, *4*(1). doi:10.1080/23311908.2017.1392230

Kenny, P. J., & Markou, A. (2001). Neurobiology of the nicotine withdrawal syndrome. *Pharmacology Biochemistry and Behavior*, *70*(4), 531–549.

Kimura, R., Ushiyama, N., & Fujii, T. (2003). Nicotine-induced Ca2+ signaling and down-regulation of nicotinic acetylcholine receptor subunit expression in the CEM human leukemic T-cell line. *Life Sciences*, *72*(18–19), 2155–2158.

King, B. A., Dube, S. R., & Tynan, M. A. (2012). Current tobacco use among adults in the United States: Findings from the national adult tobacco survey. *American Journal of Public Health*, *102*(11), e93–e100.

Kinugawa, T., Kurita, T., & Nohara, R. (2011). A case of atrial tachycardia sensitive to increased caffeine intake. *International Heart Journal*, *52*(6), 398–400.

Klatsky, A. L., Hasan, A. S., & Armstrong, M. A. (2011, Summer). Coffee, caffeine, and risk of hospitalization for arrhythmias. *The Permanente Journal*, *15*(3), 19–25.

Krebs, N. M., Chen, A., & Zhu, J. (2016, July 1). Comparison of puff volume with cigarettes per day in predicting nicotine uptake among daily smokers. *American Journal of Epidemiology*, *184*(1), 48–57. doi:10.1093/aje/kwv341

Kulak, J. A., & LaValley, S. (2018, January–June). Cigarette use and smoking beliefs among older Americans: Findings from a nationally representative survey. *Journal of Addictive Diseases*, *37*(1–2), 46–54. doi:10.1080/10550887.2018.1521255

Kuper, H., Boffetta, P., & Adami, H. O. (2002). Tobacco use and cancer causation: Association by tumour type. *Journal of Internal Medicine*, *252*(3), 206–224.

Laniado-Laborin, R. (2010). Smoking cessation intervention: An evidence-based approach. *Postgraduate Medicine*, *122*(2), 74–82. doi:10.3810/pgm.2010.03.2124

Lee, B. E., Jacob, P., & Jarvik, M. E. (1989, July). Food and nicotine metabolism. *Pharmacology Biochemistry and Behavior*, *33*(3), 621–625. doi:10.1016/0091-3057(89)90398-5

Lee, C., & Kahende, J. (2007, August). Factors associated with successful smoking cessation in the United States, 2000. *American Journal of Public Health*, *97*(8), 1503–1509.

Leone, F. T., Zhang, Y., & Evers-Casey, S. (2020, July 15). Initiating pharmacologic treatment in tobacco-dependent adults. *American Journal of Respiratory and Critical Care Medicine*, *202*(2), e5–e31. doi:10.1164/rccm.202005-1982ST

Lichtenstein, E. (1999). Nicotine anonymous: Community resource and research implications. *Psychology of Addictive Behaviors*, *13*(1), 60–68. doi:10.1037/0893-164X.13.1.60

Lichtenstein, E., Zhu, S.-H., & Tedeschi, G. J. (2010, May–June). Smoking cessation quitlines. *American Psychologist*, *65*(4), 252–261. doi:10.1037/a0018598

Lieberman, H. R., Agarwal, S., & Fulgoni, V. L. (2019). Daily patterns of caffeine intake and the association of intake with multiple sociodemographic and lifestyle factors in US adults based on the NHANES 2007–2012 surveys. *Journal of the Academy of Nutrition and Dietetics*, *19*(1), 106–114.

Liguori, A., Hughes, J. R., & Grass, J. A. (1997, November). Absorption and subjective effects of caffeine from coffee, cola and capsules. *Pharmacology Biochemistry and Behavior*, *58*(3), 721–726. doi:10.1016/S0091-3057(97)00003-8

Lindsdon-Hawley, N., Hartmann-Boyce, J., & Fanshawe, T. R. (2016, October 13). Interventions to reduce harm from continued tobacco use. *The Cochrane Database of Systematic Reviews*, *10*, CD005231. doi:10.1002/14651858.CD005231.pub3

Lindson-Hawley, N., Thompson, T. P., & Begh, R. (2015). Motivational interviewing for smoking cessation. *Cochrane Database of Systematic Reviews* (3), CD006936. doi:10.1002/14651858.CD006936.pub3

Lindson-Hawley, N., Thompson, T. P., & Ferrey, A. (2019, July 31). Motivational interviewing for smoking cessation. *Cochrane Systematic Review*, 1–2. doi:10.1002/14651856.CD006936.pub4

Loftfield, E., Freedman, N. D., & Dodd, K. W. (2016, September). Coffee drinking is widespread in the United States, but usual intake varies by demographic and lifestyle factors. *The Journal of Nutrition, 146*(9), 1762–1768. doi:10.3945/jn.116.233940

Lorist, M. M., & Tops, M. (2003). Caffeine, fatigue, and cognition. *Brain and Cognition, 53*(1), 82–94.

Maessen, G. C., Wijnhoven, A. M., & Neijzen, R. L. (2020). Nicotine intoxication by e-cigarette liquids: A study of case reports and pathophysiology. *Clinical Toxicology, 58*(1), 1–8. doi:10.1080/15563650.2019.1636994

Malaiyandi, V., Sellers, E. M., & Tyndale, R. E. (2005, March). Implications of CYP2A6 genetic variation for smoking behaviors and nicotine dependence. *Clinical Pharmacology and Therapeutics, 77*(3), 145–158. doi:10.1016/j.clpt.2004.10.011

Malson, J. L., Sims, K., & Murty, R. (2001). Comparison of the nicotine content of tobacco used in bidis and conventional cigarettes. *Tobacco Control, 10*, 181–183.

Marengo, K., & Sissons, C. (2019, January 16). Can you overdose on caffeine? *Medical News Today*, pp. 1–10.

Martyn, D., Lau, A., & Richardson, P. (2018, January). Temporal patterns of caffeine intake in the United States. *Food and Chemical Toxicology, 111*, 71–83. doi:10.1016/j.fct.2017.10.059

Massey, L. K. (1998). Caffeine and the elderly. *Drugs & Aging, 13*(1), 43–50.

Mathew, A. R., Wahlquist, A. E., & Garrett-Mayer, E. (2014, October). Affective motives for smoking among early-stage smokers. *Nicotine & Tobacco Research, 16*(10), 1387–1393. doi:10.1093/ntr/ntu093

Mattia, A. (2013, August 15–16). *Regulatory status of caffeine* (pp. 1–17). Rockville, MD: CFSAN Office of Food Additive Safety.

Maughan, R. J., & Griffin, J. (2003, December). Caffeine ingestion and fluid balance: A review. *Journal of Human Nutrition and Dietetics, 16*(6), 411–420.

Mayer, B. (2014). How much nicotine kills a human? Tracing back the generally accepted lethal dose to dubious self-experiments in the nineteenth century. *Archives of Toxicology, 88*(1), 5–7. doi:10.1007/s00204-013-1127-0

Mayo Clinic Staff. (2020, March 6). *Caffeine: How much is too much? Newsletter*. Rochester, NY: Mayo Clinic.

McKeganey, N., Russell, C., & Haseen, F. (2020). Awareness of the presence of nicotine in the JUUL brand of e-cigarettes among adolescents, young adults, and older adults in the United States. *Drugs: Education, Prevention and Policy, 27*(6), 451–461. doi:10.1080/09687637.2020.1733932

McLaughlin, I., Dani, J. A., & De Biasi, M. (2015). Nicotine withdrawal. *Current Topics in Behavioral Neurosciences, 24*, 99–123. doi:10.1007/978-3-319-13482-6_4

McLellan, T. M., Caldwell, J. A., & Lieberman, H. R. (2016). A review of caffeine's effects on cognitive, physical and occupational performance. *Neuroscience and Biobehavioral Reviews, 71*, 294–312.

Mendes, E. (2018, April 3). Coffee and cancer: What the research really shows. *ACS Research*, pp. 1–2. American Cancer Society.

Meredith, S. E., Juliano, J. L., & Hughes, J. R. (2013). Caffeine use disorder: A comprehensive review and research agenda. *Journal of Caffeine Research, 3*(3), 114–130. doi:10.1089/jcr.20123.0016

Merritt, L. L., Martin, R., & Walters, C. (2008, August). The endogenous cannabinoid system modulates nicotine reward and dependence. *Journal of Pharmacology and Experimental Therapeutics*, *326*(2), 483–492. doi:10.1124/jpet.108.138321

Mikosz, C. A., Danielson, M., & Anderson, K. N. (2019, December 20). Characteristics of patients experiencing rehospitalization or death after hospital discharge in a nationwide outbreak of E-cigarette, or vaping, product use—associated lung injury—United States, 2019. *MMWR, Morbidity and Mortality Weekly Report*, *68*, 1–7.

Mineur, Y. S., & Picciotto, M. R. (2010). Nicotine receptors and depression: Revisiting and revising the cholinergic hypothesis. *Trends in Pharmacological Sciences*, *31*(12), 580–586. doi:10.1016/j.tips.2010.09.004

Mineur, Y. S., Abizaid, A., & Rao, Y. (2011, June 10). Nicotine decreases food intake through activation of POMC neurons. *Science*, *332*(6035), 1330–1332. doi:10.1126/science.1201889

Mishra, A., Chaturvedi, P., & Datta, S. (2015). Harmful effects of nicotine. *Indian Journal of Medical Paediatric Oncology*, *36*(1, January–March), 24–31. doi:10.4103/0971-5851.151771

Mitchell, D. C., Knight, C. A., & Hockenberry, J. (2014). Beverage caffeine intakes in the U. S. *Food and Clinical Toxicology*, *63*, 136–142.

Molander, L., Hansson, A., & Lunell, E. (2001). Pharmacokinetics of nicotine in healthy elderly people. *Clinical Pharmacology and Therapeutics*, *69*(1), 57–65.

Mons, U., Muezzinler, A., & Gellert, C. (2015). Impact of smoking and smoking cessation on cardiovascular events and mortality among older adults: Meta-analysis of individual participant data from prospective cohort studies of the CHANCES consortium. *BMJ*, *350*(h1551), 1–12. doi:10.1136/bmj.h1551

Moran-Santa Maria, M. M., Flanagan, J., & Brady, K. (2014). Ovarian hormones and drug abuse. *Current Psychiatry Reports*, *16*(11), 511–522. doi:10.1007/s11920-014-0511-7

Moritz, E. D., Zapata, L. B., & Lekiachvili, A. (2019, October 28). Update: Characteristics of patients in a national outbreak of E-cigarette, or vaping, product use—associated lung injuries—United States, October 2019. *MMWR, Morbidity and Mortality Weekly Report*, *68*, 1–5.

Muraro, L., Longo, L., & Geraldini, F. (2016, October). Intralipid in acute caffeine intoxication: A case report. *Journal of Anesthesia*, *30*(5), 895–899. doi:10.1007/s00540-016-2198-x

Murray, A., & Traylor, J. (2020). *Caffeine toxicity*. Treasure Island, FL: StatPearls Publishing.

Mwenifumbo, J. C., & Tyndale, R. F. (2007). Genetic variability in CYP2A6 and the pharmacokinetics of nicotine. *Pharmacogenomics*, *8*(10), 1385–1402.

Nakajima, M., & Yokoi, T. (2005, August). Interindividual variability in nicotine metabolism: C-oxidation and glucuronidation. *Drug Metabolism and Pharmacokinetics*, *20*(4), 227–235.

Nakajima, M., Kuroiwa, Y., & Yokoi, T. (2002, November). Interindividual differences in nicotine metabolism and genetic polymorphisms of human CYP2A6. *Drug Metabolism Reviews*, *34*(4), 865–877. doi:10.1081/DMR-120015696

Nakazawa, A., Shigeta, M., & Ozasa, K. (2004). Smoking cigarettes of low nicotine yield does not reduce nicotine intake as expected: A study of nicotine dependency in Japanese males. *BMC Public Health*, *4*, 28–36. doi:10.1186/1471-2458-4-28

Nash, S. H., Liao, L. M., & Harris, T. B. (2017). Cigarette smoking and mortality in adults aged 70 years and older: Results from the NIH-AARP cohort. *American Journal of Preventive Medicine*, *52*(3), 276–283. doi:10.1016/j.ameore.2016.09.036

National Academies of Sciences, Engineering, and Medicine. (2018). *Public health consequences of E-Cigarettes*. National Academies of Sciences, Engineering, and Medicine. Washington, DC: The National Academies Press. Retrieved from https://doi.org/10.17226/24952

Nawrot, P., Jordan, S., & Eastwood, J. (2003). Effects of caffeine on human health. *Food Additives & Contaminants, 20*(1), 1–30. doi:10.1080/0265203021000007840

Nehlig, A. (2010). Is caffeine a cognitive enhancer? *Journal of Alzheimer's Disease, 20*, S85–S94. doi:10.3233/JAD-2010-091315

NIDA, National Institute on Drug Abuse. (2016, May). *Drug facts: Cigarettes and other tobacco products*. Rockville, MD: U.S. Department of Health and Human Services. Retrieved September 8, 2016, from www.drugabuse.gov/publications/drugfacts/cigarettes-other-tobacco-products

NIDDK, National Institute of Diabetes and Digestive and Kidney Diseases. (2020, July 18). Xanthine derivatives. In *Liver toxicity: Clinical and research information on drug-induced liver injury*. Bethesda, MD: National Institute of Diabetes and Digestive and Kidney Diseases.

Nides, M., Danielsson, T., & Saunders, F. (2020). Efficacy and safety of a nicotine mouth spray for smoking cessation: A randomized, multicenter, controlled study in a naturalistic setting. *Nicotine & Tobacco Research, 22*(3), 339–345. doi:10.1093/ntr/nty246

Nides, M., Oncken, C., & Gonzales, D. (2006). Smoking cessation with varenicline, a selective alpha-4 beta-2 nicotinic receptor partial agonist: Results from a 7-week, randomized, placebo- and bupropion-controlled trial with 1-year follow-up. *Archives of Internal Medicine, 166*, 1561–1568.

O'Cleirigh, C., Valentine, S. E., & Pinkston, M. (2015). The unique challenges facing HIV-positive patients who smoke cigarettes: HIV viremia, ART adherence, engagement in HIV care, and concurrent substance use. *AIDS and Behavior, 19*(1), 178–185. doi:10.1007/s10461-014-0762-7

Oh, A., & Kacker, A. (2014). Do electronic cigarettes impart a lower potential disease burden than conventional tobacco cigarettes? Review on e-cigarette vapor versus tobacco smoke. *Laryngoscope, 124*(12), 2702–2706. doi:10.1002/lary.24750

O'Keefe, J. H., Bhatti, S. K., & Patil, H. R. (2013). Effects of habitual coffee consumption on cardiometabolic disease, cardiovascular health, and all-cause mortality. *Journal of the American College of Cardiology, 62*(12), 1043–1051. doi:10.1016/j.jaoc.2013.06.035

Olsen, N. (2018, March 28). Does chocolate have caffeine? *Healthline Media*.

Pacifici, R., Pichini, S., & Graziano, S. (2015). Successful nicotine intake in medical assisted use of e-cigarettes: A pilot study. *International Journal of Environmental Research and Public Health, 12*(7), 7638–7646. doi:10.3390/ijerph120707638

Pagliaro, A. M., & Pagliaro, L. A. (2018). *Women's drug and substance abuse: A comprehensive analysis and reflective synthesis*. New York, NY: Routledge.

Pagliaro, L. A., & Pagliaro, A. M. (Eds.). (1983). *Pharmacologic aspects of aging*. St. Louis, MO: C. V. Mosby.

Pagliaro, L. A., & Pagliaro, A. M. (Eds.). (1987). *Problems in pediatric drug therapy* (2nd ed.). Hamilton, IL: Drug Intelligence Publications.

Pagliaro, L. A., & Pagliaro, A. M. (1999). *PNDR: Psychologists' neuropsychotrophic drug reference*. Philadelphia, PA: Brunner/Mazel.

Pagliaro, L. A., & Pagliaro, A. M. (2004). *Pagliaros' comprehensive guide to drugs and substances of abuse*. Washington, DC: American Pharmacists Association.

Pagliaro, L. A., & Pagliaro, A. M. (2009). *Pagliaros' comprehensive guide to drugs and substances of abuse* (2nd ed.). Washington, DC: American Pharmacists Association.

Pagliaro, L. A., & Pagliaro, A. M. (2012). *Handbook of child and adolescent drug and substance abuse: Pharmacological, developmental, and clinical considerations*. Hoboken, NJ: John Wiley & Sons.

Pagliaro, L. A., & Pagliaro, A. M. (2020). *Child and adolescent drug and substance abuse: A comprehensive reference for mental health care professionals*. New York, NY: Routledge.

Paolini, M., & De Biasi, M. (2011, October 15). Mechanistic insights into nicotine withdrawal. *Biochemical Pharmacology, 82*(8), 996–1007. doi:10.1016/j.bcp.2011.07.075

Patnode, C. D., Henderson, J. T., & Thompson, J. H. (2015a). *Behavioral counseling and pharmacotherapy interventions for tobacco cessation in adults, including pregnant women*. Rockville, MD: Agency for Healthcare Research and Quality.

Patnode, C. D., Henderson, J. T., & Thompson, J. H. (2015b, October 20). Behavioral counseling and pharmacotherapy interventions for tobacco cessation in adults, including pregnant women: A review of reviews for the U.S. Preventive services task force. *Annals of Internal Medicine, 163*(8), 608–621. doi:10.7326/M15-0171

Pelchovitz, D. J., & Goldberger, J. J. (2011). Caffeine and cardiac arrhythmias: A review of the evidence. *The American Journal of Medicine, 124*(4), 284–289. doi:10.1016/j.amjmed.2010.10.017

Perez-Paramo, Y., Watson, C., & Chen, G. (2017, April). Nicotine metabolism by the flavin monooxygenase (FMO) family of enzymes. *The FASEB Journal, 31*(1S), 1–4.

Perez-Stable, E. J., Herrera, B., & Jacob, P. (1998). Nicotine metabolism and intake in black and white smokers. *JAMA, Journal of the American Medical Association, 280*(2), 152.

Perkins, K. A., Karelitz, J. L., & Michael, V. C. (2017, August). Effects of nicotine versus placebo e-cigarette use on symptom relief during initial tobacco abstinence. *Experimental and Clinical Pharmacology, 25*(4), 249–254. doi:10.1037/pha0000134

Pfeifer, G. P., Denissenko, M. F., & Olivier, M. (2002). Tobacco smoke carcinogens, DNA damage and p53 mutations in smoking-associated cancers. *Oncogene, 21*(48), 7435–7451.

Phelps, H. M., & Phelps, C. E. (1988). Caffeine ingestion and breast cancer. *Cancer, 61*, 1051–1054.

Piper, M. E., Cook, J. W., & Schlam, T. R. (2010). Gender, race, and education differences in abstinence rates among participants in two randomized smoking cessation trials. *Nicotine & Tobacco Research, 12*(6), 647–657.

Piper, M. E., McCarthy, D. E., & Baker, T. B. (2008). Assessing dimensions of nicotine dependence. *Nicotine & Tobacco Research, 10*(6), 1009–1020. doi:10.1080/14622200802097563

Prochaska, J. J., & Hilton, J. F. (2012). Risk of cardiovascular serious adverse events associated with varenicline use for tobacco cessation: Systematic review and meta-analysis. *BMJ, 344*, e2856. doi:10.1136/bmj.e2856

Public Health Ontario. (2018, November). *Current evidence on e-cigarettes*. Toronto, ON: Queen's Printer for Ontario.

Reuters. (2015, February 25). Tobacco companies to settle smoking lawsuits for $100 million. *CNBC News*. CNBC News.

Rigotti, N. A., Chang, Y., & Tindle, H. A. (2018). Association of electronic cigarette use with smoking cessation among smokers who plan to quit after a hospitalization: A prospective study. *Annals of Internal Medicine, 168*(9), 613–620. doi:10.7326/M17-2048

RNAO, Registered Nurses' Association of Ontario. (2017, June). *Integrating tobacco interventions into daily practice*. Ottawa, ON: Registered Nurses' Association of Ontario.

Robles, G. I., Singh-Franco, D., & Ghin, H. L. (2008). A review of the efficacy of smoking-cessation pharmacotherapies in nonwhite populations. *Clinical Therapeutics, 30*(5), 800–812. doi:10.1016/j.clinthera.2008.05.010

Rogers, A. J., Denk, L. D., & Wax, P. M. (2004). Catastrophic brain injury after nicotine insecticide ingestion. *Journal of Emergency Medicine, 26*(2), 169–172.

Rom, O., Pecorelli, A., & Valacchi, G. (2015, March). Are e-cigarettes a safe and good alternative to cigarette smoking? *Annals of the New York Academy of Sciences, 1340*, 65–74. doi:10.1111/nyas.12609

Roth, G. A., Forouzanfar, M. H., & Barber, R. (2015, April 2). Demographic and epidemiologic drivers of global cardiovascular mortality. *The NEJM, 372*(14), 1333–1341. doi:10.1056/NEJMoa1406655

Safer Care Victoria. (2019, January). Nicotine poisoning. *Professional Practice Guideline*, pp. 1–3. The Royal Children's Hospital.

Schaffer, S. D., Yoon, S., & Zadezensky, I. (2009, June). A review of smoking cessation: Potentially risky effects on prescribed medications. *Journal of Clinical Nursing, 18*(11), 1533–1540. doi:10.1111/j.1365-2702.20078.02724.x

Schmidt, M., Farna, H., & Kurcova, I. (2015). Successful treatment of supralethal caffeine overdose with a combination of lipid infusion and dialysis. *American Journal of Emergency Medicine, 33*, 738.e5–738.e7. doi:10.1016/j.ajem.2014.11.002

Schoedel, K. A., Hoffmann, E. B., & Rao, Y. (2004). Ethnic variation in CYP2A6 and association of genetically slow nicotine metabolism and smoking in adult Caucasians. *Pharmacogenetics, 14*(9), 615–626. doi:10.1097/0000851-200409000-00006

Schroeder, M. J., & Hoffman, A. C. (2014, May 23). Electronic cigarettes and nicotine clinical pharmacology. *Tobacco Control* (Suppl 2), 30–35. doi:10.1136/tobaccocontrol-2013-051469

Schwartz, L., Guais, A., & Chaumet-Riffaud, P. (2010). Carbon dioxide is largely responsible for the acute inflammatory effects of tobacco smoke. *Inhalation Toxicology, 22*(7), 543–551. doi:10.3109/08958370903555909

Sharwood, L. N., Elkington, J., & Meuleners, L. (2013). Use of caffeinated substances and risk of crashes in long distance drivers of commercial vehicles: Case-control study. *BMJ, 346*. doi:10.1136/bmj.f1140

Sheen, S. J. (1988). Detection of nicotine in foods and plant materials. *Journal of Food Science, 53*(5), 1572–1573. doi:10.1111/j.1365-2621.1988.tb09328.x

Shields, P. G., Berman, M., & Brasky, T. M. (2017, August). A review of pulmonary toxicity of electronic cigarettes in the context of smoking: A focus on inflammation. *Cancer Epidemiology, Biomarkers & Prevention, 26*(8), 1175–1191. doi:10.1158/1055-9965.EPI-17-0358

Singh, S., Loke, Y. K., & Spangler, J. G. (2011). Risk of serious adverse cardiovascular events associated with varenicline: A systematic review and meta-analysis. *CMAJ, Canadian Medical Association Journal, 183*(12), 1359–1366. doi:10.1503/cmaj.110218

Sobkowiak, R., & Lesicki, A. (2013). Absorption, metabolism and excretion of nicotine in humans. *Postepy Biochemii, 59*(1), 33–44.

Solinas, M., Ferre, S., & You, Z.-B. (2002, August 1). Caffeine induces dopamine and glutamate release in the shell of the nucleus accumbens. *The Journal of Neuroscience, 22*(15), 6321–6324.

Somogyi, L. P. (2010). *Caffeine intake by the U. S. population (Subcontract number: 70000073494)* (pp. 1–85). Oakridge National Laboratory. Kensington, CA: The Food and Drug Administration.

Span, P. (2017, December 8). Some older smokers turn to vaping. That may not be a bad idea. *The New York Times*, pp. 1–4. The New York Times Company.

St Helen, G., Dempsey, D., & Wilson, M. (2013, March). Racial differences in the relationship between tobacco dependence and nicotine and carcinogen exposure. *Addiction, 108*(3), 607–617. doi:10.1111/j.1360-0443.2012.04077.x

Stead, L. F., Koilpillai, P., & Fanshawe, T. R. (2016, March 24). Combined pharmacotherapy and behavioural interventions for smoking. *The Cochrane Database of Systematic Reviews, 24*, CD008286. doi:10.1002/14651858,CD008286.pub3

Stein, M. D., Weinstock, M. C., & Herman, D. S. (2006). A smoking cessation intervention for the methadone-maintained. *Addiction, 101*(4), 599–607. doi:10.1111/j.1360-0443.2006.01406.x

Streller, S., & Roth, K. (2014a, November 4). The chemistry of tobacco—Part 2. *Chemistry Views Magazine*. Chemis in unserer Zeit/Wiley.

Streller, S., & Roth, K. (2014b, December 2). The chemistry of tobacco—Part 3.1–5. *Chemie in Unserer Zeit/Wiley*. doi:10.1002/chemv.201400117

Streller, S., & Roth, K. (2015a, January 6). The chemistry of tobacco—Part 4.1–7. *Chemie in Unserer Zeit/Wiley*. doi:10.1002/chemv.201400135

Streller, S., & Roth, K. (2015b, March 3). The chemistry of tobacco—Part 5.1–7. *Chemie in Unserer Zeit/Wiley*. doi:10.1002/chemv.201500008

Sutherland, M. T., Carroll, A. J., & Salmeron, B. J. (2013, October 1). Down-regulation of amygdala and insula functional circuits by varenicline and nicotine in abstinent cigarette smokers. *Biological Psychiatry, 74*(7), 538–546. doi:10.1016/j.biopsych.2013.01.035

Taghavi, S., Khashyarmanesh, Z., & Moalemzadeh-Haghighi, H. (2012, Winter–Spring). Nicotine content of domestic cigarettes, imported cigarettes and pipe tobacco in Iran. *Addiction and Health, 4*(1–2), 28–35.

Talhout, R., Schulz, T., & Florek, E. (2011). Hazardous compounds in tobacco smoke. *International Journal of Environmental Research and Public Health, 8*(2), 613–628. doi:10.3390/ijerph8020613

Tanner, J. A., Chenoweth, M. J., & Tyndale, R. F. (2015). Pharmacogenetics of nicotine and associated smoking behaviors. *Current Topics in Behavioral Neurosciences, 23*, 37–86. doi:10.1007/978-3-319-13665-3_3

Teekachunhatean, S., Tosri, N., & Rojanasthien, N. (2013). Pharmacokinetics of caffeine following a single administration of coffee enema versus oral coffee consumption in healthy male subjects. *ISRN Pharmacology, 2013*(147238), 1–7. doi:10.1155/2013/147238

Temple, J. L., Bernard, C., & Lipshultz, S. E. (2017, May 26). The safety of ingested caffeine: A comprehensive review. *Frontiers in Psychiatry*. doi:10.3389/fpsyt.2017.00080

Thun, M. J., Henley, S. J., & Calle, E. E. (2002, October 21). Tobacco use and cancer: An epidemiologic perspective for geneticists. *Oncogene, 21*(48), 7307–7325. doi:10.1038/sj.onc.1205807

Tomizawa, M., & Casida, J. E. (2005). Neonicotinoid insecticide toxicology: Mechanisms of selective action. *Annual Review of Pharmacology and Toxicology, 45*, 247–268.

Tonstad, S., Tonnesen, P., & Hajek, P. (2006). Effect of maintenance therapy with varenicline on smoking cessation: A randomized controlled trial. *JAMA, The Journal of the American Medical Association, 296*(1), 64–71.

Trang, J. M., Blanchard, J., & Conrad, K. A. (1982, March). The effect of vitamin C on the pharmacokinetics of caffeine in elderly men. *The American Journal of Clinical Nutrition, 35*, 487–494.

Tricker, A. R. (2003, February). Nicotine metabolism, human drug metabolism polymorphisms, and smoking behaviour. *Toxicology, 183*(1–3), 151–173.

Turnbull, D., Rodricks, J. V., & Mariano, G. F. (2017). Caffeine and cardiovascular health. *Regulatory Toxicology and Pharmacology, 89*, 165–185. doi:10.1016/j.yrtph.2017.07.025

Tutka, P., Mosiewicz, J., & Wielosz, M. (2005). Pharmacokinetics and metabolism of nicotine. *Pharmacological Reports*, *57*, 143–153.

USDHHS, U.S. Department of Health and Human Services. (2010). *How tobacco smoke causes disease: The biology and behavioral basis for smoking-attributable disease*. Centers for Disease Control and Prevention, U. S. Department of Health and Human Services. Atlanta: Office on Smoking and Health, National Center for Chronic Disease Prevention and Health Promotion. Retrieved January 17, 2018, from www.cdc.gov/tobacco/data_statistics/sgr/2010/index.htm

USDHHS, U.S. Department of Health and Human Services. (2014). *The health consequences of smoking—50 years of progress*. CDC, USDHHS. Atlanta, Georgia: Office on Smoking and Health, National Center for Chronic Disease Prevention and Health Promotion.

USDHHS, U.S. Department of Health and Human Services. (2016a). Deeming tobacco products to be subject to the Federal Food, Drug, and Cosmetic Act, as amended by the Family Smoking Prevention and Tobacco Control Act; Restrictions on the sale and distribution of tobacco products and required warning statements. *Federal Register*, *81*(Fed. Reg. 28974).

USDHHS, U.S. Department of Health and Human Services. (2016b). *E-cigarette use among youth and young adults: A report of the surgeon general*. Public Health Service, Office of the Surgeon General. Rockville, MD: USDHHS.

van Duinen, H., Lorist, M. M., & Zijdewind, I. (2005). The effect of caffeine on cognitive task performance and motor fatigue. *Psychopharmacology (Berlin)*, *180*(3), 539–547.

Varlet, V. (2016, December). Drug vaping: From the dangers of misuse to new therapeutic devices. *Toxics*, *4*(4), 29–34. doi:10.3390/toxics4040029

Verplaetse, T. L., & McKee, S. A. (2017, March). An overview of alcohol and tobacco/nicotine interactions in the human laboratory. *The American Journal of Drug and Alcohol Abuse*, *43*(2), 186–196. doi:10.1080/00952990.2016.1189927

Verster, J. C., & Koenig, J. (2018). Caffeine intake and its sources: A review of national representative studies. *Critical Reviews in Food Science and Nutrition*, *58*(8), 1250–1259. doi:10.1080/10408398.2016.1247252

Vetulani, J. (2001, May–June). Drug addiction: Part I. Psychoactive substances in the past and present. *Polish Journal of Pharmacology*, *53*(3), 201–214.

Villarroel, M. A., Cha, A. E., & Vahratian, A. (2020, April). Electronic cigarette use among U.S. adults, 2018. In *NCHS data brief* (Vol. 365, pp. 1–7). Hattsville, MD: U.S. Department of Health and Human Services.

Vu, A. T., Taylor, K. M., & Holman, M. R. (2015). Polycyclic aromatic hydrocarbons in the mainstream smoke of popular U. S. cigarettes. *Chemical Research in Toxicology*, *28*(8), 1616–1626. doi:10.1021/acs.chemrestox.5b00190

Wagener, T. L., Avery, J. A., & Leavens, E. (2021). Associated changes in e-cigarette puff duration and cigarettes smoked per day. *Nicotine & Tobacco Research*, *23*(4), 760–764. doi:10.1093/ntr/ntaa211

Wang, H., Li, X., & Guo, J. (2016, February 10). Distribution of toxic chemicals in particles of various sizes from mainstream cigarette smoke. *Inhalation Toxicology*, pp. 1–6.

Wang, T. W., Asman, K., & Gentzke, A. S. (2018, November 9). Tobacco product use among adults—United States, 2017. *MMWR, Morbidity and Mortality Weekly Report*, *67*(44), 1225–1232.

Watkins, S. S., Koob, G. F., & Markon, A. (2000). Neural mechanisms underlying nicotine addition: Acute positive reinforcement and withdrawal. *Nicotine & Tobacco Research*, *2*, 19–37.

Watson, J., Deary, I., & Kerr, D. (2002). Central and peripheral effects of sustained caffeine use: Tolerance is incomplete. *British Journal of Clinical Pharmacology, 54*(4), 400–406.

Wellman, R. J., DiFranza, J. R., & O'Loughlin, J. (2015, November). Confirmatory factor analysis of the Autonomy Over Tobacco Scale (AUTOS) in adults. *Addictive Behaviors, 50,* 217–221. doi:10.1016/j.addbeh.2015.06.033

Welsh, E. J., Bara, A., & Barley, E. (2010, January 20). *Caffeine for asthma.* Cochrane Library. *Cochrane Database of Systematic Reviews 2010*(1), CD001112. New York, NY.

Whitten, L. (2009, November 6). Studies link family of genes to nicotine addiction. *NIDA Notes, 22*(1), 10–14.

WHO, World Health Organization. (2009). *WHO study group on tobacco product regulation: Report on the scientific basis of tobacco product regulation: Third report of a WHO study group.* Geneva: World Health Organization. Retrieved October 7, 2016, from www.worldcat.org/title/who-study-group-on-tobacco-product-regulation-report-on-the-scientific-basis-of-tobacco-product-regulation-third-report-of- . . .

WHO, World Health Organization. (2020). *Health benefits of smoking cessation.* Geneva, Switzerland: World Health Organization.

Wickham, R. J. (2015). How menthol alters tobacco-smoking behavior: A biological perspective. *Yale Journal of Biology and Medicine, 88,* 279–287.

Wikoff, D., Welsh, B. T., & Henderson, R. (2017, November). Systematic review of the potential adverse effects of caffeine consumption in healthy adults, pregnant women, adolescents, and children. *Food and Chemical Toxicology, 109*(Part 1), 585–648. doi:10.1016/j.fct.2017.04.002

Willson, C. (2018). The clinical toxicology of caffeine: A review and case study. *Toxicology Reports, 5,* 1140–1152. doi:10.1016/j.toxrep.2018.11.002

Wilson, P., & Bloom, H. L. (2016). Caffeine consumption and cardiovascular risks: Little cause for concern. *JAHA, 5*(1), 1–3. doi:10.1161/JAHA.115.003089

Wu, W., Zhang, L., & Jain, R. B. (2005). Determination of carcinogenic tobacco-specific nitrosamines in mainstream smoke from U. S.-brand and non-U. S. brand cigarettes from 14 countries. *Nicotine & Tobacco Research, 7*(3), 443–451.

Yang, T. O., Crowe, B. J., & Cairns, B. J. (2015). Tea and coffee and risk of endometrial cancer: Cohort study and meta-analysis. *The American Journal of Clinical Nutrition, 101*(3), 570–578. doi:10.3945/ajcn.113.081836

Yardley, M. M., Mirbaba, M. M., & Ray, L. A. (2015). Pharmacological options for smoking cessation in heavy drinking smokers. *CNS Drugs, 29*(10), 833–845. doi:10.1007/s40263-015-0284-5

Zevin, S., & Benowitz, N. L. (1999). Drug interactions with tobacco smoking. An update. *Clinical Pharmacokinetics, 36*(6), 425–438. doi:10.2165/00003088-199936060-00004

Zhao, L.-G., Li, Z.-Y., & Feng, G.-S. (2020). Coffee drinking and cancer risk: An umbrella review of meta-analyses of observational studies. *BMC Cancer, 20*(101), 1–12. doi:10.1186/s12885-020-6561-9

Zhu, S.-H., Cummins, S. E., & Gamst, A. C. (2016, July). Quitting smoking before and after varenicline: A population study based on two representative samples of U.S. smokers. *Tobacco Control, 25*(4), 464–469. doi:10.1136/tobaccocontrol-2015-052332

Zhu, S.-H., Sun, J. Y., & Bonnevie, E. (2014). Four hundred and sixty brands of e-cigarettes and counting: Implications for product regulation. *Tobacco Control, 23,* iii43–iii9. doi:10.1136/tobaccocontrol-2014-051670

Zhuang, Y.-L., Cummins, S. E., & Sun, J. Y. (2016). Long-term e-cigarette use and smoking cessation: A longitudinal study with US population. *Tobacco Control*, *25*, i90-i95. doi:10.1136/tobaccocontrol-2016-053096

Zickler, P. (2003, March). Nicotine's multiple effects on the brain's reward system drive addiction. *NIDA Notes*, *17*(6), 1–3. Retrieved October 7, 2016, from www.ehd.org/health_tobacco_19.php

Zirakazdeh, A., Shuman, C., & Stauter, E. (2013, March). Cigarette smoking in methadone maintained patients: An up-to-date review. *Current Drug Abuse Reviews*, *6*(1), 77–84.

CHAPTER 4

CANNABIS

Many older adults in the U.S. initially began to use cannabis—illicitly—as teenagers during the 1960s. As "hippies," "flower children," and young college/university students, they generally used cannabis to "obtain psychodelic experiences," "get high," "mellow out," "party with friends," or "achieve enlightenment." These and other older adults continue to use cannabis for these desired effects, as well as to manage the anxieties and pains associated with aging. The focus of this chapter is on the use of cannabis by older adults in the U.S. during the first two decades of the new millennium.

The new millennium witnessed a literal sea change in terms of the decriminalization and legalization of cannabis across the U.S. During this brief period of time, state laws and regulations concerning cannabis cultivation, production, sale, and possession, as well as medical and licit recreational use, underwent profound transformations—the likes of which, have not been seen since the 1930s.[1] Correspondingly, in comparison to earlier years, the attitudes of adults in the U.S. toward cannabis have significantly changed during the new millennium.

- 56% of Americas believe that using marijuana is "socially acceptable;"
- 83% of Americans support the legalization of "medicinal marijuana."

(NCDAS, 2019, p. 4)

Additionally, in 2003, 34% of adults favored legalization of marijuana while 64% thought that it should remain illegal. However, as noted by the NCDAS (2019, p. 4):

> by the end of 2020, 68% favored legalization and only 32% thought that it should remain illegal.
>
> (Statistical Research Department, 2021)

We begin our overview of cannabis use by older adults in the U.S. during the new millennium with a review of the pharmacognosy and the preparation of the three principal forms of cannabis:

1. Marijuana;
2. Hashish;
3. Hashish Oil.

This subsection is followed by the pharmacology of cannabis—its pharmacodynamics; pharmacokinetics; undesired, or harmful, effects and toxicities; risks for physical and psychological dependence or use disorder; and overdosage/unintentional poisoning. We then present and discuss current trends in older adult medical prescription and illicit or licit/

1. N.B. Interestingly, the previous changes—in comparison to current trends—were in direct opposition to current changes. At that time, laws and regulations were written and implemented to restrict and criminalize the use of cannabis, which, until that time, had been legal and extensively cultivated worldwide for well over 5,000 years (Pagliaro & Pagliaro, 2004).

DOI: 10.4324/9781003010333-4

recreational use of cannabis as a result of specific state legislation concerning decriminalization and legalization. This discussion is followed by a critical review of the: (1) assessment; (2) diagnosis; and (3) treatment of cannabis dependence or use disorder among older adults. The chapter concludes with a summary of common contemporaneous diagnoses that involve cannabis dependence or use disorder.

Whereas "pharmacology" is the study of the origin, nature, chemistry, effects, and uses of drugs—a related science, "pharmacognosy" focuses specifically on the identification, recognition, extraction, and medicinal use of plants and other natural substances. For this reason, and because of the high rates of cannabis use and resultant need for production and commerce in the U.S., we begin this chapter with a section on its pharmacognosy. This section is followed by cannabis plant botany and new millennial production and commerce. We then continue with the pharmacology of cannabis with particular attention to marijuana—the most popular and, consequently, the most widely used form of cannabis in the U.S.

CANNABIS PHARMACOGNOSY

"Pharmacognosy" is the study of bioactive natural products, particularly medicinal products that are extracted or otherwise obtained (e.g., in natural dried form) from plants and other natural sources. It includes the identification, extraction, preparation, and use of these natural products. In many taxonomies, pharmacognosy is an esoteric branch of pharmacology. Of note, pharmacognosy, as a distinct discipline, generally has not been a formal part of the academic curriculum in U.S. schools of medicine, nursing, or pharmacy for over 50 years—although, some of its salient content has been incorporated into other university courses (e.g., basic pharmacology, ethnobotany, herbal medicine, holistic medicine, and traditional medicine).

Cannabis Plant Botany[2,3]

Cannabis is a genus of flowering plants found within the Cannabaceae family. It is an annual dioecious plant that is often characterized as an "herb" or "weed" and is cultivated by sowing its seeds. Indoor cultivation under controlled conditions (e.g., hydroponic "grow-ops") enable the control of the entire plant life cycle. Consequently, in comparison to harvesting a single crop per year with normal outdoor cultivation, up to four crops per year can be harvested with indoor cultivation, which commonly utilizes hydroponics.

There are several species of cannabis, including *Cannabis indica*, *Cannabis ruderalis*, and *Cannabis sativa*.[4] *Cannabis sativa* is the principal variety from which marijuana, hashish, and hashish oil are prepared. Within the species of *Cannabis sativa*, there are several varieties including *Cannabis sativa indica*, *Cannabis sativa ruderalis*, and *Cannabis sativa*.[5]

2. The study of botany is also commonly known as "phytology" or "plant science."
3. For additional information regarding cannabis botany and history, see Pagliaro and Pagliaro (2004).
4. Cannabis classifications vary. For example, the classification supported by the WHO (2018) considers cannabis to be monospecific (i.e., *Cannabis sativa L.*) with two subspecies (i.e., sativa and indica). Others (e.g., Pagliaro & Pagliaro, 2004) consider "indica," "ruderalis," and "sativa," to be varieties of *Cannabis sativa*.
5. Some botanical taxonomies classify *indica*, *ruderalis*, and *sativa* as belonging to different species of cannabis.

These three varieties differ significantly in regard to their concentration of tetrahydrocannabinol (THC)—the primary pharmacologically active cannabinoid found in the species, with the *indica* variety having the highest concentration of THC (Pagliaro & Pagliaro, 2004).

The cannabis plant—one of the world's oldest cultivated plants—has been used for over 10,000 years as a food and textile fiber, as well as a medicinal, mystic, and psychodelic substance (WHO, 2018). Early archeological evidence for use as a textile fiber comes from: (1) hemp rope imprints on shards of Chinese pottery dating back to this time; and (2) the *Shu King*, which dates back to approximately 2,350 B.C., in which the weaving of hemp into clothing is mentioned. The first medicinal use of cannabis was recorded by the Chinese emperor Shen Nung (c. 2,700 B.C.), the "Father of Chinese Medicine," who suggested its use as an herbal medicine for the treatment of many conditions including arthritis, constipation, gout, and malaria (Gumbiner, 2011a; Zuardi, 2006).

The use of cannabis in India dates back approximately 5,000 years, where it was prominently featured in the sacred Hindu texts, *The Vedas*, as one of five sacred plants (Gumbiner, 2011b).[6]

Chemical Constituents of Cannabis

Gaoni and Mechoulam (1964) chemically isolated tetrahydrocannabinol (THC) from *Cannabis sativa*. They identified its chemical structure and suggested that it was the principle psychoactive chemical in cannabis (see the related discussion in the following subsection, "Tetrahydrocannabinol"). In addition to THC, over 500 different chemicals, including more than 100 different pharmacologically active cannabinoids, or "phytocannabinoids," have been identified in cannabis (e.g., "cannabidiol" [CBD], "cannabinol" [CBN], and "tetrahydrocannabivarin" [THCV]) (WHO, 2018). Cannabinol was the first cannabinoid that was chemically isolated and identified from "charas, the excluded resin of Indian hemp" (Barlow Wood, Newton Spivey, & Hill Easterfield, 1899), followed by cannabidiol (Mechoulam & Shvo, 1963).

These cannabinoids, particularly CBD, have been largely ignored over the past 75 years because of related federal legal restrictions in the U.S. (e.g., Booth & Bohlmann, 2019; Stith, Vigil, & Brockelman, 2019). However, with the legalization of marijuana for medical and/or recreational use in most states during the new millennium, interest in CBD-containing edibles and drinks has proliferated (e.g., Lagerquist, 2019b; Scipioni, 2019). CBD, cannabichromene (CBC), and cannabigerol (CBG) are among the principal non-psychoactive cannabinoids that are being investigated for potential medical application (ElSohly, Radwan, & Gul, 2017; Smith et al., 2019).

Terpenes

In addition to cannabinoids, "terpenes" are also present in cannabis. The term, "terpene," was created in 1866 by Friedrich August Kekulé, a German organic chemist (1829–1896), to identify the group of hydrocarbons that are derived from plants and have an empirical

6. The entheogenic use of cannabis (i.e., magical, religious, shamanic, or spiritual use) is not discussed in this text. For related discussion, see Pagliaro and Pagliaro (2004).

chemical formula of $C_{10}H_{16}$. Terpenes comprise a large class of organic compounds that are produced by a variety of diverse plants—including conifers. Chemically, they are hydrocarbons that are associated with various strong aromas/odors. These smells serve to: (1) protect the plants from consumption or destruction by deterring herbivores; and (2) attract insects (e.g., bees) to promote pollination.

Over 150 different terpenes have been identified in the resin of various types of cannabis (Booth & Bohlmann, 2019). Most of these terpenes are not exclusive to cannabis. Examples of a few different terpenes found in cannabis resin include: carene,[7] lemonine,[8] myrcene,[9] pinene,[10] terpineol,[11] and terpinolene.[12]

The terpenes found in the various varieties of cannabis provide characteristic odors by which users typically distinguish a particular type of cannabis from another (Gilbert & DiVerdi, 2018)[13]—in addition to the desired effects (Pagliaro & Pagliaro, *Clinical Patient Data Files*). This appears to be quite similar to the preference for particular wines, for which aroma and flavor are significantly due to various terpenes (e.g., citronellol, geraniol, linalool, nerol) found in different types of grapes, particularly varietals of Muscat grapes, which have a higher concentration of terpenes.[14]

Tetrahydrocannabinol

THC is a lipid produced by cannabis plants, mainly by decarboxylation of its major chemical precursor—tetrahydrocannabinolic acid (THCA) (e.g., Moreno-Sanz, 2016).[15] In these plants, THC primarily serves as a natural systemic insecticide (McPartland, 1997).

Within the cannabis plant, the highest concentration of THC is found in the bracts, or small leaves, at the base of the cannabis flowers, and their resin. The next highest concentration is found in the flowering tops, and then, in decreasing order: the upper leaves (i.e., approximately 10% of that found in pistillate flowers), large stems (i.e., approximately 1% of that found in pistillate flowers), and roots (i.e., approximately 0.1% of that found in pistillate flowers) (WHO, 2018).[16] Cannabis seeds contain little, if any, cannabinoids. For

7. Also found in wood turpentine.
8. Also found in peels of citrus fruits.
9. Also found in bay and hops.
10. Also found in pine tree resin or sap.
11. Also found in pine oil and the barbed skullcap.
12. Also found in lilac and sage.
13. Terpene constitution as a phenotypic trait, in terms of type and amount/concentration, varies significantly across the different varieties of cannabis and, consequently, produces various distinct aromas.
14. Based upon our analyses of data obtained from cannabis users, collected for over 40 years, the aroma of the terpenes found in different cannabis varieties appears to also: (1) contribute to a classical, conditioned response; and (2) facilitate a placebo effect that can significantly produce mental and physical effects that are commonly attributed to cannabis.
15. The process of decarboxylation is facilitated—whether internal or external to the plant—by heat. Consequently, heating is used when: (1) drying marijuana leaves in preparation for their use; and (2) preparing edible cannabis products for ingestion (e.g., baking brownies, heating a THC-electuary prior to ingestion, quickly heating cannabis buds on buttered crackers in the microwave)—in order to maximize the conversion of any remaining THCA to THC (Pagliaro & Pagliaro, *Clinical Patient Data Files*).
16. The roots, stalks, and stems of the *Cannabis sativa* plant contain low concentrations of THC and are more fibrous than the plant leaves. Historically referred to as "hemp," these parts of the cannabis plant have been specifically cultivated and used to produce boat sails, canvas, clothing, fish nets, and paper for literally thousands of years (Pagliaro & Pagliaro, 2004). In December 2018, a bipartisan farm bill was signed into law that, as a component, formally legalized the industrial production of hemp in the

example, THC is limited to 10 mcg per gram of hemp seeds (i.e., 10 ppm) (Yang, Lewis, & Bello, 2017). Additionally, the female pistillate plants tend to have a much higher THC concentration than the male plants. Thus, the reason for advertisements and sales of tools to detect plant sex (e.g., ultraviolet lights) in drug-paraphernalia stores (i.e., headshops, hemp stores, or hydroponic grow stores), on the Internet, and in drug culture magazines (e.g., *High Times*).

The desire for higher THC concentrations also accounts for the popularity of *sinsemilla*—unfertilized female cannabis plants that are cultivated specifically for their higher THC concentration. The cultivation of *sinsemilla* is generally accomplished by planting female seeds or by destroying the male plants before pollen is produced and the female plants are fertilized. These procedures allow the unfertilized female plants to flower more abundantly and, consequently, produce more THC-containing resin.

Cannabis Preparation and THC Concentrations

The three principal forms of cannabis are: (1) marijuana, (2) hashish, and (3) hashish oil. Marijuana (i.e., "Bud," "Dope," "Grass," "Herb," "Mary Jane," "Pot," or "Weed")[17] is the dried, shredded cannabis plant form (generally, flowers and leaves).[18] It is generally a dull, grayish-green to greenish-brown color and, when compared to hashish or hashish oil, contains significantly lower concentrations of THC. Marijuana is mostly prepared for pulmonary inhalation (i.e., smoking or "toking") using methods that are similar to those used for preparing tobacco leaves for smoking. However, the preparation of marijuana generally requires less time and involvement regarding curing and drying.[19]

Fresh cannabis plants can have a moisture content of up to 80%. Drying, particularly in commercial/industrial production facilities, generally occurs in a dry, well-ventilated, dark area at approximately 25° C for 24 hours, or at 40° C for approximately 15 hours. After drying, which reduces the moisture content to 5% to 10%, the plant material is ready to be ground. The finished product is referred to as "manicured marijuana." The manicured marijuana is stored in tightly-sealed containers and kept in the dark because oxygen and light can cause degradation of THC (WHO, 2018).

Hashish (i.e., "Candy Bar," "Charas," "Hash," or "Lebanese") is prepared from the dried resin, whether crude or purified, and compressed flowers of the cannabis plant. It is

U.S. (Angell, 2018; Kasana, 2018). This bill "re-legalized" hemp, which had been extensively cultivated in the U.S. by numerous farmers since early colonization, including, for example, George Washington (Pagliaro & Pagliaro, 2004).

17. "Bang" and "ganjah" are other commonly used names for marijuana, but—to be more accurate—consist of only the flowering tops that have been obtained from female cannabis sativa plants.
18. Kif (i.e., "kaif," "keef," or "kief"), an Arabic word meaning "well-being" or "pleasure," was originally the name given to a powder that was made from the dried flowers of the female cannabis plant. Indigenous to the Rif Mountain area of northern Morocco, it was usually mixed with tobacco (i.e., one part to two parts) prior to smoking. Although the use of kif in the U.S. has been reported over the years, its use is considered to be relatively uncommon. The term is now more commonly used to denote marijuana, or hashish, that is from Morocco (Pagliaro & Pagliaro, 2004).
19. Whereas the rolled tobacco product prepared for smoking is commonly called a "cigarette," "cig," or "coffin nail," the rolled marijuana product prepared for smoking is commonly called a "doobie," "joint," "reefer," or "spliff."

generally light brown to black in color.[20] Prepared and distributed for use in compressed blocks or cubes, it has a relatively high concentration of THC.

Cannabis resin is a sticky, insoluble organic compound that contains cannabinoids and terpenes to protect the cannabis plant from insects and pests during the growing cycle. The resin is secreted by numerous glandular hairs (i.e., trichomes) that cover the cannabis plant, particularly the buds (WHO, 2018). The resin content of cannabis plants depends on their growing conditions, including humidity, hydration, lighting, and temperature.

Hashish is usually ingested or inhaled. Prior to ingestion, the hashish is heated in a variety of forms (e.g., butters, or brownies) in order to fully activate its effects (see the related discussion in the earlier subsection, Tetrahydrocannabinol—"Footnote #15"). For pulmonary inhalation, because hashish does not burn well when rolled alone in a "joint" to smoke, it is mixed with marijuana or tobacco prior to rolling, or is smoked in a pipe. Hashish also can be vaporized for pulmonary inhalation (see the related discussion in the later New Millennial Trends in Cannabis Use Among Older Adults subsection, Older Adult Illicit and Licit/Recreational Cannabis Use, Common Methods of Marijuana Use—"Vaping").

Hashish oil (i.e., "710," "Cannabinol," George W. Bush," or "Honey Oil") is prepared from hashish by the means of extraction with an organic solvent, often isopropyl alcohol (i.e., "rubbing alcohol"). It is then filtered and concentrated. Hashish oil contains the highest concentration of THC and ranges in color from clear to almost black. Food coloring is often added for color enhancement.

The THC concentrations of marijuana, hashish, and hashish oil can generally range from:

- 1% to 10% for "home grown" marijuana cigarettes;
- 12% to 25% for "commercially grown" marijuana;
- 15% to 65% for hashish;
- 30% to 90% for hashish oil.

Whereas these THC concentrations vary depending on the specific part of the plant (e.g., buds, leaves, or stems) from which the THC was obtained, it also depends on the:

1. Quality and source of the cannabis—the state, province, or country of origin (e.g., Hawaii, U.S.; British Columbia, Canada; or Mexico);
2. Cultivation techniques (e.g., hydroponic cultivation).

It is extremely important to recognize that, since the beginning of the new millennium, THC concentrations have significantly increased, on average, from 25% to 300% across the U.S. primarily depending upon the: (1) pre-millennial comparison year; (2) form of cannabis; (3) variety of cannabis; and (4) location.

On average, a high potency marijuana joint during the 1960s and 1970s contained only approximately 10 mg of THC. However, during the beginning of the new millennium, the average, high potency, marijuana joint contained approximately 150 mg of THC (e.g., Ashton, 2001; Pagliaro & Pagliaro, 2004). As the third decade of the new millennium approaches, high potency marijuana joints contain up to 300 mg of THC (i.e., the cannabis

20. Food coloring is often added to artificially modify the color of the finished product.

that older adults are using today is not the same cannabis that they had previously used during their "hippy" days) (Pagliaro & Pagliaro, *Clinical Patient Data Files*). However, regarding "apparent potency" in terms of pharmacological effects, it is important to keep in mind that the blood THC concentration achieved when smoking a marijuana joint varies significantly depending on the:

- Amount of THC in the cannabis that is smoked;
- Smoking technique used, including the rate, depth, and length of inhalation before exhaling (i.e., the "drag," "hit," or "toke");
- Amount of THC that is destroyed by pyrolysis.[21]

New Millennial Marijuana Production and Commerce

Over the new millennium, cannabis has continued to be increasingly produced worldwide as illustrated by the names given to its many varieties that are distributed and sold across the U.S. These names include, for example: "Acapulco Gold," "BC Bud," "Cambodian Red," "Hawaiian Buds," "Indian Hash," "Jamaican Ganja," "Lebanese Hash," "Moroccan Kif," "New Mexico Sinse," "Panama Gold," "Thai Sticks," and "Ukrainian Ditch Weed." In addition to worldwide distribution and sale, several states (i.e., Alabama, Alaska, Arizona, California, Hawaii, Illinois, Kentucky, Maine, North Carolina, Oregon, South Carolina, Tennessee, and West Virginia) produce cannabis to the extent that, for the last three decades, it is the most significant cash crop for these states with a combined annual revenue in excess of 35 billion dollars (Clines, 2001; Pagliaro & Pagliaro, 2009; Venkataraman, 2006; Warner, 2007).

> The domestic marijuana crop is larger than cotton in Alabama; larger than grapes, vegetables, and hay combined in California; larger than peanuts in Georgia; and larger than tobacco in both South Carolina and North Carolina.
>
> (Gettman, 2006, p. 1)

Consequently, as individual states (e.g., California, Colorado, Washington) are re-legalizing marijuana[22] for medical prescription and licit/recreational use, billions of dollars in tax revenue are being added to state tax coffers. For example, Colorado, which was the first state to legalize "recreational" marijuana use and retail sales in 2014, collected approximately $40 million in additional tax dollars in 2014 (Smith, 2017; Wyatt, 2014). However, these revenues have significantly increased in the ensuing years. As reported by the Colorado Department of Revenue (2018, p. 1), for 2016:

> Total marijuana tax revenue includes the 2.9% retail and medical marijuana sales tax, 10% retail marijuana special sales tax, 15% marijuana excise tax, and retail/medical marijuana application and license fees.

21. N.B. Given the well-documented partial degradation of THC by pyrolysis and related undesired effects and toxicities related to "smoke," several researchers (e.g., Eisenberg, Ogintz, & Almog, 2014; Gieringer, St. Laurent, & Goodrich, 2004; Hartman, Brown, & Milavetz, 2015b) studied potentially less harmful methods of use, demonstrating that vaporization is an extremely effective form of THC delivery. (See the related discussion in the later cannabis New Millennial Trends in Older Adult Marijuana Use subsections—"Vaping" and "Vaporizers.")
22. N.B. Prior to the early 20th Century, marijuana was legal and unregulated in the U.S. (see Pagliaro and Pagliaro, 2004).

The combined "marijuana tax" (i.e., taxes, licenses, and other fee revenues) for the calendar year 2017 was reported to be $247,368,473 and $302,458,426 for 2019 (Colorado Department of Revenue, 2020).

In the state of Washington, legal marijuana sales yielded over $70 million in tax revenue during the 2014/2015 fiscal year (Williams, 2015). During the 2017/2018 fiscal year, the state of Washington increased its marijuana sales tax revenue to over $320 million (Kovacevich, 2018). It has been estimated that, if marijuana sales were legalized in all 50 states, the associated tax revenue generated could exceed $3 billion annually (Ferner, 2014).[23]

In a more recent example, the tax revenue generated by medicinal and recreational cannabis use in Oregon was reported to exceed $100 million in 2020. Oregon decided to utilize this revenue windfall in support of it becoming the first state to decriminalize the use of other abusable psychotropics, including cocaine and heroin. As identified by Best (2020, p. 2):

> Instead of treating drug users as criminals, Oregon will now offer them addiction services funded by marijuana tax revenue, that is more than $100 million a year in the state.

Obviously, the licit cannabis industry is in a significant "growth" phase that is likely to continue throughout the third decade of the new millennium. Large U.S. corporations, such as Curaleaf Holdings® and Scotts Miracle-Gro® are increasingly investing hundreds of millions of dollars in the licit cannabis industry.

> Bethany Gomez, managing director for the Brightfield Group, a market research and analytics company that specializes in the cannabis industry, projects that the US recreational and medical cannabis industry will post $19 billion in sales this year [i.e., 2020] grow to $24 billion by 2021 and—with the additions of this week and likely newcomers such as New York—notch $45 billion in sales by 2025.
>
> (Wallace, 2020, p. 4)

Despite its worldwide production and commerce—and production, to varying degrees, in every state—approximately 50% of the cannabis that is illicitly used in the U.S. is smuggled in from one specific country, Mexico, particularly the area along the U.S. southern border with Mexico (Hurley, West, & Ehleringer, 2010; Pagliaro & Pagliaro, 2018). Additionally, increasing amounts of high-grade marijuana are smuggled into the U.S. from Canada, particularly along the U.S. northern border with Canada (Hurley et al., 2010; Pagliaro & Pagliaro, 2018).[24]

During the second decade of the new millennium, in addition to the widespread legalization of "medical marijuana" use in the majority of states, a related trend began that has

23. Based upon the consideration of more recent data, we believe that this prediction is an extremely conservative estimate and that the generated tax revenue could well exceed $30 billion annually by the end of the third decade of the new millennium as "legal cannabis spending is projected to reach $100 billion in the U.S. by 2029" (Bohlsen, 2019, p. 1).

24. During the first decade of the new millennium, increasing amounts of high potency marijuana (i.e., 15% to 25% THC) began to enter the U.S. from Canada. This marijuana was produced predominantly from indoor growing operations (i.e., "grow-ops") in the Province of British Columbia (i.e., "BC Bud"). This trend is expected to significantly intensify through the end of the third decade of the new millennium, and well beyond, because the possession and use of both medical and nonmedical/recreational cannabis became legalized across all of Canada in 2018 (Paperny & Saminather, 2017; Reith, 2017).

now become entrenched—state decriminalization or legalization of the "recreational" use of cannabis.[25] Associated with this trend was the rapid and increasing occurrence of the:

1. Illicit production and distribution of cannabis in states that had legalized recreational cannabis use;
2. Provision of the opportunity for transnational drug cartels to "set up shop" in these states and, consequently, facilitate the illicit distribution and sale of cannabis in states that had not legalized "recreational" use of cannabis.

(e.g., Cain, 2017; Romero, Gutierrez, & Blankstein, 2018; Shen, 2017)

> Northern California-based DEA Special Agent Casey Rettig said suspects send cash to the United States in $9,999 increments, just below the mandated reporting threshold, and receive funds from China that fly under that nation's $50,000 foreign spending limit. They then purchase homes with the help of cash lenders instead of traditional mortgage firms.
>
> (Romero et al., 2018, p. 3)

The transnational, or foreign, drug cartels—primarily from China, Cuba, and Mexico—that are involved in producing cannabis within states where "recreational" use of cannabis has been legalized, operate by: (1) concealing production within a legal environment; and (2) facilitating distribution to other states—without having to smuggle the cannabis across international borders (i.e., into the U.S. from Canada or Mexico). The methods adopted by these transnational "growers," who are operating within states where the "recreational" use of cannabis has been legalized, are quite simple. Operationally, they either purchase or lease:

1. Farms and areas of rural land to grow large cannabis crops;
2. Hundreds of homes in which to established small hydroponic "grow-ops" of up to 50 plants.

Quite often, the transnational grow-ops are operated (i.e., maintained on a day-to-day basis) by illegal immigrants—in the context of human trafficking (Pagliaro & Pagliaro, *Clinical Patient Data Files*). As noted in an NBC news investigative report:

> "There's a great profit motive in it," the DEA's Ladd said. "In Colorado, marijuana legalization has magnified the black market. The standard price per pound here is $2000, but they can get $3,500 to $4,500 by shipping it back East. The profits are great there."
>
> (Romero et al., 2018, p. 5)

CANNABIS PHARMACOLOGY

The naturally occurring chemical compounds, which have been identified in the cannabis plant, generally can be divided into three major groups:[26]

---

25. N.B. According to current U.S. federal laws (i.e., Schedule I of the Controlled Substances Act), cannabis possession, distribution, sale, and use are illegal. Although federal laws generally have precedent over related state laws, this law is generally not enforced in states that have decriminalized/legalized cannabis cultivation, possession, sales, and use.
26. See also the related discussion in the earlier subsection, "Cannabis Plant Botany—Chemical Constituents of Cannabis."

1. Cannabinoids;
2. Terpenoids;
3. Alkaloids.

Additionally, several thousand different chemicals are found in cannabis smoke, including ammonia, benz[a]anthracene, benzene, benzo[a]pyrene, carbon monoxide, cresols, cyanogen, hydrogen cyanide, nitric oxide, phenols, and tars (Graves, Johnson, & Nishida, 2020; Hitti, 2007; Sheehan, Hamnett, & Beasley, 2018; WHO, 2018).[27] Of these chemicals, approximately 100 different cannabinoids (e.g., CBD, CBN, and THC)—compounds that are only naturally found in cannabis plants and that function as exogenous ligands for the endocannabinoid system—have been identified (Weissman, 1981). (See also the related discussion in the following subsection.) Of these, the principal active cannabinoid, in terms of psychodelic actions, is THC. (See also the related discussion in the earlier cannabis pharmacognosy subsection, Cannabis Plant Botany—"Tetrahydrocannabinol.")

A variety of clearly defined dose-related effects have been associated with the psychotropic actions of THC. "Low" dosages may produce decreased intraocular pressure, drowsiness, euphoria, hypertension, increased appetite, memory impairment, reddened eyes, relaxation, tachycardia, and temporal disintegration. "Moderate" dosages may produce anxiety, decreased muscle strength and motor performance, decreased visual acuity, impaired coordination, and paranoia (Breivogel & Childers, 1998; Pagliaro & Pagliaro, 2009). "High" dosages may produce confused thinking, delusions, hallucinations, synesthesia, and toxic psychosis. (See the related discussion in the later cannabis pharmacology subsection—"Undesired, or Harmful, Effects and Toxicities.")

> The interchanging of the senses . . . the hashish eater knows what it is . . . to smell colors, to see sounds, and, much more frequently, to see feelings.
>
> (Ludlow, 1857, p. 72)

Pharmacodynamics: Mechanism of Action

This section presents and discusses several important theories regarding the mechanism of THC action, particularly those associated with the endocannabinoid system.

Endocannabinoid System

The mechanisms by which THC produces its psychodelic and other actions (e.g., analgesic and anticonvulsant) are not yet fully understood. Undoubtedly, the greatest advancement in this regard has been the identification of the endocannabinoid system—the endogenous system of cannabinoid receptors and agonists (Breivogel & Childers, 1998). Three major endogenous agonists, or ligands, of the endocannabinoid receptors have been identified:

1. Anandamide (N-Arachidonyl ethanolamine);
2. 2-Arachidonoylglycerol;
3. 2-Arachidonyl glycerol ether.

---

27. N.B. Several of these chemicals are known human carcinogens (e.g., benzo[a]pyrene, a highly carcinogenic hydrocarbon found in coal tar; cresols; phenols; and tars). (See also the later cannabis pharmacology subsection—"Undesired, or Harmful, Effects and Toxicities.")

Endocannabinoids are typically released as a result of increased intracellular calcium concentrations at postsynaptic sites—"in response to sustained synaptic activity" (Kendall & Yudowski, 2017, p. 3). The endocannabinoids elicit several pharmacologic effects that have been associated with the use of THC, including:

- Analgesia;
- Anticonvulsant;
- Antidepressant;
- Anti-emetic;
- Euphoria, mild;
- Impaired cognition;
- Impaired learning;
- Impaired memory;
- Impaired psychomotor skills;
- Pain relief;
- Polyphagia;
- Relaxation.

(Iversen, 2003; Maccarrone & Finazzi-Agro, 2002; Martin, Mechoulam, & Razdan, 1999; NIDA, 2020a; Pertwee & Ross, 2002; Singh & Budhiraja, 2006)

Important strides also have been made since the beginning of the new millennium in this regard. For example, a model of cannabinoid signaling was posited by Elphick and Egertova (2001), "in which anandamide is synthesized by postsynaptic cells and acts as a retrograde messenger molecule to modulate neurotransmitter release from presynaptic terminals" (p. 381). As explained by Wilson and Nicoll (2002, p. 678):

> In contrast to classical neurotransmitters, endogenous cannabinoids can function as retrograde synaptic messengers: They are released from postsynaptic neurons and travel backward across synapses, activating CB_1 on presynaptic axons and suppressing neurotransmitter release.

Thus, overall, the endocannabinoid system appears to primarily act as a neuromodulator of the CNS by affecting the release of several identified neurotransmitters, including:

- Acetylcholine;
- Dopamine;
- Endorphins;
- Gamma-Aminobutyric Acid (GABA);
- Glutamate;
- Noradrenaline;
- Serotonin.

(Lopez-Moreno, Gonzalez-Cuevas, & Moreno, 2008; Moreira & Lutz, 2008)

Consequently, cannabinoids share a final common neuronal action with several other drugs and substances of abuse, such as the opiate analgesics and the sedative-hypnotics (Ameri, 1999; Pagliaro & Pagliaro, 2004).

> ***Related Professional Reminder:*** ***In humans, it has been well established that all abusable psychotropics associated with physical and/or psychological dependence increase the release of dopamine in the CNS particularly in the nucleus accumbens. The nucleus accumbens is located in the basal forebrain where associative learning/memory (e.g., reward) processes occur. Dopamine activation of D_1 receptors typically results in a "reward response/behavior," while dopamine activation of D_2 receptors typically results in an "aversive response/behavior."***

CB1 And CB2 Receptors

There are two major cannabinoid G-protein coupled receptor subtypes—Subtype 1 (i.e., CB_1) receptors and Subtype 2 (i.e., CB_2) receptors (Breivogel & Childers, 1998; Pertwee, 2000). THC elicits its effects primarily by activating CB_1 receptors (Wilson & Nicoll, 2002), which are primarily present on central and peripheral neurons, predominantly within the CNS (Pertwee, 2000). These receptors appear to mediate the: (1) inhibition of adenylate cyclase (adenylyl cyclase) and various voltage-dependent calcium channels (i.e., opening of postsynaptic calcium channels followed by inhibition of presynaptic calcium influx); (2) stimulation of postsynaptic potassium channels facilitating potassium and neurotransmitter release; and (3) activation of mitogen-activated protein kinase (Ameri, 1999; Szabo & Schlicker, 2005).

The endocannabinoid activity of these receptors suggests a role in the modulation of neurotransmitter release and action (e.g., increasing dopaminergic neuronal activity in the ventral tegmental area-mesolimbic pathway) (Di Marzo, Melck, & Bisogno, 1998). However, it has since been recognized that effects on dopamine, and likely other neurotransmitters, is affected by the nature (i.e., type and degree) of THC exposure/use, particularly in the context of acute versus chronic use. For example, available data suggest that, in humans:

- Regular long-term cannabis users, particularly those who are dependent, demonstrate—via molecular imaging studies (e.g., positron emission tomography [PET] imaging)—reduced capacity for dopamine synthesis;
- Dopamine release in response to a stimulant challenge is inversely related to the level of cannabis use (i.e., from occasional to regular, long-term daily use);
- Regular, long-term cannabis users appear to have reduced dopamine transporter (DAT) density;
- Overall, cannabis users appear to have reduced presynaptic dopaminergic function;
- Repeated THC dosing may be associated with altered dopamine receptor signal transduction;
- The exposure to, or use of, THC may be related to structural abnormalities in dopamine neurons, particularly in some regions of the CNS;
- Prenatal THC exposure may produce complex postnatal changes in the CNS dopamine system.

(e.g., Ameri, 1999; Bloomfield, Ashok, & Volkow, 2016; Breivogel & Childers, 1998; Elphick & Egertova, 2001; Lopez-Moreno et al., 2008; Pagliaro, 2002)

In summary, of the variable relationships identified between cannabis/THC use or exposure, Bloomfield et al. (2016, p. 374) concluded that:

> The available evidence indicates that THC exposure produces complex, diverse, and potentially long-term effects on the dopamine system including increased nerve firing and dopamine release in response to acute THC and dopaminergic blunting associated with long-term use.

A model, which we have developed to generally account for the usual cascading sequence of events that underlie and precede the neuromodulator effects of THC (and other similar cannabinoid agonists) is represented in Figure 4.1.

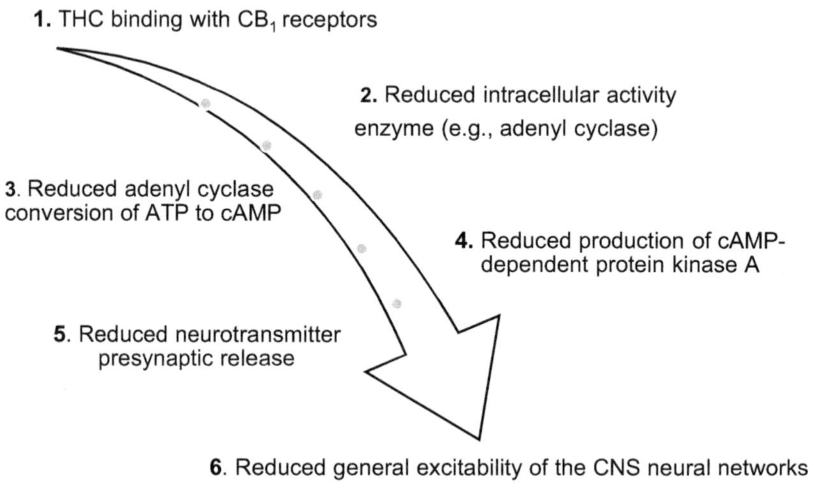

Figure 4.1 Proposed General Cascading Sequence of THC Neuromodulator Effects

As identified in Figure 4.1, activation of the CB_1 receptor[28] by THC and related agonists results in a cascade of events that culminate in reduced general excitability of the CNS neural networks[29] (i.e., inhibition of neurotransmission) ultimately by inhibiting the presynaptic release of various cholinergic, GABAergic, glutamatergic, noradrenergic, and serotonergic neurotransmitters in the CNS.[30]

CB1 Receptors

CB_1 receptors are one of the most abundant neuromodulator receptors within the CNS. They are located throughout the CNS with particularly high concentrations found in the

28. The same general proposed sequence of events also appears to be relevant and applicable in the context of THC binding to CB_2 receptors.
29. Additionally, THC decreases the inhibition normally produced by GABA neurons, which, consequently, results in increased dopamine, enhanced excitatory activity, and increased perception of the sense of pleasure. Additionally, regular long-term THC use—particularly, in the context of THC dependence, is generally associated with decreased dopamine.
30. In the peripheral nervous system, inhibition of CB_1 receptors mediates inhibition of adrenergic, cholinergic, and sensory neuroeffector transmission (Szabo & Schlicker, 2005).

basal ganglia, brainstem, cerebellum, cortex, hippocampus, neocortex, and striatum (Ameri, 1999; Wilson & Nicoll, 2002). CB_1 receptors are "also found on peripheral nerve terminals and some extra-neural sites such as the testis, eye, vascular endothelium, and spleen" (Kendall & Yudowski, 2017, p. 2). Most THC pleiotropic effects (i.e., the simultaneous influence of one gene on two or more seemingly unrelated phenotypic traits) are mediated by means of binding to the CB_1 receptor (Pagliaro & Pagliaro, 2009). For example, Cooper and Haney (2009, p. 104) identified that:

> The rewarding and positive reinforcing effects of the primary psychoactive component of smoked cannabis, delta-9-tetrahydrocannabinol (THC), are mediated by the cannabinoid CB_1 receptor. The CB_1 receptor has also been shown to mediate cannabinoid dependence and expression of withdrawal upon cessation of drug administration.

Virtually all of the psychotropic effects, and other CNS effects (e.g., analgesic and anticonvulsant), associated with the use of THC are mediated by interaction with the CB_1 receptor (Iversen, 2003).

CB2 Receptors

CB_2 receptors are primarily present on hemopoietic and immune cells, predominantly in peripheral tissues outside of the CNS (e.g., in the bone marrow and spleen) (Ameri, 1999; Klein, Lane, & Newton, 2000; Pertwee & Ross, 2002). These receptors appear to mediate the activation of mitogen-activated protein kinase and the inhibition of adenylate cyclase (Ameri, 1999).[31]

The endocannabinoid activity of these receptors (e.g., enhanced physiological response to cytokines) suggests a role in immunosuppression and anti-inflammatory action (Nocerino, Amato, & Izzo, 2000; NIDA, 2019a). In addition, although not yet confirmed, these mechanisms may play an active role in the treatment of medical disorders such as chronic neuropathic pain, which is often refractory to standard pharmacotherapeutic interventions (Eisenberg et al., 2014; Uberall, 2020; Uberall, Essner, & Mueller-Schwefe, 2019; Vuckovic, Srebro, & Savic Vujovic, 2018; Wilsey, Marcotte, & Deutsch, 2013). Most of the studies, which demonstrate efficacy, involve the oromucosal spray application of nabiximols. However, several researchers (e.g., Campbell, Hall, & Peacock, 2018; Mucke, Phillips, & Radbruch, 2018; Walitt, Klose, & Fitzcharles, 2016) have failed to confirm the efficacy of cannabis products (e.g., dronabinol, marijuana and THC) or other cannabinoids (e.g., CBD or nabilone) for the treatment of chronic neuropathic pain. As identified by Dhopeshwarkar and Mackie (2014, p. 430):

> A major limitation for the therapeutic development of compounds that directly activate CB_1 receptors is unwanted psychotropic effects. . . . In contrast, activation of CB_2 receptors does not appear to produce these psychotropic effects.

It is important to keep in mind that not all cannabinoids have the same action as agonists or antagonists of the CB_1 and/or CB_2 receptors. For example:

- THC acts as an agonist of both CB_1 and CB_2 receptors;
- CBD acts an antagonist of CB_1 and CB_2 receptor agonists;

---

31. CB_2 receptors also appear to be involved in "regulatory roles" (e.g., initiation and continuation) in the context of "drug abuse" (Kendall & Yudowski, 2017, p. 2).

- THCV acts as an agonist of CB_1 receptors at high doses and acts as an antagonist of CB_1 receptors at low doses.

(Pertwee, 2008)

Pharmacokinetics

In this section we present and discuss the absorption, distribution, metabolism, and excretion of THC among older adults. It is important to recognize that, in the cannabis plant, THC is primarily present in its non-psychoactive acid precursor form, "tetrahydrocannabinolic acid" (THCA). THCA is rapidly converted (i.e., decarboxylated) to THC by heating or burning—a process that occurs during both the extraction process and smoking (WHO, 2018).

Absorption

Cannabis and its active ingredients are generally administered by three routes: (1) pulmonary inhalation (e.g., combustion smoke and vaporization); (2) ingestion (e.g., drinking or eating); and (3) topical application to body surfaces.[32]

Following ingestion, THC bioavailability is low (i.e., approximately 10% to 15%) because of extensive first-pass hepatic metabolism (Huestis, 2007). Blood THC concentrations peak approximately two to thee hours after ingestion. Following pulmonary inhalation, THC bioavailability is much higher, having a mean of 27% (range of 17% to 37%)[33,34] due to its rapid absorption from the lungs and avoidance of first-pass hepatic metabolism.[35] Blood THC concentrations peak shortly after the pulmonary inhalation of cannabis (i.e., ~ ten minutes) (McGilveray, 2005). However, while blood THC concentrations peak at about the same time after ingestion, the bioavailability of THC following rectal administration is approximately 50% higher than that obtained by ingestion because of the greater absorption and less first-pass hepatic metabolism (Brenneisen, Egli, & ElSohly, 1996); ElSohly, Gul, & Walker, 2018). Sublingual administration of THC peaks after ~ three hours (Guy & Robson, 2003).

---

32. Topical application is used for oils and infused products such as balms, lotions, salves, and shampoos. Because significant cognitive and/or psychedelic effects are not generally associated with this route of administration, the topical application of cannabis products is not further discussed in this chapter.
33. The observed differences are primarily due to individual variability in smoking techniques (e.g., number, duration, and spacing of puffs; inhalation volume and hold time).
34. N.B. Additionally, and significantly, Spindle, Cone, and Schlienz (2018, p. 1), in their crossover trial of the acute effects obtained from either smoking or vaporizing equal doses of THC, found that:

    > Vaporized cannabis resulted in qualitatively stronger drug effects for most pharmacodynamic outcomes and higher peak concentrations of THC in blood, compared with equal doses of smoked cannabis.

35. Although "dabbing" is not a technique commonly used by older adults, it should be noted that the bioavailability of vaping THC can be increased to 75% with the use of "dabbing"—a technique in which butane hash oil (BHO) "is consumed by flash vaporization on a glowing titanium nail, followed by inhalation of the resulting vapor through a waterpipe in a single puff" (Hadener, Vieten, & Weinmann, 2019, p. 207).

Distribution

THC is approximately 97% protein bound, while its active metabolite, 11-OH-THC, is approximately 99% protein bound. The apparent volume of distribution of THC is approximately 10 liters per kg, primarily because of its high lipid solubility (Hunt, Jones, & Herning, 1981). The long-term storage of THC in body fat helps to explain the poor correlation between blood THC concentrations and clinical effects, particularly during the initial period of establishing equilibrium or hysteresis (e.g., Cone & Huestis, 1993; Goulle & Guerbet, 2014; Heather, 2001).

Metabolism

THC is primarily metabolized in the liver by the hepatic microsomal enzyme system (i.e., cytochrome P450 complex)—both CYP2C9 and CYP3A4, which are involved in the oxidative metabolism of THC.[36] Other body organs (e.g., brain, intestines, and lungs) also contain CYP450 enzymes and contribute, albeit to a significantly lesser extent, to the metabolism of THC. Once in the circulatory system, the hepatic oxidative metabolism of THC produces both an:

1. Active metabolite, 11-hydroxy-delta-9-tetrahydrocannabinol (11-OH-THC);
2. Inactive metabolite, 11-nor-hydroxy-delta-9-tetrahydrocannabinol (THCCOOH).

While the blood 11-OH-THC concentrations quickly peak following pulmonary inhalation of cannabis, the blood THCCOOH concentrations peak 1.5 to two hours after the pulmonary inhalation of cannabis and about three hours after the sublingual administration of THC.

Cannabidiol is metabolized in a manner similar to THC and is also subject to significant first-pass hepatic metabolism (Anderson & Chan, 2016; Huestis, 2007; Yamaori, Kushihara, & Yamamoto, 2010).

Excretion

Some researchers report a mean initial "alpha" distribution half-life of elimination of approximately 30 hours for THC. However, the later "beta" phase elimination half-life is about 3.5 days because of its preferential concentration and storage in the spleen and body fat (range, one to seven days). Additionally, it has long been recognized that cannabis smoke has the potential, like tobacco smoke, to induce hepatic microsomal isoenzymes. In this regard, regular, long-term cannabis users generally eliminate THC more rapidly (half-life of elimination of approximately 28 hours) than nonusers (half-life of elimination of approximately 57 hours).

Total body clearance of THC generally ranges from 750 to 1,200 ml/minute with rates being, on average, approximately 10% lower in females compared to males. The elimination half-life of its inactive metabolite, THCCOOH, is two to six days. Both metabolites

36. CYP2C9 and CYP3A4 also are primarily involved in the metabolism of CBN while CYP2C19 and CYP3A4 are involved in the metabolism of CBD.

are excreted in the urine. They are also secreted back into the gastrointestinal system by means of enterohepatic recirculation, where they are reabsorbed into the circulatory system or excreted in the feces. THC and its two major metabolites, 11-OH-THC and THCCOOH, are present in the urine as glucuronide conjugates. Low concentrations of both THC metabolites are often detected in the feces (primarily, 11-OH-THC) and urine (primarily, THC-COOH) for more than five weeks after cannabis—marijuana, hashish, or hash oil—was last used.

Tetrahydrocannabinol is subject to significant renal tubular reabsorption because of its high lipid solubility. Consequently, the renal excretion of unchanged THC is low (Sharma, Murthy, & Srinivas Bharath, 2012). Although, urinary concentrations of THC exceeding 1.5 ng/ml are suggestive of cannabis use during the previous eight hours, because of pharmacokinetic variance and extreme interindividual variability, a presumptive THC blood concentration cannot be reliably related to a specific measurable level of cognitive or behavior impairment. The blood to plasma concentration ratio for THC is 0.55.

Urine Testing for Cannabis Use

The urine tests currently used for identifying cannabis use detect concentrations of both: (1) THC; and (2) its major inactive metabolite, THCCOOH. The two general types of urinalyses involve either the use of: (1) immunoassay (IA); or (2) gas chromatography/mass spectrometry (GC/MS). Immunoassay is less expensive and easier to perform and, hence, is usually the test of first choice—often in the context of a rapid "screening" test. Immunoassay utilizes a drug-enzyme complex to determine the presence of THC metabolites in the urine. Results are binary and are qualitative in nature—either positive or negative, as indicated by the color produced. For the immunoassay test, the standard cutoff threshold for cannabinoids in the urine is typically set at 50 ng/ml in order to minimize false positive results.

Gas chromatography/mass spectrometry utilizes a more complex, or sophisticated, method of analysis that is also more time consuming and expensive. Gas chromatography, which must be conducted in a suitably equipped chemical laboratory, initially is used to separate the chemicals present in the urine sample. This is followed by the use of MS to ionize molecules present in the sample and to identify each by their specific molecular weights. The standard cutoff threshold for cannabinoids in the urine, when utilizing GC/MS, is typically set at 15 ng/ml. The major advantage of the GC/MS is that the results are quantitative. Thus, GC/MS is typically used in the context of a "confirmatory" test (i.e., following an initial, positive cannabis immunoassay test result).

The primary glucuronide conjugate of THC, THCCOOH, is predominantly detected in the urine. Levels of THCCOOH as low as 1 ng/ml of urine can be detected with good validity and reliability.[37] However, the validity of urine tests is not always accurate because false positive results can occur due to the:

1. Interference of certain other drugs or substances of abuse that may have been concurrently used (e.g., ibuprofen [Motrin®]);

37. N.B. In addition to assay sensitivity and specificity, individual factors (e.g., dosage, method of use and associated relative bioavailability, state of hydration, and rate of elimination) can significantly affect detection times (Goodwin, Darwin, & Chiang, 2008).

2. Inability of a test to differentiate between cannabis "smoke" or "vapor" that is deliberately, or directly, inhaled and that which is passively, or indirectly, inhaled (i.e., as "side stream," or "second-hand," smoke/vapor).

Additionally, the ingestion of large quantities of products that contain hemp seed oil may produce "false positive" results if the cutoff values designated by the laboratory for the urine test are too low. Urine tests also can give "false negative" results. These false negative results are much more likely to occur when the urine test sample is deliberately adulterated with an in vitro adulterant that is added to the urine sample after collection (e.g., peroxidase and peroxide, which are found in "Stealth®;" and pyridinium chlorochromate, which is found in "Urine Luck®"—products specifically developed and marketed to invalidate urine tests) (e.g., Dasgupta, 2015).

Cannabis Drug-Drug Interactions

A surprising scarcity of empirical data exists regarding drug-drug interactions involving THC. This lack of published research may be related to several variables that make quantification of potentially significant THC drug-drug interactions difficult to identify and study. These difficulties include differences in:

- THC and other cannabinoid concentrations among various natural sources (i.e., marijuana versus hashish versus hashish oil);

  THC and other cannabinoid concentrations among various synthetic sources (i.e., prescription THC formulations [i.e., dronabinol, Marinol®; nabilone, Cesamet®]);[38,39]
- Methods of cannabis use (i.e., ingestion versus pulmonary inhalation);
- Marijuana smoking techniques—such as number of "tokes" per joint, depth of inhalation, or length of time that the marijuana smoke is inhaled and retained in the lungs;
- Effects of "polycyclic aromatic hydrocarbons" (PAHs) contained in marijuana smoke.

In addition, the federal illegal status of cannabis use in the U.S. has significantly impeded related research. As states increasingly move to legalize cannabis use, this situation is expected to significantly change over the next decade.

Consequently, data concerning potentially significant THC drug-drug interactions generally are limited to theoretical questions primarily involving the cytochrome P-450 enzymes. In this regard, the cannabinoids variably act as "inducers," "inhibitors," or "substrates" of

38. Usually prescribed for the management of severe nausea and vomiting associated with cancer pharmacotherapy.
39. Additionally, nabiximols (Sativex®), which was developed in the UK, is made from a cannabis extract. Sativex®, which is available in over 30 countries, including Canada, is pending FDA approval in the U.S. primarily for the treatment of neuropathic pain. It contains an equal ratio (i.e., 1:1) of THC and CBD, as well as a variety of other cannabinoids, flavonoids, and terpenes. Sativex® is administered as an oromucosal spray (Nurmikko, Serpell, & Hoggart, 2007; Russo, Guy, & Robson, 2007).

    Epidiolex® (CBD oral solution) received FDA approval in 2018 for the treatment of the Lennox-Gastaut syndrome and Dravet syndrome—both rare forms of childhood onset epilepsy that are difficult to treat (Devinsky, Cross, & Laux, 2017; FDA, 2019; Forster, 2018; Wirrell, 2016). (See also the related discussion in the later cannabis subsection, "Medical Cannabis Use.")

the cytochrome P-450 enzymes (see the related discussion in the earlier cannabis pharmacology subsection, Pharmacokinetics—"Metabolism") (e.g., Motycka, Glinton, & Brennan, 2016; Rong, Carmona, & Lee, 2018; Stout & Cimino, 2014). For example:

1. Inducers of CYP2C9 (e.g., barbiturates, carbamazepine [Tegretol®], and phenytoin [Dilantin®]) and CYP3A4 (e.g., carbamazepine, phenytoin, and rifampin [Rifadin®]) may increase the metabolism of THC and CBD and, consequently, reduce related plasma concentrations.
2. Inhibitors of CYP2C9 (e.g., amiodarone [Cordarone®], cimetidine [Tagamet®], and fluoxetine [Prozac®]) and CYP3A4 (e.g., clarithromycin [Biaxin®], ketoconazole [Nizoral®], and verapamil [Calan®]) may decrease the metabolism of THC and CBD and, consequently, increase related plasma concentrations.
3. Marijuana and tobacco smoke induce CYP1A2. Consequently, dosage adjustments may be required with drugs that are primarily metabolized by CYP1A2 (e.g., caffeine, clozapine [Clozaril®], and theophylline [Theo-Dur®]), particularly when regular, or long-term, marijuana or tobacco smoking is initiated or discontinued.[40]
4. PAHs contained in marijuana smoke (like those contained in tobacco smoke) can induce CYP450 enzymes and, consequently, increase the metabolism of certain drugs (e.g., chlorpromazine [Thorazine®] and theophylline [Theo-Dur®]).

(Anderson & Chan, 2016; Arellano, Papaseit, & Romaguera, 2017; Horn & Hansten, 2014; Melton, 2017; Yamaori, Koeda, & Kushihara, 2012)

Undesired, or Harmful, Effects and Toxicities

There are several characteristic signs associated with cannabis use, primarily the: (1) pungent odor of cannabis smoke[41] that is often recognized on clothing and in closed areas where the cannabis has been smoked (e.g., in automobiles, bathrooms, bedrooms, and offices); and (2) reddened, or "blood shot," eyes. Whether or not older adults become "stoned," or just "mellow out," the common toxicities, which are related to the use of cannabis, can be readily divided into toxicities associated with: (1) occasional, or short-term use; and (2) regular, long-term use. However, most Americans do not appear to appreciate the significant risks associated with cannabis use. For example, the NCDAS (2019, p. 2) reported that:

72% of Americans believe that regular alcohol use is a greater health risk than regular marijuana use;

76% of Americans believe that marijuana use is less harmful than tobacco use.

Old Misbelief: Cannabis is a relatively non-toxic, natural psychodelic that is associated with little harm.

40. This effect is particularly significant among those who regularly smoke both marijuana and tobacco—a fairly common practice.
41. Thus, the common names for cannabis—"skunk" and "skunk weed" (see the related discussion of terpenes in the earlier subsection, Cannabis Plant Botany—"Chemical Constituents of Cannabis—Terpenes").

False. The following subsections address the fallacy of this misbelief with attention to occasional, or short-term cannabis use, as well as regular, long-term cannabis use.[42]

Toxicities Associated with Occasional or Short-Term Cannabis Use

Occasional or short-term cannabis use may be associated with the following undesired, or harmful, effects and toxicities (Pagliaro & Pagliaro, 2004, 2009, 2018):[43,44]

- Anxiety;
- Ataxia;
- Cognitive impairment;
- Confusion;
- Conjunctivitis;
- Delusions;
- Depersonalization;
- Dizziness;
- Executive functioning impaired;
- False memory production;[45]

---

42. N.B. During our 40 years of clinical practice with older adults, we have routinely observed a significantly higher incidence of toxicities associated with cannabis use—as well as related adverse sequelae—in comparison to that observed among younger adults. We primarily ascribe this higher susceptibility of older adults to toxicities associated with cannabis use to:

    1. Age-related diminished reserve capacity;
    2. Age-related increased number of acute and chronic medical conditions;
    3. Age-related increase in body fat;
    4. Age-related polypharmacy.

43. The occurrence and severity of these, and other undesired, or harmful, effects and toxicities, are dependent on several factors, including:

    1. THC dosage;
    2. Method of use, or route of administration;
    3. Context of use;
    4. Health status of the user;
    5. Genetics of the user.

44. Often, in addition to acting individually, these undesired or harmful effects and toxicities act in unison to produce additive or synergistic effects. For example, ataxia, cognitive impairment, dizziness, postural hypotension, psychomotor impairment, and slowed reaction time, which can occur individually, or in a myriad of possible combinations, that can place older adults at significant risk for falls and related injuries (e.g., fractured hip) (Pagliaro & Pagliaro, *Clinical Patient Data Files*). For example, in this context, Choi, Marti, and DiNitto (2018, p. 215) found that among their subjects 50 years of age or older, "marijuana use increases the likelihood of ED visits through increased injury risk." Additionally, Grewal and Loh (2020 p. E1) noted that "among older adults, cannabis consumption—including use of edibles—has been linked to greater cognitive impairment and a heightened risk of hypotension-related falls, arrhythmia and drug interactions."
45. Kloft, Otgaar, and Blokland (2020, p. 4585), in their randomized, double-blind placebo-controlled research study of the effects of cannabis on memory, found that:

    > Intoxicated participants were more susceptible to false-memory creation using a virtual-reality eyewitness scenario and virtual reality perpetrator scenario. False memory effects were mostly restricted to the acute-intoxication phase.

- Hallucinations;
- Headache;
- Hypertension;
- Increased appetite;[46]
- Memory impairment, particularly episodic, short-term, verbal, and working memory;
- Nausea;
- Panic attacks;
- Paranoia;
- Polyphagia;
- Postural (orthostatic) hypotension, particularly among older adults;
- Psychomotor impairment;
- Psychotic disorder (for further discussion, see the later subsection—"Cannabis-Induced Psychotic Disorder");
- Pulmonary irritation;
- Slowed reaction time;
- Somnolence;
- Synesthesia;
- Tachycardia;
- Temporal disintegration;
- Toxic delirium;
- Visual acuity decreased;
- Work productivity decreased.

Toxicities Associated with Regular, Long-Term Cannabis Use

Over the 1970s, 1980s, and 1990s, the potency of cannabis increased five-fold, from an average THC content of 2% to a THC content of 10% (Harrison, Backenheimer, & Inciardi, 1996). Additionally, as briefly discussed earlier in this chapter, these "standard" THC concentrations have continued to steadily and significantly increase over the first two decades of the new millennium. (See the related discussion in the earlier pharmacognosy subsection—"Cannabis Preparation and THC Concentration.") This increase in potency reflected a preferential change among users from *Cannabis (sativa) sativa* to *Cannabis (sativa) indica* and the increased selective cultivation of sinsemilla varieties (see the related discussion in the earlier Cannabis Pharmacognosy subsection—"Cannabis Plant Botany"). Consequently, several undesired, or harmful, effects and toxicities have now been associated with

46. This common effect, colloquially known as "the munchies," has been commercialized by the Jack in the Box® fast-food restaurant chain. In response to the 2018-legalization of the "recreational" use of marijuana in California, Jack in the Box® began marketing its "Merry [a reference to the common street name for cannabis, "Mary Jane"] Munchie Meal" (Gant, 2017; Morris, 2017).

the regular, long-term use of cannabis among older adults.[47] These effects and toxicities include:[48,49]

- Cannabinoid hyperemesis syndrome (CHS);[50]
- Cannabis withdrawal syndrome (relatively mild);
- Cognitive impairment;[51]
- Dysphoria;
- Immunosuppression;
- Lethargy;
- Mental depression;
- Physical dependence;
- Psychological dependence;

---

47. It may seem logical to conclude, based upon these observations, that potential cannabis users, being aware of the significant increases in the THC concentrations of current cannabis products, would take appropriate precautions (e.g., avoidance of cannabis use or reduction of dosage, or amount consumed or inhaled). However, new millennial trends—in terms of medicalization, decriminalization, and legalization of cannabis use in many cities and states across the U.S.—have significantly affected people's related attitudes (e.g., Cerda, Wall, & Keyes, 2012; Samuels, 2015).

    For example, a decreased perception of the significant risk associated with cannabis use has been identified (NIDA, 2020b). In addition, Cerda et al. (2012) noted two related and potentially problematic, but expected, trends that: (1) residents of states, which have enacted laws decriminalizing cannabis use have higher odds of cannabis use; and (2) states with legalized cannabis use have higher rates of cannabis use.
48. The intensity and clinical significance of these toxicities depend, to a significant degree, upon the: (1) amount of THC absorbed; (2) environmental setting or circumstances of use; and (3) physical, mental, and social characteristics of the user.
49. A better understanding of cannabis pharmacology (see earlier cannabis pharmacology subsection, "Mechanism of Action") provides possible explanations for many of these observed undesired, or harmful, effects and toxicities. For example, the undesired effects involving human immune response are likely mediated by interactions involving THC, or other cannabinoids, with the CB_2 receptor. The mental depression and psychosis are likely mediated by effects of the endocannabinoid system on the neurotransmitters, dopamine, and serotonin. In addition, a genetic expression of various harmful effects (e.g., development of schizophrenia), as noted by Power, Verweij, and Zuhair (2014), likely plays a significant mediating role.
50. The CHS was first identified almost 20 years ago by Allen, de Moore, and Heddle (2004). It is characterized by: (1) regular, long-term cannabis use; (2) cyclic, intractable nausea and vomiting; and (3) compulsive hot water bathing (Andrews & Bracero, 2015; Nicolson, Denysenko, & Mulcare, 2012).

    The hyperemesis phase of the CHS is self-limiting with a usual duration of one to two days (Beech, Sterrett, & Babiuk, 2015). However, continued or resumed cannabis use will generally exacerbate the signs and symptoms. Although the use of standard antiemetic pharmacotherapy is ineffective for most CHS patients, a hot bath or shower, as reported by patients, provides effective, although only temporary relief. Hospitalization may be required in cases of severe volume depletion or other acute medical contexts (Galli, Andari Sawaya, & Friedenberg, 2011).
51. As identified by van Holst and Schilt (2011)—in contrast to the neurotoxicity associated with regular, long-term alcohol or amphetamine use—the neuropsychological dysfunction (e.g., cognitive impairment and memory impairment) associated with the occasional, or short-term, use of cannabis, does not appear to persist (i.e., does not appear to be permanent) following a period of abstinence (i.e., generally a minimum of 30 days). (For further related discussion, see Chapter 1, *Alcohol*, and Chapter 2, *Amphetamines and Cocaine*.)

    However, this conclusion remains open to debate and warrants further research, particularly regarding the regular, long-term use of higher dosages/potencies of cannabis, which is attendant with the increasing legalization and availability of cannabis for "recreational use" in several states. For example, Schacht, Hutchison, and Filbey (2012) found, in their matched control study, that heavy cannabis users had significantly reduced hippocampal and amygdala volumes.

- Psychosis (see additional related discussion in the later section, "Cannabis-Induced Psychotic Disorder");
- Pulmonary irritation (e.g., cough and colds, with the eventual development of related COPD [i.e., asthma or bronchitis];[52,53]
- Suicidality (i.e., suicide ideation, suicide planning, suicide attempt, and suicide completion);[54]
- Work productivity decreased;
- Xerostomia.

(Pagliaro & Pagliaro, 2004, 2009, 2018)

---

52. N.B. Although not listed because of a paucity of available reliable published data, we have long posited (e.g., Pagliaro, 1983, 1988) that lung cancer would be an expected chronic toxicity associated with regular, long-term cannabis smoking. This toxic effect would be expected because of: (1) the presence of known human carcinogens in cannabis smoke in concentrations significantly higher than those found in tobacco cigarette smoke (e.g., Ashton, 2001); and (2) the method of smoking cannabis (i.e., inhaling the cannabis smoke deeply into the lungs and holding it in the lungs as long as possible) (e.g., Pagliaro, 1983, 1988; Pagliaro & Pagliaro, *Clinical Patient Data Files*). This smoking technique is thought to maximize the contact of the smoke with the alveoli and, hence, increase the amount of THC absorbed by the capillaries for distribution through the circulatory system. Vaporized THC significantly decreases or eliminates this risk. (See also the related discussion in the later cannabis subsections—"Pulmonary Toxicities" and "Vaping.")

    Although smoking cannabis has not yet been proven to be a definitive risk factor for the development of lung cancer, it should be noted that several studies (e.g., Aldington, Harwood, & Cox, 2008; Berthiller, Straif. & Boniol, 2008; Callaghan, Allebeck, & Sidorchuk, 2013) have supported the positive association between cannabis smoking and lung cancer. However, others (e.g., Zhang, Morgenstern, & Greenland, 2015) have found no such association. In all related studies, the major confounding variables in the interpretation of related results included: (1) small sample size; (2) concurrent nicotine tobacco use; and (3) estimated amount of cannabis used.
53. Additionally, beginning in 2019, dozens of cases of lung injury were identified and linked to "vaping." The CDC named this condition, "E-Cigarette, or Vaping, Product Use Associated Lung Injury" (EVALI). However, the exact cause (e.g., active ingredient—THC; vehicles used in vaping liquid products; frequent episodes of rapid, long-term vaping) has not been definitively identified (e.g., Perrine, Pickens, & Boehmer, 2019). More recently, the FDA (2020) analyzed vaping products, which: (1) contain THC; and (2) are associated with cases of EVALI and found that 81% contained vitamin E acetate as a diluent. Consequently, vitamin E acetate is currently widely considered to be the primary etiologic factor for EVALI (e.g., Lal, Kumar Mishra, & Kant Sahu, 2019; Splete, 2019) and, consequently, the FDA (2020, p. 5) has recommended that "vitamin E acetate should not be added to any e-cigarette, or vaping, products."

    To us, this toxicity also is reminiscent of lung damage associated with the use of crack cocaine (i.e., "crack lung"—see Chapter 2, *Amphetamines and Cocaine*). We have posited that the lung toxicity associated with THC and other vaping may be, at least partially, related to the direct irritation of the pulmonary tissue generally associated with the inhalation of large amounts of "heated vapor." See the related discussion in the later subsection, Common Methods of Marijuana use—"Vaping." See also the related discussion in Chapter 3, *Caffeine and Nicotine*, nicotine pharmacology subsection—"E-Cigarettes."

    As reported by Harrar (2019a, p. 1):

    > There have been 33 confirmed deaths [from EVALI] as of October 17 [2019]—roughly half of them in people over age 50, according to the CDC.

    See also the related discussion in the later subsection, "EVALI."
54. The relationship between regular, long-term cannabis use and suicide is reportedly positive, but modest (e.g., Borges, Bagge, & Orozco, 2016; Delforterie, Lynskey, & Huizink, 2015). However, we tend to question these findings and suggest that other underlying variables (e.g., mental depression) or other concomitant cofactors, likely play a major—if not determining—role in this reported relationship between cannabis use and suicidality. Interestingly, in comparison to states in which cannabis use was not legalized, its legal use among middle-aged men has been reportedly associated with a reduction in suicides (Anderson, Rees, & Sabia, 2014).

Although these and other toxicities associated with regular, long-term use have been extensively documented in the published literature, the relative incidence of serious toxicities directly associated with cannabis use is low. However, the available evidence—from controlled clinical studies and common sense (i.e., logical conclusions based on a knowledge of cannabis pharmacology)—point to three additional major toxicities that are directly linked to the regular, long-term use of cannabis:

1. Motor vehicle and other crashes, including airplane, train, and truck crashes;
2. Psychosis;
3. Pulmonary toxicity.

See also the later pharmacology subsection, Undesired, or Harmful, Effects and Toxicities—"Physical and Psychological Dependence.")

Motor Vehicle and Other Crashes

Motor vehicle and other crashes are a major concern for older adults who use any form of cannabis.[55]

Old Misbelief: It is relatively safe to smoke cannabis while driving a car.

False. In fact, several researchers—using large meta-analyses—found that acute cannabis intoxication results in a significant increase in the odds of being involved in a motor vehicle crash (motor vehicle collision, MVC).

For example, Li, Brady, and DiMaggio (2012, p. 65) reported that:

> The results of this meta-analysis suggest that marijuana use by drivers is associated with a significantly increased risk of being involved in motor vehicle crashes.

As found by Asbridge, Hayden, and Cartwright (2012, p. 1):

> Acute cannabis consumption is associated with an increased risk of a motor vehicle crash, especially for fatal collisions.

As noted by Hartman, Brown, and Milavetz (2015a, p. 25):

> Cannabis is the most commonly encountered non-alcohol drug in driving under the influence cases."

---

55. N.B. Interestingly, in their review of Sativex® oral mucosal spray—an extract of the cannabis sativa plant containing THC and cannabidiol (CBD) in a 1:1 ratio—Celius and Vila (2018, e00962) found that:

> The results from the THC:CBD oromucosal spray driving studies and real-world registries did not show any evidence of an increase in motor vehicle accidents associated with THC:CBD oromucosal spray.

Although not yet approved for use in the U.S. by the FDA, the combination of THC and CBD in a 1:1 ratio is referred to by the United States Adopted Name (USAN) as "nabiximols."

More recently, a 10-year AAA study of traffic deaths in Washington State revealed that the:

> Number of "stoned," or high on marijuana, drivers in deadly crashes more than doubled in Washington since 2012 [i.e., the year that Washington became the first U.S. state to legalize the recreational use of marijuana].
>
> (CBS News, 2020, p. 1)

Finally, Johnson, Mechtler, and Ali (2021), in their reanalysis of data from the *National Highway Traffic Safety Administration's Drug and Alcohol Crash Risk Study*, found that:

> Older [i.e., 64 years of age and older] THC-positive drivers were at increased risk for [a vehicle] crash.

In addition, as previously noted, when cannabis is used in combination with alcohol—a fairly common practice—the research is abundantly clear that the degree of driving impairment is significantly greater (i.e., in comparison to that caused by the use of either cannabis or alcohol alone) (e.g., Hartman et al., 2015b; Ramaekers, Berghaus, & van Laar, 2004; Sewell, Poling, & Sofuoglu, 2009).

Regular, long-term cannabis users, are at greatest risk for motor vehicle and other crashes, particularly, if they:

1. Use high potency cannabis;
2. Are drivers who concurrently abuse both cannabis and alcohol—which, can result in the deleterious, synergistic effects associated with their different mechanisms of action on driving ability;
3. Are inexperienced drivers.

(Pagliaro & Pagliaro, 2009; Stein, Caviness, & Anderson, 2014).[56]

The association between marijuana use and motor vehicle crashes has been supported by the analysis of related data from states where marijuana use has been legalized for "recreational" use (among adults). As identified by Hagler (2017, p. 11), citing data from the 2015 report entitled, *The Legalization of Marijuana in Colorado: The Impact*:

> The statistics reveal that between 2013 and 2014 there was a 45% increase in marijuana-associated impaired driving, a 32% increase in marijuana-related motor vehicle deaths (with a 92% increase from 2010 to 2014), as well as 29% and 38% increases in emergency room visits and hospital admissions secondary to marijuana use.

As cannabis use has significantly increased among drivers—coincident with its legalization—law enforcement officers now require a rapid detection quick-screen test for detecting cannabis use. The Draeger Drug Test 5000®, which is produced in Europe, is a mobile drug screening system that can be used to determine cannabis use with a simply

56. N.B. It is particularly important to recognize that the incidence of cannabis-related MVCs is increasing (e.g., Capler, Bilsker, & Van Pelt, 2017; Christophersen, Morland, & Stewart, 2016) and we fully expect it to continue to do so over the next decade as increasing numbers of states legalize marijuana use or decriminalize its possession and use. For example, Couper and Peterson (2014), in their comprehensive study of drug use and motor vehicle accidents, or MVAs—pre- and post-legalization in Washington state—found that, while other drug use remained constant, marijuana use significantly increased (i.e., from 25% to over 50%).

obtained roadside sample of the driver's saliva (Platt, 2018). The system is portable, easy to use, and provides immediate results. The Draeger Drug Test 5000® also can be used to determine the use of amphetamines, benzodiazepines, cocaine, and methadone.[57]

***Related Professional Reminder*: Without exception, drivers should not smoke or vape cannabis and drive.**

Despite this admonition, and its strong support in the published professional and scientific literature (e.g., CBS News, 2020; Hartman & Huestis, 2013), the effects of cannabis use on driving performance have not yet been ingrained into the public psyche in the U.S. To illustrate this lack of awareness, which is commonly observed among various members of the general public regarding the deleterious effects of cannabis use on motor vehicle driving performance, we share the following two anecdotal cases that we personally recently observed. In the first case, an older woman, whose driver's license was revoked because of an alcohol-related impaired driving conviction, requested that her adolescent granddaughter—a daily recreational user of marijuana—be her designated driver.

In the second case, an older man—who required a designated driver because his eyes were being dilated as part of his ophthalmological examination—was accompanied by his son in the ophthalmologist's waiting room. After a while, the son told his father that he needed to "go out for a smoke" and "stretch a bit" to relieve his "back pain." As he left the waiting room, another patient shared that he had recently lost his wife to lung cancer and that, perhaps the man's son should stop smoking. The father quickly clarified that it was "okay." His son was not going out to smoke a tobacco cigarette, but was going out to smoke his medical marijuana, which he used to manage his chronic back pain (Pagliaro & Pagliaro, *Clinical Patient Data Files*.)

The AAA study of drivers in Washington State identified that:

> 69% of residents surveyed identified as cannabis users who had driven high in the last year. Ten percent believed they actually drive better after smoking pot.
>
> (CBS News, 2020, p. 3)

As further noted by Capler et al. (2017, p. 5) in their meta-review and analysis of cannabis use and driving:

> Most cannabis users consider their driving to be only slightly impaired by cannabis use, and some believe it may be improved by cannabis use.

Additionally, among older adults who both drive and use cannabis, we have found that over 80% express little or no concern with this behavior. Typically, when questioned, they readily respond that, "since the cannabis is approved by the government and prescribed by my physician, it must be safe." Interestingly, this response and behavior, and their related effects on driving, by older adults is extremely similar to that observed among older adults who use prescription opiate analgesics for osteoarthritic pain.

---

57. N.B. In Canada, the Drager 5000® has been approved for police roadside use in the context of impaired driving. However, some concern has been raised regarding "false positive" results associated with the use of CBD—which is non-psychoactive (Boynton, 2019; Spears, 2019).

Cannabis-Induced Psychotic Disorder—Schizophrenia

Old Misbelief: Psychosis is not associated with cannabis use.

False. In fact, according to the NIDA (2020b, p. 11):

> People who have taken large doses of the drug [THC] may experience an acute psychosis, which includes hallucinations, delusions, and a loss of the sense of personal identity.

While severe mental health problems are not generally associated with cannabis use among most users, it is currently widely recognized that, for some cannabis users, it can be associated with a wide variety of schizophrenia-like effects, including "positive," "negative," and "cognitive" effects (Hall & Degenhardt, 2008; Pagliaro & Pagliaro, 1999, 2004, 2009; Wilkinson, Radhakrishnan, & D'Souza, 2014).[58]

Positive Schizophrenia-Like Effects Positive schizophrenia-like effects include:

- Abnormalities in time perception;
- Catatonic behaviors;
- Conceptual disorganization;
- Delusions, usually grandiose;
- Depersonalization;
- Derealization;
- Disorganized speech;
- Fragmented thinking;
- Grossly disorganized behavior;
- Hallucinations;
- Paranoid thoughts;
- Racing thoughts;
- Thought alienation.

Negative Schizophrenia-Like Effects Negative schizophrenia-like effects include:

- Affective flattening;
- Alogia;
- Anhedonia;
- Apathy;

58. This has not always been the case in the U.S., nor in the related published Western clinical and scientific literature. For example, we were among the first to formally identify this relationship in presentations and publications during the 1970s and 1980s (e.g., Pagliaro, 1983, 1988) based upon both our clinical experience (i.e., Pagliaro & Pagliaro, *Clinical Patient Data Files*) and a review of 100 years of related published East Indian literature from the mid-19th to the mid-20th centuries. However, we commonly received "push back" that either this observation was: (1) inaccurate; or (2) accurate and applicable in India, but not in the U.S.—due to the significant differences in cultural patterns of cannabis use.

- Avolition;
- Lack of spontaneity;
- Poverty of thought;
- Psychomotor retardation;
- Rage response decreased;
- Reduced rapport;
- Social withdrawal.

Negative Cognitive Schizophrenia-Like Effects Negative cognitive schizophrenia-like effects, include:

- Decreased attention;
- Impaired executive functioning;
- Reduced ability for abstract thought;
- Reduced problem-solving ability;
- Short-term memory deficits;
- Verbal memory deficits;
- Working memory deficits.

Depending upon the: (1) personal characteristics of the older adult (e.g., age or genetics, including gender and continental descent); (2) patterns of cannabis use (e.g., THC concentration, amount used, and frequency and method of use); and (3) concurrent use of other psychotropic drugs (e.g., alcohol or antipsychotics), these cognitive effects can range in severity from mild to severe. They also can range in duration from transient to "permanent." Thus, the various effects observed among cannabis users are neither uniform nor predictable (Pagliaro & Pagliaro, *Clinical Patient Data Files*).

Generally, although schizophrenia initially occurs among adolescents and young adults with signs and symptoms that often improve with age (Desai, Seraji, & Redden, 2010), older adults are more likely to have one or more of the listed signs and symptoms in relation to cannabis use, particularly those who are regular, long-term, high dose users of high-concentration THC. The associated clinical situation is often compounded by the presence of neurological impairment (e.g., alcoholic dementia or Alzheimer's disease).[59]

The etiological relationship between cannabis use and schizophrenia-like effects also appears to be largely mediated by a shared mechanism involving the endogenous "cannabinoid" receptor, CB_1 (Cohen, Solowij, & Carr, 2008; D'Souza, 2007; Leweke & Koethe, 2008). (Also see the earlier cannabis pharmacology subsection, "Pharmacodynamics: Mechanism of Action.")

59. In our clinical experiences, this situation is most likely to occur among older adults who have: (1) experienced the onset of schizophrenia earlier in life; and (2) been stabilized for some years on medically prescribed antipsychotic drugs (e.g., haloperidol [Haldol®]). Commonly, this scenario occurs in the context of older adults with schizophrenia being homeless and living on the streets of a major city in the U.S. (Pagliaro & Pagliaro, *Clinical Patient Data Files*).

Pulmonary Toxicities[60]

In their research to characterize the similarities and differences between cannabis smoke and tobacco smoke (i.e., a known respiratory toxin), Graves et al. (2020, p. 7160) found that:

> For tobacco and marijuana smoke, respectively, 4350 and 2575 different compounds are detected, of which, 670 and 536 (231 in common) are tentatively identified, and of these 173 and 110 different compounds (69 in common) are known to cause negative health effects through carcinogenic, mutagenic, teratogenic, or other toxic mechanisms.

Cannabis smoking, among older adults—who also smoke tobacco cigarettes, have COPD, or sleep apnea—is associated with a further compromise of pulmonary function due to additive or synergic irritation and damage to lung tissues (e.g., Hancox, Poulton, & Ely, 2010; Lee & Hancox, 2011; Pagliaro & Pagliaro, 2009; Taylor, Fergusson, & Milne, 2002).

The pulmonary toxicity identified among regular, long-term, or heavy, cannabis smokers is primarily related to the components (e.g., ammonia, hydrogen cyanide, and nitric oxide)[61] in cannabis smoke other than THC (Pagliaro, 1983, 1988; Pagliaro & Pagliaro, 2018).[62] Therefore, the severity of these pulmonary effects depends more on the:

1. Amount of cannabis smoked;
2. Smoking techniques employed;
3. Combustion properties of the materials used in the production of cannabis products (e.g., "joint" wrapping paper).

(Pagliaro & Pagliaro, 2009)[63]

---

60. See also the later Common Methods of Cannabis Use subsection—"Vaping."
61. N.B. Interestingly, the concentrations of these other "components" have been found to be five- to 20-times higher in cannabis smoke in comparison to tobacco smoke (Moir, Rickert, & Levasseur, 2008).
62. Consequently, although confirmatory empirical data currently are insufficient, we would expect that "vaping" THC would result in a reduction of the significant respiratory toxicity that is associated with "smoking a joint."
63. Over 2,500 chemicals—primarily formed by the process of pyrolysis—can be found in marijuana smoke, including many of the same chemicals that are found in tobacco smoke. As identified by Graves et al. (2020, p. 7160):

    > Tobacco and marijuana smoke particles are quantitatively similar in volatility, shape, density, and number concentration, albeit with differences in size, total mass, and chemical composition.

    When marijuana is smoked, it yields more tar than tobacco. Additionally, the tar from marijuana smoke has higher concentrations of certain carcinogens (e.g., benzo[a]pyrene) than are found in the tar from tobacco smoke. Terpenoids, also found in cannabis smoke, are possible precursors for several known carcinogens (Sheehan, Hamnett, & Beasley, 2018). Thus, it is probable that marijuana smoking will put users at a greater risk for lung cancer than tobacco smoking—currently the leading cause of lung cancer in the world.

    Based upon the chemical constituents found in the pyrolysis products of marijuana smoke versus the pyrolysis products of tobacco smoke, and comparative differences in smoking techniques for marijuana versus tobacco (i.e., smoking the entire joint and inhaling the marijuana smoke more deeply into the lungs where it is held in the lower respiratory tract for a longer period of time), we have, for several decades (e.g., Pagliaro, 1983, 1988, 1995; Pagliaro & Pagliaro, 2004, 2009, 2018) estimated that smoking one joint of marijuana subjects smokers to as much irritation and associated damage to the respiratory system, along with subsequent risk for lung cancer, as smoking one package (i.e., 20) filter-tipped tobacco cigarettes.

For example, regarding effects on airway obstruction, Aldington, Williams, and Nowitz (2007)—utilizing high-resolution computed tomography (HRCT) scanning, pulmonary function tests, and a smoking questionnaire—found that "one cannabis joint had a similar effect to 2.5–5 tobacco cigarettes" (p. 1058). Although replication studies and confirmatory data are currently lacking, we have long warned of the risk of cannabis smoking as a carcinogen or co-carcinogen contributing to lung cancer in genetically susceptible individuals. Joshi, Joshi, and Bartter (2014), in their review of the effects of marijuana smoke on the respiratory system, noted that:

> The immuno-histopathologic and epidemiologic evidence in marijuana users suggest biological plausibility of marijuana smoking as a risk for the development of lung cancer.
>
> (p. 173)

However, Tashkin (2013), as well as other researchers, suggest that the association between cannabis smoking and lung cancer is only evident with "heavy, long-term use" and not with "light or moderate [occasional or regular, short-term] use" (p. 239).

Physical and Psychological Dependence

> Old Misbelief: The regular, long-term use of cannabis does not result in the development of cannabis physical dependence.

False. In fact, although the question as to whether the regular, long-term use of cannabis results in physical dependence had been extensively studied and argued during most of the 19th and 20th centuries, the "new millennial consensus" is that it does. For example, since its 4th edition in 1994, the *Diagnostic and Statistical Manual of Mental Disorders* (DSM) (APA, 2000) has listed cannabis dependence in its taxonomy based largely upon noted tolerance and a well-recognized withdrawal syndrome. However, until the last decade of the 20th century, it was generally thought that only psychological dependence, not physical dependence, was likely to develop with the regular, long-term use of cannabis. For example, as identified by Farnsworth (1969, p. 410) in a detailed review published in the *Journal of the American Pharmaceutical Association*:

> Marijuana does not cause physiological addiction, although a psychological habit probably exists.

Currently, the DSM-5 (APA, 2013) subsumes these related conditions under the classification of "cannabis use disorder" (CUD)—the continued use of cannabis regardless of significant impairment ranging from mild to severe. (See also the related discussion in the later cannabis subsections, "Assessment and Diagnosis of Older Adult Cannabis Dependence or Use Disorder" and "Treating Older Adult Cannabis Dependence or Use Disorder.") In this regard, Volkow, Baler, and Compton (2014, p. 2219) noted that:

> Despite some contentious discussions regarding the addictiveness of marijuana, the evidence clearly indicates that long-term marijuana use can lead to addiction.

Additionally, the NIDA (2020b, p. 15) reported that:

> In 2015, about 4.0 million people in the United States met the diagnostic criteria for a marijuana [cannabis] use disorder; 138,000 voluntarily sought treatment for their marijuana use.

As noted by Halperin (2019a, p. 1), citing Aaron Weiner, Director of Addiction Services at Linden Oaks Behavioral Health Clinic:

> There is no debate that marijuana is both physiologically and psychologically addictive.

The regular, long-term, high dosage use of cannabis is clearly recognized as being associated with the development of physical dependence and psychological dependence (e.g., Budney, Roffman, & Stephens, 2007; Government of Canada, 2018; Halperin, 2019a; Jafari & Tang, 2016; Khalsa, Genser, & Francis, 2002; Maldonado & Rodriguez de Fonseca, 2002). Reflecting the classic definition of: (1) physical dependence, regular, long-term cannabis use is associated with both tolerance and withdrawal; and (2) psychological dependence, regular, long-term cannabis use is associated with craving. However, all cannabis users do not develop dependence. As recognized by Budney et al. (2007, p. 4):

> Some 9 percent of those who try marijuana develop dependence compared to, for example, 15 percent of people who try cocaine, and 24 percent of those who try heroin.

Several researchers (e.g., Lopez-Quintero, Perez de los Cobos, & Hasin, 2011; Winstock, Ford, & Witton, 2010) have identified that approximately 10% of regular cannabis users develop dependence.

Cannabis Tolerance

For some time, it has been recognized (e.g., Jones, Benowitz, & Herning, 1981; Wikler, 1976) that tolerance develops to the pharmacological actions of cannabis, including those that affect the autonomic nervous system, cardiovascular system, intraocular pressure, mood, and sleep. The development of cannabis tolerance, as related to its regular, long-term use, has been associated with the interaction of CB_1 receptors with cannabis agonists, particularly THC (Pertwee, 2008). This prolonged interaction results in the:

1. Desensitization of the receptors (i.e., a decrease in their ability to activate effector pathways);
2. Corresponding reduction in the number of related receptors.

(Kendall & Yudowski, 2017)

The observed changes are reflective of receptor down-regulation (D'Souza, Cortes-Briones, & Ranganathan, 2016; Ramaekers, Mason, & Theunisson, 2020). A break from cannabis use—whether use is for medical or recreational purposes—can "reset" CB_1 receptors and, consequently, increase sensitivity. Up-regulation begins within two days of abstinence. Depending upon the duration of THC use and its dosage, the period of time required for returning to maximum THC sensitivity generally ranges from one to four weeks (D'Souza et al., 2016).

Cannabis Withdrawal Syndrome

The cannabis withdrawal syndrome is commonly experienced following the abrupt discontinuation of the regular, long-term use of cannabis. In fact, Budney, Hughes, and Moore (2004) identified that up to 85% of cannabis users experience withdrawal after discontinuing their cannabis use.[64] The occurrence of the cannabis withdrawal syndrome is supported by two major pieces of evidence:

1. Pharmacological characterization of the endocannabinoid system (see the discussion in the earlier pharmacology subsection, Pharmacodynamics—"Mechanism of Action");
2. Acute demonstration of characteristic signs and symptoms of cannabis withdrawal when a CB_1 cannabinoid receptor antagonist is administered to an active cannabis user as part of a controlled research study (e.g., Budney & Hughes, 2006; Cooper & Haney, 2009).

The characteristic signs and symptoms, which are generally considered to be relatively mild, or non-life threatening, include:

- Aggression;
- Anger;
- Anorexia;
- Anxiety;
- Chills;
- Cramping;
- Craving for cannabis;
- Diaphoresis;
- Dreaming increased;
- Headaches;
- Hypersomnia;
- Hyperthermia;
- Insomnia;
- Irritability;
- Mental depression;
- Nausea;
- Nervousness;
- Nightmares;
- Restlessness;
- Rebound increase in rapid eye movement (REM) sleep;
- Tremor;
- Weakness;
- Weight loss.

(Bonnet & Preuss, 2017; Budney et al., 2004; Cornelius, Chung, & Martin, 2008; Pagliaro & Pagliaro, 2004)

64. N.B. The self-medication of this withdrawal syndrome (i.e., resuming cannabis use), whether performed consciously or unconsciously, has been determined to be a major factor contributing to recidivism following the discontinuation of cannabis use (Pagliaro & Pagliaro, *Clinical Patient Data Files*; Winstock et al., 2010).

The cannabis withdrawal syndrome generally has its onset within one to two days of discontinuing cannabis use and lasts for up to five days. The signs and symptoms associated with the cannabis withdrawal syndrome generally peak on day one (Pagliaro & Pagliaro, 2009; Preuss, Watzke, & Zimmermann, 2010).

Although not approved by the FDA, it has been suggested that nabiximols (i.e., a combination of THC and CBD in a 1:1 ratio) may be efficacious in ameliorating the overall severity of cannabis withdrawal and is significantly superior to placebo in this context (Allsop, Copeland, & Lintzeris, 2014). However, others (e.g., Trigo, Soliman, & Quilty, 2018) failed to discern any difference between the use of nabiximols and placebo regarding the management of the signs and symptoms of cannabis withdrawal.

It is important to note that most older adults, who experience the cannabis withdrawal syndrome, report a wide variance in the severity of the characteristic signs and symptoms. This variance appears to be associated with several factors, including the:

1. Amount and potency of the cannabis used;
2. Concurrent use of other drugs and substances of abuse;[65]
3. Duration of regular, long-term use of cannabis;
4. Genetic predisposition (e.g., single nucleotide polymorphism in the CB_1 gene [CNR1], rs2023239);
5. Presence of major depressive or psychotic disorders—this factor appears to account for most of the observed variance.

(Arendt, Rosenberg, & Foldager, 2007; Budney et al., 2004; Khan, Secades-Villa, & Okuda, 2013; Pagliaro & Pagliaro, *Clinical Patient Data Files*; Schacht et al., 2012)

***Related Professional Reminder*: Since the 1960s, the higher average potency of cannabis in the U.S. (as noted in earlier subsections), has been tremendous (i.e., a five- to ten-fold plus increase in THC concentration). This higher potency appears to have significantly increased the probability for developing cannabis "physical" dependence or CUD—and the associated recognition of the:**

1. ***Clinically significant development of tolerance, or the need to use increasing amounts of cannabis in an effort to achieve initial desired effects;***
2. ***Occurrence of the cannabis withdrawal syndrome when regular, long-term use is abruptly discontinued.***

Cannabis Overdosage/Unintentional Poisoning

Surprisingly, given the historical record of 10,000-plus years of human cannabis use (Pagliaro & Pagliaro, 2004), the toxicities associated with its use have not yet been fully

65. The use of other drugs and substances of abuse can aggravate or relieve the associated signs and symptoms of the cannabis withdrawal syndrome depending on the specific:

- Signs or symptoms;
- Particular drug or substance of abuse used;
- Dosage;
- Mental and physical characteristics of the older adult cannabis user.

evaluated. However, it appears that fatal overdosages are relatively rare. In fact, during the previous two centuries, the general medical consensus has been that the occasional use of cannabis is not particularly harmful and that the intermittent use of low potency cannabis is not generally associated with obvious signs and symptoms of toxicity (ARF/WHO, 1981).[66]

Several authors, including ourselves, have raised the concern that this situation is significantly changing during the current century because of the:

1. Availability of high THC concentration products (both for medical and licit/recreational use);
2. Widespread availability of "edible" THC products;
3. In the context of vaping, the ability to self-administer large doses of THC with relative ease.

Additionally, although several authors (e.g., Crippa, Derenusson, & Chagas, 2012; Kelly & Nappe, 2019) have recommended various pharmacotherapeutic approaches for the management of cannabis overdosage/unintentional poisoning (e.g., antagonists of CB_1, antipsychotics, beta-adrenergic blockers, and CBD), none of these approaches have consistently demonstrated clinical efficacy and none have received specific FDA approval for this indication. Fortunately, cannabis/THC overdosage is generally a non-lethal event (i.e., no $LD/_{50}$ has been established for THC in humans).[67]

> Cannabis is not associated with acute fatal overdoses.
>
> (WHO, 2018, p. 53)

---

66. Of related interest, during a recent visit to the veterinary clinic with our two St. Bernards, we met an older man who was quite distraught. Apparently, his little pug had eaten some of his edible "gummy bears" that he had just purchased from the local medical marijuana store/dispensary for the treatment of his osteoarthritic knee pain. The dog was "moving slowly" and "acting strange," so he rushed him to the clinic where the veterinarian induced vomiting that yielded some of the undigested "gummy bears." He was assured that the dog would be okay and was instructed to "just let him sleep it off," but return, if his pug's condition changes.

    Apparently, ingestion of the THC/CBD in "gummy bears" is generally not fatal for dogs, but can cause a variety of cardiovascular, neurological, and thermogenic issues—dependent upon the specific cannabinoid content and amount ingested—and a dog who has ingested it should quickly be referred to a veterinarian for appropriate assessment and treatment (Bologna, 2019; Kelley, 2020; Petrovic, 2019).

    Reportedly, the incidence of edible cannabis product consumption by pets and related poisonings has increased significantly in direct association with the decriminalization/legalization of cannabis in most states.
67. N.B. Although several authors have reported LD_{50} values for THC—for example, Hartung, Kauferstein, and Ritz-Timme (2014) estimated it to be approximately 40 mg/kg, while Canazza, Citti, and Wiley (2018), on behalf of the *WHO Expert Committee on Drug Dependence*, estimated it to be approximately 4 grams in a 70 kg human—we believe these values are erroneous. The major factors we identified in the various studies as possibly contributing to erroneous estimates, include that:

    1. Data were extrapolated from laboratory animal data;
    2. Data were based on isolated case histories that had not been adequately controlled for, and did not appear to adequately consider confounding variables;
    3. The data that were relied upon, or cited, were outdated;
    4. Data were obtained from inadequate sample sizes.

There is no known antidote for THC overdosage (Pagliaro & Pagliaro, 2004).[68] Consequently, pharmacotherapy is primarily selected on the basis of presenting signs and symptoms and applied, as needed, on a case-by-case basis. For example:

- Agitation, anxiety, or seizures can be treated with a benzodiazepine (e.g., diazepam [Valium®]);
- Acute psychosis or cannabis hyperemesis syndrome can be treated with an antipsychotic (e.g., haloperidol [Haldol®]).

Additionally, vital signs should be routinely monitored for a minimum of six hours (because of the long half-life of elimination for THC) and supported as needed. Generally, supportive care alone is sufficient to manage THC overdosage (see also the related discussion in the later subsection, Treating Older Adult Cannabis Dependence or Use Disorder—"Pharmacotherapeutic and Psychotherapeutic Approaches").[69]

NEW MILLENNIAL TRENDS IN OLDER ADULT CANNABIS USE

This section presents and discusses new trends in older adult cannabis use during the new millennium in the U.S. Particular attention is given to the medical prescription and legalized recreational use of cannabis. Also presented and discussed are trends in older adult methods of cannabis use and, for some, their illicit drug involvement.

With the increasing legalization of medicinal marijuana in the U.S. came an increased availability of many varieties of high-potency, high-percentage THC products in newly opened marijuana dispensaries. More recently, decriminalization and approval of recreational use has given rise to local neighborhood personal/recreational "herb," "pot," and "vapor" shops, which offer a variety of marijuana leaves, buds, and stems from sources throughout the world; candies and other edible cannabis "treats;" and electronic marijuana smoking devices—bongs, hookahs, and vaporizers. These changes helped, as we previously predicted—over the past four decades, to significantly increase the: (1) rates of THC use across the U.S.; and (2) variety of methods of use[70] (Pagliaro & Pagliaro, *Clinical Patient Data Files*).

> Marijuana use is becoming more prevalent in this population [i.e., older adults] and users are also at high risk for other drug use.
>
> (Han & Palamar, 2018, p. 374)

---

68. Although we found no available antidote for cannabis overdosage, we did find an example for unintentional poisoning, in which Boyles (2019, p. 1) reported a case involving a 52-year-old man, who overdosed on THC after ingesting, via an oral syringe, 330 mg—over a period of two days—in the context of the medical treatment of a brain tumor. He presented to the ED "in a state of hyperactive delirium."
69. N.B. For older adults, gastric decontamination with activated charcoal is generally ineffective after ingestion because of the delay in the onset of signs and symptoms. It is likewise ineffective in the context of pulmonary administration (Kelly & Nappe, 2019; Russo, 2018).
70. For example, an analysis of the smoking practices of adults (mean age, 45 years) revealed that:

> In terms of routes of cannabis administration, 90.8% (n=1199) of the sample reported smoking; 44% (n=587) reported eating, drinking, or ingesting; 39% (n=511) reported vaping; and 10.9% (n=144) reported skin/topical use as a route of cannabis administration in the past month.

> Cannabis use among older adults is growing faster than any other age group.
> (Bobitt, Qualls, & Schuchman, 2019, p. 1)

> Users over 65 years old are getting high more frequently than youngsters who dabble in the newly legal drug.
> (Lagerquist, 2019a, p. 1)

> Older adults are the fastest growing group of cannabis users and are out-pacing other groups as new users.
> (Baumbusch & Sloan Yip, 2021, p. 25)

And finally, as noted by the U.N. (2021, p. 1):

> When comparing past-year drug use for people aged 65 and older in the United States, the use of cannabis increased from 1.2 percent in 2012 to 5.1 percent in 2019.

Older Adult Medical Prescription Cannabis Use

> Older adults are flocking to medical marijuana.
> (Span, 2018, p. 1)

> Use of medical marijuana is increasing in the United States and older adults are the fastest growing user group.
> (Brown, Costales, & van Boemmel-Wegmann, 2020, p. 1166)

In their descriptive study of medical marijuana in the state of Florida from 2016 to 2017, Brown et al. (2020) found that 60% of registered users were older adults (i.e., 50 years of age or older). Additionally, as reported by Agronin (2021), in the U.S., the use of medical marijuana by older adults (i.e., 65 years of age and older) increased significantly from 0.5% in 2006 to 4.2% in 2018.

Cannabis, in the form of two of its chemical surrogates: (1) dronabinol—Marinol®, which is available in gel capsules, and Syndros®, which is available as an oral solution;[71,72] and (2) nabilone—Cesamet®, which is available in capsule form,[73] were approved by the FDA for the medical management of:

1. Anorexia with weight loss among patients with AIDS;
2. Mild to moderate nausea and vomiting associated with cancer chemotherapy among patients for whom conventional antiemetic treatments have failed.

Additionally, although contrary to existing U.S. federal law (Mead, 2017; Rosenthal & Pipitone, 2020), most states have individually legalized a variety of cannabis formulations (e.g., beverages, "edibles," foods, and pharmaceuticals) for the medical treatment of many physical and mental conditions, including:

> However, these were not mutually exclusive categories, and more than 50% of the sample indicated more than one administration route for past month cannabis use.
> (Cranford, Bohnert, & Perron, 2016, p. 45)

71. N.B. The oral solution of Syndros® contains alcohol.
72. Dronabinol is a synthetic form of THC.
73. Nabilone is a synthetic cannabinoid.

- Acquired immune deficiency syndrome (AIDS);
- Anorexia;
- Arthritis;
- Cachexia;
- Chronic pain;
- Glaucoma;
- Migraine headaches;
- Nausea (severe);
- Persistent muscle spasms (e.g., as related to multiple sclerosis);[74]
- Seizure disorders;
- Any other chronic or persistent medical signs or symptoms that either: (1) limit the patient's ability to conduct a major life activity as defined in the *Americans With Disabilities Act* of 1990, Public Law 101–3336; or (2) if not alleviated, may cause serious harm to the patient's safety or physical and/or mental health.[75]

Due to the significant increase in medical marijuana use by older adults in the U.S., several professional organizations have urged their members to discuss cannabis use with their older patients. For example, the American Academy of Family Physicians (AAFP) formally encourages family physicians to do so noting that:

> More people are using cannabis, this includes older adults such as baby boomers, who are in the unique position of having had more experience using one particular cannabis source—marijuana—than any preceding generation.
>
> (News Staff, 2020, p. 1)

Empirical data supporting the clinical efficacy of "medical marijuana," which have been obtained from controlled studies, are extremely limited (Gupta & Phalen, 2018). The data, which are available regarding claims of therapeutic efficacy for selected medical—and other indications—are largely anecdotal and are summarized in Table 4.1.

74. In Canada, a formulation of equal parts (i.e., 1:1) of CBD and THC was approved in 2015 for the symptomatic relief of spasticity in adults with multiple sclerosis. The formulation is referred to as "nabiximols" and is available under the trade name, "Sativex®." Sativex® is administered as a oromucosal spray (Russo, Calabro, & Naro, 2015). Nabilone (Cesamet®) is also used in Canada—as a "disease-modifying therapy"—for both multiple sclerosis-induced muscle spasms and neuropathic pain (e.g., Ko, Wine, & Tumarkin, 2006).
75. N.B. Given the growing attention to the devastating opiate analgesic epidemic in the U.S. (see the related discussion in Chapter 5, *Prescription Opiate Analgesics and Heroin*), several "cannabis proponents"—including legislators (e.g., Senator Elizabeth Warren [Granowicz, 2016]) and lay proponents (e.g., Herman, 2018; Kaplan, 2018; Lieber, 2018)—have touted the beneficial role of the medical use of cannabis in the context of reducing opioid overdosage deaths. However, related empirical evidence has been characterized as being "very weak" (Swift Yasgur, 2018). For example, as identified by Arkin and Adras (2019, p. 555) in their comprehensive review of this topic:

> Marijuana's analgesic effects are not sufficiently powerful to palliate acute pain. Marijuana is also not a reasonable analgesic for chronic pain, for several reasons. . . . Moreover, individuals who used marijuana on a near-daily basis were less likely to discontinue opioid use than participants who abstained from cannabis use. Use of marijuana during opioid treatment therefore increases the risk that opioid treatment will be unsuccessful. While further research someday might discover that one or more of marijuana's constituents could serve as a treatment for long-term chronic pain, there is no such evidence today.

Table 4.1 Evidence Supporting Claims of Cannabis/Cannabinoid Efficacy for Selected Medical Indications

MEDICAL INDICATION	EVIDENCE OF CANNABIS/CANNABINOID EFFICACY[76]
Acute pain	Subjective reports of pain relief among users have not been generally supported by human, placebo-controlled studies. Animal studies have suggested an effect on the natural analgesic system.
AIDS-related cachexia	Approved by the FDA to treat related anorexia and associated weight loss.
Alzheimer's disease	Preliminary results from animal and in-vitro studies, as well as the study of human post-mortem brain samples, suggest possible benefits.
Anxiety	May reduce anxiety among some users.
Antineoplastic related nausea and vomiting	Synthetic cannabinoids (i.e., dronabinol [Marinol® or Syndros®] and nabilone [Cesamet® or Canemes®]) have been approved by the FDA for this indication.
Glaucoma	Some studies have demonstrated that cannabis use can decrease intraocular pressure. However, results are generally short-lived, lasting for only a few hours.
Insomnia	Cannabis use, including edibles, has been associated with worsening of sleep outcomes, such as: shorter sleep duration and worse subjective sleep efficiency.
Neuropathic pain, multiple sclerosis, and related spasticity	Cannabis use may reduce the intensity of chronic neuropathic pain in a minority of users. Reduction in motor dysfunction and pain may be related to anti-inflammatory and neuroprotective endocannabinoid actions in the CNS. Cannabis use may reduce associated muscle stiffness or spasms.
Traumatic brain injury (TBI)	Animal models and limited human clinical data suggest that the endocannabinoid system is involved in the response to TBI and that agonists (both endogenous and exogenous) can decrease brain inflammation and related edema.

Sources: Canadian Pharmacists Association (2018); Kendall and Yudowski (2017); Maida and Daeninck (2016); Mayo Clinic Staff (2018); Pagliaro and Pagliaro (2004, 2009, 2018); Winiger, Hitchcock, and Bryan (2021).

Black, Stockings, and Campbell (2019), from their related meta-analysis of data concerning cannabinoid use for the treatment of mental disorders (i.e., anxiety disorders, ADHD, MDD, psychotic disorders, PTSD, and Tourette's syndrome), concluded that there was a lack of evidence to support therapeutic efficacy of cannabinoid use for any of these conditions. Interestingly, some professional and lay articles—and numerous Internet postings—suggest that CBD relieves depression (e.g., de Mello Schier, de Oliveira Ribeiro, & Coutinho, 2014; Smith, 2019; Somerset, 2018).

76. N.B. Particularly regarding cannabis use, reported efficacy also includes the contribution of any related "placebo effect," which has also been reported in relation to the use of edible cannabis products (Loflin, Earleywine, & Farmer, 2017).

Although anecdotal, and based on case reports, over the years we have encountered cases of therapeutic efficacy for the use of cannabinoids in virtually each of these mental disorders. For example, several older adults with severe anxiety related to airline travel (i.e., "fear of flying") have reported to us that they dealt with this phobia by "smoking a joint in their car at the airport parking lot and then ingesting a few THC "gummy bear" edibles during the flight—rather than having two drinks in the airport lounge while waiting for their flight to depart and two more as soon as possible after boarding the plane. Whether the reported effects, in terms of reducing their anxiety or fear of flying are due to the pharmacological actions of the cannabinoid or to a placebo effect, or both, we do not know. However, as clinicians, we are pleased with the positive therapeutic outcome.[77]

In states in which cannabis is legalized,[78] older adults—who have a medical prescription—can legally purchase, possess, and use various prescribed forms and amounts of cannabis, particularly marijuana. Marijuana also can be grown for medical or recreational use. However, it is more commonly purchased from specialized marijuana dispensaries. Currently, 41 states have some form of an active, voter-approved medical marijuana program. In these states, we have found that although some older adults use cannabis for seasonal affective disorder (SAD) and other chronic conditions,[79] it is most often prescribed and used to treat, or manage, chronic pain—generally, as an aid to deal with the tolerance associated with regular, long-term opiate analgesic (e.g., codeine [Tylenol #3®] or tramadol [Ultram®]) use (Pagliaro & Pagliaro, *Clinical Patient Data Files*). As noted by Williams, Edwards, and Rubo (2006, p. 57):

> Delta 9-tetrahydrocannabinol (Δ^9-THC) synergizes with morphine and codeine by releasing endogenous opioids. . . . Thus, the cannabinoid/opioid combination might be useful in therapeutics to enhance opioid activity, as well as to restore the efficacy of opioids.

Consequently, Cranford et al. (2016, p. 45), in their analysis of a sample of adults (mean age of 45 years), who were seeking enrolment in a medical marijuana program, found that:

> The top two reasons for seeking medical marijuana were: (1) severe and chronic pain (91.1%); and (2) severe and persistent muscle spasms (25.9%).

Similarly, in their cross-sectional survey of adults (mean age of 40 years) who were enrolled in a medical marijuana program, Cranford et al. (2016) found that medical marijuana was used primarily (i.e., 69.1%) as a substitute for other prescription drugs, primarily opiate analgesics (i.e., 35.3%).

An analysis of data obtained from the 2015–2016 *National Survey on Drug Use and Health* (NSDUH) indicated that:

> 15 percent of adults aged 50 to 64 and 23 percent of adults aged 65 and over reported that they had used the drug with a doctor's recommendation.
>
> (Ross Perlman, 2019, p. 1)

77. However, it is generally not our first choice in terms of a related therapeutic recommendation. For example, in treating "fear of flying," particularly for frequent flyers, we recommend the use of CBT that incorporates appropriate elements of education and desensitization to triggers.
78. N.B. Interestingly, the research of Smart and Liccardo Pacula (2019) revealed that state legalization of medical marijuana use "increased adult but not adolescent cannabis use" (p. 644).
79. For example, Rosenthal and Pipitone (2020, p. 1) found that medical marijuana users in Florida "most commonly used medical marijuana to treat their symptoms of anxiety, pain, and stress.

In this context, as reported by a primary care physician who has incorporated medical cannabis into his practice:

> These patients range from people in their 60s with kidney failure who can no longer take certain pain medication but still need to manage chronic pain, to patients in their 90s, who are looking for a good night's sleep and are leery of the side effects of traditional sleep medications.
>
> (Grinspoon, 2020, p, 1)

Regarding the medical use of cannabis for the treatment of severe, chronic pain (e.g., osteoarthritic pain)—particularly, in an effort to reduce opiate analgesic dosages for older adults who cannot tolerate nonsteroidal anti-inflammatory drugs (NSAIDs), including those who have severe chronic kidney disease (CKD) or gastrointestinal ulcers—we recommend, when feasible, the use of:

1. Edibles,[80] preferentially government approved purified oils to measure dosages more accurately;
2. Sublingual (SL) oils to: (1) more accurately control the dose delivered and the amount absorbed into the systemic circulation; and (2) avoid first-pass hepatic metabolism.

Additionally, for acute effects, we generally recommend the use of:

1. THC oil, usually dispensed in a dark dropper bottle, in a standardized concentration (e.g., 30 mg/ml);
2. An initial dose of 3 mg SL;
3. Use of a calibrated, 1-mg needleless oral dosage measuring syringe for SL administration;
4. Holding the dose under the tongue for 60 seconds before swallowing to maximize SL absorption;
5. Observing effects and, after 2.5 hours, adjusting the dosage, as needed;
6. Gradually, increasing the dosage, as indicated by both the level of pain relief and the occurrence of undesired, or harmful, effects and toxicities;[81]
7. Storing THC oil in a cool, dry, and dark place.[82]

---

80. Regarding cannabis, the term "edibles," generally, refers to foods and drinks to which a significant amount of THC is added for medical or recreational consumption (see discussion in the later subsection, "Common Methods of Marijuana Use"). However, through the millennia, cannabis seeds (i.e., hemp seeds) have been used as: (1) a foodstuff; and (2) a source of cold-pressed seed oil for its high alpha-omega, fatty acid content. As an oil, it is used for cooking, and it also can be directly ingested or topically applied to promote healthy hair, nails, and skin. Additionally, the hemp seeds are also rich in protein and contain no cholesterol. As identified by Yang et al. (2017, p. 274):

    > A 100-gram serving of [hemp] seeds meets up to 63% of the recommended daily value for protein.

81. Because acute fatal overdosages of THC have not been noted in humans, there appears to be a great deal of leeway for safely increasing the dosage (see the related discussion in the earlier subsection, "Cannabis Overdosage/Unintentional Poisoning") (CDC, 2018; Pagliaro & Pagliaro, *Clinical Patient Data Files*; Turner, Spurling, & Agrawal, 2020).
82. As previously noted, THC oil is usually dispensed in a dark glass dropper bottle.

For chronic effects, we generally recommend:[83]

1. 25 mg/ml CBD oil,[84] which may contain up to 2 mg of THC (or up to 0.3%);
2. Shaking CBD oil well before use;
3. CBD oil that has been described as having an "unpleasant" taste or tasting "like dirt;"
4. Generally, dosing "as needed"—either by oral ingestion or SL absorbtion;[85,86]
5. Usually beginning with 1 ml (25 mg) of CBD daily;
6. Continuing daily use for 30 days before evaluating response or adjusting dosage;
7. Storing CBD oil in a cool, dry, and dark place.

Often, the use of both THC and CBD regimens are simultaneously implemented and followed.[87] As with all psychotropic drug dosages for older adults, "start low and go slow."

> ***Related Professional Reminder:* The relatively high LD_{50} for THC generally allows older adults to obtain desired effects by increasing the THC dosage "as required" and tolerated. This behavior is generally predicated on:**
>
> ***1. Achieving desired therapeutic effects, or lack thereof;***
> ***2. Experiencing undesired, or harmful, effects and toxicities (see the earlier pharmacology subsection "Undesired, or Harmful, Effects and Toxicities").***

A special note of caution regarding cannabis dependence or use disorder is warranted based largely on the research findings of Choi and colleagues, and others. For example, Choi, DiNitto, and Marti (2017, p. 697), in their analysis of data from the *National Epidemiologic Survey on Alcohol and Related Conditions (NESARC)*, found that "32.88% of [adult] medical cannabis users, compared to 25.25% of nonmedical users, had past-year marijuana use disorder." Consequently, in their conclusion, they recommended that:

> Given the high rates of marijuana use disorder among medical users, physicians should exercise caution in recommending marijuana for medical purposes.

83. N.B. THC can also be used alone, or in combination, with CBD to treat chronic conditions (e.g., osteoarthritic pain).
84. CBD oil is available, without prescription, in most pharmacies and health-food stores in the U.S. It is also available in soft gel capsules.
85. Dosages, particularly, initial dosages that are taken at bedtime, are often guided by the nature and extent of undesired, or harmful, effects experienced by older adults, who are using CBD (e.g., blurred vision, dizziness, and headache). Caution is required because these effects may inadvertently contribute to the occurrence of psychomotor impairment and resulting falls. However, overall, CBD use is generally well-tolerated. Additional undesired or harmful effects include diarrhea, fatigue, nausea, and xerostomia.
86. Because of its high lipid solubility, CBD can be added to a number of foods (e.g., butter, olive oil, scrambled eggs, pasta sauces, and soups) to mask its unpleasant taste.
87. N.B. These recommendations are entirely based on empirical results obtained from a relatively small convenience sample of older adult patients over several years. They should be modified as dictated by individual patient response. However, as noted by Urits, Borchart, and Hasegawa (2019, p. 41):

    > While still not completely understood, the central and peripheral analgesic effects of CBD have been documented.

Older Adult Illicit/Licit Recreational[88] Cannabis Use

> Marijuana is the most frequently used illicit substance in the U.S.
>
> (Cerda Wall et al. (2012, p. 22)

> The use of cannabis in the past year by adults 65 years and older in the United States increased sharply from 0.4% in 2006 and 2007 to 2.9% in 2015 and 2016.
>
> (Han & Palamar, 2018, p. 374)

> Cannabis use in adults aged 65 and older increased from 2.4 percent to 4.2 percent in the United States, a significant increase of 75% between 2015 and 2018.
>
> (Han & Palamar, 2020, p. 609)

Although older adults have typically reported significantly lower rates of cannabis use in comparison to younger adults, during the new millennium, older adult use of marijuana has been increasingly guided by related changing trends in public attitudes toward marijuana use[89]—liberation of attitudes and the development of a generally positive and accepting perspective regarding cannabis use (e.g., Lloyd & Striley, 2018; NIDA, 2020b; Pagliaro & Pagliaro, 2018; Pagliaro & Pagliaro, *Clinical Patient Data Files*). For example, as found by Motel (2015, pp. 1–3), the changing trends supporting marijuana legalization are rapidly outpacing opposition:

- 68% of Americans say marijuana should be legalized in the U.S.;
- 70% of Americans say alcohol is more harmful to a person's health than marijuana;
- 57% of Americans would not be bothered if a store or business selling legal marijuana opened up in their neighborhood;
- 50% of Americans say they have tried marijuana;
- Most states have legalized the medical and/or recreational use of marijuana.

A logical and expected consequence of liberalized attitudes toward cannabis use is that usage will increase. For example, as reported by Halperin (2019b, p. 1):

> Older people are the fastest-growing group of cannabis users, as stigma fades and some seek an alternative to prescription drugs. As attitudes towards cannabis shift, the fastest-growing group of users is over 50—and marijuana's popularity among seniors is beginning to change the American experience of old age.

Given the consistent and growing movement toward decriminalization, medical use, and legalized recreational use of cannabis, across the U.S. during the second decade of the new millennium, we fully expect, as previously noted, that, over the next several decades, the:

88. Several states (i.e., Alaska, Arizona, California, Colorado, Illinois, Maine, Massachusetts, Michigan, Montana, Nevada, New Jersey, Oregon, South Dakota, Vermont, and Washington), as well as the District of Columbia, have legalized the recreational use of marijuana for adults. Colorado was the first state to do so in 2012 (Berke & Gould, 2020; Fuller, 2020; Lozano, 2020; Miller, 2016; Wallace, 2020).
89. For example, as noted in the AARP Newsletter (Harrar, 2019b, p. 1):

> This year, the AARP Board of Directors . . . approved a policy supporting the use of medical marijuana in the states that have legalized it.

1. Percentage of older adults, who use cannabis, will continue to increase;
2. Usage discrepancies between the genders, which have been decreasing over the new millennium, will totally "disappear."

(Pagliaro & Pagliaro, *Clinical Patient Data Files*)

These trends in marijuana use statistics are supported by extrapolating the signaling hypothesis, "which posits [that] decriminalization is a [significant] risk factor for future increases in youth marijuana prevalence and acceptance" (Miech, Johnston, & O'Malley, 2015, p. 340), to older adults. Additionally, the concomitant use of both cannabis and nicotine (i.e., smoking both marijuana "joints" and tobacco cigarettes over the past 30 days) has significantly increased in states where medical marijuana is legal compared to illegal (Wang, Ramo, & Lisha, 2016).

As identified by Azofeifa, Mattson, and Schauer (2016, p. 1)—and previously discussed earlier in this chapter:

> A decrease in the perception of great risk from smoking marijuana combined with increases in the perception of availability (i.e., fairly easy or very easy to obtain marijuana) and fewer punitive legal penalties (e.g., no penalty) for the possession of marijuana for personal use might play a role in increased use among adults.

According to a 2016 Gallup poll of over 1,000 adults in all 50 states and the District of Columbia:

> The percentage of American adults who say they currently smoke marijuana has nearly doubled since 2013. Thirteen percent of adults in the U.S. now say they currently smoke pot—up from 7 percent in 2013.
>
> (Miller, 2016, p. 3)

Additionally, a follow-up 2018 national Gallup poll found that "66% of Americans now support legalizing marijuana," including 59% of older adults (McCarthy, 2018. p. 2). It should be noted that the increase to 66% of Americans supporting the legalization of cannabis is the highest reported value since the survey started in 1969. At that time, it was 12% and has increased in a virtually linear fashion since that time.

In their systematic review of cannabis use among older adults in the 21st century, Lloyd and Striley (2018, p. 1) found that:

> The greatest increase in marijuana use was observed in the older adult population 50 years or older, and those 65 years or older had the greatest increase in marijuana use in the older adult population.

As observed by Halperin (2019b, p. 2):

> The seniors using cannabis today aren't your parents' grandparents. The generation that camped out at Woodstock is now in its seventies. They've been around grass long enough to realize it's not going to kill them and are more open to the possibility it will come with health benefits.

Additionally, as previously noted, the form and route of "cannabis" use are significantly affected by the legalization status of cannabis in individual states. For example, Borodovsky, Crosier, and Lee (2016, p. 141), in their analysis found that:

> Individuals in states in which cannabis use has been legalized had significantly higher likelihood of ever use of vaping (OR = 2.04) and edibles (OR = 1.78).

In a related context, Schauer, Njai, and Grant-Lenzy (2020, p. 107900), in their retrospective analysis of data concerning the prevalence of different modalities of cannabis use among adults in 12 states, found that:

> The prevalence of past month (current) marijuana use among adults in these states was 9.1% (males = 12.0%, females = 6.3%).[90] Among current marijuana users, 33.7% reported multiple methods of marijuana use, 90.1% reported any marijuana smoking (e.g., joints, blunts, bongs, bowls), 58.3% reported only smoking (no other modes of consumption), 24.5% reported any edible use, 4.5% reported using only edibles, 19.4% reported any marijuana vaping, 2.1% reported only vaping, 14.5% reported any dabbing (flash vaporization/inhalation of highly concentrated marijuana), and 0.4% reported only dabbing. Correlates of multimodal use are also examined.
>
> Multimodal use of marijuana is common and use of non-smoked marijuana (edibles, vaping, dabbing) often occurs in conjunction with other modes of marijuana use.

Significant increases in the numbers of older adults who use marijuana has been demonstrated by numerous epidemiological studies since the beginning of the second decade of the new millennium (e.g., DiNitto & Choi, 2011).

DiNitto and Choi (2011, p. 732), in their analysis of data from the *SAMHSA 2008 National Survey on Drug Use* found that, for adults 50 years of age and older, approximately 3% used marijuana in the past year.[91] They also found that:

> Past-year users were more likely to be younger (50–64 years old), black, and not married, and they had significantly higher psychological distress scores.

Additionally, they noted that older adults who were past year marijuana users were significantly more likely to:

- Engage in binge drinking;
- Smoke tobacco cigarettes;
- Use other illicit drugs.

Also—specifically, regarding cannabis use among older adults in the U.S.—all reports (e.g., Bobitt et al., 2019; Pagliaro & Pagliaro, 2018; Ross Perlman, 2019) indicate a significant and steadily increasing rate of use. For example:

> Baby boomers who use marijuana seem to be using it more often than in previous years, a recent survey finds—5.7 percent of respondents ages 50 to 64 said they'd tried it in the past month. The drug is also gaining popularity among people in their 70s and 80s.
>
> (Gordon, 2018, p. 1)

Common Methods of Marijuana Use

Generally, older adults use two common methods of administration: (1) ingestion; and (2) pulmonary inhalation (i.e., smoking or vaporizing). The more recent legalization of

90. Interestingly, a study of older adults of African continental descent living in the poor urban area of South Los Angeles, found that 9.1% of participants reported current cannabis use (Cobb, Bazargan, & Smith, 2019).
91. Of these older adults, approximately 25% used marijuana on at least half of the days of the previous year.

medical marijuana, as well as licit recreational cannabis use in many states, has resulted in the development of a wide variety of edible marijuana products (e.g., brownies, butters, cakes, caramels, chocolates, granola bars, "gummy bears," and lollipops).[92] These edible products can be purchased at local marijuana dispensaries along with, or as alternatives to, the extensive varieties of marijuana buds and leaves that are also legally sold in these dispensaries and neighborhood shops.

However, because the bioavailability of ingested marijuana products is low, approximately 10% (Huestis, 2007), in order to achieve equivalent actions, the required dosage of ingested products must be generally up to five times higher than that of inhaled marijuana products.[93] This difference in dosage is required because pulmonary absorption is much greater than that achieved from the GI tract (see the related discussion in the earlier cannabis pharmacology subsection, "Pharmacokinetics—Absorption"). Thus, smoking ("toking" and hookah smoking), including the use of "blunts," and inhaling vaporized cannabis (i.e., "vaping"); are the most common methods of use for all three forms of cannabis—marijuana, hashish, and hashish oil.

Vaping

Several terms are used, often interchangeably, to describe the pulmonary inhalation of a drug or substance of abuse that has been vaporized by the heat produced by an electronic device, such as a vaporizer (e.g., for nicotine, this device is usually an electric coil in an e-cigarette or e-pen). (See the related discussion in the Chapter 3, *Caffeine and Nicotine*, subsection, Undesired, or Harmful, Effects and Toxicities—"E-Cigarettes.") Various types of vaporizers also are commonly used by cannabis users, who also have developed related argot, or slang, including:

1. "Vaper," a noun that is commonly used to describe someone who vapes;
2. "Vapes," an intransitive verb used to denote the process of vaping;
3. "Vaping," a present participle of the verb "vapes."

"Vapes" and "vaping" are often used interchangeably, much like "smoke" and "smoking." These argots originated in the cannabis subculture during the 1980s and were widely adopted and used in conjunction with the introduction from China of the first commercial e-cigarette to the U.S. during the first decade of the new millennium. They have since become mainstream, with "vape" being chosen in 2014 as "the word of the year" and formally added to the Oxford Dictionary.

---

92. During the 19th century, cannabis was also ingested as candy bonbons or baked into foods, such as cookies and brownies. The ingestion of cannabis in its various forms continued through the 1950s, 1960s, and 1970—often utilizing a classic "brownie hashish fudge" recipe that was developed and popularized by Alice B. Toklas (1954).
93. Although hashish oil may be injected intravenously, this method of use is relatively rare because of the associated severe pain and inflammation—as well as the possible formation of an embolism—that may occur at the injection site secondarily to the injection of an oil. This is why, in general, injectable drugs are prepared as aqueous solutions for intravenous (IV) use or suspensions (or oils) for intramuscular (IM) use. Therefore, like other types of cannabis, hashish oil is more often ingested in edible products or inhaled by "toking"—generally in combination with cannabis or tobacco—or "vaping" (Pagliaro & Pagliaro, *Clinical Patient Data Files*).

For efficient pulmonary absorption, a drug or substance of abuse must be vaporized into an aerosolized or gaseous form. For example, inhaling: (1) volatile solvents (e.g., "sniffing" gasoline or glue); (2) smoke (e.g., smoking opium from an opium pipe or smoking a tobacco cigarette); and (3) vapor (e.g., inhaling crack cocaine from a crack pipe). Although "volatile inhalants" are generally "ready for use," in each of the examples, the volatile solvent drug or substance of abuse—prior to inhalation—must be changed in physical form from a solid or liquid to a gas. The major difference in their transformation into a gas (i.e., how much heat is required) is determined by the boiling point of the drug or substance of abuse (i.e., the temperature at which its liquid form boils and turns into a vapor).

The combustion of organic material, such as cannabis or tobacco, produces an aerosol (i.e., smoke) that contains active ingredients that can be inhaled. The temperature involved in smoking can reach close to 900° C during a puff (i.e., as drawn-in oxygen "fuels the fire" at the burning end of the cigarette/joint). Consequently, many chemicals, in addition to the "desired" drug or substance of abuse, are aerosolized, as well as formed de novo by the processes of combustion, distillation, pyrolysis, and pyrosynthesis (Dubie & Green, 1982; Streller & Roth, 2015).

Smoking can provide high enough temperatures to heat necessary aerosolized drugs and chemicals found in organic matter (e.g., marijuana and tobacco). Whereas vaporizing, which utilizes lower heat, can convert some drugs and substances of abuse (e.g., nicotine and THC) into a vapor. These drugs and substances of abuse have lower boiling points and, consequently, avoid the chemical processes of combustion, distillation, pyrolysis, and pyrosynthesis that can occur with smoking (i.e., burning).

Vaporizing cannabis involves using a commercial vaporizer to heat the cannabis and evaporate the THC into a gas that, when inhaled, delivers up to 95% of the evaporated THC to the lungs. Currently, as noted by Harrar (2019a, p. 2) on behalf of the AARP:

> 1 in 4 medical marijuana users age 50-plus vape their cannabis.

As shared by a baby-boomer, for both her and her 89-year-old father:

> Vaping flower is a flavorful, enjoyable way for older adults to inhale cannabis. It also enables them to economically sample many types of medicine to find what works best for them. But at least in the beginning, they will probably need help learning how to use their device. And those with manual dexterity issues may require assistance when loading the devices as well.
>
> (Rosner, 2019, p. 5)

***Related Professional Reminder:* In comparison to smoking cannabis, the gas associated with vaping THC has significantly less carbon monoxide and other toxins (e.g., tars found in cannabis smoke). Because the required temperature for vaporizing is significantly lower than that needed for smoking, cannabis is not burned, and, consequently, most related carcinogens are not produced.**

EVALI In 2019, the CDC began to receive reports of lung injury associated with vaping. The lung injuries appeared to be relatively rare, but serious (e.g., required hospitalization and breathing assistance).[94] The specific origin or cause of the related lung injuries were

94. As of February 18, 2020, the CDC (2020) reported a total of 2,807 EVALI hospitalized cases or deaths in the U.S.

not immediately, nor conclusively, identified (Lewis, McCaffrey, & Sage, 2019; Perrine et al., 2019).

The CDC named this "syndrome" EVALI (i.e., "E-cigarette, or Vaping, product use-Associated Lung Injury"). An acute, rather than chronic, toxicity, the signs and symptoms of EVALI generally have their onset within a few days to weeks of e-cigarette or vaping product use. Typically, related signs and symptoms include:

- Chest pain;
- Cough;
- Diarrhea;
- Fatigue;
- Fever;
- Nausea;
- Shortness of breath;
- Vomiting;
- Weight loss.

(CDC, 2019; Thielking, 2019)

The cause of the specific related pulmonary tissue damage may involve the: (1) contact time of hot "vapors" on delicate pulmonary tissues and resultant tissue damage, which may be extreme; and/or (2) vitamin E acetate (which is currently considered to be the primary cause of EVALI); or (3) other potentially irritating pharmaceutical vehicles or adjuncts found in vaping products (i.e., e-cigarette refill liquids) (CDC, 2020). However, to date, the specific origin or cause of the related lung injuries has not been conclusively identified (For further discussion, see the related discussion in the e-cigarette subsection of Chapter 3, *Caffeine and Nicotine*—"E-Cigarettes"). (See also the related discussion in the earlier subsection—"Pulmonary Toxicities.")

Vaporizers

> To see how practical vaping flower actually is for older adults, a Baby Boomer (me) and Silent Generation (my 89-year-old father) tried two vaporizers, the Pax 3, and the Flower Mate Nano.
>
> (Rosner, 2019, p. 3)

Vaporizers are generally available in two forms: (1) quasi-stationary desktop models; and (2) portable devices.[95] The desktop models (e.g., SubHERBan Art® and Volcano® forced air vaporizer) are powered by electricity provided by a standard electrical outlet. A major innovation in relation to desktop vaporizers was the development of vaporizer pods (e.g., Canna Cloud® and Wisp®). The vaporizer pods are similar in form and appearance to coffee pods and are used in much the same way as for pod coffee machines (e.g., Keurig®). Like the variety of available coffee pods, the vaporizer pods allow users to conveniently purchase

95. Vaporizers are also differentiated according to the type of product being vaporized (e.g., e-liquid vapes, dry herb vapes, and wax/oil vapes). In their study of adult "vapers," Morean, Lipshie, and Josephson (2017) found that reported preferences were as follows: hash oil (~ 45%), "THC Wax" (~ 30%), and "dried buds" (~ 35%).

and use sealed, prefilled single-use pods that are available in a variety of CBD and THC strengths and aromas/"flavors."

Portable devices (i.e., "portable vapes," "vape pens"—"Arizer Solo 2®," "Cloud Pen®," "Executive®," "Links®," "Mighty®," "Pax 3®," "Puffco®," "Puff Fog Pen®," "Solo2®," and "Zeus Arc®") are battery operated and, by far, more widely used than desktop vaporizers (Pagliaro & Pagliaro, *Clinical Patient Data Files*).

Electronic Hookahs Electronic hookahs are commonly referred to as "E-Heads," "E-Hookahs," "E-Pens" (an abbreviation for "electronic shisha pens"), "Hookah Pen," and "Vape Pens." They are disposable delivery devices about the size and general shape of a Sharpie® marking pen or an insulin pen and typically consist of three major components: (1) a rechargeable lithium battery to generate the heat necessary for vaporizing the e-liquid; (2) an atomizer that converts the e-liquid to vapor; and (3) the "e-liquid" cartridge/tank (i.e., reservoir) that contains the product to be vaporized—THC (see Figure 4.2). Inhalation through the end of the automizer turns the unit[96] on, resulting in the automatic and virtually instantaneous heating and vaporization of the THC-containing e-liquid which is, subsequently, inhaled and rapidly absorbed into the circulatory system.[97]

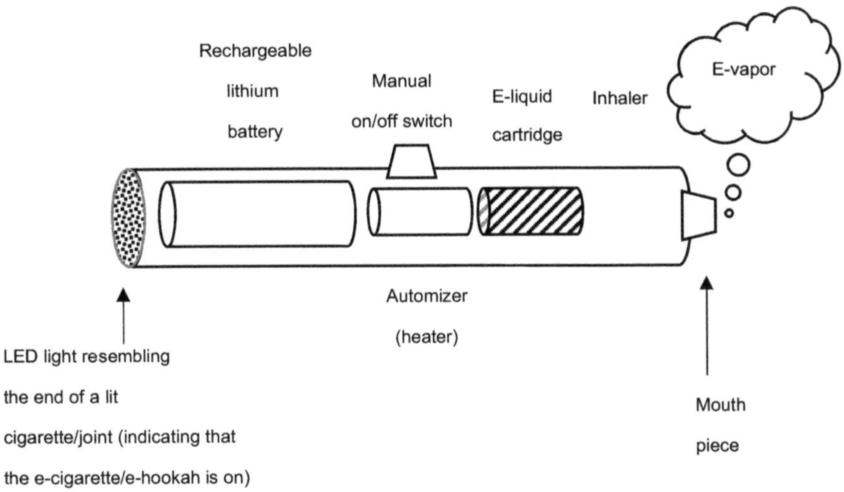

Figure 4.2 Components of an Electronic Hookah

The noted benefits of e-hookah use, according to many users, include:

- Its smaller size when compared to traditional hookahs, which makes it more convenient to carry from place to place (and conceal);

96. In some models, a button must be pressed while simultaneously inhaling in order to activate the electronic hookah.
97. Generally, the e-liquid also contains four other ingredients that function as a "vehicle" for facilitating the vaporization of the product to be vaporized and as a flavor, fragrance, or taste enhancer. These ingredients are: (1) fruit flavoring; (2) propylene glycol; (3) vegetable glycerine; and (4) water.

- Use of a battery as a heat source that produces cleaner and less toxic smoke rather than the burning charcoal, which is required with the traditional hookahs;
- Delivery of 200 to 800 puffs/hits (depending upon brand);
- Fewer associated restrictions, laws, and regulations—resulting in both more private and public use;
- Lower production of hazardous "side stream smoke."

Older Adult Illicit Drug Involvement

Older adult involvement in the illicit distribution and sale of cannabis in the U.S. exceeds their illicit involvement with all the other drugs and substances of abuse combined (Pagliaro & Pagliaro, *Clinical Patient Data Files*). In fact, involvement runs the entire gamut of illicit activities including:

- Grower of marijuana plants;
- Harvester and dryer of marijuana "buds;"
- Illicit supplier for friends/family (i.e., sharing for "free");
- Preparer of hashish and hashish oil;
- Preparer of edible marijuana products (e.g., hashish brownies);
- Seller of marijuana products from home (or from legal cannabis retail outlets);
- Smuggler of cannabis across either the Canadian or Mexican borders into the U.S.;
- Smuggler ("transporter") of cannabis from "legal" jurisdictions in the U.S. to other jurisdictions where possession and use are "illegal."

For example, many older adults become involved in drug dealing and other illicit activities to support their own cannabis use, while others may become more intensely involved as a means of obtaining their primary source of income (see earlier exemplar scenarios). Given this situation, it is disappointing that only a limited amount of published research is available regarding this widespread and perennial problem.

Regardless of the paucity of published research, it is clear to us—based on several decades of professional clinical and forensic work with older adults, who have been part of the cannabis or marijuana drug trade and other drug dealing—that the primary and virtually exclusive motivation for their involvement is "financial." Over the years the most common responses to our question, "Why are you involved in this activity?" are words to the effect that "it is easy and pays better than a "mc-job" (i.e., standing all day and working hard for a minimum wage at a local McDonalds® or Walmart®).

ASSESSMENT AND DIAGNOSIS OF OLDER ADULT CANNABIS DEPENDENCE OR USE DISORDER

> Clinicians may underestimate the likelihood of problematic substance use of a SUD among older adults. It is therefore important to conduct a comprehensive history of current and past use of substances including cannabis and cannabinoids. A comprehensive assessment is recommended when a SUD is suspected.
>
> (Conn, Rabheru, & Checkland, 2019, p. 16)

The assessment and diagnosis of cannabis dependence or use disorder (CUD) for older adults are generally achieved by means of an initial history and clinical interview with the older adult during which three major goals are achieved:

1. First, cannabis use is established;
2. Second, if established, answers are obtained to questions concerning both the qualitative and quantitative nature of the reported cannabis use;
3. Third, answers are obtained to questions concerning physical, mental, and social problems related to cannabis use—including signs and symptoms of cannabis withdrawal (see the related discussion in the earlier cannabis subsection, Physical and Psychological Dependence—"Cannabis Withdrawal Syndrome").

This section presents and discusses three approaches for achieving these goals and detecting cannabis dependence or use disorder among older adults who use cannabis: (1) DSM-5 criteria; (2) quick-Screen psychometric test, "Cannabis Use Disorder Identification Test" (CUDIT); and (3) quick-Screen psychometric test, "Cannabis Use Disorder Identification Test-Revised" (CUDIT-R). For a comprehensive overview of the general topics of assessment and diagnosis in the context of older adults AUD and SUDs, see the more detailed discussion in Chapter 1, *Alcohol*.

DSM-5 Criteria for Detecting Cannabis Use Disorder (CUD)

> Cannabis Use Disorder (CUD) is an emerging and diverse challenge among older adults . . . older adults may develop CUD in the setting of recreational and even medical use.
>
> (Bertram, Porath, & Seitz, 2020, p. 135)

Typically, endorsement of the following 11 described behaviors, which are based on DSM-5 criteria for CUD (e.g., APA, 2013; Hasin, O'Brien, & Auriacombe, 2013), are sought. Also sought is an indication of both the severity and duration of cannabis use and associated harmful effects and toxicities. In this context, older adults who acknowledge current or recent cannabis use, are asked to endorse, or not endorse, the following behaviors:

1. Continuing to use cannabis despite physical or psychological problems;
2. Continuing to use cannabis despite relationship or social problems related to use;
3. Craving for cannabis (i.e., have a longing for, or strong desire to use, cannabis);
4. Having difficulty controlling, cutting down, or discontinuing cannabis use (e.g., repeated unsuccessful attempts to quit cannabis use);
5. Giving up, or significantly reducing other activities—particularly, occupational, recreational, or social activities—in favor of cannabis use;
6. Having problems at home, or work, as a result of cannabis use;
7. Spending a lot of time on cannabis use, including obtaining cannabis or recovering from its effects;
8. Displaying tolerance to cannabis;
9. Using cannabis in hazardous situations (e.g., while supervising grandchildren or driving a motor vehicle);

10. Using more cannabis than intended, more frequently than intended, or for longer periods than intended;
11. Experiencing withdrawal when unable to obtain cannabis or when discontinuing its use.

According to DSM-5 criteria, the positive endorsement of two or more of the listed behaviors generally signify CUD with the number of endorsed items providing an indication of the severity of the CUD (i.e., "mild," two or three endorsements; "moderate," four or five endorsements; and "severe," six or more endorsements).[98]

Selected Cannabis Quick-Screen Psychometric Tests[99]

Several quick-screen psychometric tests have been developed for detecting cannabis dependence or use disorder. Generally, most of these tests are severely limited regarding available published test statistics for older adults. Additionally, none of the tests have been currently identified as a "standard" test for detecting cannabis dependence or use disorder for older adults. However, because older adults are among the largest group of new and continuing cannabis users, cannabis screening should be included in all geriatric assessments (Baumbusch & Sloan Yip, 2021; Pagliaro & Pagliaro, *Clinical Patient Data Files*). Two quick-screen psychometric tests—"Cannabis Use Disorder Identification Test" (CUDIT) and "Cannabis Use Disorder Identification Test-Revised" (CUDIT-R)—have been specifically developed to detect cannabis dependence or use disorder and have more available published test statistics than do any of the other associated tests. These two tests are presented and discussed in the following subsections.[100]

> ***Related Professional Reminder:* As with all quick-screen psychometric tests, but particularly for tests used for detecting CUD, the absence of a clinical "gold standard" diagnostic test, or "best available" benchmark, requires that suggestive positive test findings be carefully supported with appropriate clinical assessment and interview data.**

98. We, and others (e.g., Mewton, Slade, & Teesson, 2013), have shared concerns related to the DSM-5 criteria for CUD—particularly regarding the: (1) lack of distinction between social, habitual, abusive, and compulsive cannabis use; and (2) a discriminating, or cutoff, score of 2 that has the potential to make the diagnosis of CUD over-inclusive (i.e., significantly overestimated).

    Additionally, the state-by-state variance in regard to the legalization or non-legalization of medical or nonmedical/recreational cannabis use may encourage older adults to provide non-truthful responses to sensitive test items/questions that explore cannabis use and, consequently, contribute to inaccurate test results. Sznitman and Room (2018, p. 100) identified a similar concern:

    > It is possible that existing cannabis problem screening tools are not equally valid across medical and recreational users since individual screening items have different implications for recreational and medical users.

99. See also the related overview of quick-screen psychometric test selection, use, and interpretation in Chapter 1, *Alcohol*, and the description and discussion of additional nonspecific (i.e., generic) tests for the detection of SUDs in Chapter 2, *Amphetamines and Cocaine*.
100. Additionally, some general tests for detecting various SUDs have been used to detect CUD (e.g., "Severity of Dependence Scale" [SDS]). For an overview of these quick-screen psychometric tests, see Chapter 2, *Amphetamines and Cocaine*.

Cannabis Use Disorder Identification Test (CUDIT)

The CUDIT is a ten-item quick-screen psychometric test (Table 4.2) based on the "Alcohol Use Disorder Identification Test" (AUDIT). (For a discussion of the AUDIT, see Chapter 1, *Alcohol*.) Predicated on diagnostic criteria obtained from the DSM-IV, the CUDIT was developed and tested by Adamson and Sellman (2003) to detect CUD.

Scoring of the CUDIT Responses to each item of the CUDIT are given a score of 0 to 4 (see Table 4.2 for scoring criteria). The maximal score possible is 40. A discriminating cut-off score of 8 is generally considered to be equivalent to the DSM-IV diagnosis for CUD (Adamson & Sellman, 2003).

Table 4.2 The CUDIT

ITEM/QUESTION #	SCORING CRITERIA [Point Allocation]
Over the past <u>six</u> months . . .	
1. How often did you use cannabis?	Never, [0]; monthly or less, [1]; two to four times per month, [2]; two to three times per week, [3]; four or more times per week, [4]
2. How many hours were you stoned on a typical day when you had been using cannabis?	One or two, [0]; three or four, [1]; five or six, [2]; seven to nine, [3]; 10 or more, [4]
3. How often were you stoned for six or more hours?	Never, [0]; less than monthly, [1]; monthly, [2]; weekly, [3]; daily or almost daily, [4]
4. How often did you find that you were not able to stop using cannabis once you had started?	Never, [0]; less than monthly, [1]; monthly, [2]; weekly, [3]; daily or almost daily, [4]
5. How often did you fail to do what was normally expected from you because of using cannabis?	Never, [0]; less than monthly, [1]; monthly, [2]; weekly, [3]; daily or almost daily, [4]
6. How often did you need to use cannabis in the morning to get yourself going after a heavy session of using cannabis?	Never, [0]; less than monthly, [1]; monthly, [2]; weekly, [3]; daily or almost daily, [4]
7. How often did you have a feeling of guilt or remorse after using cannabis?	Never, [0]; less than monthly, [1]; monthly, [2]; weekly, [3]; daily or almost daily, [4]
8. How often have you had a problem with your memory or concentration after using cannabis?	Never, [0]; less than monthly, [1]; monthly, [2]; weekly, [3]; daily or almost daily, [4]
9. Have you or someone else been injured as a result of your use of cannabis?	No, [0]; Yes, [4]
10. Has a relative, friend, doctor or other health worker been concerned about your use of cannabis or suggested you cut down?	No, [0]; Yes, [4]

Source: Adamson and Sellman (2003).

Table 4.3 The CUDIT-R

ITEM/QUESTION #	SCORING [POINT ALLOCATION]
If you have used marijuana [cannabis] in the past six months, please answer the following questions about your cannabis use. Select the responses that are most correct for you in relation to your cannabis use over the past six months.	
1. How often do you use cannabis?	Never, [0]; monthly or less, [1]; two to four times per month, [2]; two to three times per week, [3]; four or more times per week, [4]
2. How many hours were you "stoned" on a typical day when you had been using cannabis?	Less than one, [0]; one or two, [1]; three or four, [2]; five or six, [3]; seven or more, [4]
3. How often during the last six months did you find that you were not able to stop using cannabis once you had started?	Never, [0]; less than monthly, [1]; monthly, [2]; weekly, [3]; daily or almost daily, [4]
4. How often during the last six months did you fail to do what was normally expected from you because of using cannabis?	Never, [0]; less than monthly, [1]; monthly, [2]; weekly, [3]; daily or almost daily, [4]
5. How often in the last six months have you devoted a great deal of time to getting, using, or recovering from cannabis?	Never, [0]; less than monthly, [1]; monthly, [2]; weekly, [3]; daily or almost daily, [4]
6. How often in the past six months have you had a problem with your memory or concentration after using cannabis?	Never, [0]; less than monthly, [1]; monthly, [2]; weekly, [3]; daily or almost daily, [4]
7. How often do you use cannabis in situations that could be physically hazardous, such as driving, operating machinery, or caring for children?	Never, [0]; less than monthly, [1]; monthly, [2]; weekly, [3]; daily or almost daily, [4]
8. Have you ever thought about cutting down, or stopping, your use of cannabis?	Never, [0]; Yes, but not in the past six months, [2]; Yes, during the past six months [4]

Source: Adamson et al. (2010).

Cannabis Use Disorder Identification Test-Revised (CUDIT-R)

The CUDIT-R is an eight-item, self-administered quick-screen psychometric test (Table 4.3 CUDIT-R). It was derived from the CUDIT by Adamson, Kay-Lambkin, and Baker (2010) to detect CUD among cannabis users, who have used marijuana within the past six months. The CUDIT-R is comprised of four items from the original test and four new items. It contains two items from each of the domains: "consumption;" cannabis problems/abuse;" "dependence;" and "psychological features."

Scoring of the CUDIT-R Items one to seven of the CUDIT-R are scored on a five-point Likert scale (see Table 4.3). Item eight is scored as 0, 2, or 4. The item scores are summed to give a total score of 0 to 32. A cutoff score of 8 is indicative of hazardous cannabis use, while a cutoff score of 12 is indicative of CUD.[101]

101. Australian researchers, Marshal (2013) and Bruno, Marshall, and Adamson (2013), used a cutoff score of 13 to detect: DSM-IV, "cannabis dependence;" and DSM-5, "moderate to severe CUD."

TREATING OLDER ADULT CANNABIS DEPENDENCE OR USE DISORDER

Given the extent of cannabis use among older adults in the U.S.—as well as the occurrence of cannabis dependence or use disorder in this age group—it is both surprising and disappointing that so little published research regarding treatment is currently available.[102]

> No intervention to date has proved consistently effective for the majority of those with dependence on cannabis.
>
> (Winstock et al., 2010, p. 803)

> Cannabis is the most widely used illicit psychoactive substance worldwide, yet no medication is approved for the treatment of intoxication, withdrawal, or cannabis use disorder (CUD).
>
> (Gorelick, 2016, p. 6409)

Although largely unexplored/untested for older adults in the context of CUD, SBIRT is an approach that should be considered (see Chapter 1, *Alcohol*, for a review and brief discussion of SBIRT in the context of alcohol dependence or other use disorder(s) (i.e., SUDs). As identified by Nunes, Richmond, and Marzano (2017, p. 508)—based on ten years of utilizing SBIRT—successful implementation requires:

1. Strong clinical and management advocates;
2. Full integration of services into practices' workflows, utilizing technology whenever possible;
3. Interprofessional team approaches;
4. Appropriate options for the small proportion of patients screening positive for a possible substance use disorder;
5. Cannabis screening that accounts for legalization, and interventions that acknowledge differences between alcohol and cannabis use;
6. Incorporating SBIRT into standard health care professionals' training;
7. Addressing the significant issues regarding reimbursement through private and public payers for SBIRT services.

Pharmacotherapeutic and Psychotherapeutic Approaches

As frequently noted throughout this text, the optimal treatment for alcohol or other dependence or use disorder, generally involves a selected combination of both pharmacotherapy and psychotherapy/counseling. However, for cannabis dependence or use disorder, pharmacotherapeutic approaches appear to be extremely limited.

Pharmacotherapy

Unfortunately, although several different drugs and drug classes (e.g., N-acetylcysteine, bupropion, buspirone, cannabinoids, lithium, and selective serotonin reuptake inhibitors)

102. This may be due, at least in part, to the observation that, while cannabis dependence or use disorder is likely the most common dependence or use disorder in the U.S., only a minority of older adults (i.e., approximately 10%) seek formal professional assistance for its treatment (Gates, Sabioni, & Copeland, 2016; Sherman, & McRae-Clark, 2016).

have been tested in clinical research studies for the treatment of cannabis dependence or use disorder, to date, no specific pharmacotherapeutic approach has been found to provide consistent, effective outcomes (Brezing & Levin, 2018; Copeland, 2004; Copeland & Swift, 2009; Weinstein & Gorelick, 2011). Additionally, as identified by others during the new millennium:

> Although pharmacologic treatments have shown promise, none have emerged as clearly efficacious.
>
> (Sherman & McRae-Clark, 2016, p. 511)

> Currently, the FDA has not approved any medications for the treatment of marijuana use disorder.[103]
>
> (NIDA, 2019b, p. 1; 2020b, p. 44)

> There are currently no pharmacotherapies approved for treatment of cannabis use disorder.
>
> (Nielsen, Gowing, and Sabioni (2019, p. 1)

> Although data on pharmacologic interventions for CUD are scarce, evidence exists that several drug classes, including cannabinoids and SSRIs, are ineffective.
>
> (Kondo, Morasco, & Nugent, 2020, p. 398)[104]

Psychotherapy/Counseling[105]

To date, psychotherapy/counseling has been the mainstay of treatment for cannabis dependence or use disorder (NIDA, 2019, 2020b). The major identified approaches for older adults have included:

- CBT;
- CM;
- MI;
- 12-step programs.

Each of the listed psychotherapeutic approaches has demonstrated some limited success in the treatment of cannabis dependence or use disorder (NIDA, 2019b)—as noted in several related reviews (e.g., Cooper, Chatters, & Kaltenthaler, 2015; Gates et al., 2016; Sherman & McRae-Clark, 2016). CBT—particularly, therapy that involves nine or more individual sessions—appears to be the most likely successful approach for reducing cannabis use among older adults (e.g., Copeland & Swift, 2009; Denis, Lavie, & Fatseas, 2006; Gates et al., 2016; NIDA, 2018; Sherman & McRae-Clark, 2016). However, the following

103. N.B. We would add that we are not aware of any current related "off-label" use of a pharmacotherapeutic approach—that we would recommend with a significant degree of confidence—for the treatment of cannabis dependence or use disorder among older adults.
104. Gray, Sonne, and McClure (2017, p. 249) similarly noted the ineffectiveness of N-acetylcysteine (NAC):

> There was no significant evidence that the NAC and placebo groups differed in cannabis abstinence (OR = 1.00).

105. For a discussion of each of these approaches, see the subsection in Chapter 1, *Alcohol,* Treating Older Adult Alcohol Dependence or Use Disorder—"Psychotherapy/Counseling."

major concerns must be noted and made explicit regarding the related, and largely supportive, published empirical research findings:

1. Abstinence rates post-treatment were low and unstable;
2. Sample sizes were relatively small;
3. The majority of subjects were younger adults.

Additionally, as identified by Crean, Crane, and Mason (2011, p. 5):

> The long-term executive functioning deficits associated with cannabis dependence and the associated risks for poor treatment outcome suggests that cognitively impaired cannabis users may not respond optimally to standard cognitively oriented treatment, such as CBT.

While deficits in executive function—as a result of cannabis use—are generally less likely to be apparent in users who have been abstinent for at least 30 days, the basic premise warrants clinical consideration and attention. Consequently, we recommend the administration of a neuropsychological test (e.g., "Clock Drawing Test," "Tail Making Test," or "Verbal Fluency Test"—see, for example, de Assis Faria, Veiga Dias Alves, & Charchat-Fichman, 2015) for all older adults before beginning psychotherapy/counseling for the treatment of cannabis dependence or use disorder.

Although we personally favor and have used CBT with success in the treatment of older adults, who have been diagnosed with cannabis dependence or use disorder, the aforementioned considerations/concerns and available empirical data, preclude—at least at this time—our full endorsement and recommendation for its use as a therapeutic approach for the treatment of cannabis dependence or use disorder for older adults by other mental health care professionals.

Additionally, accredited residential treatment has been recommended for older adults with cannabis dependence or use disorder, who otherwise would not be—or have not been—able to adequately respond to other treatment (e.g., Conn et al., 2019; Lemke & Moos, 2003). The available programs are generally: (1) "generic"—in terms of what type of drug or substance of abuse dependence or use disorder is being addressed; and (2) "age-integrated"—for all adults. Consequently, in the few cases in which we have both recommended this treatment and found it to be successful, the participating older adults were both: (1) younger (i.e., 50 to 60 years of age); and (2) in very good general physical health.

COMMON CONTEMPORANEOUS DIAGNOSES AMONG OLDER ADULTS

> Older individuals with psychiatric disorders are increasingly using cannabis, largely in the form of prescribed medical marijuana and cannabidiol (CBD).
>
> (Agronin, 2021, p. 2)

Although older adults are susceptible to, and may experience, virtually every form of contemporaneous diagnoses, the most often reported contemporaneous diagnosis, particularly in the context of older adult cannabis dependence or use disorder, is MDD (Pagliaro & Pagliaro, 2018; Pagliaro & Pagliaro, *Clinical Patient Data Files*; Tomko, Baker, & Hood, 2020).

Cannabis dependence or use disorder among older adults also has been commonly associated with several other mental disorders:

- Anxiety disorders;
- Alcohol Dependence or Use Disorder (i.e., AUD);
- Antisocial personality disorder (ASPD);
- Bipolar disorder (BD);
- Eating disorders;
- Psychotic disorder (e.g., schizophrenia);
- Other abusable psychotropic dependence or use disorders (i.e., SUDs).[106]

(e.g., Bahorik, Campbell, & Sterling, 2018; Lev-Ran, Le Foll, & McKenzie, 2013; Pacek, Martins, & Crum, 2013; Tomko et al., 2020)

Related Professional Reminder: ***It is important to recognize that the relationship between these disorders and cannabis use dependence or use disorder can be bi-directional. Additionally, they are not mutually exclusive and may occur in a variety of combinations. They may also occur in a variety of contexts including those involving physical medical disorders (e.g., chronic pain).***

For example, as reported by Lev-Ran et al. (2013, p. 459):

> Individuals with bipolar disorder and co-occurring CUD were at risk for nicotine dependence (Adjusted Odds Ration [AOR] = 3.8, alcohol (AOR = 6.6) and drug (AOR = 11.9) use disorders, as well as antisocial personality disorder (AOR = 2.8) compared to those without CUD.

In another example, reported by other researchers, contemporaneous diagnoses involving cannabis dependence or use disorder and MDD may commonly involve AUD (e.g., Bahorik et al., 2018; Pacek et al., 2013).

Related Professional Reminder: ***For older adults, active contemporaneous diagnoses involving alcohol or other dependence or use disorders—as well as other mental disorders—require appropriate and individualized pharmacotherapeutic and psychotherapeutic/counseling approaches with attention to the simultaneous implementation of appropriate therapeutic interventions for concurrent physical medical disorders.***

Although various prescription drugs (e.g., antidepressants and N-acetylcysteine [NAC]) have been used in an attempt to simultaneously treat both MDD and CUD, these attempts

---

106. Interestingly, and largely expected because of a number of factors previously discussed in this chapter, Choi, DiNitto, and Marti (2016)—in their secondary analysis of data from the *National Epidemiology Survey of Alcohol and Related Conditions* (NESARC-III)—found that older adult past-year marijuana users were significantly more likely to have other contemporaneous SUDs. This finding is supported by Olfson, Wall, and Liu (2018, p. 50), who found that:

> In a nationally representative sample of adults evaluated at waves 3 years apart, cannabis use was strongly associated with subsequent onset of nonmedical prescription opioid use and opioid use disorders.

have been largely unsuccessful. For example, regarding NAC, Tomko et al. (2020, p. 479)—in their secondary analysis of data from the *National Drug Abuse Treatment Clinical Trials* database—found that:

> Results do not support the use of NAC to concurrently treat co-occurring depressive symptoms and CUD in adults.

REFERENCES[107, 108, 109]

Adamson, S. J., & Sellman, J. D. (2003, September). A prototype screening instrument for cannabis use disorder: The cannabis use disorders identification test (CUDIT) in an alcohol-dependent clinical sample. *Drug and Alcohol Review*, *22*(3), 309–315. doi:10.1080/0959523031000154454

Adamson, S. J., Kay-Lambkin, F. J., & Baker, A. L. (2010). An improved brief measure of cannabis misuse: The Cannabis Use Disorders Identification Test-Revised (CUDIT-R). *Drug and Alcohol Dependence*, *110*, 137–143. doi:10.1016/j.drugalcvdfep.2010.02.017

Adlington, S., Harwood, M., & Cox, B. (2008). Cannabis use and risk of lung cancer: A case control study. *European Respiratory Journal*, *31*(2), 280–286. doi:10.1183/09031936.00065707

Agronin, M. E. (2021, March 26). The age of cannabis has arrived: Issues for older adults. *Psychiatric Times*, *38*(3), 1–7.

Aldington, S., Williams, M., & Nowitz, M. (2007). Effects of cannabis on pulmonary structure, function and symptoms. *Thorax*, *62*(12), 1058–1063.

Allen, J. H., de Moore, G. M., & Heddle, R. (2004). Cannabinoid hyperemesis: Cyclical hyperemesis in association with chronic cannabis use. *Gut*, *53*, 1566–1570.

Allsop, D. J., Copeland, J., & Lintzeris, N. (2014). Nabiximols as an agonist replacement therapy during cannabis withdrawal: A randomized clinical trial. *JAMA Psychiatry*, *71*(3), 281–291. doi:10.1001/jamapsychiatry.2013.3947

Ameri, A. (1999, July). The effects of cannabinoids on the brain. *Progress in Neurobiology*, *58*(4), 315–348.

Anderson, D. M., Rees, D. I., & Sabia, J. J. (2014). Medical marijuana laws and suicides by gender and age. *American Journal of Public Health*, *104*(12), 2369–2376. doi:10.2105/AJPH.2013.301612

107. As per publisher style, only the first three authors are listed for each reference.
108. Several times the number of references listed were found, obtained, and analyzed by the authors during the preparation of this chapter. However, only those references that were cited at least once in the body of the text are listed. Major reasons for not citing other references include that they: (1) did not provide any additional unique information or research findings; (2) were not well researched or written by their authors (i.e., were evaluated as not being valid or reliable); (3) were based predominately, or exclusively, on animal studies; (4) dealt exclusively with other population groups (e.g., children, adolescents, or young adults); (5) provided usage statistics from outside the U.S.; and/or (6) were redundant with, or not as recent as, the already cited references—unless the reference was of classical, historical, or seminal importance.
109. The reference citation, "Pagliaro & Pagliaro, *Clinical Patient Data Files*," refers to unpublished data collected, with permission, by the authors, in the formal course of their professional academic roles as clinician scientists and professors, from their patients, research subjects or participants, and students, from the 1970s to date. Most of the related data have been discussed and made public in a wide and large number of formal academic presentations, including graduate seminars, grand rounds, guest lectures, professional conferences, and undergraduate lectures.

Anderson, G. D., & Chan, L. N. (2016). Pharmacokinetic drug interactions with tobacco, cannabinoids and smoking cessation products. *Clinical Pharmacokinetics, 55*(11), 1353–1368. doi:10.1007/s40262-016-0400-9

Andrews, K. H., & Bracero, L. A. (2015). Cannabinoid hyperemesis syndrome during pregnancy: A case report. *The Journal of Reproductive Medicine, 60*(9–10), 430–432.

Angell, T. (2018, June 28). U.S. senate votes to legalize hemp after decades-long ban under marijuana prohibition. *Forbes*, pp. 1–2. Washington, DC.

APA, American Psychiatric Association. (2000). *DSM-IV, diagnostic and statistical manual of mental disorders* (4th ed.). Washington, DC: American Psychiatric Association.

APA, American Psychiatric Association. (2013). *DSM-5, diagnostic and statistical manual of mental disorders* (5th ed.). Washington, DC: American Psychiatric Association.

Arellano, A. L., Papaseit, E., & Romaguera, A. (2017). Neuropsychiatric and general interactions of natural and synthetic cannabinoids with drugs of abuse and medicines. *CNS & Neurological Disorders—Drug Targets, 16*(5), 554–566. doi:10.2174/1871527316666170413104516

Arendt, M., Rosenberg, R., & Foldager, L. (2007). Withdrawal symptoms do not predict relapse among subjects treated for cannabis dependence. *American Journal on Addictions, 16*(6), 461–467.

ARF/WHO, Addiction Research Foundation/World Health Organization. (1981). *Report of an ARF/WHO scientific (6) meeting on the adverse health and behavioral consequences of cannabis use*. Toronto: Addiction Research Foundation.

Arkin, P., & Adras, B. (2019). Opioids, overdose, and cannabis: Is marijuana an effective therapeutic response to the opioid abuse epidemic? *The Georgetown Journal of Law & Public Policy, 17*, 555–597.

Asbridge, M., Hayden, J. A., & Cartwright, J. L. (2012, February 9). Acute cannabis consumption and motor vehicle collision risk: Systematic review of observational studies and meta-analysis. *BMJ*, 344. doi:10.1136/bmj.e536

Ashton, C. B. (2001). Pharmacology and effects of cannabis: A brief review. *The British Journal of Psychiatry, 178*(2), 101–106. doi:10.1192/bjp.178.2.101

Azofeifa, A., Mattson, M. E., & Schauer, G. (2016, September 2). National estimates of marijuana use and related indicators—National survey on drug use and health, United States, 2002–2014. *MMWR, Morbidity and Mortality Weekly Report, 65*(11), pp. 1–25.

Bahorik, A. L., Campbell, C. I., & Sterling, S. A. (2018, January). Adverse impact of marijuana use on clinical outcomes among psychiatry patients with depression and alcohol use disorder. *Psychiatry Research, 259*, 316–322. doi:10.1016/j.psychres.2017.10.026

Barlow Wood, T., Newton Spivey, W. T., & Hill Easterfield, T. (1899). III. Cannabinol. Part 1. *Journal of the Chemical Society, Transactions, 75*, 20–36.

Baumbusch, J., & Sloan Yip, I. (2021). Exploring new use of cannabis among older adults. *Clinical Gerontologist, 44*(1), 25–31. doi:10.1080/07317115.2020.1746720

Beech, R. A., Sterrett, D. R., & Babiuk, J. (2015). Cannabinoid hyperemesis syndrome: A case report and literature review. *Journal of Oral Maxillofacial Surgery, 73*(10), 1907–1910. doi:10.1016/joms.2015.03.059

Berke, J., & Gould, S. (2020, January 1). Legal marijuana goes on sale today in Illinois. Here are all the states where cannabis is legal. *Business Insider*, pp. 1–5.

Berthiller, J., Straif, K., & Boniol, M. (2008, December). Cannabis smoking and risk of lung cancer in men: A pooled analysis of three studies in Maghreb. *Journal of Thoracic Oncology, 3*(12), 1398–1403. doi:10.1097/JTO.0b013e31818ddcde

Bertram, J. R., Porath, A., & Seitz, D. (2020, March). Canadian guidelines on cannabis use disorder among older adults. *Canadian Geriatrics Journal, 23*(1), 135–142. doi:10.5770/cgi.23.424

Best, P. (2020, November 4). Oregon becomes first state to decriminalize hard drugs like heroin and cocaine. *Fox News*, pp. 1–3. FOX News Network.

Black, N., Stockings, E., & Campbell, L. (2019, October 28). Cannabinoids for the treatment of mental disorders and symptoms of mental disorders: A systematic review and meta-analysis. *The Lancet Psychiatry*. doi:10.1016/S2215-0366(19)30401-8

Bloomfield, M., Ashok, A., & Volkow, N. (2016, November 17). The effects of delta-9-tetrahydrocannabinol on the dopamine system. *Nature, 539*, 369–377. doi:10.1038/nature 20153

Bobitt, J., Qualls, S. H., & Schuchman, M. (2019, May 30). Qualitative analysis of cannabis use among older adults. *Drugs & Aging, 36*, 655–666. doi:10.1007/s40266-019-00665-w

Bohlsen, M. (2019, January 9). Cannabis today and tomorrow the #1 cash crop for 2019. *Investorintel.* Investorintel Corporation.

Bonnet, U., & Preuss, U. W. (2017). The cannabis withdrawal syndrome: Current insights. *Substance Abuse and Rehabilitation, 8*, 9–37.

Booth, J. K., & Bohlmann, J. (2019, July). Terpenes in Cannabis sativa—From plant genome to humans. *Plant Science, 284*, 67–72. doi:10.1016/j.plantsci.2019.03.022

Borges, G., Bagge, C. L., & Orozco, R. (2016, May). A literature review and meta-analyses of cannabis use and suicidality. *Journal of Affective Disorders, 195*, 63–74. doi:10.1016/j.jad.2016.02.007

Borodovsky, J. T., Crosier, B. J., & Lee, D. C. (2016, October). Smoking, vaping, eating: Is legalization impacting the way people use cannabis? *International Journal of Drug Policy, 36*, 141–147. doi:10.1016/j.drugpo.2016.02.022

Boyles, S. (2019, September 12). Medical marijuana overdose sends man to ER. *Medpage Today*, p. 1.

Boynton, S. (2019, May 7). Roadside drug testing device picks up false positives from poppy seeds and tea, B.C. lawyers find. *Global News Hour*, pp. 1–4. Chorus Entertainment.

Breivogel, C. S., & Childers, S. R. (1998, December). The functional neuroanatomy of brain cannabinoid receptors. *Neurobiology of Disease, 5*(6 Part B), 417–431.

Brenneisen, R., Egli, A., & ElSohly, M. A. (1996, October). The effect of orally and rectally administered delta 9-tetrahydrocannabinol on spasticity: A pilot study with 2 patients. *International Journal of Clinical Pharmacology and Therapeutics, 34*(10), 446–452.

Brezing, C. A., & Levin, F. R. (2018). The current state of pharmacological treatments for cannabis use disorder and withdrawal. *Neuropsychopharmacology, 43*, 173–194. doi:10.1038/npp.2017.212

Brown, J. D., Costales, B., & Boemmel-Wegmann, v. (2020). Characteristics of older adults who were early adopters of medical cannabis in the Florida medical marijuana use registry. *Journal of Clinical Medicine, 18*(9), 1166. doi:10.3390/jcm9041166

Bruno, R., Marshall, S., & Adamson, S. (2013). *Screening for DSM-5 cannabis dependence using the Cannabis use identification test-revised.* NIDA Abstract Database. NIH, National Institute on Drug Abuse. Retrieved March 7, 2018, from www.drugabuse.gov/international/abstracts/screening-dsm-5-cannabis-dependence-using cannabis-use-identification-test-revised

Budney, A. J., & Hughes, J. R. (2006, May). The cannabis withdrawal syndrome. *Current Opinion in Psychiatry, 19*(3), 233–238.

Budney, A. J., Hughes, J. R., & Moore, B. A. (2004). Review of the validity and significance of cannabis withdrawal syndrome. *The American Journal of Psychiatry, 161*(11), 1967–1977.

Budney, A. J., Roffman, R., & Stephens, R. S. (2007, December). Marijuana dependence and its treatment. *Addiction Science & Clinical Practice, 4*(1), 4–16. doi:10.1151/ascp07414

Cain, P. (2017, September 22). Non-Americans barred from U.S. for smoking pot—even in states where it's legal. *Global News Online*. Global News.

Callaghan, R. C., Allebeck, P., & Sidorchuk, A. (2013, July). Marijuana use and risk of lung cancer: A 40-year cohort study. *Cancer Causes & Control, 24*, 1811–1820.

Campbell, G., Hall, W. D., & Peacock, A. (2018). Effect of cannabis use in people with chronic non-cancer pain prescribed opioids: Finding from a 4-year prospective cohort study. *Lancet Public Health, 3*(7), e341–e350. doi:10.1016/S24687-2667(18)30110-5

Canadian Pharmacists Association. (2018, January 25). Cannabis for medical purposes evidence guide: Information for pharmacists and other health care professionals. *Medical Cannabis*, pp. 1–11. Canadian Pharmacists Association.

Canazza, G., Citti, C., & Wiley, J. (2018). *Delta-9-tetrahydrocannabinol*. Geneva, Switzerland: World Health Organization.

Capler, R., Bilsker, D., & Van Pelt, K. (2017). *Cannabis use and driving: Evidence review*. Burnaby: Canadian Drug Policy Coalition.

CBS News. (2020, February 1). Number of stoned drivers in deadly crashes more than double in Washington since 2012, AAA says. *CBS News*, pp. 1–3. CBS Interactive Inc.

CDC, Centers for Disease Control and Prevention. (2018, March 7). Is it possible to "overdose" or have a "bad reaction" to marijuana? *Newsletter*, 1. U.S. Department of Health & Human Services.

CDC, Centers for Disease Control and Prevention. (2019, December 20). New cases in outbreak of e-cigarette, or vaping, use-associated lung injury (EVALI) on the decline. *CDC Newsroom Press Release*. U.S. Department of Health and Human Services.

CDC, Centers for Disease Control and Prevention. (2020, February 25). Outbreak of lung injury associated with the use of e-cigarette, or vaping, products. *Smoking & Tobacco Use*, pp. 1–2. CDC.

Celius, E. G., & Vila, C. (2018, April 6). The influence of THC:CBD oromucosal spray on driving ability in patients with multiple sclerosis-related spasticity. *Brain and Behavior, 8*(5), e00962. doi:10.1002/brb3.962

Cerda, M., Wall, M., & Keyes, K. M. (2012). Medical marijuana laws in 50 states: Investigating the relationship between state legalization of medical marijuana and marijuana use, abuse and dependence. *Drug and Alcohol Dependence, 120*(1–3), 22–27. doi:10.1016/j.drugalcdep.2011.06.011

Choi, N. G., DiNitto, D. M., & Marti, C. N. (2016, August). Older-adult marijuana users and ex-users: Comparisons of sociodemographic characteristics and mental and substance use disorders. *Drug and Alcohol Dependence, 165*, 94–102. doi:10.1016/j.drugalcdep.2016.05.023

Choi, N. G., DiNitto, D. M., & Marti, C. N. (2017, October). Nonmedical versus medical marijuana use among three age groups of adults: Associations with mental and physical health status. *American Journal of Addictions, 26*(7), 697–706. doi:10.1111/ajad.12598

Choi, N. G., Marti, C. N., & DiNitto, D. M. (2018). Older adults' marijuana use, injuries, and emergency department visits. *The American Journal of Drug and Alcohol Abuse, 44*(2), 215–223. doi:10.1080/00952990.2017.1318891

Christophersen, A. S., Morland, J., & Stewart, K. (2016). International trends in alcohol and drug use among vehicle drivers. *Forensic Science Review, 28*(1), 37–66.

Clines, F. X. (2001, February 28). Kentucky Journal: Fighting Appalachia's top cash crop, marijuana. *The New York Times, Section A*, p. 10. The New York Times.

Cobb, S., Bazargan, M., & Smith, J. (2019). Marijuana use among African American older adults in economically challenged areas of south Los Angeles. *Brain Sciences, 9*(7), 166–180. doi:10.3390/brainsci9070166

Cohen, M., Solowij, N., & Carr, V. (2008). Cannabis, cannabinoids and schizophrenia: Integration of the evidence. *Australian & New Zealand Journal of Psychiatry, 42*(5), 357–368. doi:10.1080/00048670801961156

Colorado Department of Revenue. (2018). *Colorado marijuana tax data* (pp. 1–2). Department of Revenue. Retrieved March 13, 2018, from www.colorado.gov/pacific/revenue/colorado-marijuana-tax-data

Colorado Department of Revenue. (2020, April). Marijuana tax data. *Monthly Report*, pp. 1–2. Colorado Department of Revenue.

Cone, E. J., & Huestis, M. A. (1993, December). Relating blood concentrations of tetrahydrocannabinol and metabolites to pharmacologic effects and time of marijuana use. *Therapeutic Drug Monitoring*, 527–532.

Conn, D., Rabheru, K., & Checkland, C. (2019). *Canadian guidelines on cannabis use disorder among older adults*. Toronto: Canadian Coalition for Seniors' Mental Health.

Cooper, K., Chatters, R., & Kaltenthaler, E. (2015, July). Psychological and psychosocial interventions for cannabis cessation in adults: A systematic review short report. *Health Technology Assessment, 19*(56), 1–130. doi:10.3310/hia19560

Cooper, Z. D., & Haney, M. (2009, April). Actions of delta-9-tetrahydrocannabinol in cannabis: Relation to use, abuse, dependence. *International Review of Psychiatry, 21*(2), 104–112. doi:10.1080/09540260902782752

Copeland, J. (2004, May). Developments in the treatment of cannabis use disorder. *Current Opinion in Psychiatry, 17*(3), 161–167.

Copeland, J., & Swift, W. (2009). Cannabis use disorder: Epidemiology and management. *International Review of Psychiatry, 21*(2). doi:10.1080/09540260902782745

Cornelius, J. R., Chung, T., & Martin, C. (2008). Cannabis withdrawal is common among treatment-seeking adolescents with cannabis dependence and major depression, and is associated with rapid relapse to dependence. *Addictive Behaviors, 33*(11), 1500–1505.

Couper, F. J., & Peterson, B. L. (2014). The prevalence of marijuana in suspected impaired driving cases in Washington state. *Journal of Analytical Toxicology, 38*(8), 569–574. doi:10.1093/jat/bku090

Cranford, J. A., Bohnert, K. M., & Perron, B. E. (2016, December 1). Prevalence and correlates of "vaping" as a route of cannabis administration in medical cannabis patients. *Drug and Alcohol Dependence, 169*, 41–47. doi:10.1016/j.drugalcdep.2016.10.008

Crean, R. D., Crane, N. A., & Mason, B. J. (2011, March). An evidence based review of acute and long-term effects of cannabis use on executive cognitive functions. *Journal of Addiction Medicine, 5*(1), 1–8. doi:10.1097/ADM.0b013e31820c23fa

Crippa, J., Derenusson, G. N., & Chagas, M. (2012). Pharmacological interventions in the treatment of the acute effects of cannabis: A systematic review of literature. *Harm Reduction Journal, 9*, 7–13.

Dasgupta, A. (2015, February 1). How people try to beat drug testing: Issues with urinary adulterants and their detection. *Clinical Laboratory News*, pp. 1–5.

de Assis Faria, C., Veiga Dias Alves, H., & Charchat-Fichman, C. (2015, April–June). The most frequently used tests for assessing executive functions in aging. *Dementia & Neuropsychologia*, *9*(2), 149–155. doi:10.1590/1980-57642015DN92000009

de Mello Schier, A. R., de Oliveira Ribeiro, N. P., & Coutinho, D. S. (2014). Antidepressant-like and anxiolytic-like effects of cannabidiol: A chemical compound of Cannabis sativa. *CNS & Neurological Disorders—Drug Targets*, *13*(6), 953–960.

Delforterie, M. J., Lynskey, M. T., & Huizink, A. C. (2015, May 1). The relationship between cannabis involvement and suicidal thoughts and behaviors. *Drug and Alcohol Dependence*, *150*, 98–104. doi:10.1016/j.drugalcdep.2015.02.01

Denis, C., Lavie, E., & Fatseas, M. (2006, July 19). Psychotherapeutic interventions for cannabis abuse and/or dependence in outpatient settings. *The Cochrane Database of Systematic Reviews*, *3*, CD005336.

Desai, A. K., Seraji, M., & Redden, M. (2010). Schizophrenia in older adults. *Current Psychiatry*, *9*(9), 23–29.

Devinsky, O., Cross, J. H., & Laux, L. (2017, May 25). Trial of cannabidiol for drug-resistant seizures in the Dravet syndrome. *The New England Journal of Medicine*, *376*(21), 2011–2020. doi:10.1056/NEJMoa1611618

Dhopeshwarkar, A., & Mackie, K. (2014, October). CB2 cannabinoid receptors as a therapeutic target—What does the future hold? *Molecular Pharmacology*, *86*(4), 430–437. doi:10.1124/mol.114.094649

Di Marzo, V., Melck, D., & Bisogno, T. (1998). Endocannabinoids: Endogenous cannabinoid receptor ligands with neuromodulatory action. *Trends in Neurosciences*, *21*(12), 521–528.

DiNitto, D. M., & Choi, N. G. (2011, June). Marijuana use among older adults in the U.S.A.: User characteristics, patterns of use, and implications for intervention. *International Psychogeriatrics*, *23*(5), 732–741. doi:10.1017/S1041610210002176

D'Souza, D. C. (2007). Cannabinoids and psychosis. *International Review of Neurobiology*, *78*, 289–326. doi:10.1016/S0074-7742(06)78010-2

D'Souza, D. C., Cortes-Briones, J. A., & Ranganathan, M. (2016, January). Rapid changes in CB1 receptor availability in cannabis dependent males after abstinence from cannabis. *Biological Psychiatry: Cognitive Neuroscience and Neuroimaging*, *1*(1), 60–67. doi:10.1016/j.bpsc.2015.09.008

Dubie, M. F., & Green, C. R. (1982). Methods of collection of smoke for analytical purposes. *Recent Advances in Tobacco Science*, *8*(42), 102.

Eisenberg, E., Ogintz, M., & Almog, S. (2014). The pharmacokinetics, efficacy, safety, and ease of use of a novel portable metered-dose cannabis inhaler in patients with chronic neuropathic pain: A phase 1a study. *Journal of Pain and Palliative Care Pharmacotherapy*, *28*(3), 216–225. doi:10.3109/15360288.2014.941130

Elphick, M. R., & Egertova, M. (2001, March 29). The neurobiology and evolution of cannabinoid signaling. *Philosophical Transactions of the Royal Society of London B Biological Sciences*, *356*(1407), 381–408. doi:10.1098/rstb.2000.0787

ElSohly, M. A., Gul, W., & Walker, L. A. (2018). Pharmacokinetics and tolerability of THC-hemisuccinate in a suppository formulation as an alternative to capsules for the systemic delivery of THC. *Medical Cannabis and Cannabinoids*, *1*, 44–53. doi:10.1159/0004889037

ElSohly, M., Radwan, M. M., & Gul, W. (2017). Phytochemistry of Cannabis sativa L. *Progress in the Chemistry of Organic Natural Products*, *103*, 1–36. doi:10.1007/978-3-319-45541-9_1

Farnsworth, N. R. (1969, August). Pharmacognosy and chemistry of 'cannabis sativa'. *Journal of the American Pharmaceutical Association*, *59*(8), 410–414, 440.

FDA. (2019, March 5). FDA approves new nasal spray medication for treatment-resistant depression; Available only at a certified doctor's office or clinic. *FDA News Release*.

FDA, U.S. Food and Drug Administration. (2020, January 24). Lung injuries associated with use of vaping products. *Public Health Focus*, pp. 1–8. FDA.

Ferner, M. (2014, September 22). *Marijuana tax revenue may top $3 billion a year with legalization*. Retrieved April 13, 2016, from HOFFPOST POLITICS: www.huffingtonpost.com/2014/09/22/legal-marijuana-taxes_n_5863860.html

Forster, V. (2018, June 25). FDA approves first-ever drug directly purified from cannabis. *Forbes*, pp. 1–2.

Fuller, T. (2020, December 2). Oregon decriminalizes small amounts of heroin and cocaine; Four states legalize marijuana. *The New York Times*. Oakland, CA: New York Times.

Galli, J. A., Andari Sawaya, R., & Friedenberg, F. K. (2011, December). Cannabinoid hyperemesis syndrome. *Current Drug Abuse Reviews*, *4*(4), 241–249.

Gant, M. (2017, December 29). Jack in the Box launching weed-themed Merry Munchie Meal in California. *Fox News*. FoxNews.com.

Gaoni, Y., & Mechoulam, R. (1964). Isolation, structure, and partial synthesis of an active constituent of hashish. *Journal of the American Chemical Society*, *86*(8), 1646–1647. doi:10.1021/ja01062a046-1647

Gates, P. J., Sabioni, P., & Copeland, J. (2016, May 5). Psychosocial interventions for cannabis use disorder. *The Cochrane Database of Systematic Reviews*, *5*, CD005336. doi:10.1002/14651858.CD005336.pub4

Gettman, J. (2006, December). Marijuana production in the United States (2006). *The Bulletin of Cannabis Reform*, pp. 1–28. Retrieved August 1, 2015, from www.drugscience.org/bcr/index.html

Gieringer, D., St. Laurent, J., & Goodrich, S. (2004). Cannabis vaporizer combines efficient delivery of THC with effective suppression of pyrolytic compounds. *Journal of Cannabis Therapeutics*, *4*(1), 7–27. doi:10.1300/J175v04n01_02

Gilbert, A. N., & DiVerdi, J. A. (2018). Consumer perceptions of strain differences in Cannabis aroma. *PLoS ONE*, *13*(2), e0192247. doi:10.1371/journal.pone.0192247

Goodwin, R. S., Darwin, W. D., & Chiang, C. N. (2008). Urinary elimination of 11-nor-9-carboxy-9-tetrahydrcannabinol in cannabis users during continuously monitored abstinence. *Journal of Analytical Toxicology*, *32*(8), 562–569.

Gordon, M. (2018, September 12). More older Americans are turning to marijuana. *NPR*, pp. 1–2.

Gorelick, D. A. S. (2016). Pharmacological treatment of cannabis-related disorders: A narrative review. *Current Pharmaceutical Designs*, *22*(42), 6409–6419. doi:10.2174/1381612822666160822150822.27549375

Goulle, J. P., & Guerbet, M. (2014). Tetrahydrocannabinol pharmacokinetics; new synthetic cannabinoids; road safety and cannabis. *Bulletin de l'Academie Nationale de Medecine*, *198*(3), 541–556.

Government of Canada. (2018, August). Is cannabis addictive? *Cannabis Evidence Brief*, pp. 1–6. Ottawa: Minister of Health.

Granowicz, J. (2016). Senator Elizabeth Warren asks the CDC to study marijuana as opiate alternative. *The Marijuana Times*, 1.

Graves, B. M., Johnson, T. J., & Nishida, R. T. (2020). Comprehensive characterization of mainstream marijuana and tobacco smoke. *Nature*, *10*, 7160–7174. doi:10.1038/s41598-020-63120-6

Gray, K. M., Sonne, S. C., & McClure, E. A. (2017, August 1). A randomized placebo-controlled trial of N-acetylcysteine for cannabis use disorder in adults. *Drug and Alcohol Dependence, 177*, 249–257. doi:10.1016/j.drugalcdep.2017.04.020

Grewal, J. K., & Loh, L. C. (2020). Health considerations of the legalization of cannabis edibles. *CMAJ, 192*(1), E1–E2. doi:10.1503/cmaj.191217

Grinspoon, P. (2020, April 6). Older adults and medical marijuana: Reduced stigma and increased use. *Harvard Health Blog*, pp. 1–4. Harvard University.

Gumbiner, J. (2011a, May 10). History of cannabis use in ancient China. *Psychology Today*, pp. 1–4.

Gumbiner, J. (2011b, June 16). History of cannabis in India. *Psychology Today*, pp. 1–6.

Gupta, S., & Phalen, T. (2018, January). Medical marijuana: Do the benefits outweigh the risks? *Current Psychiatry, 17*(1), 34–41.

Guy, G. W., & Robson, P. J. (2003). A phase I, double blind, three-way crossover study to assess the pharmacokinetic profile of cannabis based medicine extract (CBME) administered sublingually in variant cannabinoid ratios in normal healthy male volunteers. *Journal of Cannabis Therapeutics, 3*(4), 121–152. doi:10.1300/J175v03n04_02

Hadener, M., Vieten, S., & Weinmann, W. (2019, February). A preliminary investigation of lung availability of cannabinoids by smoking marijuana or dabbing BHO and decarboxylation rate of THC—and CBD—acids. *Forensic Sciences International, 295*, 207–212. doi:10.1016/j.forsciint.2018.12.021

Hagler, D. (2017, April). Marijuana use: Detrimental to youth. *Position Statement*, pp. 1–14. American College of Pediatricians.

Hall, W., & Degenhardt, L. (2008, June). Cannabis use and the risk of developing a psychotic disorder. *World Psychiatry, 7*(2), 68–71.

Halperin, A. (2019a, April 29). Craving cannabis: Is marijuana addictive? *The Guardian*, pp. 1–2. Guardian News & Media Limited.

Halperin, A. (2019b, January 14). The mature stoner: Why are so many seniors smoking weed? *The Guardian*, pp. 1–5. Guardian News & Media Limited.

Han, B. H., & Palamar, J. J. (2018, October). Marijuana use by middle-aged and older adults in the United States, 2015–2016. *Drug and Alcohol Dependence, 191*, 374–381. doi:10.1016/j.drugalcdep.2018.07.006

Han, B. H., & Palamar, J. J. (2020, February 24). Trends in cannabis use among older adults in the United States, 2015–2018. *JAMA Internal Medicine, 180*(4), 609–611. doi:10.1001/jamainternmed.2019.7517

Hancox, R. J., Poulton, R., & Ely, M. (2010). Effects of cannabis on lung function: A population-based cohort study. *European Respiratory Journal, 35*(1), 42–47. doi:10.1183/09031936.00065009

Harrar, S. (2019a, October 17). Vaping dangers for older adults. *Updates*, pp. 1–3. AARP, American Association of Retired People.

Harrar, S. (2019b, September 3). Marijuana: Your questions answered and what we know today. *The Daily*, pp. 1–5. AARP.

Harrison, L. D., Backenheimer, M., & Inciardi, J. A. (1996). Cannabis use in the United States: Implications for policy. In P. Cohen, & A. Sas (Eds.), *Cannabisbeleid in Duitsland, Frankrijk en de Verenigde Staten* (pp. 179–276). Amsterdam: Centrum voor Drugsonderzoek.

Hartman, R. L., & Huestis, M. A. (2013). Cannabis effects on driving skills. *Clinical Chemistry, 59*(3), 478–492. doi:10.1373/clinchem.2012.194381

Hartman, R. L., Brown, T. L., & Milavetz, G. (2015a, September). Cannabis effects on driving lateral control with and without alcohol. *Drug and Alcohol Dependence, 154*, 25–37. doi:10.1016/j.drugalcdep.2015.06.015

Hartman, R. L., Brown, T. L., & Milavetz, G. (2015b). Controlled cannabis vaporizer administration: Blood and plasma cannabinoids with and without alcohol. *Clinical Chemistry, 61*(6), 850–869. doi:10.1373/clinchem.2015.238287

Hartung, B., Kauferstein, S., & Ritz-Timme, S. (2014, April). Sudden unexpected death under acute influence of cannabis. *Forensic Science International, 237*, e11–e13. doi:10.1016/j.forsciint.2014.02.001

Hasin, D. S., O'Brien, C. P., & Auriacombe, M. (2013). DSM-5 criteria for substance use disorders: Recommendations and rationale. *American Journal of Psychiatry, 170*(8), 834–851. doi:10.1176/appi.ajp.2013.12060782

Heather, A. C. (2001, February). Pharmacology and effects of cannabis: A brief review. *The British Journal of Psychiatry, 178*, 101–106.

Herman, B. (2018, February 28). This scientist is testing a marijuana ingredient as a way to prevent relapse. *STAT*, pp. 1–5.

Hitti, M. (2007, December 14). Study shows toxins in marjuana smoke. *WebMD*, pp. 1–2. WebMD.

Horn, J. R., & Hansten, P. D. (2014, December 9). Drug interactions with marijuana. *Pharmacy Times*.

Huestis, M. A. (2007). Human cannabinoid pharmacokinetics. *Chemistry & Biodiversity, 4*(8), 1770–1804.

Hunt, C. A., Jones, R. T., & Herning, R. I. (1981, June). Evidence that cannabidiol does not significantly alter the pharmacokinetics of tetrahydrocannabinol in man. *Journal of Pharmacokinetics and Biopharmaceutics, 9*(3), 245–260.

Hurley, J. M., West, J. B., & Ehleringer, J. R. (2010). Tracing retail cannabis in the United States: Geographic origin and cultivation patterns. *International Journal of Drug Policy, 21*, 222–228. doi:10.1016/j.drugpo.2009.08.001

Iversen, L. (2003). Cannabis and the brain. *Brain, 126*, 1252–1270. doi:10.1093/brain/awg143

Jafari, S., & Tang, T. (2016, July–August). Diagnosis and treatment of marijuana dependence. *BC Medical Journal, 58*(6), 315–317.

Johnson, M. B., Mechtler, L., & Ali, B. (2021, March). Cannabis and crash risk among older drivers. *Accident Analysis & Prevention, 152*, 1–3. doi:10.1016/j.aap.2021.105987

Jones, R. T., Benowitz, N. L., & Herning, R. I. (1981). Clinical relevance of cannabis tolerance and dependence. *Journal of Clinical Pharmacology, 21*, 143S–152S.

Joshi, M., Joshi, A., & Bartter, T. (2014). Marijuana and lung diseases. *Current Opinion in Pulmonary Medicine, 20*(2), 173–179. doi:10.1097/MCP.0000000000000026

Kaplan, M. (2018, March 5). Weed is helping me quit opioids. *New York Post*, p. 1.

Kasana, M. (2018, December 21). Hemp is legal in the US now—Here's what that actually means. *Bustle*, pp. 1–2.

Kelley, B. (2020). Marijuana & edibles toxicity in dogs & cats. *Haiku Veterinary Clinic Newsletter*, p. 1. Haiku Veterinary Clinic.

Kelly, B. F., & Nappe, T. M. (2019). *Cannabinoid toxicity*. Treasure Island, FL: StatPearls Publishing.

Kendall, D. A., & Yudowski, G. A. (2017, January). Cannabinoid receptors in the central nervous system: Their signaling and roles in disease. *Frontiers in Cellular Neuroscience, 10*, 1–10. doi:10.3389/fncel.2016.00294

Khalsa, J. H., Genser, S., & Francis, H. (2002). Clinical consequences of marijuana. *Journal of Clinical Pharmacology, 42*(Suppl 11), 7S–10S.

Khan, S. S., Secades-Villa, R., & Okuda, M. (2013). Gender differences in cannabis use disorders: Results from the national epidemiologic survey of alcohol and related conditions. *Drug and Alcohol Dependence, 130*(1–3), 101–108. doi:10.1016/j.drugalcdep.2012.10.015

Klein, T. W., Lane, B., & Newton, C. A. (2000). The cannabinoid system and cytokine network. *Proceedings of the Society for Experimental Biology and Medicine, 225*(1), 1–8.

Kloft, L., Otgaar, H., & Blokland, A. (2020). Cannabis increases susceptibility to false memory. *Proceedings of the National Academy of Sciences of the United States of America, 117*(9), 4585–4589. doi:10.1073/pnas.1920162117

Ko, G. D., Wine, W. A., & Tumarkin, E. J. (2006). MS patients with neuropathic pain demonstrated improvement using the oral synthetic cannabinoid nabilone. *Practical Pain Management*, 1–6. Remedy Health Media.

Kondo, K. K., Morasco, B. J., & Nugent, S. M. (2020, March 17). Pharmacotherapy for the treatment of cannabis use disorder: A systematic review. *Annals of Internal Medicine, 172*(6), 398–412. doi:10.7326/M19-1105

Kovacevich, N. (2018, December 5). Cannabis is a tax bonanza for states. *Forbes*, pp. 1–2.

Lagerquist, J. (2019a, January 29). Women and senior cannabis users are the biggest stoners, research shows. *Yahoo/Life*, pp. 1–2. Yahoo.

Lagerquist, J. (2019b, February 25). Starbucks could be the first big chain to launch cannabis drinks. *Yahoo Finance*.

Lal, A., Kumar Mishra, A., & Kant Sahu, K. (2019). Vitamin E acetate and e-cigarette or vaping product-associated lung injury (EVALI): An update. *The American Journal of Medicine*, 1–2. doi:10.1016/j.amjmed.2019.11.005

Lee, M. H., & Hancox, R. J. (2011). Effects of smoking cannabis on lung function. *Expert Review of Respiratory Medicine, 5*(4), 537–546. doi:10.1586/ers.11.40

Lemke, S., & Moos, R. H. (2003). Outcomes at 1 and 5 years for older patients with alcohol use disorders. *Journal of Substance Abuse Treatment, 24*, 43–50.

Lev-Ran, S., Le Foll, B., & McKenzie, K. (2013, October). Bipolar disorder and co-occurring cannabis use disorders: Characteristics, co-morbidities and clinical correlates. *Psychiatry Research, 209*(3), 459–465.

Leweke, F. M., & Koethe, D. (2008). Cannabis and psychiatric disorders: It is not only addiction. *Addiction Biology, 13*(2), 264–275. doi:10.1111/j.1369-1600.2008.00106.x

Lewis, N., McCaffrey, K., & Sage, K. (2019, October 22). E-cigarette use, or vaping, practices and characteristics among persons with associated lung injury—Utah, April-October 2019. *MMWR, Morbidity and Mortality Weekly Report, 68*, 1–5.

Li, M. C., Brady, J. E., & DiMaggio, C. J. (2012). Marijuana use and motor vehicle crashes. *Epidemiologic Reviews, 34*, 65–72. doi:10.1093/epirev/mxr017

Lieber, M. (2018, April 26). Marijuana legalization could help offset opioid epidemic, studies find. *CNN*, p. 1.

Lloyd, S. L., & Striley, C. W. (2018). Marijuana use among adults 50 years of age or older in the 21st century. *Gerontology & Geriatric Medicine, 4*, 1–14. doi:10.1177/2333721418781668

Loflin, M. J., Earleywine, M., & Farmer, S. (2017, August 3). Placebo effects of edible cannabis: Reported intoxication effects at a 30-minute delay. *Journal of Psychoactive Drugs*, 1–5. doi:10.1080/02791072.2017.1354409

Lopez-Moreno, J. A., Gonzalez-Cuevas, G., & Moreno, G. (2008). The pharmacology of the endocannabinoid system: Functional and structural interactions with other neurotransmitter systems and their repercussions in behavioral addiction. *Addiction Biology, 13*(2), 160–187. doi:10.1111/j.1369-1600.2008.00105.x

Lopez-Quintero, C., Perez de los Cobos, J., & Hasin, D. S. (2011). Probability and predictors of transition from first use to dependence on nicotine, alcohol, cannabis, and cocaine: Results of the National Epidemiologic Survey on Alcohol and Related Conditions (NESARC). *Drug and Alcohol Dependence*, *115*(1–2), 120–130. doi:10.1016/j.drugalcdep.2010.11.004

Lozano, A. V. (2020, November 4). 'A tipping point': Psychedelics, cannabis win big across the country on election night. *NBC News*, pp. 1–4. NBC Universal.

Ludlow, F. H. (1857). *The hashish eater: Being passages from the life of pythagorean*. New York, NY: S. G. Rains.

Maccarrone, M., & Finazzi-Agro, A. (2002). Endocannabinoids and their actions. *Vitamins and Hormones*, *65*, 225–255.

Maida, V., & Daeninck, P. J. (2016, December). A user's guide to cannabinoid therapies in oncology. *Current Oncology*, *23*(6), 398–406.

Maldonado, R., & Rodriguez de Fonseca, F. (2002, May 1). Cannabinoid addiction: Behavioral models and neural correlates. *Journal of Neuroscience*, *22*(9), 3326–3331.

Marshal, S. E. (2013). *The Cannabis use disorder identification test—revised (CUDIT-R): Categorisation and interpretation*. Australia: University of Tasmania. Retrieved March 5, 2018

Martin, B. R., Mechoulam, R., & Razdan, R. K. (1999). Discovery and characterization of endogenous cannabinoids. *Life Sciences*, *65*(6–7), 573–595.

Mayo Clinic Staff. (2017). *Marijuana*. Mayo Clinic. Retrieved March 6, 2018

McCarthy, J. (2018, October 2). Two in three Americans now support legalizing marijuana. *Gallup*, pp. 1–6. Washington, DC: Gallup Incorporated.

McGilveray, I. J. (2005, Autumn). Pharmacokinetics of cannabinoids. *Pain Research & Management*, *10*(Suppl A), 15A–22A.

McPartland, J. M. (1997). Cannabis as repellent and pesticide. *Journal of the International Hemp Association*, *4*(2), 87–92.

Mead, A. (2017, May). The legal status of cannabis (marijuana) and cannabidiol (CBD) under U.S. law. *Epilepsy & Behavior*, *70*(Part B), 288–291. doi:10.1016/j.yebeh.2016.11.021

Mechoulam, R., & Shvo, Y. (1963, December). Hashish. I. The structure of cannabidiol. *Tetrahedron*, *19*(12), 2073–2078. doi:10.1016/0040-4020(63)85022-x

Melton, S. T. (2017, June 8). Stirring the pot: Potential drug interactions with marijuana. *MedScape*.

Mewton, L., Slade, T., & Teesson, M. (2013). An evaluation of the proposed DSM-5 cannabis use disorder criteria using Australian national survey data. *Journal of Studies on Alcohol and Drugs*, *74*(4), 614–621. doi:10.15288/jsad.2013.74.614

Miech, R. A., Johnston, L., & O'Malley, P. M. (2015). Trends in use of and attitudes toward marijuana among youth before and after decriminalization: The case of California 2007–2013. *The International Journal on Drug Policy*, *26*(4), 336–344. doi:10.1016/j.drugpo.2015.01.009

Miller, S. G. (2016, August 8). High numbers? 1 in 8 US adults smokes pot. *Live Science*, pp. 1–10.

Moir, D., Rickert, W. S., & Levasseur, G. (2008). A comparison of mainstream and sidestream marijuana and tobacco cigarette smoke produced under two machine smoking conditions. *Chemical Research in Toxicology*, *21*(2), 494–502. doi:10.1021/tx700275p

Morean, M. E., Lipshie, N., & Josephson, M. (2017, July 3). Predictors of adult e-cigarette users vaporizing cannabis using e-cigarettes and vape-pens. *Substance Use & Misuse*, *52*(8), 974–981. doi:10.1080/10826084.2016.1268162

Moreira, F. A., & Lutz, B. (2008). The endocannabinoid system: Emotion, learning and addiction. *Addictive Behaviors*, *13*(2), 196–212. doi:10.1111/j.1369-1600.2008.00104.x

Moreno-Sanz, G. (2016). Can you pass the acid test? Critical review and novel therapeutic perspectives of delta-9-tetrahydrocannabinolic acid A. *Cannabis and Cannabinoid Research*, *1*(1), 124–130. doi:10.1089/can.2016.0008

Morris, D. Z. (2017, December 26). Jack in the Box is launching a 'Munchie Meal' for stoners. *Fortune*.

Motel, S. (2015, April 14). 6 facts about marijuana. *Pew Research Center*. Retrieved April 14, 2016, from www.pewresearch.org/author/smotel/

Motycka, C., Glinton, M., & Brennan, C. (2016). Side effects and drug interactions with marijuana. *International Archives of Nursing and Health Care*, *2*(1), 1–2.

Mucke, M., Phillips, T., & Radbruch, L. (2018). Cannabis-based medicines for chronic neuropathic pain in adults. *Cochrane Database of Systematic Reviews*, *3*(3), CDO12182. doi:10.1002/14651858.CD012182.pub2

NCDAS, National Center for Drug Abuse Statistics. (2019). Marijuana addiction: Rates & usage statistics. *Report*, 1–8. NCDAS.

News Staff. (2020, March 4). Cannabis use in older adults continues upward trend. *Newsletter*, pp. 1–4. AAFP.

Nicolson, S. E., Denysenko, L., & Mulcare, J. L. (2012, May–June). Cannabinoid hyperemesis syndrome: A case series and review of previous reports. *Journal of Psychosomatics*, *53*(3), 212–219. doi:10.1016/j.psym.2012.01.003

NIDA, National Institute on Drug Abuse. (2018, June). *Marijuana*. Bethesda, MD: NIH.

NIDA, National Institute on Drug Abuse. (2019a, January 25). A whole new view of CB2. *Press Release*, pp. 1–2. NIH.

NIDA, National Institute on Drug Abuse. (2019b, December). *Available treatments for marijuana use disorders* (p. 1). Bethesda, MD: NIH.

NIDA, National Institute on Drug Abuse. (2020a, April). How does marijuana produce its effects? *Research Report*, pp. 1–2. NIH.

NIDA, National Institute on Drug Abuse. (2020b, April). Marijuana. *Research Report*, pp. 1–60. NIH.

Nielsen, S., Gowing, L., & Sabioni, P. (2019, January 28). Pharmacotherapies for cannabis dependence. *Cochrane Database of Systematic Reviews*, *1*(1), CD008940. doi:10.1002/14651858.CD008940.pub3

Nocerino, E., Amato, M., & Izzo, A. A. (2000). Cannabis and cannabinoid receptors. *Fitoterapia*, *71*(Suppl 1), S6–S12.

Nunes, A. P., Richmond, M. K., & Marzano, K. (2017). Ten years of implementing screening, brief intervention, and referral to treatment (SBIRT): Lessons learned. *Substance Abuse*, *38*(4), 508–512. doi:10.1080/08897077.2017.1362369

Nurmikko, T. J., Serpell, M. G., & Hoggart, B. (2007, August). Sativex successfully treats neuropathic pain characterised by allodynia: A randomised, double-blind, placebo-controlled clinical trial. *Pain*, 1–11. doi:10.1016/j.pain.2007.08.028

Olfson, M., Wall, M. M., & Liu, S.-M. (2018). Cannabis use and risk of prescription opioid use disorder in the United States. *The American Journal of Psychiatry*, *175*(1), 47–53. doi:10.1176/appi.ajp.2017.17040413

Pacek, L. R., Martins, S. S., & Crum, R. M. (2013, June). The bidirectional relationships between alcohol, cannabis, co-occurring alcohol and cannabis use disorders with major depression disorder: Results from a national sample. *Journal of Affective Disorders*, *148*(0), 188–195. doi:10.1016/j.jad.2012.11.059

Pagliaro, A. M., & Pagliaro, L. A. (2018). *Women's drug and substance abuse: A comprehensive analysis and reflective synthesis*. New York, NY: Routledge.

Pagliaro, L. A. (1983). Up in smoke? A brief overview of marijuana toxicity. *Kergma*, *41*, 1–4.

Pagliaro, L. A. (1988, June). Marijuana and hashish: What are the risks? *Let's Talk*, *13*, 12–14.

Pagliaro, L. A. (1995). Psychopharmacology updates: Marijuana reconsidered. *Psymposium*, *5*(2), 12–13.

Pagliaro, L. A. (2002). Drugs as human teratogens and fetotoxins. In L. A. Pagliaro & A. M. Pagliaro (Eds.), *Problems in pediatric drug therapy* (4th ed., pp. 87–200). Washington, DC: American Pharmaceutical Association.

Pagliaro, L. A., & Pagliaro, A. M. (1999). *PPDR: Psychologists' psychotropic drug reference*. Philadelphia, PA: Brunner/Mazel.

Pagliaro, L. A., & Pagliaro, A. M. (2004). *Pagliaros' comprehensive guide to drugs and substances of abuse* (1st ed.). Washington, DC: American Pharmacists Association.

Pagliaro, L. A., & Pagliaro, A. M. (2009). *Pagliaros' comprehensive guide to drugs and substances of abuse* (2nd ed.). Washington, DC: American Pharmacists Association.

Paperny, A. M., & Saminather, N. (2017, November 17). Just months away, here's how pot legalization is shaping up in Canada. (C. Reese, Ed.) *Global News*. Retrieved from https://globalnews.ca/news/3867467/marijuana-legalization-canada-progress/

Perrine, C., Pickens, C., & Boehmer, T. (2019, September 27). Characteristics of a multistate outbreak of lung injury associated with e-cigarette use, or vaping—United States, 2019. *MMWR, Morbidity and Mortality Weekly Report*, *68*, 1–5.

Pertwee, R. G. (2000). Cannabinoid receptor ligands: Clinical and neuropharmacological considerations, relevant to future drug discovery and development. *Expert Opinion on Investigative Drugs*, *9*(7), 1553–1571.

Pertwee, R. G. (2008, January). The diverse CB1 and CB2 receptor pharmacology of three plant cannabiniods: Delta9-tetrahydrocannabinol, cannabadiol and delta9-tetrahydrocannabivarin. *British Journal of Pharmacology*, *153*(2), 199–215. doi:10.1038/sj.bjp.0707442

Pertwee, R. G., & Ross, R. A. (2002). Cannabinoid receptors and their ligands. *Prostaglandins, Leukotrienes, and Essential Fatty Acids*, *66*(2–3), 101–121.

Petrovic, N. (2019, September 221). What to do if your dog eats weed edibles. *Westword*, 1. Denver: Denver Westword.

Platt, B. (2018, July 30). Federal government set to approve first device for testing drivers' saliva for cannabis. *National Post*. Ottawa: National Post.

Power, R. A., Verweij, K. J., & Zuhair, M. (2014). Genetic predisposition to schizophrenia associated with increased use of cannabis. *Molecular Psychiatry*, *19*(11), 1201–1204. doi:10.1038/mp.2014.51

Preuss, U. W., Watzke, A. B., & Zimmermann, J. (2010). Cannabis withdrawal severity and short-term course among cannabis-dependent adolescent and young adult inpatients. *Drug and Alcohol Dependence*, *106*(2–3), 133–141.

Ramaekers, J. G., Berghaus, G., & van Laar, M. (2004). Dose related risk of motor vehicle crashes after cannabis use. *Drug and Alcohol Dependence*, *73*(2), 109–119.

Ramaekers, J. G., Mason, N. L., & Theunisson, E. L. (2020, July). Blunted highs: Pharmacodynamic and behavioral models of cannabis tolerance. *European Neuropsychopharmacology*, *36*, 191–205. doi:10.1016/j.euroneuro.2020.01.006

Reith, T. (2017, November 3). Legalized marijuana presents opportunity of a lifetime for Canadian entrepreneurs. *CBC News*.

Romero, D., Gutierrez, G., & Blankstein, A. (2018, May 29). Foreign cartels embrace home-grown marijuana in pot-legal states. *NBC News*, pp. 1–5. Los Angeles, CA: NBC News.

Rong, C., Carmona, N. E., & Lee, Y. L. (2018). Drug-drug interactions as a result of co-administering delta9-THC and CBD with other psychotropic agents. *Expert Opinion on Drug Safety*, *17*(1), 51–54. doi:10.1080/14740338.2017.1397128

Rosenthal, M. S., & Pipitone, R. N. (2020). Demographics, perceptions, and use of medical marijuana among patients in Florida. *Medical Cannabis and Cannabinoids*, 1–8. doi:10.1159/000512342

Rosner, A. (2019, December 16). Vaping cannabis flower is ideal for older adults, but they might need a little help. *Forbes*, pp. 1–5. Forbes Media.

Ross Perlman, W. (2019, July 10). Drug use and its consequences increase among middle-aged and older adults. *Advancing Addiction Science*, pp. 1–3. NIH, National Institute of Drug Abuse.

Russo, E. B., Guy, G. W., & Robson, P. J. (2007). Cannabis, pain, and sleep: Lessons from therapeutic clinical trials of Sativex, a cannabis-based medicine. *Chemistry & Biodiversity*, *4*, 1729–1743.

Russo, L. (2018, January 24). Cannabinoid poisoning treatment & management. *Medscape*, pp. 1–2.

Russo, M., Calabro, R., & Naro, A. (2015, January 29). Sativex in the management of multiple sclerosis-related spasticity: Role of the corticospinal modulation. *Neural Plasticity*, 1–6. doi:10.1155/2015/656582

Samuels, A. (2015, July 16). Study: Marijuana disapproval rate down among millennials. *USA Today College News*. Retrieved from USA Today College News.

Schacht, J., Hutchison, K., & Filbey, F. (2012). Associations between cannabinoid receptor-1 (CNR1) variation and hippocampus and amygdala volumes in heavy cannabis users. *Neuropsychopharmacology*, *37*, 2368–2376. doi:10.1038/npp.2012.92

Schauer, G. L., Njai, R., & Grant-Lenzy, A. M. (2020, February). Modes of marijuana use—smoking, vaping, eating, and dabbing: Results from the 2016 BRFSS in 12 states. *Drug and Alcohol Dependence*, *209*, 107900. doi:10.1016/j.drugalcdep.2020.107900

Scipioni, J. (2019, February 28). Martha Stewart partners with pot company to develop CBD products. *Fox Business News*.

Sewell, R. A., Poling, J., & Sofuoglu, M. (2009). The effect of cannabis compared with alcohol driving. *The American Journal on Addictions*, *18*(3), 185–193. doi:10.1080/105504909027869...

Sharma, P., Murthy, P., & Srinivas Bharath, M. M. (2012, Fall). Chemistry, metabolism, and toxicology of cannabis: Clinical implications. *Iranian Journal of Psychiatry*, *7*(4), 149–156.

Sheehan, T. J., Hamnett, H. J., & Beasley, R. (2018). Chemical and physical variations of cannabis smoke from a variety of cannabis smokers in New Zealand. *Forensic Sciences Research*, *4*(2), 168–178. doi:10.1080/20961790.2018.1445937

Shen, A. (2017, December 7). US police arrest 50 Chinese in raid on US$80m illegal marijuana growing operation. *South China Morning Post*. Inkstone.

Sherman, B. J., & McRae-Clark, A. L. (2016). Treatment of cannabis use disorder: Current science and future outlook. *Pharmacotherapy*, *36*(5), 511–535. doi:10.1002/phar.1747

Singh, J., & Budhiraja, S. (2006, April). Therapeutic potential of cannabinoid receptor ligands: Current status. *Methods and Findings in Experimental and Clinical Pharmacology*, *28*(3), 177–183.

Smart, R., & Liccardo Pacula, R. (2019). Early evidence of the impact of cannabis legalization on cannabis use, cannabis use disorder, and the use of other substances: Findings from state policy evaluations. *American Journal of Drug and Alcohol Abuse*, *45*(6), 644–663. doi:10.1080/00952990.2019.1660626

Smith, A. (2017, July 19). Colorado passes a milestone for pc. *CNN.com*. CNN. Retrieved January 17, 2018, from http://money.cnn.com/2017/07/19/news/colorado-marijuana-tax-revenue/index.html

Smith, B. R. (2019, October 17). What are the benefits of CBD? *The New York Times*, pp. 1–5. The New York Times Company.

Somerset, S. B. (2018, August 27). Can CBD replace antidepressants? *Forbes*, pp. 1–3. Forbes Media.

Span, P. (2018, December 7). Older Americans are flocking to medical marijuana. *The New York Times*, pp. 1–6. The New York Times.

Spears, E. (2019, May 7). Draeger says drug testing device that produced false positives not the same as one used by police. *The Growth Op*, pp. 1–3. Postmedia Network.

Spindle, T. R., Cone, E. J., & Schlienz, N. J. (2018, November 30). Acute effects of smoked and vaporized cannabis in healthy adults who infrequently use cannabis. *JAMA Network Open*, *1*(7), 1–14. doi:10.1001/jamanetworkopen.2018.4841

Splete, H. (2019, December 23). Vitamin E acetate confirmed as likely sources of EVALI. *CHEST Physician*, pp. 1–2. Frontline Media Communications.

Statista Research Department. (2021, March 24). Americans on the legalization of marijuana 2003–2020. *Statistics Report*, pp. 1–5. New York, NY: Statista Inc. Retrieved from htpps://www.statista.com/statistics/284172/americans-on-the-legalization-of-marijuana-2003–2015/

Stein, M. D., Caviness, C. M., & Anderson, B. J. (2014). Alcohol use potentiates marijuana problem severity in young adult women. *Womens Health Issues*, *24*(1), e77–e82. doi:10.1016/j.whi.2013.10.005

Stith, S. S., Vigil, J. M., & Brockelman, F. (2019). The association between cannabis product characteristics and symptom relief. *Scientific Reports*, *9*(2712), 1–10. doi:10.1038/s41598-019-39462-1

Stout, S. M., & Cimino, N. M. (2014, February). Exogenous cannabinoids as substrates, inhibitors, and inducers of human drug metabolizing enzymes: A systematic review. *Drug Metabolism Reviews*, *46*(1), 86–95. doi:10.3109/03602532.2013.849268

Streller, S., & Roth, K. (2015, January 6). The chemistry of tobacco—Part 4. *ChemViews*, 1–10. doi:10.1002/chemv.2014.400135

Swift Yasgur, B. (2018, March 2). Legalized marijuana: Fewer risks, fewer benefits. *Medscape*, p. 1.

Szabo, B., & Schlicker, E. (2005, January). Effects of cannabinoids on neurotransmission. *Handbook of Experimental Pharmacology*, *168*(168), 327–365. doi:10.1007/3-540-26573-2_11

Sznitman, S. R., & Room, R. (2018, February). Rethinking indicators of problematic cannabis use in the era of medical cannabis legalization. *Addictive Behaviors*, *77*, 100–101. doi:10.1016/j.addbeh.2017.09.026

Tashkin, D. P. (2013). Effects of marijuana smoking on the lung. *Annals of the American Thoracic Society*, *10*(3), 239–247. doi:10.1513/AnnalsATS.201212-127FR

Taylor, D. R., Fergusson, D. M., & Milne, B. J. (2002). A longitudinal study of the effects of tobacco and cannabis exposure on lung function in young adults. *Addiction*, *97*(8), 1055–1061.

Thielking, M. (2019, October 15). Vaping-related illness has a new name: EVALI. *STAT*, pp. 1–2.

Toklas, A. B. (1954). *The Alice B. Toklas cookbook*. New York, NY: Harper Collins.

Tomko, R. L., Baker, N. L., & Hood, C. (2020). Depressive symptoms and cannabis use in a placebo-controlled trial of n-acetylcysteine for adult cannabis use disorder. *Psychopharmacology (Berlin)*, *237*(2), 479–490. doi:10.1007/s00213-019-05384-z

Trigo, J. M., Soliman, A., & Quilty, L. C. (2018). Nabiximols combined with motivational enhancement/cognitive behavioral therapy for the treatment of cannabis dependence: A pilot randomized clinical trial. *PLoS One*, *13*(1), e0190768. doi:10.1371/journal.pone.0190768

Turner, A. R., Spurling, B. C., & Agrawal, S. (2020, January 20). *Marijuana toxicity* (pp. 1–3). Treasure Island, FL: StatPearls Publishing.

Uberall, M. A. (2020). A review of scientific evidence for THC-CBD oromucosal spray (nabiximols) in the management of chronic pain. *Journal of Pain Research*, *13*, 399–410. doi:10.2147/JPR.S240011

Uberall, M. A., Essner, U., & Mueller-Schwefe, G. H. (2019, May 20). Effectiveness and tolerability of THC:CBD oromucosal spray as add-on measure in patients with severe chronic pain: Analysis of 12-week open-label real-word data provided by the German Pain e-Registry. *Journal of Pain Research*, *12*, 1577–1604. doi:10.2147/JPR.S192174

UN, United Nations. (2021, March 25). UN report warns of 'hidden epidemic' of elderly drug use. *Report*, pp. 1–2. Geneva, Switzerland: United Nations.

Urits, I., Borchart, M., & Hasegawa, M. (2019). An update of current cannabis-based pharmaceuticals in pain medicine. *Pain and Therapy*, *8*, 41–51. doi:10.1007/s40122-019-0114-4

van Holst, R. J., & Schilt, T. (2011). Drug-related decrease in neuropsychological functions of abstinent drug users. *Current Drug Abuse Reviews*, *4*(1), 42–56.

Venkataraman, N. (2006, December 20). Marijuana called top U.S. cash crop. *ABC News*, pp. 1–3. ABC News.

Volkow, N. D., Baler, R. D., & Compton, W. M. (2014). Adverse health effects of marijuana use. *The New England Journal of Medicine*, *370*(23), 2219–2227. doi:10.1056/NEJMra1402309

Vuckovic, S., Srebro, D., & Savic Vujovic, K. (2018). Cannabinoids and pain: New insights from old molecules. *Frontiers in Pharmacology*, *9*, 1259–1289. doi:10.3389/fphar.2018.01259

Walitt, B., Klose, P., & Fitzcharles, M.-A. (2016, July 18). Cannabinoids fibromyalgia. *Cochrane Database of Systematic Reviews*, *7*(7), CD011694. doi:10.1002/14651858.CD011694.pub2

Wallace, A. (2020, November 6). Legal weed won big in the election. *CNN Business*, pp. 1–4. Warner Media.

Wang, J. B., Ramo, D. E., & Lisha, N. E. (2016, September 1). Medical marijuana legalization and cigarette and marijuana co-use in adolescents and adults. *Drug and Alcohol Dependence*, *166*, 32–38. doi:10.1016/j.drugalcdep.2016.06.016

Warner, M. (2007, January 26). Marijuana is top US cash crop. *Columbia Star*, p. 1. Columbia Star.

Weinstein, A. M., & Gorelick, D. A. (2011). Pharmacological treatment of cannabis dependence. *Current Pharmaceutical Design*, *17*(14), 1351–1358.

Weissman, A. (1981). On the definition of cannabinoids: Botanical? Chemical? Pharmacological? *Journal of Clinical Pharmacology*, *21*(Suppl 8–9), 159S–165S.

WHO, World Health Organization. (2018). *Cannabis and cannabis resin*. Geneva, Switzerland: World Health Organization.

Wikler, A. (1976, December). Aspects of tolerance to and dependence on cannabis. *Annals of the New York Academy of Sciences*, *282*(1), 126–147. doi:10.1111/j.1749-6632.1976.tb49893.x

Wilkinson, S. T., Radhakrishnan, R., & D'Souza, D. C. (2014). Impact of cannabis use on the development of psychotic disorders. *Current Addiction Reports*, *1*, 115–145. doi:10.1007/s40429-014-0018-7

Williams, I. J., Edwards, S., & Rubo, A. (2006, June). Time course of the enhancement and restoration of the analgesic efficacy of codeine and morphine by delta9-tetrahydrocannabinol. *European Journal of Pharmacology*, *539*(1–2), 57–63. doi:10.1016/j.ejphar.2006.04.003

Williams, S. (2015, July 12). Washington's marijuana tax revenue tops estimates, but big problems still exist. *The Motely Fool*, pp. 1–8. Retrieved April 13, 2016, from www.fool.com/investing/general/2015/07/12/washingtons-marijuana-tax-revenue-tops-estimates-b.aspx

Wilsey, B., Marcotte, T., & Deutsch, R. (2013). Low-dose vaporized cannabis significantly improves neuropathic pain. *The Journal of Pain, 14*(2), 136–148. doi:10.1016/j.pain.2012.10.009

Wilson, R. I., & Nicoll, R. A. (2002, April 26). Endocannabinoid signaling in the brain. *Science, 296*(5568), 678–682. doi:10.1136/science.1063545

Winiger, E. A., Hitchcock, L. N., & Bryan, A. D. (2021, January). Cannabis use and sleep: Expectations, outcomes, and the role of age. *Addictive Behaviors, 112*, 1–3. doi:10.1016/j.addebeh.2020.106642

Winstock, A. R., Ford, C., & Witton, J. (2010, April 10). Assessment and management of cannabis use disorders in primary care. *BMJ, 340*, 800–804. doi:10.1136/bmj.c1571

Wirrell, E. C. (2016, June). Treatment of Dravet syndrome. *The Canadian Journal of Neurological Sciences, 43*(Suppl 3), S13–S18. doi:10.1017/cjn.2016.249

Wyatt, K. (2014, February 19). Colorado's legal marijuana market is bringing in way more tax revenue than expected. *Business Insider*, pp. 1–10. Associated Press.

Yamaori, S., Koeda, K., & Kushihara, M. (2012). Comparison in the in vitro inhibitory effects of major phytocannabinoids and polycyclic aromatic hydrocarbons contained in marijuana smoke on cytochrome P450 2C9 activity. *Drug Metabolism and Pharmacokinetics, 27*(3), 294–300.

Yamaori, S., Kushihara, M., & Yamamoto, I. (2010, June 1). Characterization of major phytocannabinoids, cannabidiol and cannabinol, as isoform-selective and potent inhibitors of human CYP1 enzymes. *Biochemical Pharmacology, 79*(11), 1691–1698. doi:10.1016/j.bcp.2010.01.028

Yang, Y., Lewis, M. M., & Bello, A. M. (2017). Cannabis sativa (hemp) seeds, delta-9-tetrahydrocannabinol, and potential overdose. *Cannabis and Cannabinoid Research, 2*(1), 274–281. doi:10.1089/can.2017.0040

Zhang, L. R., Morgenstern, H., & Greenland, S. (2015, February 15). Cannabis smoking and lung cancer risk: Pooled analysis in the International Lung Cancer Consortium. *International Journal of Cancer, 136*(4), 894–903. doi:10.1002/ijc.29036

Zuardi, A. W. (2006, June). History of cannabis as a medicine: A review. *Brazilian Journal of Psychiatry, 28*(2), 1–15. doi:10.1590/S1516-44462006000200015

CHAPTER 5

PRESCRIPTION OPIATE ANALGESICS AND HEROIN

Since the beginning of the new millennium, the illicit use of prescription opiate analgesics increased significantly among older adults across the U.S., particularly, the use of:

- Buprenorphine;
- Codeine;
- Fentanyl;
- Hydrocodone;
- Hydromorphone;
- Methadone;
- Morphine;
- Oxycodone;
- Tramadol.

For a complete list of the prescription opiate analgesics,[1] including heroin, and their subgroup category, generic name, brand/trade names, and common street names, see Table 5.1.

Primarily medically prescribed for the relief of moderate to severe pain, older adults also illicitly use prescription opiate analgesics to achieve:

1. An intense feeling of euphoria;
2. An overall warm and pleasant feeling, or "rush;"
3. A sleepy, dream-like state, commonly known as "being on-the-nod;"
4. Self-management of physical pain, often related to osteoarthritis, falls, and "just getting old;"
5. Prevention, or self-management, of the opiate analgesic withdrawal syndrome.

In addition to the increased use of prescription opiate analgesics by older adults during the past decade of the new millennium, the use of heroin increased significantly as prescription opiate analgesics became more difficult to obtain—primarily due to heightened governmental regulatory control.

We begin with the plant botany and pharmacognosy of the opium poppy. We then discuss the pharmacology of both the: (1) prescription opiate analgesics; and (2) heroin, with attention to their similarities and differences. We then present and discuss new millennial trends in older adult prescription opiate analgesic use, including both medical prescription and illicit use. The chapter concludes with an overview of the assessment and diagnosis of

1. Over the new millennium, several other prescription opiate analgesics (e.g., loperamide [Imodium®] and pentazocine [Talwin®]) were also used by older adults in the U.S. However, these opiate analgesics are less frequently now used and, thus, are not discussed in detail in this chapter. We refer readers, who require specific additional information for each of these prescription opiate analgesics, to Pagliaro and Pagliaro (2004, 2009).

DOI: 10.4324/9781003010333-5

Table 5.1 The Opiate Analgesics

CATEGORY GENERIC NAME	BRAND/TRADE NAMES[2]	COMMON STREET NAMES[3]
PURE AGONISTS—NATURAL		
Opium		"Big O," "Chinese Molasses," "Poppy"
Opium derivatives:		
Codeine[4]	Codeine Contin®, Ratio-Codeine®	"Codies," "Cough Syrup," "School Boy," "T3," "T4"
Morphine	Duramorph®, M.O.S.®, MS Contin®	"Drug Store," "Good Ole M," "Hospital Heroin," "Morph," "MS"
PURE AGONISTS—SYNTHETIC		
Fentanyl	Actiq®, Duragesic®	"Fen," "Murder 8," "Perc-O-Pop"
Heroin		"Black Tar," "Brown Sugar," "Capital H," "Charley," "China White," "Horse," "Junk," "Shit," "Smack"
Hydrocodone[5]	Hysingla®, Zohydro®	"Hydros®," "Hyke," "Tuss," "Vikes"
Hydromorphone	Dilaudid®	"Delaud," "Dillies;"
Levorphanol	Levo-Dromoran®	"Levo"
Meperidine	Demerol®	"Demmies," "Dems," "Mep"
Methadone	Dolophine®	"Adolph," "Dollies," "Done," "Wafer"
Oxycodone	OxyContin®	"Cotton," "Hillbilly Heroin," "Oxy," "Oxycotton," "Poor Boy's Heroin," "Percs"
Oxymorphone	Numorphan®, Opana®	"Blue Heaven," "Mrs. O," "Pink Lady"
Propoxyphene[6]	Darvon®	"Footballs," "Pinks," "Yellows"
Tapentadol[7]	Nucynta®, Palexia®	
Tramadol[8]	Ultram®	"Trammies," "Ultras"
MIXED AGONIST/ANTAGONISTS—SYNTHETIC		
Buprenorphine	Buprenex®, Suboxone®	"Oranges," "Tems"
Butorphanol	Stadol®	"Torb"
Nalbuphine	Nubain®	"Nubian"
Pentazocine	Talwin®	"Big T," "Ts"

2. Examples of common brand/trade names are provided, when available.
3. Partial list. When available, examples of three to five of the most common street names are provided. See Pagliaro and Pagliaro (2009) for a comprehensive listing of the drugs and substances of abuse and their common street names.
4. Usually available as one of the ingredients in a multi-ingredient product (e.g., Empirin #4 and Tylenol #4).
5. Usually available as one of the ingredients in a multi-ingredient product (e.g., Loratab® or Vicodin®).
6. In December 2010, the FDA removed propoxyphene from licit production and use within the U.S. This action followed a similar move in Europe and was in response to related risk for developing potentially serious, or even fatal, cardiac dysrhythmias associated with propoxyphene use (Gandey, 2010).
7. Also functions as a norepinephrine reuptake inhibitor.
8. Also functions as a norepinephrine reuptake inhibitor.

older adult opiate analgesic dependence or use disorder and current pharmacotherapeutic and psychotherapeutic/counseling approaches for treating older adults.

OPIUM POPPY PLANT BOTANY

The opium poppy plant (*Papaver somniferum*)—the poppy that causes sleep, is a flowering annual plant that typically grows from two to five feet in height. Its entire growth cycle is completed in approximately 120 days with the seed pod (i.e., capsule or fruit) being the only part of the poppy plant that produces opium.

The opium poppy is believed to have originated through centuries of breeding and cultivation across the eastern Mediterranean region as its use anthropogenically spread to Asia, Europe, and Northern Africa. The earliest records of its use as an analgesic and euphoriant go back over 6,000 years to ancient Sumeria. The seeds of the opium poppy also were used as a food source, a practice that continues today.[9]

Soon after the flower petals begin to fall, the unripe seed pod is lanced on two or three sides, in a vertical direction, to a depth of approximately 1 millimeter to allow the raw opium, actually a milky latex, to seep out. Often called "poppy tears," *lachryma papaveris*, the milky latex darkens upon exposure to air and turns into a gum-like brown mass as it dries. The dried latex, or resin, is scrapped off the opium poppy seed pod with a flat, short-handed, iron blade that is about 4 inches wide. The opium alkaloids[10] are then extracted from the resin by various methods (Pagliaro & Pagliaro, 2004). The average yield of raw opium, from a single poppy pod, is 80 mg (range of 10 mg to 100 mg). Raw opium contains approximately 10% morphine by weight.

OPIUM POPPY PHARMACOGNOSY

Papaver somniferum is the only poppy plant species that produces opium—a natural product that contains several alkaloids.[11] Some chemists consider alkaloids as a subclassifica-

9. The opium poppy is also commonly referred to as the "bread seed poppy" because all opium poppy varieties produce edible oil seeds. These seeds contain vegetable fats that are commonly used as a foodstuff in a variety of recipes (e.g., poppy seed bread or poppy seed cake) or pressed to produce poppy seed oil (Pagliaro & Pagliaro, 2004).
10. In addition to the opiate analgesic alkaloids of morphine (approximately 10%, range of 8% to 20%) and codeine (1.5%, range of 1% to 4.5%), opium contains over 20 other different alkaloids, including noscapine (i.e., narcotine [4% to 8%]), papaverine (1% to 3%), and thebaine (1.5%, range 1% to 5%), depending on the country of origin, climatic conditions, and the:

    1. Techniques used to lance the opium seed pod so that the opium resin, or latex, can seep out;
    2. Number of times that a pod is lanced;
    3. Amount and type of nitrogen-based fertilizers used to cultivate the opium poppy plants. (Annett, 1920; UN, 1953)

11. N.B. While opium poppy seeds contain some opium alkaloids, the seed pod is the only portion of the opium poppy plant that produces opium (Knutsen, Alexander & Barregard, 2018; Shetge, Dzakovich, & Cooperstone, 2020).

    However, poppy seeds do contain measurable amounts of morphine—usually about 10 mg/kg of washed, cleaned seeds, such as that obtained in U.S. Grocery stores, and about 100 mg/kg of unwashed/uncleaned seeds typically obtained over the Internet (Pagliaro & Pagliaro, *Clinical Patient Data Files*).

tion of amines. However, in pharmacognosy, alkaloids are defined as a naturally occurring physiologically active, nitrogen-containing organic base—like caffeine, cocaine, codeine, and morphine—that is derived from higher plants (i.e., angiosperms, gymnosperms, and pteridophytes).

The average yield of raw opium, from a single poppy pod, is 80 mg (range of 10 mg to 100 mg). Raw opium contains approximately 10% morphine by weight. Medicinally, morphine is considered the standard against which all other pure agonist natural, pure agonist synthetic, or mixed agonist-antagonist synthetic opiate analgesics are compared regarding potency and efficacy.

Sources and Distribution of Opium and Heroin

Opium cultivation and heroin production are higher than ever. Additionally, heroin is readily available in both higher concentrations and purity than at any other time in history (Ciccarone, 2009). The average concentration of injectable forms of heroin, at street level, is approximately 10% to 27%—in comparison to approximately 7% during the 1980s. The purity of street-level Colombian heroin typically ranges from 25% to 80% pure, while Mexican black tar heroin typically ranges from 14% to 60% pure with the highest purity found in cities along the U.S./Mexico border (e.g., El Paso, Texas) (Pagliaro & Pagliaro, 2018). Heroin purity, at street level, varies significantly in the U.S. from city to city and from time to time—depending upon availability and demand (Pagliaro & Pagliaro, *Clinical Patient Data Files*). For example, in 2008 heroin street-level purity in San Francisco was reported as 8.5% while in Philadelphia it was reported as 60% (Mars, Bourgois, & Karandinos, 2014).

This current situation is the result of many changing factors. One of these factors is associated with the geographical area where opium poppies are primarily grown. Another factor is their methods of cultivation. In fact, over the past 50 years, the cultivation of opium poppies has significantly changed. For example:

- During the 1970s, 1980s, and 1990s, opium production primarily occurred in the "Golden Triangle" region of Southeast Asia—specifically, the countries of Burma (Myanmar), Thailand, and Laos (DEA, 1992);
- During the first decade of the new millennium, regions in Latin America—specifically, Columbia and Mexico—significantly increased opium cultivation and heroin production (Felbab-Brown, 2017);
- During the second decade of the new millennium, the Islamic Republic of Afghanistan in Southern Asia became the world's largest cultivator and supplier of opium (Felbab-Brown, 2017);

Most of the heroin currently used in Europe is produced in France from opium poppies grown in Southeast Asia. The primary source of heroin used in the U.S. is produced from

Unwashed, unclean seeds are usually contaminated with "opiate alkaloids from poppy straw and latex in the field during harvest" (Greenthal, Lurie, & Doyon, 2021, p. 3). It has been demonstrated that the concentrations of opium alkaloids (i.e., codeine, morphine, thebaine) are significantly reduced by: (1) thermal treatment (i.e., exposure to dry heat [200° C]); and (2) by washing with water. However, baking has no significant effect on the concentration of the opium alkaloids found in poppy seeds (Shetge et al., 2020).

opium poppies grown in Latin America, with "Mexican heroin"[12] being the most prominent west of the Mississippi River, and "Columbian heroin" being the most prominent east of the Mississippi River. However, beginning at the start of the second decade of the new millennium, the opium poppy cultivation began to significantly decrease in Columbia. Consequently, "Mexican heroin" is currently the most available source of heroin and is now used throughout the U.S. The distribution and commerce of heroin in the U.S. are largely controlled by ethnically defined criminal gangs (DEA, 2018).[13, 14]

Factors that contribute to optimal opium poppy cultivation, include:

- Temperate, warm climate;
- Low humidity (to minimize damaging fungus growth);
- Moderate amounts of water (i.e., both arid conditions, and excessive moisture, adversely affect opium poppy growth);
- Long days to develop flowers because the opium poppy is a photo-responsive plant;
- Sandy loam soil (i.e., clay soils inhibit the root growth of young opium poppies; sandy soils do not retain sufficient moisture content);
- Field locations at mountain elevations over 1,000 meters, with slopes of 20 to 40 degrees, facilitate the above conditions.

It takes approximately one pound of opium poppy seeds to hand-sow one acre of land (DEA, 1992).

As identified in Figure 5.1, the process of converting raw opium resin to heroin base, or "heroin #2," involves five steps. Additional steps are required to convert the heroin base to the purer heroin HCl varieties—heroin #3 and heroin #4.

1. Step one involves dissolving the "raw (uncooked) opium resin"[15] in boiling water and screening the resulting liquid through a cheese cloth to produce an opium solution. The solution is subsequently reheated to remove excess water;
2. Step two involves dissolving the "cooked opium resin" in boiling water. Slaked lime (calcium hydroxide) is added to the cooked opium resin solution. The product is then cooled and filtered through burlap sacks. It is then reheated, without boiling,

---

12. Traditionally, Mexican heroin had generally referred to "black tar heroin" (a gummy impure mixture) that typically contains 40% to 47% heroin when sold at the retail (i.e., street) level. However, powdered heroin, brown or white, is also produced in Mexico and has a purity, on average at the wholesale level, of approximately 80% (DEA, 2018, 2021).
13. These gangs, because of their nature, composition, and structure, are more formally referred to as "transnational criminal organizations" (TCOs) (DEA, 2021). Additionally, because they currently make as much profit from human trafficking as from drug trafficking, these gangs/cartels are less frequently referred to as "drug" gangs/cartels. However, the designation "drug trafficking organizations" (DTOs) is still commonly used (e.g., Felbab-Brown, 2020).
14. For example, the importation and distribution of heroin in Seattle, Washington, is mostly controlled by Chinese gangs, utilizing front companies and working through Hong Kong. A significant amount of the retail-level heroin distribution and sales, along the northeastern coast of the U.S., is controlled by Dominican gangs, based primarily in New York City. Most of the importation and distribution of heroin from Mexico into the Southwestern U.S., is controlled by Mexican gangs (e.g., "Sinaloa Cowboys"), whereas the smuggling of heroin into the U.S. from southeastern Asia, is by Nigerian gangs based primarily in Chicago. In addition, much of the distribution of Asian heroin that is transshipped through the Port of Los Angeles, California, is controlled by Thai gangs (DEA, 2018; National Drug Intelligence Center, 2001; Pagliaro & Pagliaro, 2009; Pagliaro & Pagliaro, *Clinical Patient Data Files*).
15. Raw opium resin contains dozens of different alkaloids including morphine, which accounts for approximately 10%, by weight, of raw opium.

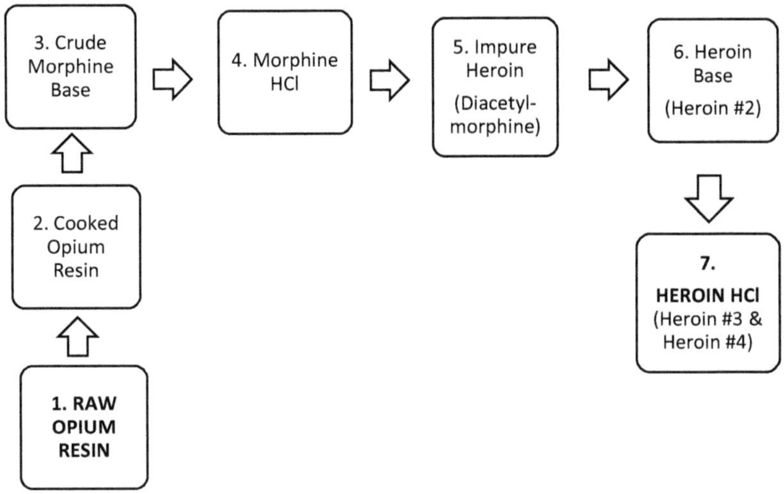

Figure 5.1 Conversion of Opium to Heroin

and ammonium chloride is added to precipitate the "crude morphine base," which is, subsequently, filtered through cloth filters;

3. Step three involves dissolving the crude morphine base in hydrochloric acid. Activated charcoal is then added and the solution is reheated and filtered to produce "morphine hydrochloride (HCl);"
4. Step four involves adding acetic anhydride[16] to form "impure heroin"—diacetylmorphine
5. Step five involves adding water to the impure heroin, along with activated charcoal and sodium carbonate (soda ash). Then, the solution is filtered and dried over a steam bath to produce "heroin base." Heroin base is also known as "Southeastern Asian Heroin #2." Southeastern Asian Heroin #2 is not water soluble and, consequently, cannot be injected IV. However, it can be smoked.

6A. To produce "Southeastern Asian Heroin #3," hydrochloric acid is added to the heroin base followed by drying (evaporating) the wet-paste mixture over a steam bath. The resultant dry coarse lumps are crushed and passed through a no. 8 mesh sieve. During the process, adulterants (e.g., caffeine, quinine, strychnine)[17] may be added

---

16. The bulk of chemicals involved in the production of heroin are shipped to Mexico from China (DEA, 2021; McKay, 2020). However, acetic anhydride has been a noted exception. As reported by Simpson, Smith, and Cattan (2020, pp. 1, 4) for *Bloomberg Businessweek*:

> During the decade-long U.S. heroin epidemic, Avantor [a $12 billion publicly traded U.S. company] has cultivated a remarkable line of business: selling acetic anhydride across Mexico in containers that are big enough to make lucrative quantities of illegal narcotics but small enough to load into the trunk of a car. Sales come via a network of distributors, online sellers, and stores spread across the country. A $324 jug of acetic anhydride, made in Mexico by publicly traded American company, is enough to produce 90,000 hits of high-grade "China white." The cartels are getting as much as they want.

17. Interestingly, up to 1 kg of caffeine can be added to each kg of crude heroin base. The quinine and strychnine are added in much smaller amounts (e.g., 5 to 15 mg per kg of crude heroin base)—primarily,

prior to achieving the finished salt form—primarily to increase volume. The color of heroin #3 crystals can range widely from purple to tan to off-white. Heroin #3 is not as pure as heroin #4 and is usually smoked.

6B. To produce "Southeastern Asian Heroin #4," water, acetic anhydride, and chloroform are added to the heroin base. The solution is then decanted, and the following ingredients are added: activated charcoal, sodium carbonate (which has been dissolved in hot water), ether, ethyl alcohol, and hydrochloric acid. The solution is then filtered through clean filter paper. The resultant heroin #4 crystals should be very white in color—hence, the street name, "China White." Asian Heroin #4 can be injected IV, smoked, or snorted.

PHARMACOLOGY

This section presents a useful and accurate categorization and overview of the prescription opiate analgesics and heroin. It is organized according to the following subsections:

- Pharmacodynamics: Mechanism of Action;
- Pharmacokinetics;
- Significant Drug-Drug Interactions;
- Undesired, or Harmful, Effects and Toxicities;
- Physical and Psychological Dependence;
- Overdosage/Unintentional Poisoning.

Pharmacologically, the opiate analgesics—for over a century—have been traditionally referred to in the U.S. as "narcotic analgesics" (i.e., reflecting their major therapeutic indication—to relieve pain).[18] They also have been simply called, "narcotics." Derived from the Greek word, "narke," narcotic means a lack of feeling or sensation—a feeling of numbness. However, the general use of the term narcotic has caused much confusion because of its "legal" meaning.

Legally, the term, narcotic, is used to denote all the various drugs and substances of abuse that are listed under the U.S. and international narcotic acts and laws. One of the first such laws in the U.S. was the Harrison Narcotics Tax Act (Ch.1, 38 Stat. 785)[19] that was approved on December 17, 1914 and took effect on March 1, 1915. This federal tax law regulated and taxed, for the first time in the U.S., the production, importation, and distribution of opiate analgesics and coca products (e.g., Coca-Cola® and Vin Mariani®—both

as "flavoring agents" (e.g., the bitter taste of quinine mimics the taste of heroin) (Klous, Lee, Hillebrand, 2006; Pagliaro & Pagliaro, *Clinical Patient Data Files*; Winek, Schweighardt, & Fochtman, 1971).

18. Opiate analgesics have been used therapeutically over several millennia to treat moderate to severe pain, both acute and chronic (Pagliaro & Pagliaro, 1986, 1999, 2004). They are, however, generally ineffective for the management of either chronic idiopathic pain (e.g., fibromyalgia) or neuropathic pain (e.g., pain associated with diabetic peripheral neuropathy or phantom limb pain) (Arner & Meyerson, 1988; Felman & Carteron, 2018; Malleson, Connell, & Bennett, 2001; Schreiber, Nones, & Reis, 2015; Wheeler, 2019)—except for the associated pain relief potentially provided by the placebo effect.
19. Hence, the basis of the derivation of the U.S. street term, "Narc" (i.e., a law enforcement officer—federal, state, or local), who enforces this and other laws regarding illicit cultivation, importation, sale, possession, or use of the various abusable psychotropics (i.e., narcotics).

of which, at that time, legally contained cocaine) (Pagliaro & Pagliaro, 2004). Under these laws, cannabis, cocaine, heroin, and lysergic acid diethylamide (LSD), for example, are all legally classified as narcotics. However, of the four drugs and substances of abuse listed in this example, only heroin is pharmacologically classified as a narcotic based upon its chemical structure and pharmacological action.

Adding to the confusion, the opiate analgesics are often referred to as "opioids"—a term that is also used to denote the: (1) opiate analgesic antagonist, naloxone (Narcan®); and (2) opiate analgesic-like substances that are naturally found in the body (i.e., endogenous opioid peptides). Consequently, in order to minimize any potential confusion associated with the use of these various terms, we selected to use the term "opiate analgesic" throughout this book for any natural (e.g., codeine) or synthetic drug (e.g., heroin) that exerts morphine-like actions on the human brain and spinal cord.

The opiate analgesics comprise three subgroups, or "families:"

1. Natural pure agonists;
2. Synthetic pure agonists;
3. Synthetic mixed agonist/antagonists.

The first, and original family, includes opium and its pure natural derivatives—codeine (Codeine Contin®)[20] and morphine (MS Contin®). The second family includes several synthetic modifications of morphine, such as fentanyl (Actiq®), heroin (diacetylmorphine), methadone (Dolophine®), and oxycodone (OxyContin®). These synthetic modifications have chemical structures and pharmacologic actions that resemble their natural parent drug, morphine. The third family comprises the synthetic, mixed agonist/antagonists—buprenorphine (Buprenex®), nalbuphine (Nubain®), and pentazocine (Talwin®).

The relative potencies of the various opiate analgesics—the average dosages that are required to generally provide equivalent pain relief, or equal efficacy—are listed in Table 5.2.

Pharmacodynamics: Mechanism of Action

The opiate analgesics have an interesting mechanism of action. Rather than raising the pain threshold to achieve analgesia—as happens, for example, with most sedative-hypnotics and general anesthetics—they modify the brain's interpretation of painful stimuli by depressing CNS activity. Thus, the sensation of pain is still experienced, but, subjectively, it does not seem to "hurt as much."

The endogenous, or natural, opioid peptides are short sequences of amino acids (i.e., pentapeptides or tetrapeptides) that were identified in the brain during the 1970s and were

20. Brand/trade names are denoted by the symbol, "®." They are included primarily for readers who comprise a wide range of health and social care professionals, who may be more familiar with brand/trade names rather than with generic names. In this regard, the inclusion of a particular brand/trade name is not meant to endorse a certain pharmaceutical opiate analgesic product, nor is it meant to suggest—unless explicitly stated otherwise—that the pharmacological and other data presented are preferentially associated with a certain brand/trade name. It is important to note that, even after a pharmaceutical company discontinues a particular named product (i.e., it has been withdrawn from the U.S. market), illicit producers and Internet vendors often continue to market and sell their products utilizing the original brand/trade name.

Table 5.2 Relative Potencies of the Prescription Opiate Analgesics[21]

OPIATE ANALGESIC **Generic and Trade/Brand Names**	**AVERAGE DOSAGE (MG) Intramuscular (IM)/Oral Ingestion (PO)**	
	IM (mg)	**PO (mg)**
Butorphanol (Stadol®)	2	—
Codeine	120	200
Fentanyl (Actiq®)	0.1	—
Hydrocodone (Hysingla®)	—	45
Hydromorphone (Dilaudid®)	1.5	7.5
Levorphanol (Levo-Dromoran®)	2	4
Meperidine (Demerol®)	75	300
Methadone (Dolophine®)	10	20
Morphine (MS Contin®)	10	30
Nalbuphine (Nubain®)	10	—
Oxycodone (OxyContin®)	15	20
Oxymorphone (Numorphan®)	1	15
Pentazocine (Talwin®)	60	180
Tramadol (Ultram®)	100	120

named, "dynorphins,"[22] "endomorphins,"[23] "endorphins,"[24] and "enkephalins." Hughes, Smith, and Kosterlitz (1975) were the first to identify enkephalins as natural ligands for opiate receptors.[25] Enkephalins were subsequently determined to be composed of two forms of pentapeptides that have subsequently become known as "metenkephalin" (i.e., Tyr-Gly-Gly Phe-Met) and "leuenkephalin" (i.e., Tyr-Gly-Gly-Phe-Leu). Various opiate analgesic G-protein coupled receptors also were discovered within the body and were extensively studied. In terms of physical structure, each of these receptors consists of: (1) an extracellular N-terminus; (2) seven transmembrane helical twists; (3) three extracellular loops; (4) three intracellular loops; and (5) an intracellular C-terminus (Trescot, Datta, & Lee, 2008).

Although the receptor classification system that evolved from this research remains incomplete, three major groups of opiate analgesic receptors were pharmacologically

21. N.B. These are single, average dosage equivalents. Consequently, for adolescents and young adults who use/abuse opiate analgesics, variability may be significant.
22. Dynorphin A and dynorphin B are formed from the metabolic cleavage of the precursor protein, prodynorphin.
23. Endomorphins are distinct from the dynorphins, endorphins, and enkephalins. Endomorphin-1 (i.e., Tyr-Pro-Trp-Phe) and endomorphin-2 (i.e., Tyr-Pro-Phe-Phe) are tetrapeptides that were discovered in 1997 (Mizusawa, 2016).
24. The name, "endorphin," was derived from a combination of the terms, "endogenous" and "morphine."
25. Their original animal research involved the use of pig brains. Enkephalin literally translates as "in the head [brain]."

characterized and named, delta, kappa, and mu.[26,27,28] These receptors, which are attached to presynaptic neurons, are found throughout the CNS. However, the highest concentrations of these cell surface receptors are found in the limbic system; midbrain, which also includes the ventral tegmental area (VTA); and spinal cord (see Figure 5.2).

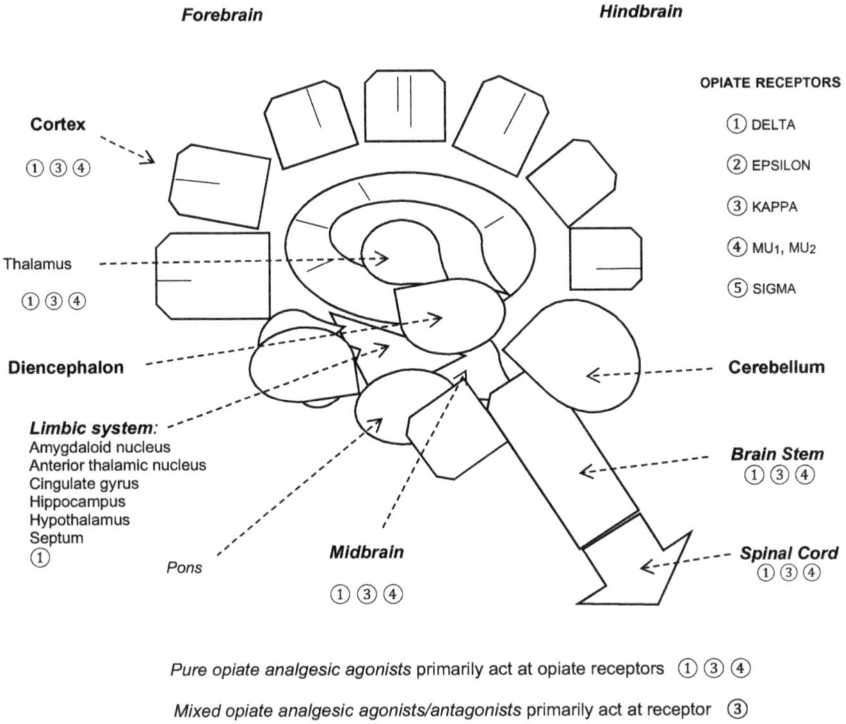

Figure 5.2 Sites of Opiate Analgesic Action in the CNS

26. Three other receptors (i.e., sigma [σ], epsilon [ε], and nociceptive [NOP] receptors) have also been identified and studied. However, their full role in regard to the mechanisms of opiate analgesic action in humans remains controversial. Nociceptive receptors, or "nociceptors," are found in the brain and spinal cord—as well as other body systems and tissues (e.g., the gastrointestinal [GI], integumentary, and muscular systems). In the context of opiate analgesic use, these receptors appear to be primarily associated with anxiety, mental depression, and the development of tolerance to opiate analgesic-related pain relief.
27. Regarding the binding of endogenous opioid peptides:

    1. Dynorphins bind to all three receptors, with their highest affinity to kappa receptors;
    2. Endomorphins bind virtually exclusively to mu receptors;
    3. Endorphins bind with a high affinity to delta, kappa, and mu receptors;
    4. Enkephalins bind to both delta and mu receptors, but with a higher affinity to delta receptors.

28. The International Union of Pharmacology (IUPHAR) designated alternative names for these receptors: OP1, or DOP, for the delta receptor; OP2, or KOP, for the kappa receptor; and OP3, or MOP, for the mu receptor (McDonald & Lambert, 2005). They also have been referred to as μOR, ΔOR, and κOR (e.g., Manglik, 2020). In the U.S., the original Greek nomenclature is generally favored and has been consistently used, by us, over the last four decades in our related articles and books—including this reference textbook.

These G-protein-coupled inhibitory receptors (i.e., delta, kappa, and mu), which mediate the inhibition of adenylyl cyclase, all preferentially couple to inhibitory G-proteins and are essential for the analgesic action of the opiate analgesics (Traynor, 2012; Zhang, Ferguson, & Barak, 1998). For example, activation of the mu receptor, by binding to an opiate analgesic, results in a variety of cellular processes, including:

1. Closing of voltage-sensitive calcium channels (VSCCs);
2. Stimulation of potassium efflux leading to hyperpolarization;
3. Reduced cyclic adenosine monophosphate (cAMP) production via inhibition of adenylyl cyclase.

Overall, this results in reduced neuronal cell excitability leading to a reduction in transmission of nerve impulses and inhibition of neurotransmitter release (McDonald & Lambert, 2005, p. 22).

Agonist-dependent processes, including receptor phosphorylation, desensitization, internalization, and down regulation, are responsible for the regulation of the opiate analgesic receptors (Zhang et al., 1998). The conformational changes induced in the receptors—as a consequence of their binding to opiate analgesics—causes "downstream signaling events" that result in associated expressed actions, including analgesia, constipation, euphoria, and respiratory depression. "Continuing activation of these signaling pathways leads to homeostatic changes that, in turn, result in [the development of] tolerance and the opiate-dependent state" (Traynor, 2012, p. 173).

The similarities and differences in the pharmacology and toxicology (i.e., undesired, or harmful, effects and toxicities) of the opiate analgesics is due primarily to their similarities and differences in selectivity for, and binding to, the delta, kappa, and mu opiate analgesic receptors (Gharagozlou, Demirci, & Clark, 2002; Inturrisi, 2002; Okada, Tsuda, & Bryant, 2002; Zuurmond, Meert, & Noorduin, 2002). For example, activation of:

- Delta receptors, which are found in high concentration regions of the forebrain (including the caudate putamen, cerebral cortex, limbic system, nucleus accumbens, olfactory bulb, and putamen) are involved in the antinociceptive/analgesic action of some opiate analgesics (e.g., pentazocine, a partial agonist). Delta receptors are also associated with dysphoric and psychotomimetic effects;
- Kappa receptors, which are found in the brain stem, limbic system, and dorsal horn of the spinal cord, are not associated with respiratory depression. However, they may produce diuresis, dysphoria, and sedation—at doses lower than those required to produce analgesia—thus, severely limiting potential therapeutic utility as an analgesic. Stimulation of the kappa receptors primarily inhibits dopamine release in the striatum;
- Mu receptors, which are found in high concentrations in the brain stem, caudate putamen, medial thalamus, and on primary afferent neurons within the dorsal horn of the spinal cord, produce significantly greater/more analgesia, euphoria, and respiratory depression than do delta or kappa receptors—which are relatively devoid of these effects other than spinal analgesia. (Bruijnzeel, 2009; Madar, Lever, & Kinter, 1996; McDonald & Lambert, 2005; Trescot et al., 2008)

"Pure" opiate analgesics (e.g., morphine) appear to exert their analgesic action primarily at the mu receptors found in the brain, spinal cord, and gastrointestinal tract. These receptors are associated with analgesia and euphoria. Mu receptors are also associated with constipation, miosis, respiratory depression, and the development of physical dependence. "Synthetic" opiate analgesics, including meperidine (Demerol®), appear to act at the delta receptors, which are located primarily in the limbic system of the brain. Delta receptors are associated with an exaggerated feeling of mental depression or unhappiness (i.e., dysphoria), hallucinations, and other "psychotomimetic" effects. They also, in conjunction with the mu receptors, are involved in the development of tolerance to the analgesic effects of the opiate analgesics. "Mixed" opiate analgesics (e.g., butorphanol [Stadol®]) act primarily at the kappa receptors, which are associated with sedation and spinal analgesia, as well as diuresis, dysphoria, and miosis (Fudin, 2018; McDonald & Lambert, 2014; Pathan & Williams, 2012; Valentino & Volkow, 2018).

Currently, although related clinical data are limited and findings are largely based on animal and in vitro laboratory studies (e.g., Kroslak, Laforge, & Gianotti, 2007), several researchers suggest that variants in the opiate analgesic receptors and/or their distribution may contribute to variability in observed effects after the administration of a particular: (1) opiate analgesic; or (2) dosage. For example, Manglik (2020) suggested that a common variant of the mu receptor "may alter pain threshold levels, sensitivity to clinically used opioids, and risk of opioid-induced respiratory depression" (p. 11).

Pharmacologically, drugs that stimulate any of the opiate analgesic receptors (i.e., delta, kappa, or mu receptors) have been designated as "agonists." Those that block the opiate analgesic receptors have been designated as "antagonists" (i.e., naloxone [Narcan®] or naltrexone [Trexan®]). Opiate analgesics that stimulate one receptor and block another have been designated as "mixed agonist/antagonists" (i.e., buprenorphine [Buprenex®]) (see Table 5.1).

The mechanism of action of the opiate analgesic antagonist, naloxone [Narcan®],[29] is particularly important regarding opiate analgesic overdosage. Naloxone can competitively bind to and block all opiate analgesic receptors and, thus, prevent opiate analgesics from attaching to the receptors and eliciting their analgesic and other (e.g., toxic) effects. However, naloxone is particularly attracted to mu receptors, to which it readily binds, reversing the respiratory depression associated with opiate analgesic overdosage. Naloxone's affinity for mu receptors is at least ten-fold higher than its affinity for kappa receptors. This greater affinity for mu receptors may explain why naloxone readily reverses the respiratory depression that occurs with opiate analgesic overdosage involving the mixed agonist/antagonists (e.g., butorphanol [Stadol®]), but only minimally reverses the analgesia that occurs with the stimulation of the kappa receptors in the spinal cord. Additionally, naloxone binding to the sigma receptor is moderate and binding to the nociceptive receptor is negligible.

Pharmacokinetics: Absorption, Distribution, Metabolism, and Excretion

The individual pharmacokinetic parameters (e.g., half-life of elimination, protein binding, and volume of distribution) vary for each of the available opiate analgesics. In addition, the opiate analgesics are available in every pharmaceutical dosage formulation and, consequently, can be administered by every possible route of administration (Pagliaro & Pagliaro, 2004;

29. See also the related discussion in the later Overdosage/Unintentional Poisoning, Acute subsection, Opiate Analgesic—"Naloxone Pharmacotherapy."

Stevens & Ghazi, 2000). These different formulations and methods of use, or administration, can significantly affect opiate analgesic pharmacokinetics—absorption, distribution, metabolism, and excretion—in several ways as discussed in the following subsections.

Absorption

Opiate analgesics can be ingested as capsules (e.g., propoxyphene, Darvon®), liquids (e.g., methadone, Dolophine®), or tablets (e.g., codeine).[30] In addition, opiate analgesics can be vaporized and inhaled into the pulmonary system by "chasing the dragon" (e.g., heroin or opium);[31] intranasally "snorted," as a powder (e.g., heroin or hydrocodone); transmucosally absorbed by sucking on a lozenge (e.g., fentanyl, Actiq®);[32] or sublingually absorbed by placing a sublingual tablet under the tongue (e.g., buprenorphine, Buprenex® or sufentanil, Dsuvia®).[33] They can be intravenously (IV) injected (i.e., "mainlined") as an aqueous solution (e.g., heroin or pentazocine, Talwin®), subcutaneously (SC) injected, or "popped" under the skin (e.g., heroin).[34] They can also be absorbed through the various skin layers (e.g., epidermis or dermis) by the application of a transdermal delivery system or "patch" (e.g., fentanyl, Duragesic®).

The absorption of the various opiate analgesics depends on their:

1. Dosage formulation (e.g., oral tablet, which has a 33% to 50% bioavailability because of extensive first-pass hepatic metabolism, versus transdermal delivery system with a bioavailability of ~ 90%);
2. Method of use/route of administration (e.g., ingestion versus IV injection, which has 100% bioavailability, or pulmonary inhalation);
3. Purity, presence of adulterants, and method of production (e.g., a tablet that is too tightly compressed, or otherwise incorrectly formulated, may not break-up or dissolve in the stomach, or intestines, when ingested, thus reducing, or preventing, the absorption of its active ingredients from the GI tract into the systemic circulation);
4. The physiochemical properties of the opiate analgesic (e.g., lipid solubility, molecular weight, and pKa).

---

30. Another method of use for the opiate analgesics involves the traditional preparation and ingestion of poppy tea, or "doda." The dried opium poppy seed pods, which generally are crushed and finely ground, are brewed as an "herbal tea." The tea is used traditionally in many parts of the world, particularly in South Asian countries and in the U.S. where Asian grocery and convenience specialty stores often stock and sell dried poppy seed pods.
31. Traditionally, opium was smoked through an opium pipe. The Chinese word for opium (i.e., "Yen") is still commonly used today to indicate a longing or yearning for something—including heroin.
32. Actiq®, the fentanyl "lollipop," is a solid drug matrix of fentanyl on a plastic stick. It was designed to facilitate easy removal from the mouth, where it is buccally, transmucosally absorbed, in the event of early signs of fentanyl overdosage (i.e., respiratory depression) during medical use. Bioavailability is ~ 50% (Stevens & Ghazi, 2020).
33. Dsuvia®—which is five to ten times more potent than its parent drug, fentanyl—delivers a sublingual dose of sufentanil by means of a disposable, prefilled single dose applicator. It was specifically designed for patients who cannot swallow oral dosage formulations or who require rapid analgesic intervention when IV access is extremely difficult or hazardous (e.g., treatment of wounded soldiers in active combat situations). In 2018, the FDA restricted approved use to certified, medically supervised health care settings. Data regarding diversion and illicit use are not currently available (FDA, 2018a).
34. The SC injection of heroin has been referred to as "chipping" (Pagliaro & Pagliaro, *Clinical Patient Data Files*). The term "chipping" also has been used to refer to occasional (e.g., once per week) heroin use (e.g., Bass, Brown, & DuPont, 1972).

Following ingestion, opiate analgesics are mainly absorbed from the intestines, where absorption can be more erratic and, consequently, less predictable and consistent than that associated with other methods of use. Absorption also is slowed and less complete from the GI tract because of first-pass hepatic metabolism. Consequently, opiate analgesic blood concentrations that are achieved after ingestion are often half, or less than half, of those achieved when the same dose of the opiate analgesic is injected IV—the only method of administration that ensures immediate and complete absorption and effects. In comparison, the other enteral route of administration, rectal administration (e.g., MS Contin® suppositories) generally has a bioavailability of ~ 33%. Additionally, as noted by Stevens and Ghazi (2000, p. 138):

> The rectal route also has several disadvantages. There may be a great deal of variation among individuals regarding the necessary dose. Normally, drugs absorbed via the interior and middle rectal veins bypass the portal system and empty into the vena cava. Thus, for the portion of drug absorbed into these veins, first-pass metabolism is avoided. The drugs absorbed via the superior rectal veins, however, are transported to the liver via the portal system. How much of the rectum is drained by these three veins is highly variable. Titration and individualization of doses are therefore necessary.

It is important to note that, when compared to IV injection, absorption following SC injection into the fatty tissues under the skin layers and IM injection into muscle tissues are both significantly more variable and produce a less rapid rise in blood concentrations than does IV injection. These and other basic pharmacological differences often affect the selection of an opiate analgesic and its dose and method of use.

In addition to IV injection, other methods of opiate analgesic use that may largely avoid first-pass hepatic metabolism, include:

- Intranasal instillation (e.g., heroin nose drops) and intranasal insufflation (e.g., crushing hydrocodone tablets and "snorting" the powder);[35]
- Pulmonary inhalation (e.g., "chasing the dragon");[36]
- SC injection (e.g., "chipping");
- Sublingual absorption from under the tongue (e.g., buprenorphine, Subutex®);
- Transdermal absorption (e.g., applying a fentanyl, Duragesic®, transdermal delivery system); or the use of an iontophoretic transdermal system, such as Ionsys®, for the delivery of fentanyl;

---

35. Transmucosal absorption also is the mechanism associated with intranasal drug delivery (e.g., nasal drops or nasal sprays). Increasingly, intranasal administration of opiate analgesics (e.g., butorphanol [Stadol NS®] or fentanyl [Lazanda®]) have been advocated and used to manage breakthrough cancer pain (Dietrich & Gums, 2012; Grassin-Delyle, Buenestado, & Naline, 2012; Vellucci, Mediati, & Gasperoni, 2017). It is also used as a route of administration of the opiate analgesic antagonist, naloxone (Narcan®). (See also the discussion in the later section—"Overdosage/Unintentional Poisoning.")
36. Of interest, although smoking opium from a pipe has been practiced for millennia, "chasing the dragon," which was developed in Hong Kong during the 1950s and quickly spread to other countries throughout the world, is currently much more preferred and used during the new millennium for the pulmonary delivery of heroin and other opiate analgesics (i.e., morphine; opium; oxycodone).

    Chasing the dragon involves: (1) placing the opiate analgesic, in liquid or powdered forms, on a piece of aluminum foil, the top of a soda can, or in an empty teapot; (2) heating the foil or can from underneath with a candle flame or cigarette lighter (the teapot is usually heated on a stove or by a Bunsen burner) to release the vapor, which resembles the wiggling tail of a dragon as it is formed, and (3) chasing the vapors while inhaling them through a straw or glass tube (Pagliaro & Pagliaro, 2004; Pagliaro & Pagliaro, *Clinical Patient Data Files*; Strang, Griffiths, & Gossop, 1997).

- Transmucosal buccal absorption (e.g., buprenorphine, Belbuca® film or the fentanyl [Actiq®] "lollipop" or "lozenge on-a-stick").

The various methods used for delivering morphine illustrate factors that may affect older adult choice and use of the various opiate analgesics. Following IV injection, morphine is readily and completely absorbed within seconds and, avoiding first-pass hepatic metabolism, quickly achieves maximal blood concentrations. However, although morphine is well-absorbed after ingestion, it takes longer to be absorbed when compared to IV injection and achieves maximal blood concentrations more slowly. In addition, only approximately 40% of the morphine that is ingested is delivered to the systemic circulation and mu receptor sites because of pre-systemic clearance (i.e., significant first-pass hepatic metabolism). Thus, to achieve morphine blood concentrations and associated desired effects that are comparable to those achieved with IV injection, an ingested dosage must generally be approximately twice as high as the IV dosage.

Distribution

Different opiate analgesics, once absorbed into the systemic circulation, have different distribution characteristics. These differences may help to explain why some users prefer one opiate analgesic over another. For example, morphine, which is not as lipophilic as heroin, does not cross the blood-brain barrier as readily and, thus, does not achieve its onset of opiate analgesic action as rapidly. Most opiate analgesics have a low to moderate degree of plasma protein binding and none are highly protein bound (i.e., > 97%) (Pagliaro & Pagliaro, 2004, 2009):

- Buprenorphine, 96% (primarily to α and β globulins, not to plasma protein);
- Codeine, 7%;
- Fentanyl, 85%;
- Hydrocodone, 30%;
- Hydromorphone, 15%;
- Methadone, 90%;
- Morphine 36%;
- Oxycodone, 45%;
- Tramadol, 20%.

Consequently, the prescription opiate analgesics are not typically involved in protein-binding mediated pharmacokinetic drug interactions (see the later pharmacology subsection Drug-Drug Interactions—"Pharmacokinetic Drug-Drug Interactions").

Metabolism and Excretion

Morphine and other opiate analgesics are largely metabolized into several inactive products by the liver before being excreted by the kidneys. Some opiate analgesics, such as small amounts of codeine and most of a dose of heroin (i.e., diacetylmorphine), are first metabolized into morphine before they are further metabolized into inactive metabolites and excreted by the kidneys. The metabolism of most opiate analgesics is relatively rapid. Thus, their duration of action, on average, is four to six hours.

Consequently, older adults, who require an opiate analgesic for the management of moderate to severe pain following an injury or a surgical procedure, generally require additional dosing every four to six hours to maintain adequate pain relief. This time frame for metabolism and excretion also helps to explain why older adults, who are physically dependent on opiate analgesics, must use them daily, at intervals as short as every three to six hours,[37] to prevent the onset of the opiate analgesic withdrawal syndrome (for further discussion, see the later section—"Physical and Psychological Dependence").

The opiate analgesics undergo metabolism predominantly by Phase I and Phase II metabolic reactions (Overholser & Foster, 2011).[38] Whereas most opiate analgesics undergo both phases: (1) hydromorphone, morphine, and oxymorphone do not undergo Phase I metabolism; and (2) fentanyl, hydrocodone, and tramadol do not undergo Phase II metabolism (DePriest, Puet, & Holt, 2015; Feng, Zhu, & Zhou, 2017; Gudin, 2012). (See also the related discussion in the later pharmacology subsection—"Drug-Drug Interactions.")

The mean half-lives of elimination of the prescription opiate analgesics range from two to 36 hours. However, most have a mean half-life of less than six hours. For example:

- Buprenorphine, two hours;
- Codeine, two hours;
- Fentanyl, seven hours;
- Hydrocodone, four hours;
- Hydromorphone, three hours;
- Methadone, 36 hours;
- Morphine, three hours;
- Oxycodone, four hours;
- Tramadol, six hours.

Urine screening for opiate analgesic use detects codeine and morphine (either as "free" drug or conjugated metabolite), as well as the active metabolites dihydrocodeine, dihydromorphine, and hydromorphone.

Old Misbelief: Finding morphine in the results of a urine drug test for an older adult confirms the recent use of morphine.

False. In fact, heroin is metabolized into morphine. Additionally, a small amount of codeine is also metabolized into morphine. Therefore, rapid screening assays cannot be used to differentially determine whether codeine, heroin, or morphine has been used.[39,40]

---

37. For example, when heroin is available, older adults, who "mainline," generally "shoot up," on average, four times per day (Pagliaro & Pagliaro, *Clinical Patient Data Files*).
38. Phase I metabolic reactions include hydrolysis and oxidation (e.g., N-demethylation, O-dealkylation, and O-demethylation). These metabolic reactions are predominately mediated by the hepatic cytochrome P450 isoenzyme system with the most important isoenzymes being CYP3A4 and CYP2D6 (Lotsch, 2005). Phase II metabolic reactions are conjugation reactions that primarily involve glucuronidation to more water-soluble metabolites. These reactions are predominantly catalyzed by glucuronosyltransferases (e.g., UGT1A3, UGT1A9, and UGT2B7).
39. To precisely determine that a certain opiate analgesic has been used, a more specific chemical assay using gas chromatography with mass spectroscopy (GC/MS) or high-pressure liquid chromatography (HPLC) must be used. These methods of chemical analysis are significantly more complex, time consuming, and costly to perform than are the rapid immunoassay screening tests. However, they are more specific and accurate.
40. Urine screening for illicit or problematic patterns of opiate analgesic use can produce both "false positive" and "false negative" results. For example, codeine is widely available in cough and cold products

Heroin has a rapid onset of action after IV injection (i.e., within ten seconds) and is a potent inducer of histamine release that dilates the blood vessels of the skin and, through this mechanism, increases feelings of body warmth—colloquially referred to in the argot of the heroin addict, as a "rush." Heroin crosses the blood-brain barrier more rapidly than morphine and produces greater euphoric effects when used in equivalent amounts. However, once in the brain, heroin is rapidly hydrolyzed back into morphine.

Heroin functions essentially as a "pro-drug" with a short half-life of elimination (i.e., two to six minutes) because it is rapidly metabolized from diacetylmorphine to 6-acetylmorphine and morphine—both of which are pharmacologically active (Clarification, 2016). Consequently, heroin does not produce a significantly superior analgesic response in comparison to morphine. Thus, the subjective reports of user preference for heroin over morphine may be largely confounded by the "rush," described above, euphorigenic, and expected placebo effects (Pagliaro & Pagliaro, *Clinical Patient Data Files*).

Drug-Drug Interactions

Opiate analgesic drug-drug interactions are relatively common (e.g., Mauer & Bartkowski, 1993; Megarbane, Gueye, & Baud, 2003; Overholser & Foster, 2011; Pergolizzi, 2011). For example, Pergolizzi, Labhsetwar, and Puenpatom (2011), in their study of patients who were receiving long-term opiate analgesic pharmacotherapy for chronic low back pain, found that the potential for drug-drug interactions involving opiate analgesics was 27%. Additionally, Pergolizzi, Ma, and Foster (2014)—utilizing data obtained from over 57,000 patients who had chronic, non-cancer pain and who were receiving a long-acting opiate analgesic for at least 30 days—found that approximately 6% were exposed to a "potentially major drug-drug interaction" (p. 467). Drug-drug interactions, including those involving opiate analgesics, occur by means of either pharmacodynamic or pharmacokinetic mechanisms (Hansten, 1986, 2002).

Pharmacodynamic Drug-Drug Interactions

Virtually all major opiate analgesic pharmacodynamic interactions involve: (1) non-opiate analgesic psychodepressants; (2) psychostimulants; or (3) serotonin reuptake inhibitors.

Non-Opiate Analgesic Psychodepressants and Opiate Analgesic Drug-Drug Interactions

Interactions involving non-opiate analgesic psychodepressants and opiate analgesics may produce additive, and potentially synergistic, CNS depressant effects that can result in a

---

and combination analgesic products. Poppy seeds also contain small amounts of morphine. If any of these products, or if enough poppy seeds are consumed, morphine can be detected in the urine for two to four days yielding positive urine screens for codeine and morphine (i.e., false positive results regarding opiate analgesic use) (Farzan, 2018; Pagliaro & Pagliaro, 2009).

False negative tests also occur. For example, increasingly, specific adulterants (e.g., Absolute Detox® and Stealth®) are being used by illicit opiate analgesic users, including those in treatment programs, to produce false negative urine test results to avoid detection of their illicit opiate analgesic use (Cody, Valtier, & Kuhlman, 2001; Dasgupta, 2015; Stolberg & Gerth, 2000). These products are widely advertised and are easily obtained by means of purchase from vendors over the Internet (Pagliaro & Pagliaro, *Clinical Patient Data Files*).

significant reduction in respiratory rate and the promotion of sedation, which, ultimately, can be fatal (e.g., Kumar, 2017; Pagliaro & Pagliaro, 2009). Given this demonstrated and well-documented concern, the FDA, for example, added a mandatory "boxed warning" on August 31, 2016 (FDA, 2016) for related drug monographs in an effort to decrease the concurrent use of opiate analgesics and benzodiazepines (see also the related discussion in Chapter 6, *Prescription Sedative-Hypnotics*).[41]

Unfortunately, this FDA warning apparently "fell on deaf ears." The published literature is replete with subsequent examples involving the specific interaction of opiate analgesics with benzodiazepines. For example, Park, Larochelle, and Saitz (2020, p. 924) studied over 63,000 adults who had received buprenorphine pharmacotherapy and found that:

1. 24% received a prescription for a benzodiazepine;
2. Combined buprenorphine and benzodiazepine treatment resulted in a 300% increased risk for fatal opiate analgesic overdosage.[42]

Psychostimulants and Opiate Analgesic Drug-Drug Interactions

Contrary to most drug-drug interactions, psychostimulant (e.g., amphetamines and cocaine) and opiate analgesic interactions are often consciously pursued—albeit in the illicit context of "recreational" opiate analgesic use—to: (1) achieve both psychodepressant and psychostimulant effects; and (2) modulate the contributory effects of each drug. Examples of this interaction include the IV injection of a: (1) "speedball," which is traditionally defined as a mixture of cocaine and heroin; or (2) "snowball," which is defined as a mixture of crack cocaine and heroin (e.g., Pagliaro & Pagliaro, *Clinical Patient Data Files*).

Selective Serotonin Reuptake Inhibitors and Opiate Analgesic Drug-Drug Interactions

A potentially significant, but decidedly less common, and less well-defined, drug-drug interaction involves the interaction between selective serotonin reuptake inhibitors (e.g., fluoxetine, Prozac®; fluvoxamine, Luvox®; paroxetine, Paxil®; sertraline, Zoloft®) and opiate analgesics, which can result in the serotonin syndrome (Gnanadesigan, Espinoza, & Smith, 2005; Houlihan, 2004; Nelson & Philbrick, 2012; Solhaug & Molden, 2017).

Pharmacokinetic Drug-Drug Interactions

Virtually all major opiate analgesic pharmacokinetic drug-drug interactions involve drugs—including various opiate analgesics themselves—that induce or inhibit the production of cytochrome P450 isoenzymes, particularly CYP3A4 and CYP2D6, which predominantly

41. N.B. On September 20, 2017, the FDA issued a related update and addendum advising that drugs used to treat opiate analgesic dependence or "addiction" (e.g., buprenorphine or methadone) "should not be withheld from patients taking benzodiazepines" because "the harm caused by untreated opioid addiction can outweigh" the related risks (FDA, 2017a, p. 1).
42. See the related discussion in the later subsection—"Overdosage/Unintentional Poisoning."

affect opiate analgesic metabolism (Feng et al., 2017; Overholser & Foster, 2011; Pagliaro & Pagliaro, 2009) (see Table 5.3). (See also the related discussion of opiate analgesic metabolism in the previous pharmacology section, Pharmacokinetics—"Metabolism.") Consequently, drugs that induce or inhibit the production of P450 isoenzymes can result in clinically significant drug interactions when used with opiate analgesics, particularly those that have a lower therapeutic index and/or are used at high dosages.

***Related Professional Reminder:* The clinical significance of all opiate analgesic drug-drug interactions, including those involving other opiate analgesics, is dependent upon several factors associated with each interacting drug: (1) dosage; (2) route of administration; (3) frequency of administration; (4) half-life of elimination; and (5) therapeutic index. Clinical significance is also dependent upon several factors associated with each recipient or user: (6) age; (7) gender; (8) concomitant medical conditions; (9) overall health status, including hepatic and renal function; and (10) genetic variability, including polymorphisms for the hepatic microsomal isoenzymes.**

Table 5.3 Major Inducers and Inhibitors of CYP3A4 and CYP2D6

CYP3A4		CYP2D6	
Inducers	***Inhibitors***	***Inducers***	***Inhibitors***
Carbamazepine	Amiodarone	Dexamethasone	Amiodarone
Fentanyl	Clarithromycin	Rifampin	Bupropion
Griseofulvin	Clotrimazole		Chlorpromazine
Methadone	Dexamethasone		Cimetidine
Modafinil	Diazepam		Citalopram
Oxycodone	Diltiazem		Clomipramine
Pentobarbital	Erythromycin		Codeine
Phenobarbital	Fluconazole		Fluoxetine
Phenytoin	Fluoxetine		Fluvoxamine
Primidone	Fluvoxamine		Haloperidol
Rifampin	Indinavir		Methadone
Ziprasidone	Itraconazole		Moclobemide
	Ketoconazole		Paroxetine
	Nefazodone		Quinidine
	Ritonavir		Ritonavir
	Valproic Acid		Sertraline
	Verapamil		Thioridazine
	Voriconazole		Valproic Acid
			Venlafaxine

Sources: FDA, 2017b; Feng et al., 2017; Gudin, 2012; Holmquist, 2009; McCance-Katz, Sullivan, & Nallani, 2010; Pagliaro & Pagliaro, 2009; Pergolizzi et al., 2014.

Undesired, or Harmful, Effects and Toxicities

> The analgesic efficacy of opioids does not have a conventional dose-related ceiling, but rather dose escalation is usually limited by the incidence of severity of adverse effects.
>
> (Trescot et al., 2008, p. S151)

A related corollary for the prescription opiate analgesics, which is axiomatic for most drugs, is that the incidence and severity of undesired, or harmful, effects and toxicities increases in direct correlation with the use of increasing dosages. For example, as found by Winn, Check, and Farkas (2020, p. 1), in their large, retrospective cohort study of over 38,000 women, 66 to 90 years of age, who received prescription opiate analgesics upon completion of active breast cancer treatment:

> Opioid use was associated with [a significantly] increased risk of adverse drug events related to substance misuse, other adverse drug events related to opioid use [e.g., falls and fractures; GI adverse events] and all-cause hospitalization. In a dose-response effect, individuals with high daily opioid doses had consistently higher risks of all study outcomes compared with individuals who had low opioid doses.

Hayes, Krebs, and Hudson (2020, p. 1098) identified an additional related clinically relevant example:

> Escalating the opioid dose for those with chronic, non-cancer pain is associated with increased risks of substance use disorder and opioid-related adverse outcomes.

We have deliberately taken the time and effort to emphasize this basic pharmacological principal associated with the "dose-response relationship" that is presented in all professional introductory pharmacology courses. In our clinical practice, we have noted, over the years, numerous examples in which the clinician focuses primarily upon the analgesic producing effects of the opiate analgesics—often at the bequest or urging of older patients, who are experiencing pain, or their family members—without paying due attention to associated adverse effects until they have occurred.

The opiate analgesics are associated with many undesired, or harmful, effects and toxicities that are generally related to their dosage and patterns of use (e.g., irregular, short-term use, or regular, long-term use).[43] The toxicities associated with the opiate analgesics can be immediate (i.e., acute) or can develop over time (i.e., chronic) (see Table 5.4). Acute toxicities occur more commonly and can be quite severe, while chronic toxicities occur less commonly and are usually relatively mild.[44] Consequently, the risk of morbidity and mortality for older adults who use the opiate analgesics is primarily associated with acute toxicity. Generally, there is little direct residual physiological damage associated with the regular, long-term use of the opiate analgesics.[45]

---

43. The difference between a "desired" pharmacological effect that is associated with the use of an opiate analgesic and an "undesired," "harmful," or "toxic" effect often is related to the context of use. For example, the development of an undesired effect, such as "constipation," for an older adult who is being successfully treated for a severe, non-productive cough with a cough syrup that contains an opiate analgesic. In another example, an older adult is being treated for severe diarrhea with an opiate analgesic, or a derivative anti-diarrheal product, for its desired constipating effects.
44. In fact, chronic toxicities associated with the opiate analgesics is generally considered to be lower than for any other psychodepressant—as well as for most of the other drugs and substances of abuse.
45. For example, although deficits in executive cognitive functioning may occur with periods of opiate analgesic use, residual impairment among former opiate analgesic users has not been reported. This

Table 5.4 Signs and Symptoms of Acute and Chronic Opiate Analgesic Toxicities

BODY SYSTEM	SIGNS & SYMPTOMS	
	Acute	**Chronic**
CNS	Cognitive impairment, headache, sedation, sleepiness, syncope	Physical dependence, psychological dependence
CV	Bradycardia; cardiac arrest; circulatory depression; orthostatic, or postural, hypotension; shock; with intravenous injection, local pain, or phlebitis at injection site	Anemia
Cutaneous	Diaphoresis; dilation of superficial blood vessels with resultant warming of the skin ("flushing"); pruritus; with subcutaneous injection, pain at injection site; urticaria	
GI	Constipation, nausea, vomiting	Constipation
Genitourinary	Impotence, reduced sexual desire, urinary retention	Reduced libido
Musculoskeletal	With intramuscular injection, pain at injection site	Diminished bone density
Ophthalmic	Miosis	
Respiratory	Central sleep apnea, decreased cough reflex, laryngospasm, respiratory arrest, respiratory depression	

> ***Related Professional Reminder:*** ***Generally, the adage, "start low and go slow," can significantly reduce the occurrence of undesired, or harmful, effects and toxicities associated with opiate analgesic pharmacotherapy, particularly for older adults. However, sufficient attention must also be given to obtaining adequate pain relief, particularly in regard to acute, severe pain.***

The risk for opiate analgesic-related morbidity and mortality among older adults can be significantly reduced by simply initiating treatment with lower dosages. We have long recommended that the starting dose for opiate analgesics, as well as other psychotropics, should be one-half of the usual dose used for younger adults (Pagliaro & Pagliaro, 1983; Pagliaro & Pagliaro, *Clinical Patient Data Files*). The dose is then gradually increased as clinically indicated and tolerated by the individual older adult (e.g., a 60-year-old man in relatively good health versus a 75-year-old woman who is frail and in poor health).

Opiate analgesics have long been known to cause the release of histamine from mast cells[46] likely by means of the direct activation of G-proteins (Barke & Hough, 1993; Moss &

observation is in stark contrast to former amphetamine users who, although abstinent, continue to display deficits in executive cognitive functioning related to their former regular, long-term amphetamine use (Ersche, Clark, & London, 2006; Pagliaro & Pagliaro, *Clinical Patient Data Files*). (Also see the related discussion in Chapter 2, *Amphetamines and Cocaine*.)

46. The mast cells display significantly different histamine release responses that depend upon: (1) specific opiate analgesic used (e.g., buprenorphine versus morphine); (2) dose; (3) frequency of use; (4) method of use, or administration (e.g., ingestion versus IV injection); and (5) tissue type/location (e.g., lung versus skin).

Roscow, 1983; Stellato, Cirillo, & de Paulis, 1992; Withington, Patrick, & Reynolds, 1993). This histamine release has been related to the "rush" experienced with the IV injection of heroin (e.g., vasodilation of most blood vessels; warming of the skin), as well as several other expected signs and symptoms, including bronchospasm, erythema, hypotension, pruritus, tachycardia, urticaria, and vomiting (e.g., Flacke, Flacke, & Bloor, 1987; Mauer, Kager, & Fellinger, 2014). In addition, the intranasal "snorting," IV injection, or pulmonary inhalation of heroin, by users who have asthma, has been associated with acute exacerbation of related nasal and respiratory signs and symptoms (e.g., congestion) (Underner, Perriot, & Peiffer, 2017; Weeks, Clark, & Mycyk, 2016).

Persistent constipation commonly occurs with regular, long-term opiate analgesic use, particularly when ingested.[47] As the opiate analgesic management of non-cancer pain significantly increased during the new millennium, the incidence of constipation related to opiate analgesic use (i.e., "opioid-induced constipation," or OIC) correspondingly increased (Weber, 2016).[48]

Significantly, relatively recent pharmacotherapeutic advances in the treatment of OIC/opioid-induced bowel dysfunction (OIBD) have primarily focused on peripheral-acting mu opiate analgesic receptor antagonists (PAMORAs) (Holder & Rhee, 2016; Leppert, 2015). For example, naloxegol (Movantik®) prevents opiate analgesics from binding to mu opiate analgesic receptors in the GI tract (Garnock-Jones, 2015). It was approved for adult oral ingestion by the FDA in September 2014 (FDA, 2014a). As such, it became the first drug in this new pharmacological classification of drugs developed for the treatment of OIC (Anantharamu, Sharma, & Gupta, 2015; Corsetti & Tack, 2015).

Known as "peripherally-acting mu opiate analgesic receptor antagonists" (PAMORAs) (Jones, Prommer, & Backstedt, 2015), these drugs are "PEGylated" derivatives of naloxone that, when ingested, are specifically developed to have negligible penetration of the CNS. Consequently, they block the constipating effects associated with the use of the opiate analgesics, but not the associated analgesic effects. Their clinical use in patients with advanced/severe OIC/OIBD symptoms, who do not respond well to traditional oral laxatives, has resulted in significant relief of adverse GI symptoms without compromising related opiate analgesia. As such, their use is particularly indicated for adults with chronic, severe pain who require opiate analgesic pharmacotherapy.[49]

Common undesired, or harmful, effects associated with naloxegol (Movantik®) include abdominal pain, diarrhea, excessive gas, and flatulence (FDA, 2014a). Additionally, the

---

47. A very unusual case related to "constipation" was reported by Greenthal et al. (2021, p. 10):

> A 54-year-old woman who reportedly ingested approximately one lb. of raw poppy seeds daily for six days, presented with stomach cramps and vomiting, and died after experiencing a massive colonic obstruction per the coroner's report. Lab tests were not reported for this case but given that opiates are known to slow gut motility, and the patient may have continued to absorb opiates from the seeds in her colon, we consider it likely that opiates from [raw] poppy [seeds] were the cause of death.

48. When additional opiate analgesic-related GI signs and symptoms (e.g., abdominal pain, bloating, gastric stasis, nausea, vomiting, and xerostomia) are combined with OIC, the resultant spectrum/syndrome of GI complaints is commonly referred to as "opioid-induced bowel dysfunction" (OIBD) (Leppert, 2015).
49. PAMORAs have also demonstrated significant therapeutic efficacy as a prophylactic against severe OIC among older adults who occasionally require an opiate analgesic for the treatment of acute pain (e.g., painful dental or medical procedure)—particularly, among those who either have previously experienced: (1) chronic constipation; or (2) severe OIC (Pagliaro & Pagliaro, *Clinical Patient Data Files*).

use of PAMORAs are associated with several undesired, or harmful, effects, which are not dose-related, including fecal impaction, bowel obstruction, and bowel perforation. Tolerance to these undesired, or harmful, effects does not develop (Jones et al., 2015).

Toxicities Associated with Opiate Analgesic Intravenous Injection

In addition to direct toxicities associated with the use of opiate analgesics, there are several significant undesired, or harmful, effects and toxicities that are specifically associated with their method of use, particularly IV injection (Bangsberg, Rosen, & Aragon, 2002; Ciccarone & Bourgois, 2003; DiGiorgio, Stein, & Morrow, 2019; Many & Drazin, 2019; Pieper & Templin, 2001; Schoener, Hopper, & Pierre, 2002).[50] These undesired effects, which specifically involve IV injection sites, include abscesses. scarring of the skin (i.e., "needle tracks" or "railroad tracks"), soft-tissue infection or inflammation (e.g., cellulitis, cutaneous venous ulcer, or necrotizing fasciitis), and thrombophlebitis. Other undesired, or harmful, effects, include:

- Aneurysms;
- Blood infections (e.g., bacteremia, sepsis, or septicemia);
- Brain and spinal cord infections;
- Cotton fever;[51]
- Endocarditis;[52]
- Gangrene;
- Muscular infection (e.g., myonecrosis, myositis, or pyomyositis);
- Osteomyelitis;
- Pulmonary abnormalities (e.g., talc granulomas);
- Spinal epidural abscesses;
- Systemic viral infections (e.g., hepatitis B virus [HBV], hepatitis C virus [HCV], or[53] HIV);
- Tetanus;
- Wound botulism.

---

50. Commonly used anatomic sites for illicit IV injection of the opiate analgesics for adults, in decreasing order of frequency of use, include the antecubital fossa, or forearm at the bend of the elbow; hands; feet, generally between the toes; leg; breast, particularly for women; groin (e.g., femoral vein); and neck (e.g., jugular vein)—which, when used, is commonly referred to as, a "pocket shot" (Pagliaro & Pagliaro, *Clinical Patient Data Files*).
51. Cotton fever is a generally benign and self-limiting febrile syndrome associated with the IV injections of solutions of heroin, or other opiate analgesics, that have been dissolved over a heat source and filtered through a cotton ball prior to injection (Xie, Pope, & Hunter, 2016). (Also see the related discussion regarding IV injection of other psychotropic drugs in Chapter 2, *Amphetamines and Cocaine*.)
52. Infective endocarditis related to intravenous injection has increased significantly during the new millennium, with the highest rates reported for men and women of European continental descent, who live in rural areas (e.g., Fleischauer, Ruhl, & Rhea, 2017). In a related study of injection and non-injection drug use and infectious disease, Keen, Khan, and Clifford (2014) found that approximately 70% of their Baltimore, Maryland sample of injection drug users were of European continental descent.
53. HCV is often a precursor to cirrhosis of the liver or hepatocellular carcinoma—either of which may be fatal or require liver transplantation (Murrell, 2018; Toshikuni, Arisawa, & Tsutsumi, 2014). The most common cause of hepatitis C in the U.S. is the sharing of contaminated needles and syringes among users of IV drugs and substances of abuse.

Not directly caused by the opiate analgesics, themselves, these infections and other undesired effects are caused by: (1) the adulterants used by dealers to "cut" the opiate analgesic to increase its weight and street value;[54] (2) crushing and injecting drugs intended for ingestion together with related excipients; (3) infection caused by using unsterile, shared needles and syringes; and (4) improper injection techniques and resultant local tissue damage. Consequently, the toxicities associated with intravenous injection of opiate analgesics are also commonly observed when other abusable psychotropics (e.g., methamphetamine) are intravenously injected. (For a related discussion, see Chapter 2, *Amphetamines and Cocaine*.)

Toxicities Associated with Opiate Analgesic Intranasal Use

Obviously, the serious complications associated with IV injection do not occur when opiate analgesics are swallowed, smoked, or "snorted." However, other methods of use also may be associated with their own undesired, or harmful, effects. For example, during the past decade, the intranasal use (i.e., "snorting) of the opiate analgesics, particularly crushed hydrocodone-acetaminophen tablets (e.g., Lortab® and Vicodin®), has been associated with:

- Bacterial infection of the nasal surfaces with a resultant rhinorrhea containing a mixture of mucopurulent exudate;
- Erosion of the lateral nasal walls, nasopharynx, and soft palate;
- Fungal invasion of the nasal surfaces;
- Inflammation of the nasal passages and sinuses;
- Perforation of the nasal septum. (Alexander, Alexander, & Valentino, 2012; Sloan & Klimkina, 2009; Yewell, Haydon, & Archer, 2002)

In addition, severe, life-threatening asthmatic attacks have been associated with the intranasal "snorting" of heroin by users who have pre-existing asthma (Krantz, Hershow, & Prachand, 2003; Pagliaro & Pagliaro, *Clinical Patient Data Files*). (For a related discussion of the significant intranasal toxicity associated with the nasal insufflation of cocaine, see Chapter 2, *Amphetamines and Cocaine*.)

More Common and More Problematic Toxicities Among Older Adults

Although all the previously noted toxicities discussed in this chapter (see Tale 5.4) can, and do, occur among older adults, several specific toxicities are generally more commonly encountered and can be potentially more problematic for this age group. These toxicities include:

- CNS impairment, particularly among older men and women who are receiving high dosages of the opiate analgesics and/or are using other prescription or nonprescription psychotropics;
- Falls and related fractures, usually involving the hip or pelvis, particularly among older women who have osteoporosis;

54. Common adulterants used in the production and commerce of heroin include caffeine, lactose, mannitol, procaine, quinine, and strychnine (DEA, 1992; Pagliaro & Pagliaro, 2004).

- Opioid-Induced Hyperalgesia (OIH), which is more commonly encountered among older adults than other age groups. It is characterized by a state of nociceptive sensitization. OIH is distinct from the development of tolerance (see the related discussion in the following subsection, "Opiate Analgesic Tolerance") and can be exacerbated by increasing the dosage of other opiate analgesics;[55]
- Suicidal behavior, including suicidal thoughts and attempts, particularly among older men, 65 years of age or older, of European continental descent with concomitant risk factors including physical and psychological pain (e.g., bereavement, chronic physical pain, or social isolation).

(Chu, Angst, & Clark, 2008; Conejero, Olie, & Courtet, 2018; McCleane, 2008; Pagliaro & Pagliaro, 1983; Pagliaro & Pagliaro, *Clinical Patient Data Files*; Ross Perlman, 2019; Saunders, Dunn, & Von Korff, 2010; Yoshikawa, Ramirez, & Smith, 2020)

Physical and Psychological Dependence

> Ms W is a 50-year-old woman being treated with methadone maintenance. She lives in Boston and has Medicare. Ms W began using heroin at age 14 years. She used intravenous heroin but has subsequently sniffed it as well. Friends of hers used the drug and she decided to try it. Initially, she did not like it, but she returned to it for reasons she cannot understand and became addicted. She supported her habit with stealing, armed robbery, and prostitution. She has been in detoxification "more than 20 times" and had repeated difficulties remaining free from heroin use. She finds that at times of stress it is very difficult to refrain from using heroin and she relapses.
>
> (O'Brien, 2008, p. 1)

Throughout the 20th century, several of the opiate analgesics, including heroin, methadone (Dolophine®), and propoxyphene (Darvon®), were specifically developed, and originally marketed to provide analgesia without causing physical or psychological dependence (Pagliaro & Pagliaro, 2004). However, it is now generally recognized that the regular, long-term use of any opiate analgesic, including the synthetic derivatives, is associated with the development of both physical and psychological dependence, characterized by: (1) tolerance; (2) an opiate analgesic withdrawal syndrome; and (3) craving (e.g., Valentino & Volkow, 2018). As identified by the National Institute on Drug Abuse:

> An estimated 2.1 million people in the United States suffer from substance use disorders related to prescription opioid pain relievers in 2012 and an estimated 467, 000 [are] addicted to heroin.
>
> (Volkow, 2014, p. 1)

***Related Professional Reminder:* Opiate analgesics that are capable of relieving pain can also cause both physical and psychological dependence.**

55. OIH is managed by several techniques, including: (1) decreasing the dosage of the opiate analgesic; (2) switching to a different opiate analgesic, preferably from a different subgroup (see Table 5.2); and (3) utilization of alternative pain relief measures, including the use of NSAIDs.

Published research over the new millennium suggests a genetic component to the physical and psychological dependence associated with the use of all opiate analgesics. Interestingly, the "genetic risk" appears to involve specific opiate analgesic receptors (see the related discussion in the earlier pharmacology subsection—"Pharmacodynamics: Mechanism of Action"). For example, Mistry, Bawor, and Desai (2014, p. 164), in their comprehensive review of the genetic contributions to the physical dependence of the opiate analgesics concluded that:

> We have observed a consistent contribution of variation within the DRD2 [D2 dopamine receptors], OPRM1 [mu receptor], OPRD1 [delta receptor], and BDNF [neurotropic factor] genes towards the development of opioid dependence, where these particular genes encode receptors and signaling molecules which play important roles in the pathophysiology of substance use disorders.

However, sufficient empirical data to enable the clinical application of these findings are not currently available.

Tolerance

"Tolerance" is the need to use increasingly higher, or more frequent doses, of an opiate analgesic in an effort to achieve the desired effects that were experienced with initial use. It appears to be physiologically moderated by means of an interaction between the delta and the mu opiate analgesic receptors (McDonald & Lambert, 2014). (See also the related discussion in the earlier pharmacology subsection—"Pharmacodynamics: Mechanism of Action.")

Tolerance develops within a few months of regular, long-term opiate analgesic use. Replacing the usual opiate analgesic with a different opiate analgesic generally does not help to achieve desired effects (e.g., analgesia or euphoria) due to the common occurrence of "cross-tolerance" (i.e., when tolerance occurs to one of the opiate analgesics, such as heroin, tolerance to the other opiate analgesics, such as morphine, also occurs). In addition, for many of the opiate analgesics, including heroin and methadone, the higher the dosage of the opiate analgesic used, the more severe the physical dependence—and the associated opiate analgesic withdrawal syndrome—when regular, long-term use is abruptly discontinued.

Old Misbelief: If older adults use their opiate analgesics exactly as medically prescribed, they can avoid the development of tolerance.

False. In fact, as noted by Volkow and McLellan (2016, p. 1) from the NIDA:

> There is lingering *misunderstanding* among some physicians about the important differences between physical dependence and addiction. The repeated administration of any opioid almost inevitably results in the development of tolerance and physical dependence.

The euphorigenic action that opiate analgesics produce among non-tolerant people is generally reduced, or eliminated, as tolerance develops. It is important to note that whereas tolerance and opiate analgesic withdrawal are two components of physical dependence,[56] "craving" is a characteristic of psychological dependence.

56. Physical dependence is associated with both: (1) the development of tolerance; and (2) a characteristic and classic opiate analgesic withdrawal syndrome, which occurs when regular, long-term use of an opiate analgesic is abruptly discontinued, and which "immediately" resolves when its use is resumed.

To once again achieve the desired euphorigenic actions, tolerant older adults, who regularly use opiate analgesics, may significantly increase the amount of the opiate analgesic they use—and, consequently, place themselves at higher risk for overdosage and death associated with severe respiratory depression. In addition, among older adults who are regular, long-term opiate analgesic users, the higher the dosage of the opiate analgesic used, the more severe the physical dependence, and, thus, the more severe the associated opiate analgesic withdrawal syndrome. Consequently, an increased desire to avoid the opiate analgesic withdrawal syndrome develops and this desire becomes a powerful, and very often persuasive, motive for continued opiate analgesic use. (See the following section for additional discussion of the opiate analgesic withdrawal syndrome.)

Withdrawal Syndrome

The opiate analgesic withdrawal syndrome occurs when regular, long-term opiate analgesic use is abruptly discontinued and is immediately relieved when opiate analgesic use is resumed. Thus, among older adults, who are physically dependent on the opiate analgesics, abrupt discontinuation of regular, long-term use, or the use of an opiate analgesic antagonist (e.g., naloxone, Narcan®), generally results in the opiate analgesic withdrawal syndrome.

Although the opiate analgesic withdrawal syndrome is not usually life threatening, the appropriate use of selected pharmacotherapeutic approaches for the management of opiate analgesic withdrawal and the monitoring of therapeutic response are generally indicated. Gradual discontinuation of the regular, long-term use of the opiate analgesic will prevent or minimize related signs and symptoms of withdrawal. A major reason to attempt to ameliorate the signs and symptoms of opiate analgesic withdrawal is to prevent relapse to resumed opiate analgesic use, which commonly occurs during unmedicated and unsupervised opiate analgesic withdrawal.

Signs and symptoms of the opiate analgesic withdrawal syndrome generally include:[57]

- Abdominal cramps and pain;
- Agitation;
- Anorexia;
- Anxiety;
- Asthenia;
- Backache;
- Chills with goose flesh (i.e., "going cold turkey");
- Diaphoresis;
- Diarrhea;
- Drug craving;
- Dysphoria;
- Fever of unknown origin;
- Hyperalgesia;

57. These signs and symptoms, which often resemble those associated with a severe case of the "flu," are not generally life-threatening (Pagliaro & Pagliaro, *Clinical Patient Data Files*).

- Hypertension;
- Hyperthermia;
- Hyperventilation;
- Insomnia;
- Irritability;
- Lacrimation;
- Muscle aches and jerks (i.e., "kicking the habit");
- Nausea;
- Nervousness;
- Piloerection;
- Restlessness;
- Rhinitis;
- Rhinorrhea;
- Shivering;
- Sneezing;
- Tachycardia;
- Tremors;
- Vomiting;
- Watery eyes;
- Worrying;
- Yawning.

Additionally, in severe cases, terrifying hallucinations, convulsions, and coma may occur.

The signs and symptoms of opiate analgesic withdrawal usually begin within eight to 16 hours following the last time that an opiate analgesic was used and resolve after two to 12 days. The occurrence and severity largely depend on the: (1) specific opiate analgesic used;[58] (2) the length of time that the opiate analgesic was regularly used; (3) dosage used (higher compared to lower); and (4) the method of use (ingestion versus IV injection). Although many users who have undergone opiate analgesic withdrawal report the experience as being extremely difficult and painful, most cases are relatively mild in terms of the pain and physical stress that is experienced.[59]

58. Reportedly, the abrupt discontinuation of methadone (Dolophine®) has been identified as resulting in the most severe withdrawal syndrome when compared to other opiate analgesics at equivalent dosages and length of use (Hiltunen & Eklund, 2002; Pagliaro & Pagliaro, 2009; Pagliaro & Pagliaro, *Clinical Patient Data Files*).
59. Despite the objective documentation of the relatively mild, undesired effects associated with the opiate analgesic withdrawal syndrome, the conscious attempt to avoid or diminish these effects is, reportedly, one of the major reasons—following, "to achieve feelings of euphoria"—for the continued regular, long-term use of opiate analgesics (Pagliaro & Pagliaro, *Clinical Patient Data Files*). As such, when their favorite opiate analgesic is not available, older adult "opiate addicts" will use whatever opiate analgesic is available to them to avoid or diminish the undesired effects, even if they would not generally otherwise use that opiate analgesic (e.g., codeine) because they "don't like it" or think it is "junk." Loperamide (Imodium®) is one-such opiate analgesic. It was developed and approved by the FDA as an antidiarrheal. Because it acts primarily at the intestinal opiate analgesic mu-receptor in the myenteric plexus of the GIT, its potential for abuse is officially labeled as "low." Consequently, it is widely available "over-the-counter," without a prescription. However, at higher dosages, it can readily

Treating the Opiate Analgesic Withdrawal Syndrome.

> It took a lot of convincing to get John Evard into rehab. He was reluctant to give up the medications he was certain were keeping his pain at bay. But ultimately, he agreed—and seven days into his stay at the Las Vegas Recovery Center, the nausea and aching muscles of opioid withdrawal are finally beginning to fade.
>
> "Any sweats?" a nurse asks him as she adjusts his blood pressure cuff. "Last night it was really bad," he tells her, "but not since I got up." Evard, who is 70, says he woke up several times in the night, his sheets drenched with sweat.
>
> (Gold, 2016, p. 1)

The opiate analgesic withdrawal syndrome is not usually fatal, even when nonmedically managed (i.e., quitting "cold turkey"). Fatalities related to opiate analgesic withdrawal are generally rare. However, when they do occur, they are usually the result of such complicating factors as concurrent use of other drugs or substances of abuse, heart disease, or mental depression leading to suicide attempts or completions.[60] Both buprenorphine and clonidine have been used to ameliorate the signs and symptoms associated with the opiate analgesic withdrawal syndrome.

Naltrexone pharmacotherapy has been available and has been used for some time in "rapid and ultra-rapid opioid detoxification" treatment centers, which promise quick, painless, same-day detoxification for people who are physically dependent on opiate analgesics (e.g., O'Connor & Kosten, 1998; Singh & Basu, 2004). However, the procedures involved in this treatment approach (e.g., administration of a general anesthetic followed by a high-dose of opiate analgesic antagonist that induces severe withdrawal with the patient having no conscious experience of it—generally pose significant risks for patients, including several documented fatalities (Hamilton, Olmedo, & Shah, 2002). Additionally, the use of naloxone has been suggested to "facilitate opiate analgesic withdrawal" (e.g., Jones, Sherwin, & Martinez, 2020). We do not recommend the use of opiate analgesic antagonists as part of opiate analgesic detoxification/withdrawal treatment.

Additionally, we generally do not recommend the use of specific pharmacotherapeutic adjuncts for the management of the heroin withdrawal syndrome because it is generally relatively mild and can usually be handled "cold turkey" (i.e., signs and symptoms of the heroin withdrawal syndrome typically resemble those of a bad case of influenza—dependent, of course, on both the amount of heroin used daily and the length of time it has been used).[61]

In contrast, the methadone withdrawal syndrome may be quite severe with convulsions and other physiological effects that require appropriate treatment under direct medical supervision, generally in the context of inpatient treatment. Even when not required medically, we strongly recommend that patients undergo methadone withdrawal in an inpatient setting, particularly patients with concomitant histories of long-standing or high-dose use of alcohol or another drug or substance of abuse, in order to provide appropriate psychological support and significantly

---

cross the blood-brain-barrier resulting in central systemic effects, including euphoria and respiratory depression—and relief the opiate analgesic withdrawal syndrome. The abuse of loperamide has been associated with physical and psychological dependence, respiratory depression, and life-threating ventricular dysrhythmias (MacDonald, Heiner, & Villarreal, 2015; Marraffa, Holland, & Sullivan, 2014; Spinner, Lonardo, & Mulamalla, 2015).

60. Except in cases of opiate analgesic withdrawal involving: (1) high dosages; or (2) methadone use—which are often reported to be significantly more severe than the withdrawal syndromes associated with other opiate analgesics (Pagliaro & Pagliaro, 2009).
61. N.B. This does not mean, nor in any way imply, that patients should be "left on their own." They should be closely monitored and appropriate therapeutic interventions—medical, pharmacological, and psychological—should always be applied as individually required to optimize clinical outcomes.

improve compliance (i.e., ensure that the patient successfully completes the withdrawal process). The average stay for people in detoxification units or centers in these situations typically is approximately three to seven days (Pagliaro & Pagliaro, *Clinical Patient Data Files*).

Craving

Craving for opiate analgesics has traditionally been conceptualized as the memory of, and the desire for, the feeling of euphoria initially experienced and, consequently, mentally associated with opiate analgesic use. As such, it appears to be a major factor underlying the: (1) concept of psychological dependence; and (2) high potential for recidivism among regular, long-term opiate analgesic users who attempt to quit their use of opiate analgesics.

In our clinical practice experience, this concept of craving and the related clinical scenario, in the context of opiate analgesic use, are particularly apropos for younger adult users—particularly those who are living "on the street." However, for older adults, craving is more often characterized in relation to a "desire" for either relief from: (1) signs and symptoms of withdrawal; or (2) pain (e.g., Ahmadi, Sefidfard Jahromi, & Ghahremani, 2018; Ashrafioun, 2016; Pagliaro & Pagliaro, *Clinical Patient Data Files*; Tsui, Lira, & Cheng, 2016). For example, as noted by Messina and Worley (2019, p. 918), "greater pain predicted greater craving" among adults with chronic pain being managed with the prescription of opiate analgesics.

> ***Related Professional Reminder:* Intervention for the opiate analgesic withdrawal syndrome should always be used as an opportunity to initiate appropriate professional treatment aimed at the cessation of opiate analgesic use and the prevention of relapsed use (i.e., recidivism).**

Overdosage/Unintentional Poisoning

This section presents and discusses published new millennial research statistics regarding opiate analgesic overdosage and unintentional poisoning in the U.S. (see also the related discussion of suicide in the later section, "Contemporaneous Diagnoses Involving Opiate Analgesics"). As identified by West, Severtson, and Green (2015, p. 117):

> Recent linear increases in rates of death and use of prescription opioids with suicidal intent among older adults have important implications as the U.S. undergoes a rapid expansion of its elderly population.

Between 1997 and 2009, the rate of hospitalizations in the U.S. related to opiate analgesic overdosage increased sharply and significantly from two hospitalizations per 100,000 U.S. population to 15 hospitalizations per 100,000 population (Unick, Rosenblum, & Mars, 2013).[62] Analyzing data from the *National Survey on Drug Use and the Health* and *National Vital Statistics System*, the CDC and FDA found that:

> During 2002–2013, heroin overdose death rates nearly quadrupled in the United States, from 0.7 deaths to 2.7 deaths per 100,000 population, with a near doubling of the rates from 2011–2013.
>
> (Jones, Logan, & Gladden, 2015, p. 719)

---

62. N.B. It is important, and clinically relevant, for health and social care professionals to keep in mind that approximately 20% of these hospitalizations—and related deaths—involve the concomitant use of

However, the highest number of annual overdosage deaths—as well as the highest rate of increase in overdosage death in the U.S. during the first decade of the new millennium (i.e., 2000 to 2011)—involved the prescription opiate analgesics, particularly oxycodone (OxyContin®) (Brown, 2011; Girion, Glover, & Smith, 2011; Rudd, 2014). The CDC identified that "prescription opioid-related overdose deaths increased sharply during 1999–2010 in the United States in parallel with increased opioid prescribing" (Guy, Zhang, & Bohm, 2017, p. 697). As noted by Nora Volkow, Director of the National Institute on Drug Abuse:

> We are seeing an increase in the number of people who are dying from overdoses, predominantly after abuse of prescribed opioid analgesics. This disturbing trend appears to be associated with a growing number of prescriptions in and diversion from the legal market.
>
> (Volkow & McLellan, 2016, p. 8)

Several others have reported similar findings. For example, as reported by Frieden and Houry (2016): "Death from prescription-opioid overdose has dramatically increased in the United States, quadrupling in the past 15 years" (p. 10). Similarly, Rudd, Aleshire, and Zibbell (2016) found that deaths associated with opiate analgesic overdosage in the U.S. increased over 200% from 2000 to 2014.[63] As noted by Galvin (2019, p. 1):

> Among adults 65 and older, the opioid-related overdose death rate soared 17.2% from 2016 to 2017, according to the CDC, and the age group was the only one to see an increase in death rate for overdoses involving prescription opioids between the two years.

Older adult heroin users also concurrently use other drugs and substances of abuse (see also the related discussion in the earlier pharmacology subsection—"Opiate Analgesic Drug-Drug Interactions"). Thus, these overdosages, as previously discussed, may also display serious synergistic effects[64] related to the use of: (1) heroin and another psychodepressant (e.g., alcohol or benzodiazepine); or (2) heroin and a psychostimulant (e.g., cocaine or methamphetamine),[65] which may have been used concurrently by the same, or by a different, method of use (Jones et al., 2014; Pagliaro & Pagliaro, 2009; Sharp & Melnik, 2015; Sporer, 1999).

Unfortunately, the rates of opiate analgesic-related hospitalizations and deaths did not abate during the second decade of the new millennium (e.g., Fleischauer et al., 2017). As identified by Williams and Bisaga (2016, p. 813):

---

alcohol (CDC, 2018; Jones, Paulozzi, & Mack, 2014). (For additional related discussion, see Chapter 1, *Alcohol*.)

63. Geographically, the highest reported increases in these opiate analgesic overdosage deaths occurred in the Appalachian and Southwestern states (Park & Bloch, 2016).
64. Synergistic drug effects occur when two or more drugs, including the drugs and substances of abuse, work together to produce, either: (1) an effect that neither drug can produce on its own; or (2) an effect size that is significantly greater than the sum of the individual drug effects when added together. For example, fatal overdosages involving either alcohol, alone, or a benzodiazepine, alone, are relatively rare. However, when both alcohol and benzodiazepines are ingested together, overdosages are much more common—including fatal overdosages (see the related discussion in Chapters 1, *Alcohol*, and 6, *Prescription Sedative Hypnotics*).
65. When injected IV, the combination of heroin and cocaine (or methamphetamine) is commonly referred to on the street as a "speedball" (also see Chapter 2, *Amphetamines and Cocaine*). The combined IV injection of a psychodepressant and psychostimulant first became popular in the 1970s (Pagliaro & Pagliaro, *Clinical Patient Data Files*). A resurgence in this pattern of use was identified during the second decade of the new millennium with reported prevalence rates "during the past six months"—among IV drug users—ranging from 20% to 50% (e.g., Al-Tayyib, Koester, & Langegger, 2017; Meacham, Strathdee, & Rangel, 2016).

> The United States is facing a vast epidemic of opioid-related deaths. More than 2.4 million Americans have a severe opioid-use disorder (OUD)[66] involving dependence on pain medications, heroin, or both, and rates of drug-overdose deaths in this country have outpaced mortality from motor vehicle accidents since 2013.

Additionally, as identified by Vivolo-Kantor, Seth, and Gladden (2018, p. 279)—on behalf of the CDC:

> During July 2016-September 2017, ED visits among those aged ≥ 11 years for opioid overdoses in the United States increased 29.7% overall and 34.5% in 16 states with high prevalence of overdose mortality. Significant rate increases were found in five Midwest region states (largest in Wisconsin [109%]) and three Northeast region states (largest in Delaware [105%]).

Seth, Scholl, and Rudd (2018, p. 349), again on behalf of the CDC, identified that:

> Drug overdose deaths in the United States increased 11.4% from 2014 to 2015 resulting in 52,404 deaths in 2015, including 33,091 (63.1%) that involved an opioid. The largest rate increases from 2014 to 2015 occurred among deaths involving synthetic opioids other than methadone (synthetic opioids) (72.2%).

Approximately 16,000 people in the U.S. die annually because of a prescription opiate-analgesic overdosage and an additional number of approximately 8,000 people die annually because of heroin-related overdosages (i.e., approximately 65 people daily) (NIDA, 2015b). As noted by Soelberg, Brown, and Du Vivier (2017, p. 1675):

> The United States is in the midst of a devastating opioid misuse epidemic leading to over 33,000 deaths per year for both prescription and illegal opioids. Roughly, half of these deaths are attributable to prescription opioids.

In 2018, the director of the National Institutes of Health reiterated this observation:

> Every day, more than 115 Americans die after overdosing on opioids, that is a fourfold increase since 2000, and the numbers continue to climb.
>
> (NIH, 2018, p. 1).

As reported by Schroeder (2019, p. 1):

> Among people 65 and older, opioid-related emergency room visits were up 74 percent from 2010 to 2015 and opioid-related emergency room visits were up 74 percent. . . . In 2015, there were 124,300 opioid-related hospital admissions of patients 65 and up in the U.S.

The CDC identified that "in 2017, 47,600 persons died from drug overdoses involving opioids" (Guy, Haegerich, & Evans, 2019, p. 1). We expect that these numbers will continue to increase significantly over the next 20 years, together with related prescription opiate analgesic deaths and ED visits, as increasing numbers of baby boomers reach age 65+ (Colliver, Compton, & Gfroerer, 2006; Gossop & Moos, 2008; Han, Gfroerer, & Colliver, 2009a, 2009b; Nordrum, 2016; Wu & Blazer, 2011).

Particularly tragic, in this context, is the observation by Doctor, Nguyen, and Lev (2018, p. 588) that:

> Most opioid prescription deaths occur among people with common conditions for which prescribing risks outweigh benefits.

66. This term is used in the 5th edition of the DSM (APA, 2013) taxonomy.

Also, tragic, and avoidable, was the significant increase in opiate analgesic-related overdosage deaths and suicides that occurred in 2020 during the COVID-19 pandemic "shutdown." These deaths were directly associated with the government policy/response to COVID-19 that included:

- Closure of local physician offices;
- Closure of walk-in clinics;
- Closure of needle exchange programs;
- Cancellations of in-person support group meetings;
- Social distancing and isolation policies;
- Increased stress related to concerns regarding contracting COVID-19;
- Increased stress due to lack of social services;
- SAMHSA temporary allowance of treatment programs to provide patients with two to four weeks of methadone doses—instead of daily doses;
- "Shortage" of street heroin due to the closure of U.S. borders—particularly, the Mexico-U.S. border;
- Disruption of global supply chains for street heroin and fentanyl due to international travel restrictions;
- Increased stress due to unemployment.

(Cousins, 2020; Erdman, 2020; Kaur, 2020; Pagliaro & Pagliaro, *Clinical Patient Data Files*; Patterson Silver Wolf, 2020; Schulz, 2020)

Early in the pandemic, Becker and Fiellin (2020, p. 1) expressed the following concern:

> We are gravely concerned that COVID-19 will increase already catastrophic opioid overdose rates.

As noted by the head of emergency medicine at a major city hospital:

> The pandemic itself is driving people to use more drugs (and) to be more reckless in their use of drugs. We were encouraging users to never use alone, because that's when people die of opioid overdoses, but now some of our substance users are afraid to use at . . . the safe injection sites or even with friends, so it sets them up for a deadly situation of using alone.
>
> (Cousins, 2020, p. 1)

> Franklin County had seen a 50% increase in fatal overdoses from January to April 15. Sixty-two people died of overdoses in the month of April alone.
>
> (Bruner, 2020, p. 1)

> Niagara County in New York reported last month that drug overdoses spiked 35% from January 1 to April 6, compared to the same time last year.
>
> (Kaur, 2020, p. 1)

> A report released earlier this month by the Well Being Trust predicted as many as 75,000 Americans could die because of drug or alcohol misuse and suicide as a result of the coronavirus pandemic.
>
> (Erdman, 2020, p. 1)

The signs and symptoms of acute opiate analgesic overdosage are listed in Table 5.5. As shown, several major organ systems may be involved.

Table 5.5 Signs and Symptoms of Acute Opiate Analgesic Overdosage

BODY SYSTEM	ACUTE OPIATE ANALGESIC OVERDOSAGE SIGNS & SYMPTOMS
Cardiovascular	Hypotension or shock.
Central nervous	Stupor or coma. Seizures may occur with meperidine (Demerol®) or propoxyphene (Darvon®). Seizures may also occur with hypoxemia.
Gastrointestinal	Diminished or absent bowel sounds or constipation.
Peripheral nervous	Reflex arc effects, including diminished or absent reflexes (e.g., abdominal reflex, ankle jerk reflex, quadriceps knee jerk reflex, and radial brachialis reflex).
Ophthalmic	Miosis. Mydriasis may occur with meperidine (Demerol®) and with extreme hypoxia.
Pulmonary	Apnea, hypopnea, hypoxia, or non-cardiogenic pulmonary edema.
Thermoregulatory	Hypothermia.

***Related Professional Reminder*: Opiate analgesic overdosage is a life-threatening medical emergency that generally requires: (1) immediate administration of naloxone; (2) monitoring of respirations and provision of any required respiratory support; and (3) detection and treatment of any other suspected concurrent overdosage involving other drugs and substances of abuse (e.g., alcohol or methamphetamine).**

Before proceeding to the treatment of opiate analgesic overdosage, it is appropriate to briefly discuss "unintentional" poisoning. Research and, consequently, related published data have focused primarily on fatal, or potentially fatal, opiate analgesic overdosages in the context of the opiate epidemic that has occurred during the new millennium (see the related discussion earlier in this section). However, "accidental," or "unintentional opiate poisoning" has occurred in the context of the ingestion of poppy seeds (see the related discussion of poppy seeds in the earlier sections—"Opium Poppy Plant Botany" and "Opium Poppy Pharmacognosy").

Poppy seeds are primary ingested in the U.S. in three circumstances:

1. As raw seeds—generally to achieve some direct, related effects(s) (e.g., to get "high," to relieve opiate analgesic withdrawal, to relieve pain, or to facilitate sleep);
2. As a baked food product, such as poppy seed bread or cake—generally for nutrition or taste;
3. As poppy seed tea—generally to relax or to obtain other desired effects (see ingestion of raw seeds above). (Pagliaro & Pagliaro, *Clinical Patient Data Files*).

In the U.S., overdosages, as well as lesser forms of toxicity, have been associated with the ingestion of opium poppy tea (Haber, Pergolizzi, & LeQuang, 2019; Pagliaro & Pagliaro, 2004; Spyres, van Wijk, & Lapoint, 2018). For example, Seyani, Green, and Daniel (2017) reported a rather typical case of a 64-year-old woman, who was found unresponsive and in respiratory arrest. Fortunately, she responded well to the administration of naloxone. Later, it was determined that she had brewed and ingested opium poppy tea that she had made from opium buds that she had picked. In the majority of reported cases, as well as in our own clinical practice, overdosages can also occur from the "unwashed" opium poppy seeds obtained through Internet orders on Amazon® or eBay® (Pagliaro & Pagliaro, *Clinical Patient Data Files*).

Fortunately, these types of exposures occur rarely. However, they can result in death (e.g., Bailey, Richards-Waugh, & Clay, 2010; Greenthal et al., 2021; Swortwood, 2017).[67] For example, Greenthal et al. (2021, p. 2), in their retrospective analysis of data from the American Association of Poison Control Centers' *National Poison Data System* (NPDS), from 2000 to 2018, found that:

> NPDS included 18 overdoses and three deaths likely attributable to poppy, most involving poppy seed tea . . . including previously reported cases, there are now at least 19 U.S. deaths associated with poppy seeds in the literature. We recommend that practitioners working in opioid treatment and recovery be alert to the use of poppy to treat pain and symptoms of withdrawal.

Treating Opiate Analgesic Overdosage: Naloxone Pharmacotherapy

Naloxone (Narcan®) is a relatively inert drug that has no significant actions other than to competitively bind to, and block, endogenous opiate analgesic receptor sites—primarily, mu receptor sites—where it subsequently prevents the opiate analgesic from binding to the site and eliciting its expected desired therapeutic and undesired, or harmful, effects. (See also the related discussion in the earlier pharmacology subsection, "Pharmacodynamics: Mechanism of Action.") Naloxone is the only essentially pure opiate analgesic antagonist currently available for the treatment of opiate analgesic overdosage. The use of naloxone can literally bring an older adult, who has overdosed on an opiate analgesic, "back from death's doorstep."[68] Naloxone has:

1. A usual duration of action of one to two hours;
2. A serum half-life of elimination of approximately 60 minutes (range of 30 to 90 minutes);

---

67. In some related cases a co-intoxicant (e.g., alcohol) was also ingested. In this case, the co-intoxicant was a benzodiazepine.
68. N.B. It is extremely important to be mindful that naloxone only reverses the actions of the opiate analgesics. Naloxone does not reverse the actions of any other drug, including any other drug or substance of abuse (e.g., alcohol or cocaine) that may also be involved in the overdosage. Other drugs and substances of abuse that are suspected to be involved in the overdosage must be appropriately identified and individually addressed—for example, with activated charcoal, gastric lavage, or a specific antidote as per established clinical protocols. As noted in an analysis of related data by the CDC and FDA:

    > Overall, 96% of past-year heroin users reported use of at least one other drug during the past year, and 61% reported using at least three different drugs.
    >
    > (Jones et al., 2015, p. 721)

    Additionally, it should be kept in mind that naloxone is not a "magic bullet" for opiate analgesic overdosage. CPR and other supportive care are also required, as indicted by patient circumstances and response.

3. Rapid equilibrium between the plasma and brain (i.e., approximately 6.5 minutes to achieve 50% equilibrium);
4. The ability to bind to all endogenous opioid receptors, but preferentially to mu receptors;
5. No pharmacologic action, other than its antagonism of the opiate analgesic agonists;
6. Not been associated with overdosage toxicity;
7. Virtually no contraindications for its use. However, cautious use is indicated because, along with its rapid reversal of the respiratory depression associated with opiate analgesic overdosage, it also can precipitate an acute opiate analgesic withdrawal syndrome when administered to those who are physically dependent on opiate analgesics.

Naloxone, which is not well absorbed from the GI tract, is therapeutically administered by a variety of other routes, including endotracheal (ET) instillation—for intubated patients, IM injection, nasal inhalation (IN), IV injection or infusion, and SC injection. Absorption following IV and ET administration is generally rapid. However, absorption may be slow and the related onset of action delayed with IM or SC injection (Dowling, Isbister, & Kirkpatrick, 2008). Consequently, we generally recommend that naloxone be administered by IV injection whenever possible.[69]

The generally recommended injectable dosage of naloxone is 0.1 mg/kg. The dosage can be repeated, if needed, within a couple of minutes.[70] Thereafter, dosages generally are repeated at hourly intervals (i.e., commensurate with the half-life of elimination of naloxone).[71] A constant IV infusion of naloxone, although generally not required, may also be initiated (Kauffman, Banner, & Blumer, 1990; Pagliaro & Pagliaro, 1999). (See also the related discussion in the earlier section, "Overdosage/Unintentional Poisoning.")

Although naloxone has generally become more widely available, death due to acute heroin overdosage is a relatively common event that, as noted earlier, has been increasing since the early1990's—from less than 1,000 deaths per year to more than 10,000 deaths per year (NIDA, 2015b; Ochoa, Hahn, & Seal, 2001; Rudd, 2014). As identified by Jones et al. (2015, p. 1), "Heroin use and overdose deaths have increased significantly in the United States"—quadrupling from 2002 to 2013 (Nordrum, 2015) and more than tripling from 2010 to 2014 (Rudd et al., 2016).

As previously noted, naloxone is poorly absorbed following ingestion (i.e., $F < 0.02$) (Smith, Hopp, & Mundin, 2012). Thus, it has been traditionally administered by IV, IM, or SC injection. However, because opiate analgesic users comprise a high-risk population

---

69. N.B. Administration into a central vein is the most efficient method. The use of peripheral veins can be problematic in cases of opiate analgesic overdosage because of, for example, collapsed veins, hypotension, trauma, and vasoconstriction. In these cases, when a central vein is not easily accessible, the IM, IN, or ET routes are generally recommended.
70. N.B. A significant number of overdosage patients (i.e., up to 50%) require more than one dose of naloxone.
71. N.B. If clinically indicated, the dose can be repeated at more frequent intervals—particularly when treating overdosages involving very high doses of the opiate analgesics or those (e.g., buprenorphine or fentanyl) that have a high binding affinity for the endogenous endorphin receptors. Additionally, a larger dosage of naloxone may be indicated (Rzasa Lynn & Galinkin, 2018). For example, Moss, McCabe Pryor, and Baillie (2020) note that "results suggest that the current doses of naloxone (2 mg IM or 4 mg IN) may be inadequate for rapid reversal of toxicity due to [high dose] fentanyl exposure" (p. e0234683). Consequently, they recommend a naloxone dose of 5 mg or 10 mg IM.

for HIV, hepatitis, and other serious infections, concern was raised regarding possible needle-stick injuries among medical staff members who injected naloxone into opiate analgesic users who had overdosed. As a result of this concern, researchers explored other methods of naloxone administration that would be both expedient and safe.

In response, the FDA approved the use of a hand-held naloxone auto-injector (Evzio®) in 2014 (FDA, 2014b). Formulated for IM or SC use, it is indicated for the management of opiate analgesic overdosage (A naloxone, 2014). The single dose naloxone autoinjector (Evzio®) is available by prescription for use by family members or caregivers for the emergency treatment of known or suspected cases of opiate analgesic overdosage. It is available in a carton containing two doses to allow for and facilitate repeated dosing, if required. The injector has an automatically retracting needle and consequently, significantly reduces the risk of accidental needlestick injury. A single 2 mg IM[72] or SC dose of naloxone is injected with a 0.4 ml pre-filled, hand-held auto-injector. Use is facilitated by verbal instructions provided to the user by an electronic voice instruction system—once the unit has been turned on—similar to the verbal instructions provided by some automated external defibrillators (AEDs). Additional doses can be administered, utilizing a new autoinjector, at two- to three- minute intervals as indicated by patient response (i.e., failure to respond to the initial dose or response to the initial dose followed by relapse into respiratory depression).

Another related development was the production of a "needleless" intranasal (IN) method of naloxone administration that appears to be effective in approximately 75% of pre-hospital treatment cases (Robinson & Wermeling, 2014; Weber, Tataris, & Hoffman, 2012). In November 2015, the FDA approved this route of administration and made it available to care givers, family members, and first responders under the formulation and product name of "Narcan Nasal Spray®" (FDA, 2015; NIDA, 2015a). Narcan Nasal Spray® is dispensed in a box containing two individual doses of naloxone (4 mg each in a 0.1 ml of nasal spray solution) in self-contained, single use disposable nasal spray units (Nordrum, 2016).[73]

However, concern has been raised about the bioavailability of the intranasal dose (i.e., F ~ 0.5) (Ryan & Dunne, 2018). For example, Dietze, Jauncey, and Salmon (2019), in a "double-blind, double-dummy randomized clinical trial" that compared the efficacy of the administration of equal IM and IN doses of naloxone, they found that significantly more subjects who received IN naloxone required a rescue dose 10 minutes after the initial dose due to the reduced bioavailability of the IN route in comparison to the IM route.

These observations may be related to the "time course" of effects of intranasal naloxone. Johansson, Hirvonen, and Lovro (2019) used PET scans to investigate the brain availability of intranasally administered naloxone at the mu receptors in human subjects. They found, regarding the occupancy of the mu receptors by naloxone, that the:

- Time taken to achieve 50% occupancy was approximately ten minutes;
- Maximal receptor occupancy occurred in less than 60 minutes;

72. It is recommended that the IM injection of naloxone be made into the anterolateral aspect of the thigh (i.e., quadriceps femoris or vastus lateralis muscles), through clothing, if necessary, for older adults.
73. In most states, Narcan Nasal Spray® can be purchased directly from a pharmacist without a prescription.

- Half-life of receptor occupancy was approximately 60 minutes;
- Peak plasma concentration following intranasal naloxone administration ranged from 15 to 80 minutes (mean of 25 minutes).

Consequently, when the IN route is used for naloxone pharmacotherapy, we regularly recommend that:

1. Initially, the 4 mg dose is administered into one nostril;
2. The 4-mg dose is repeated in the opposite nostril, every two to three minutes, as indicated by clinical response.[74]

***Related Professional Reminder*: Intranasal naloxone bioavailability is limited (i.e., approximately 50% in comparison to IM administration). However, additional factors can further limit nasal absorption, including:**

- ***Nasal congestion;***
- ***Abundant nasal secretions;***
- ***Presence of dried blood in the nostrils;***
- ***Topical vasoconstriction caused by the use of decongestants or intranasally administered cocaine;***
- ***Significant nasal polyps.***

The presence of these factors must be taken into consideration and may favor the use of different non-IV routes (e.g., the use of the FDA-approved IM autoinjector).

Over the last 30 years, increasingly pure supplies of heroin (i.e., higher relative concentrations of heroin in actual street samples) became generally available in the U.S. These supplies of heroin were associated with literally thousands of deaths as previously noted in this chapter.[75] From 2012 to 2015, heroin was the most frequently mentioned drug associated with overdosage deaths in the U.S. (Hedegaard, Bastian, & Trinidad, 2018). In many of these cases, the deaths were the result of users not making allowances for the increasingly pure supplies of heroin that they were obtaining (i.e., they failed to reduce their usual dosages in response to increasing heroin concentrations).

Additionally, while a significant increase in overdosage deaths was identified among IV heroin users in the U.S. during the second decade of the new millennium, the chemical analyses—which were conducted by both the CDC and DEA—determined that fentanyl and its analogs, which were added to the street heroin, were the most frequent cause for the significant increase in overdosage deaths (Gladden, Martinez, & Seth, 2016; Peterson, Gladden, & Delcher, 2016).[76]

---

74. The lowest effective dose of naloxone is generally recommended because of the possible precipitation of the opiate analgesic withdrawal syndrome. (See the related discussion in the earlier pharmacology subsection, Physical and Psychological Dependence—"Withdrawal Syndrome.") However, doses of up to 2 mg/kg IV have been safely administered (Rzasa Lynn, & Galinkin, 2018).
75. N.B. Not only has the "number" of heroin-related overdosage deaths increased significantly in the U.S., but also has the "rate" of heroin-related overdosage deaths. (See the related discussion in the earlier section, "Overdosage/Unintentional Poisoning.")
76. Generally, in national statistical reports, overdosage deaths are not identified separately for individual opiate analgesics (e.g., fentanyl overdosages are not distinguished from those involving oxycodone and

In 2016, fentanyl was the most frequently mentioned drug that was involved with overdosage deaths in the U.S. (Hedegaard et al., 2018). The NIH (2018, p. 1), based upon an analysis of data from their searchable internal database, *CDC Wonder*, found that:

> Among the more than 72,000 drug overdose deaths estimated in 2017, the sharpest increase occurred among deaths related to fentanyl and fentanyl analogs (synthetic opioids) with nearly 30,000 overdose deaths.

The highest increase in these fentanyl-related overdosage deaths occurred in eight "high burden" states—Florida, Kentucky, Maine, Maryland, Massachusetts, New Hampshire, North Carolina, and Ohio. Overall, the number of fentanyl-related overdosage deaths in the U.S. increased significantly from approximately 3,000 deaths in 2010, to approximately 6,000 deaths in 2014. (Also see the related discussion in the later section, "Fentanyl.") Additionally, Althoff, Leifheit, and Park (2020, p. 108321), in their analysis of "shifting patterns" of fentanyl-related overdose mortality in the U.S. from 2013 to 2017, found that:

> Among older (≥ 55 years) adults, only urban NH [non-Hispanic] Black Americans had an increase in overdose-related mortality rate (87% increase). Urban NH Black Americans also experienced the greatest increase in the percent of fentanyl-involved deaths (65% in younger, 61% in older).

As part of the concerted action of the government to combat the growing epidemic of opiate analgesic deaths, HHS recommended, in December 2018, that clinicians consider the routine prescription of naloxone for patients who are at high risk for overdosage. Specifically, the HHS (2018, p. 5) recommended that:

In order to reduce the risk of overdose deaths, clinicians should strongly consider prescribing or co-prescribing naloxone, and providing education about its use for the following patients who are at risk of opioid overdose:

- Patients prescribed opioids who:
  - Are receiving opioids at a dosage of 50 morphine milligram equivalents (MME) per day or greater;
  - Have respiratory conditions such as COPD or obstructive sleep apnea (regardless of opioid dose);
  - Have been prescribed benzodiazepines (regardless of opioid dose);
  - Have a non-opioid substance use disorder, report excessive alcohol use, or have a mental health disorder (regardless of opioid dose).
- Patients at high risk for experiencing or responding to an opioid overdose, including individuals:
  - Using heroin, illicit synthetic opioids, or misusing prescription opioids;
  - Using other illicit drugs such as stimulants, including methamphetamine and cocaine, which could potentially be contaminated with illicit synthetic opioids like fentanyl;

---

heroin overdosages frequently are not distinguished from those involving all combined prescription opiate analgesic overdosages).

- ◦ Receiving treatment for opioid use disorder, including medication-assisted treatment with methadone, buprenorphine, or naltrexone;
- ◦ With a history of opioid misuse that were recently released from incarceration or other controlled settings where tolerance to opioids has been lost.

Despite this specific and directed admonition, as reported by the CDC, "only one naloxone prescription was dispensed for every 69 high-dose opioid prescriptions" (Guy, Haegerich, & Evans, 2019, p. 1). This finding appears to be supported by others. For example, Sohn, Brinkman, and Wellman (2020, p. 82), in their cross-sectional study of data from extant U.S. datasets (i.e., *National Ambulatory Medical Care Survey*; *National Hospital Medical Care Survey*), noted that:

> The rates of naloxone co-prescribing with opioids were extremely low [i.e., < 1%] in office-based and ED settings in the U.S.

However, it has been demonstrated that appropriate "take-home naloxone" practices can yield significant positive results. For example, Katzman, Takeda, and Greenberg (2020, p. 1), in a year-long cohort study of the use of take-home naloxone doses for adults with OUD who were being discharged from an outpatient treatment program, found that:

> Seventy-three of the 395 study participants (18.0%) performed 114 overdose reversals in the community. All community reversals were heroin related. Most study participants (86.8%) stated that the person on whom they performed an overdose reversal was a friend, relative, acquaintance, or significant other.

***Related Professional Reminder*: Following successful intervention, patients who have been treated for opiate analgesic overdosage in the ED should always be referred for: (1) appropriate treatment of their opiate dependence or use disorder; and (2) assessment and, if necessary, treatment for suicidality.**

This reminder is particularly salient considering the related research by Weiner, Baker, and Bernson (2020). As highlighted by Tobin (2020, p. 1), the major results of the study were that:

- About one in 20 patients treated for a nonfatal opioid overdose in an ED died within one year of their visit, many within two days;
- Two-thirds of these deaths were directly attributed to subsequent opioid-related overdoses;
- Immediate treatment for substance use disorder in the ED that continues after discharge is needed to reduce opioid-related deaths.

NEW MILLENNIAL TRENDS IN OLDER ADULT PRESCRIPTION OPIATE ANALGESIC AND HEROIN USE

During the new millennium, the use of "prescription" (e.g., oxycodone) and "non-prescription" (e.g., heroin) opiate analgesics increased significantly among older adults with the licit use of prescription drugs often preceding the illicit use of heroin and fentanyl. This section presents and discusses:

- Medical prescription use;
- Illicit/"recreational" (i.e., non-medical) prescription use;
- Illicit heroin use.

Medical Prescription Use

Prescription opiate analgesics for older adults are medically prescribed for several medical indications:[77]

1. Treatment of severe, nonproductive cough;
2. Management of diarrhea;
3. Preoperative sedation;
4. Relief of moderate to severe pain due to, for example, acute injury, surgery, or cancer.

The medical prescription of opiate analgesics grew exponentially over the first two decades of the new millennium. As reported by Manchikanti (2007, p. 399):

> Opioid pill prescribing grew 533% from 1997–2005 with hydrocodone becoming the leading prescribed medication and oxycodone the top retailed opioid by weight in the United States.

While much of this growth was due to the medical management of moderate to severe cancer pain, it also was due to the largely inappropriate management of chronic, nonmalignant pain.[78]

For example, Jauregui, Nutt, and Margolis (2020, p. 210), in the context of conducting a comprehensive retrospective chart review, noted that:

> National guidelines created by the Agency for Healthcare Research and Quality (AHRQ), the American College of Emergency Physicians (ACEP), and American College of Physicians (ACP) support the use of nonsteroidal anti-inflammatory drugs (NSAIDs) over opioids when treating acute low back pain . . . [However,] despite the current evidenced-based guidelines by the AHRQ, ACEP, and ACP against opioid prescribing for acute low back pain, more subjects received an opioid prescription at discharge than a prescription for an NSAID.
>
> Americans, constituting only 4.6% of the world's population, have been consuming 80% of the global opioid supply, and 99% of the global hydrocodone supply.
>
> (Manchikanti & Singh, 2008, p. 563)

Specifically, regarding older adults:

> "Older Americans are among those unseen in this epidemic," said Sen. Robert P. Casey Jr. (PA), the top Democrat on the panel. "In 2016, one in three people with a Medicare

77. Although opiate analgesics are capable of inducing sleep, they are not generally used for this indication because of their high potential for physical and psychological dependence and the availability of the safer and more effective sedative-hypnotic drugs (see Chapter 6, *Prescription Sedative-Hypnotics*).
78. N.B. Papaleontiou, Henderson, and Turner (2010), in their meta-analysis of the treatment of chronic non-cancer pain among older adults (i.e., 60 years of age or older), reported that "the occurrence of adverse effects prompted opioid discontinuation in up to 31% of cases" (p. 1353).

> prescription drug plan received an opioid prescription. This puts baby boomers and our oldest generation at great risk."
>
> (Davidson, 2018, p. 1)

As further noted by Chang and Compton (2016, p. 21):

> Liberal opioid drug prescribing on the part of well-meaning clinicians has in part fueled this epidemic, being correlated to opioid death and addiction treatment admission rates . . . the fastest growing age group for opioid drug misuse/abuse is older (ages 50 to 64).

The pharmaceutical industry, specifically the "$13 billion-a-year opioid industry" has not been only complicit, but has played a major, direct, and contributing role in initiating and sustaining the new millennial opiate analgesic epidemic in the U.S. (e.g., AP, 2018; Hadland, Cerda, & Li, 2018; Haffajee & Mello, 2017; Pagliaro & Pagliaro, *Clinical Patient Data Files*). The manufacturers of prescription opiate analgesics (e.g., Purdue Pharma L. P.—the manufacturer of OxyContin®) used several specific advertising techniques to increase the demand for and sustain the use of opiate analgesics in the U.S. starting in the mid-1990s and continuing throughout the new millennium (e.g., Lyapustina & Alexander, 2015; Pagliaro & Pagliaro, *Clinical Patient Data Files*). These techniques included:

1. Advocating the prescription of opiate analgesics for chronic pain management;[79]
2. Using advertising that deliberately omitted, or minimized, concerns regarding possible physical and psychological dependence;
3. Aggressive marketing (e.g., promotion campaigns)—specifically directed at prescribing physicians—including, the use of free patient samples, gifts for prescribers, and all-expenses-paid continuing education (CE) conferences and programs;
4. An unprecedented increase in production that far exceeded the amounts required to fill legitimate prescription needs in the U.S.

These "predatory" techniques were widely identified in numerous related articles that appeared in both the lay and professional press during the second decade of the new millennium. For example:

> As tens of thousands of Americans die from prescription opioid overdoses each year, an exclusive analysis by CNN and researchers at Harvard University found that opioid manufacturers are paying physicians huge sums of money—and the more opioids a doctor prescribes, the more money he or she makes. In 2014 and 2015, opioid manufacturers paid hundreds of doctors across the country six-figure sums for speaking, consulting and other services. Thousands of other doctors were paid over $25,000 during that time. Physicians who prescribed particularly large amounts of the drugs were the most likely to get paid. . . .

79. This recommendation—by the pharmaceutical industry—was particularly injurious to older adults in the U.S. because over 20% of older adults experience chronic pain and opiate analgesics are not indicated for the management of chronic, nonmalignant pain (e.g., Galvin, 2019; Pagliaro & Pagliaro, 1999, 2018; Reid, Eccleston, & Pillemer, 2015). As emphasized by Eisler (2014, p. 1):

> They kept saying, "How did you get so much?" recalls Van Amburgh, 68, who'd been on an increasingly potent mix of medications since a series of back surgeries 20 years earlier. "The doctors just kept prescribing them. It was always, do you have pain? Let me give you a prescription. . . . But I got addicted. I was a zombie."

> More than 200,000 doctors who wrote opioid prescriptions received payments from pharmaceutical companies that make opioids . . .
>
> The Harvard researchers said it's not clear whether the payments encourage doctors to prescribe a company's drug or whether pharmaceutical companies seek out and reward doctors who are already high prescribers.
>
> "I don't know if the money is causing the prescribing or the prescribing led to the money, but in either case, it's potentially a vicious cycle. It's cementing the idea for these physicians that prescribing this many opioids is creating value," said Dr. Michael Barnett, assistant professor of health policy and management at the Harvard T. H. Chan School of Public Health.
>
> (Kessler, Cohen, & Grise, 2018, pp. 1, 3)

As reported by Satterfield and Nelson (2018, pp. 2, 4):

> Purdue funded the creation of advocacy groups, including the American Pain Society and the American Pain Foundation, and then gave those same groups grants for marketing campaigns, the lawsuit showed.
>
> Purdue would then pay for "educational" pamphlets and brochures with titles such as "In the Face of Pain" and "Partners Against Pain"—all of which cited the advocacy groups as authority on the safety of opioids for chronic pain. . . .
>
> Purdue told its sales staffers to "have a specific business plan in place" for nursing homes and other long term care facilities—"maximizing demand" for OxyContin and Ryzolt, Purdue's brand of the narcotic-like pain reliever tramadol.
>
> Purdue Pharma offers $10–12 billion to settle opioid claims.
>
> (Strickler, 2019, p. 1)

> Purdue Pharma, drug maker accused of fueling the opioid epidemic, files for bankruptcy.
>
> (Rowland, 2019, p. 1)

In partial response to the continuing and escalating epidemic of prescribed opiate analgesic use, the CDC released new guidelines for the prescription of opiate analgesics (Dowell, Haegerich, & Chou, 2016). In a follow-up investigation of "long-term opioid use"—which was based on the *CDC Guideline for Prescribing Opioids for Chronic Pain*—Shah, Hayes, and Martin (2017, p. 265) found that:

> In a representative sample of opioid naïve, cancer-free adults who received a prescription for opioid pain relievers, the likelihood of chronic opioid use increased with each additional day of medication supplied starting with the third day. . . . The highest probability of continued opioid use at 1 and 3 years was observed among patients who started on a long-acting opioid.

In a large international study, Winstock (2016, p. 19) found that prescription opiate analgesic use was highest in the U.S. He also reported a somewhat unexpected finding for which he provided a related recommendation:

Our study showed that less than 50% of patients in receipt of prescription opioids had ever been warned about the risks of addiction,[80] so [as a request to my medical colleagues], please have that conversation upfront when you start prescribing. Informed patients are safer patients.

---

80. Others, prior to and since Pagliaro and Pagliaro (1983), have reported similar findings. For example, Fadulu (2018, pp. 1, 3) reported that:

> A recent poll suggests many doctors aren't warning elderly patients of the risks when prescribing painkillers. . . . You don't often see the elderly as a population at risk for developing substance-use disorders.

As shared by Eisler (2014, p. 2) in a report regarding a 68-year-old patient:

Schroeder (2019, p. 1), citing data from the Agency for Healthcare Research and Quality, reported that:

> 1 in 3 seniors enrolled in a Medicare prescription drug plan received prescription opioids and a substantial number received higher dosages than recommended for prolonged periods of time.

***Related Professional Reminder:* As we have repeatedly encountered, while consulting on drug and substance abuse among older adults over the past 40 years, and have recently reported, chronic pain—untreated or undertreated—contributes significantly to drug and substance abuse among older adults (Pagliaro & Pagliaro, Clinical Patient Data Files). Untreated or undertreated chronic nonmalignant pain (e.g., that associated with arthritis or osteoarthritis) commonly leads to:**

1. ***Abuse of prescribed opiate analgesics;***
2. ***Mental depression that leads to the abuse of several different abusable psychotropics, including alcohol (see Chapter 1, "Alcohol") and psychostimulants (see Chapters 2, "Amphetamines and Cocaine" and 3, "Caffeine and Nicotine")—often in the context of "self-medication" (i.e., in an unconscious attempt to ameliorate related signs and symptoms of mental depression).***

Consequently, it is never appropriate for health and social care professionals to consider or accept that the chronic pain being experienced (and unrelieved) by appropriate opiate analgesic prescription must simply be endured or accepted as part of "getting old." Alternate pain relief strategies (e.g., acupuncture, counter-irritants, NSAIDs, physiotherapy, or transcutaneous electrical nerve stimulation [TENS] therapy) must be evaluated and appropriately implemented for each individual older patient with chronic pain.

In this context, we should note that we are "old school," both literally and figuratively, regarding the therapeutic management of pain—mild, moderate, or severe. We believe that pain should always be actively addressed and, following attention to emergent conditions, primary attention should be directed at pain relief. Early, quickly effective intervention both relieves acute distress that the patient is experiencing and, perhaps more importantly, demonstrates to patients that significant pain relief is achievable and places them in a "better state of mind" to address other clinical concerns including, in many cases, the cause of the pain (Pagliaro & Pagliaro, *Clinical Patient Data Files*).[81] Although we tend to favor pharmacotherapeutic approaches to treat pain, we always consider the wide array of approaches that are currently available as either primary or auxiliary treatments for pain. These approaches include:

- Acupressure;
- Acupuncture;
- Anti-calcitonin gene-related peptide monoclonal antibodies (e.g., for migraine headaches);

> Through two decades of back pain, she saw general practitioners, orthopedists, pain specialists. Each would assess her drug regimen, maybe switch a narcotic, tweak a dosage. "No one ever told me to cut back," she says.

81. This psychological concept contributed to the successful development and use of patient-controlled analgesia (PCA) utilizing infusion pumps during the 1980s (Graves, Foster, & Batenhorst, 1983; Owen, Mather, & Rowley, 1988; Pagliaro & Pagliaro, 1986).

- Anticonvulsants (e.g., carbamazepine [Tegretal®] or gabapentin [Neurontin®]) for the treatment of neuropathic pain;
- Bioelectric therapy;
- Biofeedback;
- Botox injections (e.g., for migraine headaches);
- Chiropractic manipulation;
- Cognitive therapy;
- Cold packs;
- Counter irritants (e.g., for arthritic pain);
- Desensitization;
- Distraction;
- Epidural anesthesia (e.g., as an adjunct to general anesthesia);
- Exercise (e.g., swimming, walking, or yoga);
- Guided imagery;
- Heat packs (e.g., for muscular pain);
- Hydrotherapy;
- Hypnosis;
- Intra-articular hyaluronan injections;
- Local steroid injections (e.g., for arthritic joint pain);[82]
- Local topical anesthesia (e.g., lidocaine [Xylocaine®]);
- Massage therapy (e.g., for muscle pain);
- Meditation;
- Mild exercise (e.g., swimming or tai chi—for mild to moderate arthritic pain);
- Music therapy;
- Nerve block (e.g., trigeminal nerve block);
- Neurostimulation, including transcutaneous nerve stimulation (TENS);
- Nonprescription, non-NSAID analgesics (e.g., acetaminophen (Tylenol®);
- Nonsteroidal anti-inflammatory drugs (NSAIDs);[83]
- Occupational therapy;
- Pastoral counseling;
- Physical therapy;
- Pet therapy;
- Radiation therapy;
- Relaxation techniques;
- Spinal cord stimulation (implant);
- Surgery;

82. Although this approach is commonly used, we have long avoided its recommendation due to the consideration of potential long-term joint damage (Pagliaro & Pagliaro, 1986; Pagliaro & Pagliaro, *Clinical Patient Data Files*).
83. Although generally efficacious for the relief of mild to moderate pain and the reduction of inflammation, the use of NSAIDS must be implemented with extreme caution in older adults because of the associated significant risks for: (1) cardiovascular toxicities (e.g., congestive heart failure or hypertension); (2) gastrointestinal toxicities (e.g., GI ulceration); and (3) renal toxicities (e.g., those associated with CKD) (Pagliaro & Pagliaro, 1983; Pagliaro & Pagliaro, *Clinical Patient Data Files*).

- Therapeutic touch;
- Trigger point injections of local anesthetics;
- Weight loss (for obese patients).

While it is beyond the scope of this text to discuss the strengths and weaknesses—and optimal clinical therapeutic applications of each of these pain relief approaches—we can categorically state that, over the years, we have successfully used each of these techniques[84] for the management of pain, in lieu of, or in conjunction with, the opiate analgesics. We also have found that the success of these approaches is largely dependent upon selecting the appropriate clinical context for their use with consideration of:

1. Pain location;
2. Pain severity;
3. Suspected cause of the pain;[85]
4. Concurrent physical and mental disorders;
5. The personal characteristics of each patient.

***Related Professional Reminder*: When appropriately selected, these approaches can result in diminished pain and a reduction in the opiate analgesic dosage. Thus, preventing, or at least significantly reducing, the risk for the development of opiate analgesic dependence or use disorder.**

Whenever considering opiate analgesic dosage and adjustments, or the implementation of auxiliary pain relief modalities, we use the opportunity to evaluate reasons to reduce or discontinue opiate analgesic pharmacotherapy. In this context, clinical patient outcome measures to consider, as suggested by HHS (Dowell, Jones, & Compton, 2019, p. 1), include:

- The patient's pain improves;
- The patient requests dosage reduction or discontinuation of opiate analgesic pharmacotherapy;
- The patient's pain and function are not meaningfully improved;
- The patient is receiving higher opiate analgesic doses without evidence of benefit from the higher dose;
- The patient has current evidence of opiate analgesic misuse;
- The patient experiences side effects that diminish quality of life or impair function;
- The patient experiences an overdose, or other serious event (e.g., hospitalization or injury), or has warning signs (e.g., confusion, sedation, or slurred speech) for an impending event;
- The patient is receiving prescription drugs (e.g., benzodiazepines) or has diagnosed medical conditions (e.g., advanced age, fall risk, kidney disease, liver disease, lung disease, or sleep apnea) that increases risk for adverse outcomes;
- The patient has been treated with opiate analgesics for a prolonged period (e.g., years) and the current benefit-harm balance is unclear.

84. Usually, through referral to clinicians who specialize in the specific modality (e.g., acupuncturists, chiropractors, clergy, hypo-therapists, or massage therapists).
85. Among older adults, common sources of pain include inflammation (e.g., inflammatory arthropathies or tissue injury), compression (e.g., low back pain), neurologic issues (e.g., headaches), and neuropathies (e.g., diabetic neuropathy or postherpetic neuralgia).

To help clinicians identify, a priori, the risk for opiate analgesic dependence or use disorder among patients who are prescribed opiate analgesics for the management of chronic pain, Webster and Webster (2005, p. 432) developed a brief screening tool, the "Opioid Risk Tool" (ORT):[86]

> The Opioid Risk Tool (ORT) is a brief, self-report screening tool designed for use with adult patients in primary care settings to assess risk for opioid abuse among individuals prescribed opioids for treatment of chronic pain. Patients categorized as high-risk are at increased likelihood of future abusive drug-related behavior. The ORT can be administered and scored in less than 1 minute and has been validated in both male and female patients, but not in non-pain populations.[87]

The ORT (Table 5.6) is a commonly used, patient self-administered, five-item test that can be quickly completed. It is generally administered during the patient's initial visit.

Eliminating the question dealing with preadolescent sexual abuse, Cheatle, Compton, and Dhingra (2019) revised and further developed the ORT. The revised ORT is now touted to be superior to the original ORT in predicting opiate analgesic dependence or use disorder among patients with chronic, nonmalignant pain who are receiving long-term opiate analgesic pharmacotherapy.

Additionally, as identified by Brott and Cascella (2020), several other tools have now been developed for clinical assistance in predicting opiate analgesic dependence or use disorder among patients with chronic, nonmalignant pain who are receiving long-term opiate analgesic pharmacotherapy. These tools include, the: "Diagnosis, Intractability, Risk, and Efficacy Score (DIRE)," "Screening Instrument for Substance Abuse Potential (SISAP)," and "Screener and Opioid Assessment for Patients with Pain" (SOAPP).

***Related Professional Reminder:* The abrupt discontinuation of opiate analgesic use, or the rapid reduction of an opiate analgesic dosage, may result in the opiate analgesic withdrawal syndrome among patients who are physically dependent on opiate analgesics (see the related discussion in the earlier pharmacology subsection, Undesired, or Harmful, Effects and Toxicities—"Opiate Analgesic Withdrawal Syndrome").[88] Consequently, we recommend a more gradual reduction of dosage—except in cases involving life-threatening issues, such as acute overdosage.**

Illicit/Recreational (Non-Medical) Prescription Use

As reported by the SAMHSA (2009, p. 1), based on national data:

> Nearly 2 million individuals in the U.S. have opioid abuse or dependence, with the majority reporting abuse of prescription opioids.

---

86. N.B. The safety and efficacy of the use of opiate analgesics for the treatment of chronic non-cancer pain is still widely debated. We, as noted earlier in this chapter and elsewhere, have consistently recommended that the use of opiate analgesics, particularly long-term high-dosage pharmacotherapy, should not be used for the treatment of chronic non-cancer pain.
87. N.B. Two separate studies (i.e., Barclay, Owens, & Blackhall, 2014; Ma, Horton, & Hwang, 2014) evaluated the utility of the ORT to help screen for abuse risk among cancer patients receiving prescription opiate analgesics for pain management. It is interesting to note that each study found that approximately 25% of their patient samples were deemed high-risk based on ORT results.
88. This withdrawal syndrome is also commonly accompanied by an acute exacerbation of any associated pain and, consequently, an increase in patient distress—including suicidal ideation.

Table 5.6 The Opioid Risk Tool (ORT)

This tool should be administered to patients upon an initial visit prior to beginning opioid therapy for pain management. A score of 3 or lower indicates low risk for future opioid abuse, a score of 4 to 7 indicates moderate risk for opioid abuse, and a score of 8 or higher indicates a high risk for opioid abuse.

	Female	**Male**
	Scoring Criteria	
	Circle each item that applies:	
FAMILY HISTORY OF SUBSTANCE ABUSE:		
• Alcohol	1	3
• Illegal drugs	2	3
• Rx drugs	4	4
PERSONAL HISTORY OF SUBSTANCE ABUSE:		
• Alcohol	3	3
• Illegal drugs	4	4
• Rx drugs	5	5
AGE BETWEEN 16–45 YEARS:	1	1
HISTORY OF PREADOLESCENT SEXUAL ABUSE:	3	0
PSYCHOLOGICAL DISEASE:		
• ADD, OCD, bipolar, schizophrenia	2	2
• Depression	1	1
Scoring totals		

Modified from: Webster & Webster, 2005.

Generally, most older adults appropriately use opiate analgesics as prescribed by their physicians for the management of acute pain and other indications (e.g., diarrhea or non-productive cough) and do not develop harmful patterns of use. However, other older adults inappropriately use prescribed opiate analgesics by using them more frequently and/or in larger amounts than prescribed. Additionally, still others illicitly obtain and nonmedically use prescription opiate analgesics. Consequently:

> The face of the nation's opioid epidemic increasingly is grey and wrinkled . . . while opioid abuse declined in younger groups between 2002 and 2014, the epidemic almost doubled among Americans over age 50.
>
> (Davidson, 2018, p. 1)

During the new millennium, the medical prescription of opiate analgesics significantly increased among every demographic in the U.S. (Brady, McCauley, & Back, 2016; Pagliaro & Pagliaro, 2009; Pagliaro & Pagliaro, *Clinical Patient Data Files*). Specific patient factors related to the medical prescription, and subsequent abuse of prescription opiate analgesics, include:

- Chronic, non-cancer pain, including arthritis and back pain;
- Concurrent affective disorders (e.g., depression);
- Current, acute moderate to severe pain;
- History of alcohol abuse;
- Inability to fall and/or stay asleep;
- Increased severity of pain. (Barth, Moran-Santa Maria, & Lawson, 2013; Jamison, Ross, & Michna, 2010; Shah, Hayes, & Martin, 2017; Tsui, Herman, & Kettavong, 2010)

In the U.S., older adults, particularly those who meet several of these factors, are significantly more likely to engage in the practice of "double-doctoring," or "physician shopping." This practice is commonly used by older adults to obtain multiple opiate analgesic prescriptions from several different prescribers for the same medical condition (e.g., back pain—real or feigned). In a comprehensive study of data obtained from over 146 million opioid prescriptions dispensed by 76% of U.S. retail pharmacies during 2008, McDonald and Carlson (2013) found that "doctor shoppers:"

- Comprised approximately 1% of all prescription purchases;
- On average, obtained 32 prescriptions for opiate analgesics;
- On average, filled their prescriptions for opiate analgesics at ten different pharmacies;
- Bought approximately 2% of all opiate analgesic prescriptions (4% of "weighed amounts");
- Often paid for their prescriptions in cash to avoid detection.

In addition, as identified by Stanos, Bruckenthal, and Barkin (2012, p. 683):

> A study of prescription opioid abusers in a drug rehabilitation program found that 80% tampered with opioid tablets to accelerate drug release by chewing the tablet or by administering the drug intranasally or intravenously.

Health Care Professionals Acting Unprofessionally[89]

Although a thorough discussion of this issue goes beyond the scope of this text, it would be negligent not to mention that some (fortunately, relatively few) corrupt and unethical health and social care providers (primarily from the professions of pharmacy and medicine) have played a major contributory role in the perpetuation of the opiate analgesic abuse epidemic in the U.S. during the new millennium. As identified by DuBois, Chibnall, and Anderson (2016, p. 457):

> Improper prescribing of controlled substances contributes to opioid addictions and death by overdose.

Dineen and DuBois (2016, p. 7) characterize these prescribers as being either "careless, corrupt, or compromised by impairment."

89. See also the related discussion in the later subsection, "Older Adult Involvement in Illicit Drug Dealing and Trafficking."

Medical and pharmacy boards[90] across the U.S. have routinely documented these relatively common transgressions regarding the inappropriate prescribing of opiate analgesic and filling of related prescriptions—usually based on pecuniary motives (Fox, 2018; Pagliaro & Pagliaro, *Clinical Patient Data Files*). As illustrated by the lay press:

> The more opioids doctors prescribe, the more money they make.
> (Kessler, Cohen, & Grise, 2018, p. 1)
>
> 16 doctors and medical professionals charged in fraud and opioid takedown in Texas.
> (Finnegan, 2019, p. 1)
>
> Doctor facing life in prison for thousands of opioid doses, contributing to crisis.
> (Rankin, 2019, p. 1)
>
> Doctor gets 40 years in prison for prescribing over 500,000 opioid doses.
> (Guardian Staff, 2019, p. 1)

Unfortunately, as we have routinely observed during over 40 years of both academic and clinical practice, the cited incidents are only the "tip of the iceberg." For example, in the vast majority of cases, related boards and colleges of medicine and pharmacy routinely, in over 90% of cases, dismiss all related complaints or simply issue a "warning" to the offending health care professional—sometimes with a minor fine or short period of "probationary" practice. In their systematic review of criminal and administrative cases involving "physicians charged with opioid analgesic prescription offenses" in the U.S., Goldenbaum, Christopher, and Gallagher (2008, p. 737) found that "criminal or administrative charges and sanctions for prescribing opioid analgesics are rare." Only in particularly egregious cases are more severe sanctions (e.g., revocation of "narcotic" prescribing privileges or removal from the professional practice register) imposed (Pagliaro & Pagliaro, *Clinical Patient Data Files*).[91]

Prescription Opiate Analgesics Commonly Abused by Older Adults

The four prescription opiate analgesics most commonly abused by older adults during the new millennium—from highest to lowest—are:

1. Oxycodone;
2. Hydrocodone;
3. Buprenorphine;
4. Fentanyl.

Each of these prescription opiate analgesics are presented and discussed in the following subsections along with new millennial trends in their use by older adults. Before proceeding, we think that it is germane and important to consider the finding of Schepis, Wastila, and Ammerman (2020) regarding the "motives" for prescription opiate analgesic misuse by

90. See also the related discussion in the Preface of this text regarding the profession of nursing.
91. Having served on several professional regulatory boards (e.g., Dentistry, Medicine, Nursing, Pharmacy, and Psychology) during our 40+ years of professional service, these issues and concerns are not new, nor unique, to medicine. Rather, they reflect those which have become implicit in the nature and practice of professional self-regulation—as noted by several authors (e.g., Bertkau, Halpern, & Yadla, 2005; Motluk, 2019; Pagliaro & Pagliaro, *Clinical Patient Data Files*).

older adults in the U.S. In their analysis of data from the *National Survey on Drug Use and Health* (NSDUH), a nationally representative U.S. survey, they found that:

> POM [prescription opioid misuse] motivated solely by physical pain relief increased from 35.1% in young adults to 65.4% in older adults; in older adults, 84.7% of POM episodes involved pain relief as a motive.
>
> (p. 2237)

Oxycodone

Oxycodone (OxyContin®) is one of the most widely abused prescription opiate analgesics in the U.S. (Cicero, Inciardi, & Munoz, 2005). Illicitly used to primarily achieve euphoric effects, or a "rush," and to prevent or manage the opiate analgesic withdrawal syndrome and associated toxicities, the abuse of oxycodone "skyrocketed" during the 1990s and has remained high ever since. It has been estimated that, during the new millennium, 99% of the world's production of oxycodone, as well as hydrocodone, was consumed in the U.S. (Winstock, 2016).

The extended-release formulation of oxycodone, "OxyContin®," was approved by the FDA in 1995. Although initially considered to have a lower abuse potential because of its slow-release properties—and marketed as such—its widespread use began in 2000 and continued throughout the first decade of the new millennium. Almost immediately, users discovered that crushing and "snorting" the extended-release tablets enabled them to achieve a rapid release of the OxyContin® and resultant high blood oxycodone levels (Aquina, Marques-Baptista, & Bridgeman, 2009; Cicero, Inciardi, & Munoz, 2005; Pagliaro & Pagliaro, 2009). In 2010, the most potent strength tablet of OxyContin® (i.e., 160 mg) was discontinued and a new formulation was introduced that made crushing and dissolving the extended-release tablets more difficult (MacLaren, 2015). These changes resulted in only a temporary and moderate degree of success in terms of decreasing OxyContin® abuse.

During the first decade of the new millennium, the use of oxycodone was highest in rural and suburban regions of the western U.S. (Cicero, Surratt, & Inciardi, 2007). In an earlier study, Carise, Dugosh, and McLellan (2007) analyzed data obtained from approximately 28,000 participants, who were admitted to 157 addiction treatment programs in the U.S., from 2001 to 2004. The researchers found that only approximately 5% used OxyContin® that was obtained predominantly from nonmedical sources. More recently, in an analysis of trends in the nonmedical use of OxyContin® in the U.S.—from 2000–2013—Jones, Muhuri, and Lurie (2017, p. 452) found that:

> In 2013, the percentage of past-year nonmedical use of OxyContin® among people 12 years of age and older in the United States was 0.5%.

Hydrocodone

Hydrocodone (e.g., Hycodan®, Hysingla ER®, and Vicodin®), like oxycodone, is another prescription opiate analgesic that is widely abused in the U.S. (Cicero, Inciardi, & Munoz, 2005). It is a semisynthetic opiate analgesic that can be derived from a number of precursors, including codeine, morphine, and thebaine. Hydrocodone is extensively metabolized in the liver, primarily by CYP3A4, to several metabolites, including the active metabolite, hydromorphone. When ingested, hydrocodone potency closely approaches that of ingested morphine or oral oxycodone and is approximately ten times greater than that of oral codeine (Oyler, Cone, & Joseph, 2000; Pagliaro & Pagliaro, 2004). Hydrocodone is commonly available for use in a combination analgesic product (i.e., Vicodin®) that contains both hydrocodone and acetaminophen.[92]

Between 2014 and 2015, the FDA approved two "extended-release" formulations of hydrocodone—Hysingla ER® and Zohydro ER®—for the medical management of chronic, severe pain (Extended-Release, 2014, 2015). To address the potential risk for the abuse of these products, they were formulated with several "abuse-deterrent" properties. For example, whether the tablets were coarsely or finely ground, the resultant powder was formulated to fall out of the nostrils when intranasally insufflated, or "snorted." In addition, when attempts were made to dissolve the tablets for IV injection, a viscous gel is formed that is difficult to inject. As part of a *Risk Evaluation and Mitigation Strategy* (REMS) program, the FDA also mandated that pharmaceutical manufacturers make training programs for the optimal use of these formulations available to prescribers.

Buprenorphine

Buprenorphine (Buprenex®) is a synthetic opiate analgesic that was synthesized in the late 1970s for the medical management of moderate to severe pain. Acting primarily as an agonist, it has a high affinity to bind to, and slowly separate from, mu receptors. Consequently, buprenorphine produces expected opiate analgesic agonist effects, particularly at low to moderate dosages. However, at higher dosages, it can reach a ceiling effect and, subsequently, acts as an opiate analgesic antagonist (Buprenorphine, 2016).

Buprenorphine also acts as an antagonist at kappa receptors. Because of its mixed agonist/antagonist actions, it is FDA approved for the medical management of acute opiate analgesic detoxification, stabilization, and long-term maintenance of resumed nonuse of opiate analgesics (Connery, 2015; Greenwald, Comer, & Fiellin, 2014; Hard, 2014; Soyka, 2015) (see the related discussion in the later "Pharmacotherapy" section). Naloxone (see the related discussion in the earlier pharmacology subsection, Undesired, or Harmful, Effects and Toxicities—"Opiate Analgesic Overdosage/Unintentional Poisoning") is generally combined with a sublingual formulation of buprenorphine (e.g., Suboxone®, sublingual film; Zubsolv®, sublingual tablet) to minimize the risk for buprenorphine diversion or abuse (Smith, Bailey, & Woody, 2007).

Combination buprenorphine and naloxone continues to be diverted and illicitly used in the U.S. primarily to self-manage the signs and symptoms of the opiate analgesic withdrawal syndrome (Schuman-Olivier, Albanese, & Nelson, 2010; Yokell, Zaller, & Green, 2011). Those, who use buprenorphine tend to be younger and of European descent (Pagliaro & Pagliaro, *Clinical Patient Data Files*). Among buprenorphine users, who seek drug and substance abuse treatment in the U.S., 6% reported injecting buprenorphine to get "high" (Cicero, Surratt, & Inciardi, 2007). Interestingly, whereas buprenorphine users are more likely to be "injection drug users," those who use the buprenorphine/naloxone combination product are more likely to be "non-injection drug users" (Bazazi, Yokell, & Fu, 2011). Dart (2011) found

92. It is also commonly available in the combination antitussive (i.e., Hycodan®), which contains hydrocodone bitartrate and homatropine hydrobromide.

that 45.5% of "intravenous" buprenorphine users and 16.3% of combination buprenorphine/naloxone users reported use within the previous month.

The abuse of buprenorphine, particularly combination buprenorphine/naloxone, is significantly limited in the U.S. by the ready availability—"on the street"—of high-quality heroin. As found by Cicero, Ellis, and Surratt (2014b, p. 98):

> Buprenorphine is rarely preferred for its inherent euphorigenic properties, but rather serves as a substitute for other drugs, particularly heroin, or as a drug used, preferable to methadone, to self-medicate withdrawal sickness or wean off opioids.

(See also the related discussion of buprenorphine in the later subsection—"Treating Older Adult Opiate Analgesic Dependence or Use Disorder.")

Fentanyl

Fentanyl is an extremely potent prescription opiate analgesic that is 50 to 100 times more potent than morphine (see Table 5.2). It is currently approved by the FDA for the management of surgical/postoperative pain, severe pain, and breakthrough cancer pain.[93]

Fentanyl is licitly available in eight different formulations in various dosages that are produced by pharmaceutical manufacturers and dispensed by pharmacists:

1. Soluble buccal film (Onsolis®);
2. Effervescent buccal tablet (Fentora®), that uses the OraVescent® drug delivery system;
3. Injectable formulation for IM or IV use (Sublimaze®);
4. Intranasal spray (Lazanda®), available in both aqueous solution and pectin-based mucus-adhesive system;
5. Sublingual spray (Subsys®);
6. Sublingual tablet (Abstral® or Vellofent®);
7. Transdermal delivery system (Duragesic®), designed to continuously deliver a specific dosage of fentanyl over a period of 72 hours (i.e., "fentanyl patch"), as well as a relatively newer "iontophoretic transdermal" system (Ionsys®);
8. Transmucosal lozenge for buccal absorption (Actiq®), a solid drug matrix on a handle (i.e., "fentanyl lollipop"), that, in the event of signs and symptoms of overdosage, facilitates removal of the lozenge from the mouth.

Fentanyl is less often prescribed for non-hospitalized, or outpatients, because of its high potency and associated risk for overdosage. However, illicitly manufactured fentanyl is readily available and easily obtained "on the street" in the U.S.—the current primary source for this "prescription" opiate analgesic. In this context of use, illicitly produced fentanyl is generally:

1. Primarily produced in China—or in the U.S. from precursor chemicals that are predominantly manufactured in and imported from China (often by mail) (DEA, 2020);[94]

93. Fentanyl is also indicated for the adjuvant management of general anesthesia. For use in major surgeries and at higher dosages, fentanyl requires the concurrent use of artificial ventilation.
94. N.B. Perhaps surprisingly, most of these mail shipments are: (1) less than 1 kg in weight; and (2) over 90% pure (DEA, 2020).

2. Almost always clandestinely mixed with street heroin by opiate analgesic dealers prior to its sale—without the consent or knowledge of the buyer/user (Gladden et al., 2016; Pagliaro & Pagliaro, *Clinical Patient Data Files*; Peterson et al., 2016);
3. Also produced in Mexico, it is usually transported—often by mail[95]—across the U.S./Mexican border, where it is distributed throughout the U.S. by Mexican transnational drug cartels (e.g., the New Generation Jalisco and Sinaloa cartels);
4. Bought and sold at the "wholesale" level, in 10-gram units that are customarily referred to as "fingers."

Fentanyl, because of its potency and variety of available formulations, has been widely abused in the U.S. It also is often clandestinely: (1) added to heroin to increase the potency and "kick" of heroin; and (2) falsely represented and sold as alprazolam, hydrocodone, oxycodone, and other drugs and substances of abuse. As noted by the NIDA, "The fake pills are much cheaper than the real versions" (NDA, 2016, p. 1).

More importantly, because buyers are generally unaware of what they are purchasing, "hundreds of people have overdosed on fentanyl across the nation since 2013, often because of using heroin that has been 'laced' with the much stronger substance" (NIDA, 2015b, p. 1). Consequently, drug-related overdosages have significantly increased during the second decade of the new millennium. As reported by Seth et al. (2018), the fentanyl-related deaths increased 100% in the U.S. from 2015 to 2016. O'Donnell, Halpin, and Mattson (2017), in their analysis for the CDC of "5,152 opioid-overdosage deaths in 10 states during July-December 2016," found that over 50% involved fentanyl (p. 1197).[96]

A warning shared by a current heroin user in regard to fentanyl use:

> Be careful. It's got a lotta bodies on it [i.e., it's so strong its killing people].
>
> (Carroll, Marshall, & Rich, 2017, pp. 136–137)

We now turn to the illicit opiate analgesic, "Heroin."

Illicit Heroin Use

Heroin (diacetylmorphine) was first synthesized at St. Mary's hospital in London in 1874. Soon, thereafter, it was produced and marketed by the German pharmaceutical company, Bayer. In the U.S., heroin was extensively used at the end of the 19th century to treat the "great army of suffering—veterans of the U.S. Civil War, who, as a result of

95. Increasingly, starting at the beginning of the second decade of the new millennium, Mexican drug cartels have been producing wholesale quantities of "illicit fentanyl pills" and smuggling them into the U.S. (DEA, 2020).
96. N.B. Because of its physical characteristics, it is much easier to add fentanyl to powdered heroin (e.g., "China White") than to "black tar heroin"—which is a significantly less refined "tarry, opium-like substance." Consequently, fentanyl overdosages are much more likely to occur in areas of the U.S. where powdered heroin is predominantly available (e.g., the east coast) and less common in areas of the U.S. where "black tar heroin" is predominantly available (e.g., the southwest region). As noted by a young adult heroin user who wanted to avoid fentanyl use because of its associated increased risk for fatal overdosage:

> Black tar heroin I feel safer doing. It's harder to cut. It's not powder. Powder you can add anything to. . . . Black tar heroin, in order to cut it, you have to do all this stuff to it, cook it, and it's a lot harder to cut, so I feel safer doing that
>
> (Carroll et al., 2017, p. 140).

the use of morphine for the treatment of their painful war injuries, including amputations, had become addicted to morphine. Interestingly, at that time, heroin was marketed and believed to be a cure for "morphinism" (i.e., morphine dependence) (Pagliaro & Pagliaro, 2004).

This subsection presents and discusses illicit heroin and opium use among older adults during the new millennium with attention to: (1) the extent and patterns of heroin use in the U.S.; and (2) older adult involvement in drug dealing and trafficking.

Extent and Patterns of Heroin Use in the U.S

Across the U.S., during the new millennium, the ready availability of purer, powdered heroin—rather than the more commonly available, and less pure, black-tar heroin—resulted in:

1. Increased accessibility to heroin;
2. Lower street cost per dose;
3. Increased intranasal use (i.e., "sniffing" or "snorting");
4. Increased use among older adults.

(Chhatre, Cook, & Mallik, 2017; Huhn, Strain, & Tompkins, 2018; Niles, Gudin, & Radcliff, 2021; Pagliaro & Pagliaro, 2004; Pagliaro & Pagliaro, *Clinical Patient Data Files*; Tarabar & Nelson, 2003)

Old Misbelief: In the U.S., the typical opiate analgesic "addict" is a young man of non-European descent with a criminal history, and who is often "on welfare" or "living on the street."

False. In fact, as identified by Cicero, Ellis, and Surratt (2014a, p. 821):

> The abuse of heroin has migrated from low-income urban areas with large minority populations to more affluent suburban and rural areas with primarily white populations.

Additionally, Marsh, Park, and Lin (2018, p. 79) noted that:

> Women are increasing heroin use at a faster rate than men [in the U.S.].

The rapid rise in heroin use has been largely due to the "unanticipated consequences" of government interventions[97] set in the context of a "perfect storm" (i.e., the convergence of several individual factors that, together, strongly encouraged and supported increases in heroin use). As reported by the National Institute on Drug Abuse (NIDA, 2014, p. 1):

> For a few years, NIDA and other Federal partners have been sounding the alarm over the rise in heroin use, particularly among people with addictions to prescription opioids who switch to heroin because it is cheaper and easier to obtain. Half a million Americans are now

97. Specifically, responding to an epidemic of opiate analgesic use, the FDA issued several rules, and Congress passed several laws, intended to limit the illicit production and often inappropriate over-prescription, of opiate analgesics, particularly oxycodone (OxyContin®). (See the related discussion in the previous section, "Common Prescription Opiate Analgesic Abused by Older Adults—"Oxycodone.")

> addicted to heroin, and four out of five recent heroin initiates had previously used prescription opioids non-medically.

Similarly, Case and Deaton (2015, p. 15081) identified that:

> Tighter controls on opioid prescription brought some substitution into heroin and, in this period, the U.S. saw falling prices and rising quality of heroin, as well as availability in areas where heroin had been previously largely unknown.

A decade into the new millennium, Holscher, Reissner, and Di Furia (2010) identified that, in the U.S., there was no gender difference between men and women regarding the age of onset of regular, long-term heroin use.[98] Regarding older adults, Rosen, Hunsaker, and Albert (2011, p. 2) found that:

> Heroin is already the second most frequently cited primary substance of abuse (after alcohol) for all admissions to substance abuse treatment by adults over the age of 50. . . . Part of the reason for this increase in heroin addiction amongst older adults is the high rates of substance abuse in the baby-boom cohort.

In addition, pooling data from the annual *National Survey on Drug Use and Health* (NSDUH) for 2002 through 2011, Muhuri, Gfroerer, and Davies (2013, p. 1) found that the:

> Heroin incidence rate was 19 times higher among those who reported prior nonmedical pain reliever [i.e., prescription opiate analgesic] use than those who did not.

Older Adult Involvement in Illicit Drug Dealing and Trafficking

Older adults, despite their significant involvement in the opiate analgesic epidemic in the U.S.—as both users and victims—are generally not as significantly involved in opiate analgesic drug dealing and trafficking as are younger-aged cohorts. However, several related cases have been reported in the literature. For example:

> Federal immigration authorities seized 1.2 kilos of fentanyl—enough to kill hundreds of thousands of people—from a former sheriff's deputy and his son in West Virginia as part of an ongoing narcotics investigation, an Immigration and Customs Enforcement (ICE) press release says.
>
> 45-year-old Dale McCallister and his 76-year-old father, Larry McCallister—a retired Cabell County deputy sheriff—have been indicted "with various drug and gun crimes" after federal agents seized around 1.2 kilograms of fentanyl, 300 grams of methamphetamine, over $8,000 in cash, and a .357 magnum revolver, the release says. $4,000 of the seized cash was from an earlier undercover purchase of fentanyl.
>
> (Madden, 2019, p. 1)

> An 81-year-old woman was arrested on Wednesday after allegedly attempting to smuggle 92 pounds of heroin across the U.S.-Mexico border.
>
> (Merrett, 2018, p. 1)

98. Research in this area often presents seemingly contradictory results (i.e., that men still significantly outnumber women in terms of heroin use in the U.S.). However, these apparent discrepancies are largely related to study design and sampling procedures (e.g., sampling within specific ethnic communities or specific age groups or variable definitions of heroin use from daily use to lifetime use).

Older adults are at particular risk to:

1. Act as "mules" in direct response to financial pressures (e.g., living on a fixed retirement income);
2. Be targeted and victimized by Internet and telephone phishing scams.

As identified by the Canada Border Services Agency (CBSA):

> These scams are aimed at seducing individuals by influencing emotional vulnerability. The most common are romance scams, inheritance scams, and offering fake business opportunities which include mandatory travel and paid expenses.
>
> (Harris, 2018, p. 1)

The concealment and transport of illicit drugs and substances of abuse across high-security ports of entry (e.g., airport customs and immigration screens) by these older adults usually involves one of several common methods:

1. Hiding illicit drugs and substances of abuse within the lining of their clothes and luggage, as well as vehicles (e.g., car door, trunk, and upholstery);
2. Hiding illicit drugs and substances within secret cabinets, under floors, or other "safe places" in their boats, cars, planes, and trucks;
3. Hiding illicit drugs and substances by dissolving them in a licit liquid—alcohol or gasoline;
4. Hiding illicit drugs and substances within the body by "body packing."

Body packing involves placing illicit drugs and substances within the body. In this method, the drugs and substances of abuse are usually placed into supposedly airtight, water-tight packets (e.g., balloons, condoms, and latex glove fingers). After the illicit drugs and substances of abuse are placed in the packet, a knot is tied, and the packet is placed into another empty packet and tied—for extra safety. The filled packets are either swallowed or digitally inserted into the vagina or rectum.

The rapid detection of drug packets that are concealed in body cavities is necessary to both:

- Decrease illicit drug transportation (i.e., in a forensic context);
- Adequately address the clinical needs of older adults who present in the ED with signs and symptoms of potential drug toxicity or overdosage, which may be related to the internal leaking of concealed body packings.

Typically, X-rays of the abdomen are used to facilitate the identification and approximate number of concealed illicit drug or substance abuse packets. As noted by Abedzadeh, Iqbal, and Al Bastaki (2019, p. 632):

> One of the noninvasive, rapid, and widely available radiological examinations to rule out a body packer is plan abdominal X-ray. It is a relative accessible and low-cost method for screening and diagnosing body packers with accuracy of 40%-90%.

However, because newer packaging and masking methods can decrease the detection rate associated with the use of plain abdominal x-rays, when possible, the use of a CT abdominal examination is noted to be significantly more accurate in detecting body packers—although it delivers comparatively high radiation doses (Abedzadeh et al. (2019).

Before proceeding it should be noted that older adults do not function only as "drug mules"—in the context of illicit opiate analgesic trafficking—but also as "for profit dealers."

> ***Related Professional Reminder*****:** ***Older adults in the U.S. of all ages and socioeconomic status—including pharmacists and physicians—have been and are currently involved in the distribution and sale (i.e., trafficking) of opiate analgesics. Consequently, factors such as age, gender, race, and socioeconomic status should not be relied upon to decrease suspicion of involvement in drug trafficking.***

> An 81-year-old Delaware County pharmacist is accused of selling drugs to at least two women in exchange for sexual services. A review from the DEA revealed that the pharmacy was the largest purchaser of oxycodone, fentnayl and related drug products in the 19063 zip code, according to officials.
>
> (Chang, 2021, pp. 1, 3)

The following are a few related additional examples that have been obtained from recent DEA Press Releases:

> Michael Don Robertson, 68, a former Anchorage psychiatrist, was sentenced on January 6, 2021, by the U.S, District Court. . . . Robertson issued 465 prescriptions of meperidine to 30 different recipients, totaling 32,109 meperidine pills, knowing that the recipients did not truly need the medication for legitimate medical purposes. The investigation revealed that Robertson issued the meperidine prescriptions as part of a conspiracy in which the recipients filled the meperidine prescriptions and, then, distributed the meperidine to Robertson. In exchange for the recipients diverting the meperidine to Roberson, Robertson provided prescriptions for controlled substances, including fentanyl and oxycodone, to the recipients.
>
> (Tarentino & Underwood, 2021, p. 1)

> Agents arrested Perry Funchess, 56, and Jamal Johnson, 50, both of Brooklyn, New York after . . . agents and officers recovered the two bags, which appeared to contain approximately seven and a half kilograms of suspected fentanyl and heroin pressed into brick form (over 16 pounds) and more than 50,000 filled individual dose glassine envelopes suspected to contain heroin and fentanyl.
>
> (Donovan & Mulvey, 2021, p. 2)

> Thomas Parker III, aka "June," age 52, of Washington, D.C., pleaded guilty yesterday to federal charges. . . . Parker and his co-conspirators distributed heroin, fentanyl, and powder and crack cocaine to drug users and distributors in the Maryland and D.C. area.
>
> (Forget, 2021a, p. 1)

> Keith Jordan, also known as "Knowledge," 52 of Waterbury, was sentenced today by U.S. District Judge. . . . Court documents revealed that Jordan was receiving large quantities of heroin from various suppliers and selling the drug to other drug distributors and several street-level customers.
>
> (Boyle & Desmond, 2021, p. 1)

> Alexis Garcia Cabrera, 51, of Newark, is charged with possessing over 400 grams of fentanyl with intent to distribute. Law enforcement officers executed a search warrant at Garcia Cabrera's residence and found multiple freezer-type bags containing suspected heroin as well as a large quantity of loose narcotics that were in the processing stage. Law enforcement officers also found equipment used to process and "cut" heroin, including grinders, sifters, and chemical cutting agents, and large quantities of materials designed to package heroin for street-level distribution, including 1,000 glassine envelops. Agents located multiple "bricks,"

> or packages of 50 individual doses, of suspected heroin, which are intended for street-level distribution. Subsequent lab tests revealed that the suspected heroin also contained fentanyl.
>
> (Gibson & McMahon, 2021, p. 1)

> Two of the five defendants charged as part of a conspiracy that trafficked heroin from Maryland to Virginia leading to at least one fatal and one non-fatal overdose were sentenced yesterday in U.S. District Court. . . . Norma Lynda Kidwell, 56, was sentenced to 100 months in federal prison. Craig Allen Kidwell, 54 was sentenced yesterday to 100 months in federal prison.
>
> (Forget, 2021b, p. 1)

> A federal grand jury returned a two-count indictment today against Alfredo Garcia Jr, 27, Eva Romero, 53 [Garcia's mother] and Leo Torres, 30. Garcia, Romero, and Torres conspired to smuggle heroin and methamphetamine into the Fresno County Jail for further distribution among inmates.
>
> (Rettig, 2021, p. 1)

> U.S. District Judge George L. Russell, III today sentenced David Robinson, age 51, of Baltimore, Maryland, to 171 months in federal prison, followed by three years of supervised release, for the federal charges of conspiracy to distribute oxycodone and alprazolam and for murder for hire. . . . Robinson, formerly a licensed pharmacist who owned and operated the Frankford Family Pharmacy . . . pleaded guilty to a federal drug conspiracy involving the distribution of oxycodone and alprazolam outside the scope of professional practice and not for a legitimate medical purpose.
>
> (Forget, 2021c, p. 1)

ASSESSMENT AND DIAGNOSIS OF OPIATE ANALGESIC DEPENDENCE OR USE DISORDER

The assessment and diagnosis of opiate analgesic dependence or use disorder among older adults involves an initial clinical interview during which:

1. Opiate analgesic use is established;
2. Answers are obtained to questions concerning both the qualitative and quantitative nature of reported opiate analgesic use (e.g., particular opiate analgesic[s] used, history or pattern of use [amount and frequency of use, route of administration, or method of use], attempts to quit, or previous treatment approaches);
3. Answers are obtained to questions concerning harmful consequences of use (e.g., physical, psychological, and social harm, including arrest[s], divorce, effects on health, job loss, related amount of money spent, and restrictions on grandchild visits).

Assessment and diagnosis may also involve the use of: (1) DSM-5 criteria and scoring for the opioid use disorder (OUD) and its severity; (2) other approaches, including the use of SBIRT; and (3) use of appropriate quick-screen psychometric tests.

DSM-5 Criteria for Detection and Severity of OUD

OUD is a creation of the DSM-5 (APA, 2013). It combines the previous DSM-IV diagnoses of "opioid dependence" and "opioid abuse" with the deletion of a single item, "legal problems"

(Compton, Dawson, & Goldstein, 2013; Hasin, O'Brien, & Auriacombe, 2013).[99] The eleven criteria measure four factors:

1. Impaired control (criteria 1 through 4);
2. Social impairment (criteria 5 through 7);
3. Risky use (criteria 8 and 9);
4. Pharmacological properties (criteria 10 and 11) (Table 5.7, see p. 446).

A contextual predicate of the DSM-5 diagnosis of OUD is that "legitimate medical use" of the opiate analgesics invalidates the diagnosis (APA, 2013). We take extreme umbrage with this biased, dated, and profoundly unscientific view of opiate analgesic dependence or use disorder. Quite simply, "physical" dependence or use disorder, is a biophysiological process (i.e., is characterized by a physical withdrawal syndrome when regular long-term opiate analgesic medical or nonmedical/illicit use is: (1) abruptly discontinued; and (2) immediately relieved when use is resumed) that has no inherent moral or psychological basis—it has no conscious component. Thus, the development of physical dependence equally occurs whether an opiate analgesic is used as prescribed by a physician for a legitimate medical indication or for a nonmedical/illicit purpose. Consequently, when we use the DSM-5 criteria for OUD, we simply ignore this aspect—for example, regarding the DSM footnotes for criteria 10, "tolerance," and criteria 11, "withdrawal" (Pagliaro & Pagliaro, *Clinical Patient Data Files*).

Screening, Brief Intervention, and Referral to Treatment (SBIRT)

SBIRT[100] is widely endorsed by many groups. Unfortunately, the use of SBIRT—particularly to screen older adults for heroin and other opiate analgesic dependence or use disorder(s)—has not been widely adopted. This lack of adoption is likely due, to a significant extent, to the lack of available, quick-screen psychometric tests specifically formulated for detecting opiate analgesic dependence or use disorder among older adults. Additionally, it may also be due to implicit ageism in which many clinicians do not typically "visualize" an older adult as being an "opiate addict" (Pagliaro & Pagliaro, *Clinical Patient Data Files*).

In this context, Thiesset, Schliep, and Stokes (2020, p. 200) conducted an interesting research study using a random sample of 368 surgical patients. In the premise of their published study, they noted that:

1. "A majority of surgical patients are prescribed an opiate analgesic for pain management;"
2. "Patients who used opiate analgesics prior to surgery are at increased risk of developing OUD after surgery."

Subsequently, they found and reported that:

1. Preoperative screening for opioid use is uncommon;
2. Only 7% of patients were screened preoperatively for opioid use.

---

99. The concordance between DSM-IV "opioid dependence" and DSM-5 "opioid use disorder" is high. For example, Boscarino, Rukstalis, and Hoffman (2011) reported an associated kappa value of 0.87.
100. For a detailed discussion of SBIRT, see Chapter 1, *Alcohol*.

Table 5.7 DSM-5 Criteria and Scoring for Opioid Use Disorder

ITEM #	DSM-5 CRITERIA & SCORING
1.	Opioids are often taken in larger amounts or over a longer period than was intended
2.	There is a persistent desire or unsuccessful efforts to cut down or control opioid use
3.	A great deal of time is spent in activities necessary to obtain the opioid, use the opioid, or recover from its effects
4.	Craving or a strong desire to use opioids
5.	Recurrent opioid use resulting in a failure to fulfill major role obligations at work, school, or home
6.	Continued opioid use despite having persistent or recurrent social or interpersonal problems caused or exacerbated by the effects of opioids
7.	Important social, occupational, or recreational activities are given up or reduced because of opioid use
8.	Recurrent opioid use in situations in which it is physically hazardous
9.	Continued opioid use despite knowledge of having a persistent or recurrent physical or psychological problem that is likely to have been caused or exacerbated by opioids
10.	Tolerance,* as defined by either of the following: (a) Need for markedly increased amounts of opioids to achieve intoxication or desired effect (b) Markedly diminished effect with continued use of the same amount of opioid
11.	Withdrawal,* as manifested by either of the following: (a) Characteristic opioid withdrawal syndrome (b) The same opioid (or a closely related) opioid is taken to relieve or avoid withdrawal symptoms
SCORING	According to DSM criteria: The presence of at least two of these symptoms within a 12-month period indicates an opioid use disorder (OUD). Additionally, the severity of the OUD is defined as: "Mild," the presence of two or three symptoms; "Moderate," the presence of four or five symptoms; or "Severe," the presence of six or more symptoms.

Source: APA, 2013.

* Patients who are prescribed opioid medications for analgesia may exhibit these two criteria (withdrawal and tolerance) but would not necessarily be considered to have a substance use disorder (i.e., the criterion is not met if the opioid is taken solely under appropriate medical supervision).

They also found and reported that the most common perceived barriers to preoperative screening were:

- Insufficient clinical time;
- Logistics of who should screen/not required as part of their clinical workflow;
- Not perceiving screening as a priority;
- Lack of expertise in the area of chronic opioid use and OUD.

Quick-Screen Psychometric Tests for Detecting Older Adult Opiate Analgesic Dependence or Use Disorder

Other chapters of this text generally include an overview and discussion of relevant quick-screen psychometric tests that have been developed for the particular abusable psychotropic(s) presented in the chapter. Unfortunately, no such tests have been specifically developed and evaluated for the detection of opiate analgesic dependence or use disorder among older adults. However, the *Severity of Dependence Scale* (SDS) has been developed—as the name implies—not to detect, but to help generally ascertain the "severity" of abusable psychotropic dependence or use disorder(s) (Gossop, Drake, & Griffiths, 1995).

The SDS is short and easy to administer and has been endorsed by several organizations, including, the WHO. The scale also has been evaluated with several different abusable psychotropics (e.g., Woody, Cottler, & Cacciola, 1993). Additionally, it has been tested with older adults, 65 to 90 years of age, and was determined to be a valid and reliable tool (Cheng, Siddiqui, & Gossop, 2019). (See Chapter 2, *Amphetamines and Cocaine*, for a copy of the SDS and additional related discussion.)

Other, more recently developed screening tests, such as *The Rapid Opioid Dependence Screen* (RODS), developed by Wickersham, Azar, and Cannon (2015), have been suggested for use. However, outside of the developers, these tests generally have not been widely used or validated by others. Consequently, very little psychometric test data are available and, thus, at least at this time, we cannot recommend their use in the context of assessment and diagnosis of opiate analgesic dependence or use disorder among older adults.

TREATING OLDER ADULT OPIATE ANALGESIC DEPENDENCE OR USE DISORDER

In their "retrospective, comparative effectiveness research study" of 40,885 individuals with OUD—of which 40% were 54 years of age and older—Wakeman, Larochelle, and Ameli (2020), found, overall, that:

- 59% received non-intensive outpatient counseling (i.e., "non-intensive behavioral health" only);
- 16% received inpatient detoxification or residential services;
- 13% received buprenorphine or methadone pharmacotherapy;
- 5% received intensive outpatient counseling (i.e., "intensive behavioral health");
- 5% received no documented treatment;
- 2% received naltrexone pharmacotherapy.

Meta-analyses regarding specific treatment outcomes for opiate analgesic dependence or use disorder for sample groups of adults—both young and old—have been completed by several researchers (e.g., Carew & Corniskey, 2018). However, most of these studies failed to separate adults by age (e.g., younger adults versus older adults). Consequently, we are currently left with a situation in which treatment approaches for older adults must be guided primarily by the outcomes of these combined samples. With these limitations in mind, we present current findings for the treatment of opiate analgesic dependence or use disorder for older adults, particularly: (1) pharmacotherapeutic approaches; and (2) psychotherapeutic/counseling approaches.

Pharmacotherapeutic Approaches[101]

Advances in the pharmacotherapeutic treatment of opiate analgesic dependence or use disorder are quite diverse. For example, the use of: methadone (Dolophine®) for opiate analgesic maintenance (i.e., methadone maintenance) (Fareed, Casarella, & Amar, 2010); and buprenorphine (Buprenex®) as an aid for opiate analgesic detoxification (Flassing, 2010; Kovas, McFarland, & McCarty, 2007). Other related pharmacotherapeutic approaches for the treatment of opiate analgesic dependence or use disorder are presented and discussed in the following sections:[102]

1. Opiate analgesic abuse-deterrent technologies;
2. Opiate analgesic maintenance, replacement, or substitution;
3. Opiate analgesic withdrawal syndrome;[103]
4. Opiate analgesic relapse prevention.

Abuse-Deterrent Technologies

An area of active pharmaceutical research and development over the new millennium has involved the pharmaceutical alteration of: (1) dosage formulations;[104] and (2) drug delivery systems. These efforts are aimed at both discouraging the use of a particular drug or substance of abuse, or its method of use, and to avoid or reduce associated harm. As noted by the FDA:

> Most abuse deterrent technologies developed to date are intended to make manipulation more difficult or to make abuse of the manipulated product less attractive or less rewarding.
> (USDHHS, 2015, p. 3)

> Old Misbelief: Newer altered drug formulations totally prevent the abuse of opiate analgesics while maintaining their desired pain-relieving effects.

False. In fact, the FDA-approved pharmaceutical formulations, which have been developed and implemented for use in the U.S., are designed to "deter" abuse. They are not designed to make use impossible. Thus, they do not fully prevent abuse. However, there is growing evidence that supports their efficacy in terms of deterring, or reducing, some opiate analgesic abuse.

---

101. The clinical efficacy of selected pharmacotherapies is significantly enhanced by concurrent psychotherapy/counseling. To achieve optimal outcomes, we also consistently recommend the coordinated application of both approaches (see the related discussion in the later subsection, "Psychotherapy/Counseling").
102. For the treatment of opiate analgesic overdosage/unintentional poisoning, see the earlier subsection, Treating Older Adult Opiate Analgesic Overdosage/Unintentional Poisoning—"Naloxone Pharmacotherapy."
103. For the treatment of the opiate analgesic withdrawal syndrome, see the earlier subsection, "Treating the Opiate Analgesic Withdrawal Syndrome."
104. These formulations, which differ significantly, are often referred to as "abuse-deterrent formulations," or ADFs (Schaeffer, 2012).

As a result of the steep increase in abuse, misuse, and both fatal and non-fatal overdoses involving prescription opioids in the U.S., over the new millennium (see the earlier related discussion in this chapter), the focus of developmental research within the area of "abuse-deterrent formulations" has been primarily directed at opiate analgesic abuse, including the preparation of "tamper resistant formulations."[105] Several examples of abuse-deterrent technologies and formulations are presented and discussed in the following subsections. We begin with a highly successful approach that involved the development of combination buprenorphine/naloxone sublingual tablets (Bunavail® and Suboxone®) to prevent the illicit intravenous use of buprenorphine. Other examples of this approach include EMBEDA®, as well as oxycodone, in controlled release/extended release (CR/ER) formulations (e.g., OxyContin® CR/ER).

Buprenorphine/Naloxone Sublingual Tablets

Illicit IV use of buprenorphine has been significantly reduced in the U.S. with an abuse-deterrent pharmacological/pharmaceutical strategy. The addition of naloxone to the buprenorphine sublingual tablet formulation prevents illicit intravenous use of buprenorphine by an interesting, and rather simple, mechanism.

When used sublingually, the naloxone is poorly absorbed and, thus, has virtually no effect on the analgesic action of buprenorphine—as clinically intended. However, if the combination tablet is illicitly crushed, dissolved, and injected IV, the naloxone is immediately and completely absorbed blocking the desired action of the buprenorphine at the endogenous CNS opiate analgesic receptors (Connery, 2015; Hard, 2014). (See also the related discussion in the later subsection, "Opiate Analgesic Maintenance, Replacement, or Substitution—Buprenorphine/Naloxone Combination.")

Embeda®

Embeda® is an extended-release combination of morphine and naltrexone in capsular form. Within the capsule are morphine pellets that contain a core of sequestered naltrexone. The analysis of post-marketing data regarding undesired, or harmful, effects and toxicities associated with approximately 97,000 prescriptions for EMBEDA®, indicated a significant reduction in abuse (Badalamenti, Buckley, & Smith, 2012).

This finding was consistent with the results of a related naltrexone bioavailability study by Johnson and Setnik (2011), who found that when the capsules are crushed, the naltrexone is immediately released "mitigating morphine-induced effects," including

---

105. As noted by Passik, Hays, and Eisner (2006), in their study sample of adults who abused prescription drugs and who were entering drug rehabilitation, 80% reported tampering with prescription opiate analgesic tablets by chewing them or administering them by intranasal or intravenous routes. Interestingly, in another laboratory observational study of adults—who abused prescription opiate analgesics and were tasked with attempting to modify "crush-resistant" opiate analgesic prescription formulations to enable self-administration by either the intranasal or intravenous routes—Vosburg, Jones, and Manubay (2012, p. 206) found that:

> No particularly unique tools were requested for tampering purposes. Intranasal abusers worked primarily with a hammer, razor, and wax paper; while intravenous abusers primarily employed a razor, spoon, lighter, hammer, syringe and cotton, cookers, and water.

related "drug liking" scores (p. 391). However, as emphasized by Smith (2011), in a related review: "No product is likely to be abuse-proof in the hands of clever and determined abusers" (p. 1111).

Oxycodone CR/ER

In August 2010, oxycodone CR/ER—including OxyContin®—tablets were reformulated in the U.S. with a polymer coating to reduce non-oral methods of use. When the tablets are crushed and, subsequently, attempted to be dissolved in water for intranasal or IV use, the polymer coating turns into a gel that deters intranasal and IV use.

As identified by Butler, Cassidy, and Chilcoat (2013, p. 351), preliminary analysis of "a sentinel surveillance sample of 140,496 individuals assessed for substance abuse treatment at 357 U.S. centers" indicated that the reformulated product was associated with a significant reduction (i.e., 41%) in abuse when compared to the original oxycodone product. However, the same research group—in a subsequent study involving "232,874 adults, at 437 facilities"—failed to detect a significant reduction in the abuse of the oxycodone CR/ER product (Cassidy, DasMahapatra, & Black, 2014, p. 440).

In another study, Havens, Leukefeld, and DeVeaugh-Geiss (2014), utilizing structured interviews of 189 adults with histories of opiate analgesic abuse, reported "mixed" results regarding the abuse of the OxyContin® CR/ER) formulations (i.e., significant amounts of abuse, but significantly lower amounts than reported for the original, immediate-release [IR] formulations). Others (e.g., Michna, Kirson, & Shei, 2014; Sellers, Perrino, & Colucci, 2013) have reported similar findings.

Maintenance, Replacement, or Substitution

Maintenance, replacement, or substitution (MRS) pharmacotherapy[106] for opiate analgesic dependence or use disorder is based on the principle of harm reduction (Collins, Clifasefi, & Logan, 2012). As such, MRS pharmacotherapy involves replacing an opiate analgesic, and/or its method of use, with another opiate analgesic or method of use that is, in comparison, less harmful. This section focuses on two such opiate analgesics: (1) buprenorphine, which is used alone or in combination with naloxone; and (2) methadone, which is most often used for older adults who use heroin.

Before beginning this discussion, we note that in a few other countries (e.g., Australia, Canada, England, Germany, and Switzerland), a third opiate analgesic (i.e., heroin) is also used for this indication, but not in the U.S. (Clarke, 1999; Knopf, 2019; Purdon & Palleja, 2019; Uchtenhagen, 2011; Vikander, 2020). For example, in the context of MRS, heroin has been officially approved in the U.K. since 1926, to "treat opiate dependence." Although, "heroin cigarettes" and powdered heroin, which is often vaporized (see earlier discussion of "chasing the dragon"), can be used, most of the country's heroin is prescribed for use in "safe injection sites" under the supervision of trained nurses (Gordon, 2018; Stimson &

106. MRS pharmacotherapy is also referred to by the FDA as "medication-assisted treatment" (MAT).

Metrebian, 2003).[107] We do not support or recommend this "therapeutic" use of heroin (Pagliaro & Pagliaro, *Clinical Patient Data Files*).

Even if legally available in the U.S. for MRS pharmacotherapy, we would not recommend heroin for this use. A number of studies (e.g., Ferri, Davoli, & Perucci, 2011; Hartnoll, Mitcheson, & Battersby, 1980; Magwood, Salvalaggio, & Beder, 2020; Perneger, Giner, & del Rio, 1998) have indicated that, as logically expected, whereas heroin maintenance may reduce involvement in criminal activities, which would otherwise be required to maintain one's heroin habit, it perpetuates the status quo (i.e., opiate analgesic dependence or use disorder as a lifelong condition). Still, several studies recommend the use of heroin maintenance for those individuals who are refractory to traditional interventions.

For example, some municipal jurisdictions in the U.S. (e.g., Seattle, Washington), while not providing heroin directly to homeless patients, encourage heroin use by:

1. Providing heroin "pipes" (i.e., "Bubbles," "Hammers," and "Stems") for free;
2. Distributing "information" brochures that promote the rectal administration of heroin and providing related kits (i.e., "Booty Bumping Kits") (Rantz, 2021).

The rationale for these actions is, in accordance with the principal of "harm reduction," to mitigate the harm associated with the IV injection of heroin.

More recently, the Canadian government has admitted their inability to successfully curtail the opiate analgesic overdose epidemic, particularly among indigenous peoples. Consequently, they expanded their related harm reduction program to include—in addition to heroin: needle exchange programs, safe injection sites, and safe supply prescriptions. The safe supply component (i.e., part of the MRS approach) now includes the dispensing of injectable hydromorphone (Dilaudid®).

> She's been on oral morphine and suboxone in the past but the change to the safe supply guidelines mean she's been able to get a prescription for hydromorphone for the first time. That prescription also allows her to have "carries," meaning the pharmacy will give her a supply to take home and "carry" her through the day.
>
> (Bellrichard, 2020, p. 3)

Similar to our related recommendation regarding the use of heroin in the context of MRS—and for the same reasons—we do not recommend the use of hydromorphone for MRS.

Buprenorphine

Buprenorphine has been found effective for both the: (1) management of acute opiate analgesic detoxification; and (2) long-term opiate analgesic maintenance pharmacotherapy (e.g., Kovas et al., 2007; Pagliaro & Pagliaro, 2009).

---

107. The approach noted and utilized in these other countries is generally based on federal drug policies that are predicated upon "four pillars:"

    1. Harm reduction;
    2. Treatment;
    3. Prevention;
    4. Repression (i.e., law enforcement).

In late 2017, the FDA approved the use of an injectable, extended-release form of buprenorphine (BUP-XR) for the treatment of opiate analgesic dependence or use disorder. BUP-XR is available under the trade name of Sublocade® and is administered once monthly as an IM injection. In early 2019, results of a randomized, double-blind study indicated that:

> Both BUP-XR regimens led to substantial proportions of participants achieving abstinence from opioids, relief of withdrawal symptoms, and control of craving without the need for daily medication adherence or supplemental buprenorphine.
>
> (NIDA, 2019, p. 1)

Buprenorphine also has been found to be safer than methadone in cases of overdosage and is associated with a less severe opiate analgesic withdrawal syndrome when regular, long-term use is abruptly discontinued (Raisch, Fye, & Boardman, 2002).

Buprenorphine/Naloxone Combination

In an effort to curtail the widespread use of buprenorphine associated with the increasing opiate analgesic epidemic across the U.S. during the new millennium, the FDA endorsed the marketing of combination drug products that contained both buprenorphine (2 mg) and naloxone (5 mg) (e.g., Suboxone®).

Buprenorphine, a mixed opiate analgesic agonist/antagonist (i.e., partial mu-receptor agonist and full kappa-receptor antagonist), is preferentially administered sublingually (absorption F = 0.5; half-life of elimination, approximately 30 hours). Naloxone, an opiate analgesic antagonist, also can be administered sublingually (absorption F = 0.1; half-life of elimination, approximately 1 hour) (Chiang & Hawks, 2003; Pagliaro & Pagliaro, 2009; Robinson, 2006). Thus, the pharmacokinetics of these two drugs, particularly their difference in bioavailability (i.e., F), allows their combination as a mixed opiate analgesic agonist/antagonist in different buccal or sublingual formulations that can be dosed once daily:

- Buccal film (Bunavail®);
- Sublingual film (Suboxone® Film);
- Sublingual tablet (Suboxone® or Subutex®).

When the combined product is intravenously injected, absorption is 100% for both buprenorphine and naloxone (i.e., F=1) resulting in the desired euphoric and analgesic effects of buprenorphine being totally blocked by the naloxone. In addition to the expected undesired effects and toxicities associated with the use of buprenorphine, the buccal/sublingual formulations have been associated with numbness and redness of the mouth and tongue pain. In the U.S. since 2000, physicians are required to:

1. Apply for a license to prescribe combination buprenorphine/naloxone opiate analgesic MRS pharmacotherapy on an outpatient basis;
2. Undergo a training course.

However, as noted by Williams and Bisaga (2016, p. 814), in their editorial regarding the "vast epidemic of opioid-related deaths," facing the U.S.:

> In 40% of U.S. counties there is currently no physician authorized to prescribe buprenorphine, and the majority of authorized providers actually treat few or no patients.

Additionally, as identified by Wakeman et al. (2020, p. 2):

> Medication [i.e., buprenorphine; methadone] for opioid use disorder is effective and improves mortality [rates], treatment retention, and remission, but most people with OUD remain untreated.

For older adults, the initial "induction" dose of buprenorphine/naloxone is 2 mg/0.5 mg SL on day one with incremental dose increases of 2mg/0.5 mg SL until achievement of the suppression of the signs and symptoms associated with the opiate analgesic withdrawal syndrome (see also the earlier pharmacology subsection, Undesired, or Harmful, Effects and Toxicities—"Opiate Analgesic Withdrawal Syndrome"). The generally recommended target dosage is 16 mg/4 mg once daily with a maximum dose of 24 mg/6 mg per day.

Tapering-Off Buprenorphine/Naloxone Combination

If a decision, in consultation with the patient, is made to discontinue buprenorphine/naloxone combination, then a tapering protocol should be initiated. Generally, the more gradual the taper (i.e., six to 12 months), the more successful the outcome. The following is an example of such a tapering protocol that was modified from Wyman and Radhakrishnan (2018, p. 8):

- Decrease dose by small amounts (e.g., 2 mg);
- Leave at least two weeks between dose decreases;
- Put the taper "on hold" at the patient's request, or if the patient experiences withdrawal symptoms or craving;
- Return to the original dose if the patient begins using opioids again, even in small amounts or intermittently;
- Regularly provide support and encouragement.

Methadone Methadone (Dolophine®), a long-acting opiate analgesic, has been used in the U.S. as a legal form of pharmacotherapy for opiate analgesic maintenance for almost 60 years. It is indicated for patients, who are: (1) "addicted" to heroin; and (2) have been unable to successfully complete opiate analgesic detoxification. In this context of use, methadone has long been the "gold standard" of opiate analgesic maintenance therapy. However, as identified by Rosen et al. (2011, p. 9), in their review of the related literature, "Research on . . . methadone treatment among older adults is scant."

Additionally, over the last decade, methadone maintenance has been associated with a disproportionate number of deaths related to prescription opiate analgesic overdosages. As noted by Faul, Bohm, and Alexander (2017, p. 320):

> Methadone accounted for approximately 1% of all opioids prescribed for pain but accounted for approximately 23% of all prescription opioid deaths in 2014.

These overdosages have been reported particularly among patients who have been prescribed methadone in place of oxycodone for the management of chronic pain (Faul et al., 2017;

Pagliaro & Pagliaro, *Clinical Patient Data Files*). As reported by Collins (2010), many of these deaths, appear to be iatrogenic, specifically involving the:

1. Inappropriate use of conversion tables for dosing methadone;
2. Prescription of too high a dosage of methadone for initiating methadone maintenance (i.e., 80 mg/day as opposed to 30 mg/day).

Prescribed in dosages that generally do not produce euphoria or other desired psychotropic effects, methadone maintenance holds off, or keeps at bay, the signs and symptoms of the opiate analgesic withdrawal syndrome. Despite its associated limitations and problems, methadone remains the "gold standard" for opiate analgesic maintenance pharmacotherapy (Connery, 2015).

Methadone maintenance pharmacotherapy for older adults, who are dependent on heroin, is guided by the following goals:

- Cessation of the illicit use of heroin;
- Enhancement of the abilities to lead a more normal and, consequently, less harmful, and more productive life than that generally associated with heroin use.

Methadone maintenance pharmacotherapy offers several benefits:

1. Ingested once daily, it eliminates the hazards associated with the need to obtain illegal heroin, which is generally injected at least four times per day;
2. Prevents the harmful effects associated with heroin IV injection (e.g., HIV infection or overdosage) (see also the earlier related pharmacology subsection, Undesired, or Harmful, Effects and Toxicities—"Toxicities Associated with Intravenous Injection of Opiate Analgesics");
3. Decreases craving for heroin;
4. Avoids, or significantly diminishes, the occurrence of euphoria and excessive sedation;
5. Is legally available at a relatively low cost;
6. Is more conveniently and safely obtained at licensed neighborhood pharmacies.

Methadone maintenance has been associated with a significant reduction in "hustling" and other related behaviors that are commonly associated with older adult heroin use, including imprisonment and overdosage death. It also has been associated with increased abilities to participate in psychotherapy and other tertiary prevention approaches and maintain effective personal and social responsibilities (e.g., Farrell, Ward, & Mattick, 1994; Joseph, Stancliff, & Langrod, 2000).

Relapse Prevention[108]

Several pharmacological approaches involving opiate analgesic antagonists have been developed in an effort to ensure continued abstinence (i.e., relapse prevention) among opiate analgesic-dependent older adults, who have discontinued opiate analgesic use. In this

108. See also the earlier discussion in the related section, "Opiate Analgesic Maintenance, Replacement, or Substitution."

context, relapse prevention pharmacotherapy generally attempts to ensure abstinence by means of blocking associated "rewarding" stimuli when opiate analgesics are used.

Naltrexone, a long-acting oral opiate antagonist, was originally developed and marketed in the U.S. in 1984 under the brand name, Trexan®, for the treatment of opiate analgesic dependence, or "addiction"—particularly among practicing physicians and other health care professionals (e.g., Greenstein, Arndt, & McLellan, 1984; Kirchmayer, Davoli, & Verster, 2000; Pagliaro & Pagliaro, *Clinical Patient Data Files*).

The oral dosage form of naltrexone can be administered once daily without regard to meals or the ingestion of other foods and beverages. However, compliance has been problematic (Pagliaro & Pagliaro, *Clinical Patient Data Files*). In an effort to improve compliance and therapeutic outcomes, an injectable form of naltrexone was made available (Garbutt, Kranzler, & O'Malley, 2005; Gastfriend, 2014). The injectable form of naltrexone (Vivitrol®) is an extended-release suspension formulation that can be injected IM[109] once monthly by a health care professional. While found to significantly improve compliance for some patients, for others, poor patient compliance and low treatment retention rates continue (e.g., Minozzi, Amato, & Vecchi, 2011). For example, in a sample of over 300 community-living, ex-prisoners, who had limited use of heroin within the 30 days prior to the commencement of the research study, Lee, Friedmann and Kinlock (2016) found that—even when extended-release naltrexone (Vivitrol®)[110] was used in combination with relapse-prevention counseling and community support—monthly injections of naltrexone demonstrated significant efficacy only during the first six months of therapy. Several studies (e.g., NIDA, 2017; Orciari Herman, 2017; Tanum, Solli, & Latif, 2017), compared the naltrexone injection formulation with the oral buprenorphine and naloxone combination formulation with the general finding that the two approaches were therapeutically equivalent.

The most common undesired effect associated with the use of naltrexone is nausea. However, its long-term safety and efficacy have not yet been clearly established and the FDA has added a "Boxed Warning" to its official monograph stating that:

> Naltrexone may cause liver damage when taken in large doses [i.e., several times the normal recommended daily dose for an extended period].
>
> (Naltrexone, 2009, p. 1)

In addition, as previously noted, naltrexone—being an opiate analgesic antagonist—can precipitate the opiate analgesic withdrawal syndrome among regular, long-term users of opiate analgesics, including those who are being medically managed for moderate to severe chronic pain (e.g., chronic cancer pain). Thus, caution must be exercised when naltrexone pharmacotherapy is initiated for opiate analgesic relapse prevention for those patients who would also require alternative pain relief measures (e.g., acupuncture/acupressure; non-opiate analgesics, such as acetaminophen [Tylenol®]; NSAIDs [e.g., aspirin, ibuprofen]; local anesthetic, such as topical lidocaine; regional nerve block) (Pagliaro & Pagliaro, 1999; Pagliaro & Pagliaro, *Clinical Patient Data Files*; Volpicelli, Clay, & Watson, 1995).

---

109. Intramuscular injection of naltrexone has been associated with injection site reactions, including dark scabbing, erythema, induration, intense pain, lumps, open wounds, pruritus, swelling, and tenderness. On occasion, these reactions can be severe enough to warrant surgical or other therapeutic intervention. Thus, naltrexone IM injection pharmacotherapy requires appropriate, routine monitoring of injection sites.
110. Vivitrol® is also approved for the treatment of alcohol dependence or use disorder. For further discussion, see Chapter 1, *Alcohol.*

Psychotherapeutic/Counseling Approaches

Although virtually every form of psychotherapy/counseling has been used to treat older adults who have opiate analgesic dependence or use disorder, CBT is the generally accepted mainstay of this therapeutic approach (e.g., McHugh, Votaw, & Barlow, 2017; Moore, Fiellin, & Cutter, 2016; Pagliaro & Pagliaro, *Clinical Patient Data Files*). (See also the related discussion in the "Psychotherapeutic/Counseling" section of Chapter 1, *Alcohol.*)

In December 2018, the FDA approved the use of a CBT-related mobile "app" to be used in conjunction with a formal treatment program for OUD:

> The reSET-O app is a prescription cognitive behavioral therapy intended to be used in addition to outpatient treatment under the care of a health care professional, in conjunction with treatment that includes buprenorphine and contingency management. . . .
>
> The reSET-O is an app that can be downloaded directly to a patient's mobile device [e.g., from Google Play®] after they receive a prescription to do so from their doctor. It is intended to be used while participating in an outpatient OUD treatment program.
>
> (FDA, 2018b, p. 1)[111]

The reSET-O® app was developed by the biotech company Pear Therapeutics, and is marketed by Novartis and Sandoz Pharmaceuticals. After downloading the app to a smartphone, the patient unlocks it with a "passcode" that has been provided by his/her clinician. The patient then has access to the app for 12 consecutive weeks and is expected to complete four modules per week. Each module utilizes a combination of audio, video, and text messaging/interaction and incorporates a variety of contingency rewards to help maintain continued app usage. Currently, reSET-O® is the first and only FDA authorized prescription digital therapeutic (PDT). However, additional related products are under development.

CONTEMPORANEOUS DIAGNOSES INVOLVING OPIATE ANALGESICS

Several common contemporaneous, or concurrent, diagnoses have been identified among older adults who use opiate analgesics. These diagnoses include alcohol and other dependence or use disorders, particularly, nicotine dependence or use disorder; other mental disorders (e.g., adjustment disorder, anxiety disorders, orMDD); numerous physical medical disorders (PMDs), particularly pain disorders—both acute and chronic; and somatic symptom disorder (SSD) (Pagliaro & Pagliaro, *Clinical Patient Data Files*; Trafton, Oliva & Horst, 2004; Verdurmen, Videler, & Kamperman, 2017; Wolitzky-Taylor, Castriotta, & Lenze, 2010). (See also the following related discussion.)

The concurrent use of other drugs and substances of abuse with opiate analgesics also depends largely on availability, reason for use, and context of use. For example, older adults who use heroin typically drink alcohol and smoke or vape cannabis and/or tobacco. "Homeless" older adults use opiate analgesics, whenever available—along with virtually any and

111. The use of the reSET-O® program has been demonstrated to increase program retention, but not efficacy in comparison to buprenorphine pharmacotherapy and contingency management alone (FDA, 2018b, p. 2).

all other available drugs and substances of abuse. Additionally, older adults may use prescription opiate analgesics to deal with acute or chronic pain related to work or other, primarily recreational, activities (e.g., bicycling, bowling, golfing, or running)[112]—at least until the availability of their opiate analgesics ceases, at which time they may increase their use of alcohol and/or switch to heroin. (See also the related discussion in the following subsection.)

Pain Disorders

Several contemporaneous diagnoses involving opiate analgesic dependence or use disorder, as would be expected, include various PMDs, particularly pain disorders—both acute and chronic (i.e., the major reason why opiate analgesics are initially prescribed for most older adults). However, as noted by Katz, Rosenbloom, and Fashler (2015, p. 165):

> For the first time in more than 30 years, the most recent edition of the DSM no longer includes a pain-specific mental disorder. DSM-5 SSD with predominant pain replaces DSM-IV pain disorder but it is *not* recommended for people with chronic pain, because it lacks validity, and is overly inclusive and stigmatizing. Instead, *adjustment disorder* remains the most appropriate, accurate, and acceptable diagnosis for people who are overly concerned about their pain.

Suicide or Suicidal Behavior Disorder

> The combined number of deaths among Americans from suicide and unintentional [opiate analgesic] overdose increased from 41,364 in 2000 to 110,749 in 2017.
>
> (Bohnert & Ilgen, 2019, p. 71)

Although, suicide has no single cause, opiate analgesic dependence or opioid use disorder (OUD) have been associated with suicidal ideation or "suicidal behavior disorder"[113] among older adults.[114] In fact, older adults who use opiate analgesics—whether medically prescribed or illicitly used—are at significantly increased risk for suicide (Pagliaro & Pagliaro, *Clinical Patient Data Files*). Contributory factors, which significantly increase this risk, include:

- Concomitant use of additional psychodepressants;
- Longer duration of medical or illicit opiate analgesic use;
- Long-term chronic pain;
- Long-term disability;
- Use of higher dosages of opiate analgesics;
- Discontinuation of medical or illicit opiate analgesic use;

---

112. Sports injuries often lead to regular, long-term opiate analgesic use particularly when injuries are not given enough time to heal. "Acute pain" frequently converts to "chronic pain," often along with an anxiety disorder or major depressive disorder that requires additional pharmacotherapy, such as antidepressants and sedative-hypnotics, including antianxiety drugs (e.g., benzodiazepines, Ativan®; diazepam, Valium®). (See also Chapter 6, *Prescription Sedative-Hypnotics.*) The increasing complexity of pharmacotherapy also increases the risk for drug-drug interactions and other dependence or use disorders.
113. Suicidal behavior disorder has been proposed in DSM-5 (Oquendo & Baca-Garcia, 2014).
114. See also the related discussion in the earlier pharmacology subsection, "Opiate Analgesic Overdosage/Unintentional Poisoning."

- One or more of the following mental disorders:
  - Concurrent alcohol dependence or use disorder (AUD);
  - Concurrent MDD;[115]
  - Concurrent PTSD.

In our long clinical practice, we have noted that, in the absence of related clinical indicia (e.g., a suicide note), it is often extremely difficult to determine if the noted death associated with an overdosage of opiate analgesics is "accidental" (i.e., unintentional) or "deliberate" (i.e., an intentional suicide). Additionally, some older adults, particularly those with disabling chronic pain and incurable inadequately relievable conditions, may consciously (or unconsciously) seek a "medical" remedy (i.e., overdosage) to end their "misery" (Pagliaro & Pagliaro, *Clinical Patient Data Files*).

These observations appear to be particularly apropos and clinically relevant in the current context of the growing acceptance and use of physician-assisted suicide (also commonly referred to as "medical aid in dying" [MAID] over the new millennium. This practice is legal in several countries (e.g., Canada and the United Kingdom) and in a growing number of U.S. states (e.g., California, Colorado, Hawaii, Oregon, and Washington) (Collier, 2017; Gopal, 2015; Meisel, 2019; Rizzo, 2000).[116]

Interestingly, in their analysis of data from a large national adult cohort from the *U.S. National Longitudinal Mortality Study*, Aram, Johnson, and Ting Lee (2020, p. 769) found that, in comparison to employed adults (i.e., primarily younger adults), older adults who were "disabled," "unemployed," and/or "retired" were three to six times more likely to experience a drug-related overdosage death.

***Related Professional Reminder*: Health care professionals should be cognizant that older adults who use opiate analgesics, particularly those with opiate analgesic dependence or OUD, are considered to be at significant risk of suicide.**

For example, as emphasized by the U.S. Department of Veterans Affairs (2020, p. 1):

> People with opioid use disorder (OUD) are 13 times more likely than those who do not have the disorder to die by suicide, and Veterans Health Administration (VHA) patients are seven times more likely than commercially insured patients to be diagnosed with OUD.

Additionally, and largely unexpected by many health and social care professionals, risk for opiate analgesic-related suicide has been noted to be extremely high upon discontinuation of opiate analgesic treatment (Demidenko, Dobscha, & Morasco, 2017; Oliva, Bowe, & Manhapra, 2020).

Managing Contemporaneous Diagnoses[117]

An appropriate combination of both pharmacotherapeutic and psychotherapeutic approaches for the management of contemporaneous diagnoses involving opiate analgesic dependence

115. MDD—which is significantly correlated with suicide, is not used as a reliable predictive criterion in this regard because most of the people with MDD do not attempt or commit suicide (e.g., McGirr, Renaud, & Seguin, 2008).
116. For the record, while we attempt to remain nonjudgmental in this context of practice—we do not personally or professionally support or partake in this practice because of our contrary philosophical and religious beliefs.
117. For a general overview of contemporaneous diagnoses and their general management, see the related discussion in Chapter 1, *Alcohol*.

or use disorder is an integral component of the medical, psychological, and other health and social care services required by older adults. In addition, as noted by several researchers (e.g., McCarthy & Anderson, 2005), failure to adequately treat other involved mental disorders may significantly contribute to—following successful treatment outcomes for opiate analgesic dependence or use disorder—a significantly increased risk for relapsed opiate analgesic use.

Three major general approaches are commonly used in the treatment of older adults with contemporaneous diagnoses. These approaches have been categorized by Smith and Randall (2012) as:

1. Sequential;
2. Parallel;
3. Integrated.

The "sequential" approach is based largely on the hypothesis that a single clinician can optimally focus on, or address, a single dependence or use disorder.[118] This selected dependence or use disorder is treated first while largely ignoring—or delaying—the treatment of the concurrent dependence or use disorder(s) or other mental or physical medical disorders. A related corollary is that once the single selected dependence or use disorder is treated and is under "control/remission," another dependence or use disorder (or other mental or physical medical disorder) can be successfully treated (i.e., is more amenable to intervention).

In the "parallel" approach, specific treatment approaches for opiate analgesic and or other dependence or use disorder, mental disorder, or physical medical disorder are often delivered separately, but simultaneously, by different clinicians, frequently, in different facilities. Given that significant deficits in coordination and communication are the major reasons for the therapeutic failures associated with the parallel approach, careful attention must be given to the:

1. Coordination and communication between older adult patients and clinicians. For example, when one clinician says something in terms of the cause of the condition, the preferred therapeutic approach, or the necessary length of treatment to an older adult patient and another clinician(s) says something else;
2. Coordination and communication between and among the treating clinicians, which is particularly apt to be lacking when they are *not* part of the same clinic or treatment unit/site (e.g., clinic or university hospital).

In the "integrated" approach, treatment is delivered in a similar way to the parallel approach, but by a single health care professional. This is our preferred approach for the treatment of contemporaneous diagnoses. We have consistently used this approach with great success over the decades as well as recommended its use to others. However, it is the most difficult approach to successfully employ because of the absolute requirements for a skilled, knowledgeable, and clinically experienced clinician or therapist who, when needed, is able to obtain appropriate consultation, collaboration, and referral as needed, which is

118. Unfortunately, in this situation, the order of treatment is almost always chosen on an "ad hoc" basis predicated primarily on the background, knowledge, and clinical strengths of the clinician as opposed to the individual needs of the specific patient who is seeking treatment, and the relationship between, or among, the presenting concurrent disorders.

extremely beneficial to the treatment outcomes. In the majority of "difficult" or previously "failed" cases that have been referred to us over the years, the most common problem has been the use of non-professionally educated para-professional therapists, usually recovering from their own opiate analgesic or other dependence or use disorders, who have experience with and strengths in group therapy and other related skills, but are ill-prepared to plan and deliver complex therapeutic treatment that tends to be far beyond their abilities when confronted with contemporaneous disorders involving opiate analgesic and other dependence or use disorders, and often multiple other medical disorders (OMDs) and PMDs (Pagliaro & Pagliaro, *Clinical Patient Data Files*).

Additionally, we have frequently observed, particularly among older adult patients who are extremely socially-economically (i.e., financially) or educationally successful, that therapeutic success is significantly hindered when the patient thinks that he or she is "superior" to the individual providing the therapeutic intervention. For example, in our clinical experience, successful older adults, such as bank managers, corporate executives, dentists, lawyers, and physicians, respond best to a therapist who they both respect and implicitly trust. Consequently, therapeutic success with the older adults who have opiate analgesic or other dependence or use disorder(s), and/or multiple OMDs and/or PMDs is generally minimal when the therapist is, for example, a recovering alcoholic or heroin addict with little or no formal advanced education/clinical experience.[119]

REFERENCES[120,121,122]

A naloxone. (2014, June 9). A naloxone auto-injector (Evzio). *The Medical Letter*, *56*(1444), 45–46.

Abedzadeh, A., Iqbal, S., & Al Bastaki, U. (2019). New packaging methods of body packers: Role of advanced imaging in their detection. A case study. *Radiology Case Reports*, *14*(5), 627–633. doi:10.1016/j.radcr.2019.03.002

Ahmadi, J., Sefidfard Jahromi, M., & Ghahremani, D. (2018, December 10). Single high-dose buprenorphine for opioid craving during withdrawal. *BMC Trials*, *19*(1), 675. doi:10.1186/s13063-018-3055-z

119. This observation can also be related to differences in IQ—in which, the potential for successful therapeutic intervention is minimized when the IQ of the older adult who has a contemporaneous diagnosis involving opiate analgesic or other dependence or use disorder(s), and/or multiple OMDs and PMDs—is significantly higher than that of the therapist.
120. As per publisher style, only the first three authors are listed for each reference.
121. Several times the number of references listed were found, obtained, and analyzed by the authors during the preparation of this chapter. However, only those references that were cited at least once in the body of the text are listed. Major reasons for not citing other references include that they: (1) did not provide any additional unique information or research findings; (2) were not well researched or written by their authors (i.e., were evaluated as not being valid or reliable); (3) were based predominately, or exclusively, on animal studies; (4) dealt exclusively with other population groups (e.g., children, adolescents, or young adults); (5) provided usage statistics from outside the U.S.; and/or (6) were redundant with, or not as recent as, the already cited references—unless the reference was of classical, historical, or seminal importance.
122. The reference citation, "Pagliaro & Pagliaro, *Clinical Patient Data Files*," refers to unpublished data collected, with permission, by the authors, in the formal course of their professional academic roles as clinician scientists and professors, from their patients, research subjects or participants, and students, from the 1970s to date. Most of the related data have been discussed and made public in a wide and large number of formal academic presentations, including graduate seminars, grand rounds, guest lectures, professional conferences, and undergraduate lectures.

Alexander, D., Alexander, K., & Valentino, J. (2012). Intranasal hydrocodone-acetaminophen abuse induced necrosis of the nasal cavity and pharynx. *Laryngoscope*, *122*(11), 2378–2381. doi:10.1002/lary.23542

Al-Tayyib, A., Koester, S., & Langegger, S. (2017, July 3). Heroin and methamphetamine injection: An emerging drug use pattern. *Substance Use & Misuse*, *52*(8), 1051–1058. doi:10.1080/10826084.2016.1271432

Althoff, K. N., Leifheit, K. M., & Park, J. N. (2020, November 1). Opioid-related overdose mortality in the era of fentanyl: Monitoring a shifting epidemic by person, place, and time. *Drug and Alcohol Dependence*, *216*, 108321. doi:10.1016/j.drugalcdep.2020.108321

Anantharamu, T., Sharma, S., & Gupta, A. K. (2015). Naloxegol: First oral peripherally acting mu opioid receptor antagonists for opioid-induced constipation. *Journal of Pharmacology and Pharmacotherapeutics*, *6*(3), 188–192. doi:10.4103/0976-500X.162015

Annett, H. E. (1920). Factors influencing alkaloidal content and yield of latex in the opium poppy (Papaver somniferum). *Biochemical Journal*, *14*(5), 618–636.

AP, Associated Press. (2018, February 10). OxyContin maker will stop marketing opioids to doctors, company says. *The Guardian*, 1.

APA, American Psychiatric Association. (2013). *DMS-5, diagnostic and statistical manual of mental disorders* (5th ed.). Washington, DC: American Psychiatric Association.

Aquina, C. T., Marques-Baptista, A., & Bridgeman, P. (2009). OxyContin abuse and overdose. *Postgraduate Medicine*, *121*(2), 163–167. doi:10.3810/pgm.2009.03.1988

Aram, J., Johnson, N. J., & Ting Lee, M. (2020, November 1). Drug overdose mortality is associated with employment status and occupation in the National longitudinal mortality study. *American Journal of Drug and Alcohol Abuse*, *46*(6), 769–776. doi:10.1080/009552990.2020.1820018

Arner, S., & Meyerson, B. A. (1988, April). Lack of analgesic effect of opioids on neuropathic and idiopathic forms of pain. *Pain*, *33*(1), 11–23.

Ashrafioun, L. (2016, September 18). Prescription opioid-craving: Relationship with pain and substance use—Related characteristics. *Substance Use & Misuse*, *51*(11), 1512–1520. doi:10.1080/10826084.2016.1188948

Badalamenti, V. C., Buckley, J. W., & Smith, E. T. (2012). Safety of EMBEda (morphine sulfate and naltrexone hydrochloride) extended-release capsules: Review of postmarketing adverse events during the first year. *Journal of Opioid Management*, *8*(2), 115–125.

Bailey, K., Richards-Waugh, L., & Clay, D. (2010, October). Fatality involving the ingestion of phenazepam and poppy seed tea. *Journal of Analytical Toxicology*, *34*(8), 527–532. doi:10.1093/jat/34.8.527

Bangsberg, D. R., Rosen, J. I., & Aragon, T. (2002). Clostridial myonecrosis cluster among injection drug users: A molecular epidemiology investigation. *Archives of Internal Medicine*, *162*(5), 517–522.

Barclay, J. S., Owens, J. E., & Blackhall, L. J. (2014). Screening for substance abuse risk in cancer patients using the Opioid Risk Tool and urine drug screen. *Supportive Care in Cancer*, *22*, 1883–1888.

Barke, K. E., & Hough, L. B. (1993). Opiates, mast cells and histamine release. *Life Sciences*, *53*(18), 1391–1399.

Barth, K. S., Moran-Santa Maria, M., & Lawson, K. (2013). Pain and motives for use among non-treatment seeking individuals with prescription opioid dependence. *The American Journal on Addictions*, *22*(5), 486–491. doi:10.1111/j.1521-0391.2013.12038.x

Bass, U. F., Brown, B. S., & DuPont, R. L. (1972). The use of heroin by an offender population: A report over time. *Corrective Psychiatry & Journal of Social Therapy, 18*(4), 24–30.

Bazazi, A. R., Yokell, M., & Fu, J. (2011). Illicit use of buprenorphine/naloxone among injecting and non-injecting opioid users. *Journal of Addiction Medicine, 5*, 175–180.

Becker, W. C., & Fiellin, D. A. (2020, April 2). When epidemics collide: Coronavirus disease 2019 (COVID-19) and the opioid crisis. *Annals of Internal Medicine*, 1–2. doi:10.7326/M20-1210

Bellrichard, C. (2020, May 12). B.C. moves to 'safe supply' as overdose deaths spike during COVID-19 pandemic. *CBC News*, 1–3. CBC/Radio-Canada.

Bertkau, A., Halpern, J., & Yadla, S. (2005, April). The privileges and demands of professional self-regulation. *Virtual Mentor*, *7*(4), 1–2.

Bohnert, A. S., & Ilgen, M. A. (2019). Understanding links among opioid use, overdose, and suicide. *The New England Journal of Medicine, 380*(1), 71–79. doi:10.1056/NEJMra1802148

Boscarino, J. A., Rukstalis, M. R., & Hoffman, S. N. (2011). Prevalence of prescription opioid-use disorder among chronic pain patients: Comparison of the DSM-5 vs. DSM-4 diagnostic criteria. *Journal of Addictive Diseases, 30*(3), 185–194.

Boyle, B. D., & Desmond, T. (2021, January 27). Waterbury heroin trafficker sentenced to 10 years in prison. In *DEA press release, new England division*. Washington, DC: U.S. Department of Justice.

Brady, K. T., McCauley, J. L., & Back, S. E. (2016). Prescription opioid misuse, abuse, and treatment in the United States: An update. *The American Journal of Psychiatry, 173*(1), 18–26. doi:10.1176/appi.ajp.2015.15020262

Brott, N. R., & Cascella, M. (2020, January 8). *Opioid risk tool*. Treasure Island, FL: StatPearls.

Brown, E. (2011, November 1). *Prescription painkillers outpace heroin, cocaine in OD deaths. Los Angeles Times*, pp. 1–2. Retrieved from http://articles.latimes.com/2011/nov01/news/la-heb-prescription-drug-overdose-deaths-2 . . .

Bruijnzeel, A. W. (2009). Kapa-opioid receptor signaling and brain reward function. *Brain Research Reviews, 62*(1), 127–146. doi:10.1016/j.brainresrev.2009.09.008

Bruner, B. (2020, May 4). Franklin county had more than 28 overdose calls in 24 hours. *The Columbus Dispatch*, pp. 1–2. Gannett Company.

Buprenorphine buccal film (Belbuca) for chronic pain. (2016). *The Medical Letter, 58*(1492), 47–48.

Butler, S. F., Cassidy, T. A., & Chilcoat, H. (2013). Abuse rates and routes of administration of reformulated extended-release oxycodone: Initial findings from a sentinel surveillance sample of individuals assessed for substance abuse treatment. *The Journal of Pain, 14*(4), 351–358. doi:10.1016/j.jpain.2012.08.008

Carew, A. M., & Corniskey, C. (2018). Treatment for opioid use and outcomes in older adults: A systematic literature review. *Drug and Alcohol Dependence, 182*, 48–57.

Carise, D., Dugosh, K. L., & McLellan, A. T. (2007). Prescription OxyContin abuse among patients entering addiction treatment. *American Journal of Psychiatry, 164*(11), 1750–1756.

Carroll, J. J., Marshall, B., & Rich, J. D. (2017). Exposure to fentanyl-contaminated heroin and overdose risk among illicit opioid users in Rhode Island: A mixed methods study. *International Journal of Drug Policy, 46*, 136–145. doi:10.1016/j.drugpo.2017.05.023

Case, A., & Deaton, A. (2015, December 8). Rising morbidity and mortality in midlife among White non-Hispanic Americans in the 21st Century. *Proceedings of the National Academy of Science, 112*(49), 15078–15083. Retrieved from www.pnas.org/cgi/doi/10.1073/pnas.1518393112

Cassidy, T. A., DasMahapatra, P., & Black, R. A. (2014). Changes in prevalence of prescription opioid abuse after introduction of an abuse-deterrent opioid formulation. *Pain Medicine*, *15*(3), 440–451. doi:10.1111/pme.12295

CDC, Centers for Disease Control and Prevention. (2018, February 21). *Alcohol screening and brief intervention for people who consume alcohol and use opioids*. Atlanta, GA: National Center for Injury Prevention and Control.

Chang, D. (2021, November 2). 81-year-old Delaware county pharmacist accused of selling drugs for sex. *NBC News,* Channel 10, pp. 1–6. NBC News, Philadelphia, PA.

Chang, Y.-P., & Compton, P. (2016). Opioid misuse/abuse and quality persistent pain management in older adults. *Journal of Gerontological Nursing*, *42*(12), 21–30. doi:10.3928/00989134-20161110-06

Cheatle, M. D., Compton, P. A., & Dhingra, L. (2019). Development of the revised opioid risk tool to predict opioid use disorder in patients with chronic nonmalignant pain. *Journal of Pain*, *20*(7), 842–851. doi:10.1016/j.jpain.2019.01.011

Cheng, S., Siddiqui, T., & Gossop, M. (2019). The severity of dependence scale detects medication misuse and dependence among hospitalized older patients. *BMC Geriatrics*, *19*(article 174), 1–5.

Chhatre, S., Cook, R., & Mallik, E. (2017). Trends in substance use admissions among older adults. *BMC Health Services Research*, *17*(1), 584–592. doi:10.1186/s12913-017-2538-z

Chiang, C. N., & Hawks, R. L. (2003). Pharmacokinetics of the combination tablet of buprenorphine and naloxone. *Drug and Alcohol Dependence*, *70*(Suppl 2), S39–S47.

Chu, L., Angst, M. S., & Clark, D. (2008, July–August). Opioid-induced hyperalgesia in humans: Molecular mechanisms and clinical considerations. *The Clinical Journal of Pain*, *24*(6), 479–496. doi:10.1097/AJP.0b013e31816b2f43

Ciccarone, D. (2009). Heroin in brown, black and white: Structural factors and medical consequences in the US heroin market. *International Journal of Drug Policy*, *20*(3), 277–282.

Ciccarone, D., & Bourgois, P. (2003). Explaining the geographical variation of HIV among injection drug users in the United States. *Drug and Substance Misuse*, *38*(14), 2049–2063.

Cicero, T. J., Ellis, M. S., & Surratt, H. L. (2014, September 1). Factors contributing to the rise of buprenorphine misuse: 2008–2013. *Drug and Alcohol Dependence*, *142*, 98–104. doi:10.1016/j.drugalcdep.2014.06.005

Cicero, T. J., Inciardi, J. A., & Munoz, A. (2005). Trends in abuse of oxycontin and other opioid analgesics in the United States: 2002–2004. *The Journal of Pain*, 662–672.

Cicero, T. J., Surratt, H. L., & Inciardi, J. (2007). Use and misuse of buprenorphine in the management of opioid addiction. *Journal of Opioid Management*, *3*, 302–308.

Clarification: Half-life of heroin. (2016). *The Medical Letter*, *58*(1489), 32.

Clarke, H. (1999). Public provision of heroin for addicts. *Agenda*, *6*(3), 195–210.

Cody, J. T., Valtier, S., & Kuhlman, J. (2001). Analysis of morphine and codeine in samples adulterated with Stealth. *Joural of Analytical Toxicology*, *25*, 572–575.

Collier, R. (2017, January 23). Assisted death gaining acceptance in US. *CMAJ*, *189*(3), E123. doi:10.1503/cmaj.109-5366

Collins, S. E., Clifasefi, S., & Logan, D. E. (2012). Current status, historical highlights, and basic principles of harm reduction. In G. A. Marlatt, M. E. Larimer, & K. Witkiewitz (Eds.), *Harm reduction: Pragmatic strategies for managing high-risk behaviors* (pp. 3–35). New York: Guilford Press.

Collins, T. R. (2010, February 8). Deaths from methadone overdose disproportionate to number of prescriptions. *Medscape Medical News*. Retrieved from www.medscape.com/viewarticle/716603_print

Colliver, J. D., Compton, W. M., & Gfroerer, J. C. (2006). Projecting drug use among aging baby boomers in 2020. *Annals of Epidemiology, 16*, 257–265.

Compton, W. M., Dawson, D. A., & Goldstein, R. B. (2013, September). Crosswalk between DSM-IV dependence and DSM-5 substance use disorders for opioids, cannabis, cocaine and alcohol. *Drug and Alcohol Dependence, 132*, 387–390. doi:10.1016/j.drugalcdep.2013.02.036

Conejero, I., Olie, E., & Courtet, P. (2018). Suicide in older adults: Current perspectives. *Clinical Interventions in Aging, 13*, 691–699.

Connery, H. S. (2015). Medication-assisted treatment of opioid use disorder: Review of the evidence and future directions. *Harvard Review of Psychiatry, 23*(2), 63–75. doi:10.1097/HRP.0000000000000075

Corsetti, M., & Tack, J. (2015). Naloxegol: The first orally administered, peripherally acting, mu opioid receptor antagonist, approved for the treatment of opioid-induced constipation. *Drugs of Today (Barcelona), 51*(8), 474–489. doi:10.1358/dot.2015.51.8.2364896

Cousins, B. (2020, April 22). B.C. emergency doctor worries of possible rise in opioid deaths due to COVID-19. *CTV News*, pp. 1–2. Toronto, ON: CTV.

Dart, R. C. (2011). *5th annual scientifica meeting presentation.* Evaluation of ADFs Using RADARS System Data. Retrieved from www.radars.org/Home2/Annual Meeting/RADARSSystem2011AnnualMeeting.aspx

Dasgupta, A. (2015, February 1). How people try to beat drug testing. *Clinical Laboratory News,* pp. 1–5. AACC, Washington, DC.

Davidson, J. (2018, May 25). Unseen face of the opioid epidemic: Drug abuse among the elderly grows. *The Washington Post*, pp. 1–2.

DEA, Drug Enforcement Administration. (1992, September). *Opium poppy cultivation and heroin processing in Southeast Asia.* Office of Intelligence. Washington, DC: U.S. Department of Justice.

DEA, Drug Enforcement Administration. (2018, October). *2018 national drug threat assessment.* Washington, DC: U.S. Department of Justice.

DEA, Drug Enforcement Administration. (2020, January). Fentanyl flow to the United States. *DEA Intelligence Report*, pp. 1–4. Washington, DC: U.S. Department of Justice.

DEA, Drug Enforcement Administration. (2021, March). *2020 National drug threat assessment.* Washington, DC: U.S. Department of Justice.

Demidenko, M. I., Dobscha, S. K., & Morasco, B. J. (2017, July). Suicidal ideation and suicidal self-directed violence following clinician-initiated prescription opioid discontinuation among long-term users. *General Hospital Psychiatry, 47*, 29–35. doi:10.1016/j.genhosppsych.2017.04.011

DePriest, A. Z., Puet, B. L., & Holt, A. C. (2015, July). Metabolism and disposition of prescription opioids: A review. *Forensic Science Review, 27*(2), 115–145.

Dietrich, E., & Gums, J. G. (2012). Intranasal fentanyl spray: A novel dosage form for the treatment of breakthrough cancer pain. *Annals of Pharmacotherapy, 46*(10), 1382–1391. doi:10.1345/aph.1R069

Dietze, P., Jauncey, M., & Salmon, A. (2019, November 13). Effect of intranasal vs intramuscular naloxone on opioid overdose: A randomized clinical trial. *JAMA Network Open*, 1–12. doi:10.1001/jamanetworkopen.2019.14977

DiGiorgio, A. M., Stein, R., & Morrow, K. D. (2019). The increasing frequency of intravenous drug abuse-associated spinal epidural abscesses: A case series. *Neurosurgical Focus*, *46*(1), E4. doi:10.3171/2018.10.FOCUS18449

Dineen, K. K., & DuBois, J. M. (2016). Between a rock and a hard place: Can physicians prescribe opioids to treat pain adequately while avoiding legal sanction? *The American Journal of Law & Medicine*, *42*(1), 7–52.

Doctor, J. N., Nguyen, A., & Lev, R. (2018, August 10). Opioid prescribing decreases after learning of a patient's fatal overdose. *Science*, *361*, 588–590.

Donovan, R. P., & Mulvey, E. (2021, January 8). Over 20 kilograms of suspected fentanyl, heroin and cocaine seized in Ozone Park, Queens: Three arrested. *DEA Press Release, New York Division*, 1–5. Washington, DC: U.S. Department of Justice.

Dowell, D., Haegerich, T. M., & Chou, R. (2016, March 18). CDC guideline for prescribing opioids for chronic pain—United States, 2016. *MMWR, Morbidity and Mortality Recommendations and Reports*, *65*(1), 1–49. doi:10.15585/mmwr.rr6501e1

Dowell, D., Jones, C., & Compton, W. (2019, October). HHS Guide for Clinicians on the Appropriate Dosage Reduction or Discontinuation of Long-Term Analgesics. *HHS Guide*, pp. 1–6. U.S. Department of Health and Human Services.

Dowling, J., Isbister, G. K., & Kirkpatrick, C. M. (2008, August). Population pharmacokinetics of intravenous, intramuscular, and intranasal naloxone in human volunteers. *Therapeutic Drug Monitoring*, *30*(4), 490–496. doi:10.1097/FTD.0b013e3181816214

DuBois, J. M., Chibnall, J. T., & Anderson, E. E. (2016, October). A mixed-method analysis of reports on 100 cases of improper prescribing of controlled substances. *Journal of Drug Issues*, *46*(4), 457–472. doi:10.1177/0022042616661836

Eisler, P. (2014, May 22). Older American hooked on Rx: 'I was a zombie'. *USA Today*, pp. 1–5.

Erdman, S. L. (2020, May 21). Opioid drug overdose deaths are down in US, study finds, but COVID-19 could change that. *CNN News*, pp. 1–3. Turner Broadcasting System.

Ersche, K. D., Clark, L., & London, M. (2006). Profile of executive and memory function associated with amphetamine and opiate dependence. *Neuropsychopharmacology*, *31*(5), 1036–1047. doi:10.1038/sj.npp.1300889

Extended-Release hydrocodone (Hysingla ER) for pain. (2015). *The Medical Letter*, *57*(1468), 71–72.

Extended-Release hydrocodone (Zohydro ER) for pain. (2014). *The Medical Letter*, *56*(1444), 45–46.

Fadulu, L. (2018, August 31). A simple reason so many older Americans are overdosing on opioids. *The Atlantic*, pp. 1–5. The Atlantic Monthly.

Fareed, A., Casarella, J., & Amar, R. (2010). Methadone maintenance dosing guideline for opioid dependence: A literature review. *Journal of Addictive Diseases*, *29*(1), 1–14.

Farrell, M., Ward, J., & Mattick, R. (1994, October 15). Methadone maintenance treatment in opiate dependence: A review. *BMJ*, *309*, 997–1001.

Farzan, A. (2018, August 8). Yes, you can fail a drug text by eating a poppy seed bagel. *The Washington Post*, pp. 1–4. The Washington Post, Washington, DC.

Faul, M., Bohm, M., & Alexander, C. (2017, March 31). Methadone prescribing and overdose and the association with Medicaid preferred drug list policies—United States 2007–2014. *MMWR, Morbidity and Mortality Weekly Report*, *66*(12), 320–323.

FDA, U.S. Food and Drug Administration. (2014a, September 16). Press announcements > FDA approves Movantik for opioid-induced constipation. *FDA.gov*. Retrieved October 3, 2016, from www.fda.gov/NewEvents/Newsroom/PressAnnouncements/ucm414620.htm

FDA, U.S. Food and Drug Administration. (2014b, April 3). FDA approves new hand-held auto-injector to reverse opioid overdose. *FDA News Release*.

FDA, U.S. Food and Drug Administration. (2015, November 18). FDA News Release. In *FDA moves quickly to approve easy-to-use nasal spray to treat opioid overdose*. Retrieved from htp://www.fda.gov/NewsEvents/Newsroom/PressAnnouncements/ucm473505.htm

FDA, U.S. Food and Drug Administration. (2016a, August 31). FDA drug safety communication: FDA warns about serious risks and death when combining opioid pain or cough medicines with benzodiazepines: Requires its strongest warning. *Safety Announcement.*

FDA, U.S. Food and Drug Administration. (2017a, September 20). FDA drug safety communication: FDA urges caution about withholding opioid addiction medications from patients taking benzodiazepines or CNS depressants: Careful medication management can reduce risks. *Safety Announcement.*

FDA, U.S. Food and Drug Administration. (2017b, November 14). *Drug development and drug interactions: Table of substrates, inhibitors and inducers*. Silver Springs, MD: FDA.

FDA, U.S. Food and Drug Administration. (2018a, November 2). Statement from FDA commissioner Scott Gottlieb, M.D., on agency's approval of Dsuvia and the FDA's future consideration of new opioids. *Statement.*

FDA, U.S. Food and Drug Administration. (2018b, December 10). FDA clears mobile medical app to help those with opioid use disorder stay in recovery programs. *FDA News Release.*

Felbab-Brown, V. (2017, November 21). Afghanistan's opium production is through the roof—why Washington shouldn't overreact. *Brookings*, pp. 1–5. The Brookings Institution.

Felbab-Brown, V. (2020, July 22). Fending off fentanyl and hunting down heroin: Controlling opioid supply from Mexico. *Brookings*, pp. 1–4. The Brookings Institute.

Felman, A., & Carteron, N. (2018, January 5). Everything you need to know about fibromyalgia. *Medical News Today*, pp. 1–5. Healthline Media.

Feng, X., Zhu, L., & Zhou, Q. (2017). Opioid analgesics-related pharmacokinetic drug interactions: From the perspectives of evidence based on randomized controlled trials and clinical risk management. *Journal of Pain Management, 10*, 1225–1239.

Ferri, M., Davoli, M., & Perucci, C. A. (2011, December 7). Heroin maintenance for chronic heroin-dependent individuals. *Cochrane Database of Systematic Reviews, 12*, CD003410. doi:10.1002/14651858.CD003410.pub4

Finnegan, J. (2019, September 18). 16 doctors and medical professionals charged in fraud and opioid takedown in Texas. *FierceHealthcare*, p. 1. FiercePracticeManagement.

Flacke, J. W., Flacke, W. E., & Bloor, B. C. (1987). Histamine release by four narcotics: A double-blind study in humans. *Anesthesia and Analgesia, 66*(8), 723–730.

Flassing, J. (2010). Buprenorphine: A more accessible treatment for opioid dependence. *Journal of the American Academy of Physician Assistants, 23*(9), 40–43.

Fleischauer, A. T., Ruhl, L., & Rhea, S. (2017, June 9). Hospitalizations for endocarditis and associated health care costs among persons with diagnosed drug dependence—North Carolina, 2010–2015. *Morbidity and Mortality Weekly Report, 66*(22), 569–573.

Forget, J. A. (2021a, February 19). Final defendant—A drug supplier in D.C. and Prince George's county drug conspiracy—pleads guilty. *DEA Press Release, Washington, D.C. Division*, pp. 1–2. Washington, DC: U.S. Department of Justice.

Forget, J. A. (2021b, February 9). Two sentenced for role in Maryland-to-Virginia heroin pipeline & overdose death. *DEA Press Release, Washington, D.C. Division*, pp. 1–2. Washington, DC: U.S. Department of Justice.

Forget, J. A. (2021c, March 4). Pharmacist sentenced to more than 14 years in federal prison for a drug distribution conspiracy and for murder for hire. *DEA Press Release, Washington, D.C. Division*, pp. 1–3. Washington, DC: U.S. Department of Justice.

Fox, M. (2018, September 10). Doctors gave no reason for a third of opioid prescriptions study finds. *NBC News*, p. 1. NBC.

Frieden, T. R., & Houry, D. (2016, March 15). *Reducing the risks of relief—The CDC opioid-prescribing guideline [Epub ahead of print]*. PubMed—NCBI. Retrieved April 7, 2016, from www.gov.nih.gov/pubmed/?term=frieden+houry

Fudin, J. (2018, January 6). Opioid agonists, partial agonists, antagonists: Oh my! *Pharmacy Times*, pp. 1–8.

Galvin, G. (2019, April 16). Addiction among older adults poses complex challenges. *U.S. News & World Report*, pp. 1–2. U.S. News & World Report.

Gandey, A. (2010, November 9). Propoxyphene withdrawn from US market. *Medscape*, pp. 1–2. WebMD.

Garbutt, J. C., Kranzler, H. R., & O'Malley, S. S. (2005). Efficacy and tolerability of long-acting injectable naltrexone for alcohol dependence: A randomized controlled study. *JAMA, The Journal of the American Medical Association, 293*, 1617–1625.

Garnock-Jones, K. P. (2015). Naloxegol: A review of its use in patients with opioid-induced constipation. *Drugs, 75*(4), 419–425. doi:10.1007/s40265-015-0357-2

Gastfriend, D. R. (2014). A pharmaceutical industry perspective on the economics of treatments for alcohol and opioid use disorders. *Annals of the New York Academy of Sciences, 1327*, 112–130. doi:10.1111/nyas.12538

Gharagozlou, P., Demirci, H., & Clark, J. D. (2002). Activation profiles of opioid ligands in HEK cells expressing delta opioid receptors. *BMC Neuroscience, 3*(1), 19.

Gibson, S. A., & McMahon, M. (2021, February 5). Essex county man indicted for operating heroin mill in his apartment. *DEA Press Release*. U.S. Department of Justice, Washington, DC.

Girion, L., Glover, S., & Smith, D. (2011, September 17). Drug deaths now outnumber traffic fatalities in U.S., data show. *Los Angeles Times*, pp. 1–3. Retrieved from http://articles.latimes.com/2011/sep/17/local/la-me-drugs-epidemic-20110918

Gladden, R. M., Martinez, P., & Seth, P. (2016, August 26). Fentanyl law enforcement submissions and increases in synthetic opioid-involved overdose deaths—27 states, 2013–2014. *MMWR, Morbidity & Mortality Weekly Report, 65*(33), 837–843. doi:10.15585/mmwr.mm6533a2

Gnanadesigan, N., Espinoza, R. T., & Smith, R. (2005, July–August). Interaction of serotonergic antidepressants and opioid analgesics: Is serotonin syndrome going undetected? *Journal of the American Medical Directors Association, 6*(4), 265–269.

Gold, J. (2016, December 20). Opioids can derail the lives of older people, too. *NPR*, pp. 1–2.

Goldenbaum, D. M., Christopher, M., & Gallagher, R. M. (2008, September). Physicians charged with opioid analgesic-prescribing offenses. *Pain Medicine, 9*(6), 737–747. doi:10.1111/j.1526-4637.2008.00482.x

Gopal, A. A. (2015). Physician-assisted suicide: Considering the evidence, existential distress, and an emerging role for psychiatry. *The Journal of the American Academy of Psychiatry and the Law, 43*(2), 183–190.

Gordon, E. (2018, September 27). In Canada, some doctors are prescribing heroin to treat heroin addiction. *Public Radio International*, pp. 1–5. PRI.

Gossop, M., & Moos, R. (2008). Substance misuse among older adults: A neglected but treatable problem. *Addiction, 103*, 347–348.

Gossop, M., Drake, S., & Griffiths, P. (1995). The Severity of Dependence Scale (SDS): Psychometric properties of the SDS in English and Australian samples of heroin, cocaine and amphetamine users. *Addiction, 90*(5), 607–614.

Grassin-Delyle, S., Buenestado, A., & Naline, E. (2012). Intranasal drug delivery: An efficient and non-invasive route for systemic administration: Focus on opioids. *Pharmacology & Therapeutics*, *134*(3), 366–379. doi:10.1016/j.pharmthera.2012.03.003

Graves, D. A., Foster, T. S., & Batenhorst, R. L. (1983, September 1). Patient-controlled analgesia. *Annals of Internal Medicine*, *99*(3).

Greenstein, R. A., Arndt, I. C., & McLellan, A. T. (1984). Naltrexone: A clinical perspective. *The Journal of Clinical Psychiatry*, *45*(9, part 2), 25–28.

Greenthal, E., Lurie, P., & Doyon, S. (2021, January 12). Opioid exposure associated with poppy consumption reported to poison control centers and the U.S. Food and Drug Administration. *Clinical Toxicology*, 1–14. doi:10.1080/15563650.2020.1866766

Greenwald, M. K., Comer, S. D., & Fiellin, D. A. (2014, November 1). Buprenorphine maintenance and mu-opioid receptor availability in the treatment of opioid use disorder: Implications for clinical use and policy. *Drug and Alcohol Dependence*, *144*, 1–11. doi:10.1016/j.drugalcdep.201 . . .???

Guardian Staff. (2019, October 3). Doctor gets 40 years in prison for prescribing over 500,000 opioid doses. *The Guardian*, pp. 1–3.

Gudin, J. (2012, December). Opioid therapies and cytochrome P450 interactions. *Journal of Pain and Symptom Management*, *44*(6S), S4–S14. doi:10.1016/j.jpainsymman.2012.08.013

Guy, G. P., Haegerich, T. M., & Evans, M. E. (2019, August 6). Vital signs: Pharmacy-based naloxone dispensing—United States, 2012–2018. *MMWR, Morbidity and Mortality Weekly Report*, pp. 1–5. CDC.

Guy, G. P., Zhang, K., & Bohm, M. K. (2017, July 7). Vital signs: Changes in opioid prescribing in the United States. 2006–2015. *MMWR, Morbidity and Mortality Weekly Report*, *66*(26), 697–704.

Haber, I., Pergolizzi, J., & LeQuang, J. A. (2019, June). Poppy seed tea: A short review and case study. *Pain Therapy*, *8*(1), 151–155. doi:10.1007/s40122-019-0113-5

Hadland, S. E., Cerda, M., & Li, Y. (2018). Association of pharmaceutical industry marketing of opioid products to physicians with subsequent opioid prescribing. *JAMA Internal Medicine*, *178*(6), 861–863.

Haffajee, R. L., & Mello, M. M. (2017, December 14). Drug companies' liability for the opioid epidemic. *The New England Journal of Medicine*, *377*, 2301–2305.

Hamilton, R. J., Olmedo, R. E., & Shah, S. (2002). Complications of ultrarapid opioid detoxification with subcutaneous naltrexone pellets. *Academic Emergency Medicine*, *9*(1), 63–68.

Han, B., Gfroerer, J. C., & Colliver, J. D. (2009a). *An examination of trends in illicit drug use among adults aged 50 to 59 in the United States*. Rockville, MD: Substance Abuse and Mental Health Services Administration, Office of Applied Studies.

Han, B., Gfroerer, J. C., & Colliver, J. D. (2009b). Substance use disorder among older adults in the United States in 2020. *Addiction*, *104*(1), 88–96.

Hansten, P. D. (1986). Drug interactions. In A. M. Pagliaro, & L. A. Pagliaro (Eds.), *Pharmacologic Aspects of Nursing* (pp. 170–179). St. Louis, MO: C. V. Mosby.

Hansten, P. D. (2002). Pediatric drug interactions. In L. A. Pagliaro, & A. M. Pagliaro (Eds.), *Problems in pediatric drug therapy* (4th ed., pp. 315–346). Washington, DC: American Pharmaceutical Association.

Hard, B. (2014, November 28). Management of opioid painkiller dependence in primary care: Ongoing recovery with buprenorphine/naloxone. *BMJ Case Reports*, 207308. doi:10.1136/bcr-2014-207308

Harris, K. (2018, November 18). Scammed senior citizens being recruited as drug mules: CBSA. *CBC News*, pp. 1–2. CBC News.

Hartnoll, R. L., Mitcheson, M. C., & Battersby, A. (1980). Evaluation of heroin maintenance in controlled trial. *Archives of General Psychiatry*, *37*(8), 877–884. doi:10.1001/archpsy.1980017802100035003

Hasin, D. S., O'Brien, C. P., & Auriacombe, M. (2013). DSM-5 criteria for substance use disorders: Recommendations and rationale. *The American Journal of Psychiatry*, *170*(8), 834–851. doi:10.1176/appi.ajp.2013.12060782

Havens, J. R., Leukefeld, C. G., & DeVeaugh-Geiss, A. M. (2014, June 1). The impact of a reformulation of extended-release oxycodone designed to deter abuse in a sample of prescription opioid abusers. *Drug and Alcohol Dependence*, *139*, 9–17. doi:10.1016/j.drugalcdep.2014.02.018

Hayes, C. J., Krebs, E. E., & Hudson, T. (2020). Impact of opioid dose escalation on the development of substance use disorders, accidents, self-inflicted injuries, opioid overdoses and alcohol and non-opioid drug-related overdoses: A retrospective cohort study. *Addictions*, *115*(6), 1098–1112. doi:10.1111/add.14940

Hedegaard, H., Bastian, B. A., & Trinidad, J. P. (2018, December). Drugs most frequently involved in drug overdose deaths: United States, 2011–2016. *National Vital Statistics Reports*, *67*(9), 1–14.

HHS, Health and Human Services. (2018, December 19). HHS recommends prescribing or co-prescribing naloxone to those at high risk for an opioid overdose. *HHS Press Release*, pp. 1–5.

Hiltunen, A. J., & Eklund, C. (2002). Withdrawal from methadone maintenance treatment. Reasons for not trying to quit methadone. *European Addiction Research*, *8*(1), 38–44.

Holder, R. M., & Rhee, D. (2016, March 6). Novel oral therapies for opioid-induced bowel dysfuntion in patients with chronic noncancer pain [Epub ahead of print]. *Pharmacotherapy*. doi:10.1002/phar.1711

Holmquist, G. L. (2009). Opioid metabolism and effects of cytochrome P450. *Pain Medicine*, *10*(S1), S20–S29. doi:10.1111/j.1526-4637.2009.00596.x

Holscher, F., Reissner, V., & Di Furia, L. (2010). *Differences between men and women in the course of opiate dependence: Is there a telescoping effect? 260*(3), 235–241. doi:10.1007/s00406-009-0053-x

Houlihan, D. J. (2004). Serotonin syndrome resulting from coadministration of tramadol, venlafaxine, and mirtazapine. *The Annals of Pharmacotherapy*, *38*(3), 411–413.

Hughes, J., Smith, W., & Kosterlitz, H. W. (1975, December). Identification of two related pentapeptides from the brain with potent opiate agonist activity. *Nature*, *258*, 577–579. doi:10.1038/258577a0

Huhn, A. S., Strain, E. C., & Tompkins, D. A. (2018, December 1). A hidden aspect of the U.S. opioid crisis: Rise in first-time treatment admissions for older adults with opioid use disorder. *Drug and Alcohol Dependence*, *193*, 142–147. doi:10.1016/j.drugalcdep.2018.10.002

Inturrisi, C. E. (2002). Clinical pharmacology of opioids for pain. *The Clinical Journal of Pain*, *18*(4 Suppl), S3-S13.

Jamison, R. N., Ross, E. L., & Michna, E. (2010). Substance misuse treatment for high risk chronic pain patients on opioid therapy: A randomized trial. *Pain*, *150*(3), 390–400. doi:10.1016/j.pain.2010.02.033

Jauregui, J. E., Nutt, R. J., & Margolis, A. M. (2020). Frequency of opioid prescribing for acute low back pain in a rural emergency department. *Advanced Emergency Nursing Journal*, *42*(3), 210–214. doi:10.1097/TME.0000000000000310

Johansson, J., Hirvonen, J., & Lovro, Z. (2019). Intranasal naloxone rapidly occupies brain mu-opioid receptors in human subjects. *Neuropsychopharmacology*, 1–7. doi:10.1038/s41386-010-0368-x

Johnson, F., & Setnik, B. (2011). Morphine sulfate and naltrexone hydrochloride extended-release capsules: Naltrexone release, pharmacodynamics, and tolerability. *Pain Physician, 14*(4), 391–406.

Jones, C. M., Logan, J., & Gladden, R. M. (2015, July 10). Vital signs: Demographic and substance use trends among heroin users—United States, 2002–2013. *MMWR, Morbidity and Mortality Weekly Report, 64*, 719–725.

Jones, C. M., Muhuri, P. K., & Lurie, P. G. (2017). Trends in the nonmedical use of OxyContin, United States, 2006 to 2013. *The Clinical Journal of Pain, 33*(5), 452–461. doi:10.1097/AJP.0000000000000426

Jones, C. M., Paulozzi, L. J., & Mack, K. A. (2014). Alcohol involvement in opioid pain reliever and benzodiazepine drug abuse—Related emergency department visits and drug-related deaths—United States, 2010. *Morbidity and Mortality Weekly Report (MMWR), 63*(40), 881–885.

Jones, J. D., Sherwin, E., & Martinez, S. (2020, January). Naloxone-induced withdrawal in individuals with and without fentanyl-positive urine samples. *American Journal of Addiction, 29*(1), 51–56. doi:10.1111/ajad/12979

Jones, R., Prommer, E., & Backstedt, D. (2015, July 6). Naloxegol: A novel therapy in the management of opioid-induced constipation. *American Journal of Hospice and Palliative Care*, Epub ahead of print. Retrieved March 12, 2016, from www.ncbi.nim.nih.gov/pubmed/26150678

Joseph, H., Stancliff, S., & Langrod, J. (2000, October-November). Methadone maintenance treatment (MMT): A review of historical and clinical issues. *The Mount Sinai Journal of Medicine, New York, 67*(5–6), 347–364.

Katz, J., Rosenbloom, B. N., & Fashler, S. (2015). Chronic pain, psychopathology, and DSM-5 somatic symptom disorder. *Canadian Journal of Psychiatry, 60*(4), 160–167. doi:10.1177/070674371506000402

Katzman, J. G., Takeda, M. Y., & Greenberg, N. (2020, February 5). Association of take-home naloxone and opioid overdose reversals performed by patients in an opioid treatment program. *JAMA Network Open, 3*(2), e2001127. doi:10.1001/jamanetworkopen.20230.0117

Kauffman, R. E., Banner, W., & Blumer, J. L. (1990, September). Naloxone dosage and route of administration for infants and children: Addendum to emergency drug doses for infants and children. *Pediatrics, 86*(3), 484–485.

Kaur, H. (2020, May 10). The opioid epidemic was already a national crisis. COVID-19 could be making things worse. *CNN News*, pp. 1–4. Warner Media.

Keen, L., Khan, M., & Clifford, L. (2014, September). Injection and non-injection drug use and infectious disease in Baltimore city: Differences by race. *Addictive Behaviors, 39*(9), 1325–1328. doi:10.1016/j.addbeh.2014.04.020

Kessler, A., Cohen, E., & Grise, K. (2018, March 12). CNN exclusive: The more opioids doctors prescribe, the more money they make. *CNN Health*, pp. 1–10. CNN.

Kirchmayer, U., Davoli, M., & Verster, A. (2000). Naltrexone maintenance treatment for opioid dependence. *Cochrane Database of Systematic Reviews, 2*, CD001333.

Klous, M. G., Lee, W. C., & Hillebrand, M. (2006, January-February). Analysis of diacetylmorphine, caffeine, and degradation products after volatilization of pharmaceutical heroin for inhalation. *Journal of Analytical Toxicology, 30*(1), 6–13. doi:10.1093/jat/30.1.6

Knopf, T. (2019, January 21). From abroad. *North Carolina Health News*, pp. 1–12. Zurich and Geneva, Switzerland: North Carolina Health News.

Knutsen, H. K., Alexander, J., & Barregard, L. (2018, May 16). Update of the scientific opinion on opium alkaloids in poppy seeds. *EFSA Journal*, *16*(5), e05243. doi:10.2903/j.efsa.2018.5243

Kovas, A. E., McFarland, B. H., & McCarty, D. J. (2007). Buprenorphine for acute heroin detoxification: Diffusion of research into practice. *Journal of Substance Abuse Treatment*, *32*(2), 199–206.

Krantz, A. J., Hershow, R. C., & Prachand, N. (2003). Heroin insufflation as a trigger for patients with life-threatening asthma. *Chest*, *123*(2), 510–517.

Kroslak, T., Laforge, K. S., & Gianotti, R. J. (2007, October). The single nucleotide polymorphism A118G alters functional properties of the human mu opioid receptor. *Journal of Neurochemistry*, *103*(1), 77–87. doi:10.1111/j.1471-4159.2007.04738.x

Kumar, R. (2017). Association between concurrent use of prescription opioids and benzodiazepines and overdose: Retrospective analysis. *BMJ*, *356*, 760.

Lee, J. D., Friedmann, P. D., & Kinlock, T. W. (2016). Extended-release naltrexone to prevent opioid relapse in criminal justice offenders. *New England Journal of Medicine*, *374*(13), 1232–1242. doi:10.1056/NEJMoa1505409

Leppert, W. (2015, April 16). Emerging therapies for patients with symptoms of opioid-induced bowel dysfunction. *Drug Design, Development and Therapy*, *9*, 2215–2231. doi:10.2147/DDDT.S32684

Lotsch, J. (2005, May). Opioid metabolites. *Journal of Pain and Symptom Management*, *29*(Suppl 5), S10–S24. doi:10.1016/j.jpainsymman.2005.01.004

Lyapustina, T., & Alexander, G. C. (2015, June 13). The prescription opioid addiction and abuse epidemic: How it happened and what we can do about it. *The Pharmaceutical Journal*, *294*(7866). doi:10.1211/PJ.2015.20068579

Ma, J. D., Horton, J. M., & Hwang, M. (2014). A single-center, retrospective analysis evaluating the utilization of the opioid risk tool in opioid-treated cancer patients. *Journal of Pain & Palliative Care Pharmacotherapy*, 1–6. doi:10.3109/15360288.2013.869647

MacDonald, R., Heiner, J., & Villarreal, J. (2015). Loperamide dependence and abuse. *BMJ Case Reports, pii*, brc2015209705. doi:10.1136/bcr-2015-209705

MacLaren, E. (2015). Oxycodone history and statistics. Drugabuse.com, pp. 1–23. Retrieved March 12, 2016, from http://drugabuse.com/library/oxycodone-history-and-statistics/

Madar, I., Lever, J. R., & Kinter, C. M. (1996, September). Imaging of delta opioid receptors in human brain by N1'([11C]naltrindole and PET. *Synapse*, *24*(1), 19–28. doi:10.1002/(SICI)1098-2396(199609)24:1

Madden, N. (2019, August 20). A single ICE bust seizes enough fentanyl to kill'750,000 people,' prosecutor says. *Conservative Review*, 1.

Magwood, O., Salvalaggio, G., & Beder, M. (2020, January 16). The effectiveness of substance use interventions for homeless and vulnerable housed persons: A systematic review of systematic reviews on supervised consumption facilities, managed alcohol programs, and pharmacological agents for opioid use disorder. *PLoS One*, 1–31. doi:10.1371/journal.pone.0227298

Malleson, P. N., Connell, H., & Bennett, S. M. (2001). Chronic musculoskeletal and other idiopathic pain syndromes. *Archives of Disease in Childhood*, *84*, 189–192.

Manchikanti, L. (2007). National drug control policy and prescription drug abuse. *Pain Physician*, *10*, 399–424.

Manchikanti, L., & Singh, A. (2008). Therapeutic opioids: A ten-year perspective on the complexities and complications of the escalating use, abuse, and nonmedical use of opioids. *Pain Physician, 11*(Suppl 2), S63–S88.

Manglik, A. (2020, January 1). Molecular basis of opioid action: From structures to new leads. *Biological Psychiatry*, 6–14. doi:10.1016/j.biopsych.2019.08.028

Many, G. M., & Drazin, D. (2019). Is the rise in spinal infections an unexpected consequence of the opioid epidemic? *Neurosurgical Focus, 46*(1), 1–2. doi:10.3171/2018/10.FOCUS18449

Marraffa, J. M., Holland, M. G., & Sullivan, R. W. (2014). Cardiac conduction disturbance after loperamide abuse. *Clinical Toxicology (Philadelphia), 52*(9), 952–957. doi:10.3109/15563650.2014.969371

Mars, S. G., Bourgois, P., & Karandinos, G. (2014, March). "Every 'never' I ever said came true": Transitions from opioid pills to heroin injecting. *International Journal on Drug Policy, 25*(2), 257–266. doi:10.1016/j.drugpo.2013.10.004

Marsh, J. C., Park, K., & Lin, Y.-A. (2018, April). Gender differences in trends for heroin use and nonmedical prescription opioid use, 2007–2014. *Journal of Substance Abuse Treatment, 87*, 79–85. doi:10.1016/j.jsat.2018.01.001

Mauer, P. M., & Bartkowski, R. R. (1993). Drug interactions of clinical significance with opioid analgesics. *Drug Safety, 8*(1), 30–48.

Mauer, U., Kager, C., & Fellinger, C. (2014, February 27). Risk of anaphylaxis in opioid dependent persons: Effects of heroin versus substitution substances. *Substance Abuse Treatment, Prevention, and Policy, 9*, 12. doi:10.1186/1747-597X-9-12

McCance-Katz, E. F., Sullivan, L., & Nallani, S. (2010). Drug interactions of clinical importance among the opioids, methadone and buprenorphine, and other frequently prescribed medications: A review. *The American Journal on Addictions, 19*(1), 4–16. doi:10.1111/j.1521-0391.2009.00005.x

McCarthy, D. M., Tomlinson, K. L., & Anderson, K. G. (2005). Relapse in alcohol and drug disordered adolescents with comorbid psychopathology. *Psychology of Addictive Behaviors, 19*, 28–34.

McCleane, G. (2008, May). Pain perception in the elderly patient. *Clinics in Geriatric Medicine, 24*(2), 203–211.

McDonald, D. C., & Carlson, K. E. (2013, July 17). Estimating the prevalence of opioid diversion by "Doctor Shoppers" in the United States. *PLoS One, 8*(7), 1–25, e69241. doi:10.1371/journal.pone.0069241

McDonald, J., & Lambert, D. G. (2005, February). Opioid receptors. *Continuing Education in Anaesthesia, Critical Care & Pain, 5*(1), 22–25. doi:10.1093/bjaceaccp/mki004

McDonald, J., & Lambert, D. G. (2014). Opioid receptors. *Continuing Education in Anaesthesia, Critical Care & Pain*, 1–6. doi:10.1093/bjaceaccp/mku041

McGirr, A., Renaud, J., & Seguin, M. (2008, May 31). Course of major depressive disorder and suicide outcome: A psychological autopsy study. *The Journal of Clinical Psychiatry, 69*(6), 966–970. doi:10.4088/jcp.v69n0612

McHugh, R. K., Votaw, V. R., & Barlow, D. H. (2017, September). Development of an integrated cognitive behavioral therapy for anxiety and opioid use disorder: Study protocol and methods. *Contemporary Clinical Trials, 60*, 105–112. doi:10.1016/j.cct.2017.07.006

McKay, H. (2020, November 12). Chinese 'cartels' quietly operating in Mexico, aiding US drug crisis. *Fox News*, pp. 1–14. Mexico City, Mexico: Fox News.

Meacham, M. C., Strathdee, S. A., & Rangel, G. (2016). Prevalence and correlates of heroin-methamphetamine co-injection among persons who inject drugs in San Diego, California, and Tijuana, Baja California, Mexico. *Journal of Studies on Alcohol and Drugs, 77*, 774–781.

Megarbane, B., Gueye, P., & Baud, F. (2003, November). Interactions between benzodiazepines and opioids. *Annales de Medicine Interne*, *154*(Spec No 2), S64–S72.

Meisel, A. (2019, November 19). A history of the law of assisted dying in the United States. *SMU Law Review*, 1–64. University of Pittsburgh. Retrieved from https://ssrn.com/abstract=3491401

Merrett, R. (2018, August 10). 81-year-old woman tried to smuggle 92 lbs. of heroin across US-Mexico border: Police. *Yahoo News*, pp. 1–2. Yahoo.

Messina, B. G., & Worley, M. J. (2019). Effects of craving on opioid use are attenuated after pain coping counseling in adults with chronic pain and prescription opioid addiction. *Journal of Consulting and Clinical Psychology*, *87*(10), 919–926. doi:10.1037/ccp0000399

Michna, E., Kirson, N. Y., & Shei, A. (2014). Use of prescription opioids with abuse-deterrent technology to address opioid abuse. *Current Medical Research and Opinion*, *30*(8), 1589–1598. doi:10.1185/03007995.2014.915803

Minozzi, S., Amato, L., & Vecchi, S. (2011). Oral naltrexone maintenance treatment for opioid dependence. *Cochrane Database of Systematic Reviews*, *4*, CD001333. doi:10,1002/14651858.CD001333.pub4

Mistry, C. J., Bawor, M., & Desai, D. (2014). Genetics of opioid dependence: A review of the genetic contribution in opioid dependence. *Current Psychiatry Reviews*, *10*(2), 156–167.

Mizusawa, K. (2016). Subchapter 7D—Endomorphin. In *Handbook of hormones* (pp. 62–63). Amsterdam, Netherlands: Elsevier. doi:10.1016/B978-0-12-801028-0.00120-3

Moore, B. A., Fiellin, D. A., & Cutter, C. J. (2016, December). Cognitive behavioral therapy improves treatment outcomes for prescription opioid users in primary-care based buprenorphine treatment. *Journal of Substance Abuse Treatment*, *71*, 54–57. doi:10.1016/j.jsat.2016.08.016

Moss, J., & Roscow, C. E. (1983, October). Histamine release by narcotics and muscle relaxants in humans. *Anesthesiology*, *59*(4), 330–339.

Moss, R. B., McCabe Pryor, M., & Baillie, R. (2020). Higher naloxone dosing in a quantitative systems pharmacology model that predicts naloxone-fentanyl competition at the opioid mu receptor level. *PLos One*, *15*(6), e0234683. doi:10.1371/journal.pone.0234683

Motluk, A. (2019, July 30). Self-regulation in health care professions comes under scrutiny. *CMAJ News*, pp. 1–2. CMAJ.

Muhuri, P. K., Gfroerer, J. C., & Davies, M. C. (2013, August). *Associations of nonmedical pain reliever use and initiation of heroin use in the United States*. Retrieved March 3, 2016, from CBHSQ (Center for Behavioral Health Statistics and Quality) Data Review: http://archive.samhsa.gov/data/2k13/DataReview/DR006/nonmedical-pain-reliever-use-2013.htm

Murrell, D., & Case-Lo, C. (2018, May 29). Cirrhosis and hepatitis C: Their connection, prognosis, and more. *Healthline Media*, pp. 1–3.

Naltrexone. (2009, February 1). *Medline Plus*, pp. 1–4. Retrieved from www.nlm.nih.gov/medlineplus/druginfo/meds/a685041.html

National Drug Intelligence Center. (2001, May). *Heroin. California central district dug threat assessment* (pp. 1–8). National Drug Intelligence Center. Retrieved from www.justice.gov/ndic/pubs0/668/heroin.htm

Nelson, E. M., & Philbrick, A. M. (2012, December 12). Avoiding serotonin syndrome: The nature of the interaction between tramadol and selective serotonin reuptake inhibitors. *Annals of Pharmacotherapy*.

NIDA, National Institute on Drug Abuse. (2014, June 24). *What can we do about the heroin overdose epidemic?* (pp. 1–6). Retrieved June 26, 2014, from www.drugabuse.gov/about-nida/noras-blog/2014/06/what-can-we-do-about-heroin-o . . .

NIDA, National Institute on Drug Abuse. (2015a, November 18). *FDA approves naloxone nasal spray to reverse opioid overdose* (pp. 1–4). Retrieved January 12, 2016, from www.drugabuse.gov/news-events/news-releases/2015/11/fda-approves-naloxone-nas . . .

NIDA, National Institute on Drug Abuse. (2015b, December). *Overdose death rates*. Retrieved February 21, 2016, from www.drugabuse.gov/related-topics/trends-statistics/overdose-death-rates

NIDA, National Institute on Drug Abuse. (2016, May 5). *Fake prescription drugs laced with fentanyl* (pp. 1–2). National Institute on Drug Abuse (NIDA). Retrieved May 5, 2016, from www.drugabuse.gov/emerging-trends/fake-prescription-drugs-laced-fentanyl?utm_source=NIDA+Emerging+Trends&utm_campaign=abd868b77 . . .

NIDA, National Institute on Drug Abuse. (2017, November 14). Opioid treatment drugs have similar outcomes once patients initiate treatment. *Press Release*. Bethesda, MD: National Institutes of Health.

NIDA, National Institute on Drug Abuse. (2019, February 19). Monthly buprenorphine injections effective for opioid use disorders. *News Release*. National Institutes of Health.

NIH, National Institute on Drug Abuse. (2018, August). Overdose death rates. *Advancing Addiction Science*, pp. 1–4. NIH.

Niles, J. K., Gudin, J., & Radcliff, J. (2021, February). The opioid epidemic within the COVID-19 pandemic: Drug testing in 2020. *Population Health Management*, *24*(S1), S43–S51. doi:10.1089/pop.2020.0230

Nordrum, A. (2015, July 7). Deaths from heroin overdoses have quadrupled over past decade in US, CDC says. *IBTimes*. Retrieved March 19, 2016, from www.ibtimes.com/deaths-heroin-overdoses-have-quadrupled-over-past-decade-us-cdc-says-1998702?rel=rel2

Nordrum, A. (2016, January 21). Addiction 2016: As heroin use escalates, a new drug to reverse overdoses hits US drugstores. *IBTimes.com*. Retrieved from http:www/ibtimes.com/addiction-2016-heroin-use-escalates-new-drug-reverse-overdoses-hits-us-drugstores-2271924

O'Brien, C. P. (2008, July 16). A 50-year-old woman addicted to heroin. *JAMA*, *300*(3), 1–14. doi:10.1001/jama.300.1.jrr80005

Ochoa, K. C., Hahn, J. A., & Seal, K. H. (2001). Overdosing among young injection drug users in San Francisco. *Addictive Behaviors*, *26*(3), 453–460.

O'Connor, P. G., & Kosten, T. R. (1998). Rapid and ultrarapid opioid detoxification techniques. *JAMA*, *279*(3), 229–234. doi:10.1001/jama.279.3.229

O'Donnell, J. K., Halpin, J., & Mattson, C. L. (2017, November 3). Deaths involving fentanyl, fentanyl analogs, and U-47700–10 states, July-December 2016. *MMWR, Morbidity and Mortality Weekly Report*, *66*(43), 1197–1202.

Okada, Y., Tsuda, Y., & Bryant, S. D. (2002). Endomorphins and related opioid peptides. *Vitamins and Hormones*, *65*, 257–279.

Oliva, E. M., Bowe, T., & Manhapra, A. (2020, March 4). Associations between stopping prescriptions for opioids, length of opioid treatment, and overdose or suicide deaths in US veterans: Observational evaluation. *BMJ Open Access*, *368*(m283), 1–10. doi:10.1136/bmj.m283

Oquendo, M. A., & Baca-Garcia, E. (2014, June). Suicidal behavior disorder as a diagnostic entity in the DSM-5 classification system: Advantages outweigh limitations. *World Psychiatry*, *13*(2), 128–130. doi:10.1002/wps.20116

Orciari Herman, A. (2017, October 19). Extended-release naltrexone seems as effective as standard treatment for opioid dependence. *NEJM Journal Watch*. NEJM.

Overholser, B. R., & Foster, D. R. (2011). Opioid pharmacokinetic drug-drug interactions. *The American Journal of Managed Care*, *17*, S276–S287.

Owen, H., Mather, L. E., & Rowley, K. (1988, November). The development and clinical use of patient-controlled analgesia. *Anaesthesia and Intensive Care*, *16*(4), 437–447.

Oyler, J. M., Cone, E. J., & Joseph, R. E. (2000, October). Identification of hydrocodone in human urine following controlled codeine administration. *Journal of Analytical Toxicology*, *24*, 530–535.

Pagliaro, A. M., & Pagliaro, L. A. (Eds.). (1986). *Pharmacologic aspects of nursing*. St. Louis: C. V. Mosby.

Pagliaro, A. M., & Pagliaro, L. A. (2018). *Women's drug and substance abuse: A comprehensive analysis and reflective synthesis*. New York, NY: Routledge.

Pagliaro, L. A., & Pagliaro, A.M. (Eds.). (1983). *Pharmacologic aspects of aging*. St. Louis: C. V. Mosby.

Pagliaro, L. A., & Pagliaro, A. M. (1999). *PNDR: Psychologists' neuropsychotropic drug reference*. Philadelphia, PA: Brunner/Mazel.

Pagliaro, L. A., & Pagliaro, A. M. (2004). *Pagliaros' comprehensive guide to drugs and substances of abuse*. Washington, DC: American Pharmacists Association.

Pagliaro, L. A., & Pagliaro, A. M. (2009). *Pagliaros' comprehensive guide to the drugs and substances of abuse* (2nd ed.). Washington, DC: American Pharmacists Association.

Papaleontiou, M., Henderson, C. R., & Turner, B. J. (2010). Outcomes associated with opioid use in the treatment of chronic non-cancer pain among older adults: A systematic review and meta-analysis. *Journal of the American Geriatrics Society*, *58*(7), 1353–1369. doi:10.1111/j.1532-5415.2010.02920.x

Park, H., & Bloch, M. (2016, January 19). How the epidemic of drug overdose deaths ripples across America. *The New York Times*. Retrieved July 16, 2016, from www.nytimes.com/interactive/2016/01/07/us/drug-overdose-deaths-in-the-us.html

Park, T. W., Larochelle, M. R., & Saitz, R. (2020). Associations between prescribed benzodiazepines, overdose death and buprenorphine discontinuation among people receiving buprenorphine. *Addiction*, *115*(5), 924–932. doi:10.1111/add.14886

Passik, S. D., Hays, L., & Eisner, N. (2006). Psychiatric and pain characteristics of prescription drug abusers entering drug rehabilitation. *Journal of Pain and Palliative Care Pharmacotherapy*, *20*(2), 5–13.

Pathan, H., & Williams, J. (2012, February). Basic opioid pharmacology: An update. *British Journal of Pain*, *6*(1), 11–16. doi:10.1177/2049463712438493

Patterson Silver Wolf, D. A. (2020, May 20). Real-time data are essential for COVID-19. They're just as important for the opioid overdose crisis. *STAT*, pp. 1–5. STAT.

Pergolizzi, J. V. (2011, September 20). Quantifying the impact of drug-drug interactions associated with opioids. *The American Journal of Managed Care*, *17*, S288–S292.

Pergolizzi, J. V., Labhsetwar, S. A., & Puenpatom, R. A. (2011). Prevalence of exposure to potential CYP450 pharmacokinetc drug-drug interactions among patients with chronic low back pain taking opioids. *Pain Practice*, *11*(3), 230–239.

Pergolizzi, J. V., Ma, L., & Foster, D. R. (2014). The prevalence of opioid-related major potential drug-drug interactions and their impact on health care costs in chronic pain patients. *Journal of Managed Care & Specialty Pharmacy*, *20*(5), 467–476.

Perneger, T. V., Giner, F., & del Rio, M. (1998, July 4). Randomised trial of heroin maintenance programme for addicts who fail in conventional drug treatments. *BMJ*, *317*(7150), 13–18. doi:10.1136/bmj.317.7150.13

Peterson, A. B., Gladden, R. M., & Delcher, C. (2016, August 26). Increases in fentanyl-related overdose deaths—Florida and Ohio, 2013–2015. *MMWR, Morbidity and Mortality Weekly Report*, *65*(33), 844–849. doi:10.15585/mmwr.mm6533a3

Pieper, B., & Templin, T. (2001). Chronic venous insufficiency in persons with a history of injection drug use. *Research in Nursing & Health, 24*(5), 423–432.

Purdon, N., & Palleja, L. (2019, June 19). Free heroin? Unusual clinic offers 'chance at being human again'. *CBC News*, pp. 1–11. CBC.

Raisch, D. W., Fye, C. L., & Boardman, K. D. (2002). Opioid dependence treatment, including buprenorphine/naloxone. *Annals of Pharmacotherapy, 36*(2), 312–321.

Rankin, S. (2019, September 28). Doctor facing life in prison for thousands of opioid doses, contributing to crisis. *The Globe and Mail*, pp. 1–5. Associated Press.

Rantz, J. (2021, February 22). Seattle homeless shelter buys heroin pipes with city funds, teaches rectal injection method. *KTTH News 770*, pp. 1–12. KTTH News.

Reid, M. C., Eccleston, C., & Pillemer, K. (2015). Management of chronic pain in older adults. *BMJ, 350*, h532.

Rettig, C. (2021, March 25). Plot to smuggle heroin and methamphetamine into Fresno county jail results in charges against inmate, mother and associate. *DEA Press Release, San Francisco Division*, pp. 1–2. Washington, DC: U.S. Department of Justice.

Rizzo, R. F. (2000). Physician-assisted suicide in the United States: The underlying factors in technology, health care and palliative medicine. *Theoretical Medicine and Bioethics, 21*(3), 277–289. doi:10.1023/a:1009948715185

Robinson, A., & Wermeling, D. P. (2014, December 15). Intranasal naloxone administration for treatment of opioid overdose. *American Journal of Health-Systems Pharmacy, 71*(24), 2129–2135. doi:10.2146/ajhp130798

Robinson, S. E. (2006). Buprenorphine-containing treatments: Place in the management of opioid addiction. *CNS Drugs, 20*(9), 697–712.

Rosen, D., Hunsaker, A., & Albert, S. M. (2011). Characteristics and consequences of heroin use among older adults in the United States: A review of the literature, treatment implications, and recommendations for further research. *Addictive Behaviors, 36*(4), 279–285. doi:10.1016/j.addbeh.2010.12.012

Ross Perlman, W. (2019, July 10). *Drug use and its consequences increase among middle-aged and older adults* (pp. 1–2). Bethesda, MD: NIH.

Rowland, C. (2019, September 15). Purdue Pharma, drugmaker accused of fueling the opioid epidemic, files for bankruptcy. *The Washington Post*, pp. 1–3.

Rudd, R. A. (2014, October 3). Increases in heroin overdose deaths—28 States, 2010 to 2012. *MMWR, Morbidity and Mortality Weekly Report, 63*(39), 849–854.

Rudd, R. A., Aleshire, N., & Zibbell, J. E. (2016). Increases in drug and opioid overdose deaths—United States, 2000–2014. *MMWR, Morbidity and Mortality Weekly Report, 64*(50), 1378–1382.

Ryan, S. A., & Dunne, R. B. (2018). Pharmacokinetic properties of intranasal and injectable formulations of naloxone for community use: A systematic review. *Pain Management, 8*(3), 231–245.

Rzasa Lynn, R., & Galinkin, J. L. (2018, January). Naloxone dosage for opioid reversal: Current evidence and clinical implications. *Therapeutic Advances in Drug Safety, 9*(1), 63–88. doi:10.1177/2042098617744161

SAMHSA, Substance Abuse and Mental Health Services Administration, Office of Applied Studies. (2009). *Results from the 2008 national survey on drug use and health: National findings* (HHNSDUH Series H-36, HHS Publication No. SMA 09–4434). Rockville, MD.

Satterfield, J., & Nelson, K. L. (2018, July 16). OxyContin maker used subterfuge to sell public on safety, targeted veterans, elderly, suit says. *Knox News*, pp. 1–4. Knoxville, TN: Knox News.

Saunders, K. W., Dunn, K. M., & Von Korff, M. (2010). Relationship of opioid use and dosage levels to fractures in older chronic pain patients. *Journal of General Internal Medicine*, *25*(4), 310–315. doi:10.1007/s11606-009-1218-z

Schaeffer, T. (2012). Abuse-deterrent formulations, an evolving technology against the abuse and misuse of opioid analgesics. *Journal of Medical Toxicology*, *8*, 400–407. doi:10.1007/s13181-012-0270-y

Schepis, T. S., Wastila, L., & Ammerman, B. (2020). Prescription opioid misuse motives in US older adults. *Pain Medicine*, *21*(10), 2237–2243. doi:10.1093/pm/pnz304

Schoener, E. P., Hopper, J. A., & Pierre, J. D. (2002). Injection drug use in North America. *Infectious Disease Clinics of North America*, *16*(3), 535–551.

Schreiber, A. K., Nones, C., & Reis, R. C. (2015, April 15). Diabetic neuropathic pain: Physiopathology and treatment. *World Journal of Diabetes*, *6*(3), 432–444. doi:10.4239/wjd.v6.i3.432

Schroeder, M. O. (2019, January 29). Addressing prescription drug addiction in older adults. *U.S. News & World Report*, pp. 1–3. U.S. News & World Report.

Schulz, P. (2020, May 22). Let's not forget the ongoing epidemic of overdose deaths. *Edmonton Journal*, p. A1.

Schuman-Oilivier, Z., Albanese, M., & Nelson, S. E. (2010). Self treatment: Illicit buprenorphine use by opioid-dependent treatment seekers. *Journal of Substance Abuse Treatment*, *39*(1), 41–50.

Sellers, E. M., Perrino, P. J., & Colucci, S. V. (2013). Attractiveness of reformulated OxyContin(R) tablets: Assessing comparative preferences and tampering potential. *Journal of Psychopharmacology*, *27*(9), 808–816. doi:10.1177/0269881113493364

Seth, P., Scholl, L., & Rudd, R. A. (2018, March 30). Overdose deaths involving opioids, cocaine, and psychostimulants—United States, 2015–2016. *MMWR, Morbidity and Mortality Weekly Report*, *67*(12), 349–358.

Seyani, C., Green, P., & Daniel, L. (2017, April 28). An interesting case of opium tea toxicity. *The BMJ, Case Report*, 1–3. doi:10.1136/bcr-23016-218971

Shah, A., Hayes, C. J., & Martin, B. C. (2017, March 17). Characteristics of initial prescription episodes and likelihood of long-term opioid use—United States, 2006–2013. *MMWR, Morbidity and Mortality Weekly Report*, *66*(10), 265–269.

Sharp, M. J., & Melnik, T. A. (2015). Poisoning deaths involving opioid analgesics—New York State, 2003–2012. *MMWR Morbidity and Mortality Weekly Report*, *64*(14), 377–380.

Shetge, S. A., Dzakovich, M. P., & Cooperstone, J. L. (2020, May 6). Concentrations of the opium alkaloids morphine, codeine, and thebaine in poppy seeds are reduced after thermal and washing treatments but are not affected when incorporated in a model baked product. *Journal of Agricultural and Food Chemistry*, *68*(18), 5241–5248. doi:10.1021/acs.jafc.0c01681

Simpson, C., Smith, M., & Cattan, N. (2020, August 26). Heroin's hidden ingredient is a chemical made by US companies. *Bloomberg Businessweek*, pp. 1–21. Bloomberg L.P.

Singh, J., & Basu, D. (2004). Ultra-rapid opioid detoxification: Current status and controversies. *Journal of Postgraduate Medicine*, *50*(3), 227–232.

Sloan, P. A., & Klimkina, O. (2009). Intranasal abuse of prescription hydrocodone/acetaminophen results in oronasal fistula: A case report. *Journal of Opioid Management*, *5*(6), 383–385.

Smith, H. S. (2011). Morphine sulfate and naltrexone hydrochloride extended release capsules for the management of chronic, moderate-to-severe pain, while reducing morphine-induced subjective effects upon tampering by crushing. *Expert Opinion on Pharmacotherapy*, *12*(7), 1111–1125. doi:10.1517/14656566.2011.571205

Smith, J. P., & Randall, C. L. (2012). Anxiety and alcohol use disorders: Comorbidity and treatment considerations. *Alcohol Research: Current Reviews*, *34*(4), 414–431.

Smith, K., Hopp, M., & Mundin, G. (2012). Low absolute bioavailability of oral naloxone in healthy subjects. *International Journal of Clinical Pharmacology and Therapeutics*, *50*(5), 360–367.

Smith, M. Y., Bailey, J. E., & Woody, G. E. (2007). Abuse of buprenorphine in the United States: 2003–2005. *Journal of Addictive Diseases*, *26*(3), 107–111.

Soelberg, C. D., Brown, R. E., & Du Vivier, D. (2017, November). The US opioid crisis: Current federal and state legal issues. *Anesthesia and Analgesia*, *125*(5), 1675–1681. doi:10.1213/ANE.0000000000002403

Sohn, M., Brinkman, R., & Wellman, G. S. (2020, March). Coprescription of opioid and naloxone in office-based practice and emergency department settings in the United States. *Public Health*, *180*, 82–84. doi:10.1016/puhe.2019.11.014

Solhaug, V., & Molden, E. (2017, October). Individual variability in clinical effect and tolerability of opioid analgesics- Importance of drug interactions and pharmacogenetics. *Scandinavian Journal of Pain*, *17*, 193–200. doi:10.1016/j.sjpain.2017.09.009

Soyka, M. (2015). Buprenorphine-naloxone buccal soluble film for the treatment of opioid dependence: Current Update. *Expert Opinion on Drug Delivery*, *12*(2), 339–347. doi:10.1517/17425247.2014.953479

Spinner, H. L., Lonardo, N. W., & Mulamalla, R. (2015). Ventricular tachycardia associated with high-dose chronic loperamide use. *Pharmacotherapy*, *35*(2), 234–238. doi:10.1002/phar.1540

Sporer, K. A. (1999). Acute heroin overdose. *Annals of Internal Medicine*, *130*(7), 584–590.

Spyres, M. B., van Wijk, X. M., & Lapoint, J. (2018). Two cases of severe opiate toxicity after ingestion of poppy seed tea. *Toxicology Communications*, *2*(1), 102–104. doi:10.1080/24734306.2018.1540178

Stanos, S. P., Bruckenthal, P., & Barkin, R. L. (2012). Strategies to reduce the tampering and subsequent abuse of long-acting opioids: Potential risks and benefits of formulations with physical or pharmacologic deterrents to tampering. *Mayo Clinic Proceedings*, *87*(7), 683–694.

Stellato, C., Cirillo, R., & de Paulis, A. (1992, November). Human basophil/mast cell releasability. IX. Heterogeneity of the effects of opioids on mediator release. *Anesthesiology*, *77*(5), 932–940.

Stevens, R. A., & Ghazi, S. M. (2000, March/April). Routes of opioid analgesic therapy in the management of cancer pain. *Cancer Control*, *7*(2), 132–141.

Stimson, G. V., & Metrebian, N. (2003). *Prescribing heroin: What is the evidence?* Water End, York: Joseph Rowntree Foundation.

Stolberg, S. G., & Gerth, J. (2000, November 16). High-tech stealth being used to sway doctor prescriptions. *The New York Times, Section A*, p. 1.

Strang, J., Griffiths, P., & Gossop, M. (1997). Heroin smoking by 'chasing the dragon': Origins and history. *Addiction*, *92*(6), 685–695.

Strickler, L. (2019, August 27). Purdue Pharma offers $10–12 billion to settle opioid claims. *NBC News*, pp. 1–3.

Swortwood, M. (2017, October 10). Home-brewed poppy seed tea can be lethal. *Sam Houston State University Press Release*, pp. 1–4.

Tanum, L., Solli, K. K., & Latif, Z. E. (2017, October 18). The effectiveness of injectable extended-release naltrexone vs daily buprenorphine-naloxone for opioid dependence: A randomized clinical noninferiority trial. *JAMA Psychiatry*. doi:10.1001/jamapsychiatry.2017.3206

Tarabar, A. F., & Nelson, L. S. (2003, April). The resurgence and abuse of heroin by children in the United States. *Current Opinion in Pediatrics, 15*(2), 210–215.

Tarentino, F., & Underwood, J. (2021, January 6). Anchorage doctor sentenced for prescribing medically unnecessary opioids in health care fraud scheme. *DEA Press Release, Seattle Division*, pp. 1–2. Washington, DC: U.S. Department of Justice.

Thiesset, H. F., Schliep, K. C., & Stokes, S. M. (2020, August). Opioid misuse and dependence screening practices prior to surgery. *Journal of Surgical Research*, 200–205. doi:10.1016/j.jss.2020.03.015

Tobin, S. C. (2020, April 2). *Many people treated for opioid overdose in emergency departments die within 1 year* (pp. 1–5). NIDA Notes. Bethesda, MD: NIDA.

Toshikuni, N., Arisawa, T., & Tsutsumi, M. (2014, March 21). Hepatitis C-related cirrhosis—strategies for the prevention of hepatic decompensation, hepatocarcinogenesis, and mortality. *World Journal of Gastroenterology, 20*(11), 2876–2887. doi:10.3748/wig.v20.i11.2876

Trafton, J. A., Oliva, E. M., & Horst, D. A. (2004). Treatment needs associated with pain in substance use disorder patients: Implications for concurrent treatment. *Drug and Alcohol Dependence, 73*(1), 23–31. doi:10.1016/j.drugalcdep.2003.08.007

Traynor, J. (2012). Mu-opioid receptors and regulators of G protein signaling (RGS) proteins: From a symposium on new concepts in mu-opioid pharmacology. *Drug and Alcohol Dependence, 121*(3), 173–180. doi:10.1016/j.drugalcdep.2011.10.027

Trescot, A. M., Datta, S., & Lee, M. (2008). Opioid pharmacology. *Pain Physician, 11*(Special Issue), S133–S153.

Tsui, J. I., Herman, D. S., & Kettavong, M. (2010). Physician introduction to opioids for pain among patients with opioid dependence and depressive symptoms. *Journal of Substance Abuse Treatment, 39*(4), 378–383. doi:10.1016/j.jsat.2010.06.012

Tsui, J. I., Lira, M. C., & Cheng, D. M. (2016, September 1). Chronic pain, craving, and illicit opioid use among patients receiving opioid agonist therapy. *Drug and Alcohol Dependence, 166*, 26–31. doi:10.1016/j.drugalcdep.2016.06.024

U.S. Department of Veterans Affairs. (2020). *Opioid use and suicide risk*. Washington, DC: Veterans Health Administration.

Uchtenhagen, A. A. (2011, March). Heroin maintenance treatment: From idea to research to practice. *Drug and Alcohol Dependence, 30*(2), 130–137. doi:10.1111/j.1465-3362.2010.00266.x

UN, United Nations. (1953, March 1). *The opium alkaloids* (pp. 13–14). Geneva, Switzerland: UN.

Underner, M., Perriot, J., & Peiffer, G. (2017, July-August). Asthma and heroin use. *La Presse Medicale, 46*(7–8 (Part 1)), 660–675. doi:10.1016/j.lpm.2017.06.002

Unick, G. J., Rosenblum, D., & Mars, S. G. (2013). Intertwined epidemics: National demographic trends in hospitalizations for heroin- and opioid-related overdoses, 1993–2009. *PloS One, 8*, e54496.

USDHHS, U.S. Department of Health and Human Services. (2015). *Abuse-deterrent opioids—evaluation and labeling: Guidance for industry*. USDHHS, Division of Drug Information. Silver Springs: Food and Drug Administration.

Valentino, R. J., & Volkow, N. D. (2018). Untangling the complexity of opioid receptor function. *Neuropsychopharmacology, 43*, 2514–2520. doi:10.1038/s41386-018-0225-3

Vellucci, R., Mediati, R. D., & Gasperoni, S. (2017). Assessment and treatment of breakthrough cancer pain: From theory to clinical practice. *Journal of Pain Research, 10*, 2147–2155. doi:10.2147/JPR.S135807

Verdurmen, M. J., Videler, A. C., & Kamperman, A. M. (2017, September 1). Cognitive behavioral therapy in later life: A prospective comparative explorative pilot study in two clinical populations. *Dovepress, 2017:13*, 2331–2339. doi:10.2147/NDT.S141208

Vikander, T. (2020, April 16). Coronavirus prompts Canada to roll out safe drugs for street users. *Reuters*, pp. 1–4. Vancouver, Canada: Reuters.

Vivolo-Kantor, A. M., Seth, P., & Gladden, R. M. (2018, March 9). Vital signs: Trends in emergency department visits for suspected opioid overdoses—United States, July 2016—September 2017. *MMWR, Morbidity and Mortality Weekly Report*, *67*(9), 279–285.

Volkow, N. D. (2014, May 14). *America's addiction to opioids: Heroin and prescription drug abuse*. National Institute on Drug Abuse (NIDA). Retrieved March 12, 2016, from www.drugabuse.gov/about-nida/legislative-activities/testimony-to-congress/2016/americas-addiction-to-opioids-heroin-prescription-drug-abuse

Volkow, N. D., & McLellan, A. T. (2016, March 31). *Opioid abuse in chronic pain*. Retrieved March 30, 2016, from NEJM Resident E-Bulletin: resebulletin@nejm.org

Volpicelli, J. R., Clay, K. L., & Watson, N. T. (1995). Naltrexone in the treatment of alcoholism: Predicting response to naltrexone. *The Journal of Clinical Psychiatry*, *56*(Suppl 7), 39–44.

Vosburg, S. K., Jones, J. D., & Manubay, J. M. (2012). Assessment of a formulation designed to be crush-resistant in prescription opioid abusers. *Drug and Alcohol Dependence*, *126*, 206–215. doi:10.1016/j.drugalcdep.2012.05.013

Wakeman, S. E., Larochelle, M. R., & Ameli, O. (2020, February 5). Comparative effectiveness of different treatment pathways for opioid use disorder. *JAMA Network Open*, *3*(2), 1–12. doi:10.1001/jamanetworkopen.2019.20622

Weber, H. C. (2016). Opioid-induced constipation in chronic noncancer pain. *Current Opinion in Endocrinology, Diabetes and Obesity*, *23*(1), 11–17. doi:10.1097/MED.0000000000000220

Weber, J. M., Tataris, K. L., & Hoffman, J. D. (2012). Can nebulized naloxone be used safely and effectively by emergency medical services for suspected opioid overdose? *Prehospital Emergency Care*, *16*(2), 289–292. doi:10.3109/10903127.2011.640763

Webster, L. R., & Webster, R. M. (2005, November). Predicting aberrant behaviors in opioid-treated patients: Preliminary validation of the opioid risk tool. *Pain Medicine*, *6*(6), 432–442. doi:10.1111/j.1526-4637.2005.00072.x

Weeks, M. A., Clark, E. P., & Mycyk, M. B. (2016). Characteristics of heroin-dependent patients seeking asthma care in the ED. *The American Journal of Emergency Medicine*, *34*(5), 896–898. doi:10.1016/j.ajem.2016.02.005

Weiner, S. G., Baker, O., & Bernson, D. (2020). One-year mortality of patients after emergency department treatment for nonfatal overdose. *Annals of Emergency Medicine*, *5*(1), 13–17.

West, N. A., Severtson, S. G., & Green, J. L. (2015). Trends in abuse and misuse of prescription opioids among older adults. *Drug and Alcohol Dependence*, *149*, 117–121. doi:10.1016/j.drugalcdep.2015.01.027

Wheeler, T. (2019). *Neuropathic pain management* (pp. 1–2). New York, NY: WebMD.

Wickersham, J. A., Azar, M. M., & Cannon, C. M. (2015). Validation of a brief measure of opioid dependence: The rapid opioid dependence screen (RODS). *Journal of Correctional Health*, *21*(1), 12–26. doi:10.1177/1078345814557513

Williams, A. R., & Bisaga, A. (2016). From AIDS to opioids—how to combat an epidemic. *The New England Journal of Medicine*, *375*(9), 813–815.

Winek, C. L., Schweighardt, F. K., & Fochtman, F. W. (1971). Quinine in urinalysis for heroin. *JAMA*, *217*(9), 1243–1244. doi:10.1001/jama.1971.03190090065017

Winn, A. N., Check, D. K., & Farkas, A. (2020). Association of current opioid use with serious adverse events among older adult survivors of breast cancer. *JAMA Network Open, 3*(9), 1–7. doi:10.1001/jamanetwork open.2020.16858

Winstock, A. R. (2016, January 12). *The global drug survey 2015 findings—what did we learn from GDS2015?* (pp. 1–27) Global Drug Survey. Retrieved from www.globaldrugsurvey.com/the-global-drug-survey-2015-findings/

Withington, D. E., Patrick, J. A., & Reynolds, F. (1993). Histamine release by morphine and diamorphine in man. *Anaesthesia, 48*(1), 26–29.

Wolitzky-Taylor, K. B., Castriotta, N., & Lenze, E. J. (2010). Anxiety disorders in older adults: A comprehensive review. *Depression and Anxiety, 27*, 190–211.

Woody, G. E., Cottler, L. B., & Cacciola, J. (1993). Severity of dependence: Data from the DSM-IV field trials. *Addiction, 88*(11). doi:10.1111/j.1360-0443.1993.tb03144.x

Wu, L.-T., & Blazer, D. G. (2011, April). Illicit and nonmedical drug use among older adults: A review. *Journal of Aging and Health, 23*(3), 481–504. doi:10.1177/0898264310386224

Wyman, J., & Radhakrishnan, A. (2018, November). Opioid use disorder (OUD) tool. In *Practice tools* (pp. 1–10). Toronto, ON: Centre for Effective Practice.

Xie, Y., Pope, B. A., & Hunter, A. J. (2016). Cotton fever: Does the patient know best? *Journal of General Medicine, 31*(4), 442–444. doi:10.1007/s11606-015-3424-1

Yewell, J., Haydon, R., & Archer, S. (2002). Complications of intranasal prescription narcotic abuse. *The Annals of Otology, Rhinology, and Laryngology, 111*(2), 174–177.

Yokell, M. A., Zaller, N. D., & Green, T. C. (2011). Buprenorphine and buprenorphine/naloxone diversion, misuse, and illicit use: An international review. *Current Drug Abuse Reviews, 4*(1), 28–41.

Yoshikawa, A., Ramirez, G., & Smith, M. L. (2020). Opioid use and the risk of falls, fall injuries and fractures among older adults: A systematic review and meta-analysis. *Journals of Gerontology: Medical Sciences, 75*(10), 1989–1995. doi:10.1093/gerona/glaaa038

Zhang, J., Ferguson, S., & Barak, L. S. (1998, June). Role for G protein-coupled receptor kinase in agonist-specific regulation of mu-opioid receptor responsiveness. *Proceedings of the National Academy of Sciences of the United States of America, 95*, 7157–7162.

Zuurmond, W. W., Meert, T. F., & Noorduin, H. (2002). Partial versus full agonists for opioid-mediated analgesia—focus on fentanyl and buprenorphine. *Acta Anaesthesiologica Belgica, 53*(3), 193–201.

CHAPTER 6

PRESCRIPTION SEDATIVE-HYPNOTICS

Over the last century and into the first two decades of the new millennium, prescription sedative-hypnotics, a subclass of the psychodepressants, have been increasingly used by older adults—primarily for the management of anxiety disorders and insomnia. They also have been widely abused and medically misused for nursing home "crowd control." Pharmacologically, all of the prescription drugs discussed in this chapter are classified as "sedative-hypnotics." However, some of these drugs—because of their pharmaceutical company-directed development and marketing, as well as FDA approval—may also be classified according to their indications for use as:

1. "Anxiolytics;"
2. "Anticonvulsants;"
3. "Muscle relaxants."

However, regardless of their general classification or indication for use, all prescription sedative-hypnotics are "abusable psychotropic psychodepressants."

Two subclasses of the prescription sedative-hypnotics—"benzodiazepines" and "z-drugs"[1]—are the primary focus of this chapter because of their extensive use by older adults during the new millennium in the U.S. (Table 6.1).[2,3] We first present and discuss the benzodiazepines, followed by the z-drugs, giving special attention to their:

1. Pharmacology—"pharmacodynamics," or mechanism of action; "pharmacokinetics," or absorption, distribution, metabolism, and excretion; "drug-drug interactions;" and "undesired, or harmful, effects and toxicities;"
2. Physical and psychological dependence;
3. Overdosage/unintentional poisoning;
4. Trends in older adult use during the new millennium;
5. Assessment and diagnosis of older adult dependence or use disorder;
6. Treating older adult dependence or use disorder.

---

1. Because both of these subclasses of sedative-hypnotics interact at the same receptor site (see the later related discussion in the Benzodiazepine subsection, benzodiazepine pharmacology, Pharmacodynamics: Mechanism of Action—"Benzodiazepine Receptors") some clinicians and researchers (e.g., Conn, Rabheru, & Checkland, 2019; Pottie, Thompson, & Davies, 2018) classify both subclasses together as "benzodiazepine receptor agonists" (BZRAs). While this is a logical and acceptable classification, we have used the more traditional—and widely accepted classification—sedative-hypnotics (see, for example, Pagliaro & Pagliaro, 1998, 1999, 2004, 2009). Consequently, we discuss the two subclasses as being very closely related pharmacologically, but molecularly/chemically distinct.
2. Other prescription sedative-hypnotics, including the: (1) "barbiturates" (e.g., pentobarbital [Nembutal®], phenobarbital [Luminal®], and secobarbital [Seconal®]); and (2) "miscellaneous sedative-hypnotics" (e.g., chloral hydrate [Noctec®] or suvorexant [Belsomra®]), which were more commonly used in the U.S. from the late 1800s and throughout most of the 1900s, are not discussed in this chapter. For related detailed information and discussion, see Pagliaro and Pagliaro (1998, 2004, 2009).
3. For an overview and discussion of the "non-prescription" sedative-hypnotic that is used mostly by older adults, see Chapter 1, *Alcohol*.

DOI: 10.4324/9781003010333-6

Table 6.1 Prescription Sedative-Hypnotics Commonly Used by Older Adults in the U.S.

CATEGORY Generic Name	BRAND/TRADE NAMES,[4,5]	COMMON STREET NAMES[6]
BENZODIAZEPINES		
Alprazolam	Xanax®	"Bars," "Xan," "Zannies"
Bromazepam	Lectopam®	
Chlordiazepoxide[7]	Librium®	"Libs," "Libbies"
Clobazam	Onfi®	
Clonazepam	Klonopin®, Rivotril®	"Clo," "Klonnies," "K-Pin"
Clorazepate	Tranxene®	
Diazepam	Valium®	"Blues," "Mother's Little Helper," "Vs"
Estazolam	ProSom®	"Sleepies"
Flunitrazepam[8]	Rohypnol®	"Forget Me Pill," "*La Roche*," "Mexican Valium," "*Papas*," "Roofies"
Flurazepam	Dalmane®	
Halazepam	Paxipam®	
Lorazepam	Ativan®	"Zzz"
Midazolam	Versed®	"Dormo," "Hypno"
Nitrazepam	Mogadon®	"Dons," "Moggies"
Oxazepam	Serax®	"Ser"
Prazepam	Centrax®	
Quazepam	Doral®	
Temazepam	Restoril®	"Green Devils," "Temmies"
Triazolam	Halcion®	"Halcyon," "Halcyon Daze"
Z-DRUGS		
Eszopiclone	Lunesta®	
Zaleplon	Sonata®	
Zopiclone	Imovane®, Zimovane®	"Zim-Zims"
Zopidem	Ambien®, Edluar®, Lunata®, Zolpimist®	"Nappien," "No-Go," "Tic-Tacs," "Zim"

4. When available, examples of common brand/trade names are provided.
5. Some brand/trade names (e.g., Serax®) have been officially discontinued by the manufacturer but are still available through the Internet.
6. Partial list. Examples of three to five of the most common street names are provided, when available.
7. Chlordiazepoxide is also available in two combination products (i.e., chlordiazepoxide/clindinium [Librax®] and chlordiazepoxide/amitriptyline [Limbitrol®]).
8. Although not legally produced in the U.S., flunitrazepam is widely available worldwide under the brand/trade name, "Rohypnol®." It is commonly known and used as a date-rape drug.

BENZODIAZEPINES

The benzodiazepine molecule[9] was synthesized in the late 1950s as a pharmacotherapeutic alternative to the barbiturates (i.e., derivatives of barbituric acid), which had dominated the sedative-hypnotic market for the previous 100 years. In 1960, chlordiazepoxide (Librium®) became the first benzodiazepine to be approved by the FDA for use in the U.S. Its introduction was soon followed by diazepam (Valium®) (Pagliaro & Pagliaro, 2004). Over the last 60 years, several hundred different benzodiazepine derivatives were developed. During this time, the benzodiazepines were widely advertised and marketed as being the safest drugs available for managing anxiety and insomnia because, in comparison to the barbiturates, they possessed a significantly higher therapeutic index. For this reason, and because the benzodiazepines were found to be relatively safe and effective for use in clinical practice—they rapidly became the most widely medically-prescribed, and abused, sedative-hypnotics in the U.S.—as well as throughout the rest of the world (Barden Schallemberger & de Fatima Colet, 2016; Pagliaro & Pagliaro, 2004; Yeung, Chung, & Zhang, 2017).

The first benzodiazepine, "chlordiazepoxide" (Librium®), was synthesized in the early 1950s by Leo Sternbach (1908–2005), a chemist working at a branch of the Swiss pharmaceutical company, Hoffmann-La Roche, in New Jersey. However, its potential use was not immediately recognized, and it sat on a shelf in the laboratory for several years until, by chance and with the help of a laboratory assistant, Sternbach discovered its efficacy as a sedative-hypnotic. Subsequently, chlordiazepoxide was aggressively marketed as an effective sedative-hypnotic without abuse potential.[10] It was an immediate marketing success. By 1963, a "chemical sister," diazepam (Valium®) joined the market and, over the following decade, more than two dozen additional "chemical cousins" (i.e., drugs that utilize the basic benzodiazepine structure [see footnote #9] with a slight chemical modification) were synthesized, developed, and marketed. (For further related discussion, see Pagliaro & Pagliaro, 2004.)

The use of the benzodiazepines peaked, worldwide, during the late 1970s. However, inappropriately high rates of prescription and nonprescription/illicit use continued throughout the first two decades of the 21st century, particularly among older adults (Gerlach, Wiechers, & Maust, 2018; Pagliaro & Pagliaro, 1983, 2004, 2009). As identified by Guina and Merrill (2018a, p. 17):

> Despite recommendations against long-term benzodiazepine use. . . . Total benzodiazepine use actually increased from 1999 to 2014, largely driven by increases in long-term use.

Olfson, King, and Schoenbaum (2015, p. 136), in their analysis of benzodiazepine prescription in the U.S. during the first decade of the new millennium, found that:

> In 2008, approximately 5.2% of US adults aged 18 to 80 years used benzodiazepines. The percentage who used benzodiazepines increased with age from 2.6% (18–35 years) to

---

9. The core chemical structure of the benzodiazepines consists of a seven-member heterocyclic diazepine ring fused to a benzene ring.
10. Chlordiazepoxide (Librium®) is not unique in this false claim. Throughout the modern history of pharmaceutical synthesis and marketing of various drugs, it seems that whenever a new psychotropic drug—particularly, one with psychodepressant actions—was developed (e.g., heroin, pentazocine [Talwin®], or zopiclone [Imovane®]), it was, initially, aggressively marketed as being "non-habit forming." In fact, initially, heroin was specifically marketed by Bayer Pharmaceuticals during the late 19th century as a cure for "morphinism" (morphine addiction) (Pagliaro & Pagliaro, 2004)—see Chapter 5, *Prescription Opiate Analgesics and Heroin*.

> 5.4% (36–50 years) to 7.4% (51–64 years) to 8.7% (65–80 years). Benzodiazepine use was nearly twice as prevalent in women as men. The proportion of benzodiazepine use that was long term increased with age from 14.7% (18–35 years) to 31.4% (65–80 years).

Additionally, Gerlach, Maust, and Leong (2018, p. 1560) identified that:

> Benzodiazepine use among older adults is common despite evidence for many potential risks. While treatment guidelines recommend short-term use of benzodiazepines, up to one-third of use is long term, which is most common among older adults.

Although the benzodiazepines continue to be widely used for their desired sedative-hypnotic actions, their use is now being increasingly replaced by the more recently developed z-drugs. In fact, the z-drugs are rapidly becoming the most medically prescribed and abused sedative-hypnotics in the U.S. (see the later section—"Z-Drugs").[11]

Benzodiazepine Pharmacology

The benzodiazepines and their active metabolites share similar sedative and hypnotic actions with no one benzodiazepine being reported to be significantly superior to any other benzodiazepine.[12] However, some older adults may react differently to various benzodiazepines, particularly regarding associated undesired, or harmful, effects and toxicities. These effects and toxicities are discussed in the following subsections, along with other related basic pharmacological principles and concepts. It is important to note that the variability in individual response may be, in large part, due to a "placebo effect."[13] We begin with the pharmacodynamics of the benzodiazepines and their mechanism of psychodepressant action.

Pharmacodynamics: Mechanism of Action

Although the benzodiazepines have been commercially available since the late 1950s, the precise sites and specific mechanisms of their sedative and hypnotic actions, even now, are not fully understood. It is thought that the benzodiazepines act in the CNS, in concert with gamma-aminobutyric acid (GABA), to inhibit neurotransmission, particularly in the cerebral cortex and the limbic system, including the amygdala and the thalamus

---

11. N.B. Although the use of the z-drugs has significantly increased in popularity during the new millennium (see later discussion), there are no current available data that support their significant superiority in terms of clinical efficacy, or safety, over the benzodiazepines.
12. However, the benzodiazepines do significantly differ regarding their anticonvulsant actions. Generally, only clobazam (Onfi®), clonazepam (Rivotril®), clorazepate (Tranxene®), diazepam (Valium®), lorazepam (Ativan®), and midazolam (Versed®) are used to pharmacologically manage seizure disorders. Additionally, clonazepam is probably more appropriately primarily classified as an anticonvulsant, rather than as a sedative-hypnotic, because of its pharmacologic actions and primary medical use.
13. The placebo effect is a psychological mechanism of drug action that applies to all drugs, whether pharmacologically active (e.g., opiate analgesic) or not (e.g., sugar tablet or normal saline injection). Placebo and other drug actions are not mutually exclusive. In fact, as observed in our clinical experience, they generally occur together with the use of most drugs (e.g., the headache relief that is often obtained within seconds after swallowing an aspirin tablet with a glassful of water—prior to its complete absorption and attainment of therapeutic blood concentrations). Only the percentage of response due to the placebo effect differs from individual to individual and from drug to drug—based largely on several variables that are related to the patient, prescriber, drug, and clinical context of use (see the related discussion in this chapter).

(Bergman, 1986). These areas are particularly associated with effects on various specific CNS-mediated functions:

- Amygdala:[14] anger, attention, facial recognition, fear, memory (particularly, episodic-autobiographical memory), pain, pleasure, and social processing;
- Cerebellum: balance, coordination of voluntary motor movements, coordination of eye movements and speech, and learning motor behaviors;
- Cerebral Cortex: arousal, awareness, consciousness, emotional response, executive function, hearing, intellect, language, memory, movement, perception, personality, senses, speech, temperature, and vision;
- Hippocampus: cognition, emotional response, learning, and memory (particularly long-term memory and spatial memory);
- Limbic System: attention, consciousness, emotions, learning, memory, motivation, olfaction, punishment, and reward;
- Reticular Formation: alertness, arousal, cardiovascular control, consciousness, pain modulation, sleep, and somatic motor control;
- Thalamus: alertness, consciousness, mood, motivations, pain modulation, sensory modulation (except for olfaction), and sleep.

Gamma Aminobutyric Acid (GABA)

GABA, a naturally occurring four-carbon, non-protein amino acid, is produced by conversion from glutamate (i.e., glutamic acid)—a major excitatory neurotransmitter—by the enzyme glutamate decarboxylase and the cofactor pyridoxal phosphate (i.e., the active form of vitamin B_6 [pyridoxine]). Chemically, GABA exists in a rather unusual form as a "zwitterion" (i.e., a molecule that contains an equal number of negatively and positively charged functional groups) (Jewett & Sharma, 2020).[15]

Additionally, GABA is the most common inhibitory neurotransmitter found in the CNS with particularly high concentrations in the cerebral cortex, limbic system, and spinal cord. As such, it is associated with several effects, such as amnestic analgesia, anticonvulsant, anxiolytic, hypnotic, muscle relaxant, and sedative effects (Enna & McCarson, 2006; Howard, Twycross, & Shuster, 2014; Pagliaro & Pagliaro, 2004, 2009; Zeilhofer, Neumann, & Munro, 2019). GABA was originally identified in the brains of humans, as well as amphibians (i.e., frogs) and several other animals (e.g., guinea pigs, mice, rabbits, and rats) by Roberts and Frankel (1950). However, its biological activity and significance were not recognized for almost a decade (Spiering, 2018).

GABA RECEPTOR COMPLEX. A GABA receptor complex has been identified, at which the benzodiazepines appear to enhance GABA-mediated chloride influx through chloride ion channels (see Figure 6.1). Consequently, the inhibitory effect of a given concentration of GABA, which is present in the neuronal membrane, is significantly augmented (Bergman, 1986; Cheng, Wallace, & Ponteri, 2018).

14. Generally, the "amygdala," "hippocampus," and "thalamus" are considered to be part of the limbic system.
15. This is in contrast to most ions that predominantly exist in either a negatively charged (i.e., anion) or a positively charged (i.e., cation) form.

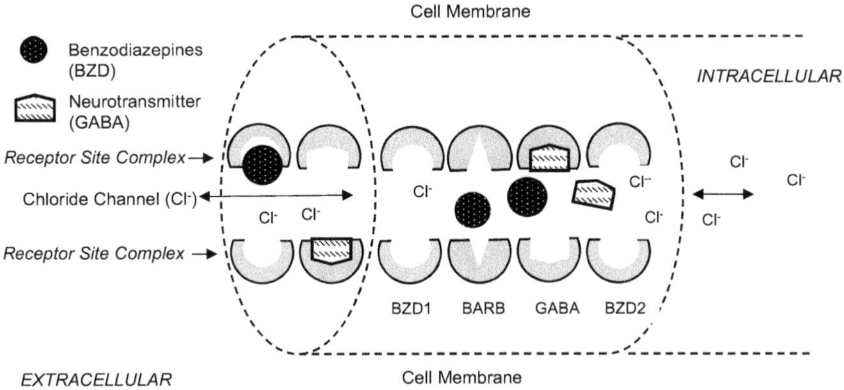

Figure 6.1 The GABA Benzodiazepine Receptor

Over 50 years ago, three GABA receptors were identified in all regions of the brain (Olsen & DeLorey, 1999). They were designated as "$GABA_A$," "$GABA_B$," and "$GABA_C$."[16] However, their importance was not fully realized until the early 1970s. The $GABA_A$ receptor is the most important and the most studied of the three GABA receptors and is primarily localized on post-synaptic membranes. More appropriately conceptualized as a receptor complex, $GABA_A$ is comprised of five glycoprotein subunits, which are arranged in a specific pentameric order/structure, surrounding a central trans-cell membrane ion pore, or channel, that is permeable to chloride and other anions (Nutt & Malizia, 2001; Pagliaro & Pagliaro, 2004; Sieghart, 1994). Consequently, the $GABA_A$ receptor is considered to be an ionotropic receptor that functions in concert with a cys-loop ligand-gated chloride receptive ion (i.e., anion) channel.[17,18] The $GABA_A$ receptor is the principal receptor in the CNS with which the benzodiazepines, and other sedative-hypnotics, interact (Cheng et al., 2018; Griffin, Kaye, & Rivera-Bueno, 2013; Samardzic & Strac, 2016).

The endogenous ligand for the $GABA_A$ receptor, as indicated by its name, is GABA. Thirty different isoforms of the $GABA_A$ receptor have been identified that contain the alpha (α) (1–6), beta (β) (1–3), and gamma (γ) (1–3) subunits in different combinations that are arranged in a unique pentameric order. The biological complexity of the $GABA_A$ receptors is largely accounted for by the numerous diverse combinations of the receptor subunits. The most common isoform for the $GABA_A$ receptor contains the α, β, and γ subunits arranged in the following pentameric order—"α_1, β_2, α_1, β_2, and γ_2." Each $GABA_A$ receptor complex has two GABA-binding sites and one benzodiazepine-binding site. (See Figures 6.2 and 6.3.)

16. The $GABA_C$ receptor is often considered to be an isoform of the $GABA_A$ receptor rather than a separate receptor (Sigel & Steinmann, 2012).
17. The cys-loop ligand-gated ion channel receptors, which are characterized by a loop formed by a disulfide bond between two cysteine residues, are considered to be a super family of receptor subtypes and include the nicotinic acetylcholine receptor (see the related discussion in the Chapter 3, *Caffeine and Nicotine*, pharmacology subsection—"Mechanism of Action").
18. Conversely, the $GABA_B$ receptor is considered to be a G protein-coupled receptor (i.e., a metabotropic receptor).

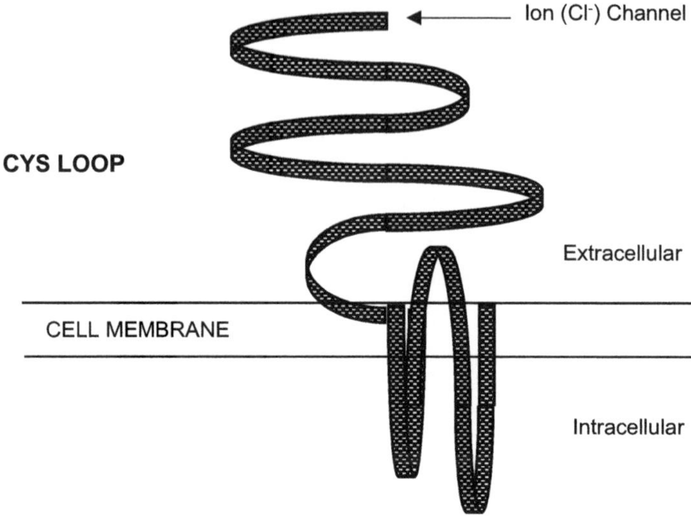

Figure 6.2 Typology of the Cys-Loop $GABA_A$ Receptor

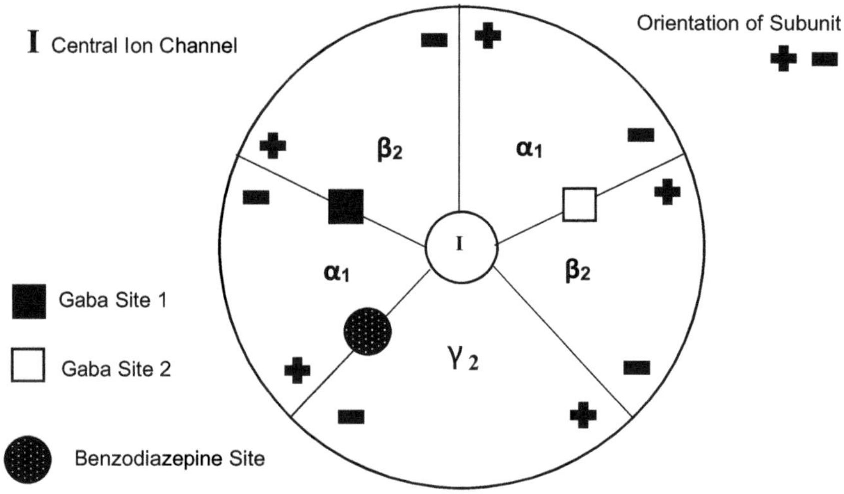

Figure 6.3 Major Isoform of $GABA_A$ Receptors, α_1, β_2, and γ_2: A Transverse Perspective

Several exogenous chemicals (e.g., bicuculline[19] and muscimol[20]), which can bind directly to the $GABA_A$ receptor, have been developed—primarily for laboratory research purposes (Olsen & DeLorey, 1999). Additionally, the $GABA_A$ receptor protein complex

19. Bicuculline is a synthetic antagonist of the $GABA_A$ receptor. It was originally identified as a pharmacologically active plant alkaloid found naturally in the family *Papaveraceae*, subfamily *Fumarioideae*.
20. Muscimol is one of the principal active components found naturally in the psychedelic mushroom, *Amanita muscaria*. It is a potent agonist of the $GABA_A$ receptor.

contains several allosteric binding sites that can modulate the activity of the $GABA_A$ receptor. Examples of sedative-hypnotics that bind to these allosteric sites include alcohol, barbiturates, benzodiazepines, chloral hydrate, and z-drugs.

Benzodiazepine Receptors

The benzodiazepines bind primarily, in a nonspecific manner, to two receptors that have been commonly referred to as the benzodiazepine 1 (BZD1) and benzodiazepine 2 (BZD2) receptors.[21] BZD1 receptors, which are concentrated in the cerebral cortex, cerebellum, and thalamus, contain α_1, β_1, β_2, β_3, and γ_2 subunits. BZD2 receptors, which are concentrated in the limbic system, motor neurons, and the dorsal horn of the spinal cord, contain α_2, α_3, α_5, β_1, β_2, β_3, and γ_2 subunits (Atack, 2005; Crestani, Low, & Keist, 2001; Griffin et al., 2013; Sieghart, 1994). For example, regarding the alpha subunits:[22]

- The α_1 subunit is the most distributed subunit in the CNS;
- Agonistic action involving the α_1 subunit is primarily related to the production of sedation, hypnosis, and anterograde amnesia—and some anticonvulsant activity;
- The α_1 subunit also plays a role in addiction;
- The α_2 and α_3 subunits are more closely related to the effects of anxiolysis, muscle relaxation, sleep regulation, and spinal analgesia;
- The α_4 subunit rejects benzodiazepine binding;
- The α_5 subunit is involved with anterograde amnesia, anxiolytic activity, and some muscle relaxation;
- The α_6 subunit rejects benzodiazepine binding.

(Cheng et al., 2018; Dias, Wayne, & Sheppard, 2005; Gunja, 2013b; Howard et al., 2014; Zeilhofer et al., 2019)

Although it has been clearly demonstrated that the benzodiazepines have a high affinity for binding at the GABA receptor complex,[23] it has not yet been proved that this action is directly, and solely, responsible for their observed pharmacologic actions in humans. For example, these effects also may be related to the direct modulatory actions of endogenous pregnane neurosteroids (e.g., allopregnanolone and tetrahydrodeoxycorticosterone)[24] at

---

21. To be more precise, it is generally agreed that the benzodiazepines do not bind to specific "benzodiazepine receptors," but rather to allosteric modulatory regions near the GABA receptor complex (i.e., between the alpha and gamma subunits) (Samardzic & Strac, 2016). Thus, the benzodiazepines are commonly referred to as "positive allosteric modulators"—although this description is not uniformly agreed upon (Cheng et al., 2018).
    The reasoning for the conclusion that the benzodiazepine binding sites are not considered to be true receptors is based primarily upon the observation that, in the absence of GABA, benzodiazepines do not elicit their associated psychodepressant effects (Bergman, 1986; Sieghart, 1994). Consequently, the "benzodiazepine receptors" are currently more appropriately referred to as, "benzodiazepine binding sites."
22. Most of the data concerning alpha subunit effects were obtained from both in vivo and in vitro animal laboratory studies.
23. Endogenous ligands for the benzodiazepine-binding site (i.e., the "brain's Valium") are known as "endozepines" and consist of a group, or family, of neuropeptides. The major identified ligands in this family include: (1) nonpeptidic endozepines; (2) oleamides; and (3) diazepam-binding inhibitor.
24. These neurosteroids are naturally occurring metabolites of endogenous steroid hormones (e.g., progesterone and deoxycorticosterone, respectively).

the $GABA_A$ receptor (Belelli & Lambert, 2005; Hosie, Wilkins, & da Silva, 2006; Samba Reddy, 2010; Usami, Yamamoto, & Shintani, 2002).

Pharmacokinetics: Absorption, Distribution, Metabolism, and Excretion

The basic pharmacokinetics of the benzodiazepines—the processes of absorption, distribution, metabolism, and excretion—are described and discussed in the following subsections. We begin with "absorption."

Absorption

The benzodiazepines are administered by a wide variety of routes, including intramuscular (IM), intranasal (IN), intravenous (IV), oral (PO), rectal (PR), subcutaneous (SC), and sublingual (SL). Each of these routes of administration, or methods of use, can affect the bioavailability of the benzodiazepine that is delivered to the systemic circulation (Pagliaro & Pagliaro, 2004).

Following IV injection,[25] peak blood benzodiazepine concentrations are achieved within 15 minutes with F = 1.0. After IM injection,[26] peak blood concentrations usually occur within one hour with bioavailability generally being equivalent to PO administration. Although eventually complete, the IM absorption of both chlordiazepoxide and diazepam is slow and erratic (Griffin et al., 2013; Sellers, 1978).

The benzodiazepines are generally well-absorbed after being ingested (80% to 90%). However, the ingestion of food can sometimes delay the rate of absorption, but not the extent of absorption. For example, diazepam (Valium®) is virtually completely absorbed after ingestion and can achieve peak concentrations within one to two hours. However, in comparison to ingestion, the SL administration of alprazolam, diazepam, lorazepam, and triazolam is generally more rapid, while the extent of absorption is similar (Crevoisier, Delisle, & Joseph, 2003; Garzone & Kroboth, 1989; Howard et al., 2014).

Distribution

The benzodiazepines are highly bound (i.e., > 96%) to plasma proteins (e.g., albumin) and are widely distributed throughout body tissues (Sellers, 1978). However, because they are highly lipophilic, the benzodiazepines—and their metabolites—readily cross the blood-brain, and other biological, "barriers," with resultant accumulation in the CNS and adipose tissue (Griffin et al., 2013; Pagliaro & Pagliaro, 2004). The volume of distribution of the benzodiazepines is generally significantly larger for both women and all adults over 70 years of age, primarily due to increased adipose tissue, and, consequently, total body

25. Absorption is immediate and, by definition, 100% following intravenous injection (i.e., F = 1.0—for all IV-injected drugs).
26. Absorption may be erratic (i.e., increased or decreased) following IM injection, depending largely on blood flow to the specific muscle injection site. The IM absorption of chlordiazepoxide and diazepam is often slow and erratic. However, IM absorption of lorazepam and midazolam appears to be rapid and complete (Griffin et al., 2013).

Table 6.2 Benzodiazepines: Half-Lives of Elimination

BENZODIAZEPINE	$T_{½}$—HOURS [RANGE] PARENT BENZODIAZEPINE	$T_{½}$—HOURS [RANGE] {ACTIVE METABOLITE(S)}
Alprazolam	12 [7–16]	—
Bromazepam	15 [8–19]	—
Chlordiazepoxide	10 [5–30]	≤ 100 {nordiazepam, oxazepam}
Clobazam	18 [10–30]	50 [36–100] {N-desmethyl-clobazam}
Clonazepam	23 [10–50]	—
Clorazepate	≤ 2	≤ 100 {nordiazepam}
Diazepam	43 [24–48]	≤ 100 {nordiazepam, oxazepam}
Estazolam	18 [13–35]	—
Flunitrazepam	15 [10–30]	[10–16] {7-amino-flunitrazepam} [23–33] {N-desmethyl-flunitrazepam}
Flurazepam	2 [1–3]	75 [50–100] {desakyl-flurazepam}
Halazepam	14 [10–30]	≤ 100 {nordiazepam}
Lorazepam	14 [10–20]	—
Midazepam	2.5 [1.5–3.0]	1 {α-hydroxymidazolam}
Nitrazepam	25 [18–30]	—
Oxazepam	8 [6–11]	—
Prazepam	1–3	≤ 100 {nordiazepam}
Quazepam	36	≤ 100 {2-oxoquazepam, N-desalkyl-2-oxoquazepam}
Temazepam	10 [3.5–18]	—
Triazolam	3 [1.5–5]	—

clearance is slower. This slower rate of elimination contributes to drug accumulation and a longer half-life of elimination in women and older adults (Pagliaro & Pagliaro, 1983; Pagliaro & Pagliaro, 2004; Sellers, 1978). (See also the following subsection, "Metabolism and Excretion.")

Metabolism and Excretion

Most of the benzodiazepines are primarily metabolized in the liver by the hepatic microsomal enzyme system, predominantly by CYP3A4.[27] Thus, hepatic disease or dysfunction (e.g., cirrhosis of the liver or hepatitis) can slow benzodiazepine metabolism and, consequently, increase toxicity. Some benzodiazepines, including flurazepam (Dalmane®), undergo extensive first-pass hepatic metabolism.[28] Other benzodiazepines, such as lorazepam (Ativan®), oxazepam (Serax®), and temazepam (Restoril®), are metabolized primarily by urinary conjugation to more water-soluble (i.e., polar) glucuronide derivatives that are, subsequently, excreted in the urine.

The benzodiazepines can have rapid, intermediate, or slow elimination profiles (Pagliaro & Pagliaro, 2004). The half-life of elimination is directly related to the elimination profile.

The benzodiazepines that have "rapid" elimination profiles (i.e., are "short-acting") include:

- Midazolam (Versed®);
- Triazolam (Halcion®).

The benzodiazepines that have "intermediate" elimination profiles include:

- Alprazolam (Xanax®);
- Clonazepam (Rivotril®);
- Estazolam (Prosom®);
- Lorazepam (Ativan®);
- Oxazepam (Serax®);
- Temazepam (Restoril®).

The benzodiazepines that have "slow" elimination profiles (i.e., are "long-acting") are those that produce active metabolites, either from: (1) parent drugs; or (2) inactive pro-drugs.

---

27. Diazepam and temazepam also are metabolized by CYP2C19. Although a relatively minor metabolic pathway for these drugs, it may contribute to significant variance in both therapeutic and undesired effects because of its associated genetic polymorphism. In the U.S., approximately 3% of people who are of European continental descent, and 20% of people who are of Asian continental descent, have absent or reduced CYP2C19 enzyme activity. Consequently, they are considered to be "poor metabolizers" of diazepam and temazepam (Dean, 2016).
28. Following ingestion, a drug is transported to the liver by way of the portal venous system before it is released into the general systemic circulation. As it passes through the liver, some, or occasionally most, of the drug is metabolized to a less active or completely inactive form. The amount metabolized, on this single pass through the liver, is commonly referred to as the "hepatic extraction ratio" and the entire process is called "first pass hepatic metabolism," or the "first-pass effect." The first-pass effect does not occur when abusable psychotropics are administered by other common routes that allow them to immediately enter the systemic circulation, such as buccal placement between the inner cheek and gum; IM, IV, and subcutaneous (SC) injection; pulmonary inhalation; rectal insertion; SL placement under the tongue; and transdermal and transmucosal delivery.

1. Benzodiazepines that produce long-acting active metabolites[29] from active parent drugs include:
   - Chlordiazepoxide (Librium®);
   - Diazepam (Valium®);
   - Flurazepam (Dalmane®).
2. Benzodiazepine inactive pro-drugs that produce long-acting active metabolites[30] include:
   - Clorazepate (Tranxene®);
   - Prazepam (Centrax®).

See also Table 6.2 for a list of benzodiazepine half-lives ($T_{1/2}$) of elimination.

Drug-Drug Interactions

Drug-drug interactions that involve the benzodiazepines can be characterized as being either: (1) pharmacodynamic; or (2) pharmacokinetic (Pagliaro & Pagliaro, 1998). Pharmacodynamic interactions occur at the receptor sites and generally result in the modification (i.e., increase or decrease) of the effect(s) of the benzodiazepines. For example, psychostimulants (e.g., caffeine, cocaine, and nicotine), when used concurrently with benzodiazepines, can reduce many of the psychodepressant effects of the benzodiazepines. Conversely, psychodepressants (e.g., alcohol, opiate analgesics, or z-drugs)—when used concurrently with benzodiazepines—can increase the psychodepressant effects of the benzodiazepines, particularly toxic effects (see the related discussion in the following benzodiazepine pharmacology subsection—"Undesired, or Harmful, Effects and Toxicities").

In this drug-drug interaction category, the interaction between benzodiazepines and opiate analgesics is particularly noteworthy. This combination has been associated with significant risk for falls and respiratory impairment among older adults. Additionally, risk of suicidality is significantly increased (see the related discussion in the following benzodiazepine pharmacology subsection, Undesired, or Harmful, Effects and Toxicities—"Suicides"). In spite of these adverse effects, benzodiazepines and opiate analgesics are still commonly co-prescribed to older adults in the U.S. in emergency departments for the treatment of pain and anxiety and in outpatient settings for the treatment of osteoarthritis (Alamanda, Wally, & Seymour, 2020; Pourmand, Lombardi, & Roberson, 2020). (See also the related discussion in Chapter 5, *Prescription Opiate Analgesics and Heroin*.)

Pharmacokinetic interactions occur when the concurrently used drug or substance of abuse affects the absorption, distribution, metabolism, or excretion of the benzodiazepine. Most of these interactions, which can result in clinically significant effects, involve the metabolism of the benzodiazepines. Because many of the benzodiazepines (e.g., alprazolam, chlordiazepoxide, clonazepam, diazepam, midazolam, temazepam, and triazolam)

29. These metabolites primarily include nordiazepam (i.e., desmethyldiazepam) and oxazepam for chlordiazepoxide and diazepam, and hydroxyethylflurazepam for flurazepam.
30. Desmethyldiazepam (i.e., nordiazepam) is the principal long-acting active metabolite of these inactive prodrugs. Nordiazepam is subsequently further metabolized to another, but shorter-acting active metabolite, oxazepam.

are primarily metabolized by the hepatic microsomal enzyme CYP3A4, there is significant risk for the following two types of benzodiazepine metabolic drug-drug interactions:

1. Drugs[31] that strongly "inhibit" CYP3A4 (e.g., clarithromycin, ketoconazole, nefazodone, or ritonavir), which may necessitate a decrease in the benzodiazepine dosage;
2. Drugs that moderately "induce" CYP3A4 (e.g., carbamazepine, phenytoin, or rifampin), which may necessitate an increase in the benzodiazepine dosage.[32]

Undesired, or Harmful, Effects and Toxicities

As noted earlier in this chapter, the benzodiazepines have a relatively high therapeutic index. Even so, several undesired, or harmful, effects and toxicities have been associated with their use. These effects can generally be classified as: "acute" effects; "chronic" effects; and "other" effects.

Acute Effects

Acute effects include ataxia, blurred vision, bradypnea, diplopia, dizziness, dysarthria, lethargy, muscle weakness, psychomotor impairment, slurred speech, and somnolence. They also include amnesias, particularly anterograde amnesia,[33] and other memory impairments, such as those affecting long-term, explicit (episodic) and implicit (procedural) memory and short-term (active) memory.

These acute harmful effects often occur together (e.g., blurred vision, cognitive impairment, confusion, and dizziness). Consequently, they contribute to a higher risk for psychomotor impairment and related injury (e.g., falling down a flight of stairs and suffering, for example, a serious head injury; being involved in a motor vehicle crash [MVC]; and slipping in a bathtub and breaking a hip) (e.g., Brandt & Leong, 2017; McDonald & Caslangen, 2019; Pagliaro & Pagliaro, 1983, 2004, 2009; van Strien, Koek, & van Marum, 2013).

Other acute harmful effects include aggressive, or violent, behavior. Often considered to be idiosyncratic personality effects, these actions are, more likely, a consequence of benzodiazepine-induced disinhibition among individual older adults who have pre-existing aggressive tendencies or personalities (Pagliaro & Pagliaro, *Clinical Patient Data Files*). (See also the related discussion in the later benzodiazepine subsection, Physical and Psychological Dependence—"Fatalities.")

Regarding the management of the related acute, unavoidable, undesired, or harmful, effects and toxicities commonly associated with the medical prescription use of benzodiazepines (and other sedative-hypnotics) for older adults, we recommend—in the context of hypnotic use—the: (1) correction of related concurrent medical conditions (e.g., restless

31. Some other products (e.g., grapefruit juice) can also inhibit CYP3A4 (Hukkinen, Varhe, & Olkkola, 1995; Sugimoto, Araki, & Ohmori, 2006).
32. See also Chapter 5, *Prescription Opiate Analgesic and Heroin*, Table 5.3, "Major Inducers and Inhibitors of CYP3A4 and CYP2D6," for a more comprehensive list.
33. This action of the benzodiazepines is used both therapeutically (e.g., to provide amnesia of surgical events for patients requiring surgery) and criminally (e.g., to facilitate crimes including robbery and date rape—see later subsection, "Sexual Assault"). In some contexts of use, the benzodiazepine-related memory impairment resembles alcoholic "blackouts" (see Chapter 1, *Alcohol*, for further discussion).

leg syndrome or sleep apnea); and (2) implementation of helpful sleep hygiene practices, as tolerated, including:

- Avoid afternoon naps (i.e., after 2 pm) and limit naps to a maximum of 30 minutes;
- Avoid caffeine after lunch time;
- Avoid foods that cause dyspepsia, particularly at dinner and before bedtime;
- Avoid tobacco smoking before bedtime;
- Control room temperature to avoid being too cold or too hot;
- Encourage exposure to natural light, as appropriate and available, during the day;
- Establish a regular sleep routine;[34]
- Exercise as tolerated—up to 2 hours before bedtime;
- Have a warm decaffeinated beverage or warm milk at night—being cognizant to limit fluid volume (see recommendation below);
- Increase daytime activity;
- Reduce ambient light and sound;
- Restrict fluid intake, as appropriate, before bedtime;
- Use a comfortable mattress, pillows, and sheets.

Chronic Effects

Regular, long-term use of the benzodiazepines is associated with several adverse effects, including apathy, cognitive decline/impairment,[35] decreased impulse control, diminished sleep quality,[36] emotional instability, falls and associated hip fractures or other injuries, lethargy, memory impairment,[37] mental depression, and rebound anxiety.[38] Regular, long-term use of the benzodiazepines also is associated with physical and psychological dependence characterized by tolerance, craving, and the benzodiazepine withdrawal syndrome (see the

34. For example: (1) go to sleep and get up at the same time every day (e.g., use an alarm clock, if necessary, to awaken at the same time every morning); (2) close window curtains or shades to minimize ambient light and noise; and (3) limit fluids and use the toilet before going to bed to minimize related need to get up during the night.
35. The noted cognitive decline/impairment, which is commonly associated with the use of benzodiazepines, is often exacerbated in older adults because of: (1) concurrent use of other abusable psychotropics, particularly other psychodepressants (e.g., alcohol or opiate analgesics); and (2) contemporaneous diagnoses such as Alzheimer's disease or MDD (Gregory, Torres, & Ge, 2020; Pagliaro & Pagliaro, 2018).
36. A decrease in sleep quality appears to be related, at least in part, to the development of the signs and symptoms of mental depression among chronic benzodiazepine abusers (Bourgeois, Elseviers, & Van Bortel, 2014b; Pagliaro & Pagliaro, *Clinical Patient Data Files*).
37. The use of benzodiazepines, particularly long-acting benzodiazepines for six months or longer, is commonly believed to be associated with the development of Alzheimer's disease or other dementias among older adults (e.g., Billioti de Gage, Moride, & Ducruet, 2014; Ha, Chen, & Wu, 2019; Tapiainen, Taipale, & Tanskanen, 2018). However, several studies (e.g., Imfeld, Bodmer, & Jick, 2015; Saarelainen, Taipale, & Koponen, 2016) have failed to support this association. See the related discussion in the later benzodiazepine subsection, "Alzheimer's Disease."
38. Rebound anxiety occurs when the regular, long-term (i.e., over 30 days) use of a sedative hypnotic for its anxiolytic effects is abruptly discontinued. In this situation, the anxiety that was initially being treated returns, generally at a much greater degree. (See the related discussion in the later benzodiazepine subsection, Physical and Psychological Dependence—"Benzodiazepine Withdrawal Syndrome.")

later benzodiazepine subsection—"Physical and Psychological Dependence"). As identified by Gould, Coulson, and Patel (2014, p. 98):

> The long-term use of benzodiazepines has been advised against in older people owing to adverse outcomes, including increased risks of cognitive impairment, falls, fractures, traffic accidents, delirium, and dependence.

Concern for the significant undesired, or harmful, effects and toxicities, which are associated with the regular, long-term use of benzodiazepines, was emphasized by the FDA in 2020 with the insurance of a stronger "boxed warning" for all formal benzodiazepine pharmaceutical monographs (FDA, 2020). As noted by Young (2020):

> The FDA is requiring that boxed warnings for benzodiazepines be updated to emphasize the risks for misuse, addiction, physical dependence, and withdrawal symptoms, even when the drugs are taken at the recommended dosages.

Other Effects

Other effects associated with benzodiazepine abuse include fatalities, sexual assaults, and suicides. These and other related effects (e.g., Alzheimer's Disease) are discussed in the following subsections.

Fatalities Potentially fatal harmful effects and toxicities have been associated with the concurrent use of benzodiazepines and other drugs and substances of abuse, particularly, "alcohol" (see Chapter 1, *Alcohol*) and/or opiate analgesics (see Chapter 5, *Prescription Opiate Analgesics and Heroin*). As noted in the CBHSQ report from SAMHSA:

> Combining benzodiazepines with opioid pain relievers or alcohol significantly increases the risk of serious ED [emergency department] visit outcome for all age groups.
>
> (Day, 2014, p. 1)

The sedative-hypnotic actions of the benzodiazepines are potentiated by the actions of all other psychodepressants (e.g., alcohol, opiate analgesics, and z-drugs). In fact, the concurrent use of benzodiazepines and alcohol has resulted in a number of deaths due to associated respiratory depression (Pagliaro & Pagliaro, 2009; Tanaka, 2002). (See also the later benzodiazepine pharmacology subsection—"Overdosage/Unintentional Poisoning.")

Sexual Assaults Over the last three decades, the benzodiazepines—alone, or in combination with alcohol and other drugs and substances of abuse—have frequently been used to facilitate the perpetration of "drug-facilitated sexual assaults" (DFSA) (Bechtel & Holstege, 2007; Dowd, Strong, & Janicak, 2002; Gautam, Sharratt, & Cole, 2014; Grela, Gautam, & Cole, 2018; Montgomery, 2010; Pagliaro & Pagliaro, 2009, 2018). In this context of illicit use, the benzodiazepines, and other sedative-hypnotics (e.g., z-drugs, particularly zolpidem [Ambien®]), have been increasingly referred to as:

- "Acquaintance rape drugs;"
- "Date rape drugs" (the most commonly used term);
- "Drug-assisted rape drugs;"
- "Intimate partner rape drugs;"
- "Sexual assault drugs."

(NIDA, 2008; Pagliaro & Pagliaro, 2009, 2018)

It is estimated that the use of date rape drugs is involved in up to 50% of all rape cases in the U.S. (Madea & Musshoff, 2009; Pagliaro & Pagliaro, 2009, 2018). Unfortunately, the use of benzodiazepines in the perpetration of sexual assaults appears to be increasing. In fact, flunitrazepam (Rohypnol®)—"Forget Me Drug," "Mexican Valium," *Papas*, or "Roofie,"—is the benzodiazepine that is most often involved in cases of date rape, being easily slipped into the victim's beverage—without her (or his) knowledge—to induce drowsiness, or sleep, in order to facilitate the sexual assault. Benzodiazepines also induce anterograde amnesia (see the earlier related discussion in the benzodiazepine subsection—"Acute Effects") which helps the perpetrator to avoid successful prosecution by preventing the victim from:

1. Clearly remembering details of the sexual assault;
2. Identifying the perpetrator;
3. Testifying under oath, in a court of law, that consent was not given for sexual contact or other related events that may have occurred or did not occur.

(Daderman & Edman, 2001; Daderman, Fredriksson, & Kristiansson, 2002; Pagliaro & Pagliaro, *Clinical Patient Data Files*)

As emphasized by Ireton (2019, p. 1), regarding a recent study of sexual assault:

> The study also uncovered more than 900 cases of elder sexual abuse. "There hasn't been a study before looking at sexual assault across the lifespan . . . all the way up to elder abuse over 70 years old, amongst men and women."

Although "overall, older women report lower lifetime and past year rates of physical and sexual assault," these phenomena are significantly increasing among the cohort of aging baby boomers (Cook, Dinnen, & O'Donnell, 2011, p. 1075). As reported to the U.S. Department of Justice:

> This exploratory, hypothesis-generating study provided evidence that adults ages 60 and older may be victims of sexual abuse in their own homes, in nursing homes, and in the community and implies that age is no protection against sexual victimization.
>
> (Burgess, 2006, p. 4)

Additionally, date-rape is occurring more often as increasing numbers of older adults—often following the loss (e.g., by death or divorce) of their spouses or other long-term partners—find themselves dating "strangers,"[39] who they often meet through popular "senior-oriented" dating sites (e.g., "J-Date, "Our Time," "Senior Friend Finder," or "Silver Singles") (Pagliaro & Pagliaro, *Clinical Patient Data Files*).

Related Professional Reminder**: *Among older adults, the use of date-rape drugs to facilitate sexual assault commonly occurs in long-term care facilities (e.g., nursing homes) where "caregivers" take advantage of older adults who: (1) may already be experiencing some cognitive impairment; and (2) are further compromised by their routinely prescribed nightly prescription sedative-hypnotic.***

39. N.B. Most of these "strangers" who perpetrate date rape are older men.

Suicides Many of the deaths associated with benzodiazepine use have resulted from deliberate suicides. As identified by Dodds (2017, p. 1):

> Benzodiazepines appear to cause an overall increase in the risk of attempting or completing suicide. Possible mechanisms of presuicidal effects may include increases in impulsivity or aggression, rebound or withdrawal symptoms, and toxicity in overdose.

Mental health professionals should be aware that the risk for suicide attempts among older adults who abuse benzodiazepines is significantly higher for those who use higher dosages of the benzodiazepines and concurrently have other mental disorders, including:

- AUD;
- BPD;
- MDD;
- OUD.

(Bellivier, Yon, & Luquiens, 2011; Lekka, Paschalis, & Beratis, 2002; Pagliaro & Pagliaro, *Clinical Patient Data Files*; Voaklander, Rowe, & Dryden, 2008)[40]

This significant risk has been identified and documented in literally thousands of autopsies and case reports during the new millennium. To appreciate the significance of this risk more fully, consider the following findings.

Analyzing their data from U.S. adults, 50 years of age and older—who participated in the 2015 to 2016 National Survey on Drug Use and Health—Schepis, Simoni-Wastila, and Esteban McCabe (2019, p. 122) found that:

> While 2.2% of US older adults not engaged in either opioid or benzodiazepine misuse reported past-year suicidal ideation, 25.4% of those who misused both medication classes endorsed such suicidality (AOR = 4.73, 95% CI = 2.07–10.79).
>
> Both past-year prescription opioid and benzodiazepine misuse are associated with past-year suicidal ideation in US older adults.

Ross Perlman (2019, p. 1), on behalf of the NIDA, similarly concluded that:

> Prescription opioid and benzodiazepine misuse increased older adults' risk of suicidal thoughts.
>
> Those [older adults] who misused both prescription opioids and benzodiazepines were 10 times more likely than those who did not to report that they "thought seriously about killing" themselves during the past year.

Related Professional Reminder: ***The co-prescription of both a sedative-hypnotic and an opiate analgesic is commonly encountered in clinical practice involving older adults, and most clinicians are aware of the significant additive risks for the occurrence of both CNS and respiratory depression. However, clinicians must be***

40. N.B. Older age, living alone, and chronic medical illnesses are other contributing factors that are associated with suicides among older adults.

equally aware that, even at lower dosages, which do not pose significant risk of CNS or respiratory depression, the potential for suicidal ideation is significantly elevated among older adults who simultaneously use both a sedative-hypnotic and an opiate analgesic.

See the previous list of additional factors that contribute to high risk in these clinical situations. See also the related discussion in the later s-drug subsection, Undesired, or Harmful, Effects and Toxicities—"Chronic Toxicities."

Alzheimer's Disease Throughout most of the first two decades of the new millennium, it was widely postulated that the use of the benzodiazepines, particularly among older adults, posed a significant risk for the development, or exacerbation, of Alzheimer's disease and other dementias (e.g., vascular dementia) (e.g., Billioti de Gage et al., 2014). This issue is of particular concern because of the common use of benzodiazepines to treat behavioral symptoms associated with dementia (Defrancesco, Marksteiner, & Fleischhacker, 2015; Rochon, Vozoris, & Gill, 2017).

In a case-controlled analysis, which matched newly diagnosed cases of dementia with dementia-free controls, Imfeld et al. (2015) found a significant association when the benzodiazepines were used during the prodromal phase (i.e., less than one-year before the onset of the symptoms of dementia). However, long-term benzodiazepine use was not associated with an increased risk for dementia.

In contrast, in a similar review, Ha et al. (2019) came to a different conclusion (i.e., finding an association between benzodiazepine use and dementia among older adults). Additionally, they noted that, "this association is stronger in people using long-acting BDZs for longer durations" (p. 9).

Salzman (2020, p. 476), in another systematic review of the related published data, reported that:

> The preponderance of data available to date do not support a causal relationship between low therapeutic benzodiazepine use and the development of Alzheimer's or other dementias, despite the well-known mild and reversible memory impairment associated with benzodiazepine doses that occurs in some individuals.

Similarly, Osler and Balslev Jorgensen (2020, p. 497), in a large Danish study of over 230,000 adults with affective disorders, who received prescription benzodiazepines or z-drugs and were followed for incident dementia for a median of six years, found that:

> This large cohort study did not reveal associations between use of benzodiazepines or Z-drugs and subsequent dementia, even when exposures were cumulated or divided into long- and short-acting drugs.

<u>Related Professional Reminder</u>: Even if benzodiazepine pharmacotherapy does not cause Alzheimer's disease, benzodiazepine pharmacotherapy requires cautious use for older adults who have Alzheimer's disease, or any other dementia, because it can:

1. ***Cause cognitive impairment;***
2. ***Complicate, or obscure, the monitoring of both related disease progression and treatment interventions.***

Benzodiazepine Physical and Psychological Dependence

The benzodiazepines have a low to moderate potential for physical dependence and a moderate to high potential for psychological dependence (Pagliaro & Pagliaro, 2009; Weaver, 2015). It has long been recognized that psychological dependence can develop with the regular, long-term use of the benzodiazepines at both lower and higher dosages. However, from the time that the benzodiazepines were introduced into medical practice in the 1960s and through the 1980s, it was generally thought that physical dependence, in the strictest sense, did not occur. Available data now indicate that the regular, long-term use of the benzodiazepines, even within therapeutic dosage ranges, can lead to a true, or classic, physical dependence in a significant number of people (Pagliaro & Pagliaro, 2009), particularly those who have a past personal or family history of alcoholism.

Some general indicators of benzodiazepine physical and psychological dependence, include:

- Regular use of a benzodiazepine extending over 30 days;
- An expressed craving for the benzodiazepine;
- A need to increase the dosage of the benzodiazepine to achieve, or maintain, the desired effect(s);[41]
- Characteristic signs and symptoms of the benzodiazepine withdrawal syndrome that occur when the use of the benzodiazepine is abruptly discontinued for any reason, such as:
    - Inability to renew a prescription;
    - Lack of funds to buy more of the drug;
    - Inability to ingest dosages because of illness, including nausea or vomiting.

(Also see the later benzodiazepine pharmacology subsection, Undesired, or Harmful, Effects and Toxicities—“Benzodiazepine Withdrawal Syndrome.”)

***Related Professional Reminder*: Benzodiazepine dependence, including the development of tolerance to the benzodiazepine and a withdrawal syndrome if the use of the benzodiazepine is abruptly discontinued, is rarely a problem when the benzodiazepine is used at an appropriate dosage for less than four weeks.**

As identified by Canham, Gallo, and Simoni-Wastila (2014, p. 873):

> 35% of persons who take benzodiazepines regularly for four weeks or longer will develop dependence; after 4 to 6 months of daily use, the majority of users will develop dependence.

As noted by Span (2018, p. 1):

> Jessica Falstein began taking Klonopin [clonazepam] for an anxiety disorder in 1992. She spent the last five years trying to wean herself from some of her medications. . . . Now 67,

41. In this context, a generally related indicator of benzodiazepine dependence or use disorder is a pattern of increasing requests for early refills for benzodiazepine prescriptions (Pagliaro & Pagliaro, *Clinical Patient Data Files*).

> with her health and stamina in decline, Ms. Falstein has been diligently working to wean herself from both medications, part of the class called benzodiazepines that is widely prescribed for insomnia and anxiety. "They turn on you," she said.

Nevertheless, the inappropriate and excessive prescription of benzodiazepines for older adults in the U.S. has continued—virtually unabated. As recognized by the Mayo Clinic in a continuing medical education review:

> The American Geriatrics Society (AGS) placed benzodiazepines on a list of medications that should be avoided in patients over 65 years of age. Several major psychiatric associations also advise against using benzodiazepines for generalized anxiety disorder and insomnia in the elderly. Despite these recommendations, benzodiazepines continue to be prescribed to a group [i.e., older adults] with the highest risk of serious adverse effects from these medications.
>
> (Markota, Rummans, & Bostwick, 2016, pp. 1632–1633)

The AGS go on to posit several possible reasons for this situation:

> Primary care physicians prescribe the largest absolute number of long-term benzodiazepines, likely because they see the greatest number of elderly patients. However, in relative numbers, primary care physicians do not prescribe benzodiazepines at a higher rate than psychiatrists. There are several independent reasons why doctors are unable to change their benzodiazepine prescription patterns. Some are intrinsic to physicians, including insufficient recognition of adverse effects, conviction that the risk to benefit ratio favors the latter, perceived lack of skills and training on how to respond to problems that occur during a taper, resource constraints such as limited time and a resultant decision to focus on other important medical issues in this population, fear of jeopardizing the doctor-patient relationship or fear of push-back leading to patients finding other doctors, unwillingness to question other colleagues' prescription rationales, and opinion that discontinuation could be too stressful for an elderly user with a limited life expectancy. Other reasons are external to physicians, such as patients' resistance to change, health systems with insufficient reimbursement for the invested time and effort, limited availability of psychotherapists, absence of scheduled medication reviews, or inability to access support from psychiatrists in a timely fashion.
>
> (Markota et al., 2016, p. 1633)

Old Misbelief: Drugs and substances of abuse, including the benzodiazepines and z-drugs, do not cause physical dependence when medically prescribed by a physician for an appropriate and active clinical condition.

False. In fact, the "misprescription" of benzodiazepines has long been widely associated with a false and dangerous belief that the drugs and substances of abuse are not addicting when they are prescribed by a physician—and taken exactly "as directed." As expressed by a psychiatrist, who published a review article on the benzodiazepines:

> It is important to distinguish between addiction to and normal physical dependence on benzodiazepines. . . . Due to the chronic nature of anxiety, long-term low-dose benzodiazepine treatment may be necessary for some patients; this continuation of treatment should not be considered abuse or addiction.[42]
>
> (O'Brien, 2005, p. 28)

42. N.B. This statement is a classic example of the logical fallacy: "a distinction without a difference."

Unfortunately, this erroneous and clearly unscientific view has become "enshrined" by psychiatrists in the 5th edition of the classification scheme for mental disorders, the *Diagnostic and Statistical Manual for Mental Disorders* (DSM-5):

> According to Charles O'Brien, Chair of the Substance-related Disorders Work Group, the term dependence is misleading because it is often confused with addiction, when in fact the tolerance and withdrawal patients experience are normal responses. . . . So, we're eliminating that bad terminology.
>
> (Cassels, 2010, p. 2)

> the diagnosis of dependence caused much confusion. Most people link dependence with "addiction" when in fact dependence can be a normal body response to a substance.
>
> (APA, 2013, p. 1)

While, to some, this issue may appear to be "just a matter of semantics," we would like to remind readers of the extremely germane words of William Shakespeare (1564–1616) in *Romeo and Juliet*, written in 1594: *What's in a name? That which we call a rose by any other name would smell as sweet.*

We call attention to this particular "view" of addiction because it also concerns the prescription of other drugs and substances of abuse (e.g., opiate analgesics, see Chapter 5, *Prescription Opiate Analgesics and Heroin*). Health and social care professionals should be aware of this situation and use this knowledge in their own practices, particularly when working with older adults whose harmful use of prescription psychotropics may be related, at least initially, to an "iatrogenic" cause.

Regardless of one's personal/professional "view of addiction," it is patently obvious that users of benzodiazepines—whether prescribed, or not, or whether used for a "legitimate" medical indication, or not—commonly display "addict-like" behaviors, or "behavioral correlates of benzodiazepine dependence." As identified by Soyka (2017, p. 1151):

> People who have become dependent on therapeutic doses of benzodiazepines usually have several of the following characteristics:

- They have taken benzodiazepines in prescribed "therapeutic" (usually low) doses for months or years;
- They have gradually come to "need" benzodiazepines to carry out normal day-to-day activities;
- They have continued to take benzodiazepines even though the original indication for the prescription has disappeared;
- Because of withdrawal symptoms, they have difficulty stopping use of the drug or reducing the dose;
- Those taking short-acting benzodiazepines have anxiety between doses or a craving for the next dose;
- They contact their doctor regularly to obtain repeat prescriptions;
- They become anxious if the next prescription is not readily available; they may carry their tablets around with them and may take an extra dose before an event that is anticipated to be stressful or before spending the night in a strange bed;
- They may have anxiety symptoms, panic attacks, agoraphobia, insomnia, depression, or increasing physical symptoms, despite continuing to take benzodiazepines;

- Doctor-shopping, emergency visits, and lost prescriptions are common;
- They use private prescriptions rather than those for which the cost would be reimbursed by health insurance;
- They take hypnotic agents during the day.

***Related Professional Reminder:* Mental health care professionals need to be aware of the possible occurrence of iatrogenic physical and psychological dependence related to prescribed sedative-hypnotics (and other abusable psychotropics), particularly among older adults, and be attentive to its prevention and management.**

Benzodiazepine Tolerance

Tolerance to the actions of the benzodiazepines (i.e., the need to use more of the drug more frequently to achieve desired actions) is a complex process that generally develops within several days, weeks, or months of initial, daily use—regardless of the dosage range (i.e., low to high) or if medically prescribed or not. As well known for some time (e.g., Busto & Sellers, 1991), the rate of the development of tolerance varies from: (1) individual to individual; (2) benzodiazepine to benzodiazepine; and (3) pharmacological action to pharmacological action (e.g., generally, tolerance develops more quickly to the hypnotic effects of the benzodiazepines than to their anxiolytic effects).

It also has been noted that, for most patients, tolerance to the anticonvulsant and muscle relaxant effects of the benzodiazepines generally occurs within a few weeks of the initiation of continued daily use. As explained by Vinkers and Olivier (2012, p. 1):

> Tolerance develops relatively quickly for the sedative and anticonvulsant actions of benzodiazepines, whereas tolerance to anxiolytic and amnesic effects probably does not occur at all.

The development of benzodiazepine tolerance among older adults is a cause for clinical concern for two major reasons:

1. It may be a sign of physical dependence;
2. It is commonly associated with an increase in dosage, whether prescribed or not, and this increased dosage is associated with an increase in both the incidence and severity of adverse effects.

Benzodiazepine Withdrawal Syndrome

The characteristic signs and symptoms of the benzodiazepine withdrawal syndrome are widely documented in the context of the abrupt discontinuation of regular, long-term benzodiazepine use (e.g., Bateson, 2002).[43] Usually, mild to moderate in intensity, the signs and symptoms of the benzodiazepine withdrawal syndrome may include:

- Agitation;
- Agoraphobia;

43. Interestingly, the signs and symptoms of the benzodiazepine withdrawal syndrome also have been noted with the discontinuation of concurrent pharmacotherapy that inhibits the cytochrome P450 isoenzymes responsible for the metabolism of the benzodiazepines. The discontinuation allows the benzodiazepines to

- Anorexia;
- Anxiety;
- Blurred vision;
- Catatonia (uncommon);
- Chest pain;
- Cognitive impairment;
- Confusion;
- Delirium (uncommon);
- Delusions (uncommon);
- Diaphoresis;
- Diarrhea;
- Difficulty swallowing or a sensation of choking;
- Disorientation;
- Dizziness;
- Dysphoria;
- Dyspnea;
- Flushing;
- GI distress;
- Hallucinations (uncommon);
- Headaches;
- Hypertension;
- Impaired concentration;
- Insomnia;
- Irritability;
- Lightheadedness;
- Muscle aches/spasms;
- Nausea;
- Nervousness;
- Nightmares;
- Palpitations;
- Panic attacks;
- Paresthesia;
- Psychosis (uncommon);
- Restlessness;
- Seizures (uncommon, but may be severe);
- Sensory hypersensitivity;
- Shaking;
- Suicidal ideation (uncommon);

---

be more quickly metabolized and, consequently, eliminated from the body more rapidly (Ninan, 2001). (See the related discussion in the earlier benzodiazepine pharmacology subsection—"Drug-Drug Interactions.")

- Tachycardia;
- Tremors;
- Vertigo.

(Brett & Murnion, 2015; FDA, 2020; Greenberg, 2001; Pagliaro & Pagliaro, 2009; Pagliaro & Pagliaro, *Clinical Patient Data Files*; Petursson, 1994; Soyka, 2017; Sparks & Cohen, 2019)

These characteristic signs and symptoms, which, generally, are the opposite of the desired effects associated with the benzodiazepines, are more likely to occur with:

1. Short-acting benzodiazepines (e.g., alprazolam [Xanax®], lorazepam [Ativan®], or triazolam [Halcion®]);[44]
2. Higher dosages of benzodiazepines;
3. Regular, daily use of benzodiazepines for four months, or longer;
4. Abrupt discontinuation of benzodiazepines after regular, daily use.

The signs and symptoms of benzodiazepine withdrawal syndrome are widely recognized in numerous studies and reports (e.g., Pagliaro & Pagliaro, 2018, 2020) to be a major factor in dissuading patients (and some clinicians) from discontinuing prescribed benzodiazepine use. Additionally, these signs and symptoms often contribute to the resumed use of the benzodiazepines (Pagliaro & Pagliaro, *Clinical Patient Data Files*; Tannenbaum, 2015). Although benzodiazepine users commonly handle their withdrawal syndromes "cold-turkey"—without medical care or adjunctive pharmacotherapy, we generally recommend that the benzodiazepine withdrawal syndrome be medically managed with the substitution of an equivalent dose of a long-acting benzodiazepine (e.g., diazepam [Valium®]) that is gradually reduced over a period of two to 12 weeks (Pagliaro & Pagliaro, 2009).[45] (See also the related discussion in the later benzodiazepine subsection, "Deprescribing or Tapering, Benzodiazepine Dosage.")

The time course (i.e., onset, peak, and duration) of the signs and symptoms associated with the benzodiazepine withdrawal syndrome is directly related to whether the benzodiazepine is short-acting or long-acting (Figure 6.4). See also the table of half-lives of elimination for the benzodiazepines (Table 6.2).

***Related Professional Reminder:* Benzodiazepine withdrawal should always be medically managed with close monitoring in order to: (1) increase patient**

44. Short-acting benzodiazepines are more likely to produce insomnia when they are abruptly discontinued than are long-acting benzodiazepines. Long-acting benzodiazepines are less likely to produce insomnia, or the other signs and symptoms of withdrawal, when they are abruptly discontinued probably because of their longer half-life of elimination. In this context, it is generally thought that the longer half-life of elimination may provide a "built-in" tapering-off effect.
45. Some clinicians and researchers (e.g., Hood, Norman, & Hince, 2014) suggest the use of a low dose "infusion" of the benzodiazepine antagonist, "flumazenil" (Anexate® or Romazicon®), for the treatment of benzodiazepine withdrawal. However, finding insufficient data to support the efficacy of this pharmacotherapeutic intervention, we do not recommend it—particularly for older adults. In addition, others (e.g., Lin, 2014) have advocated the use of acetylcholinesterase inhibitors (e.g., donepezil or rivastigmine)—for the rapid detoxification of benzodiazepine (or z-drug) dependence. As we also noted regarding the suggested use of flumazenil in this context, insufficient supportive data are available for us to recommend this pharmacotherapeutic use of the acetylcholinesterase inhibitors.

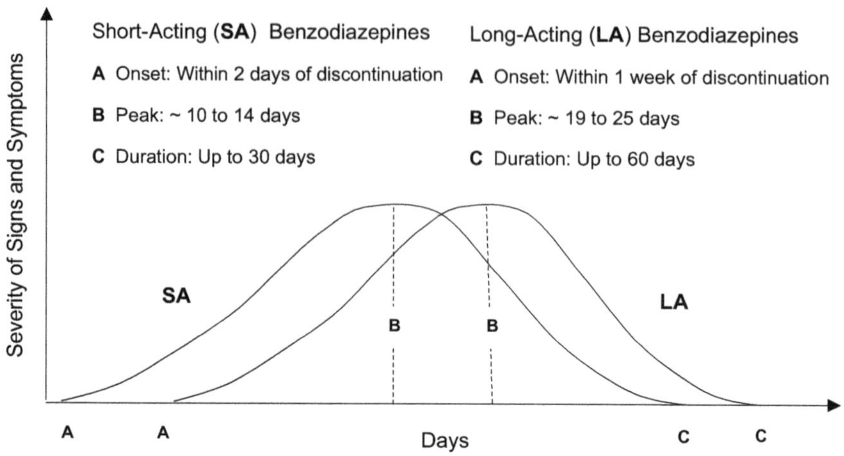

Figure 6.4 General Onset, Peak, and Duration of the Benzodiazepine Withdrawal Syndrome

compliance; (2) avoid serious withdrawal reactions (e.g., seizures); and (3) minimize other withdrawal reactions. Also ensure that supportive related mental and social health care are available to help prevent, as required, the resumed use of the benzodiazepine (i.e., recidivism).

> When Ms. Falstein [67 years of age] began experiencing "jelly legs," that left her too weak to stand for long, increased panic attacks, extreme fatigue, and other health problems, she and her psychopharmacologist agreed that she should begin tapering off her benzos.
>
> "I thought I'd be off them in a year, maybe two," Ms. Falstein said. But it has taken five so far, with the support of a Facebook group and a "taper friend" she speaks to almost daily. Using a method called liquid titration, she has been able to discontinue Ativan and cut back to less than a daily milligram of Klonopin.
>
> Though she suffered a variety of debilitating symptoms, "I was determined," she said. "I'm going as quickly but as safely as I can." She figures she has two years to go.
>
> (Span, 2018, p. 2)

A quick-screen psychometric test, which has been developed to facilitate the recognition/diagnosis of benzodiazepine withdrawal among benzodiazepine-dependent adults, is presented in the following subsection.

Benzodiazepine Withdrawal Symptom Questionnaire (BWSQ)

The BWSQ (Table 6.3) is a 20-item, self-report questionnaire that detects the symptoms of benzodiazepine withdrawal among adults, young and old, who have benzodiazepine dependence or use disorder. The BWSQ is the only specific self-report tool for indicating benzodiazepine withdrawal and is widely recognized as the leading psychometric tool for assessing benzodiazepine withdrawal symptoms (Baillie, 1996; Ratcliffe, 2012).

For over 30 years, the questionnaire, which was developed by Tyrer, Murphy, and Riley (1990), has been used in a number of studies—both quantitative studies and clinical practice cases—of benzodiazepine withdrawal programs in several countries, including:

Table 6.3 Benzodiazepine Withdrawal Symptom Questionnaire (BWSQ)

SYMPTOM	NO, ABSENT	YES, MODERATE	YES, SEVERE
Feeling unreal	0	1	2
Very sensitive to noise	0	1	2
Very sensitive to light	0	1	2
Very sensitive to smell	0	1	2
Very sensitive to touch	0	1	2
Peculiar taste in mouth	0	1	2
Pains in muscles	0	1	2
Muscle twitching	0	1	2
Shaking and trembling	0	1	2
Pins and needles	0	1	2
Dizziness	0	1	2
Feeling faint	0	1	2
Feeling sick	0	1	2
Feeling depressed	0	1	2
Sore eyes	0	1	2
Feeling of things moving when they are still	0	1	2
Seeing or hearing things that are not really there—hallucinations	0	1	2
Unable to control your movements	0	1	2
Loss of memory	0	1	2
Loss of appetite	0	1	2
Any additional symptoms? (describe each symptom below and select the score rating)			
1.	0	1	2
2.	0	1	2
3.	0	1	2
4.	0	1	2

Source: Modified from Tyrer et al., 1990.

- Belgium (e.g., Bourgeois, Elseviers, & Van Bortel, 2014);
- China (e.g., Yeung et al., 2017);
- The Netherlands (e.g., Couvee & Zitman, 2002);
- The United Kingdom (e.g., Seivewright & Dougal, 1993);
- The U.S. (e.g., Guina & Merrill, 2018b).

Scoring of the BWSQ Each of the twenty items on the BWSQ is rated from 0 to 2 to yield a maximum possible score of 40. If, for an individual questionnaire, the respondent either: (1) scores over 20; or (2) repots several "additional" symptoms, then general practitioners are advised to "seek special medical help" (Tyrer et al., 1990, p. 60). Additionally, a positive change score of 3 or greater—from an earlier administration of the BWSQ—is indicative of withdrawal.

As identified by Couvee and Zitman (2002, p. 337), "low scores [on the BWSQ] during withdrawal predicted more limited future use of the benzodiazepines." Additionally, Seivewright and Dougal (1993, p. 15) added that:

> Greater severity of benzodiazepine withdrawal symptoms on the BWSQ was significantly associated with high dosage, the use of multiple benzodiazepines, and oral, rather than injected, use.

Available Test Statistics and Recommendations The BWSQ has been demonstrated by several researchers (e.g., Couvee & Zitman, 2002; Guina & Merrill, 2018b), to have high, or acceptable validity (i.e., construct validity or predictive validity) and reliability (i.e., test-retest reliability). Reported reliability coefficients ranged from 0.84 to 0.88 and test-retest correlations were between 0.75 and 0.88. Although available psychometrics for the BWSQ, overall, are limited, it is the leading tool for the assessment of benzodiazepine withdrawal symptoms and has been available for over 30 years.

Although the BWSQ can be entirely self-administered, we generally request older adults to self-administer the questionnaire in our presence so that we can clarify any related questions that they may have. The BWSQ is routinely integrated into the general assessment of older adults who use benzodiazepines. We tend to utilize the self-assessment process to both: (1) introduce the topic of benzodiazepine dependence; and (2) begin our initial therapeutic intervention as indicated.

Benzodiazepine Overdosage/Unintentional Poisoning

> Non-medical use of prescription benzodiazepines has been a long-established problem that has been associated with a large number of overdose deaths worldwide. Most recently, the concomitant use of benzodiazepines and opioids has been linked to a number of deaths that occurred in the recent opioid crisis, featuring in a rising number of fatalities and adverse events in North America and in Europe.
>
> (UNODC, 2017, p. 3)

During the new millennium, older adults in the U.S., have been involved in a significant number of overdosages and emergency department visits associated with a combination of a benzodiazepine—primarily, alprazolam [Xanax®])—and an opiate analgesic—primarily, oxycodone [Oxycontin®]) (Preidt, 2014; Sharp & Melnik, 2015).[46]

> The estimated number of ED visits involving nonmedical use of benzodiazepines increased from 143,500 in 2004 to 271,700 in 2008 (i.e., 89%).
>
> (CDC, 2010, p. 706)

---

46. N.B. Alcohol use is frequently an additional significant cofactor (Pagliaro & Pagliaro, *Clinical Patient Data Files*).

Factors associated with increasing risk for prescription sedative-hypnotic overdosage/unintentional poisoning among older adults, include:

- Advanced age;
- AUD;
- Chronic medical conditions (e.g., cancer, immobility, or pain);
- Concurrent alcohol use;
- Concurrent opiate analgesic use;
- History of previous overdosage/suicide attempt;
- Low levels of religiosity;
- MDD;
- Polypharmacy;
- Social isolation;
- SUD;
- Suicidal ideation.

(Cho, Spence, & Niu, 2020; Gahlinger, 2020; Garg, Fulton-Kehoe, & Franklin, 2017; NIDA, 2021; Pagliaro & Pagliaro, *Clinical Patient Data Files*; Paulozzi, Kilbourne, & Shah, 2012; Zoorob, 2018)

Among older adults, unintentional poisonings, involving the benzodiazepines, increased during the first decade of the new millennium. Additionally, during the second decade of the new millennium (see the related discussion in the following "z-drug" section), the medical use of z-drugs increased. These trends encouraged Kaufmann, Spira, and Alexander (2017, p. 1414) to analyze data regarding ED visits that involved the use of benzodiazepines (BZDs) and non-benzodiazepine receptor agonists (nBZRAs), or z-drugs. They found that:

> Nineteen percent of visits involving other sedative-hypnotics, 28% involving BZDs-only, 20% involving nBZRAs-only, and 48% involving a combination of BZDs and nBZRAs resulted in a serious disposition. Compared to visits involving other sedative-hypnotics, visits involving BZDs-only had 86% greater odds and visits involving a combination of BZDs and nBZRAs had almost four times increased odds of a serious disposition. Results were similar across age groups.

Signs and symptoms of benzodiazepine overdosage/unintentional poisoning, include:

- Ataxia;
- Blurred vision;
- Coma;
- Confusion;
- Decreased deep tendon reflexes;
- Diminished reflexes;
- Dizziness;
- Drowsiness;
- Hypotension;

- Hypotonia;
- Impaired mental status;
- Incoordination;
- Nystagmus;
- Respiratory impairment;
- Slurred speech;
- Somnolence;
- Weakness.

(Gahlinger, 2020; Gresham, 2020; Pagliaro & Pagliaro, 2009)

Respiratory arrest occurs more commonly: (1) with short-acting benzodiazepines (e.g., alprazolam [Xanax®], midazolam [Versed®], or triazolam [Halcion®]); and (2) when benzodiazepines (e.g., diazepam [Valium®]) are administered by IV injection.[47]

Benzodiazepine overdosage[48] is not usually fatal because the benzodiazepines have a high therapeutic index, or $LD_{50.}$[49] (See also the related earlier discussion, in the benzodiazepine pharmacology subsection—"Fatalities.") Of note, alprazolam (Xanax®)—is reported to be "relatively more toxic than others in overdosage" (Gresham, 2020, p. 5). It also is the benzodiazepine that is most often encountered in ED visits (Kang, Galuska, & Ghassemzadeh, 2020).

Treatment of Benzodiazepine Overdosage/Unintentional Poisoning

Regardless of which specific benzodiazepine is involved in the overdosage, benzodiazepine overdosage requires emergency medical support of body systems—particularly, maintenance of a patent airway. Gastric lavage and gastric decontamination with the administration of activated charcoal are generally of limited benefit and, consequently, are not recommended (Kang et al., 2020; Pagliaro & Pagliaro, 2009).[50]

The benzodiazepine competitive antagonist, "flumazenil" (Anexate®, Mazicon®, or Romazicon®), is an effective antidote and may be required. However, some caution is warranted because flumazenil antagonism may precipitate the benzodiazepine withdrawal syndrome among older adults who are physically dependent on the benzodiazepines.

47. Parenteral administration of diazepam (Valium®) or lorazepam (Ativan®) also is accompanied by the risk for propylene glycol poisoning/toxicity. Propylene glycol is used as a diluent and vehicle for injectable solutions of the benzodiazepines—usually in a concentration of 400 mg/ml. Although propylene glycol is "generally recognized as safe" (GRAS) by the FDA, extremely large doses or rapid IV injections can rarely cause significant toxicity, including cardiac dysrhythmias, coma, hemolysis, hypotension, lactic acidosis, and skin and soft tissue necrosis (Kang et al., 2020). Treatment of propylene glycol toxicity is primarily supportive and may include the administration of sodium bicarbonate to correct metabolic acidosis and hemodialysis to correct severe hyperosmolality.
48. N.B. This refers to cases in which a benzodiazepine is the only drug or substance of abuse involved in the overdosage. The involvement of other drugs and substances of abuse (e.g., alcohol or opiate analgesics), as previously noted, significantly increases the potential severity of the overdosage.
49. The LD_{50} is the median lethal dose, or the dose that would be fatal for one-half of the population. Although commonly used in the context of human pharmacology, it is more often associated with toxicology testing with population samples of laboratory animals (e.g., Sprague-Dawley albino rats).
50. N.B. However, these procedures may be of benefit in cases of mixed drug overdosage (i.e., the co-ingestion of a benzodiazepine and one or more other abusable psychotropics).

***<u>Related Professional Reminder</u>*: In this context of flumazenil use, mental health care professionals should anticipate this event and be prepared to appropriately manage the associated signs and symptoms of the benzodiazepine withdrawal syndrome (see the earlier subsection, "Benzodiazepine Withdrawal Syndrome").**

Additionally, by antagonizing the actions of the benzodiazepines, the seizure threshold decreases.[51] Mental health care professionals also should recognize that flumazenil is a relatively short-acting competitive inhibitor of benzodiazepine receptor activity with a half-life of elimination of approximately one hour (Pagliaro & Pagliaro, 1999, 2009). This observation is clinically significant because it explains why overdosages with long-acting benzodiazepines often require management with subsequent additional doses of flumazenil.

Flumazenil is available as an injectable solution (0.1 mg/ml). The initial usual IV dose is 0.2 mg over 15 to 30 seconds—preferably in a large vein to minimize pain.[52] If no response, administer 0.5 mg IV over 30 seconds at one-minute intervals to a maximum cumulative dose of 3 mg/hour. If re-sedation[53] subsequently occurs, additional doses may be administered at 20-minute intervals to a maximum of 1 mg/dose or 3 mg/hour.

Additionally, as noted earlier, benzodiazepine overdosage frequently involves the concomitant use of other psychodepressants (e.g., alcohol or opiate analgesics) (Jones, Paulozzi, & Mack, 2014) that are not amenable to the antagonist effects of flumazenil (Pagliaro & Pagliaro, 2009; Sharp & Melnik, 2015). As identified by the FDA, overall "overdose deaths that involved both opioid analgesics and benzodiazepines [increased significantly] in the U.S. from 2004 to 2011" (Jones & McAninch, 2015, p. 493). It is important to remember that alcohol is involved in a significant number of opiate analgesic and benzodiazepine related ED visits and drug-related deaths (Jones et al., 2014, p. 881).

New Millennial Trends in Older Adult Benzodiazepine Use

> Alprazolam (e.g., Xanax), lorazepam (e.g., Ativan), clonazepam (e.g., Klonopin), diazepam (e.g., Valium), and temazepam (e.g., Restoril) are the five most prescribed, as well as the most frequently encountered benzodiazepines on the illicit market.
>
> (DEA, 2019, p. 1)

This subsection presents and discusses two trends in older adult benzodiazepine use during the new millennium: (1) medical prescription use; and (2) nonmedical/illicit use. We begin with medical prescription use.

---

51. Consequently, the FDA has added a Black Box warning to the flumazenil monograph to caution about possible seizures:

    > Seizures: Benzodiazepine reversal has correlations with seizures. Seizures may happen more frequently in patients who have been on benzodiazepines for long-term sedation or in patients who are showing signs of severe tricyclic antidepressant overdose. The required dosage of Flumazenil should be measured and prepared by the practitioners to manage seizures. Flumazenil use requires caution in patients relying on a benzodiazepine for seizure control.
    >
    > (Sharbaf Shoar, Bistas, & Saadabadi, 2020, p. 4)

52. Although the IV route of administration is preferred, flumazenil has also been administered by the IM, IN, and PR routes.
53. Re-sedation commonly occurs among patients who have received a single large dose, or cumulative doses, of benzodiazepines.

Medical Prescription Use

> The use of benzodiazepines is increasing among older adults and they form the largest group of users for these drugs. These agents are effective in treating some clinical symptoms, but their use is fraught with serious side effects and addiction potential among older adults.
>
> (Gupta, Bhattacharya, & Balaram, 2021, p. 5)

> Nearly half of the prescriptions for benzodiazepine among older adults are potentially inappropriate.
>
> (Tampi & Bennett, 2021, p. 1)

Since the benzodiazepines were first synthesized in the 1950s, they have been medically used for their psychodepressant actions. This subsection presents an overview of the medical use of these prescription sedative-hypnotics. The use of benzodiazepines are currently approved by the FDA for the treatment of several medical conditions, including:

- Anxiety disorders, including panic attacks and social anxiety disorders (e.g., alprazolam [Xanax®] or diazepam [Valium®]);
- Insomnia (e.g., flurazepam [Dalmane®] or temazepam [Restoril®]);[54]
- Lower back pain—as a skeletal muscle relaxant (e.g., diazepam [Valium®]);
- Management of prescription sedative-hypnotic withdrawal syndromes (e.g., diazepam [Valium®]);
- Management of seizures associated with the alcohol withdrawal syndrome (i.e., long-acting benzodiazepines, such as chlordiazepoxide [Librium®] or diazepam [Valium®]);
- Pre-medication for medical procedures or surgical adjunct to anesthesia (e.g., lorazepam [Ativan®] or midazolam [Versed®]);[55]
- Seizure disorders (e.g., clonazepam [Rivotril®] or diazepam [Valium®]). (Holbrook, Crowther, & Lotter, 1999; Pagliaro & Pagliaro, 2009; Sparks & Cohen, 2019)

Concerns regarding an "over-medicated society" increased during the second decade of the new millennium and resulted in a re-evaluation of the prescribing practices of physicians. Although the benzodiazepines were generally approved for short-term pharmacotherapy, this limited duration of continuous use became, in practice, the "exception"—rather than the "rule." As illustrated in a rather typical case history by Tannenbaum (2015, p. E27):

> A 72-year-old woman with a psychiatric history of anxious depression and insomnia is receiving ongoing pharmacotherapy and psychotropic management. Her mood disorder has been stable with escitalopram (10 mg/d) for 3 years. She has been taking lorazepam (1 mg nightly) since the death of her husband 12 years ago.

As a result of the increasing expressions of concern, the use of benzodiazepines (and other sedative-hypnotics) generally declined. For example, concerned about the increased risks for

---

54. N.B. Chronic insomnia is common affecting approximately 60% of older adults in the U.S. Consequently, more sedative-hypnotic prescriptions are written for this indication than for all of the other medical conditions combined (Abad & Guilleminault, 2018; Conn & Madan, 2006).
55. Lorazepam (Ativan®) and midazolam (Versed®) are commonly used as pre-medications to both: (1) decrease anxiety among patients undergoing surgery; and (2) to produce anterograde amnesia so that patients do not later recall potentially stressful or distressing surgical experiences.

cognitive impairment, delirium, falls, and MVCs, the American Geriatric Society has urged clinicians, since 2012, to avoid the use of benzodiazepines for older adults (Ault, 2018). Unfortunately, even though the use of benzodiazepines (and other sedative-hypnotics) has generally declined, benzodiazepines continue to be widely prescribed in the U.S.[56] Additionally, they continue to be among the most widely, over-prescribed and "mis-prescribed" drugs in the world. (See the earlier related discussion in the benzodiazepine pharmacology subsection, Undesired, or Harmful, Effects and Toxicities—"Physical and Psychological Dependence.")

> In 2008, approximately 5.2% of US adults aged 18 to 80 years used benzodiazepines. The percentage who used benzodiazepines increased with age from 2.6% (18–35 years) to 5.4% (36–50 years) to 7.4% (51–64 years) to 8.7% (65–80 years). Benzodiazepine use was nearly twice as prevalent in women as men. The proportion of benzodiazepine use that was long term increased with age from 14.7% (18–35 years) to 31.4% (65–80 years).
>
> (Olfson et al., 2015, p. 136)

> [In 2015 and 2016] A total of 30.6 million adults (12.6%) reported past-year benzodiazepine use—25.3 million (10.4%) as prescribed and 5.3 million (2.2%) misuse. Misuse accounted for 17.2% of overall use. Adults ages 50–64 had the highest prescribed use (12.9%).
>
> (Maust, Lin, & Blow, 2019, p. 97)

Guidelines for the Prescription of Sedative-Hypnotics for Older Adults[57]

> Based on current estimates, up to a third of all benzodiazepine prescriptions may not be clinically necessary. Moreover, a third of the elderly patients who are prescribed benzodiazepines end up using them long-term. Educating prescribers on appropriate indications and the use of benzodiazepines in elderly individuals is necessary to prevent indiscriminate use of these agents that are likely to cause significant adverse effects in this population.
>
> (Gupta et al., 2021, p. 5)

As presented in the previous subsection, and confirmed in virtually every related systematic review, benzodiazepines are widely and commonly over prescribed for older adults in the U.S. For example, as noted by Gerlach, Wiechers, and Maust (2018, p. 264):

> This systematic review suggests that BZD prescribing to older adults is significantly in excess of what the available evidence suggests is appropriate.

Given the continuing over-prescription of benzodiazepines for older adults during the second decade of the new millennium—and related adverse consequences—several organizations (e.g., American Geriatric Society and Canadian Coalition for Seniors' Mental Health) have recommended that the use of benzodiazepines be either avoided or minimized. For example, as recommended by Conn et al. (2019, p. 9):

> Long-term use of BZRAs [benzodiazepines and z-drugs receptor agonists] (> 4 weeks) in older adults should be avoided for most indications because of their minimal efficacy and risk of harm. Older adults have increased sensitivity to BZRAs and decreased ability to metabolize some longer-acting agents, such as diazepam. All BZRAs increase the risk of cognitive

---

56. For example, in 2008, according to the CDC, the most prescribed benzodiazepine in the U.S. was alprazolam (Xanax®) (Cai, Crane, & Poneleit, 2010).
57. N.B. Older adults, who are receiving hospice, palliative, or other end-of-life care, are generally considered to be exempt from these prescription guidelines.

impairment, delirium, falls, fractures, hospitalizations, and motor vehicle crashes. Alternate management strategies for insomnia, anxiety disorders, and the behavioral and psychological symptoms of dementia are recommended.

<u>Related Professional Reminder</u>: When considering the prescription of benzodiazepines for older adults, prescribers should keep in mind the following general guidelines:

1. ***Avoid the use of benzodiazepines for older adults who are already taking opiate analgesics;***
2. ***Before initiating benzodiazepine pharmacotherapy, check for possible clinically significant drug-drug interactions;***
3. ***For most older adults, particularly those who are frail or of advanced age, initiate benzodiazepine therapy with half of the usual adult dose and titrate—up-or-down—according to individual patient response;***
4. ***Advise patients that only short-term benzodiazepine use is indicated;***
5. ***Limit daily, or near daily, benzodiazepine use to 30 days;***[58]
6. ***Educate patients to monitor for, avoid, and report potential related undesired, or harmful, effects and toxicities associated with benzodiazepine use (e.g., ataxia; confusion; dizziness; and mental depression).***

Because the current status of prescribing sedative-hypnotics among older adults has been so problematic for so long, we constructed a flowchart (Figure 6.5) for approaching the short-term management of insomnia among older adults. This flow chart is predicated on current knowledge and clinical practice guidelines. It concludes with: (1) identified prescription sedative-hypnotics that can be utilized for the short-term management of specific types of insomnia; and (2) initial suggested starting doses for most older adults.

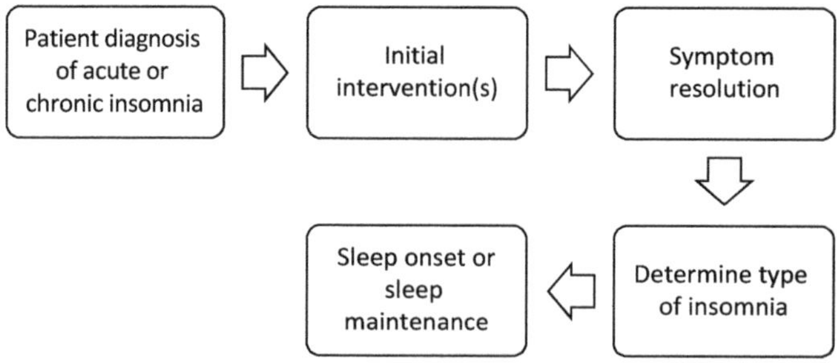

Figure 6.5 Suggested Flowchart for the Short-Term Management of Insomnia Among Older Adults

The selection of which specific sedative-hypnotic to use, as well as the ideal dosage, must be predicated on each older adult's individual characteristics (e.g., hepatic function,

58. N.B. Some clinical protocols recommend that daily benzodiazepine use be limited to a maximum of two weeks.

Table 6.4 Benzodiazepine and Z-Drug Oral Dose Equivalents for Diazepam (Valium®) 5 mg[59]

CATEGORY **Generic Name**	**Brand Name®**	**Approximate Equivalent Dose for Diazepam (Valium®) 5 mg**
BENZODIAZEPINES		
Alprazolam	Xanax®	0.5 mg
Bromazepam	Lectopam®	4 mg
Chlordiazepoxide	Librium®	10 mg
Clobazepam	Frisium®	10 mg
Clonazepam	Klonopin®	0.25 mg
Clorazepate	Tranxene®	7.5 mg
Diazepam	Valium®	5 mg
Estazolam	ProSom®	1 mg
Flunitrazepam[60]	Rohypnol®	1 mg
Flurazepam	Dalmane®	15 mg
Halazepam	Paxipam®	10 mg
Lorazepam	Ativan®	1 mg
Midazolam	Versed®	5 mg
Nitrazepam	Mogadon®	5 mg
Oxazepam	Serax®	15 mg
Prazepam	Centrax®	7.5 mg
Quazepam	Doral®	7.5 mg
Temazepam	Restoril®	10 mg
Triazolam	Halcion®	0.25 mg
Z-DRUGS[61]		
Eszopiclone	Lunesta®	2 mg
Zaleplon	Sonata®	10 mg
Zolpidem	Ambien®	10 mg
Zopiclone	Imovane®	7.5 mg

concomitant pharmacotherapy [e.g., opiate analgesic pharmacotherapy, which poses a relative contraindication to the use of benzodiazepines for older adults], and concurrent physical [e.g., sleep apnea] and mental disorders [e.g., MDD]).

59. N.B. Health and social care professionals should recognize that these dosage equivalents are approximate and that individual variations, particularly regarding: (1) genotype or genetic makeup; and (2) hepatic function (see the related discussion in the earlier benzodiazepine pharmacology subsection, Pharmacokinetics—"Metabolism"), may require adjustment or modification of the listed equivalent dosages. Additionally, health and social care professionals should recognize that differences in the half-lives of elimination (see Table 6.2) may require alteration or modification in the dosage schedule.
60. Flunitrazepam is not legally available in the U.S.
61. See the related discussion in the later section, "Z-Drugs."

Deprescribing, or Tapering, Benzodiazepine Dosage[62]

Tapering benzodiazepine dosage may be performed in order to:

- Decrease risk for undesired, or harmful, effects and toxicities (e.g., cognitive impairment or falls);
- Improve quality of life (e.g., increase cognitive alertness and energy);
- Manage benzodiazepine dependence or use disorder.

> Transfer to diazepam followed by gradual withdrawal is an effective way of discontinuing chronic benzodiazepine use.
>
> (Zitman & Couvee, 2001, p. 317)

> We recommend that deprescribing, or slowly tapering, of BZRAs [i.e., benzodiazepine receptor agonists] be offered to elderly adults (≥ 65 years) who take BZRAs, regardless of duration of use.
>
> (Pottie et al., 2018, p. 339)

> To reduce the risk of acute withdrawal reactions, use a gradual taper to reduce the dosage or to discontinue benzodiazepines. No standard benzodiazepine tapering schedule is suitable for all patients; therefore, create a patient-specific plan to gradually reduce the dosage, and ensure ongoing monitoring and support as needed to avoid serious withdrawal symptoms or worsening of the patient's medical condition.
>
> (FDA, 2020, p. 2)

Several different approaches for tapering patients off of their benzodiazepine have been suggested, as noted by Ogbonna and Lembke (2017, p. 607):

> There are three basic approaches to a benzodiazepine taper: (1) use the same medication for tapering; (2) switch to a longer-acting equivalent; and (3) use adjunctive medications to help mitigate potential withdrawal symptoms.

However, when tapering benzodiazepine dosages, we generally recommend:

1. Use a diazepam (Valium®) dosage equivalent to the benzodiazepine dosage currently being used by the patient (see Table 6.4). A single daily dose at bedtime is generally recommended because diazepam has a long half-life of elimination;[63]
2. Slowly taper the dosage (e.g., equivalent to 5 mg of diazepam per week or 10% of the dosage per week—whichever is less);[64]

---

62. The successful discontinuation of benzodiazepine pharmacotherapy—and the continuation of resumed nonuse, once obtained—can be increased with the concurrent use of appropriate cognitive behavioral therapy (CBT) in conjunction with the tapering protocol selected (Ahmed, Westra, & Stewart, 2008; Baillargeon, Landreville, & Verreault, 2003; Darker, Sweeney, & Barry, 2015; Morin, Bastien, & Guay, 2004; Otto, McHugh, & Simon, 2010; Otto, Pollack, & Meltzer-Brody, 1992).
63. For managing the benzodiazepine tapering process, some clinicians in Australia and Canada (e.g., Brett, 2015; Conn et al., 2019) recommend the use of a benzodiazepine with a shorter half-life of elimination (e.g., alprazolam [Xanax®] or lorazepam [Ativan®]). However, we generally do not concur with this recommendation.
64. Generally, the tapering is accomplished over a period of approximately three months. However, up to six months can be used for older adults who either have been: (1) maintained on benzodiazepines for six months or longer; or (2) received particularly high dosages of the benzodiazepines.

3. Monitor for undesired, or harmful, effects and toxicities (e.g., anxiety or seizures) and—as clinically indicated—be prepared to appropriately treat these effects and toxicities by restoring the previous benzodiazepine dosage;
4. As part of patient education, ensure that older adult patients understand the reasons for tapering the benzodiazepine dosage, the anticipated benefits, and the projected time schedule;
5. Use an explicit tapering schedule and not an ad hoc approach;
6. Monitor patient clinical response with weekly follow-up appointments, as indicated;
7. At each follow-up appointment, assess and inquire about the occurrence of specific related signs and symptoms (e.g., anxiety, craving, insomnia, irritability, or seizures) and the older adult patient's subjective evaluation of the tapering process;
8. Depending on individual patient characteristics (e.g., personality and willingness to comply with therapy), consider writing new prescriptions every one to two weeks—with particular attention to current changes in dosages;
9. Utilize nonpharmacological approaches (e.g., cognitive therapy) to manage the occurrence of anxiety, insomnia, or other related troubling effects as needed;
10. At the completion of the tapering process, schedule a follow-up appointment within one week of completion and schedule subsequent appointments, as needed, to help to prevent recidivism, or relapsed use.

Regarding benzodiazepine tapering, Gold (2020, p. 48) suggested the following additional recommendations:

- Provide patient with clear, written instructions for taper:
  - Discuss how prescription will be written, the quantity provided, and appropriate refill date;
  - Consider having patient sign a treatment agreement including information on consequences related to early refill requests, prescriptions from other providers, or misuse of other substances.
- Converting to a long-acting agent for the duration of the taper is not absolutely necessary but may mitigate withdrawal symptoms compared with short-acting agents;
- It is okay to stay at a dose for longer than expected, but do not increase the dose once a taper has started;
- Avoid as-needed use of benzodiazepines during the taper;
- Provide a seven- to 14-day supply of medication;
- Obtain urine drug screen prior to starting taper and periodically thereafter:
  - Repeat urine drug screen if patient has noticeable changes in behavior, misses follow-up appointments, or requests early refills;
  - Monitor for use of other substances to replace benzodiazepine or to manage withdrawal symptoms;
  - Also monitor gamma-glutamyl transferase (GGT) for alcohol use.

As supported by several published reviews (e.g., Gould et al., 2014; Ng, Le Couteur, & Hilmer, 2018; Reeve, Ong, & Wu, 2017), deprescribing benzodiazepines, utilizing the methods and approaches presented in this subsection, can prove successful for a majority of older adults. For example:

> Discontinuation of chronic BZD/Z [benzodiazepine/z-drug] use is feasible in the nursing home setting without noticeable withdrawal symptoms without a switch in medication use, without detrimental effect on quality of life and with a positive effect on the self-perceived sleep quality.
>
> (Bourgeois, Elseviers, & Van Bortel, 2014a, p. 1251)

> When benzodiazepine discontinuation is managed judiciously and individually, success rates can be 70% to 80%.
>
> (Guina & Merrill, 2018b, p. 8)

Related Professional Reminder: ***Nearly all nonmedical/illicit benzodiazepine use among older adults originates with inappropriate medical prescription benzodiazepine use (i.e., is primarily iatrogenic) and in this context, is specifically related to:***

1. ***Inappropriate prescribing;***
2. ***Inadequate monitoring.***

Consequently, prevention and treatment of inappropriate medical prescription benzodiazepine use among older adults primarily involves:

- ***Reducing medical use of benzodiazepines for older adults, overall;***
- ***Whenever clinically feasible and appropriate, carefully considering and using non-benzodiazepine pharmacotherapeutic and psychotherapeutic approaches;***
- ***Increasing the monitoring of all benzodiazepine use for older adults;***
- ***Planning for and implementing dosage tapering, as necessary, for older adults for whom the abrupt discontinuation of benzodiazepine use may be problematic (e.g., result in the benzodiazepine withdrawal syndrome).***

Nonmedical/Illicit Use

The overall nonmedical/illicit use of the benzodiazepines significantly decreased from the high levels observed during the end of the last century. However, during the first decade of the new millennium, their use continued to be significant as indicated by reports from both addiction treatment centers and hospital emergency departments across the U.S. (e.g., Forrester, 2006; O'Brien, 2008; Schmitz, 2016)—with alprazolam (Xanax®), clonazepam (Rivotril®), diazepam (Valium®), and lorazepam (Ativan®) accounting for many of these reports.[65] In addition, a significant number of older adults who sought assistance from addic-

65. Interestingly, Maust et al. (2019), in their review of data from the *National Survey on Drug Use and Health* (NSDUH), found that for adults 50 years of age and older, the four most commonly

tion counselors for alcohol or opiate analgesic dependence or use disorder, also were found to have issues with benzodiazepine dependence or use disorder. (See also the related discussion in the earlier benzodiazepine pharmacology subsection—"Benzodiazepine Overdosage/Unintentional Poisoning.")

As noted by the DEA (2019, p. 1):

> Individuals abusing benzodiazepines obtain them by getting prescriptions from several doctors, forging prescriptions, or buying diverted pharmaceutical products on the illicit market.

However, in our clinical experience, the most common source of illicit benzodiazepines for older adults, is their medical prescriber (see the related discussion in the previous subsection, "Medical Prescription Use"). Additionally, as noted by Maust et al. (2019), another common source of illicit benzodiazepines for older adults is their friends or relatives.

Of interest, Canham et al. (2014, p. 872) conducted a phenomenological study of the perceptions of benzodiazepine dependence or use disorder among older adults—specifically, older women 65 years of age and older. The major themes they identified, include:

- Benzodiazepine dependence is similar to dependence on diabetes or blood pressure medications;
- Dependence is distinctive from addiction/abuse;
- Addiction/abuse is perceived as worse than dependence;
- Concerns about addiction/abuse result in low-dose benzodiazepine use.

They concluded that these themes reflect the general medicalization of benzodiazepine dependence among older adults and the associated need for the appropriate education of prescribers—and, in turn—their patients.

Assessment and Diagnosis of Benzodiazepine Dependence or Use Disorder

The assessment and diagnosis of benzodiazepine dependence or use disorder generally involves conducting a detailed patient history and clinical interview concerning benzodiazepine use.[66] In addition, as recommended by Conn et al. (2019, p. 7):

> All older adults should be asked about current and past consumption of substances that might lead to substance use disorders, including BZRA [benzodiazepines and z-drug receptor agonists] during periodic health examinations, admissions to facilities or services, perioperative assessments when considering the prescription of a BZRA, and at transitions in care.

---

misused benzodiazepines were alprazolam (56.4%), clonazepam (13.6%), diazepam (30.5%), and lorazepam (26.0%).

66. A more comprehensive overview and discussion of professional assessment and diagnosis of older adult alcohol or other dependence or use disorders can be found in the Chapter 1, *Alcohol*, subsection—"Assessment and Diagnosis of Alcohol Dependence or Use Disorder."

Additionally, Conn et al. (2019, p. 8) recommend that:

> Assessment of older adults suspected of having a BZRA use disorder should include indication, dose, duration, features indicative of BZRA use disorder, readiness to change, and presence of both medical and psychiatric comorbidities, including any other past or current substance use or misuse.[67]

Unfortunately, little research has been directed at the specific development and testing of quick-screen psychometric tests and other tools to assist health and social care professionals with their assessment and diagnosis of benzodiazepine dependence or use disorder among older adults. However, the data collection procedures can be generally facilitated by the use of the:

1. "Benzodiazepine Dependence Questionnaire" (BDEPQ);
2. DSM-5 criteria for the detection and severity of the "Sedative, Hypnotic, or Anxiolytic Use Disorder" (SHAUD);
3. "Severity of Dependence Scale" (SDS).

Each of these tools are presented and discussed in the following subsections.

Benzodiazepine Dependence Questionnaire

Extended from the master's degree thesis of its developer, Baillie (1992), the BDEPQ (Table 6.5)[68] is a quick-screen psychometric test that was designed to measure dependence on benzodiazepines and other sedative-hypnotics (Baillie, 1996). The 30-item, self-report questionnaire was created with the use of a convenience sample of 267 Australians (mean age of 61 years of age). The items, or questions, of the BDEPQ specifically refer to the past month and cover all aspects of benzodiazepine dependence, except benzodiazepine withdrawal. Each item is rated on a four-point Likert scale.

Available Test Statistics and Recommendations Although psychometrics are limited, test statistics regarding specificity and sensitivity, and validity and reliability, are available for the BDEPQ. These statistics are presented and discussed in the following subsections along with limitations and recommendations for supporting its use.

Regarding, specificity and sensitivity, Minaya, Fresan, and Cortes-Lopez (2011), using a sample of 150 Mexican patients, who met DSM-IV diagnostic criteria for benzodiazepine dependence, found that: (*continued*, p. 524; see 1. and 2.)

---

67. We recommend that, minimally, the assessments of older adults also include a:

    1. Comprehensive list of prescription and non-prescription drugs—including illicit drugs and substances of abuse, such as cocaine, and over-the-counter (OTC) drugs, such as acetaminophen (Tylenol®)—primarily, to identify possible drug-drug interactions (e.g., alcohol and benzodiazepine);
    2. Baseline assessment of the indications (e.g., anxiety disorder or insomnia) for which the benzodiazepine or z-drug was originally prescribed;
    3. History of undesired, or harmful, effects and toxicities associated with the previous use of the benzodiazepine or z-drug (e.g., injuries associated with falls; memory impairment).

68. Wording has been slightly modified (see the related discussion in the subsection—"Recommendations").

Table 6.5 Benzodiazepine Dependence Questionnaire (BDEPQ)

Instructions: *In the questions that follow you will be asked about your experience using benzodiazepines. When answering the questions please think about your experiences over the last month. Place a mark in the box below the response that best suits your experience in the last month.*

1. In the last month, have you taken another benzodiazepine as soon as the effects of the previous one began to wear off?

Never	**Sometimes**	**Often**	**Always**
☐	☐	☐	☐

2. Have you taken benzodiazepines in the last month because you like the way they make you feel?

Always	**Often**	**Sometimes**	**Never**
☐	☐	☐	☐

3. In the last month, have you felt that you cannot face anything out of the ordinary without a benzodiazepine?

Never	**Sometimes**	**Often**	**Everyday**
☐	☐	☐	☐

4. Do you feel that you cannot get through the day without the help of your benzodiazepines?

Never	**Sometimes**	**Often**	**Everyday**
☐	☐	☐	☐

5. Do you need to carry your benzodiazepines with you?

Always	**Often**	**Sometimes**	**Never**
☐	☐	☐	☐

6. Have you tried to reduce the number of benzodiazepines you take because they interfered with your life?

A great deal	**Somewhat**	**A little**	**No**
☐	☐	☐	☐

7. Have you found that you needed to take more benzodiazepines to get the same effect in the last month compared to when you first took them?

No	**Sometimes**	**Often**	**Always**
☐	☐	☐	☐

8. Do you need to take benzodiazepines to deal with the problems in your life?

Never	**Sometimes**	**Often**	**Everyday**
☐	☐	☐	☐

9. Do you feel terrible if you do not take a benzodiazepine?

Everyday	**Often**	**Sometimes**	**Never**
☐	☐	☐	☐

(*Continued*)

Table 6.5 (Continued)

10a. In the last month have you been worried that your doctor might not continue to prescribe the benzodiazepines you are taking?

Never	Sometimes	Often	A lot
☐	☐	☐	☐

10b. How strong has this worry been?

Mild	Moderate	Severe
☐	☐	☐

11. Could you stop taking benzodiazepines tomorrow without any difficulties?

- ☐ No, it would be impossible
- ☐ Perhaps, with a lot of difficulty
- ☐ Yes, with some difficulty
- ☐ Yes, without difficulty

12. Do you count down the time until you can take your next benzodiazepine?

Always	Often	Sometimes	Never
☐	☐	☐	☐

13a. Have you experience relief when you have taken benzodiazepines in the last month?

Never	Sometimes	Often	Always
☐	☐	☐	☐

13b. How strong is that relief?

Mild	Moderate	Intense
☐	☐	☐

14a. In the last month, have you felt bad or sick as the effects of benzodiazepine wore off?

- ☐ **Yes** *Answer the next question* ("# 14b")
- ☐ **No** *Skip to question 15*

14b. Have you taken another benzodiazepine to reduce these unpleasant after-effects?

Never	Sometimes	Often	Always
☐	☐	☐	☐

15. In the last month, have you taken benzodiazepines against your doctor's advice or more frequently than recommended?

Never	Occasionally	Sometimes	Often
☐	☐	☐	☐

16. Are you concerned about the number of benzodiazepines you have taken in the last month?

A great deal	A lot	A little	Not at all
☐	☐	☐	☐

17. Have you taken more benzodiazepines in one day or night than you planned to?

Everyday	Often	Sometimes	Never
☐	☐	☐	☐

18a. Have you found the effects of benzodiazepines pleasant?

Never	Sometimes	Often	Always
☐	☐	☐	☐

18b. How strong is the pleasant feeling?

Mild	Moderate	Intense
☐	☐	☐

19. Have you taken benzodiazepines for a longer period than you intended to when you started?

Never	Sometimes	Often	A lot
☐	☐	☐	☐

20a. Have you felt tense or anxious as your prescription for benzodiazepines began to run out?

Never	Sometimes	Often	Every time
☐	☐	☐	☐

20b. How strong have these feelings been?

Mild	Moderate	Severe
☐	☐	☐

21a. Have you felt an urge or a desire take benzodiazepines in the last month?

Never	Sometimes	Often	Everyday
☐	☐	☐	☐

21b. How strong is that urge or desire?

Mild	Moderate	Intense
☐	☐	☐

22. Have you taken benzodiazepines in the last month when you did not really need them?

Never	Sometimes	Often	Everyday
☐	☐	☐	☐

Instructions: *In the next set of questions please tick the box below the answer that matches what you think.*

23. I feel powerless to prevent myself from taking a benzodiazepine when I am anxious, uptight, or unhappy.

Strongly disagree	Somewhat disagree	Somewhat agree	Strongly agree
☐	☐	☐	☐

24. I would not be able to handle my problems unless I take a benzodiazepine.

Strongly agree	Somewhat agree	Somewhat disagree	Strongly disagree
☐	☐	☐	☐

25. I get so upset over small arguments, that I need to take a benzodiazepine.

Strongly agree	Somewhat degree	Somewhat disagree	Strongly disagree
☐	☐	☐	☐

Source: Modified from Baillie, 1996.

Scoring the BDEPQ As noted by Baillie (1996, p. 8):

> In general, higher scores are associated with greater risk of future withdrawal symptoms, of continued BZD use, and are more likely to be associated with positive CIDI [*WHO-WMH-CIDI, The World Health Organization World Mental Health Composite International Diagnostic Interview*] diagnoses of BZD dependence.

Scoring of the BDEPQ is relatively easy if the steps presented in Table 6.6 are adhered to.

Table 6.6 Six Steps for Scoring the BDEPQ

THE 6 STEPS	SCORING PROCEDURES
	The BDEPQ is relatively easy to score if the following 6 steps are adhered to:
1.	Score most items as: 0 1 2 3 ☐ ☐ ☐ ☐
2.	Except for items 2, 5, 6, 9, 12, 16, 17, and 23, which are reversed. Score these as: 3 2 1 0 ☐ ☐ ☐ ☐
3.	Score the second part (b) of two-part items (items 10a & b, 18a & b, 20a & b, 21a & b) as 0 if the first part (a) is scored 0.
4.	Ignore item 14a.
5.	Score item 11 as: ☐ **3** No, it would be impossible ☐ **2** Perhaps, with a lot of difficulty ☐ **1** Yes, with some difficulty ☐ **0** Yes, without difficulty
6.	Sum the items to give a total score. ***Additionally, "subscale scores" can be calculated as follows:*** a. Sum items, 1, 6, 7, 10a, 10b, 14b, 15, 16, 17, 19, 20a, 20b, 21a, and 22 to give a score on the *General Dependence* subscale. b. Sum items 2, 13a, 13b, 18a, 18b, and 21b to give a score on the *Pleasant Effects* subscale. c. Sum items 3, 4, 5, 8, 9, 11, 12, 23, 24, and 25 to give a score on the *Perceived Need* subscale.

1. Strong alpha values were obtained for both the subscales and total score;
2. A cut-off value of 23 was associated with most stable specificity and sensitivity values.

Regarding validity and reliability, the face validity of the BDEPQ appears to be high. The 30 items selected for inclusion were based primarily upon factor analysis from an original list of 68 items. The selected test items were found to have a Cronbach's alpha coefficient of 0.922 (Baillie, 1996), demonstrating a high reliability, or internal consistency. The four-month, test-retest correlation was 0.88 (Baillie, 1996). This high correlation suggests that, regarding benzodiazepine dependence, a state rather than a trait is being measured.

Regarding recommendations, as reported by Baillie and Mattick (1996, p. 276), the BDEPQ appears to be "a reliable and valid self-report instrument for the assessment of benzodiazepine dependence." The BDEPQ has also been found "to be a useful instrument for the early recognition of benzodiazepine dependence in clinical populations" (Minaya et al., 2011, p. 874). Thus, based on its: (1) good face validity; (2) supporting, although limited, published psychometric data; and (3) development and testing that included older adults, we generally recommend the use of the BDEPQ as a quick-screen psychometric test for detecting benzodiazepine dependence among older adults.

However, we have noted, as has Baillie (1996), that some older adults have difficulty completing the BDEPQ because of its confusing presentation and wording. Thus, we suggest that older adults complete the questionnaire in the presence of the tester so they can clarify any confusion encountered while completing the BDEPQ. We also suggest that testers review the questionnaire for completeness (e.g., questions that have been left unanswered) and any obvious response bias (e.g., a check mark placed in the first square for each question). Testers are also encouraged to consider rewording the original instructions below, replacing them with the "revised instructions" which follow:

> *Instructions: In the questions that follow you will be asked about your experience using medications known as sleeping pills, sedatives, hypnotics, 'benzos' or minor tranquillisers [sic]. These medications are also known by their trade names of 'Valium', 'Serepax', 'Mogadon', 'Normison', and 'Rohypnol' to list a few. All of these will be called sedatives, tranquillisers [sic] or sleeping pills in the questions.*
>
> (Baillie, 1996, p. 60)

Revised Instructions: "In the questions that follow, you will be asked about your experience using benzodiazepines (e.g., Ativan®; Halcion®; Valium®)."[69]

DSM-5

Benzodiazepine dependence or use disorder is classified, according to the DSM-5 (APA, 2013), as "Sedative, Hypnotic, or Anxiolytic Use Disorder" (SHAUD). The revised criteria, which is utilized in the DSM-5, combines the previous related DSM-IV diagnoses of "abuse" and "dependence" with the elimination of the single criteria related to "legal problems" (Hasin, O'Brien, & Auriacombe, 2013; Saunders, 2017).

The assessment and diagnosis of SHAUD usually involves an initial clinical interview with the older adult during which: (1) benzodiazepine use is established and, if established; (2) questions are asked to obtain answers concerning: the benzodiazepine used; the history, or pattern of use; attempts to quit; and previously explored treatment approaches. Gill (2015, p. 35) suggests the use of the following 11 questions:

Thinking back, is there a 12-month period of time where you could answer YES to any of these questions?

1. Do you find that you use more often, or for a longer time, than you planned?
2. Do you want to cut back or stop; or have you ever tried and failed to cut back or stop your use?
3. Do you spend a great deal of time obtaining, taking, or recovering from your use?
4. Do you experience strong desires or cravings to use?

69. The wording for each of the BDEPQ questions is also revised accordingly from "sedatives, tranquillisers [sic], or sleeping pills" to "benzodiazepines."

5. Have you repeatedly failed to fulfill major obligations at work, at home, or at school because of your use?
6. Do you continue to use even though you suspect, or even know, that it creates or worsens interpersonal or social problems?
7. Have you given up or reduced important social, occupational, or recreational activities because of your use?
8. Do you repeatedly use in situations in which it is physically hazardous to yourself or others, such as smoking in bed, driving a car, operating a machine, or being at work while intoxicated, impaired, or under the influence?
9. Do you continue to use, even though you suspect, or even know, that it creates or worsens problems with your mind and body?
10. Do you find that you need to use more than in the past in order to achieve the same desired effect, or that you feel less of an effect from the same amount than in the past?
11. Do you find when you stop or reduce your use, that you experience any withdrawal symptoms, or have you ever taken another substance to prevent or reduce withdrawal symptoms?

Four factors are measured by the 11 criteria listed in Table 6.7:

1. Impaired control (Criteria 1 through 4);
2. Social impairment (Criteria 5 through 7);
3. Risky use (Criteria 8 and 9);
4. Pharmacological properties (Criteria 10 and 11).

A contextual predicate of the DSM-5 diagnosis of sedative, hypnotic, or anxiolytic use disorder is that "legitimate medical use" of the sedatives, hypnotics, and anxiolytics invalidates the diagnosis (APA, 2013). We take extreme umbrage with this biased, outdated, and profoundly unscientific view of dependence. Physical dependence or use disorder—a biophysiological process that is characterized by a "physical" benzodiazepine withdrawal syndrome when regular long-term medical or nonmedical/illicit benzodiazepine use is abruptly discontinued and is immediately relieved when use is resumed—has no inherent moral or psychological basis, nor does it have a conscious component as does "psychological" dependence. Consequently, physical dependence occurs irrespective of whether a benzodiazepine is used for a legitimate medical indication or for a nonmedical/illicit purpose. Because of the noted considerations, when we do use these DSM-5 criteria, we simply ignore the DSM-5 footnotes for criteria 10, "tolerance," and criteria 11, "withdrawal" (Pagliaro & Pagliaro, *Clinical Patient Data Files*).

Severity of Dependence Scale (SDS)

The SDS was developed by Gossop, Darke, and Griffiths (1995). Since that time, it has demonstrated acceptable psychometric properties ("test-retest reliability," or "good internal consistency" [i.e., Cronback's alpha ranging from 0.80 to 0.90]—0.89 over a one-day interval—[Gossop et al., 1995; Gossop, Best, & Marsden, 1997]; and "validity and reliability" [Ferri, Marsden, & de Araujo, 2000]) for a variety of abusable psychotropics (e.g., amphetamines, benzodiazepines, cocaine, and heroin) in several different countries (e.g., Australia, Brazil, and the U.S.).

The SDS consists of five items that are each scored on a 4-point Likert scale (0–3). Summation of the individual scores provides the total score (range of 0–12).

Table 6.7 DSM-5 Criteria and Scoring for Sedative, Hypnotic, or Anxiolytic Use Disorder (SHAUD)

ITEM #	DSM-5 SYMPTOM CRITERIA FOR SHAUD
1.	Benzodiazepines/Z-drugs are often taken in larger amounts or over longer periods of time than was intended
2.	There is a persistent desire or unsuccessful efforts to cutdown or control benzodiazepine/z-drug use
3.	A great deal of time is spent in activities necessary to obtain the benzodiazepine/z-drug, use the benzodiazepine/z-drug, or recover from its effects
4.	Craving or a strong desire to use benzodiazepines/z-drugs
5.	Recurrent benzodiazepine/z-drug use resulting in a failure to fulfill major role obligations at work, school, or home
6.	Continued benzodiazepine/z-drug use despite having persistent or recurrent social or interpersonal problems caused or exacerbated by the effects of benzodiazepines/z-drugs
7.	Important social, occupational, or recreational activities are given up or reduced because of benzodiazepine/z-drug use
8.	Recurrent benzodiazepine/z-drug use in situations in which it is physically hazardous
9.	Continued benzodiazepine/z-drug use despite knowledge of having a persistent or recurrent physical or psychological problem that is likely to have been caused or exacerbated by benzodiazepines/z-drugs
10.	Tolerance,[70] as defined by either of the following: (a) Need for markedly increased amounts of benzodiazepines/z-drugs to achieve intoxication or desired effect (b) Markedly diminished effect with continued use of the same amount of benzodiazepine/z-drug
11.	Withdrawal,[71] as manifested by either of the following: (a) Characteristic benzodiazepine/z-drug withdrawal syndrome (b) The same benzodiazepine/z-drug (or other "sedative, hypnotic, or anxiolytic") taken to relieve or avoid withdrawal symptoms
SCORING	According to DSM-Criteria: The presence of at least two of these symptoms within a 12-month period indicates a "sedative, hypnotic, or anxiolytic" disorder. Additionally, the severity of the disorder is defined as: "Mild," the presence of two or three symptoms; "Moderate," the presence of four or five symptoms; or "Severe," the presence of six or more symptoms.

Source: Modified from APA, 2013.

The average self-completion time for the SDS is approximately 1 minute and its use is currently endorsed by the World Health Organization (WHO, 2020). See Chapter 2, *Amphetamines and Cocaine*, for additional related discussion and a copy of the SDS.

70. Patients, who are prescribed benzodiazepines/z-drugs, may exhibit these two criteria (tolerance and withdrawal) but would not necessarily be considered to have a substance use disorder (i.e., the criterion is not met if the benzodiazepine/z-drug is taken solely under appropriate medical supervision). N.B. See the text for our rationale and recommendation to ignore these "exemptions" that are stipulated in DSM-5.

71. N.B. See also the subsection, "DSM-5 Criteria for Detection and Severity of OUD," which is found in Chapter 5, "Prescription Opiate Analgesics and Heroin."

Available Test Statistics and Recommendations Additionally, several health and social care providers and researchers, including ourselves, have found the SDS to be an adequate psychometric tool and recommend its use for this purpose. For example, de las Cuevas, Sanz, and de la Fuente (2000) found the SDS to be highly valid and reliable when a cutoff score of 6 is used to determine benzodiazepine dependence. Additionally, they found that the SDS had, as a screening tool for benzodiazepine dependence, a specificity of 94.2% and a sensitivity of 97.9%. In another example, Cheng, Ghazal Siddiqui, and Gossop (2019) evaluated the efficacy of the SDS using a sample of 100 older adults, 65 to 90 years of age, who were identified as chronic, long-term users of benzodiazepines, opiate analgesics, or z-drugs, and found that the SDS, in comparison to DSM-IV criteria, was a valid and reliable diagnostic tool.

Treating Older Adult Benzodiazepine Dependence or Use Disorder[72]

Meta-analyses regarding specific treatment outcomes for sample groups of adults—both young and old—have been completed by several researchers (e.g., Conn et al., 2019; Darker et al., 2015; Fluyau, Revadigar, & Manobianco, 2018). However, most of these studies failed to separate adults by age (e.g., younger adults versus older adults). Consequently, we are currently left with a situation in which treatment approaches for older adults must be primarily guided by the outcomes of these combined samples. With these limitations in mind, we present current findings for the treatment of benzodiazepine dependence or use disorder for older adults, particularly: (1) pharmacotherapeutic approaches; and (2) psychotherapeutic/counseling approaches.

Pharmacotherapeutic Approaches

No specific pharmacotherapeutic approaches for the treatment of benzodiazepine dependence or use disorder have received FDA approval. However, pharmacotherapy has been approved and has long been available for the management of:

1. Benzodiazepine overdosage/unintentional poisoning (see the related discussion in the earlier benzodiazepine pharmacology subsection—Overdosage/Unintentional Poisoning—"Treatment of Benzodiazepine Overdosage");
2. Facilitation of benzodiazepine discontinuation/withdrawal (see the related discussion in the earlier benzodiazepine subsection, "Tapering Benzodiazepine Dosage").

In addition to the well-established, previously discussed, and related pharmacotherapy (i.e., flumazenil for benzodiazepine overdosage and diazepam for benzodiazepine discontinuation), a number of diverse drugs (e.g., baclofen, clonidine, carbamazepine, gabapentin, hydroxyzine, imipramine, melatonin, progesterone, propranolol, tiagabine, trazadone, Valerian, and valproic acid) have been utilized and evaluated for the treatment of benzodiazepine dependence or use disorder.

72. See also the related discussion in the earlier benzodiazepine subsection, "Tapering Benzodiazepine Dosage."

Several retrospective database reviews (e.g., Darker et al., 2015; Fluyau et al., 2018; Sabioni, Bertram, & Le Foll, 2015; Welsh, Tretyak, & McHugh, 2018) have been conducted to collect and evaluate the efficacy of these proposed pharmacotherapeutic treatment approaches. The consensus, as concisely and succinctly stated by Fluyay, Revadigar, and Manobianco (2018, p. 147), is that: "The efficacy of these medications is not robust." In support of this conclusion, Baandrup, Ebdrup, and Rasmussen (2018, p. 3)—in a systematic review of 38 randomized controlled studies involving 2,543 patients diagnosed with benzodiazepine dependence (average age 50 years)—found that:

> Given the low or very low quality of the evidence for the reported outcomes, and the small number of trials identified with a limited number of participants for each comparison, it is not possible to draw firm conclusions regarding pharmacological interventions to facilitate benzodiazepine discontinuation in chronic benzodiazepine users.

Psychotherapeutic/Counseling Approaches[73]

Psychotherapeutic/counseling approaches, particularly CBT, have demonstrated significant benefit when used for older adults diagnosed with benzodiazepine dependence or use disorder. CBT provides education and training in the development of patient coping and social skills. As an intended result, older adults are better able to deal with anxiety and life's stressors. In turn, benzodiazepine use can be reduced and, once reduced, ceased, and resumed use prevented (i.e., prevention of relapsed use) (Soyka, 2017). Additionally, as concluded by Baillargeon et al. (2003, p. 1015):

> A combination of cognitive-behavioral therapy and benzodiazepine tapering was superior to tapering alone in the management of patients with insomnia and chronic benzodiazepine use.

(See also the related discussion in the earlier benzodiazepine subsection, "Tapering Benzodiazepine Dosage.")

We now turn to the "Z-Drugs."

Z-DRUGS

The z-drugs are rapidly becoming the most frequently medically prescribed sedative-hypnotics in the U.S. This subgroup of the prescription sedative-hypnotics is comprised of four major drugs:

1. Zaleplon (Sonata®);
2. Zolpidem (Ambien®);
3. Zopiclone (Imovane®);
4. Eszopiclone (Lunesta®).[74]

73. See the related discussion of these approaches in the Chapter 1, *Alcohol* subsection, "Psychotherapeutic/ Counseling Approaches."
74. Eszopiclone is a stereoisomer of zopiclone. An isomer is a closely related chemical that has the exact same molecular formula, but a different physical structure (e.g., one drug may be "dextro," or "right-handed," and the other drug may be "levo," or "left-handed"). Health and social care professionals

Z-Drug Pharmacology

Z-drugs have been used since the early 1990s in the U.S. for the short-term treatment of insomnia. However, since the beginning of the second decade of the new millennium, the medical use of the z-drugs has increased significantly. FDA approved and legally produced by pharmaceutical manufacturers, primarily in capsule or tablet formulations for ingestion,[75] they are now prescribed more than any other prescription sedative-hypnotic in the U.S.

The z-drugs have a relatively rapid onset (i.e., they reduce sleep latency, or the time it takes to fall asleep after going to bed) and a relatively short duration of hypnotic actions. Consequently, they generally are purported to be associated with minimal "next day," or "hangover" effects. Although their chemical structures are different from the basic benzodiazepine molecular structure, they have a virtually identical spectrum of pharmacological actions—given that they elicit their effects by means of binding to "benzodiazepine" receptors (i.e., "omega binding sites")[76] (see the related discussion in the later pharmacology subsection—"Pharmacodynamics: Mechanism of Action").

Generally, the use of z-drugs is contraindicated for older adults with the following conditions:

- AUD;
- Complex sleep behaviors (i.e., parasomnias);
- Concurrent use of a benzodiazepine;
- Concurrent use of an opiate analgesic;
- Concurrent use of another z-drug;
- Hepatic failure;
- Hepatic impairment (severe);
- History of a z-drug-related complex sleep behavior;
- Hypersensitivity (i.e., z-drug use-related angioedema);
- MDD (severe, untreated);
- Myasthenia gravis;
- Other abusable psychotropic dependence or use disorder (SUD);
- Sleep apnea (severe).

Zaleplon (Sonata®) Zaleplon shares many features with the benzodiazepine, triazolam (Halcion®), and another z-drug, zolpidem (Ambien®). However, in comparison to zolpidem, zaleplon appears to produce less sedation and memory impairment (Drover, Lemmens, & Naidu, 2000; Ebbens & Verster, 2010; Rush, Fry, & Griffiths, 1999). Zaleplon selectively binds to the brain omega-1 site situated on the alpha subunit of the GABA receptor complex.

should be aware that a difference in physical structure may result in a significant difference in actions, particularly when the site of action is a stereospecific drug receptor site.

75. Some z-drugs are also available as oral spray and sublingual tablet formulations. Additionally, they have been also administered intranasally in the context of nonmedical/illicit use.
76. Consequently, z-drugs are also known—as are the benzodiazepines—as benzodiazepine receptor agonists (BZRAs).

Zolpidem (Ambien®) Zolpidem is a short-acting z-drug that is available in tablet form for ingestion. Zolpidem (Ambien®) was introduced into clinical practice in the U.S. in 1992 as a sleeping aid with the belief that it had little risk for physical or psychological dependence. However, its use for the short-term symptomatic medical management of insomnia has now been associated with both physical and psychological dependence—particularly, when prescribed and used in higher dosages, or for longer periods of time than recommended. It also is the most widely prescribed sedative-hypnotic in the U.S., and, although its pharmacological actions are very similar to the benzodiazepines, it is chemically distinct (Holm & Goa, 2000).

Zopiclone (Imovane®) Imovane, also a short-acting z-drug, shares a virtually identical spectrum of pharmacological actions with the benzodiazepines. Zopiclone became commercially available in Europe in 1986 and in the U.S. in 2005. Currently, it is one of the most widely used sedative-hypnotics in the U.S., and throughout the world (Brandt, Alessi-Severini, & Singer, 2019).

Eszopiclone (Lunesta®) Eszopiclone was approved in Europe in 1992 and later approved for use in the U.S. in 2004. It is the levorotatory isomer of zopiclone. The tablet forms of both drugs are generally orally ingested, often with an alcoholic beverage to enhance their euphoric or stress-reducing actions. Zopiclone and eszopiclone have been demonstrated to reduce sleep latency, decrease the number of nocturnal awakenings, and increase total sleep time (Najib, 2006). However, because of their longer half-life of elimination, their use for older adults may also be associated with "hangover" effects—"residual sedative or diminished cognitive effects" (Greenblatt & Zammit, 2012, p. 1609). Eszopiclone is particularly unique among the z-drugs because it has been approved for the long-term treatment of insomnia and is reportedly effective for up to six months (Brielmaier, 2006). Nevertheless, we do not recommend the long-term use of eszopiclone for older adults because its prolonged use can be associated with:

1. Decreased efficacy;
2. Increased undesired, or harmful, effects, which can be serious (e.g., falls).

Pharmacodynamics: Mechanism of Action

As noted, the z-drugs are not benzodiazepines. However, current data suggest that all of the z-drugs act at the benzodiazepine receptor. More specifically, the z-drugs appear to act at the benzodiazepine recognition site of the $GABA_A$ receptor complex, particularly, the omega-1 receptor at its alpha subunit (Agravat, 2018; Sanger, 2004). Working in concert with the inhibitory neurotransmitter GABA, the z-drugs appear to potentiate the GABA-evoked chloride current. A noted placebo-effect also appears to play a significant role in their ability to produce sleep among those who have insomnia (Pagliaro & Pagliaro, *Clinical Patient Data Files*). Although the z-drugs are equally as efficacious as the benzodiazepines for the treatment of insomnia, they display significantly less anxiolytic and anticonvulsant activity—presumably because of their selective binding to the BZD1 receptor (see the related discussion in the earlier benzodiazepine pharmacology subsection, Mechanism of Action—"Benzodiazepine Receptors"). For additional related discussion of the mechanism of action, see the earlier Benzodiazepine pharmacology subsection—Pharmacodynamics: Mechanism of Action."

Pharmacokinetics: Absorption, Distribution, Metabolism, and Excretion

The z-drugs are rapidly absorbed following ingestion and achieve peak blood concentrations and related effects within one to two hours. However, absorption is delayed when zolpidem is ingested with food, particularly high fat foods or large meals. Additionally, the AUC can be decreased by 15% to 30%. The half-life of elimination for the Z-drugs usually ranges from one to five hours. Typically, less than 5% of an oral dose is excreted in unchanged form in the urine. Thus, renal impairment, including that associated with normal aging, does not usually affect z-drug: (1) dosing; (2) half-life of elimination; (3) possible accumulation in the body; or (4) occurrence of undesired, or harmful, effects and toxicities. The z-drugs are extensively metabolized in the liver by the hepatic microsomal (isoenzyme) system, particularly CYP3A4.[77]

In the following z-drug subsections, we consider the pharmacokinetics of each of the z-drugs, beginning with zaleplon.

Zaleplon (Sonata®) Zaleplon is rapidly absorbed following ingestion and achieves peak serum concentrations within one hour (Dooley & Plosker, 2000). However, because of its extensive first-pass hepatic metabolism, its oral bioavailability is limited (i.e., F = 0.3) (Pagliaro & Pagliaro, 2004). Additionally, a high fat meal may delay oral absorption by up to two hours and reduce the maximal serum concentration by one-third.

Regarding distribution, approximately 60% of zaleplon is bound to plasma proteins and its apparent volume of distribution is 1.4 L/kg—indicating significant distribution into extravascular tissues (Rosen, Fournie, & Darwish, 1999). Zaleplon undergoes extensive metabolism to several inactive metabolites. The metabolism primarily involves the aldehyde oxidase enzyme and, to a lesser extent, the hepatic microsomal enzyme CYP3A4. Less than 1% of zaleplon is excreted in unchanged form in the urine. Total body clearance is ~ 1 L/kg/hr. The hepatic extraction ratio of zaleplon is ~ 0.7 (as is consistent with its extensive first-pass hepatic metabolism). The half-life of elimination is approximately one hour (Drover et al., 2000; Gunja, 2013b) and, because of its short half-life of elimination and lack of active metabolites, zaleplon is associated with fewer residual "hang-over" effects (Drover, 2004). The rapid onset of action of zaleplon and its short half-life of elimination make it useful in treating older adults who have difficulty falling asleep. The pharmacokinetics of

77. N.B. In addition, CYP3A4 is involved in the metabolism of various benzodiazepines (e.g., alprazolam [Xanax®], midazolam [Versed®], and triazolam [Halcion®]). CYP3A4 is significantly inhibited by the selective serotonin reuptake inhibitors (SSRIs)—fluoxetine (Prozac®), fluvoxamine (Luvox®), and sertraline (Zoloft®). It also may be inhibited by the ingestion of grapefruit juice. The consequence of this "inhibition" of CYP3A4 is a significant increase in the blood concentrations of the z-drugs and the benzodiazepines—without any changes in their dosages (see the related discussion in the later subsection, "Drug-Drug Interactions Involving Z-Drugs").

zaleplon for healthy older adults, up to 85 years of age, does not significantly differ from that for younger adults.

Zolpidem (Ambien®) Zolpidem is rapidly and moderately well-absorbed (F = 0.7) following ingestion (Drover, 2004). It achieves peak concentrations within 1.5 hours. However, ingesting zolpidem with food delays and decreases its absorption. Zolpidem oral spray is rapidly absorbed from both the oral mucosa and the GI tract. Peak concentrations occur more rapidly (i.e., ~ one hour), but overall bioavailability is equivalent to that obtained following ingestion (i.e., ~ 70%). Sublingual administration results in bioavailability that is essentially equivalent to that obtained following the ingestion of conventional tablets.

Zolpidem is approximately 92% bound to plasma proteins and has an apparent volume of distribution of 0.7 L/kg (Salva & Costa, 1995). It is metabolized extensively in the liver and its metabolites are primarily excreted in the urine. Less than 1% of zolpidem is excreted in unchanged form in the urine. Metabolism is dependent on the mixed cytochrome P450 isoenzymes, particularly the hepatic isoenzyme, CYP3A4, but also involves CYP2D6, CYP2C9, and CYP1A2 (Gunja, 2013b). Total body clearance is ~ .25 ml/kg/minute. The mean elimination half-life is ~ 2.5 hours (Drover et al., 2000). The half-life of elimination ($T_{1/2}$) may be prolonged in older adults with hepatic dysfunction (e.g., hepatitis), but is not significantly affected by renal dysfunction. The reported pharmacokinetics of zolpidem are significantly modified in older adults (i.e., area under the curve [AUC], maximum plasma concentration [Cmax], and $T_{1/2}$ are significantly increased). Consequently, the normal dosage is reduced from 10 mg to 5 mg and is orally administered once daily at bedtime.

Following ingestion, Vlase, Popa, and Neag have examined potential pharmacokinetic interactions between zolpidem and other drugs, including carbamazepine and ciprofloxacin. Regarding carbamazepine (Tegretol®), they found that the bioavailability of zolpidem is decreased by ~ 60% and that the mean half-life of elimination of zolpidem is reduced from 2.3 hours to 1.6 hours (Vlase, Popa, & Neag, 2011a). Regarding ciprofloxacin (Cipro®), they found that the bioavailability of zolpidem increased by ~ 50% and that the mean half-life of elimination of zolpidem increased from 2.4 hours to 3.3 hours (Vlase, Popa, & Neag, 2011b).

Zopiclone (Imovane®) Zopiclone is rapidly and well-absorbed following ingestion (F = 0.75) and reaches peak blood concentrations in approximately two hours. However, the ingestion of foods that are high in fat content may delay reaching peak blood concentrations and associated psychodepressant actions. Zopiclone is weakly bound to plasma proteins (i.e., approximately 80%) (Fernandez, Gimenez, & Thuillier, 1999) and is widely distributed in the body with an apparent volume of distribution of approximately 110 L.

Zopiclone is extensively metabolized in the liver, principally by the hepatic isoenzymes CYP3A4 and CYP2E1, to several metabolites, particularly zopiclone-N-oxide (inactive) and N-desmethylzopiclone (active). Total body clearance is 232 ml/min. Only 5% of zopiclone is excreted in unchanged form in the urine. Zopiclone has a mean elimination half-life of approximately five hours. Its longer half-life, in comparison to other z-drugs, may contribute to its greater efficacy in terms of maintaining a full night's sleep, with fewer "wake-up" periods (Drover, 2004), making it effective for patients who experience nocturnal awakenings. However, the longer half-life of elimination may also contribute to residual "hang-over" effects in the morning upon awakening. Fernandez and colleagues (e.g., Fernandez et al., 1999; Fernandez, Maradeix, & Gimenez, 1993; Fernandez, Martin, & Gimenez, 1995) have noted that the pharmacokinetics of zopiclone are stereoselective and that the half-life of elimination differs for the levorotatory enantiomer (i.e., ~ 3.5 hours) versus the dextrorotatory enantiomer (i.e., ~ 6.5 hours).

Eszopiclone (Lunesta®) Eszopiclone is rapidly and well-absorbed following ingestion and achieves peak plasma levels within one hour. Eszopiclone is weakly bound to plasma proteins (~55%) and has a volume of distribution of approximately 90 L. It is extensively metabolized in the liver, primarily by the hepatic microsomal enzymes CYP3A4 and CYP2E1. Less than 10% is excreted as racemic zopiclone in the urine. Eszopiclone has a mean elimination half-life of ~ six hours in younger adults, but may be prolonged in older adults, particularly, those who either: (1) have hepatic impairment; or (2) are taking CYP3A4 inhibitors (Greenblatt & Zammit, 2012; Najib, 2006). (See the related discussion in the following subsection, "Drug-Drug Interactions Involving Z-Drugs.") Consequently, older adults—particularly upon awakening—may be at risk for hangover effects that place them at significant risk for falls.

> ***Related Professional Reminder:* Health care professionals are reminded that, for all z-drugs, renal impairment does not affect dosing, half-life of elimination, potential accumulation in the body, or associated undesired, or harmful, effects and toxicities. However, hepatic impairment can significantly affect the serum concentration. Consequently, no dosage adjustment is required for older adults with mild to moderate renal impairment, but it is required for those with mild to moderate hepatic impairment.**[78]

Drug-Drug Interactions Involving Z-Drugs

Additive psychodepressant effects occur whenever z-drugs are concurrently used with other psychodepressants (e.g., alcohol, benzodiazepines, or opiate analgesics). When combined with these other psychodepressants, the risk for respiratory depression, coma, suicidal ideation, and death significantly increases (Iversen, 2013; McCall, Benca, & Rosenquist, 2017; Pagliaro & Pagliaro, 2009), particularly when large dosages are used (see the later z-drug subsection, "Z-Drug Overdosage/Unintentional Poisoning").

---

78. N.B. All older adults, including those without any renal or hepatic impairment, should initially receive half of the usual adult dose, which, subsequently, is adjusted as required based upon patient response.

Also, because the z-drugs are primarily metabolized by the hepatic microsomal enzyme CYP3A4:

1. Z-drugs generally should not be concurrently used with drugs that strongly "inhibit" CYP3A4 (e.g., clarithromycin, diltiazem, erythromycin, itraconazole, ketoconazole, nefazodone, ritonavir, or verapamil);[79]
2. Z-drugs may require an increase in dosage if concurrently used with drugs that moderately "induce" CYP3A4 (e.g., carbamazepine, dexamethasone, modafinil, phenytoin, or rifampin).

(Hesse, van Moltke, & Greenblatt, 2003;
Pagliaro & Pagliaro, 1999, 2009, 2020)

(See also the related discussion in the earlier z-drug pharmacology subsection, Pharmacokinetics—"Zolpidem.")

Undesired, or Harmful, Effects and Toxicities

The spectrum of undesired, or harmful, effects and toxicities associated with the z-drugs appears to be similar to those associated with the benzodiazepines.[80,81] In this regard, the z-drugs have been associated with both "acute" and "chronic" toxicities, including physical and psychological dependence, and are often associated with serious accidents (e.g., falls or MVCs) (Nevriana, Moller, & Laflamme, 2017; Pagliaro & Pagliaro, 2018, 2020; Schroeck, Ford, & Conway, 2016; Sparks & Cohen, 2019; Stranks & Crowe, 2014).[82] These undesired, or harmful, effects and toxicities are summarized in the following subsections. The noted incidence and severity of these effects and toxicities are significantly increased by the concomitant use of additional abusable psychotropics, particularly psychodepressants (e.g., alcohol, benzodiazepines, or opiate analgesics)—see the related discussion in the previous pharmacology subsection—"Drug-Drug Interactions Involving Z-Drugs."

In 2019, the American Geriatrics Society (AGS, 2019, p. 13) updated their 2015 *Beers Criteria for Potentially Inappropriate Medication Use in Older Adults*[83] (i.e., for adults

---

79. Grapefruit juice is also an inhibitor of CYP3A4 (Hanley, Cancalon, & Widmer, 2011).
80. N.B. Overall, the z-drugs are not "safer" than the benzodiazepines.
81. For example, z-drug use among older adults has been associated with the development of Alzheimer's disease. However, as per the benzodiazepines, this association has not been confirmed. As noted by Osler and Balslev Jorgensen (2020, p. 504):

> This large cohort study [based on data from the *Danish National Patient Registry*] did not reveal associations between use of benzodiazepines or Z-drugs and subsequent dementia, even when exposures were cumulated or divided into long- and short-acting drugs.

See also the related discussion in the earlier Benzodiazepine pharmacology subsection, Undesired, or Harmful Effects and Toxicities—"Alzheimer's Disease."

82. The use of z-drugs has been significantly associated with falls and hip fractures, particularly among older women residing in nursing homes (Barry, Lee, & Cai, 2013; Donnelly, Bracchi, & Hewitt, 2017; Gnjidic, Wilson, & Hilmer, 2013; Ryba & Rainess, 2020; Treves, Perlman, & Kolenberg Geron, 2018). However, it has been suggested by Tom, Wickwire, and Park (2016) that this risk for falls is lower with the use of eszopiclone.
83. The currently modified (i.e., updated) *AGS Beers Criteria* was originally developed as a guide, over 30 years ago, based upon a consensus statement from the UCLA Division of Geriatric Medicine that

65 years of age and older) and found, based on a comprehensive systematic review of related data, that:

> Nonbenzodiazepine, benzodiazepine receptor agonist hypnotics (i.e., Z-drugs) have adverse events similar to those of benzodiazepines in older adults (e.g., delirium, falls, fractures); increased emergency room visits/hospitalizations; motor vehicle crashes; minimal improvement in sleep latency and duration.

Consequently, the AGS strongly recommended that the use of the z-drugs—as well as benzodiazepines—for older adults (except for those in hospice and palliative care settings) be avoided (Fixen, 2019). While we do not fully endorse this recommendation, it should serve as a cautionary note.

Acute Toxicities

The acute toxicities associated with the use of the z-drugs are primarily dose-related. Although generally uncommon (i.e., occurring in less than 5% of patients), the z-drugs share the risk for a general spectrum of acute complex sleep behaviors (i.e., parasomnias), including sleep cooking, sleep driving, sleep eating, sleep violence, and sleep walking (Chen, Lin, & Choiu, 2013; Gunja, 2013a; Harcourt, Nevo, & Zhang, 2020; Matheson & Hainer, 2017). Amnesia often accompanies these behaviors. Consequently, patients may not remember these behaviors when they awake the following morning. In response to significant concerns regarding these behaviors and associated undesired, or harmful, effects, the FDA added on April 30, 2019 a related boxed warning for the risk of serious injury and death resulting from complex sleep behaviors that may occur in relation to z-drug use (FDA, 2019):

- Sleep walking;
- Sleep driving;
- Engaging in other activities while not fully awake.

Other warnings included:

- Complex sleep behaviors have occurred in patients with and without a history of such behaviors and can occur even at recommended doses and after just one dose of these drugs;
- Discontinue drug if a complex sleep behavior occurs.

<u>Related Professional Reminder</u>: Prior to the initial prescription and dispensing of z-drugs for older adults, the potential for the occurrence of complex sleep behaviors should be discussed with them and, as appropriate, their family members and caregivers. Older adults who received prescriptions for z-drugs need to be aware of the possible occurrence of complex sleep behaviors and how to appropriately monitor for their occurrence in order to avoid or minimize possible related sequelae if they do occur. Additionally, it should be noted that a history of having previously experienced complex sleep behaviors is a contraindication to the subsequent use of a z-drug.

---

was developed to reduce inappropriate drug therapy among older adult nursing home residents (Beers, Ouslander, & Rollingher, 1991).

Other acute toxicities associated with particular z-drugs include:

- Zaleplon (Sonata®) has been associated with several acute toxicities, such as abdominal pain, abnormal thinking, anterograde amnesia, asthenia, ataxia, behavioral changes, cognitive impairment, dizziness, falls, hallucinations/illusions (generally, visual, and short-lived), headaches, lightheadedness, nausea, psychomotor impairment, somnolence, and xerostomia.
- Zolpidem (Ambien®) has been associated with several similar acute toxicities, including anterograde amnesia, asthenia, ataxia, blurred vision, cognitive impairment, confusion, constipation, delirium, diarrhea, dizziness, dyspepsia, falls, hallucinations (i.e., visual, particularly with extremely high dosages), "hangover" effects, headaches, impaired judgment, increased appetite, memory impairment, particularly verbal memory nausea, nightmares, red eyes, sleep driving (i.e., sleep-deprived, or drowsy, driving), somnambulism, somnolence, suicidal ideation, tinnitus, tremors, and xerostomia.
- Zopiclone (Imovane®) also is significantly associated with several acute toxicities. These toxicities include anterograde amnesia, anxiety, asthenia, ataxia, bitter metallic taste, cognitive impairment, confusion, constipation, daytime fatigue, dizziness, dyspepsia, falls, grogginess and cognitive impairment upon awakening (e.g., "hangover" effects), headache, memory impairment (particularly verbal memory), psychomotor impairment, somnambulism, somnolence, suicidal ideation, and xerostomia.
- Eszopiclone (Lunesta®)-related toxicities, among older adults (65 to 86 years of age), include abnormal dreams, accidental injury, anxiety, bitter metallic taste, diarrhea, dizziness, dyspepsia, falls, headache, nausea, neuralgia, pruritus, psychomotor impairment, skin rash, suicidal ideation, and xerostomia. (Brielmaier, 2006; McCrae, Ross, & Stripling, 2007; Pagliaro & Pagliaro, 2009)

Chronic Toxicities

The major chronic toxicity associated with both zaleplon and zopiclone is mental depression. Zopiclone also shares a similar profile of undesired, or harmful, effects and toxicities with its levorotatory isomer, eszopiclone. Both zopiclone and eszopiclone also have been associated with increased reports of: (1) extended hangover effects lasting over 11 hours; and (2) impaired driving skills. As a result, in 2014, the FDA recommended the reduction of the starting dosage of eszopiclone to 1 mg for adults and the discontinuation of the 3-mg evening dosage (Abramowicz, 2014).

In 2006, the FDA noted that an increased risk of suicidal ideation and behavior were linked to the use of the z-drugs and changed the official package inserts for the z-drugs to include the following statement:

> In primarily depressed patients, worsening of depression, including suicidal thoughts and actions (including completed suicides), has been reported in association with the use of sedative/hypnotics.
>
> (Southworth, 2006, p. 1)

As a guide to help decrease the risk for, and incidence of, toxicities associated with z-drug use—including suicide ideation and attempts—see Table 6.8.

Table 6.8 Suggested Steps to Decrease Toxicities—Including Suicide Risk—Associated with Z-Drug Use

STEP #	SUGGESTIONS
1	Following FDA guidelines, prescribe the lowest possible effective dosage—generally start with one-half of the normal adult dosage.
2	Avoid prescribing a dosage higher than the FDA-recommended maximum dosage for older adults (i.e., eszopiclone, 2 mg; zaleplon, 10 mg; zolpidem, 5 mg IR/6.25 mg ER; zopiclone, 5 mg).
3	Instruct older adults to avoid combining a z-drug with alcohol, particularly when close to bedtime.
4	Avoid prescribing a z-drug with other medications that have CNS depressant or sedative-hypnotic effects.
5	Avoid prescribing a z-drug for older adults with severe, untreated MDD.
6	Instruct older adults to take their z-drug at a time of day that would maximize the probability of sleeping.[84]
7	Instruct older adults to go to bed with the intention of sleeping within 15 minutes after dosing.
8	Instruct older adults not to take the z-drug (i.e., skip the dose) if there is insufficient time for drug elimination between their planned bedtime and their planned rising time.
9	Discontinue the z-drug if there are new episodes of parasomnia.

Source: Modified from McCall et al., 2017.

Z-Drug Physical and Psychological Dependence

When originally marketed in the U.S., the z-drugs were widely touted as being essentially "non-addictive," and, consequently, a safer alternative to their precursors—the dependence producing benzodiazepines. However, since then, both physical and psychological dependence have been generally associated with the regular, long-term use of various z-drugs (e.g., Atkin, Comai, & Gobbi, 2018; Flynn & Cox, 2006; Schifano, Chiappini, & Corkery, 2019; Victorri-Vigneau, Dailly & Veyrac, 2007). For example:

- The regular, long-term use of zaleplon (Sonata®) has been associated with a low potential for physical dependence and a low to moderate potential for psychological dependence. However, as the dosage increases, the risk/incidence for dependence correspondingly increases. Additionally, older adults with a history of alcohol or other dependence or use disorder are at significantly increased risk of dependence, both physical and psychological. In case reports, identified signs and symptoms include: anxiety, insomnia, irritability, mood swings, muscle cramps, nausea, restlessness, and vomiting (FDA, 2013);
- The regular, long-term use of zolpidem (Ambien®) has been associated with the development of low to moderate physical dependence and moderate psychological

84. Under the circumstances of a socially normative sleeping schedule (i.e., between 9 pm and 1 am) the homeostatic sleep drive would be at its highest and the circadian alerting signal at its lowest.

dependence. In a study evaluating z-drug dependence among long-term users of either zolpidem or zopiclone, Yen, Yen, and Ko (2015) found that:

  - Zolpidem users reported more severe dependence than did zopiclone users;
  - Severe dependence, which was reported, was significantly correlated with reports of severe mental depression.

- A zolpidem withdrawal syndrome has been associated with the abrupt discontinuation of its regular, long-term use. Like the benzodiazepine withdrawal syndrome (see earlier benzodiazepine pharmacology subsection, Physical and Psychological Dependence—"Benzodiazepine Withdrawal Syndrome"), the zolpidem withdrawal syndrome is characterized, in severe cases, by: (1) seizures; and (2) drug-induced psychosis (Cubala & Landowski, 2007; Mattoo, Gaur, & Das, 2011; Pagliaro & Pagliaro, 2009). The standard seven-day diazepam (Valium®) withdrawal program, which gradually tapers diazepam dosages, has been used to successfully manage the zolpidem withdrawal syndrome;
- The regular long-term use of zopiclone (Imovane®) has been associated with low potential for physical dependence and low to moderate potential for psychological dependence. However, health care professionals are reminded that individual differences in drug response may occur. A zopiclone withdrawal syndrome, like the alcohol and benzodiazepine withdrawal syndromes, has been observed upon abrupt discontinuation of its regular, long-term medical or nonmedical/illicit use (e.g., Cimolai, 2007; Iversen, 2013; Pagliaro & Pagliaro, 2009; Pong Wong, Chun Chiu, & Wing Chu, 2005). This withdrawal syndrome is characterized by agitation, anxiety, confusion, delirium, diaphoresis, flushing, hallucinations, headache, irritability, nightmares, palpitations, rebound anxiety, rebound insomnia, seizures (rare, at recommended dosages), tachycardia, and tremor. The abrupt discontinuation of the regular long-term use of eszopiclone can produce a similar withdrawal syndrome. Regular, long-term use should be gradually discontinued in order to avoid the occurrence of this syndrome.

> A 76-year-old married woman with a history of recurrent depressive disorder had been prescribed zopiclone in increasing doses for insomnia related to a recurrence of depression. Eventually, for some months she was consuming up to 9 X 7.5 mg per day in three divided doses. She described symptoms consistent with dependence, including increased tolerance. Withdrawal phenomena such as agitation, tremor, and speech difficulties began five to six hours after the previous dose.
>
> Two days after abrupt withdrawal of the drug she had three tonic-clonic seizures. She was admitted to hospital and managed with symptomatic anti-epileptic treatment. The daily dose of zopiclone was gradually reduced over a one-week period, without further adverse effects.
>
> (Flynn & Cox, 2006, p. 898)

Related Professional Reminder: ***Generally, at this time, z-drugs should be considered to have the same abuse potential as benzodiazepines. Additional clinical data, gathered over the next decade, should further clarify any individual differences in the relative abuse potential of the z-drugs. What is currently known is that the incidence of toxicities (e.g., falls or memory impairment) among older adults increases for both the z-drugs and the benzodiazepines, in direct response to increased dosage.***

For examples and a discussion of recommended approaches for safely tapering the use of z-drugs by older adults, who have developed physical or psychological dependence, see the related discussion in the earlier benzodiazepine subsection, Medical Prescription Use—"Deprescribing, or Tapering, Benzodiazepine Dosage."

Z-Drug Overdosage/Unintentional Poisoning

Overdosages involving the z-drugs are generally associated with ataxia, confusion, dizziness, hypotension, lethargy, respiratory depression, and somnolence. Zolpidem overdosage is also associated with miosis.[85] In cases of severe overdosage, impaired consciousness, ranging from drowsiness to light coma, also can occur. However, being pharmacologically similar to the benzodiazepines (Gunja, 2013a), overdosages involving the z-drugs are rarely fatal—except in the context of overdosages that involve the concurrent use of other drugs and substances of abuse, particularly, other psychodepressants (e.g., alcohol or opiate analgesics) (AGS, 2019; Zosel, Osterberg, & Mycyk, 2011). It is important to note that overdosages involving a deliberate suicide attempt often involve the ingestion of additional drugs and substances of abuse (Forrester, 2007). Fatalities can also be associated with the risky behavior that often accompanies z-drug overdosage (Pagliaro & Pagliaro, 2009). For example: (1) driving under the influence (DUI); and (2) sleep driving (Pagliaro & Pagliaro, 2018; Pressman, 2011).[86]

> ***Related Professional Reminder:* The concurrent use of a z-drug with other psychodepressants, including alcohol, benzodiazepines, opiate analgesics, or other z-drugs, can significantly increase the risk for fatal overdosage.**

Overdosages involving zolpidem require emergency medical support of body systems, with particular attention to: (1) decreasing zolpidem absorption (e.g., appropriate use of activated charcoal, syrup of ipecac, or gastric lavage); and (2) maintaining adequate respiratory function (Kurta, Myers, & Krenzelok, 1997). Hemodialysis is not of clinical utility in cases of zolpidem overdosage. There is no known antidote. The benzodiazepine antagonist, "flumazenil" (Anexate® or Romazicon®), reportedly, may be of some benefit in the management of zolpidem overdosage (Gunja, 2013b). However, caution is required because the use of flumazenil may precipitate a benzodiazepine-like withdrawal syndrome among older adults who are physically dependent on zolpidem.

Overdosages involving zopiclone or eszopiclone, alone, are generally not life-threatening. Signs and symptoms associated with zopiclone or eszopiclone overdosage include ataxia, coma, confusion, dysarthria, hallucinations, hypotension, hypotonia, hypoxia, lethargy, respiratory depression, somnolence, tachycardia, and vomiting. Zopiclone has been reported to have many more serious harmful effects and toxicities related to overdosage/unintentional poisoning or suicide attempts than those reported for zolpidem (Schifano et al., 2019). Both zopiclone and eszopiclone overdosages require emergency medical support

85. N.B. Miosis is also a common feature of opiate analgesic use and overdosage (see Chapter 5, *Prescription Opiate Analgesics and Heroin*, pharmacology subsection, Undesired, or Harmful, Effects and Toxicities—"Prescription Opiate Analgesic and Heroin Overdosage/ Unintentional Poisoning").
86. For too many older adults, the use of z-drugs, and/or benzodiazepines, may also be associated with severe illness or death as the result of a sedative-hypnotic-induced fall and resultant hip fracture, with commonly related sequelae (e.g., hospitalization, pneumonia, or death) (Ostbye, Walton & Steenhuis, 2004; Pagliaro & Pagliaro, 2004, 2018; Pagliaro & Pagliaro, *Clinical Patient Data Files*; Wolinsky, Fitzgerald & Stump, 1997).

of body systems, with attention to maintaining cardiac and respiratory function (Schifano et al., 2019). The benzodiazepine antagonist, flumazenil (Anexate® or Romazicon®), may be of assistance (Gunja, 2013b). However, caution is required because the use of flumazenil may precipitate an alcohol- or benzodiazepine-like withdrawal syndrome among older adults who are physically dependent on zopiclone or eszopiclone.

Fatal overdosages involving zaleplon, alone, have not been reported. As noted in the product monograph "individuals have fully recovered from zaleplon overdosages of greater than 200 mg" (i.e., 20 times the upper recommended dose for older adults) (Wyeth Pharmaceuticals, 2007, p. 2). In cases of overdosage, signs and symptoms of CNS depression, ranging from drowsiness to coma, may be observed, including ataxia, hypotonia, hypotension, lethargy, loss of consciousness, mental confusion, and respiratory depression. Vital signs should be monitored, and treatment is generally symptomatic and supportive. The benzodiazepine antagonist, flumazenil (Anexate® or Romazicon®), may be of assistance (Gunja, 2013b), but is rarely required.

New Millennial Trends in Older Adult Z-Drug Use

This z-drug subsection presents and discusses the medical and nonmedical/illicit use of z-drugs by older adults. We begin with the medical use of z-drugs.

Medical Prescription Use

Based on data from controlled clinical studies, the z-drugs have received FDA approval for the short-term management of insomnia (i.e., for less than five consecutive weeks).[87,88,89] Unfortunately, since the beginning of the new millennium, prescribers have largely ignored the well-known and well-documented pharmacotherapeutic limitations and precautions associated with the use of zolpidem and other z-drugs. For example, as noted in the review, "Prescrire International:"

> Loss of efficacy can occur after a few weeks of treatment with zolpidem and zopiclone.
> (Hypnotic dependence, 2001, p. 15)

<u>Related Professional Reminder</u>: Whenever the prescription of z-drugs is being considered for older adults, we recommend that health and social care professionals keep in mind the following general considerations:

1. ***Z-drugs are not inherently safer or more efficacious than benzodiazepines. Consequently, older adults should not be automatically or routinely switched from benzodiazepines to z-drugs;***

87. Whenever z-drug, or other prescription sedative-hypnotic pharmacotherapy is considered or deemed necessary for older adults with sleep disorders, we recommend that it be implemented only after adequate sleep hygiene and appropriate cognitive behavioral therapy have been implemented.
88. N.B. Many clinicians, as well as related professional organizations and pharmaceutical company guidelines (i.e., as published in official drug monograph/package inserts), recommend a maximum of four consecutive weeks of use—including the time required for tapering-off (i.e., discontinuing use).
89. Eszopiclone is a noted exception and has been approved for long-term use (i.e., up to six months) by the FDA.

2. ***Z-drugs are only approved for the management of insomnia;***[90]
3. ***Z-drugs are generally considered to be "high-risk" when used for older adults;***
4. ***The previous occurrence of complex sleep behaviors (e.g., sleep driving or sleepwalking) is a contraindication to the use of z-drugs;***
5. ***Use the lowest effective dosage. For older adults, particularly those who are frail or of advanced age, generally initiate pharmacotherapy with half of the usual adult dosage and titrate according to patient response;***
6. ***Advise patients that the z-drugs are generally approved by the FDA for short-term treatment of insomnia (i.e., less than 30 days). (See footnote #89 for a noted exception).***

Nonmedical/Illicit Use

In their comprehensive examination of related reports to the *European Medicines Agency Database*, Schifano et al. (2019, p. 270) found "firm and large-scale evidence that z-drugs may be abused for recreational purposes." Generally, in this context of use, the tablet formulations of the z-drugs are orally ingested—often with an alcoholic beverage—to enhance their desired euphoric and stress-reducing actions (Pagliaro & Pagliaro, *Clinical Patient Data Files*).

In the U.S., older adults use the z-drugs for their psychodepressant actions—to achieve an alcohol-like disinhibitory euphoria, or "high," and to reduce anxiety or stress. They also use them to prevent or self-manage respective z-drug withdrawal syndromes. The z-drugs are generally obtained by medical prescription. However, they also are illicitly obtained on the street or from Internet vendors.

In the following z-drug subsection, we consider more specific trends in older adult use of z-drugs. We begin with zaleplon.[91]

Zaleplon (Sonata®)

During the new millennium in the U.S, older adult zaleplon use almost always began with a medical prescription to treat insomnia. Although generally prescribed for "short-term use only," older adults typically continued to use their zaleplon well beyond the prescribed time-frame while often increasing their original daily prescribed dosages by five to 10 times (or more) (see the earlier related discussion in this subsection). Typically, older adults, concurrently use their zaleplon with other drugs and substances of abuse, including alcohol. While most ingest their capsules (i.e., primary pharmaceutical dosage formulation) and tablets,

90. N.B. In contrast to the very closely related benzodiazepines (see the earlier benzodiazepine section of this chapter), the z-drugs are not clinically approved by the FDA for use as either anxiolytics or anticonvulsants.
91. N.B. Because of the paucity of published survey and research studies regarding older adult use of the z-drugs in the U.S., many of the references used in the following subsections were obtained from: (1) published European surveys and studies—where clinical experience with the z-drugs is longer and more extensive than that in the U.S.; and (2) our own clinical experience with z-drug use in this population group.

some older adults—in order to obtain "quick results"—choose to empty their capsules, or pulverize their tablets, and intranasally (IN) "snort" the resultant fine powder in a manner similar to snorting cocaine, heroin, or other drugs and substances of abuse. The IN method of use of the z-drugs, including zaleplon have been infrequently reported in published professional literature (e.g., Paparrigopoulos, Tzavellas, & Karaiskos, 2008). However, we have had this method of use shared with us by older adults, who report a more rapid onset and greater intensity of desired effects in comparison to oral use. We have posited that the reported effects are probably due to rapid nasal absorption and/or avoidance of first-pass hepatic metabolism.

Zolpidem (Ambien®)

Known on the street as "A-minus," "No-Go,"[92] "Nappien," or "Tic-Tacs," zolpidem is used to achieve an alcohol-like disinhibitory euphoria, or "high," and optical, or visual, illusions. The tablet is usually crushed and snorted for quick IN absorption. Rarely, it is "cooked"—dissolved in a warm liquid and cooled—for IV injection (Pagliaro & Pagliaro, *Clinical Patient Data Files*). Generally, zolpidem is initially prescribed for older adults by their physicians to manage anxiety or sleep disorders. However, because of acquired tolerance, they use higher dosages than prescribed for longer periods of time than recommended (e.g., Madrak & Rosenberg, 2001). As physical dependence develops, older adults use zolpidem to prevent or self-manage the zolpidem withdrawal syndrome.

Zopiclone (Imovane®)

Known on the street as "Zim-Zims," zopiclone is used to achieve an alcohol-like euphoria, or "high." It may also be used to manage the zopiclone withdrawal syndrome, or the withdrawal syndrome related to the use of another sedative hypnotic. Although reportedly relatively few in numbers (e.g., Hajak, Muller, & Wittchen, 2003), older adults who use zopiclone, generally share the following two characteristics:

1. Began use as a medically prescribed drug to facilitate sleep;
2. Are concurrent users of other drugs and substances of abuse. (e.g., Kuntze, Bullinger, & Mueller-Spahn, 2002; Morinan & Keaney, 2010; Pagliaro & Pagliaro, *Clinical Patient Data Files*; Sikdar, 1998)

Assessment, Diagnosis, and Treatment of Older Adult Z-Drug Dependence or Use Disorder

No specific quick-screen psychometric tests have been developed to assist in the assessment and diagnosis of z-drug dependence or use disorder among older adults. However, the DSM-5 criteria can be generally used for the detection of all sedative, hypnotic, and

92. Zolpidem is used in the military of the U.S., and other countries, to facilitate sleep and readiness between missions among pilots and special operations personnel. Formal use in the U.S. Air Force is accompanied by a six-hour restriction on subsequent flight operations. Hence, the military argot denoting zaleplon as "no go pills."

anxiolytic use disorders. Likewise, no specific pharmacotherapeutic or psychotherapeutic/counseling approaches have been approved for the treatment for older adults diagnosed with z-drug dependence or disorder.

However, because the z-drugs, although differing in chemical structure, are closely related to the benzodiazepines, several clinicians and researchers (e.g., Pagliaro & Pagliaro, *Clinical Patient Data Files*; Pagliaro & Pagliaro, 2020; Pardal, Praksh, & Konwar, 2011; Tyrer & Silk, 2012) have suggested using benzodiazepine assessment, diagnosis, and treatment protocols for older adults who use z-drugs and are suspected of being dependent on them. Thus, for general guidance, readers are referred to the earlier related benzodiazepine subsections—"Assessment and Diagnosis of Older Adult Benzodiazepine Dependence or Use Disorder" and "Treatment of Older Adult Benzodiazepine Dependence or Use Disorder."

REFERENCES[93,94,95]

Abad, V. C., & Guilleminault, C. (2018). Insomnia in elderly patients: Recommendations for pharmacological management. *Drugs & Aging*, *35*(9), 791–817. doi:10.1007/s40266-018-0569-8

Abramowicz, M. (2014). Lowering the dose of Lunesta. *The Medical Letter on Drugs and Therapeutics*, *56*(1444), 48.

Agravat, A. (2018). 'Z'-hypnotics versus benzodiazepines for the treatment of insomnia. *Progress in Neurology and Psychiatry*, *22*(2), 26–29.

AGS, American Geriatrics Society. (2019). American geriatrics society 2019 updated AGS Beers Criteria for potentially inappropriate medication use in older adults. *Journal of the American Geriatrics Society*, 1–21. doi:10.1111/jgs.15767

Ahmed, M., Westra, H. A., & Stewart, S. H. (2008). A self-help handout for benzodeiazepine discontinuation using cognitive behavioral therpay. *Cognitive and Behavioral Practice*, *15*(3), 317–324. doi:10.1016/j.cbpra.2007.05.003

Alamanda, V. K., Wally, M. K., & Seymour, R. B. (2020). Prevalence of opioid and benzodiazepine prescriptions for osteoarthritis. *Arthritis Care & Research*, *72*(8), 1081–1086. doi:10.1002/acr.23933

APA, American Psychiatric Association. (2013). Substance-related and addictive disorders. *Press Release*, pp. 1–2.

93. As per publisher style, only the first three authors are listed for each reference.
94. Several times the number of references listed were found, obtained, and analyzed by the authors during the preparation of this chapter. However, only those references that were cited at least once in the body of the text are listed. Major reasons for not citing other references include that they: (1) did not provide any additional unique information or research findings; (2) were not well researched or written by their authors (i.e., were evaluated as not being valid or reliable); (3) were based predominately, or exclusively, on animal studies; (4) dealt exclusively with other population groups (e.g., children, adolescents, or young adults); (5) provided usage statistics from outside the U.S.; and/or (6) were redundant with, or not as recent as, the already cited references—unless the reference was of classical, historical, or seminal importance.
95. The reference citation, "Pagliaro & Pagliaro, *Clinical Patient Data Files*," refers to unpublished data collected, with permission, by the authors, in the formal course of their professional academic roles as clinician scientists and professors, from their patients, research subjects or participants, and students, from the 1970s to date. Most of the related data have been discussed and made public in a wide and large number of formal academic presentations, including graduate seminars, grand rounds, guest lectures, professional conferences, and undergraduate lectures.

Atack, J. R. (2005). The benzodiazepine binding site of GABAA receptors as a target for the development of novel anxiolytics. *Expert Opinion on Investigational Drugs*, *14*(5), 601–618. doi:10.1517/13543784.14.5.601

Atkin, T., Comai, S., & Gobbi, G. (2018, April). Drugs for insomnia beyond benzodiazepines: Pharmacology, clinical applications, and discovery. *Pharmacological Reviews*, *70*(2), 197–245. doi:10.1124/pr.117.014381

Ault, A. (2018, August 24). Warnings about benzodiazepine use in the elderly go unheeded. *Medscape*, pp. 1–2.

Baandrup, L., Ebdrup, B., & Rasmussen, J. (2018, March 15). Pharmacological interventions for benzodiazepine discontinuation in chronic benzodiazepine users. *Cochrane Database of Systematic Reviews*, 1–10. doi:10.1002/14651858.CD011481.pub2

Baillargeon, L., Landreville, P., & Verreault, R. (2003). Discontinuation of benzodiazepines among older insomniac adults treated with cognitive-behavioural therapy combined with gradual tapering: A randomized trial. *CMAJ*, *169*(10), 1015–1020.

Baillie, A. J. (1992). *The measurement of dependence on benzodiazepines*. Kensington, Australia: School of Psychology, University of New South Wales.

Baillie, A. J. (1996, February 26). *Manual for the benzodiazepine dependence questionnaire (BDEPQ)*. National Drug and Alcohol Research Centre. Darlinghurst, NSW: University of New South Wales.

Baillie, A. J., & Mattick, R. P. (1996, September). The benzodiazepine dependence questionnaire: Development, reliability and validity. *The British Journal of Psychiatry*, *169*(3), 276–281. doi:10.1192/bjp.169.3.276

Barden Schallemberger, J., & de Fatima Colet, C. (2016). Assessment of dependence and anxiety among benzodiazepine users in a provincial municipality in Grande do Sul, Brazil. *Trends in Psychiatry and Psychotherapy*, *38*(2), 63–70. doi:10.1590/2237-6089-2015-0041

Barry, S. D., Lee, Y., & Cai, D. (2013, May). Nonbenzodiazepine sleep medication use and hip fractures in nursing home residents. *JAMA Internal Medicine*, *173*(9), 754–761. doi:10.1001/jamaintermed.2013.3795

Barry, S. D., Lee, Y., & Dore, D. (2013, May 13). Nonbenzodiazepine sleep medication use and hip fractures in nursing home residents. *JAMA Internal Medicine*, *173*(9), 754–761. doi:10.1001/jamainternmed.2013/3795

Bateson, A. N. (2002). Basic pharmacologic mechanisms involved in benzodiazepine tolerance and withdrawal. *Current Pharmaceutical Design*, *8*(1), 5–21.

Bechtel, L. K., & Holstege, C. P. (2007, May). Criminal poisoning: Drug-facilitated sexual assault. *Emergency Medical Clinics of North America*, *25*(2), 499–525.

Beers, M. H., Ouslander, J. G., & Rollingher, I. (1991). Explicit criteria for determining inappropriate medication use in nursing home residents. *Archives of Internal Medicine*, *151*, 1825–1832.

Belelli, D., & Lambert, J. J. (2005). Neurosteroids: Endogenous regulators of the GABAA receptor. *Nature Reviews in Neuroscience*, *6*, 565–575.

Bellivier, F., Yon, L., & Luquiens, A. (2011). Suicidal attempts in bipolar disorder: Results from an observational study (EMBLEM). *Bipolar Disorders*, *13*(4), 377–386.

Bergman, S. A. (1986, September–October). The benzodiazepine receptor. *Anesthia Progress*, *33*(5), 213–219.

Billioti de Gage, S., Moride, Y., & Ducruet, T. (2014). Benzodiazepine use and risk of Alzheimer's disease: Case-control study. *BMJ*, *349*, 1–10. doi:10.1136/bmj.g5205

Bourgeois, J., Elseviers, M. M., & Van Bortel, L. (2014a). Feasibility of discontinuing chronic benzodiazepine use in nursing home residents: A pilot study. *European Journal of Pharmacology, 70*(10), 1251–1260. doi:10.1007/s00228-014-1725-7

Bourgeois, J., Elseviers, M. M., & Van Bortel, L. (2014b). One-year evolution of sleep quality in older users of benzodiapines: A longitudinal cohort study in Belgian nursing home residents. *Drugs and Aging, 31*(9), 677–682. doi:10.1007/s40266-014-0203-3

Brandt, J., & Leong, C. (2017). Benzodiazepines and z-drugs: An updated review of major adverse outcomes reported on in epidemiologic research. *Drugs, 17*, 493–507. doi:10.1007/s40268-017-0207-7

Brandt, J., Alessi-Severini, S., & Singer, A. (2019). Novel measures of benzodiazepine & z-drug utilisation trends in a Canadian provincial adult population (2001–2016). *Journal of Population Therapeutics & Clinical Pharmacology, 26*(1), 1–4. doi:10.2374/1710-6222.26.1.3

Brett, J., & Murnion, B. (2015). Management of benzodiaepine misuse and dependence. *Australian Prescriber, 38*(5), 152–155. doi:10.1877/austprescr.2015.055

Brielmaier, B. D. (2006). Eszopiclone (Lunesta): A new nonbenzodiazepine hypnotic agent. *Baylor University Medical Center Proceedings, 19*(1), 54–59. doi:10.1080/08998280.2006.119 28127

Burgess, A. W. (2006). *Elderly victims of sexual abuse and their offenders*. Office of Justice Programs, National Institute of Justice. Washington, DC: U.S. Department of Justice.

Busto, U., & Sellers, E. M. (1991). Pharmacologic aspects of benzodiazepine tolerance and dependence. *Journal of Substance Abuse Treatment, 8*(1–2), 29–33.

Cai, R., Crane, E., & Poneleit, K. (2010, June 18). Emergency department visits involving nonmedical use of selected prescription drugs—United States, 2004–2008. *MMWR, Morbidity and Mortality Weekly Report, 59*(23), 705–709.

Canham, S. L., Gallo, J. J., & Simoni-Wastila, L. (2014). Perceptions of benzodiazepine dependence among women age 65 and older. *Journal of Gerontological Social Work, 57*(8), 872–888. doi:10.1080/01634372.2014.901470

Cassels, C. (2010, February 10). APA releases proposed draft of the DSM-5. *Medscape Medical News*, pp. 1–4. Retrieved from www.medscape.com/viewarticle/716807?sssdmh=dml.588982&src=nldne&uac=144544HX

CDC, Centers for Disease Control and Prevention. (2010). Emergency department visits involving nonmedical use of selected prescription drugs—United States, 2004–2008. *MMWR, Morbidity and Mortality Weekly Report, 59*(23), 705–709.

Chen, L.-F., Lin, C.-E., & Choiu, Y.-C. (2013). A comparison of complex sleep behaviors with two short-acting z-hypnosedative drugs in nonpsychotic patients. *Neuropsychiatric Disease and Treatment, 9*, 1159–1162. doi:10.2147/NDT.S48152

Cheng, S., Ghazal Siddiqui, T., & Gossop, M. (2019). The Severity of Dependence Scale detects medication misuse and dependence among hospitalized older patients. *BMC Geriatrics, 19*(174), 1–8. doi:10.1186/s12877-019-1182-3

Cheng, T., Wallace, D. M., & Ponteri, B. (2016, May 23). Valium without dependence? Individual GABAA receptor subtype contribution toward benzodiazepine addiction, tolerance, and therapeutic effects. *Dovepress, 2018*, 1351–1361. doi:10.2147/NDT.S164307

Cho, J., Spence, M. M., & Niu, F. (2020). Risk of overdose with exposure to prescription opioids, benzodiazepines, and non-benzodiazepine sedative-hypnotics in adults: A retrospective cohort study. *Journal of General Internal Medicine, 35*, 696–703. doi:10.1007/s11606-019-05545-y

Cimolai, N. (2007). Zopiclone: Is it a pharmacologic agent for abuse? *Canadian Family Physician, 53*(12), 2124–2129.

Conn, D. K., & Madan, R. (2006). Use of sleep-promoting medications in nursing home residents: Risks versus benefits. *Drugs & Aging, 23*(4), 271–287.

Conn, D. K., Rabheru, K., & Checkland, C. (2019). *Canadian guidelines on benzodiazepine receptor agonist use disorder among older adults* (pp. 1–25). Ottawa, ON: Canadian Coalition for Seniors' Health.

Cook, J. M., Dinnen, S., & O'Donnell, C. (2011, July). Older women survivors of physical and sexual violence: A systematic review of the quantitative literature. *Journal of Women's Health, 20*(7), 1975–1081. doi:10.1089/jwh.2010.2279

Couvee, J. E., & Zitman, F. G. (2002). The benzodiazpeine withdrawal symptom questionnaire: Psychometric evaluation during a discontinuation program in depressed chronic benzodiazepine users in general practice. *Addiction, 97*(3), 337–345. doi:10.1046/j.1360-0443.2002.00081.x

Crestani, F., Low, K., & Keist, R. (2001). Molecular targets for the myorelaxant action of diazepam. *Molecular Pharmacology, 59*(3), 442–445.

Crevoisier, C., Delisle, M. C., & Joseph, I. (2003). Comparative single-dose pharmacokinetics of clonazepam following intravenous, intramuscular and oral administration to healthy volunteers. *European Neurology, 49*, 173–177. doi:10.1159/000069089

Cubala, W. J., & Landowski, J. (2007, March 30). Seizure following sudden zolpidem withdrawal. *Progress in Neuro-Psychopharmacology and Biological Psychiatry, 31*(2), 539–540. doi:10.1016/j.pnpbp.2006.07.009

Daderman, A. M., & Edman, G. (2001). Flunitrazepam abuse and personality characteristics in male forensic psychiatric patients. *Psychiatry Research, 103*(1), 27–42.

Daderman, A. M., Fredriksson, B., & Kristiansson, M. (2002). Violent behavior, impulsive decision-making, and anterograde amnesia while intoxicated with flunitrazepam and alcohol or other drugs: A case study in forensic psychiatric patients. *The Journal of the American Academy of Psychiatry and the Law, 30*(2), 238–251.

Darker, C. D., Sweeney, B. P., & Barry, J. M. (2015). Psychosocial interventions for benzodiazepine harmful use, abuse or dependence. *Cochrane Database of Systematic Reviews* (5), CD009652. doi:10.1002/14651858.CD009652.pub2

Day, C. (2014, December 18). Benzodiazepines in combination with opioid pain relievers or alcohol: Greater risk of more serious ED visit outcomes. *The CBHSQ Report*.

de las Cuevas, C., Sanz, F. J., & de la Fuente, J. A. (2000). The Severity of Dependence Scale (SDS) as screening test for benzodiazepine dependence: SDS validation study. *Addiction, 95*(2), 245–250. doi:10.1046/j.1360-0443.2000.95224511.x

DEA, Drug Enforcement Administration. (2019, December). *Benzodiazepines* (p. 1). Washington, DC: Drug Enforcement Administration.

Dean, L. (2016, August 25). Diazepam therapy and CYP2C19 genotype. (V. Pratt, H. McLeod, & W. Rubinstein, Eds.) *Medical Genetics Summaries*, pp. 1–3.

Defrancesco, M., Marksteiner, J., & Fleischhacker, W. W. (2015, September). Use of benzodiazepines in Alzheimer's disease: A systematic review of literature. *International Journal of Neuropsychopharmacology, 18*(10), 1–11. doi:10.1093/ijnp/pyv055

Dias, R., Wayne, F., & Sheppard, R. (2005, November 16). Evidence for a significant role of alpha3-containing GABAA receptors mediating the anxiolytic effects of benzodiazepdines. *Journal of Neuroscience, 25*(46), 10682–10688. doi:10.1523/JNEUROSCI.1166-05.2005

Dodds, T. J. (2017, March). Prescribed benzodiazepines and suicide risk: A review of the literature. *Primary Care Companion for CNS Disorders, 19*(2), 1–5. doi:10.4088/PCC.16r02037

Donnelly, K., Bracchi, R., & Hewitt, J. (2017). Benzodiazepines, z-drugs and the risk of hip fracture: A systematic review and meta-analysis. *PLoS One*, *12*(4), e0174730. doi:10.1371/journal.pone.0174730

Dooley, M., & Plosker, G. L. (2000, August). Zaleplon: A review of its use in the treatment of insomnia. *Drugs*, *60*(2), 413–445.

Dowd, S. M., Strong, M. J., & Janicak, P. G. (2002). The behavioral and cognitive effects of two benzodiazepines associated with drug-facilitated sexual assault. *Journal of Forensic Sciences*, *47*(5), 1101–1107.

Drover, D. R. (2004). Comparative pharmacokinetics and pharmacodynamics of short-acting hypnosedatives: Zaleplon, zolpidem and zopiclone. *Clinical Pharmacokinetics*, *43*(4), 227–238. doi:10.2165/00003088-200443040-00002

Drover, D. R., Lemmens, H., & Naidu, S. (2000). Pharmacokinetics, pharmacodynamics, and relative pharmacokinetic/pharmacodynamic profiles of zaleplon and zolpidem. *Clinical Therapeutics*, *22*(12), 1443–1461.

Ebbens, M. M., & Verster, J. C. (2010). Clinical evaluation of zaleplon in the treatment of insomnia. *Nature and Science of Sleep*, *2*, 115–126. doi:10.2147/nss.s6853

Enna, S. J., & McCarson, K. E. (2006). The role of GABA in the mediation and perception of pain. *Advances in Pharmacology*, *54*, 1–27. doi:10.1016/s1054-3589(06)54001-3

Farzampour, Z., Reimer, R. J., & Huguenard, J. (2015). Endozepines. *Advances in Pharmacology*, *72*, 147–164. doi:10.1016/bs.apha.2014.10.005

FDA, Food and Drug Administration. (2013, April). *Sonata medication guide* (pp. 1–3). Bethesda, MD: FDA.

FDA, Food and Drug Administration. (2019, April 30). FDA adds warning for risk of serious injuries caused by sleepwalking with certain prescription insomnia medicines. In *FDA drug safety communication* (pp. 1–8. Bethesda, MD: Food and Drug Administration.

FDA, Food and Drug Administration. (2020, September 23). FDA requiring boxed warning updated to improve safe use of benzodiazepine drug class: Includes potential for abuse, addiction, and other serious risks. In *FDA drug safety communication* (pp. 1–10). Bethesda, MD: Food and Drug Administration.

Fernandez, C., Gimenez, F., & Thuillier, A. (1999, January). Stereoselective binding of zopiclone to human plasma proteins. *Chirality*. doi:10.1002/(SICI)1520-636X(1999)11

Fernandez, C., Maradeix, V., & Gimenez, F. (1993, November-December). Pharmacokinetics of zopiclone and its enantiomers in Caucasian young healthy volunteers. *Drug Metabolism and Disposition*, *21*(6), 1125–1128.

Fernandez, C., Martin, C., & Gimenez, F. (1995, December). Clinical pharmacokinetics of zopiclone. *Clinical Pharmacokinetics*, *29*(6), 431–441. doi:10.2165/00003088-199529060-00004

Ferri, C. P., Marsden, J., & de Araujo, M. (2000). Validity and reliability of the Severity of Dependence Scale (SDS) in a Brazilian sample of drug users. *Drug and Alcohol Reviews*, *19*, 451–455.

Fixen, D. R. (2019, November 1). 2019 AGS Beers Criteria for older adults. *Pharmacy Today*, pp. 42–51.

Fluyau, D., Revadigar, N., & Manobianco, B. E. (2018). Challenges of the pharmacological management of benzodiazepine withdrawal, dependence, and discontinuation. *Therapeutic Advances in Psychopharmacology*, *8*(5), 147–168. doi:10.1187/2045125317753340

Flynn, A., & Cox, D. (2006, June). Dependence on zopiclone. *Addiction*, *101*(6), 898. doi:10.1111/j.1360-0443.2006.01448.x

Forrester, M. B. (2006). Flunitrazepam abuse and malicious use in Texas, 1998–2003. *Substance Use & Misuse*, *41*(3), 427–439.

Forrester, M. B. (2007). Eszopiclone ingestions reported to Texas poison control centers, 2005 2006. *Human & Experimental Toxicology*, *26*(10), 795–800.

Gahlinger, P. M. (2020, July). Benzodiazepine overdose: Symptoms, diagnosis and treatment. *BMJ Best Practice*, pp. 1–6.

Garg, R. K., Fulton-Kehoe, D., & Franklin, G. M. (2017, July). Patterns of opioid use and risk of opioid overdose death among medicaid patients. *Medical Care*, *55*(7), 661–668. doi:10.1097/MLR.0000000000000738

Garzone, P. D., & Kroboth, P. D. (1989, June). Pharmacokinetics of the newer benzodiazepines. *Clinical Pharmacokinetics*, *16*(6), 337–364.

Gautam, L., Sharratt, S. C., & Cole, M. D. (2014). Drug facilitated sexual assault: Detection and stability of benzodiazepines in spiked drinks using gas chromatography-mass spectrometry. *PLos One*, *9*(2), e89031. doi:10.1371/journal.pone.00S9031

Gerlach, L. B., Maust, D. T., & Leong, S. H. (2018). Factors associated with long-term benzodiazepine use among older adults. *JAMA Internal Medicine*, *178*(11), 1560–1562.

Gerlach, L. B., Wiechers, I. R., & Maust, D. T. (2018, August 31). Prescription benzodiazepine use among older adults: A critical review. *Harvard Review of Psychiatry*, *26*(5), 264–273. doi:10.1097/hrp.0000000000000190

Gill, P. A. (2015). How and why to diagnose substance use disorders under DSM-5. *MOJ Addiction Medicine & Therapy*, *1*(2), 34–35. doi:10.15406/mojamt.2015.01.00009

Gnjidic, D., Wilson, N., & Hilmer, S. N. (2013). Understanding drug effects in older people: The role of pharmacology. *JAMA Internal Medicine*, *173*(20), 1930. doi:10.1001/jamainternmed.2013.9782

Gold, J. (2020, March). Approaches to managing benzodiazepines. *Pharmacy Today*, pp. 41–54.

Gossop, M., Best, D., & Marsden, J. (1997). Test-retest reliability of The Severity of Dependence Scale. *Addiction*, *92*(3), 353.

Gossop, M., Darke, S., & Griffiths, P. (1995). The Severity of Dependence Scale (SDS): Psychometric properties of the SDS in English and Australian samples of heroin, cocaine and amphetamine users. *Addiction*, *90*(5), 607–614.

Gould, R. L., Coulson, M. C., & Patel, N. (2014). Interventions for reducing benzodiazepine use in older people: Meta-analysis of randomised controlled trials. *The British Journal of Psychiatry*, *204*, 98–107. doi:10.1192/bjp.bp.113.126003

Greenberg, M. I. (2001). Benzodiazepine withdrawal: Potentially fatal, commonly missed following benzodiazepine cessation, withdrawal symptoms may begin within 24 hours or take up to two weeks to develop. *Emergency Medicine News*, *23*(12), 18–22. doi:10.1097/01.EEM.0000292622.83311.c3

Greenblatt, D. J., & Zammit, G. K. (2012). Pharmacokinetic evaluation of eszopiclone: Clinical and therapeutic implications. *Expert Opinion on Drug Metabolism & Toxicology*, *8*(12), 1609–1618. doi:10.1517/17425255.2012.741588

Gregory, E., Torres, I. J., & Ge, R. (2020, September 1). Predictors of cognitive impairment in treatment-resistant depression. *Journal of Affective Disorders*, *274*, 593–601. doi:10.1016/j.jad.2020.05.101

Grela, A., Gautam, L., & Cole, M. D. (2018, November). A multifactorial critical appraisal of substances found in drug facilitated sexual assault cases. *Forensic Science International*, *292*, 50–60. doi:10.1016/j.forsciint.2018.08.034

Gresham, C. (2020, January 23). Benzodiazepine toxicity. *Medscape*, pp. 1–5.

Griffin, C. E., Kaye, A. M., & Rivera Bueno, F. (2013, Summer). Benzodiazepine pharmacology and central nervous system-mediated effects. *The Ochsner Journal*, *13*(2), 214–223.

Guina, J., & Merrill, B. (2018a). Benzodiazepines I: Upping the care on downers: The evidence of risks, benefits and alternatives. *Journal of Clinical Medicine*, *7*(2), 17–22. doi:10.3390/jcm7020017

Guina, J., & Merrill, B. (2018b). Benzodiazepine II: Waking up on sedatives: Providing optimal care when inheriting benzodiazepine prescriptions in transfer patients. *Journal of Clinical Medicine*, *7*(20), 1–18. doi:10.3390/jcm7020020

Gunja, N. (2013a). In the Zzz Zone: The effects of Z-drugs on human performance and driving. *Journal of Medicine and Toxicology*, *9*, 163–171. doi:10.1007/s13181-013-0294-y

Gunja, N. (2013b, June). The clinical and forensic toxicology of z-drugs. *Journal of Medical Toxicology*, *9*(2), 155–162. doi:10.1007/s13181-013-0292-0

Gupta, A., Bhattacharya, G., & Balaram, K. (2021). Benzodiazepine use among older adults. *Neurodegenerative Disease Management*, *11*(1), 5–8. doi:10.2217/nmt-2020-0056

Ha, Q., Chen, X., & Wu, T. (2019). Risk of dementia in long-term benzodiazepine users: Evidence from a meta-analysis of observational studies. *Journal of Clinical Neurology*, *15*(1), 9–19.

Hajak, G., Muller, W. E., & Wittchen, H. U. (2003). Abuse and dependence potential for the non-benzodiazepine hypnotics zolpidem and zopiclone: A review of case reports and epidemiological data. *Addiction*, *98*(10), 1371–1378.

Hanley, M. J., Cancalon, P., & Widmer, W. W. (2011). The effect of grapefruit juice on drug disposition. *Expert Opinion in Drug Metabolism and Toxicology*, *7*(3), 267–286. doi:10.1517/17425256.2011.553189

Harcourt, K., Nevo, O. N., & Zhang, R. (2020). Association of eszopiclone, zaleplon, or zolpidem with complex sleep behaviors resulting in serious injuries, including death. *Pharmacoepidemiology and Drug Safety*, *29*(6), 684–691. doi:10.1002/pds.5004

Hasin, D. S., O'Brien, C. P., & Auriacombe, M. (2013). DSM-5 criteria for substance use disorders: Recommendations and rationale. *American Journal of Psychiatry*, *170*(8), 834–851. doi:10.1176/appi.ajp.2013.12060782

Hesse, J. M., von Moltke, L. L., & Greenblatt, D. J. (2003). Clinically important drug interactions with zopiclone, zolpidem and zaleplon. *CNS Drugs*, *17*(7), 513–532.

Holbrook, A. M., Crowther, R., & Lotter, A. (1999). Meta-Analysis of benzodiazepine use in the treatment of acute alcohol withdrawal. *CMAJ, Canadian Medical Association Journal*, *169*(5), 649–655.

Holm, K. J., & Goa, K. L. (2000). Zolpidem: An update of its pharmacology, therapeutic efficacy and tolerability in the treatment of insomnia. *Drugs*, *59*(4), 865–889.

Hood, S. D., Norman, A., & Hince, D. A. (2014). Benzodiazepine dependence and its treatment with low dose flumazenil. *British Journal of Clinical Pharmacology*, *77*(2), 285–294. doi:10.1111/bcp.12023

Hosie, A. M., Wilkins, M. E., & da Silva, H. (2006, November 23). Endogenous neurosteroids regulate GABAA receptors through two discrete transmembrane sites. *Nature*, *444*, 486–489.

Howard, P., Twycross, R., & Shuster, J. (2014, May 1). Benzodiazepines. *Journal of Pain and Symptom Management*, *47*(5), 955–964. doi:10.1016/j.jpainsymman.2014.03.001

Hukkinen, S. K., Varhe, A., & Olkkola, K. T. (1995, August). Plasma concentrations of triazolam are increased by concomitant ingestion of grapefruit juice. *Clinical Pharmacology and Therapeutics*, *58*(2), 127–131. doi:10.1016/0009-9236(95)90188-4

Imfeld, P., Bodmer, M., & Jick, S. S. (2015). Benzodiazepine use and risk of developing Alzheimer's disease or vascular dementia: A case-control analysis. *Drug Safety*, *38*(10), 909–919. doi:10.1007/s40264-015-0319-3

Ireton, J. (2019, July 19). 15-year study tallies toll of sexual assault in Ontario. *CBC News*. Ottawa: CBC/Radio-Canada.

Iversen, L. (2013). *Z-Drugs: A review of the evidence of misuse and harm*. London, UK: ACDM, Advisory Council on the Misuse of Drugs.

Jewett, B. E., & Sharma, S. (2020). *Physiology, GABA*. Treasure Island, FL: StatPearls Publishing.

Jones, C. M., & McAninch, J. K. (2015). Emergency department visits and overdose deaths from combined use of opioids and benzodiazepines. *American Journal of Preventive Medicine*, *49*(4), 493–501.

Jones, C. M., Paulozzi, L. J., & Mack, K. A. (2014). Alcohol involvement in opioid pain reliever and benzodiazepine drug abuse—Related emergency department visits and drug-related deaths—United States, 2010. *Morbidity and Mortality Weekly Report (MMWR)*, *63*(40), 881–885.

Kang, M., Galuska, M. A., & Ghassemzadeh, S. (2020). *Benzodiazepine toxicity*. Treasure Island, FL: StatPearls Publishing.

Kaufmann, C. N., Spira, A. P., & Alexander, G. C. (2017). Emergency department visits involving benzodiazepines and non-benzodiazepine receptor agonists. *The American Journal of Emergency Medicine*, *35*(10), 1414–1419. doi:10.1016/j.ajem.2017.04.023

Kuntze, M. F., Bullinger, A. H., & Mueller-Spahn, F. (2002). Excessive use of zopiclone: A case report. *Swiss Medical Weekly*, *132*, 523.

Kurta, D. L., Myers, L. B., & Krenzelok, E. P. (1997). Zolpidem (Ambien): A pediatric case series. *Journal of Toxicology. Clinical Toxicology*, *35*(5), 453–457.

Lekka, N. P., Paschalis, C., & Beratis, S. (2002). Suicide attempts in high-dose benzodiazepine users. *Comprehensive Psychiatry*, *43*(6), 438–442.

Lin, S. K. (2014, July). Rapid detoxification of benzodiazepine or Z-drugs dependence using acetylcholinesterase inhibitors. *Medical Hypotheses*, *83*(1), 108–110. doi:10.1016/j.mehy.2014.03.032

Madea, B., & Musshoff, F. (2009, May). Knock-out drugs: Their prevalence, modes of action, and means of detection. *Deutsches Arzteblatt International*, *106*(20), 341–347. doi:10.3238/arztebl.2009.0341

Madrak, L. N., & Rosenberg, M. (2001, August 1). Zolpidem abuse. *The American Journal of Psychiatry*, *1330a*. doi:10.1176/appi.ajp.158.8.1330-a

Markota, M., Rummans, T. A., & Bostwick, J. M. (2016). Benzodiazepine use in older adults: Dangers, management, and alternative therapies. *Mayo Clinic Proceedings*, *91*(11), 1632–1639. doi:10.1016/j.mayocp.2016.07.024

Matheson, E., & Hainer, B. L. (2017, July). Insomnia: Pharmacologic therapy. *American Family Physician*, *96*(1), 29–35.

Mattoo, S. K., Gaur, N., & Das, P. P. (2011, November–December). Zolpidem withdrawal delirium. *Indian Journal of Pharmacology*, *43*(6), 729–730. doi:10.4103/0253-7613.89838

Maust, D. T., Lin, L. A., & Blow, F. C. (2019). Benzodiazepine use and misuse among adults in the United States. *Psychiatric Services*, *70*(2), 97–106. doi:10.1176/appi.ps.201800321

McCall, W. V., Benca, R. M., & Rosenquist, P. B. (2017, January). Hypnotic medications and suicide: Risk, mechanisms, mitigation, and the FDA. *American Journal of Psychiatry*, *174*(1), 18–25. doi:10.1176/appi.ajp.2016.16030336

McCrae, C. S., Ross, A., & Stripling, A. (2007). Eszopiclone for late-life insomnia. *Clinical Interventions in Aging*, *2*(3), 313–326.

McDonald, E. M., & Caslangen, J. (2019). Benzodiazepine use and falls in older adults: Is it worth the risk? *Research in Gerontological Nursing*, *12*(5), 214–216. doi:10.3928/19404921-20190813-01

Minaya, O., Fresan, A., & Cortes-Lopez, J. L. (2011). The benzodiazepine dependence questionnaire (BDEPQ) validity and reliability in Mexican psychiatric patients. *Addictive Behaviors*, *36*(8), 874–877. doi:10.1016/j.addbeh.2011.03.007

Montgomery, M. A. (2010, January). The use of benzodiazepines to facilitate sexual assault. *Forensic Science Review*, *22*(1), 33–40.

Morin, C. M., Bastien, C., & Guay, B. (2004). Randomized clinical trial of supervised tapering and cognitive behavior therapy to facilitate benzodiazepine discontinuation in older adults with chronic insomnia. *The American Journal of Psychiatry*, *161*(2), 332–342. doi:10.1176/appi.ajp.161.2.332

Morinan, A., & Keaney, F. (2010). Long-term misuse of zopiclone in an alcohol dependent woman with a history of anorexia nervosa: A case report. *Journal of Medical Case Reports*, *4*, 403–408.

Najib, J. (2006). Eszopiclone, a nonbenzodiazepine sedative-hypnotic agent for the treatment of transient and chronic insomnia. *Clinical Therapeutics*, *28*(4), 491–516. doi:10.1016/j.clinthera.2006.04.014

Nevriana, A., Moller, J., & Laflamme, L. (2017). New, occasional, and frequent use of zolpidem or zopiclone (alone and in combination) and the risk of injurious road traffic crashes in older adult drivers. *CNS Drugs*, *31*(8), 711–722. doi:10.1007/s40263-017-0445-9

Ng, B. J., Le Couteur, D. G., & Hilmer, S. N. (2018, June). Deprescribing benzodiazepines in older patients: Impact of interventions targeting physicians, pharmacists, and patients. *Drugs & Aging*, *35*(6), 493–521. doi:10.1007/s40266-018-0544-4

NIDA, National Institute of Drug Abuse. (2008, August). Club drugs (GHB, Ketamine, and Rohypnol). *InfoFacts*, pp. 1–3. NIDA.

NIDA, National Institute on Drug Abuse. (2021, February 3). Benzodiazepines and opioids. *Opioids*, pp. 1–3. Washington, DC: National Institutes of Health.

Ninan, P. T. (2001). Pharmacokinetically induced benzodiazepine withdrawal. *Psychopharmacology Bulletin*, *35*(4), 94–100.

Nutt, D. J., & Malizia, A. L. (2001). New insights into the role of the GABAA-benzodiazepine receptor in psychiatric disorder. *British Journal of Psychiatry*, *179*, 390–396.

O'Brien, C. P. (2005). Benzodiazepine use, abuse, and dependence. *Journal of Clinical Psychiatry*, *66*(Suppl 2), 28–33.

O'Brien, M. P. (2008, June). Epidemiological trends in drug abuse. In *Proceedings of the community epidemiology work group. Volume 1: Highlights and executive summary*. Bethesda, MD: National Institute on Drug Abuse, US Department of Health and Human Services.

Ogbonna, C. I., & Lembke, A. (2017, November). Tapering patients off of benzodiazepines. *American Family Physician*, *96*(9), 606–608.

Olfson, M., King, M., & Schoenbaum, M. (2015). Benzodiazepine use in the United States. *JAMA Psychiatry*, *72*(2), 136–142. doi:10.1001/jamapsychiatry.2014.1763

Olsen, R. W., & DeLorey, T. M. (1999). GABA receptor physiology and pharmacology. In G. J. Siegel, B. W. Agranoff, & R. W. Albers (Eds.), *Basic neurochemistry: Molecular, cellular, and medical aspects* (6th ed., pp. 1–5). Philadelphia, PA: Lippincott-Raven.

Osler, M., & Balslev Jorgensen, M. (2020). Associations of benzodiazepines, z-drugs, and other anxiolytics with subsequent dementia in patients with affective disorders: A nationwide cohort and nested case-control study. *American Journal of Psychiatry*, *177*(5), 497–505. doi:10.1176/appi.ajp.2019.19030315

Ostbye, T., Walton, R. E., & Steenhuis, R. (2004, Fall). Predictors and sequelae of fractures in the elderly: The Canadian Study on Health and Aging (CSHA). *Canadian Journal on Aging*, *23*(3), 247–253.

Otto, M. W., McHugh, R. K., & Simon, N. (2010, July). Efficacy of CBT for benzodiazepine discontinuation in patients with panic disorder: Further evaluation. *Behaviour Research and Therapy*, *48*(8), 720–727. doi:10.1016/j.brat.2010.04.002

Otto, M. W., Pollack, M. H., & Meltzer-Brody, S. (1992). Cognitive-behavioral therapy for benzodiazepine discontinuation in panic disorder patients. *Psychopharmacology Bulletin*, *28*(2), 123–230.

Pagliaro, A. M., & Pagliaro, L. A. (2018). *Women's drug and substance abuse: A comprehensive analysis and reflective synthesis*. New York, NY: Routledge.

Pagliaro, L. A., & Pagliaro, A. M. (1983). *Pharmacologic aspects of aging*. St. Louis, MO: C.V. Mosby.

Pagliaro, L. A., & Pagliaro, A. M. (1998). *The pharmacologic basis of psychotherapeutics: An introduction for psychologists*. Washington, DC: Brunner/Mazel.

Pagliaro, L. A., & Pagliaro, A. M. (1999). *PPDR: Psychologists' psychotropic drug reference*. Philadelphia, PA: Brunner/Mazel.

Pagliaro, L. A., & Pagliaro, A. M. (2004). *Pagliaros' comprehensive guide to drugs and substances of abuse* (1st ed.). Washington, DC: American Pharmacists Association.

Pagliaro, L. A., & Pagliaro, A. M. (2009). *Pagliaros' comprehensive guide to drugs and substances of abuse* (2nd ed.). Washington, DC: American Pharmacists Association.

Pagliaro, L. A., & Pagliaro, A. M. (2020). *Child and adolescent drug and substance abuse: A comprehensive reference for mental health care professionals*. New York, NY: Routledge.

Paparrigopoulos, T., Tzavellas, E., & Karaiskos, D. (2008). Intranasal zaleplon abuse. *The American Journal of Psychiatry*, *165*(11), 1489–1490. doi:10.1176/appi.ajp.2008.08030452

Pardal, P. K., Praksh, J., & Konwar, R. (2011, October). Zolpidem dependence. *Delhi Psychiatry Journal*, *14*(2), 388–389.

Paulozzi, L. J., Kilbourne, E. M., & Shah, N. G. (2012). A history of being prescribed controlled substances and risk of drug overdose death. *Pain Medicine*, *13*, 87–95.

Petursson, H. (1994). The benzodiazepine withdrawal syndrome. *Addiction*, *89*(11), 1455–1459. doi:10.1111/j.1360-0443.1994.tb03743.x

Pong Wong, C., Chun Chiu, P. K., & Wing Chu, L. (2005, September). Zopiclone withdrawal: An unusual cause of delirium in the elderly. *Age and Ageing*, *34*(5), 526–527. doi:10.1093/ageing/afi132

Pottie, K., Thompson, W., & Davies, S. (2018, May). Deprescribing benzodiazepine receptor agonists. *Canadian Family Physician*, *64*, 339–350.

Pourmand, A., Lombardi, K. M., & Roberson, J. (2020). Patterns of benzodiazepine administration and prescribing to older adults in U.S. emergency departments. *Aging Clinical and Experimental Research*, *32*(12), 2621–2628. doi:10.1007/s40520-020-01496-1

Preidt, R. (2014, May 22). Sharp rise in ER visits tied to abuse of sedative, study finds. *U.S. News and World Report*, pp. 1–2. Retrieved June 28, 2014, from http://health.usnews.com/health-news/articles/2014/05/22/sharp-rise-in-er-visits-tied-to-ab . . .

Pressman, M. R. (2011). Sleep driving: Sleepwalking variant or misuse of z-drugs? *Sleep Medicine Review*, *15*(5), 285–292. doi:10.1016/j.smrv.2010.12.004

Ratcliffe, S. (2012, October). *The clinical assessment of withdrawal* (pp. 1–22). Cambridge, MA: Pfizer Pharmaceuticals.

Reeve, E., Ong, M., & Wu, A. (2017). A systematic review of interventions to deprescribe benzodiazepines and other hypnotics among older adults. *European Journal of Clinical Pharmacology*, *73*, 927–935. doi:10.1007/s00228-017-2257-8

Roberts, E., & Frankel, S. (1950). Gamma-aminobutyric acid in brain: Its formation from glutamic acid. *The Journal of Biological Chemistry*, *187*, 55–63.

Rochon, P. A., Vozoris, N., & Gill, S. S. (2017, April). The harms of benzodiazepines for patients with dementia. *CMAJ*, *189*(4), E517–E518. doi:10.1503/cmaj.170193

Rosen, A. S., Fournie, P., & Darwish, M. (1999, April). Zaleplon phamacokinetics and absolute bioavailability. *Biopharmaceutics & Drug Disposition*, *20*(3), 1–3. doi:10.1002/(SICI)1099-081X(199904)20:3

Ross Perlman, W. (2019, July 10). Drug use and its consequences increase among middle-aged and older adults. *NIDA Notes*, pp. 1–3. Bethesda, MD: NIDA, National Institute on Drug Abuse.

Rush, C. R., Frey, J. M., & Griffiths, R. R. (1999). Zaleplon and triazolam in humans: Acute behavioral effects and abuse potential. *Psychopharmacology*, *145*(1), 39–51.

Ryba, N., & Rainess, R. (2020). Z-drugs and falls: A focused review of the literature. *The Senior Care Pharmacist*, *35*(12), 549–554. doi:10.4140/TCP.n2020.549

Saarelainen, L., Taipale, H., & Koponen, M. (2016). The incidence of benzodiazepine and related drug use in persons with and without Alzheimer's disease. *Journal of Alzheimer's Disease*, *49*, 809–818. doi:10.3233/JAD-150630

Sabioni, P., Bertram, J., & Le Foll, B. (2015). Off-label use of medications for treatment of benzodiazepine use disorder. *Current Pharmaceutical Design*, *21*(23), 3306–3310. doi:10.2174/1381612821666150619092039

Salva, P., & Costa, J. (1995, September). Clinical pharmacokinetics and pharmacodynamics of zolpidem. Therapeutic implications. *Clinical Pharmacokinetics*, *29*(3), 142–153. doi:10.2165/00003088-199529030-00002

Salzman, C. (2020, June). Do benzodiazepines cause Alzheimer's disease? *American Journal of Psychiatry*, *177*(6), 476–478. doi:10.1176/appi.ajp.2020.20040375

Samardzic, J., & Strac, D. (2016). *Benzodiazepines and anxiety disorders: From laboratory to clinic* (pp. 23–45). Intech. doi:10.5772/64959

Samba Reddy, D. (2010). Neurosteroids: Endogenous role in the human brain and therapeutic potentials. *Progress in Brain Research*, *186*, 113–137. doi:10.1016/B978-0-444-53630-3.00008-7

Sanger, D. J. (2004, January). The pharmacology and mechanisms of action of new generation, non-benzodiazepine hypnotic agents. *CNS Drugs*, *18*(Suppl 1), 9–15. doi:10.2165/00023210-200418001-00004

Saunders, J. B. (2017). Substance use and addictive disorders in DSM-5 and ICD 10 and the draft ICD 11. *Current Opinion in Psychiatry*, *30*, 1–10. doi:10.1097/YCO.0000000000000332

Schepis, T. S., Simoni-Wastila, L., & Esteban McCabe, S. (2019). Prescription opioid and benzodiazepine misuse is associated with suicidal ideation in older adults. *International Journal of Geriatric Psychiatry*, *34*(1), 122–129. doi:10.1002/gps.4999

Schifano, F., Chiappini, S., & Corkery, J. M. (2019). An insight into z-drug abuse and dependence: An examination of reports to the European medicines agency database of suspected adverse drug reactions. *International Journal of Neuropsychopharmacology*, *22*(4), 270–277.

Schmitz, A. (2016, June). Benzodiazepine use, misuse, and abuse: A review. *Mental Health Clinics*, *6*(3), 120–126. doi:10.9740/mhc.2016.05.120

Schroeck, J. L., Ford, J., & Conway, E. L. (2016, November). Review of safety and efficacy of sleep medicine in older adults. *Clinical Therapeutics*, *38*(11), 1–23. doi:10.1016/j.clinthera.2016.09.010

Seivewright, N., & Dougal, W. (1993, March). Withdrawal symptoms from high dose benzodiazepines in polydrug users. *Drug and Alcohol Dependence*, *32*(1), 15–23. doi:10.1016/0376-8716(93)90018-L

Sellers, E. M. (1978, June 24). Clinical pharmacology and therapeutics of benzodiazepines. *CMAJ, 118*, 1533–1538.

Sharbaf Shoar, N., Bistas, K. G., & Saadabadi, A. (2020, September 3). Flumazenil. *StatPearls [Internet]*, 1–6. Treasure Island, FL: StatPearls Publishing.

Sharp, M. J., & Melnik, T. A. (2015, April 17). Poisoning deaths involving opioid analgesics—New York State, 2003–2013. *MMWR, Morbidity and Mortality Weekly Report, 64*(14), 377–380.

Sieghart, W. (1994). Pharmacology of benzodiazepine receptors: An update. *Journal of Psychiatry & Neuroscience, 19*(1), 24–29.

Sigel, E., & Steinmann, M. E. (2012, November 23). Structure, function, and modulation of GABAA receptors. *Journal of Biological Chemistry, 287*(48), 40224–40231. doi:10.1074/jbc.R112.386664

Sikdar, S. (1998). Physical dependence on zopiclone. *BMJ, 317*, 146. doi:10.1136/bmj.317.7151.146

Southworth, M. R. (2006). Zaleplon, eszopiclone, zolpidem: Suicidal ideation and attempts, completed suicides. In *Drug safety post-marketing safety review*. Silver Spring, MD: Division of Drug Risk Evaluation, Center for Drug Evaluation and Research, Food and Drug Administration.

Soyka, M. (2017, March 23). Treatment of benzodiazepine dependence. *New England Journal of Medicine, 376*(12), 1147–1157. doi:10.1056/NEJMra1611832

Span, P. (2018, March 16). A quiet drug problem among the elderly. *The New York Times*, pp. 1–2.

Sparks, A., & Cohen, A. (2019, January). *Benzodiazepine and Z-drug safety guidelines*. Seattle, WA: Kaiser Foundation Health Plan of Washington.

Spiering, M. J. (2018, December 7). The discovery of GABA in the brain. *Journal of Biological Chemistry, 293*(49), 19159–19160. doi:10.1074/jbc.CL.118.006591

Stranks, E. K., & Crowe, S. F. (2014). The acute cognitive effects of zopiclone, zolpidem, zaleplon, and eszopiclone: A systematic review and meta-analysis. *Journal of Clinical and Experimental Neuropsychology, 36*(7), 691–700. doi:10.1080/13803395.2014.928268

Sugimoto, K., Araki, N., & Ohmori, M. (2006, March). Interaction between grapefruit juice and hypnotic drugs: Comparison of triazolam and quazepam. *European Journal of Clinical Pharmacology, 62*(3), 209–215. doi:10.1007/s00228-005-0071-1

Tampi, R. R., & Bennett, A. (2021). Benzodiazepine use and the risk of dementia. *Psychiatric Times, 38*(1), 1–10.

Tanaka, E. (2002). Toxicological interactions between alcohol and benzodiazepines. *Journal of Toxicology. Clinical Toxicology, 40*(1), 69–75.

Tannenbaum, C. (2015, May). Inappropriate benzodiazepine use in elderly patients and its reduction. *Journal of Psychiatry & Neuroscience, 40*(3), E27–E28. doi:10.1503/jpn.140355

Tapiainen, V., Taipale, H., & Tanskanen, A. (2018, August). The risk of Alzheimer's disease associated with benzodiazepines and related drugs: A nested case-control study. *Acta Psychiatrica Scandinavica, 138*(2), 91–100. doi:10.1111/acps.12909

Tom, S. E., Wickwire, E. M., & Park, Y. (2016). Nonbenzodiazepine sedative hypnotics and risk of fall-related injury. *Sleep, 1*(39), 1009–1014. doi:10.5665/sleep.5742

Treves, N., Perlman, A., & Kolenberg Geron, L. (2018). Z-drugs and risk for falls and fractures in older adults: A systematic review and meta-analysis. *Age and Aging, 47*(2), 201–208. doi:10.1093/ageing/afx167

Tyrer, P., Murphy, S., & Riley, P. (1990). The benzodiazepine withdrawal symptom questionnaire. *Journal of Affective Disorders, 19*(1), 53–61. doi:10.1016/0165-0327(90)90009-W

Tyrer, P., & Silk, K. R. (2012). Treatment of sedative-hypnotic dependence. In *Effective treatments in psychiatry* (pp. 109–117). Cambridge: Cambridge University Press. doi:10.1017/CBO9780511993503.017

UNODC, United Nations Office on Drugs and Crime. (2017, September). Non-medical use of benzodiazepines: A growing threat to public health? *Global Smart Update*, *18*, 1–11.

Usami, N., Yamamoto, T., & Shintani, S. (2002). Substrate specificity of human 3(20)alpha-hydroxysteroid dehydrogenase for neurosteroids and its inhibition by benzodiazepines. *Biological and Pharmaceutical Bulletin*, *25*(4), 441–445.

van Strien, A. M., Koek, H. L., & van Marum, R. J. (2013). Psychotropic medications, including short acting benzodiazepines, strongly increase the frequency of falls in elderly. *Maturitas*, *74*(4), 357–362. doi:10.1016/j.maturitas.2013.01.004

Victorri-Vigneau, C., Dailly, E., & Veyrac, G. (2007, August). Evidence of zolpidem abuse and dependence: Results of the French centre for evaluation and information on pharmacodependence (CEIP) network survey. *British Journal of Clinical Pharmacology*, *64*(2), 198–209. doi:10.1111/j.1365-2125.2007.02861.x

Vinkers, C. H., & Olivier, B. (2012). Mechanisms underlying tolerance after long-term benzodiazepine use: A future for subtype-selective GABAA receptor modulators? *Advances in Pharmacological Sciences*, *2012*(416864), 1–15. doi:10.1155/2012/416864

Vlase, L., Popa, A., & Neag, M. (2011a). Pharmacokinetic interaction between zolpidem and carbamazepine in healthy volunteers. *Journal of Clinical Pharmacology*, *51*(8), 1233–1236. doi:10.1177/0091270010383690

Vlase, L., Popa, A., & Neag, M. (2011b, January). Pharmacokinetic interaction between zolpidem and ciprofloxacin in healthy volunteers. *European Journal of Drug Metabolism and Pharmacokinetics*, *35*(3–4), 83–87. doi:10.1007/s13318-010-0014-9

Voaklander, D. C., Rowe, B. H., & Dryden, D. M. (2008). Medical illness, medication use and suicide in seniors: A population-based case-control study. *Journal of Epidemiology & Community Health*, *62*(2), 138–146.

Weaver, M. F. (2015). Prescription sedative misuse and abuse. *Yale Journal of Biology and Medicine*, *88*, 247–256.

Welsh, J., Tretyak, V., & McHugh, R. K. (2018, August 1). Review: Adjunctive pharmacologic approaches for benzodiazepine tapers. *Drug and Alcohol Dependence*, *189*, 189–196. doi:10.1016/j.drugalcdep.2018.04.028

WHO, World Health Organization. (2020). Severity of dependence scale (SDS). In *Management of substance abuse*. Geneva, Switzerland: World Health Organization.

Wolinsky, F. D., Fitzgerald, J. F., & Stump, T. E. (1997). The effect of hip fracture on mortality, hospitalization, and functional status: A prospective study. *American Journal of Public Health*, *87*(3), 398–403.

Wyeth Pharmaceuticals. (2007, November). Sonata. *Approved Labeling Text*, pp. 1–15. Philadelphia, PA.

Yen, C. F., Yen, C. N., & Ko, C. H. (2015). Correlates of dependence and beliefs about the use of hypnotics among zolpidem and zopiclone users. *Substance Use & Misuse*, *50*(3), 350–357. doi:10.3109/10826084.2014.980955

Yeung, W.-F., Chung, K.-F., & Zhang, Z.-J. (2017). Electroacupuncture for tapering off long-term benzodiazepine use: Study protocol of randomized controlled trial. *Complementary and Alternative Medicine*, *17*(183), 1–9. doi:10.1186/s12906-1692-5

Young, K. (2020, September 24). Benzodiazepines get stronger boxed warning on misuse risk. *NEJM Journal Watch*, p. 1. NEJM Group.

Zeilhofer, H. U., Neumann, E., & Munro, G. (2019, August). Spinal GABAA receptors for pain control: Back to the future? *British Journal of Anaesthesia, 123*(2), e176–e179. doi:10.1016/j.bja.2019.01.030

Zitman, F. G., & Couvee, J. E. (2001). Chronic benzodiazepine use in general practice patients with depression: An evaluation of controlled treatment and taper-off: Report on behalf of the Dutch Chronic Benzodiazepine Working Group. *The British Journal of Psychiatry, 178*(4), 317–324. doi:10.1192/bjp.178.4.317

Zoorob, M. J. (2018, March). Polydrug epidemiology: Benzodiazepine prescribing and the drug overdose epidemic in the United States. *Pharmacoepidemiology and Drug Safety, 27*(5), 1–5. doi:10.1002/pds.4417

Zosel, A., Osterberg, E. C., & Mycyk, M. B. (2011). Zolpidem misuse with other medications or alcohol frequently results in intensive care unit admission. *American Journal of Therapeutics, 18*(4), 305–308. doi:10.1097/MJT.0b013e3181d169ed

ENDNOTE

As we complete this book, perhaps our last, we reflect upon our long professional academic careers and wonder why we spent the preponderance of our adult lives teaching and writing. Perhaps the answer is best summarized by four simple words uttered by Senecca the Younger (4BC-AD65): *Docendo disco, scribendo cogito* (I learn by teaching, I think by writing).

INDEX[1,2,3,4,5,6]

1. f, followed by the figure number, indicates that the index entry is to be found within the identified figure.
2. fn, followed by the footnote number, indicates that the index entry is to be found within the identified footnote at the bottom of the identified page.
3. t, followed by the table number, indicates that the index entry is to be found within the identified table.
4. Quotation marks around a word indicate that it is a commonly used "street name" for the associated drug or substance of abuse.
5. ® indicates a registered proprietary brand/trade name.
6. Italics signifies a term that is part of the addictions argot.

www.ingramcontent.com/pod-product-compliance
Ingram Content Group UK Ltd.
Pitfield, Milton Keynes, MK11 3LW, UK
UKHW022016180926
475701UK00005B/871
9780367445508